Peter Apps is global affairs commentator at Reuters, a British Army reservist and executive director of pop-up think tank the Project for Study of the 21st Century (PS21). Peter has reported from across the world as Reuters political risk and global defence correspondent, and was appointed a Reuters columnist in 2016. He undertook reserve military training with both the British and U.S. armies and more recently as a UK specialist army reservist, providing advice, analysis and training and serving two full-time tours of duty during the Covid-19 pandemic and Ukraine war. He is the author of two successful Kindle Singles, Before Ebola (2014) and Churchill in the Trenches (2015).

Praise for *Deterring Armageddon*:

Deterring Armageddon is far from a dry historical record.
A Reuters foreign correspondent and specialist Army
Reservist, the author combines the detailed research and
insight of a historian with the vivid prose of a professional
journalist, the access of a high-ranking diplomat and the
practicality of a soldier. — *British Army Review*

Hugely impressive. — *Independent*

An impressive chronicle, rich in anecdote, of Nato's history
from its uncertain founding amid the wreckage of post-second
world war Europe to the present day . . . Several themes recur
in Apps' well-paced narrative of the backroom deals, political
posturing, big personalities, and recurring crises that have
tested Nato ever since. — *Financial Times*

Fascinating . . . We should be very grateful to Peter
Apps . . . for writing a thorough history of NATO
from birth in 1949 to today. — *Daily Mail*

Excellent . . . Peter Apps's account is longer and more
comprehensive, in effect providing a history of the big
transatlantic policy debates since 1945, with surprisingly
little left out. He covers the ground efficiently, enlivening
the discussion with vivid pen portraits of the key characters.
— Lawrence Freedman, *THE TLS*

Explains in absorbing detail the conception, birth and life [of
NATO] so far . . . an astonishingly fine history. — *Country Life*

A masterful portrait of an organisation often misunderstood
but absolutely central to much of contemporary international
politics . . . expertly crafted. — *Irish Independent*

A well-researched, highly readable account of the military,
strategic – and indeed personal – twists and turns in

NATO's history . . . fascinating and enthralling . . .
relevant and important. — Lord Robertson, former
NATO Secretary General, *The House magazine*

Utterly eye-opening - compelling, haunting and continually
illuminating. As Peter Apps so brilliantly demonstrates in this
gripping book, the story of the NATO alliance is in many
ways a parallel global history of the last 75 years. As well as
all the outbreaks of seething tension between the US and its
European allies – and the counter-moves of rival powers – this
is also an account of just how often in those postwar years that
we all stood on the edge of the most terrible abyss. With
mesmerising fluency, and dazzling research, Apps follows the
criss-crossing threads of the Cold War and beyond. Those
threads converge in our shadowed present, and the conflict
in Ukraine. In order to fathom today's dark world, Apps has
explored a labyrinth of once-classified history, and he brings
dazzling clarity. — Sinclair McKay

Peter Apps takes us on a journey through NATO's history
with the kind of storytelling flair that one would expect from
someone steeped in the art of journalism – and an eye for the
kind of anecdote that brings engagingly to life what could too
easily be a dry bureaucratic subject. — Engelsberg Ideas

Peter Apps has created a quintessential guide for understanding
NATO, from its historical development to its future path-
ways . . . *Deterring Armageddon* is a must-read as we enter a
new era of heightened global risk and shock events.
— Dr Maha Hosain Aziz

Compelling and informative – a must-read for anyone serious
about understanding both the history and future of Western
military strategy. — Anna-Joy Rickard, the Great British
Foreign Affairs Podcast

Deterring Armageddon

A Biography of NATO

PETER APPS

WILDFIRE

First published in hardback in 2024 by WILDFIRE an imprint of
HEADLINE PUBLISHING GROUP LIMITED

This paperback edition published in 2025

2

Cataloguing in Publication Data is available from the British Library

Paperback ISBN 978 1 0354 0579 4

Typeset in Baskerville MT Pro by Jouve (UK), Milton Keynes

Printed and bound in Great Britain by Clays Ltd, Elcograf S.p.A.

Headline's policy is to use papers that are natural, renewable
and recyclable products and made from wood grown in sustainable forests.
The logging and manufacturing processes are expected to conform
to the environmental regulations of the country of origin.

HEADLINE PUBLISHING GROUP
An Hachette UK Company
Carmelite House
50 Victoria Embankment
London EC4Y 0DZ

The authorized representative in the EEA is Hachette Ireland, 8 Castlecourt
Centre, Castleknock Road, Castleknock, Dublin 15, D15 YF6A, Ireland

www.headline.co.uk
www.hachette.co.uk

To those I've worked with, served with and loved.

Table of Contents

Part 7: The Road to 2049

Introduction

Those who founded the North Atlantic Treaty Organisation and built its first civilian and military structures believed they knew exactly what its mission was. 'I regard NATO as the all-important organisation today in the world,' NATO's first Deputy Supreme Allied Commander, Field Marshal Viscount Bernard Montgomery, told students at NATO's new Defence College in 1953. 'It is my very firm belief that if NATO had come into being earlier, there would have been no Second World War . . . It is also my belief that in the strengthening of NATO lies the best hope of preventing a Third.'[1]

Montgomery had been shot and nearly killed in World War One, defeated Hitler's best general Erwin Rommel in the desert during World War Two and led British and Commonwealth forces in mainland Europe after D-Day. These were individuals who knew what war was like, and believed the advent of atomic weapons meant any future global conflict could end the human race. They saw the banding together of European and North American democracies in mutual self-defence as the best way to prevent catastrophe in Europe. As the first generation of NATO ambassadors looked back on its first forty years, they noted it had outlasted all but one significant long-term international alliance in history. The only past historic rival to its record by that point was the ancient Delian League, the Athenian-dominated group of city-states formed against the Persians in 478 BC and dismantled seventy-four years later having created the building blocks of modern Greece.

Italian diplomat Egido Ortona wrote in 1985 that NATO came into existence because of a sense of danger. The result, he said, was 'an alliance that is even more necessary and unavoidable today than when it was created'.[2] As long-serving Belgian ambassador to NATO André de Staercke put it, also in the 1980s: 'I for my part can think of no other democratic alliance that has ever succeeded, in times of peace and for an indefinite period, in building anything approaching a common political or military policy.'[3]

NATO is, even its greatest supporters will concede, a very imperfect institution, one perpetually beset by divisions and where decision-making by consensus can sometimes lead to choices not being made at all. Zach Wolfraim, a former NATO official who wrote his PhD on national narratives within the North Atlantic Council, notes that countries often conform to the most basic stereotypes in their discussions and approaches.[4] Plenty of those who have worked within its structures admit to finding much infuriating. It has unquestionably made mistakes, particularly in its longest war in Afghanistan and other interventions. For all that, since the moment of the treaty NATO has proved remarkably effective at ensuring that 'not a single inch' of its territory in the North Atlantic area has fallen to a foreign power (the 'NATO area' does not extend south of the Tropic of Cancer nor into the Pacific, excluding most colonial territories like the British Falklands). While it has faced conflicts outside its borders in the Balkans, Afghanistan and Libya, within NATO's member nations whole generations have been able to grow up largely in peace without the global conflicts that tore the world apart from 1914 and 1939.

The scale of fighting in Ukraine from 2022 takes the alliance again into uncharted waters, a situation where a major war is raging on the European continent and might yet escalate to something worse. It has sent NATO back firmly to its roots, to the defence of its most vulnerable members and borders.

Cold War confrontations like Berlin and Cuba showed the

complexities of an alliance between democracies of very different size and power. Even in a world where the US called the shots, it has not always been obvious who was actually in charge. At times, decisions intended to make accidental war less likely may have had the opposite effect. More such challenges are almost certainly on the way. Those who built NATO believed that without it, the Soviet Union would almost certainly have attempted to overrun at least part of Western Europe in the early 1950s, just as the Soviet-backed North invaded South Korea. Many in Eastern Europe today similarly believe that had they not gained alliance membership in the 1990s and 2000s, they too might already have found themselves attacked. Recent history suggests the United States, Russia and a rising China are all becoming much more unpredictable, as is European politics, with the alliance caught somewhere in the middle.

As NATO turns seventy-five in 2024, it has finally outlasted the Delian League, its position as the world's longest-lasting multinational alliance no longer open to debate. As incoming US Defense Secretary Jim Mattis told a newly elected Donald Trump in 2017, it would be necessary to invent it if it did not exist already.[5] But it now faces multiple new questions, not least what to do about Ukraine and whether it can survive if the US turns isolationist.

NATO only got where it is today through leadership and vision. US Air Force General Lauris Norstad recalled that one of the reasons Dwight D. Eisenhower was so effective as NATO's first supreme military commander was that he believed in individuals, ideas and institutions, impressing on every member of the alliance his belief that it could work even when he privately had his doubts.[6] Other NATO leaders since have picked up that task with varying effect.

The coming years may be as dangerous – perhaps more – than anything that has come before. If NATO is the conflicted, flawed protagonist of a multi-decade struggle to stop a global war beginning once again in Europe – and this book argues that it is – then that work is very far from over.

Part 1:
The Shock of Ukraine

1

'A Sense of Threat and Fear' (2022–2023)

'Is Estonia next? Well . . . we are
doing our maximum to prevent it.'

Estonian Defence Minister
Hanno Pevkur, 16 February 2023[1]

It was the twelfth month after Russia's full-scale invasion of Ukraine, and the sound of gunfire echoed through the trees of central Estonia. In wood-lined trenches, soldiers snapped magazines into automatic rifles, scanning the forest for infantry and advancing armour. British Challenger 2 tanks charged down woodland tracks, draped with camouflage branches and white sheets to match the snow and pines. Somewhere nearby waited a squadron of slightly smaller Danish Leopards crewed by the Jutland Dragoons. In support were Alpine infantry from France, their winter and mountain warfare skills now tested in the Baltic.

'The scenario is that there's been an enemy incursion into Estonia,' said Major Nick Bridges, Chief of Staff of the UK-led 'enhanced Forward Presence' (eFP) NATO battle group in Estonia. 'They have penetrated quite far to the west – and this is us trying to launch a counter-attack.' As soldiers knelt in shallow snow, a Chinook helicopter touched down, blasting clouds of whiteness upwards. This was just an exercise – but one taken very seriously.[2] Almost a thousand miles to the south-west, Ukraine's army had been fighting for national survival against the Kremlin for almost a year.

For the bullish, grey-bearded commander of Estonia's First Infantry Brigade, Colonel Andrus Merilo, Exercise WINTER CAMP was a chance to show enemies and allies that his country would be just as tough to conquer – and to ensure that Estonian troops and their NATO allies were fully prepared for fighting in the freezing cold of winter if they had to. Events in Ukraine had given his troops 'confidence that so far what we have done has been right,' Merilo said. 'Russia has been our neighbour for centuries. We have been practising for this one.'[3]

Ever since seizing their renewed independence as the Soviet Union collapsed in 1991, many in the Baltic states had warned that only strong defences and NATO membership could protect Lithuania, Latvia, Estonia and the other new democracies of Eastern and Central Europe. As they signed up to join in 2002, Latvian President Vaira Vīķe-Freiberga described alliance membership as the only guarantee that Baltic citizens could 'go to bed and not worry about someone knocking on the door and putting you on a train for Siberia'.[4]

Vladimir Putin's February 2022 invasion of Ukraine offered further proof of that, Estonia's Prime Minister Kaja Kallas told journalists at NATO's HQ in Brussels sixteen months later. When Ukraine was loosely invited to join the alliance but denied an immediate path to membership in 2008, it had been left in a vague 'grey zone' between East and West. The world was now facing the cost of that decision, Kallas said – and had Estonia itself not been allowed to join in 2004, it too would almost certainly be facing 'some really dark times'. 'Any grey zone in Europe is a source of conflict,' she said. 'The only security guarantee that really works is NATO.'[5]

*

For the alliance, the 2022 Ukraine invasion was a shot of adrenaline that would kickstart its most ambitious planning and activity since the early 1950s. 'NATO relies on momentum,' said former US intelligence official Andrea Kendall-Taylor. 'And a lot of the momentum is generated by a sense of threat and fear.'[6] It was a dynamic NATO's founders would have recognised.

As the scope of the new alliance became clear during the 1948 discussions for its creation, US ambassador to Britain Lewis Douglas wondered whether the US was 'biting off more than we can chew'. A British general at the same meeting conceded that binding their nations together was 'a risk', but warned the 'worse risk was to allow one country after another to be picked off'.[7] As NATO's first Secretary General Hastings Ismay later wrote, that was exactly what Hitler had done in the run-up to 1939, and the alliance was intended to stop it from happening again.[8]

As representatives of twelve nations signed the North Atlantic Treaty in Washington in April 1949, President Harry S. Truman described it as a 'simple document' that, if it had existed earlier, might have prevented two world wars. 'In this Treaty we seek to establish freedom from oppression and from the use of force in the North Atlantic community,' he told the signatories. 'To protect this area against war will be a long step toward permanent peace in the whole world.'[9] The fourteen articles of the NATO treaty, modern-day NATO officials say, have offered just the right balance of clarity and vagueness to keep the alliance going, providing both flexibility and a sense of mission. US diplomat Lucius Battle, one of the last surviving witnesses to the signing, described it as a 'superb idea, and it turned out to be a superb accomplishment'. But, he noted fifty years later, 'there was by no means universal agreement that it was the right way to go'.[10]

'Universal agreement' has rarely occurred since either. NATO's survival and effectiveness have never been something it or its members could take for granted. Its history, in many respects, is one of successive crises, both internal and external – and in an organisation run entirely through 'consensus', where one country's veto can sometimes block agreement, even a relatively minor disagreement or misunderstanding can stop anything happening at all. 'Just by reading the newspapers or watching the television you can see that NATO allies disagree on many issues,' Secretary General Jens Stoltenberg told a press conference in Washington for the alliance's seventieth anniversary in April 2019, describing trade, climate change and Iran as among the largest issues that year. '[But] the strength of NATO is that despite these differences we have always been able to unite around our core task, and that is to protect and defend each other.'[11]

*

In the aftermath of the Ukraine invasion, many – particularly those from Eastern Europe – believe the alliance has again reached a critical inflection point, where it once again must adapt and rebuild to protect its members. 'Aggression cannot pay off,' said Estonian Prime Minister Kallas in December 2022, arguing that any nation that attacked another should be punished rather than allowed to walk away with more territories or resources. 'We have agreed in the international rules-based order that it's illegal to attack another country.'[12]

In barely four months following February 2022, NATO's policy planning team under Stoltenberg's direction drew up its first new strategic concept since 2010. Whereas the previous version had talked of the Euro–Atlantic area being 'at peace', this explicitly said the opposite. It described Russia's invasion as having 'shattered peace and gravely altered our security environment', further exacerbating a security environment already defined by 'pervasive instability, rising strategic competition and advancing authoritarianism'. NATO's three core tasks, it said, were now: 'deterrence and defence', 'crisis prevention and management' and 'cooperative security'.[13] Officials talked of a new feeling of urgency and purpose. 'There's no question of the sense of mission,' said one official.[14] 'NATO is more unified than I've ever seen NATO unified before,' General Christopher G. Cavoli, commanding the US Army in Europe and soon to take on Eisenhower's old role as NATO's supreme commander, told reporters in Poland shortly after the invasion. 'I've been working since I was a second lieutenant in 1988, and I can tell you, I've never seen the resolve . . . it's remarkable.'[15]

'He [Putin] made a big mistake by invading Ukraine because he totally underestimated Ukrainians, their strengths, their resilience and their courage,' said Secretary General Stoltenberg. 'He totally underestimated NATO and NATO allies . . . NATO is the most successful alliance in history because of our unity and because of our ability to adapt. When the world changes, NATO changes.'[16]

For anyone wondering whether a modern Western democracy could fight off a concerted, brutal attack from an authoritarian state like Russia, Ukraine's success in surviving the initial onslaught was inevitably encouraging. But the sheer scale of the war – and the resulting human losses – outstripped anything the alliance had considered possible in its recent history. UN reports of some 8,500 civilian casualties in the first year of the war were, the officials who drew them up acknowledged, likely a dramatic underestimate.[17] Associated Press used civilian satellite footage to track more than 10,000 new graves in the coastal city of Mariupol alone following its devastating siege and capture – and warned many more bodies were likely buried where they lay as Russian bulldozers razed neighbourhoods. Some local sources put the true number of dead at 25,000 in that city alone, others three times that.[18] By August 2023, US officials estimated almost 200,000 troops had lost their lives on both sides, with approximately two-thirds of them Russian and the remainder from Ukraine, plus another 300,000 wounded.[19] Later US estimates would reduce their number of suspected Russian fatalities to around 60,000 in the first two years – but the truth appeared to be that no one really knew.[20]

Other more localised reports were equally disturbing. As Ukrainian troops re-entered the Kyiv suburb of Bucha in April 2022, they discovered dozens of bodies in the streets, many with hands tied behind their backs. The Ukrainian government later put the death toll at 458. Those planning alliance defence now had an appalling, visual indicator of what even a limited war in Europe might look like. 'This is the biggest war on the European continent since World War Two,' said one senior NATO official. 'There cannot be a Bucha [style massacre] on NATO territory. Ever.'[21]

*

Former US ambassador to NATO Donald Rumsfeld once said that the alliance had a lucky habit of being 'saved' once a decade by a new crisis between the West and Kremlin.[22] Following the 2022 invasion of Ukraine, NATO appeared to embrace action and reform on a scale not seen since the early 1950s.

For the first year of its existence after the 1949 signing of the treaty, the alliance had no permanent structures at all to speak of, just a series of meetings with ministers and generals. For months, increasingly concerned military commanders contrasted Kremlin military preparations with their own and warned that if the Soviets attacked, Western defences might crumble fast. When war came, however, it was on the far side of the world. NATO was barely a year old when North Korean troops launched a massive and unexpected assault across the 38th parallel in June 1950, almost overrunning the entire peninsula before being halted by the US and its allies. Events in Korea would change NATO forever. President Truman recalled Eisenhower, the architect of Allied victory in Europe in World War Two, to the US Army, and immediately appointed him NATO's first Supreme Allied Commander Europe (SACEUR). In the space of barely a year, 'Ike' and many of the team that had planned the D-Day landings built what remains the basis for NATO's modern military machine.

During the 1990s and 2000s, many of those at the top of the alliance shifted to viewing Russia as much a partner as a potential foe, with NATO refocusing 'out of area' as a tool of intervention in first the Balkans and then Afghanistan. Like its later 2011 war in Libya, these were often controversial actions. Some within the alliance talk of an awkward search for relevance during the years the Russian threat appeared diminished. But that is not a problem now.

Concern over Russia's actions began growing from 2007, when Estonia found itself under a suspected Russian cyber attack, further intensifying through Russia's 2008 war with Georgia and a series of increasingly aggressive Russian military exercises in Eastern Europe – including some that simulated nuclear strikes against eastern NATO members. The annexation of Crimea in 2014 and fighting in eastern Ukraine that followed re-orientated NATO firmly back towards 'classical deterrence', sending the first eFP battle groups to Eastern Europe. By the time the Covid-19 pandemic hit in March 2020 the US was committed to a series of annual DEFENDER exercises moving forces across the Atlantic to continental Europe; a twenty-first-century equivalent of the Cold War-era REFORGER drills that had defined the 1970s and 1980s. Stoltenberg described the alliance as 'actually quite prepared' for the 2022 invasion, 'partly because we had very precise intelligence, but also partly because the Russian invasion was part of a pattern that started in Chechnya and then Georgia, and then Crimea . . . We may as people be shocked by the brutality, but we should not be surprised by the fact that President Putin invaded Ukraine.'[23]

*

As the pandemic eased in April 2021, the Russian military began moving more than 100,000 troops towards the Ukraine border. Most Russian units returned to their bases from the start of May, but there was little let-up in rhetoric from the Kremlin, increasingly questioning Ukraine's right to exist as an independent state. From November 2021 Putin's army headed back in even greater numbers, with US and British spies increasingly convinced that this was not an exercise. When global leaders met in Glasgow for the COP climate summit later that month, senior US officials told Ukrainian President Volodymyr Zelensky they believed his country was about to face invasion.

As Putin's attack preparations reached their final stages, US intelligence officials did what they had done for every major international crisis since Cuba in 1962: fly in US experts to brief NATO's North Atlantic Council and to prepare alliance members for what might happen next. As throughout alliance history, predictable divisions fast became apparent. There was, those involved say, scepticism from several European nations, mutterings over past US errors on Iraqi weapons of mass destruction, and doubt the Kremlin would truly launch a major war.[24]

NATO's eastern members – particularly the Baltic states and Poland – were much more openly alarmed, lobbying for more alliance troop deployments to further deter an attack on them.[25] In September 2021 they had watched Western forces quit Afghanistan in chaos after two decades of 'ironclad' commitment from the alliance. Now they were watching embassies flee Kyiv.

As always in a crisis, all eyes turned to the United States. As he boarded the Marine One helicopter outside the White House in December 2021, President Biden made it clear that sending US forces to defend Ukraine was 'not on the table'. Those nations already inside the alliance, however, would be defended to the hilt. Both assertions were to be repeated on multiple occasions in the coming weeks. 'We have a moral obligation and a legal obligation to our NATO allies if [Russia] were to attack,' Biden said. 'It's a sacred obligation. That obligation does not extend . . . to Ukraine.'[26]

*

Throughout the eight decades since 1945 the US has always been by far the most powerful NATO member. Its importance stems from its simultaneous political, economic and military strength, its status as the first Western atomic power, and its history as the 'arsenal of freedom' that came late to both world wars before being critical to victory. Ending that isolationist tradition was top of the agenda for those who built the alliance, locking the US into a binding commitment to the defence of Europe in a way previous American generations had always avoided.

That has not been enough to stop decades of discussions in Washington and beyond over whether the US bears an unfair burden. Several US presidential candidates have favoured withdrawing troops from Europe over the decades, while senators and congressmen have attempted to pass bills to achieve the same. Most recently, Donald Trump's dismissal of NATO as 'obsolete' and his rows with almost every member prompted some to ask if the alliance could survive. Even in more united times, the power imbalance between Washington and other capitals has always been a source of tension, with smaller allies accusing the US and other major powers of making decisions behind their backs. In fact, the Trump era saw the US increase its military contribution to the alliance – although whether the president was aware of this remains another question.

From February 2022, the Biden administration showed its colours as even more resolutely transatlanticist. The US has deliberately placed itself at the heart of a Western strategy to support Ukraine with weapons, punish Russia diplomatically and economically, and shore up NATO's own defences. That might only be a temporary rebalancing. November 2024 could see Trump returned to the White House, while the Republican primaries showed isolationism, if anything, growing within the party. Even amongst Americans committed to engaging with the world, priorities are shifting firmly to the Pacific, with some warning of conflict sparked by an invasion of Taiwan as soon as 2027. 'For the US, Russia is a regional power, a pain but not the centre of their attention,' said former French ambassador to Washington DC Gerard Ardaud. 'They want to put an end to the war in Ukraine as soon as possible to face the real threat: China.'[27] How European states and NATO itself might respond to that long-term US shift away from Europe remains unclear.

*

Initially, few in Russia or the West expected Ukraine's government to survive the 2022 invasion. An airborne assault and armoured thrust from Belarus was expected to overrun Kyiv and 'decapitate' its military and civilian leadership. As the US, Britain, the Baltic states and Poland poured rocket launchers and other hand-held weapons into the country, they expected to be supporting an insurgency against a Russian occupation, not a functioning Ukrainian state.

As Russia initiated its offensive in the early hours of 24 February, Stoltenberg and his NATO team had already planned their immediate response. They scheduled an immediate meeting of ambassadors of the North Atlantic Council, also ordering the mobilisation of 40,000 troops to locations across Eastern Europe. The next day, thirty NATO national leaders – together with other partners including the European Union, Sweden and Finland – held an emergency virtual summit, condemning Russia's 'senseless' war and committing again to the alliance principles of mutual aid and self-defence.[28]

Next, Stoltenberg and alliance military leaders moved to demonstrate just how much force the alliance could muster in a hurry. Within days, NATO had increased the number of operational forces under its direct command to 140 ships at sea, 32,000 ground troops on the eastern flank, and 135 aircraft devoted to NATO operations.[29] Expectations that the Kyiv government would prove an easy victim were swiftly overturned. Russian airborne troops failed to secure Hostomel airport near the capital, while its troops advancing from Belarus struggled to move forward.[30] Cities that Russia had expected to take readily – such as the predominantly Russian-speaking university town of Kharkiv and the coastal steel-manufacturing centre Mariupol – instead offered fierce resistance. 'We meet here at the NATO headquarters facing the most serious security crisis in a generation,' Stoltenberg told reporters as leaders arrived in Brussels for an emergency summit a month after the invasion. He announced a 'new sense of urgency' to build up alliance defences, and a decision to send further eFP battle groups to Romania, Bulgaria, Hungary and Slovakia.[31]

Like every other foe that it had faced, from Stalin to the Taliban, Putin hoped the alliance would fracture under pressure. 'Putin was banking on NATO being split,' said Biden. 'In my early conversations with him in December and early January, it was clear to me he didn't think we could sustain this cohesion. NATO has never, never been more united than it is today. Putin is getting exactly the opposite of what he intended.'[32] On 26 April 2022, the sixty-second day of fighting, more than forty nations met at Ramstein Air Base in south-west Germany to coordinate arms shipments and supply. 'Putin never imagined that the world would rally behind Ukraine so swiftly and surely,' said US Defense Secretary Lloyd Austin.[33]

Of course, the fact the war was happening at all was a sign of NATO and wider Western failure. As he lobbied for weapons, Ukraine's Zelensky noted diplomatically that leaving his country in the fragile 'grey zone' between membership and abandonment was perhaps a long-term recipe for trouble. Others blamed the mayhem of the Trump era and earlier US-led Middle East interventions for creating a narrative of strategic weakness. Without the chaotic fall of Kabul and the unravelling of the US and NATO Afghan machine in August 2021, some suggested Putin might not have had the confidence to launch the Ukraine invasion just six months later.

These were now uncharted waters. Never before had NATO members been so directly involved in arming and supporting a major European state at existential war with Russia. When it came to arming Ukraine, countries struck deals directly with the Kyiv government through the US-coordinated Ramstein process. NATO's involvement was limited, although it was able to use its structures to support mass purchasing of artillery shells. Without the existence of the alliance, however – and specifically its 'Article 5' mutual defence guarantee – insiders say that few of its Eastern and Central European members would have felt so confident to support Ukraine, nor that they could have done so without facing some form of attack by Russia. 'The invasion of Ukraine has broken the taboo on the state-on-state use of force in Europe,' said an Eastern European diplomat. 'NATO is fulfilling its role . . . by managing escalation, by providing a safe space for the help effectively to be delivered.'[34] 'I really think this will come to be seen as NATO's finest hour,' said former Assistant Secretary General for Operations Stephen Evans. 'Without it, I don't believe Ukraine could have been supported as it has.'[35]

*

NATO members had never truly contemplated a sustained war in Europe on the scale of present-day Ukraine. By 2023, the Kyiv government was estimated to be spending 34 per cent of gross domestic product on defence, ten times its pre-war levels, while many NATO members were still struggling to reach their long-running target of just 2 per cent.[36] As the war progressed, the realisation grew in Western capitals that it could last for years. The government in Kyiv had halted male citizens fleeing the country to conscript them for the front, a step few had felt possible in the hyper-connected, hyper-mobile modern age.

Now, NATO's most exposed nations felt they had to prepare themselves for such a potential conflict while also continuing to support Ukraine. The level of firepower being used by both sides outstripped anything Western states had previously considered. Within the first two months of the war Ukraine used up a significant proportion of the entire Western consignment of Stinger hand-held anti-aircraft missiles, with manufacturers struggling to restock supplies.[37] Ukrainian officials reported Russian artillery firing up to 600,000 shells a month in the first months of conflict, equivalent to an entire year of European defence industry pre-war production output.[38] At the height of the Cold War, US strategists calculated the US military needed to set aside artillery shells for no more than sixty days of high-intensity fighting before a conflict either stopped or became nuclear and apocalyptic. European states had never been persuaded to match those stocks, running down supplies even further after the fall of the Berlin Wall.

The US, the ally with by far the biggest arsenals, delivered a million shells by the end of 2022, but only by breaking into strategic stockpiles held outside Europe in Israel and South Korea.[39] The European Union pledged another million shells, itself an unprecedented step. One NATO official called the allied effort to deliver Ukraine ammunition as an 'incredible, unforeseen strain on the supply system' – but a 'military necessity'.[40] In US artillery production plants that had barely changed since the 1950s, manufacturing lines were now running 24 hour days throughout the working week as officials and defence executives scoped out locations for new sites and recruited a new generation of munitions workers. Alongside such 'old-fashioned' mass-production warfare sat equally dramatic demand for high-tech drones, missiles, microchips and satellite communications, not to mention all the requirements of continuous cyber and information warfare.

'The magnitude of this war is incredible,' NATO's SACEUR Cavoli told a Swedish military audience in January 2023. 'The Russians have lost almost 2000 tanks . . . the scale dwarfs all our recent thinking but it is real and we must contend with it.'[41] 'People need to be aware that this is a long fight,' said another NATO official. 'This is not a crisis. This is not some small incident somewhere that can be managed. This is an all-out war. It's treated that way now by politicians all across Europe and across the alliance, and that's absolutely appropriate.'[42]

With most of Russia's forces bogged down in Ukraine, Central and Eastern European states were, by mid-2023, temporarily less nervous about an imminent attack. Their worry, however, was that once that war was paused or over, a humiliated Kremlin might re-arm and come for them. 'I don't think this war will weaken Russia so much that it would stop being a threat,' said Latvian Defence Minister Artis Pabriks. Latvia's National Security Adviser Jānis Kažociņš, a former spy chief, described Russia as a problem to be handled 'for ever': 'There's no imminent sense of crisis, but there is a sense of danger.'[43] Most NATO officials had a similar diagnosis. 'We are convinced that the Russians are going to reconstitute,' said NATO Military Committee Chairman Admiral Robert Bauer, previously defence chief for the Netherlands.[44]

'For years and years, time was on our side,' said Bauer. 'We thought for a while that if we have mutual relationships with a nation that we trade with, and economic interdependency, there will never be war again. Well, that has been proved wrong.'[45]

2

A Very Political Alliance (2023)

'People think of NATO as a military alliance, but everything here is political – even the military decisions.'

Eastern European diplomat, 2023[1]

NATO's seventy-fourth birthday, 4 April 2023, was cold and clear in Brussels. Outside NATO's vast steel and glass HQ, a single new and empty flagstaff stood erect and ready for its latest member: Finland. As foreign ministers arrived in limousines, Secretary General Jens Stoltenberg described the moment as a personal failure for Putin, and a direct consequence of his invasion of Ukraine. 'He wanted less NATO along his borders,' he told reporters, his comments translated almost immediately into Ukrainian and Russian for the NATO website. 'He is getting exactly the opposite.'[2]

With the addition of Finland, NATO's total population stood at 955 million across almost 25,000,000 km². If it were a single and unified nation state – and some of its founders hoped that it might be that by now – it would be by far the richest in the world, the third most populous after India and China, and the geographically largest country in history, surpassing for the first time the total area of the Soviet Union at its height.[3] Even after the Cold War ended, it had remained relatively unthinkable that either Finland or Sweden might join the alliance – such a move was simply not popular enough within their countries. The February 2022 invasion of Ukraine, however, upended that reality.

At NATO's military Supreme Headquarters Allied Powers Europe (SHAPE) in the Belgian city of Mons and across the Atlantic at its Allied Command Transformation in Norfolk, Virginia, work was soon afoot to defend both countries and integrate them into wider military plans. That would include using the Swedish–Finnish road and rail network to move forces fast in times of trouble, either to defend the Baltic states or potentially threaten Russia. Sweden and Finland might have remained neutral through the first Cold War, but they had built powerful militaries optimised for self-defence. That now included Finland's F-35 Joint Strike Fighters, 250,000 military reservists and Sweden's cutting-edge submarines. NATO officers integrating the potential new arrivals into the alliance described it as 'a huge step forward' from a military perspective.[4] But almost immediately after the May 2022 announcement that Finland and Sweden had applied to join, a stumbling block emerged as Turkey announced it would veto them.[5] It was a stark reminder of one of NATO's 'core realities'. If it wished, a single nation could leave decision-making deadlocked by refusing to agree – and the North Atlantic Treaty offered no way to stop them, let alone evict them if required.

Persuading Turkey to agree to Finland's membership took almost a year of focused diplomacy. Over multiple meetings between Turkish, Finnish and Swedish officials, several deals emerged, including an agreement from the two Nordic nations to clamp down on Kurdish militants and lift arms embargoes on the government in Ankara. In March 2023, Turkish President Recep Tayyip Erdoğan announced Finland had done enough to join – but still not Sweden. There were, he said, several reasons – including the Stockholm government's tolerance of 'blasphemy' over the burning of the Qur'an at a far-right demonstration.[6] That incident would later turn out to have been organised by a journalist with links to Kremlin-funded media, prompting suggestions it was a deliberate provocation.[7] The dispute was, some warned, undermining NATO credibility. 'Any fissure, any lack of solidarity provides an opportunity for those who would oppose the alliance,' said former US ambassador to NATO Douglas Lute.[8] 'NATO has set up Swedish membership to be one of the jewels of the crown of that summit,' said a diplomat in Brussels. 'If it cannot deliver it, that will inevitably raise questions.'[9]

The other unanswered long-term question was what to do about Ukraine. As Finland's flag rose outside NATO HQ in April 2023, several dozen protesters chanted and waved banners. 'Ukraine is Europe!' they chanted, still loud enough to be heard even after being moved away by the police. 'Give us weapons! Ukraine in NATO! Ukraine in NATO!'[10]

*

From its inception in April 1949, squaring such political circles has been at the heart of the job for those running the alliance. Of the roughly 4,000 who come to work each day in the sprawling civilian HQ by Brussels airport, which some refer to as the 'Death Star', approximately half work for the national delegations of its members. Another 500 military personnel make up its International Military Staff, with several hundred more from other partner countries or organisations. Then there are the one thousand 'international staff', the core team including those around the secretary general tasked with keeping it all together.[11]

Some parts of NATO have a reputation for being somewhat sedentary. International NATO jobs are well remunerated and its staff do not pay tax, prompting some incumbents to stay for years. In 2020, the average age of NATO staff was forty-seven,[12] and there have long been jokes about the ineffectiveness of parts of its bureaucracy (asked how many people worked for NATO, its longest-serving Secretary General Joseph Luns is once said to have replied: 'About half.')[13]

At the centre of the alliance, however – particularly those working with the secretary general – the pace has always been relentless, and as the alliance has expanded it has increased further. Particularly during a ministerial meeting, dozens of decision-makers can be seen striding through the building, surrounded by their staff: young, earnest men, power-dressing women, officers in uniform and a multinational crowd of journalists, all clutching their smart phones. Former NATO secretary generals have complained at the 'tiny' size of the central bureaucracy compared to other major institutions like the European Union or International Monetary Fund, blaming the constituent members of the alliance for failing to provide the proper resources. George Robertson, who ran the alliance from 1999 until 2003, describes it as being 'as weak as the . . . nation states want to make it or as strong as they want to make it'. 'I could decide to go to Moscow and negotiate with President Putin,' Robertson said after leaving office. 'I could go to the White House and negotiate with President Bush. But I couldn't upgrade a gardener or a security guard, and I couldn't move a single euro from one of the budget heads to the other [without the agreement of all members].'[14]

That relentless necessity to get multinational sign-off is a constant across many NATO structures. As well as its main HQ, the alliance has centres, operations rooms and offices in almost every member, including several dozen 'centres of excellence' on everything from cyber security to military veterinary medicine. Their staff include NATO's Young Professionals, usually in their early to mid-twenties, on three-year schemes that moves them between different alliance institutions – and often countries – every year. Then there are the tens of thousands of service personnel and smaller numbers of civilians who pass through other NATO structures, exercises, courses and validation programmes, all aimed at helping them work together.

The political dynamics shape all else that happens. 'What you realise when you work in NATO is that there are all sorts of unwritten ground rules that unite the nations of the alliance,' said British General Sir James Everard, Deputy Supreme Allied Commander Europe from 2017 to 2020. 'Most of them are about mutual respect and impeccable politeness.'[15]

*

As Winston Churchill persuaded Defence Minister Lord Hastings Ismay to become NATO's first secretary general in February 1952, he told him that the alliance offered the best chance of securing global peace – but that to do so, it needed to be run and managed properly.[16] Some of NATO's most sophisticated diplomats have since struggled to find the language for what that really means. In 1969 US NATO ambassador Harlan Cleveland described the alliance to a newly elected President Richard Nixon as an 'organised controversy' attempting to resolve sometimes almost irreconcilable and enduring differences between its members.[17]

Cleveland was attempting to explain to Nixon – accurately, as it turned out – why achieving what he wished to within the alliance would be hard. In May 1984, US ambassador to the UN Jeane Kirkpatrick reached for a more human metaphor, describing NATO as 'a colossal success, the greatest single success of the post-World War Two years', but also as 'not a perfect marriage'.[18] Few of these metaphors really work in detail. If NATO is a marriage, it is an unusually complex partnership, more a polyamorous commune with multiple overlapping relationships and atomic arms. Certainly, its multimember nature and internal drive for consensus make it an eternal challenge to direct and mould. 'Some folks are more transactional – "I want this for that" – and you can work with that,' said one senior NATO official. 'Sometimes there is an absolute bedrock principle and they won't budge at all. Then you look for ways of bridging the gap . . . finding the middle ground. Consensus isn't everyone saying yes. It's no one saying no.'[19]

Times of tension have sometimes delivered unity, but also savage rows. Rows over how to tackle the building of the Berlin

Wall in 1961 prompted Secretary General Dirk Stikker to warn his US colleagues that the alliance could 'not stand many more scenes like that of last Friday'.[20] More minor frictions and diplomatic wrangling are endemic. One present-day senior diplomat at the headquarters described her first encounter with NATO committee work as 'absolutely horrendous', with alliance members battling incessantly over individual words and punctuation. 'Only years later do you realise what you've learned,' she said.[21] 'The glue that holds this whole thing together is that there is an extremely strong conviction in every capital that the purpose of NATO is really worthwhile fighting for – and so unity is usually reached at the end of the day,' said another diplomat based in Brussels. 'That can take a very long time – it's the slowest boat in the convoy, so to speak, that decides how fast this organisation can move.'[22]

Resources are another permanent constraint. When most journalists or academics talk about 'NATO forces', they are often referring to the totality of all military units under the control of alliance nations. On paper, that is a vast number – statistics website Statista calculates that, in total, NATO alliance nations have some 3.35 million regular service personnel and another 1.7 million reservists.[23] Only a relatively small proportion of those, however, are allocated to NATO at any particular point in peacetime. When it wants to achieve something significant militarily, the alliance must either go back to its members or react smartly with what it has. That means the limited number of military assets the alliance directly controls at any given time – such as the handful of AWACS airborne early warning planes operated by the alliance since the 1970s – can find themselves deployed a lot to deliver useful headlines and presence.[24]

If it is to defend itself, it must also keep its secrets – and that has often been another challenge. During the Cold War, NATO was penetrated several times, with more than one senior official spying for the Eastern bloc. The Balkan and Afghan wars brought their own leaks, while the modern era has added cyber attacks to a growing list of threats.

*

It was March 2023, and NATO was making a quite deliberate show of force around the platforms of Norway's largest offshore gas field, Troll. Over the year since the Ukraine invasion, Norway had increased production of natural gas, feeding an anxious Europe missing the cheap Russian energy on which it had become increasingly dependent. Those resources, however, were under mounting threat, including from drones and submersibles 'actively mapping' critical infrastructure, including on the seabed. 'The Russians are more active than we've seen in years in this domain,' NATO Assistant Secretary General for Intelligence and Security David Cattler told reporters, describing Russian vessels – some with armed guards on board – taking 'more risks' in the North and Baltic seas.

Surrounded by a gaggle of reporters, Secretary General Jens Stoltenberg, European Commission President Ursula von der Leyen and Norwegian Prime Minister Jonas Gahr Støre disembarked from helicopters in yellow overalls and white hard hats. In the background cruised several warships from NATO's Standing Maritime Group, providing a signal of commitment to protect critical offshore infrastructure from a growing number of new threats. 'We have seen how President Putin has tried to use energy as a weapon,' said Stoltenberg. 'Norwegian gas has helped us respond to that [but] since these structures are so vital, they are also vulnerable.'[25] By May 2023 NATO's new 'cell' to track these risks was up and running, led by Germany's Lieutenant General Hans-Werner Wiermann. 'We have increased our vigilance and surveillance activities,' he said. 'We have significantly increased the number of ships patrolling . . . but we need to do more.'[26] It was a classic piece of NATO action – some smart use of military forces already allocated to the alliance, and some slick PR, including inviting TV crews aboard warships of

NATO nations and a briefing in Brussels – coupled with some genuinely useful coordination. Defending the entire continent against a concerted Russian assault, however, would be a very different matter.

At the Madrid summit in June 2022, NATO's national leaders authorised the alliance to take its most recent military thinking – dubbed 'Defence and Deterrence of the Euro–Atlantic Area' (DDA) – and supercharge it through actionable regional defence plans. They also approved a new NATO force structure, with three 'tiers' of readiness: 100,000 troops supposedly ready to move into action within ten days; another 200,000 at ten to thirty days' notice; and another 500,000 who could be mobilised in between one and six months.[27] Efforts to turn those plans into reality began immediately after, with the aim to get at least some ready for review in Vilnius a year later. The result was arguably the most concerted, urgent burst of military planning since the years following NATO's creation.

When Dwight D. Eisenhower arrived in Europe in January 1951, the only forces the new SACEUR had were twelve combat-ready divisions, compared to 175 on the Soviet side. The result was a challenge each NATO Supreme Commander and secretary general would face: how to construct a credible narrative of deterrence and defence with limited means and political constraints. But, as Eisenhower wrote to White House adviser Averell Harriman later in that year: 'The last thing that a leader may be is pessimistic if he is to achieve success.'[28] Leading NATO has always required that balance – an optimistic approach, and a willingness to act creatively. It has also required a lot of political awareness, particularly when it comes to reassuring vulnerable-feeling members that their territory will not be readily surrendered. As NATO's third Supreme Allied Commander Alfred Gruenther put it in 1953: 'I am charged with defending all of Western Europe, not merely the easy portions.'[29] Expansion since has only made that harder.

Throughout most of the Cold War NATO's war plans and

exercises were fiendishly complex, allocating tens of thousands of troops, hundreds of aircraft and entire naval forces including nuclear weapons. Their aim was twofold: to prepare for any fight, and to be seen as sufficiently credible by the Kremlin in order to deter aggressive action. That, NATO leaders agreed in Madrid in 2022, was needed once again. Few were blunter than Estonian Prime Minister Kaja Kallas. Her mother was six months old when she and her entire family were deported to Siberia after the Soviet invasion of 1940, returning only ten years later. Visiting Brussels shortly before Madrid in June 2022, she told journalists that her country would be 'wiped from the map' under current NATO planning, which lacked the forces to put up a concerted defence against a serious attack on the scale of that launched against Ukraine. As an aside, she said she had spoken to NATO soldiers of the UK-led force in Estonia – in the case of an invasion, she believed they knew they would be overrun, and that they did not like the idea any more than she did.[30]

As of mid-2023 NATO had around 10,000 service personnel deployed in Eastern Europe as part of its eight eFP groups in Estonia, Latvia, Lithuania, Poland, Bulgaria, Romania, Hungary and Slovakia. In the aftermath of the Ukraine invasion, SACEUR Cavoli ordered the eFP battle groups to increase their readiness so they could be prepared to 'fight tonight' – a tacit admission that that was not currently the case.[31] In Madrid, NATO agreed each battle group should be prepared to triple its strength to a full brigade in times of crisis – something the Baltic states, Poland and Romania argued should be done as fast as possible. 'This change will move us from an alliance that is optimised for out-of-area contingency operations to an alliance built on the purpose of large-scale operations to defend every inch of the alliance's territory,' Cavoli said. 'This is necessitated by the new realities we face.'[32]

Ever since Eisenhower first took the role in 1951, every SACEUR has been American – and, from his departure in

1952, also explicitly 'double-hatted', as the commander of all US forces on the continent. Critically, in times of war, that status should give them relatively unrestricted access to US intelligence and resources, as well as atomic weapons. Several other critical roles are also US-held – including the command of air and land forces across the alliance, as well as NATO forces in the Mediterranean. Others are divided across the rest of the alliance: Britain commands maritime forces while a French officer leads the long-range planning Allied Transformation Command in Norfolk, Virginia. The permanent chair of NATO's Military Committee responsible for bringing national defence chiefs together to make key decisions is also always a European or Canadian.

But since the job was created in 1952, it has been the secretary general that sets the tone for NATO more than any other individual. In its first seventy-five years, thirteen men have held the role – although there is a growing feeling it is time a woman had the job. Past holders include three Britons, three Dutchmen, two Belgians and one Italian, German, Spaniard and Dane – and the current incumbent, Stoltenberg from Norway. A more activist and larger NATO has often inherently found itself more controversial. Former Spanish physicist turned foreign minister Javier Solana, who led the alliance through the 1999 war in Kosovo, described the role of secretary general as being a 'catalyst for consensus'.[33] But he found that approach pushed to its very limit by the Kosovan conflict, in which the alliance almost tore itself apart.

Stoltenberg's father was UN ambassador, defence and foreign minister, and Stoltenberg himself was once termed 'Norway's Tony Blair'. As prime minister, he bolstered defences in the Arctic, sent Norwegian forces to Afghanistan and Libya – and negotiated with the Kremlin to end a border dispute that had run for decades. When Anders Breivik launched Norway's worst ever terror attack in July 2011, killing seventy-seven, his response was regarded as just the right blend of empathy and strength, securing his global 'brand'. At NATO's ministerial and national meetings, Stoltenberg's timekeeping and that of his team is ruthless, whether clapping his hands together to hasten a photoshoot or calling the meeting to order before evicting reporters. While some criticised him for his assiduous handling of Donald Trump during his years in office, others credit his management of that relationship – sometimes dubbed 'Trump-whispering' – with holding NATO together. Stoltenberg describes the sometimes tough bilateral and group negotiations as 'part of being secretary general . . . It is also part of being a politician. I've been a prime minister for ten years, I've been a minister for several years before that in the 1990s. Part of that is to take positions and negotiate and agree with people from other parties or from other countries.'[34] Taking over from Denmark's Anders Fogh Rasmussen in 2014, he also has the advantage of a single defining theme: his tenure has been dominated by mounting confrontations with the Kremlin.

In July 2023 his tenure was yet again extended for another year, postponing once again the endless diplomatic parlour game of guessing who comes next. As always, diplomats and officials remarked, the appointment would be made through a deeply untransparent process of negotiation between the major powers, and ultimately decided by the United States. 'What usually happens is you get agreement first,' said one diplomat at NATO. 'Then you have a meeting, and the US ambassador says: this person would be good. And everyone agrees.'[35]

Stitching up such deals in advance has long been an alliance habit. 'Ideally, you only call a meeting when you already know what decision will be made,' said Jamie Shea, who first joined NATO as a junior official in 1980 before retiring as Deputy Assistant Secretary General for Emerging Security Challenges in 2018, noting an element of theatre to many interactions.[36] The larger the alliance has become, however, the more difficult those deals can prove to be.

*

Just off the vast main hallway of the new Brussels HQ sits the chamber of the North Atlantic Council – universally known within the alliance as the NAC – and its supreme decision-making body. It is, most agree, the best home the NAC has ever had – dominated by a giant oval table, open in the middle to allow media photographers to take pictures at the start of otherwise secret sessions. At one end sits the secretary general – and next to him, when present, the Supreme Allied Commander Europe. Giant screens allow speakers – such as Ukraine's President Zelensky, who refused to leave his country in the first months of the war – to address the NAC remotely. Illuminated signs remind all that discussions are classified 'NATO SECRET'. Mobile phones must be left outside.

Inevitably, given the size of the alliance, NAC meetings that reach critical decisions often only do so after diplomatic shepherding, both by NATO officials and the more powerful delegations. Most of the day-to-day sessions – and there can be multiple each week on different topics – are attended by national ambassadors or their deputies, holding discussions as stepping-stones to the gatherings of foreign and defence ministers. These in turn now occur several times each year, both virtually and in person, building to summits of national leaders. The frequency of the latter has varied wildly over NATO's history, but it now seems increasingly established that they occur each summer.

As well as the actions of its enemies, much of the drama in NATO's history has come from the contest for influence and status between member nations and individual leaders. The national delegations at the headquarters are at the forefront of handling what that really means.

With thirty-one members, speakers often only have three minutes to address the NAC. Less formally documented are the bilateral and group discussions between the member states. They too often cluster in groups. France and Germany often work together, their positions frequently supported by Italy,

Spain and other Western EU nations – all of whom are sometimes accused by Eastern and other Central European members of being too soft or naïve about the Kremlin. Southern European states often stick together – a position formalised under the new regional defence plans. Those in the Balkans and the Black Sea complain their regions have been excessively ignored, while Britain periodically asserts a leadership position despite widespread speculation – largely consistent since 1945 – that its influence is terminally in decline.

Several nations – most recently Bulgaria, the Czech Republic and Slovakia – have shown a recent trend of alternating between pro and anti-NATO governments, a trend that some suspect might soon also become the norm with the United States. As illustrated with the potential expansion to Sweden and Finland, however, it is Turkey and to a lesser extent Hungary that have won the most significant reputations as the most disruptive states.

The NAC has often struggled to make decisions – and, with increased membership, in the early 2020s that situation is arguably becoming worse. Some in NATO suggest this is not necessarily a problem, providing consensus can be reached and all remain agreed on the need to defend each other, but that belief has not always been universal. NATO's second secretary general, former Belgian Prime Minister Paul-Henri Spaak, argued throughout his career that the right to veto by permanent members of the Security Council had wrecked the United Nations, and was unwelcome elsewhere.[37] In the 2020s some Eastern and Central European NATO members suggested that, in the event of an attack on any member, the triggering of the Article 5 self-defence clause should be a 'self-evident fact', even if not every alliance delegation was willing to vote to that effect.[38] Whether that 'self-evident fact' is enough for nervous nations to count on is another question. Quietly, over the last decade, some of NATO's members have begun to plan for what to do if the alliance proved unable to agree to 'play' in a time of crisis.

While NATO's regional war plans are – theoretically, at least – intended to provide the backbone of Western preparations, they are not the only options. Each nation that feels threatened has the option of negotiating its own bilateral and often secret deals with other allies, including the US – although whether an isolationist US administration would fight or not remains another question. Such secret plans have existed throughout NATO's history. There are also other structures – including the Joint Expeditionary Force (JEF), a UK-led military structure that also includes Estonia, Latvia, Lithuania, Denmark, Finland, the Netherlands, Norway and Sweden. 'The JEF is particularly important to us,' said one official from the Baltic states, where it is seen as a potential 'last-ditch' alliance should they be abandoned by the US and Western Europe.[39]

Whatever happens, Eastern and Central European states would likely fight in the event of a Russian attack. Poland, in particular – seen as the fastest-rising major military power in Europe following the invasion of Ukraine – could almost certainly emulate the Kyiv government in battling on alone if necessary.[40]

Even if no such conflict comes to pass, as NATO approached the Vilnius summit in the summer of 2023 there was also mounting discussion of what Europe's 'security architecture' might look like once the fighting in Ukraine ceased – with little agreement on whether Ukraine itself should join the alliance once the war was over.

It was a topic on which divisions would become more obvious in the run-up to Vilnius in July 2023, with Eastern and Nordic members committed to bringing Ukraine into NATO fast, but the US and others still reluctant. 'Ukrainian people deserve to hear what we think,' said Lithuanian Foreign Minister Gabrielius Landsbergis, one of the strongest supporters of Ukrainian membership. 'We have to have an answer for them.'[41]

Even more important, others warned, was that the alliance looked suitably serious if it came to a real fight. 'We will not have sustainable peace in Europe unless there is credible deterrence in Europe,' said Sinikukka Saari, an expert on Russian foreign policy and research director at the Finnish Institute of International Affairs. 'That is the bottom line ... even if the [Ukraine] war ends soon there will be no going back.'[42]

It was the same challenge NATO's founders faced after 1945, as those that had lived through two world wars worked desperately to stop a third.

Part 2:
Conception and Birth

Part 2

Conception and Birth

3

From the Ruins of Dunkirk (1945–1948)

'We have before us the prospect of two or three monstrous super-states, each possessed of a weapon by which millions of people can be wiped out in a few seconds . . . in a permanent state of "Cold War" with its neighbours.'

George Orwell, October 1945[1]

Hitler had been dead less than two weeks, and Winston Churchill was already planning for the next major European conflict. The Second World War itself was not yet over − but having won in Europe, the US was now firmly pivoting to Asia to defeat Japan. Following Franklin D. Roosevelt's unexpected death the previous month, the US now had a new, untested president in Harry Truman, a man neither the British nor the Soviets yet felt they had the measure of. Mainland Western Europe was in ruins, its military forces practically non existent and its citizens almost starving. The Soviet Union under Stalin had just conquered most of Eastern Europe, and Churchill believed it could keep as many as 200 divisions − several million soldiers − mobilised and ready to push further west.[2] 'I am profoundly concerned about the European situation,' Churchill cabled Truman on 12 May 1945. 'I learn that half the American Air Force in Europe has already begun to move to the Pacific theatre. The newspapers are already full of the movement of American armies out of Europe . . . In a short space of time our armed power on the Continent will have vanished, except for moderate forces to hold down Germany . . . Meanwhile, what is to happen about Russia?'

Within five years, the North Atlantic Treaty would be signed, locking the US, Canada and Western Europe into a lasting alliance that would hold back the Kremlin for three-quarters of a century. Conflict might rage around the rest of the world, from Korea to Angola, but not an inch of alliance territory would be lost between 1949 and the present day. But none of that was inevitable in 1945, with millions already watching their hopes of post-war freedom crushed under Kremlin rule. 'An iron curtain is drawn down upon their front,' Churchill wrote to Truman of the areas under Russian domination, using for the first time the phrase he would make famous in a speech in 1946. 'We do not know what is going on behind.' Without consulting allies, Churchill ordered his commanders to draw up Operation UNTHINKABLE, a unilateral British plan to launch an immediate pre-emptive war against the Soviet Union in mid-1945.[3]

How seriously it was considered remains impossible to truly know. British demobilisation – the release of UK soldiers, sailors and airmen back to their civilian lives – slowed notably and perhaps deliberately that May and June, perhaps a sign of official consideration that they might be required elsewhere.[4] Field Marshal Montgomery – thrown overnight from commanding Britain and Canada's armies to finding himself military governor of a swathe of Germany – later reported being ordered that May to cease destruction of German military weaponry 'in case they might be needed . . . for whatever reason'.[5] As its name suggested, UNTHINKABLE was a little mad. The plan's controversial willingness to turn Nazi Germany's only-just-defeated military into an ally was just one reason its existence remained classified until the 1980s.

*

The Potsdam 'big three' meeting in July 1945 was Truman's first true foray into great power politics. The 'little man from

Missouri' had never expected to be president. Returning from service as an artillery officer in World War One, he first went into business and then local politics before entering the Senate, remaining largely unknown overseas until he was picked as Roosevelt's running mate in 1944. Shortly after the Potsdam summit began on 17 July there was another shock, as Churchill and his Conservative government were swept from power, bringing more untested participants to the table. They would include the man who would strike the initial spark that started NATO. The elitist world of international diplomacy had never seen anything like him before, and arguably, it has not since.

Born in 1881 to a single mother in rural Somerset, Ernest Bevin had started work as an unskilled labourer aged eleven before founding Britain's most powerful labour body, the Transport and General Workers' Union. His early years, which included the Great War and Depression, all left him with a distrust for the ruling classes. But in 1922 he had returned from an international socialist conference in Berlin with an even deeper distaste for the Soviet state and its brand of communism. 'It is contrary absolutely to our concept of democracy,' he told a union conference afterwards.[6] From 1940, Bevin ran much of Britain's Second World War 'home front' as Minister for Labour in Churchill's coalition government. Following the election, he expected to take a short break in Devon with his wife before taking on another domestic role. Instead, he found himself in Potsdam.[7] New Labour Prime Minister Clement Attlee appointed Bevin as his Foreign Secretary specifically to stand up for Britain and a devastated Europe against the Kremlin. 'I thought affairs were going to be pretty difficult,' Attlee told Bevin's first biographer Alan Bullock years later. 'And a heavy tank was what was going to be required rather than a sniper.'[8]

The new US president wondered quietly whether the loss of Churchill might make it easier for him to cut a deal with Stalin. He was not impressed with Bevin or Attlee – describing them in a letter to his daughter as 'sourpusses' and commenting on Bevin's weight.[9] While Truman found Bevin's relentless anti-Soviet positioning annoying in Potsdam, he eventually concluded it was reasonable. After leaving office, Truman would describe his own mindset at the time as naïve, calling himself 'an innocent idealist' who had 'liked the little son-of-a-bitch' Stalin. In private conversation in Moscow on his return, Stalin told his deputy Nikita Khrushchev that the new US president was 'useless'.[10] Truman could be forgiven for having other matters on his mind. Throughout the Potsdam conference, secret communications kept him updated as the cruiser USS *Indianapolis* carried the atomic weapon 'Little Boy' to a Pacific air strip. On 31 July 1945, he gave the order for its use against Japan.[11] America's status as the sole possessor of the atomic bomb would, in the short term at least, mitigate at least some of Churchill's concerns of an imminent Russian attack. The Kremlin, meanwhile, was already doing everything it could to ensure America's nuclear monopoly would not last.

Three days after the formal Japanese surrender, on 5 September 1945, Soviet cipher clerk Igor Gouzenko defected in Ottawa. He handed initially sceptical Canadian officials documentary evidence of the scale of Soviet efforts to steal Allied atomic and other secrets. Over the following months, his revelations would kickstart a generation of US 'red scare' spy hunts, hastening the descent into what some already termed a new 'Cold War'. The battlelines of that confrontation were already forming. Defeated Germany was divided into occupation zones by the 'big three', soon to be joined there by France. French leader Charles de Gaulle would never forgive his allies for not inviting him to Potsdam, but he won his newly liberated country a zone of Germany to administer and a place at future four-way foreign ministerial meetings with the US, Soviets and British largely through force of character. These meetings, timetabled to take place several times a year from Potsdam onwards, were intended to keep the East–West wartime alliance functioning, but would instead become a venue for mounting confrontation and distrust.

As Churchill had feared, the military balance shifted fast. On VE Day in 1945, US armed strength on the ground in Europe was 3.1 million, falling to 391,000 by May 1946. Canada's 299,000 troops had gone entirely, leaving the UK as the largest Western military player in Europe with less than half a million personnel, also heavily committed across the unravelling British Empire.[12] The Soviet Union also demobilised – but it maintained three-fifths of its wartime strength of more than five million armed personnel.[13] Unlike Western states, it continued to plough huge proportions of its industry into armaments, building vast stockpiles of shells and ammunition that the West would never match, weapons that the Kremlin would still be turning to decades later in Ukraine.

The war's end had left the Red Army master of most of Eastern Europe – from the Baltic states and Poland through Hungary and Romania to the Black Sea. In October 1945, the first four-way council of Soviet, US, French and British foreign ministers in London was acrimonious, the participants unable to agree on the fate of multiple European nations. The following month, Soviet-backed Communists seized power in Romania's election through fraud and intimidation. 'It was now fairly clear we were heading for trouble in a big way,' noted Britain's Field Marshal Bernard Montgomery, now commanding occupation troops in Germany.[14] The Soviets there were stripping everything of value from their sector, he noted, while their conversion of East German railways to the wider Russian gauge suggested plans for permanent occupation.[15]

Repression was particularly harsh in the Baltic states. Estonia, Latvia and Lithuania were swiftly annexed into the USSR as Soviet republics, ceasing to exist as independent nations. 'Forest Brothers' partisans would fight for several years, prompting an even more brutal crackdown. As many as 200,000 people – 10 per cent of the entire adult Baltic population – would be deported to labour camps inside the Soviet Union. In their place, the Kremlin settled ethnic Russians, determined to entrench control forever. Absorbing the rest of Eastern Europe into the Soviet state was judged too complex – and likely to antagonise the US and Western Europe. Instead, other nations in the Soviet bloc became 'People's Republics', a formulation the USSR had first used in 1926 for Outer Mongolia.[16] Some were more independent than others – Soviet troops temporarily left Czechoslovakia in their entirety, while Marshal Tito's Yugoslavia also avoided outright Russian dominance.

Most, however, would be firmly under Moscow's grip. In the immediate years that followed 1945, hundreds of 'monuments to gratitude' would be erected across the Eastern bloc, many of Soviet soldiers commemorating their victory over Nazi Germany. But in Poland in particular, partisan resistance would continue for several years. Modern researchers believe around 200,000 Poles were engaged in active armed resistance immediately following the war, more than had fought the Nazis during the war itself. The last significant organised Polish combat units surrendered in the early 1950s, while the last partisan to die in combat against Soviet-led forces did so in 1963.[17]

*

That the post-war United States would remain globally engaged was not inevitable. As late as spring 1940, opinion polls had shown that 96.4 per cent of Americans opposed entering World War Two, and a return to isolationism remained genuinely plausible. Nor was a future as a military superpower encoded in its DNA. The US Army in 1939 had been the seventeenth largest in the world, with 189,839 officers and men. By 1945, it stood at 11 million – but many of them now wanted to go home.[18]

Within the US government, the first major post-war consideration of relations with the Kremlin came from George Kennan, a senior diplomat at the US embassy in Moscow. His

8,000-word 'long telegram' of February 1946 warned that the Soviet state had no intent – or even, in its current Stalinist state, ability – to embrace 'peaceful cooperation' with the West. Its strategy, he predicted, would be to undermine Western powers by fomenting unrest, deliver 'no-holds-barred' support to violent struggles in the developed world, and pursue the overthrow of governments when the USSR's leadership believed it necessary. Kennan stopped short of predicting outright war, but he made it clear that Washington should view itself in an era of worldwide and potentially bloody strategic competition.[19]

Churchill shared such beliefs. Now out of power, he accepted an invitation to visit Truman in his home state of Missouri. On 5 March 1946, with the US president beaming beside him, Britain's wartime leader unleashed his historic 'Iron Curtain' speech, laying into the Soviet Union for its domination of Eastern Europe and arguing that the future for the West lay in forging unbreakable alliances. Truman had seen the content in advance, telling Churchill it would 'do nothing but good' and 'make a stir'. But the response from the American press was extremely hostile. The *Wall Street Journal* warned that the United States had no need for alliances with any other nation, while the *Nation* described Truman as being 'remarkably inept' in associating himself with the occasion. Political commentator Walter Lippmann called the speech an 'almost catastrophic blunder'.[20] Back in Washington, a shocked Truman backed away from Churchill's words, telling reporters – incorrectly – that he had not known what Churchill was about to say. To placate a furious Stalin – who denounced the speech as 'a call to war' – Truman offered to send the battleship *Missouri* to bring Stalin to the United States and accompany him to the same state to give a speech.[21]

For those in Europe, the need for unity was increasingly unmistakable. Back in London in May 1946 as Chief of the Imperial General Staff – the professional head of the British Army – Montgomery told his staff to view 'a strong Western bloc' as central to any future war.[22] As the US approached mid-term elections in November 1946, it was clear America was at a fork in the road when it came to European affairs. 'In testing our mettle so often, the Russians are trying to find out . . . if we really mean to stay in Europe with both feet,' wrote *New York Times* reporter Edwin James.[23]

Not everybody believed America should. In September, Commerce Secretary Henry A. Wallace – FDR's previous vice president – made a deeply isolationist speech. He told an audience in New York it was the responsibility of the West to make the Soviet Union feel comfortable and safe, to agree guarantees of security 'even at the expense of risking epithets of appeasement'.[24] For Europe, this was terrifying stuff – but it would prove to be a turning point, forcing the White House to double down on previously lukewarm commitments to defend its allies. In a 20 September presidential statement Truman announced that Wallace's views on foreign policy and those of his administration – 'the latter shared, I am confident, by the great body of our citizens' – were in 'fundamental conflict', and asked Wallace to resign.[25] Europeans knew they had dodged a bullet. If Democratic Party heavyweights had not persuaded Roosevelt to drop Wallace from the vice presidential slot in 1944, he would have been America's first post-war president – and Europe would almost certainly have been abandoned.

The November mid-terms would see the Republicans take both houses of Congress, seen as a rebuke for Truman that pushed him to build a firmer cross-partisan consensus on the US's global role. As 1946 came to a close, Truman appointed George Marshall as Secretary of State. As America's army chief during the war, he had overseen the forty fold expansion of its military. Now, he would give his name to the Marshall Plan that would fund the rebuilding of Europe and set the stage for NATO's birth.

*

The winter of 1946–47 was one of the coldest in Europe in a generation, deepening the misery of a continent that in many places continued to get poorer. But it was also to mark the moment the United States and its European allies began finally working together in earnest to build a partnership against the Kremlin. For that, the initial energy would come from Britain – and Ernest Bevin in particular. Revitalising the Anglo – French partnership had been a key ambition of Bevin's since taking office, but relations with de Gaulle had made it difficult. The general had resented his dependence on London and Washington during the war, and was determined to chart an independent path. In November 1944, shortly after the Allies had liberated France, de Gaulle had even met Stalin in the apparent hope of reigniting the historic French alliance with Russia to counterbalance Britain and America.[26] In January 1946, however, de Gaulle had resigned as head of the provisional government, believing that by doing so, he could force a constitutional referendum that would give him proper power. But those leading the post-war Fourth Republic refused to consider such a notion. In December 1946 seventy-four-year-old concentration camp survivor and Socialist politician Léon Blum became prime minister of France. Almost immediately, British ambassador to Paris Alfred Duff Cooper suggested a much deeper alliance.[27]

Both nations were desperately short of fuel. In late January power shortages forced Britain to shut down swathes of heavy industry for weeks, something even German bombing had not done. However, the Attlee government was willing to use whatever resources it had for diplomatic leverage. When Blum wrote to Attlee requesting coal from both Britain and the US and British-occupied German Ruhr, he was immediately invited to London.[28] Bevin's lack of French hamstrung negotiations – partly remedied, according to Ambassador Duff Cooper, by his habit of telling 'a number of not very funny vulgar stories which were difficult to translate but at which Blum laughed very loudly'. Two days later, Britain agreed France would receive coal from the British zone in Germany, and Bevin had his initial agreement on a two-nation treaty.[29]

Within weeks Blum was replaced as premier by Paul Ramadier. Georges Bidault, the new foreign minister and a former head of the Resistance, was keen to move ahead but adamant that any pact should be explicitly against German aggression rather than referring to the USSR.[30] In part, this was intended to avoid antagonising Stalin – but it was also a measure of growing French nervousness that Germany might recover faster from the war and once again present a threat. Both Britain and France were also negotiating their own peace treaties with the Kremlin; formulaic and ultimately meaningless documents they still hoped might minimise the clearly growing danger of conflict. Diplomatically, these agreements also focused on the risk of war with Germany. The French suggested the new treaty with Britain should use almost identical language – particularly if it was to be completed before the next four-way foreign ministerial meeting in Moscow in March 1947.[31] Bevin was recovering from a heart attack, his condition serious enough for Washington to be asked to consider delaying that meeting's start. Britain was also struggling in the face of its own economic crisis. On 21 February, British embassy officials told their US counterparts the UK could no longer afford to bankroll Greece and Turkey, forcing Washington to plug the gap or lose the eastern Mediterranean to Communism. US officials refused to delay the Moscow meeting for Bevin's health.

The foreign secretary was determined to push ahead. Bevin and his entourage would head to Moscow by train, stopping on the way to sign the hastily written defence agreement with France on 4 March in the sub-prefecture office at Dunkirk. As in much of Europe, rebuilding had scarcely started in the town, pounded by the Germans in 1940 and the RAF in 1944. French Foreign Ministry chief Jean Chauvel later described it as 'destroyed to the point of resembling the excavations of the less preserved Greek cities'. Having holidayed on nearby beaches as a child, he scarcely recognised the place.[32] Another attendee recalled squalls of wind blowing in from the North Sea as a defining memory of the day. But he would also recall the enthusiasm of the remaining population of Dunkirk.[33] A film crew from Pathé caught footage of them waving Union Jacks and tricolours, clad in overcoats, mufflers and scarves amid the snow-blown ruins. As Bevin noted in his speech, the location inevitably brought 'profound memories', a reminder of the inescapable horror of the 'two great wars'.[34] On the French side, Chauvel had reservations over the Dunkirk location with its connotations of defeat.[35] Bidault was more upbeat, arguing it was an opportunity to banish such ghosts for ever.

Inside the civic offices, benches were set up for journalists and officials. Bidault and Bevin entered the room, then sat awkwardly in silence. The car of the British Foreign Office official carrying the treaty had become lost in the still-chaotic ruins. Soon, however, they arrived, and the signing went ahead.[36] The delegations headed to the beach where history had been made in 1940, each pledging that this time their alliance was 'for all time'.[37] As he passed through Brussels shortly after, a journalist asked Bevin if he favoured a similar pact with Belgium. 'I hope to sign a similar one with Belgium and all our good neighbours in the West,' Bevin later described himself as replying. '[Britain] will do everything possible to prevent a new conflict in the West, whether it comes from Germany or elsewhere.'[38] At least in Bevin's head, NATO was on its way to being born.

*

So too was modern Europe. In January 1947 Bevin had convinced the US to sign off the merger of American and British zones of occupation within Germany to form the single 'bizone' administrative unit. It was a significant economic gamble, leaving London theoretically responsible for funding half the bizone's costs. It would prove a critical step in the creation of West Germany.[39]

For all his upbeat comments, Bevin was depressed as he

headed towards Moscow, struggling with both his own health and the strategic situation. But March 1947 and the months that followed would finally see the US recommit itself to Europe, opening the door to NATO and the North Atlantic Treaty. On 12 March, as the foreign ministers began what would become a seven-week marathon in Moscow, Truman announced $400 million for Turkey and Greece. Outlining what would become known as the Truman Doctrine, he declared that Washington stood firmly against Soviet efforts to expand the Eastern bloc by violence or subversion. From the start, US officials realised wider support was desperately needed across Europe. With US Secretary of State Marshall in Moscow, his deputy Dean Acheson – a former governor of Illinois with close relations with the president – told congressmen that if those first two countries fell, others would follow like 'dominoes'.[40]

A whole generation of Americans were now persuading themselves of the urgent need for US leadership. As Marshall's Undersecretary of State for Economic Affairs, William Clayton, toured Europe, he concluded it risked a comprehensive economic and political unravelling. 'It is now obvious that we grossly underestimated the destruction to the European economy by the war,' he wrote. 'Europe is steadily deteriorating . . . millions of people in the cities are slowly starving . . . Without further prompt and substantial aid from the United States, economic, social and political disintegration will overwhelm Europe.'[41]

Travelling with the US delegation to Moscow were several Republican foreign policy heavyweights, including future Secretary of State John Foster Dulles and Arthur Vandenberg, chair of the Senate Foreign Relations Committee. A tougher line with Russia had bipartisan support – and the US team was designed to signal isolationism would not be coming back. Prospects for a serious strategic deal between France and Moscow were also on the rocks, much to the relief of the Americans and British. Persuaded perhaps in part by the Treaty of Dunkirk, the Kremlin now believed France was too deep within the Western camp to be extracted.[42] Back stateside in June 1947, Marshall presented the new US economic rescue package in a speech at Harvard University. US aid, both he and Truman made clear, was open to the Soviet Union and countries of the Eastern bloc – but it required recipients to open their economies to outside reporting and to US trade, conditions they knew Stalin and the Soviets would publicly reject.

Bidault and Bevin swiftly agreed to accept the offer, coordinating with the US to convene a conference in Paris for European states. Russia prevented Czechoslovakia and Poland from sending delegations. Stalin ordered Soviet Foreign Minister Vyacheslav Molotov to attend and then walk out after several days, hoping the Marshall Plan itself could be delayed or blocked through Soviet objections. The strategy swiftly failed, as the US made it clear conditions for the aid were non-negotiable. When Czechoslovakia still proved eager to explore the US offer, Stalin summoned pro-Soviet Prime Minister Klement Gottwald to Moscow to threaten him, making it clear to all Eastern European nations that taking American assistance would have consequences. Early in 1948, a pro-Soviet coup brought Czechoslovakia back into the Russian orbit, where it would remain until 1989.[43] 'The disappearance of Czechoslovakia as a free democratic state was the last straw on the camel's back – or, if you prefer, the flash of lightning which forced open the most stubborn eyes,' then Belgian Foreign Minister and later NATO Secretary General Paul-Henri Spaak said later. 'Everyone in Western Europe understood – and fortunately also in the New World – that if we wanted to prevent the continuing unbounded development of Soviet imperialism . . . then the Western countries had to unite, to draw together.'[44]

In September 1947, Canadian Secretary of State for External Affairs Louis S. St Laurent raised again the prospect of a defence alliance, telling the United Nations General Assembly that Western nations must band together. 'If forced,' he said, 'these nations may seek greater safety in an association of democratic and peace-loving states willing to accept more specific international obligations in return for a greater measure of national security.'[45] By December 1947 Bevin was determined to broaden the Dunkirk treaty structure to include other European nations. A defensive treaty, he said in a memorandum to the British ambassador in Washington early the next year, would 'create confidence and energy on one side' – the Western democracies – and 'respect and caution on the other'.[46]

Bevin's first attempt to pitch the plan to Marshall, in a late-night meeting at the end of the three-week December 1947 foreign ministers' conference in London, was somewhat unsuccessful. It had been an exhausting year of continuous travel, and the US secretary of state struggled to understand the detail. Returning from the meeting, Marshall called Jack Hickerson, state department director of European Affairs, instructing him to consult the Foreign Office the next morning and find out what Bevin really meant. Hickerson did so, and officials there outlined what they understood of their boss's thinking. References to 'circles' that had so baffled Marshall referred to suggested defensive groups of countries, a solid inner band of European nations – initially Britain, France and the Benelux nations of Belgium, the Netherlands and Luxembourg – supported by a wider network including the US and Canada. 'That is the first mention I ever heard of an Atlantic Pact,' Hickerson later said. 'Bevin didn't call it an Atlantic Pact . . . that was worked out later, but that was it.'[47]

Bevin's initial approach to Marshall brought no immediate success – the US secretary of state was still focused on getting economic aid to Europe agreed by Congress. Not until the start of 1948 would momentum build in Washington. But British officials now wasted as little time as possible creating a wider European security structure from the Dunkirk treaty. After the coup in Czechoslovakia, the smaller Benelux states needed little encouragement to join, and work was well underway by

Christmas 1947. On 17 March 1948 the Treaty of Brussels would be signed by heads of state as well as foreign ministers, including Britain's King George VI, Queen Wilhelmina of the Netherlands, Charlotte, Grand Duchess of Luxembourg and Prince Charles of Belgium.

That August, the Brussels treaty members would create the Western Union Defence Organisation, with military headquarters at Fontainebleau near Paris. Chairmanship of the Military Committee was offered to Montgomery, with its major subordinate commands split between French and British officers. This was the structure around which NATO's own military commands would eventually be built. By then, however, work on transforming the Brussels treaty into a truly transatlantic concept was already underway. The first faltering steps towards NATO might have been a mostly European affair, predominantly led by Britain, but the next chapter in its story would be written firmly in America.

4

Airlift and Alliance (1948–1949)

'A general stiffening of morale in free Europe is needed, and it can come only from action by this country . . . Willingness to fight for liberty is closely related to the strength of the help available.'

Memorandum from Jack Hickerson to Secretary of State George Marshall, 8 March 1948[1]

In the mid-afternoon of 31 December 1947, the US Director of European Affairs, Jack Hickerson, strode into the State Department office of his deputy Theodore Achilles and announced that the two of them were about to change the world.

'I don't care whether entangling alliances have been considered worse than original sin ever since George Washington's time,' Achilles later quoted his boss as saying, describing him as 'well mellowed' by drinks at the nearby Metropolitan Club. 'We've got to negotiate a military alliance with Western Europe in peacetime, and we've got to do it quickly.' A forty-nine-year-old Texan with a fascination for Europe, Hickerson believed that the Truman-era policies that counted were made by mid-level officials like himself. The Marshall Plan, in his opinion, was more the product of Undersecretary for Economic Affairs Will Clayton than the secretary of state whose name it bore.[2] Now, Hickerson was determined to create and shepherd what would become the North Atlantic Treaty through the complexities of the Washington bureaucracy.

'Fine,' said Achilles, the forty-two-year-old nephew of a

former governor of Hawaii. 'When do we start?' 'I already started,' said Hickerson. 'Now it's your baby.' In reality it would be a joint effort, with Hickerson firmly in the driving seat. 'It was a one-man Hickerson treaty,' Achilles told the Truman Presidential Archive in 1972 as he, Hickerson and other players gave a blow-by-blow account of how the treaty was delivered. 'It would be a long time before anyone would admit publicly that we were even considering a treaty,' Achilles told the archivists. 'But Jack and I knew clearly from the beginning what we were working for.'[3] Diplomats at the British embassy in Washington, told by London that their top priority was ending American isolationism for good, were similarly determined to involve the United States. 'Insofar as America was concerned, the leading [UK] objective was to help America become involved in a political and military alliance with Europe,' said William Edwards, heading up the British Information Services division in Washington from 1946 to 1949. 'When that actually was signed, I did feel I had seen a complete revolution in American public opinion in my short life.'[4]

Behind closed doors, Hickerson and Achilles hoped for something even bigger. According to Achilles, both had read *Union Now*, a 1939 book by Clarence Streit that argued the world's leading democracies should form a federal union – effectively a single country – to safeguard and promote governance and human rights. Both men privately hoped that creating the alliance might prove a key step on that road. 'We shared enthusiasm for negotiating a military alliance . . . as a basis for further progress towards unity,' Achilles later told the archive.[5] For Hickerson and Achilles, the first priority was to effectively overwrite Bevin's plan for a series of overlapping defence treaties and networks with something much more structured and coordinated.

Bevin's initial scheme, as he had suggested to the journalist while passing through Brussels in March 1947, was to create a larger version of the Treaty of Dunkirk to lock together the 'core' states of Western Europe, initially bringing together Britain, France, Belgium, the Netherlands and Luxembourg. Like the Dunkirk treaty, he initially intended to keep the alliance theoretically focused against future German aggression for ease of drafting and to avoid antagonising Russia. Writing to Marshall, Hickerson described Bevin's ambition as 'magnificent' but also a 'highly dubious' approach. He quoted a recent telegram from Belgian Prime Minister Paul-Henri Spaak arguing that a European defence structure without US membership was 'without practical value'. 'In my opinion a European Pact modelled on the Treaty of Rio de Janeiro is the best answer to the security problem for Western Europe,' wrote Hickerson. 'For such a pact to be really effective, the United States would have to adhere. I believe that this country could and should adhere to such a treaty if it were clearly lined up with the UN.'[6]

The 'Inter-American Treaty of Reciprocal Assistance' – known as the Rio Treaty – was a 'hemispheric defence' agreement, in which all signatories agreed to treat an attack on one as an attack on all. It had been signed in September 1947 by nineteen nations from across the Americas, and Hickerson and Achilles were soon determined to take it as a model to build their own Atlantic structure. Some senior US officials were openly opposed. George Kennan, now back from Moscow and director of the State Department policy planning staff, was dismissive of the idea of a wider military alliance, describing it as 'of little value', and suggested political structures to deliver greater US–European unity should come first, with military ones to follow.[7] It was, with hindsight, a strange argument – any such structure would have been much more complex and controversial than Hickerson's military alliance.

Hickerson lobbied furiously for the Rio Treaty formulation, going over the heads of some senior officials to propose it directly to the British. Meeting British ambassador Lord Inverchapel on 21 January 1948, Hickerson was cautious in terms of US commitments, but lit a flame of expectation that there might be more to come. The US was happy to see 'freedom-loving' European states come together, he said, with or without the United States. But providing such a structure was built in line with the United Nations Charter, the US might also be interested in playing a leading role.[8] In creating the UN in 1945, the wartime allies had hoped for an institution that would guarantee international cooperation. The UN Charter had also effectively outlawed wars of aggression – only the Security Council could endorse military action. That body, however, was now blocked by Russian veto.

The difference between the two institutions was quite striking. In building the UN, the US and its allies had taken what many hoped was a first step to a truly globalised, peaceful world. NATO would be a very different type of body, committed to defensive action only but built for confrontation.[9]

*

Addressing the House of Commons on 22 January 1948, Bevin made it clear he was still thinking of a much looser architecture of overlapping alliances, suggesting Britain's arrangements with different allies might be varied.[10] Simultaneously, however, both US officials and Belgian Prime Minister Spaak were now pushing much more aggressively for a more fully realised regional organisation.

Spaak had fought in World War One, then fled occupied Europe hidden in a truck in 1940. Now, he was among the most enthusiastic advocates of both European unity and a transatlantic alliance. 'He is more than willing to sign a secret military alliance with concrete promises on all sides for immediate action . . . if the United States is associated in some form with them, but he is afraid of a "high sounding treaty" with nothing effective behind it,' read a US diplomatic cable.[11] On 17 February 1948 the Benelux countries issued a joint note describing the idea of multiple variations on the Dunkirk treaty as 'inadequate' and instead called for a 'regional organisation of Western

Europe', with a Rio-style self-defence clause. 'The idea of a strong Western Europe to ensure peace, but without cherishing any aggressive thought against anyone, is an idea which opens up a way full of promise,' the tripartite statement read.[12] Britain and Bevin might have lit the spark for the alliance, particularly the Brussels Treaty, but it was now also being fuelled by other sources.

As the likely signatories met in Brussels to discuss the treaty at the start of March 1948, French officials told their US counterparts they wanted the agreement to have teeth. Foreign Minister Georges Bidault wrote to Marshall. 'The moment has come,' he said, 'to strengthen on the level, as soon as possible, on a military level, the collaboration of the Old and New World.' France was determined to do everything in its power to defend democratic Europe, he said, but needed US and Allied help.[13] Both diplomatically and domestically, the mood music was shifting NATO's way, prompted heavily by events in Europe. In Czechoslovakia, the February 1948 coup that swept from power the Prague government that had flirted with the Marshall Plan was followed by the 'suicide' in March of Foreign Minister Jan Masaryk, sending a shiver of apprehension across the continent. As local Communist parties contested elections in France and Italy, Finland was gripped by fear of an imminent Communist takeover; a spy scandal in Norway added to the tension.

In a top-secret memo to Marshall on 8 March, Hickerson expressed concern that more Western European governments might turn Communist, or that the Soviet Union might inadvertently start a war by underestimating US commitment to the defence of Europe. The best way to avoid this, he suggested, would be for Marshall to gauge Truman's openness to American membership of what he termed a 'North Atlantic–Mediterranean defence pact'.[14] The lobbying campaign was now relentless and increasingly multisided. On 11 March, the Dutch ambassador to the US told a senior US official the Brussels Pact would mean little without US support, and that a strong display of American commitment was vital to the morale of Europe.[15]

Things were particularly edgy in Berlin. From the start of the Allied occupation in 1945, it had been clear that the Kremlin wanted other nations out of the shattered German capital. At the very first parade of Allied troops, the Russian contingent marching alongside the British, French and US infantry battalions pointedly included a battalion of heavy tanks. Intimidation got steadily worse from there, with Soviet propaganda aggressively pushing the idea that the other allies would eventually quit the city altogether.[16] The Western allies were determined not to go. By early 1948 the US, Britain and France were advancing secret plans to create a democratic state of West Germany from the 'bizone', French territory and the allied sectors of West Berlin. When the Soviets discovered this in March, they furiously withdrew from the Allied Control Council that administered the city.

In Washington, Hickerson and Achilles focused on the bureaucratic process of building a larger treaty, and the political manoeuvrings to ensure that it passed into law. In 1919 the League of Nations treaty had at the last minute failed to win congressional approval, and the American diplomats were determined their new charter would not suffer the same fate. From Europe, Spaak and other European officials kept their US counterparts firmly abreast of negotiations on their new defence pact. On 17 March 1948, the same day King George VI and the Benelux royalty signed the Treaty of Brussels, Truman told Congress: 'I am sure that the determination of the countries of Europe to protect themselves will be matched by an equal determination on our part to help them.' Committing the US to taking every 'wise and necessary step' to achieve that aim, he warned it would require military investment, cooperation and a willingness to 'pay the costs of war'.[17] It was a critical presidential endorsement, both domestically and internationally. Writing on behalf of the Brussels Treaty powers later that day, Bevin and

Bidault described the speech as 'encouraging' and 'impressive', asking the US to provide clarity on the next steps.[18]

By now secret negotiations were already underway in Washington between British, US and Canadian officials, hosted in the basement of the Pentagon. Their explicit objective was a 'security pact for the North Atlantic area, plus an extension of the Brussels agreement'. The US should be a member of this pact, they agreed, together with potentially all nations bordering the North Atlantic – and perhaps also Italy. Future West German membership was specifically favourably mentioned, the next stage in turning it from a country under occupation back into a major European power. Creating what would become NATO, US officials believed, should be the beginning of a global network of alliances that could encompass other key US allies including Iran and currently neutral Scandinavia.[19] While the initial US–UK–Canadian talks were kept secret from most allies, they may not have been so from the Russians. In the room for almost every meeting was British diplomat Donald Maclean, based in the UK embassy to Washington but shortly to defect to Moscow. 'The Russians must have been getting a daily play-by-play account,' Achilles later said.[20]

By mid-April 1948 those proposals were in front of the US National Security Council.[21] European allies kept up the diplomatic pressure. If war came back to Europe, Bevin told US officials, there was no way Britain would be able to fight alone for more than two years, as she had from 1939. A transatlantic alliance was therefore the only way to avoid rapid, permanent defeat.[22] Churchill – now leader of the opposition – advocated even more radical action to US ambassador Lewis Douglas. Returning to the theme of Operation UNTHINKABLE, he argued the US and its allies should threaten the Soviets directly, warning them 'if they do not retire from Berlin and abandon Eastern Europe, withdrawing to the Polish frontier, we will raze their cities'. If such action was not taken, he said, a Soviet offensive in Western Europe was inevitable as soon as Stalin had the atomic bomb. Douglas noted diplomatically that he disagreed with Churchill on that plan – and, indeed, with Churchill's more limited suggestion to respond to any Russian action in Berlin by blocking their shipping from the Panama and Suez canals. On the broader fundamental point, however, the ambassador believed the old warrior was sound: 'We cannot appease, conciliate or provoke the Soviet,' wrote Douglas. 'We can only arrest and deter them by a real show of resolution.'[23]

Within Washington Hickerson and Achilles were directly engaging legislators. On the boat back from London at the end of 1947 Hickerson had persuaded Republican heavyweight John Foster Dulles of the value of alliance, and they had done a deal. Dulles would schmooze and win over his fellow Republicans on Capitol Hill, while Hickerson focused on the Truman administration.[24] Throughout the war, the State Department had wooed Senator Vandenberg, the sixty-four-year-old Foreign Relations Committee chair whose 1920s isolationism had been converted to invaluable support for the UN and other new international institutions. Vandenberg began working closely with Hickerson and Achilles, delivering the June 'Vandenberg Resolution' authorising the negotiation of a transatlantic treaty. Hickerson would refer to the Vandenberg Resolution as the 'springboard for the North Atlantic Treaty'. The text was drafted by Achilles, but with heavy input from both Hickerson and the senator, who wanted multiple references to the UN Charter to remind anyone who doubted that the US remained committed to those UN structures. It was an exacting process – Vandenberg demanded that the final text to be able to fit on a single page of paper, something that ultimately took shrinkage of font and margins to achieve.[25]

From March 1948, each train and truck leaving East Berlin for the West was searched by the Communist authorities, prompting US General Lucius Clay – the governor of the US zone – to order the US Berlin garrison be reinforced by air. Interference with road traffic continued through the spring, as

Soviet military aircraft 'buzzed' allied transport planes flying to and from the city. On 5 April a Soviet fighter collided with a British European Airways Vickers Viking, killing all aboard both planes. Behind the scenes the US, France and Britain braced for confrontation. Secretly, they were now preparing to issue a new 'Deutschmark' currency across the Allied sectors, including Berlin, effectively bringing a West German economy into existence overnight. It was another quite deliberate step on West Germany's path to statehood – and it was bound to infuriate the Kremlin. On 13 June, less than a week before the currency rollout, Clay warned Washington that Berlin was indefensible if the Soviets attacked – but that the US had no choice but to stay. 'Our remaining in Berlin is essential to our prestige in Germany and in Europe,' he wrote. 'Whether for good or bad, it has become a symbol of the American intent.'

The day after the 18 June announcement of the Deutschmark, Soviet guards halted traffic along the autobahn through East Germany to Berlin. As the currency was introduced two days later, a US military supply train was stopped and sent back to the west. The Soviets launched their own currency in East Germany including East Berlin, and warned that coming 'economic and administrative sanctions' would force West Berliners to accept it. On 25 June they moved to cut off West Berlin entirely. With roads, rail links and canals closed – and electricity cables severed – two million occupants of the US, British and French sectors now faced starvation and the collapse of basic services.

According to those who worked with him, the mercurial Clay barely stopped to consult the Pentagon, going direct to legendary US bomber commander Curtis LeMay, now commanding America's air forces on the continent. LeMay had coordinated the US aerial offensives against Japan, and would soon oversee the massive expansion of the nuclear-carrying Strategic Air Command. 'We're going to keep the city alive,' Clay told the incredulous airman as the general told him the most vital mission for his aircraft would now be 'hauling coal'.[26]

No logistics exercise on this scale by air had ever been attempted. On 26 June the US launched Operation VITTLES, the beginning of an airlift that would last 323 days. The RAF joined two days later. For those involved, it was exhausting and dangerous. Russian fighters would sometimes fly directly at US and British aircraft, daring them to swerve away. In total, the airlift would cost 101 lives, including 40 Britons and 31 Americans, with the loss of 25 aircraft.

Most of the aircrews had flown against Germany as an enemy before 1945, but US pilot Gail Halvorsen said he did not hear a single complaint. 'It was a time to heal the wounds of war,' he recalled in the 1990s, describing it as the 'pivotal point' of the early Cold War. 'The Berlin blockade brought the British and Americans and French and Germans together and brought them to a common goal.'[27] Behind the scenes Clay's aides said he briefly considered more aggressive action, potentially sending US troops to break the blockade on the autobahn to West Berlin, or US military engineers to forcibly fix a bridge the Soviets claimed was broken. He would make such a suggestion in writing in early July, but was rebuffed by a Pentagon desperate to avoid an outright war.[28]

As the airlift got underway in earnest, so did the secret discussions that would write the NATO treaty, the confrontation in Berlin delivering an added sense of drama. 'We met every working day from the beginning of July to the beginning of September,' Achilles recalled. 'That was before the days of air conditioning, and we all worked with our coats off. Most of us were already on a first-name basis, and we all were by the third day . . . The "NATO spirit" was born in that working group.' What that meant, he said, was an informal agreement that all members of the group, whatever country they were from, would work primarily for the good of the fledgling alliance. If they believed their individual nations were giving them instructions that would not work, delegates would go back to their government and try to get them changed.

The 1948 US election was now also underway – and one of the reasons for the heightened secrecy was to ensure the question of an alliance did not become an election issue. The initial official paperwork setting up talks made it clear no steps would be taken to write a treaty into law until January 1949. 'A leak, particularly during the political campaign . . . might throw the whole enterprise into jeopardy,' Secretary of State Robert Lovett told the group.[29]

From the start, the later-declassified minutes make it clear participants believed history was being made. The United States, Lovett said, had previously hoped for 'peace through weakness but that after many heartbreaks it had reversed its policy and was seeking to deter aggression by proof of determination'.[30] Multiple decisions were made that would shape the long-term future of the NATO alliance. Initially, the treaty was never expected to be indefinite in duration – the US team felt the Senate would decline to ratify anything longer than a decade, while France wanted a duration of fifty years like the Dunkirk and Brussels pacts.[31] The resulting compromise – an open-ended agreement that any party could call for a review after ten years and leave after twenty – was unexpected by all sides, but vital for NATO's long-term growth. A shorter-lifespan treaty might never have survived the Cold War, let alone its aftermath.

Not everyone appreciated the US dominance of the treaty-writing process. The British delegation wanted concrete early promises on US arms for Europe, which the US refused before more structures were in place to defend the continent. In private messages to London, British ambassador Sir Oliver Franks described the US as acting like 'a kind of fairy godmother handing out favours to the less fortunate Western European countries.'[32]

*

By September 1948 the working group had the beginnings of a treaty – but was entering a waiting game. As Hickerson later noted, the Truman administration was expected to be swept from power in the November vote, so any decisions would be best left to its successor.[33]

In Berlin, the airlift continued to intensify. At its height one aircraft landed every forty-five seconds in Berlin's Tempelhof Airport. 'None of us really expected it to last . . . for more than three or four weeks,' remembered aviation pioneer and pilot Sir Freddie Laker. 'It would either collapse or there would be war . . . But then it became like a crusade.'[34] As US and British authorities threw every available transport aircraft at Berlin, the US moved decisively to bolster Europe's additional defences. British Prime Minister Clement Attlee agreed to let US B-29 nuclear-armed Superfortress bombers – the aircraft that had dropped atomic bombs on Japan less than three years earlier – fly from British bases. An initial thirty-day deployment was extended to sixty days, becoming a permanent presence for the defence of Europe and setting the tone for decades of future military reassurance.

Montgomery's Western Union headquarters in Fontainebleau – UNIFORCE – was tasked to plan for the realities of war and deliver exercises that built capability and signalled Western resilience and intent. Resources, however, were severely lacking, with personality clashes worsening the problem. Montgomery had always been a challenge for contemporaries and seniors, clashing repeatedly with Eisenhower and others through much of World War Two. Now, his relationship with his French deputy was particularly bad – but he was also seriously worried that he lacked the troops to defend Europe if he needed. His outspokenness would sometimes prove extremely counter-productive, but it was central to his ethos, worldview and reputation with his troops. 'My present instructions are to hold the line at the Rhine,' Montgomery told London in an early cable shared by British officials with their US counterparts. 'Presently available Allied forces might enable me to hold the tip of the Brittany peninsular for three days. Please instruct further.' A reply is not recorded.[35]

*

The 1948 election produced one of the most unexpected upsets in US political history, with Truman confounding the predictions of pollsters and pundits that he would fail to retain the White House. Not only did he win the election, his Democratic Party took control of both houses of Congress. That brought a new complication to slow things down. Hickerson's ally, the Republican Vandenberg, lost his majority chairmanship of the Senate Foreign Affairs Committee to Democrat Tom Connally. The latter now also needed to be won over for the North Atlantic Treaty, something Truman handled with a personal charm offensive.[36] In January 1949 Truman appointed Dean Acheson as secretary of state. Acheson was popular with US lawmakers and foreign diplomats, coincidentally voted the best-dressed man in America that year. He would also prove critical to getting the treaty passed.[37]

As treaty drafts bounced between potential alliance members and congressional committees, Hickerson, Achilles and Acheson wrote and rewrote the text to find wording acceptable to all. The most important element of the treaty – the Article 5 'self-defence clause' – would also prove the most contentious. As well as declaring an attack on one nation an attack on all, some earlier drafts committed all members to taking 'such action as may be necessary to repel [it]'. Senators would not accept this, arguing that only the Senate could declare war. 'As *may be* necessary' was replaced with 'such action *as it deems* necessary'. This was enough to persuade US lawmakers they retained their agency, but the Europeans found it weak. Achilles and Hickerson told them bluntly that if the Senate could not agree, there would be no treaty at all. 'More than any other human being, Jack was responsible for the nature, content and form of the treaty,' said Achilles later. 'He insisted that it be short, simple and flexible, permitting maximum freedom of evolution.'[38]

The next significant questions were over who would join. Throughout 1948 it had become clear that multiple other European powers were extremely keen. While many of the Brussels powers would rather have kept the alliance tight, the US was particularly open to expansion, with France wanting Italy to provide another Mediterranean member from the start.[39]

Mindful of the Battles of the Atlantic in both world wars, there was a desire to get Atlantic islands to act as bases, particularly Iceland, Danish-owned Greenland and the Portuguese Azores. Discussions with neutral Ireland came to nothing – the Irish government said it would only consider joining NATO if Britain gave up Northern Ireland.[40] Portuguese officials were sceptical, according to Achilles, primarily because they feared French and British designs on their African colonies – but were won over with a message written by Achilles sent personally from Truman to Portuguese dictator António Salazar. Norway was in a particular hurry, having come under pressure from Moscow earlier in the year to sign a non-aggression treaty similar to that which had just locked post-war Finland in a neutral no man's land. Along with Denmark and Iceland, the Oslo government was in the midst of negotiating a defence pact with also-neutral Sweden – but this now fell apart. NATO membership was a step too far for 1940s Sweden, but it enquired whether in the event of war it could receive NATO military aid without joining the organisation. '[We] told them that they would of course be eligible, if there was anything left after everyone else's needs had been taken care of,' said Achilles. The Swedes declined to take the discussions further.[41]

By and large, those drafting the NATO treaty had avoided explicitly stating that decisions would require consensus. The exception was allowing new nations to enter the alliance, stated to require the agreement of each member. In 1949, the only country to be vetoed would be Spain, blocked by Britain's Labour government's opposition to dictator Francisco Franco.[42]

The geographic limits of the treaty were also heatedly debated. From the start, there had been questions over whether it might include US territories in the Pacific, or European colonial possessions in Africa and Asia. France wanted to include the latter, perhaps hopeful of additional forces to fight its own colonial wars, while US officials and senators demanded that they should be explicitly excluded. Eventually, the North Atlantic Charter was limited to what was defined as the 'North Atlantic Area', coming down from the North Pole to the Tropic of Cancer.[43]

*

At 2 p.m. Eastern Standard Time on Sunday 20 March 1949, the US National Broadcasting Corporation began a new eight-part series, produced in conjunction with the State Department. Its title made clear the scale of its ambition: '*The United States in World Affairs.*'

'Last Friday, the United States and seven other countries concluded the negotiations of a new treaty called the North Atlantic Pact,' Washington correspondent Richard Harkness told his listeners. 'The treaty will probably be signed here in Washington in a couple of weeks. After that, it will go to the Senate. Now is the time for the American public to study the purposes of the treaty, weigh its advantages, make up their minds about it – and let their senators know what they think.' Then he turned to Assistant Secretary of State Dean Rusk and asked him why the US needed a new treaty with seven other nations when it had only just established the United Nations, which was intended to protect every country in the world.[44]

Luckily, Rusk had plenty of talking points with which he could respond. The allegation that the North Atlantic Treaty undermined the UN was something the new allies were prepared for. On 31 March the Soviet Union wrote what was seen as a threatening memorandum to all twelve prospective signatories, arguing just that. A coordinated reply from all twelve nations came two days later, pointing to the text of the treaty and its repeated references to the UN Charter. The North Atlantic Treaty was intended solely to defend their members against aggression, they said, and did not identify any specific foe.[45]

European governments, however, were keen to leave their people in no doubt over what it meant. In a radio broadcast, French Foreign Minister Robert Schuman told listeners: 'We have today obtained what we hoped for in vain between the wars. The United States has recognised that there can be no peace or security for America if Europe is in danger.'[46]

On 4 April the twelve nations came together in the vast 'interdepartmental auditorium' on Constitution Avenue. The ceremony went without a hitch, save that the speech by the Portuguese delegate was so mangled that no one realised he was speaking English – and the English translator followed immediately with the same speech pronounced in a way that it could be understood. ('Nobody but the Portuguese knew the difference,' Achilles recalled later.)[47] The Marine Band played, Truman watched Acheson sign for the United States, Bevin for Great Britain and the other foreign ministers for their respective countries. For those who had worked to deliver it, this was a moment of high emotion. 'The United States was for the first time formally entering into the outside world, abandoning isolationism,' said William Edwards at the British embassy.[48] Privately, Bevin had warned his Cabinet colleagues barely two months earlier that final drafts of the treaty looked excessively 'feeble', including Article 5 which he said fell short of British hopes for a definite commitment to go to war if Europe was attacked. But even a weakened treaty was better than none at all. He pronounced himself satisfied with the eventual version, and basked in US and European praise for getting it started in the first place.[49]

A few hours later Hickerson and Achilles were in the basement bar of the Hotel Willard with a US Air Force sergeant
(implied by Achilles to be female) who had helped them coordinate security. 'After fifteen months of effort, worry and tension,
the treaty was a fact,' said Achilles. 'We could relax, grin at
each other, and really enjoy a couple of bourbons.'[50] It was not,
they knew, the end of the process – the treaty required ratifica-
tion by its various parliaments and the US Senate. The media
campaign was part of that – but Acheson had also been making
visits once or twice a week to Capitol Hill throughout the final
month of negotiations, talking both Democrats and Republicans through each detail of the treaty. He now steered it through
the Senate approval process.[51]

The Senate voted to ratify the treaty on 21 July. Sitting with
Acheson in his office after watching the Senate give approval,
Achilles suggested the treaty might be the start of a much larger
process. 'Dean, now we got this one wrapped up, let's go for a
full Atlantic federal union,' said Achilles. Acheson agreed. 'I'd
rather start with Britain, Canada and ourselves,' he said. A
committee between the three nations was set up shortly after to
discuss the prospect, but never gained real traction, leaving one
of the great 'what ifs' of history.[52]

For now, however, there was little structure at all behind the
commitments in the charter – no military command system,
little beyond the agreement for the North Atlantic Council and
subsidiary committees to meet. NATO had no troops, the
Western Union's forces were still weak, and only the US atomic
deterrent made European states feel anything close to safe. The
night before the ceremony, Secretary of Defense Louis Johnson
told Truman and Acheson, 'Neither the signing of the Atlantic
Pact nor any initial US military aid programme is going to
enable us to hold the Rhine line.' Truman concurred, warning
that 'Western nations are practically disarmed and have no
power sufficient to prevent . . . Soviet divisions from overrunning Western Europe and most of Asia.'[53]

Some countries, of course, were already overrun. In New York, Estonian envoy Johannes Kaiv wrote to the US State Department, describing the creation of NATO as a 'courageous move in the interests of universal peace'. Only the fact it was occupied by the Soviets, he said, prevented Estonia from joining the pact immediately itself. Similar letters were written by Latvian and Lithuanian counterparts, presumably coordinated. 'This expression of interest . . . on behalf of the Estonian people is appreciated,' Assistant US Secretary of State Rusk wrote back in May 1949. 'The United States, together with the other signatories . . . firmly believes that the treaty will contribute to the preservation of world peace as well as strengthen the devotion of freedom-loving peoples everywhere to the ideals of liberty and independence.'[54]

There was no pledge of any kind of support for those behind the Iron Curtain. It would be fifty-five years to the day until the Baltic states would join for real.

Part 3:
The First Cold War

5

Putting the 'O' in NATO (1949–1951)

*'As things stand . . . there would be scenes of
appalling and indescribable confusion in Western Europe
if we were ever attacked by the Russians.'*

Field Marshal Bernard Montgomery, June 1951[1]

On 29 August 1949, less than a month after the NATO treaty
had been ratified by the US Senate, the Soviet Union detonated
its first atomic bomb at a test range in Kazakhstan. The US
nuclear monopoly had lasted barely half a decade. Initially,
Truman was reluctant to believe the Russian breakthrough. As
NATO foreign ministers reconvened in Washington on 17 September, US scientists were still checking the data, preparing for
a public announcement later in the month.

The first formal ministerial meeting of the North Atlantic
Council in September 1949 lasted little more than thirty minutes;
its primary outcome the agreement of ministers to set up further
committees and events. Shortly afterwards, a communiqué was
issued with the letters 'NATO' proudly emblazoned on top of
every page, the first time it had been used.[2] The mood among
the senior attendees was mixed. If such decisions could be made
so easily, why had they been summoned to Washington in the
first place?

The answer, Hickerson and Achilles realised, was that they
had prepared 'too well', ironing out every detail beforehand
through the member embassies. Writing his memoirs later,

Achilles was unapologetic. 'It would help if more meetings were that well-prepared,' he wrote. But he was also, he conceded, at the point of absolute exhaustion, briefly referring himself to Bethesda Naval Hospital. The challenges of decision-making – particularly as long as the alliance lacked its own administrators – were fast becoming clear. As the alliance's Military Committee met for the first time at the Pentagon in October, all the staff work had to be done by US officers. A scheme to set up a military planning team of British, American and French officers in Washington prompted immediate complaints from Italy and Belgium, but would ultimately prove a starting point for future NATO structures.[3]

In mainland Europe the Western Union was now coming to the end of its first year of military activity, with US B–29 bombers training alongside British, French, Belgian and Dutch aircraft, tanks and troops. But secretly, Western officials worried about strategic credibility.[4] A US intelligence assessment prepared in 1949 warned that Russian military forces could overrun all of Western Europe and the Middle East as far as Cairo within six months, subject Britain to severe air and missile bombardment, wage serious submarine warfare in the Atlantic and launch 'a number of one-way bomber sorties' against the United States. Within five years, Soviet capability was predicted to have increased to the point where they could launch 'serious' air attacks against the US, deploy nuclear, biological and chemical weapons and permanently absorb Europe into the Soviet-controlled bloc.[5] Multiple NATO nations and the fledgling CIA set up secret armies to fight on in the event of Soviet occupation – embracing as they did so a number of dubious characters and entities, from the Italian Mafia to former Nazi elements. Rumours of this would emerge from the 1970s onwards, and be confirmed by officials in multiple countries from the 1990s, often to the detriment of the alliance's reputation.[6]

NATO's own first 'strategic concept for the defence of the North Atlantic area' landed on 19 October 1949. The US nuclear monopoly, the document stated, meant that it would be responsible for ensuring NATO had access to atomic arms in times of war. European nations were envisaged holding the primary responsibility for countering enemy ground and air offensives in Europe, with the US in a supporting role – something that would never really happen. Britain and the US would keep the sea lanes open, and other nations would be responsible for defending key support areas and bases.[7] Soon, a further 'medium-term defence plan' was underway, to be employed by the alliance by the middle of the decade. It committed the alliance to defending as much of its territory as possible – as attempts to recapture it afterwards might be impossible against a nuclear-armed foe. Again, how this would be coordinated remained unclear.[8]

The foreign ministers of the North Atlantic Council met four times between October 1949 and the following May, each session a major undertaking in terms of bringing the ministers and their staff together – and failing to break the mounting feeling that the alliance might be going nowhere. In its first year of existence, the increase in military force across the alliance was negligible. The November 1949 meeting saw an agreement to establish a Defence Financial and Supply Committee, with a host of commitments to standardise equipment and supply chains – but even those involved questioned whether progress was really being made.[9]

For the first time, NATO now had a small number of planners in London supporting those committees, located in two houses in Belgrave Square. The capability to deliver serious coordination, however, remained limited – while worries over the Soviet threat grew rapidly. An April report from the US Army quoted one senior Western official describing the world situation as 'gradually deteriorating'. 'Probably our greatest military danger for the next several years is that the Russian army will overrun Western Europe,' the authors of the report wrote, warning this might produce a 'prolonged war of many years'.[10] By 1950 the Soviet Union still had some four million troops under arms, and was able to call on a further 800,000 from across the Eastern bloc. The entire US military strength was now down to less than 1.5 million, spread across the globe, barely 10 per cent of that in 1945. Those forces available to NATO in Europe were described as 'a handful . . . ill-equipped and uncoordinated'.[11] That produced an alarming logic – if the Soviet Union were to attack, it might be wise to do so imminently, before Western strength recovered. 'In 1950, I began to think that the Russians would invade Europe in 1953,' British Chief of the Imperial General Staff Viscount Slim told a US interviewer in the 1960s. Quietly, Slim ordered preparations for a 'Group Z' call-up, designed to mobilise simultaneously all those with military experience, including those who served during World War Two.[12]

*

For all the worries of looming conflict within Western government circles, Western Europe's population was much more focused on rebuilding. The public appeared to be losing interest in NATO, while a new European project had now seized the attention of the US, European and British press. On 9 May 1950, French Foreign Minister Robert Schuman proposed a 'European Coal and Steel Community', wrapping together France, West Germany, Italy, the Netherlands, Belgium and Luxembourg. It was a crucial step towards what would become the European Union, a journey that had started exactly a year earlier with the creation of the Council of Europe in the Treaty of London between those six countries and Britain. Pooling coal and steel production would raise living standards and improve political stability. But it would also tie the hands of coming generations and make a future war between France and Germany, in the words of its founders: 'not merely unthinkable, but materially impossible'.[13]

The difference in ambition between the coal and steel

community and where NATO seemed to be heading was quite apparent – although the European desperation to keep the US involved in Europe stopped the NATO project from looking as irrelevant as it might against the new European scheme. For all the talk of greater political integration, the US, British and Canadian officials who had started the ball rolling on the alliance saw it primarily as a tool to defend the status quo. Those building what would become the EU wanted something much greater, a structure that would change the face of the continent forever.

Stuck somewhere in the middle was the Western Union, the still extant defence body of Britain, France and the Benelux nations. Its military chief, Montgomery, was now becoming deeply jaded, warning that in its current form the Western Union's forces and structure left Europe 'indefensible'.[14] Within ten days of Montgomery writing to his superiors to that effect, war erupted for real – but on the far side of the world. At 4 a.m. local time on the morning of 25 June 1950, North Korean artillery began a devastating barrage as its army poured into South Korea, supported by up to 200 Russian-supplied aircraft. Within hours, the kind of chaos Montgomery had feared in Europe was unfolding across the entire central Korean peninsula. South Korea's handful of aircraft were destroyed on the ground, while its outnumbered troops lacked armour, anti-tank weapons and howitzers. There was panic and retreat, with millions of South Korean civilians caught up in the crossfire.[15] Recent research suggests Stalin only agreed to let Kim II Sung attack South Korea because stolen US documents gave him the impression Washington would not defend its Asian allies. To use the more recent language of Estonian PM Kallas and Ukraine's Zelensky, he believed South Korea was in a 'grey zone'.[16]

Western leaders at the time believed the very creation of NATO a year earlier had already made Europe safer from attack. Now, the challenge was to make their defences credible enough so that Russia would not dare attack any member state either as a consequence of escalation in Korea, or once that conflict ended.

The US *was* almost completely unprepared for combat in Korea, lacking in relevant intelligence and with only limited forces on the ground. But in Washington and beyond, a strong feeling soon emerged that, like West Berlin, the peninsula could not simply be abandoned.[17] 'If South Korea falls,' US broadcaster Ed Murrow told his listeners, 'it is only reasonable to expect . . . that there will be other and bolder ventures.'[18]

Fresh from his success with NATO, Jack Hickerson was now running the State Department UN desk. With the Soviet Union attempting to delegitimise the UN by ceasing to engage with the Security Council, Hickerson and the New York delegation decided to push through an immediate resolution condemning the invasion and authorising a US-sponsored UN force to protect South Korea. Nothing like it would ever happen again at the United Nations – the Kremlin would never risk boycotting it again, instead turning back to its Security Council veto to block actions it opposed. A year earlier, the Atlantic Treaty negotiations had touched upon whether NATO membership short-circuited the constitutional right of Congress to declare war. This time, the Hill was barely consulted as the US raced to move troops and reinforce the peninsula. Truman was determined to defend not just South Korea but also the exiled Chinese nationalists now running their own government in Taiwan, sending the Sixth Fleet into the South China Sea to deter any attacks that might be mounted. It was a turning point for the alliance too. 'The Korean War did not so much change NATO as give urgency to ideas that already existed,' wrote historian Timothy A. Sayle in 2019.[19]

*

The May 1950 meeting of the North Atlantic Council had made one additional and critical decision – to constitute a

Council of Deputies in London, a body that would sit permanently in session. This was designed to facilitate decision-making in a crisis, and those who designed it hoped it would attract some of the most respected and high-profile individuals of each member nation. First choice for US deputy was William Averell Harriman, wartime US ambassador to both London and Moscow and now an adviser to Truman at the White House. During World War Two, he had conducted a high-profile and scandalous affair with Pamela Churchill, wife to the prime minister's eldest son – which Churchill had found it politic to ignore. In the bureaucratic world, Achilles described his reputation as 'a runner-up to God Almighty . . . The other governments would have had to produce at least ex-prime ministers or ex-foreign ministers to match him.' But Harriman did not wish to leave the White House, and no one of similar prominence could be persuaded to take the job. As the council met for the first time in July, most of its members were civil servants, many veterans of the 'working group' that had hammered out the Atlantic Treaty in secret sessions that hot Washington summer of 1948. They would provide the first iteration of the permanent NATO ambassadors and representatives that still endure today. Leading the first permanent US delegation was Charles 'Chuck' Spofford, a New York lawyer soon elected to chair the NAC itself, with Achilles as his deputy.

Despite the initial opposition of the US delegation, NATO now added further international staff. First was an administrative secretary, then an accountant, a spokesman and a deputy. Global attention, however, remained firmly fixed on the drama in Korea. Getting attention for the alliance in Europe and the US was proving difficult. In July 1950, Spofford hosted a dinner for American correspondents and broadcasters, asking them what it might take for NATO to become a regular feature on the world's front pages. 'It takes a person,' said one reporter, suggesting the alliance needed a military megastar as a high-profile leader. 'Get a top Supreme Allied Commander and you'll get publicity.'[20]

The speed of events in Korea continued to bring mounting shock. In the first two months of the war US-led forces were forced back to a perimeter around the port of Pusan, which was packed with refugees and encircled by the continuously attacking North Korean forces. Montgomery's warnings that the forces of the Western Union might only be able to hold the tip of the Brittany peninsula no longer looked histrionic. US forces, however, were able to maintain air superiority and keep the port facilities open, shipping in tens of thousands of Allied troops and finally breaking out from the enclave in late September.

If a Soviet offensive came to Europe, the war would be lost or won in West Germany, not yet part of the alliance. For many in the Pentagon and State Department that made West German rearmament a top priority, a view shared by Chancellor Conrad Adenauer. Mayor of Cologne on and off since 1917, fired by both the Nazis and British occupiers for his independent-mindedness and imprisoned by the Gestapo, Adenauer would not take no for an answer. 'The fate of the world will not be decided in Korea but in the heart of Europe,' he announced, calling events on the peninsula a 'dress rehearsal' for a European war.[21] In Washington, the White House and Pentagon told the State Department it needed to do whatever necessary to ensure West Germany could rearm, either as an independent nation or – perhaps less controversially – through integrating its forces into a larger European structure.[22]

The idea burst into public barely a week later, on 11 August, in a speech to the Council of Europe by Churchill, still out of office as the leader of the opposition but whose words – particularly with the Labour government now on its last legs – were still very closely listened to 'We should make a gesture of practical and constructive guidance by declaring ourselves in favour of the immediate creation of a European army under a unified command, and in which we should all play a worthy and honourable part,' he told the Council, shortly before it adopted a UK-written resolution to that effect. Britain's wartime leader more often favoured keeping Britain out of any unified European structures, and the implication that British troops should join such a structure was the closest he would ever come to explicitly favouring ceding such sovereignty to the mainland.[23]

In September 1950, Acheson opened a NATO ministerial meeting in New York announcing that only a militarily strong Germany could make Western defences credible and unveiling America's proposals for a rearmed Federal Republic. Unusually, the announcement had not been trailed in advance, and European representatives were left shocked and angry. French Defence Minister Jules Moch – whose Resistance fighter eldest son had been killed by a Nazi firing squad – announced immediately that German rearmament would only happen over his dead body. French Foreign Minister Schuman said that it would never pass the French Assembly, but pledged to find a way to move things forward,[24] a week later proposing a 'European Defence Community' including German troops within an international force in groups of squad-level size – around ten men. Under this plan Germany would have no national staff or military organisation, rendering its re-emergence as a military power impossible. The concept was approved as a basis for study – as, more importantly, was the peacetime appointment of a supreme allied commander from the US military.[25] Belgium's Spaak argued bluntly that the armies of Western Europe had been crushed outright in 1940, and only American leadership would be credible. 'Europeans have no confidence in their national military establishments,' he said.[26]

Events in Korea, meanwhile, continued to overshadow those in Europe. In September 1950, to relieve pressure on the Pusan perimeter, US-led forces conducted amphibious landings around Incheon, well over 160 kilometres (100 miles) behind North Korean lines, which signalled the start of a UN counter-offensive that soon seized back much of South Korea. On 1 October, as UN forces crossed into North Korea, Kim Il Sung requested China intervene with force – and fast. On 25 October the Chinese offensive began. As commander on the ground, General Douglas MacArthur openly called for the use of US nuclear weapons, only to be publicly rebuffed by Truman. It was, some in Europe believed, a concerning sign that the US might be similarly reluctant to use the atomic bomb in the event of a Russian offensive there, choosing to hold it back for the defence of the continental United States.[27] This was a worry that would never truly go away.

*

From the start, there was little disagreement between the United States and European allies over the preferred choice of SACEUR. On Monday 23 October 1950 Dwight D. Eisenhower – a civilian since stepping down as head of the US Army in February 1948 and now president of New York's Columbia University – received a message to phone the White House. He was immediately put through to Truman, who, Eisenhower later related in his diary, said, 'He should like to have me come to Washington for a conversation, to talk in general terms about an assignment for me involving a command for the Atlantic pact defensive forces.' By Friday 27 October, he was on a military aircraft flying to DC for talks. According to Lauris Norstad, at the time deputy head of plans and operations for the US Air Force who had worked with Eisenhower during the war, Ike was initially reluctant – not least because he had just promised his wife Marnie they could move to a ranch near Gettysburg.[28] 'They want me [for NATO] . . . because nobody else wants it,' Eisenhower told Norstad and another officer sent by the Pentagon to New York to get his views. 'Nobody else believes that it's going to work.'

'There's no one else can swing it.' Norstad told him: 'It won't work unless you take it on.'[29] Worried that events on the Korean peninsula might repeat themselves around the world, Eisenhower decided that he would take the job if given sufficient authority and directly ordered by the president. Truman said he would prefer that Eisenhower treated the offer as a 'request'. Eisenhower asked again that it be rewritten as a presidential order – possibly so he could tell his wife that was what it was – and he got his way.[30] During the war in Europe, Eisenhower had had a widely reported close relationship with his female army driver – something both always denied was a physical affair – but he had put considerable effort into resurrecting his marriage in the years that followed.[31]

The official decision on a NATO supreme commander came from the North Atlantic Council meeting in Brussels on 18 December 1950. The response was immediate. 'I am authorised by the president to say that before this day is out he will place under the command of the supreme commander the United States forces in Europe,' Secretary of State Acheson told the Brussels meeting. 'We hope that this action will be matched as soon as possible by other governments.' This was exactly the kind of grand theatre NATO needed to reinforce its narrative and deliver publicity and credibility. 'His name was associated with victory in the minds of millions and millions of people,' Lord 'Pug' Hastings Ismay, Churchill's former military assistant (about to enter NATO's story in his own right), later wrote. 'His appointment was a tremendous psychological asset to the alliance.'[32] Simultaneous to appointing Eisenhower, the NATO nations also accepted the proposal for a European Defence Community – providing it did not delay the rearmament of Germany. Other organisational reforms included broadening the Military Committee in Washington with representatives from each member state – precisely what the US had initially tried to avoid – and a new Standing Group Liaison Office in London to support the deputies.[33]

NATO's new US personnel were not wasting time. By the next day, Colonel Robert Brown – who had built Eisenhower's World War Two HQ before D-Day – was on the ground at the Hôtel Astoria in Paris telling his superiors that all he needed was 'a pocketful of dough'. He got funds from the Pentagon's European Command, together with several truckloads of US troops driving down from Heidelberg to lift boxes, furniture and equipment.[34] British Foreign Secretary Bevin, now extremely sick, was delighted with the outcome. 'It is given to few men to see their dreams fulfilled,' he said after the meeting. 'Three times in the last year I know I have nearly died, but I kept myself alive because I wanted to see this North Atlantic Alliance properly launched. This has been done today.'[35] As his biographer Alan Bullock wrote, Bevin's journey from a farm boy born in 1881 was quite unprecedented – no other senior Western statesman of the nuclear age had come from anything like such humble origins. His death was announced on 14 April 1951, and his burial followed in Westminster Abbey; Bevin was laid to rest alongside medieval kings and Victorian patricians.[36] In his tribute, Attlee described the Brussels and Atlantic Treaties as 'largely due to his initiative. He rightly regarded the establishment of the Atlantic Treaty as one of his greatest achievements, and history will confirm that.' For Churchill, Bevin was a 'valiant spirit' and 'wartime comrade', while Truman called him 'the embodiment of rugged honesty and the ancient English virtues'. Reuters reported that Radio Moscow made no comment, but Bevin's death was the final item on its news.[37]

6

The Eisenhower 'Spiral of Strength Going Upwards' (1951–1952)

'I rather look on this effort as about the last remaining chance for the survival of Western civilisation.'

Dwight D. Eisenhower, 1951[1]

On 1 January 1951, Eisenhower left New York for Washington for talks with Truman and the military chiefs before flying to Europe to build his new command. Writing to friends and relatives, he made it clear he felt the imminent threat to Europe was great enough that it might be the most important job that he would ever do.

Secretary of State Acheson outlined the task in front of Eisenhower in a memo to the president. 'The first fifteen months of the existence of the North Atlantic Treaty have been spent largely in creating the necessary organisational structure and developing plans,' he wrote. 'The time has now come . . . when plans must be translated into action.'[2] On the Korean peninsula, US, Australian and British troops fought savagely against advancing Chinese and North Korean troops. In the skies above, snatches of radio traffic in Russian and the arrival of new pilots with much better flying skills left Allied aircrew suspecting their Soviet counterparts had entered the war. Later evidence would prove those suspicions correct – the first Soviet squadrons arrived in November 1950, their jets carrying Chinese and North Korean markings.

Shortly after Eisenhower arrived in Paris, Montgomery told

him he believed Korea had distracted the Kremlin, and it would be unable to launch an offensive in Europe in 1951. 'In my view the most dangerous time will be in 1952,' the British general said. Eisenhower sketched out to Montgomery his battle plan in the event of any Soviet assault: he intended to reinforce mainland Europe, and build up huge reserves of airpower in the Atlantic and Mediterranean on multiple aircraft carriers commanded by NATO. Montgomery thought such plans and for now imaginary massive force unworkable, but appears – unusually – to have kept quiet.[3] In Paris, what would become the Supreme Headquarters Allied Powers Europe (SHAPE) was receiving its first senior staff, the vast majority American. Many had served with Eisenhower since the middle of the Second World War – and would guide NATO through much of its first decade.

Eisenhower would not formally take command until April, when he would officially move to Paris with his wife. In Washington, he had been frustrated to discover that the US had already launched consultations with the other NATO allies as to what SHAPE's command structure might look like. Eisenhower told Lieutenant-General Alfred Gruenther – his wartime staff officer known as 'the brain' for his grasp of detail, now appointed chief of staff – that this would just bring trouble. Eisenhower noted in his diary: 'We are going to find (as always) that our system will make everyone a bit angry, but now we've given them the right to advise and suggest, so we are going to make them believe we have violated their considered opinions instead of their casually expressed comments. In 1944, the British and Monty situation was not unlike this one.'[4]

How to use Montgomery this time round was another decision Ike would have to make. The two had corresponded in the autumn, Eisenhower sending the British general best wishes for his birthday in November 1950, Montgomery replying with his assessment of Europe's strategic situation: 'We need you badly:

to get the nations to cooperate genuinely, and to give firm decisions on which everyone will act. At present there is no genuine cooperation, and no decision.' Soon, Eisenhower was back in the air, embarking on a whistlestop tour of European capitals. The eighteen months that followed would often only merit a few pages in his future biographies, sandwiched between his defeat of Nazi Germany and ascent to the White House, but they would set the tone for the following seven decades of NATO history.

*

Born in 1890 and raised by devout Mennonite Christians, Eisenhower had chosen to join the army and attend its West Point military academy in part because there were no fees. Disappointed to miss a posting to the front during America's two years in World War One, he instead found himself as an acting lieutenant colonel running training for the new US Army Tank Corps – then demoted again to major in 1919 as the US military shrank dramatically in size.

It was a rank he would hold for another sixteen years, but that time brought unique and good experience. Major Eisenhower found himself taking US Army vehicles across the American continent from Washington to San Francisco – on appallingly maintained roads. He worked closely with several US generals, including Marshall and MacArthur, serving with the latter as he cleared 'Hooverville' protesters from DC in 1932 and then as a full colonel in the Philippines as war returned to Europe in 1939. Summoned to Washington after Pearl Harbor by his mentor Marshall, now head of the fast-expanding US Army, Eisenhower's rise became meteoric. Having received his first 'star' as a brigadier general in October 1941, he now rocketed through more senior roles as deputy chief of Pacific defences, deputy then head of war plans, and then assistant chief of staff running the new Operations Division. In June 1942, he was posted to London as Commanding General, US European

Theatre Operations, a three-star lieutenant general and the top US soldier taking the fight to Hitler. From the first US landings in North Africa to the fall of Berlin, Eisenhower led first US and then all Allied forces across the European continent. It was a fearsome responsibility and challenge that required managing complex personalities, including Churchill, de Gaulle, General George S. Patton and Montgomery.

Before landing in North Africa, Eisenhower had never heard a shot fired in anger – a measure of America's limited international engagement in the previous three decades, and a situation never close to being replicated in any senior US military career since. It was a reality Montgomery in particular – who had commanded in the trenches in France in 1940, and whose five-star field marshal rank from 1944, in theory, put him above Eisenhower, despite the latter being his immediate commander – could never quite forget. In the bigger picture, it did not seem to matter – and by the end of the war, Eisenhower was a five-star 'General of the Army'. In the eyes of almost everyone, he was a master of diplomacy and coalition-building, the architect of victory on the European continent and an infinitely safer and more reliable pair of hands than the mercurial General MacArthur would prove in Asia.

At Potsdam in 1945, Truman had offered to help Eisenhower get any job he wanted, including the Democratic presidential nomination in 1948. He repeated the suggestion two years later, offering to run as his vice president if MacArthur – whose presidential ambitions were never secret – secured the Republican nomination.[5] It was a remarkable suggestion, perhaps unparalleled in US presidential history – but it was also an acknowledgement that as a candidate Eisenhower might be impossible to beat. For Eisenhower himself, questions over a presidential run had begun during the war and would never stop. 'I do not want a political career,' he wrote in his diary on 1 January 1950, noting that he also did not wish to be associated with either political party.[6] Already, however, there were signs that this position might be shifting. At Columbia, he began to speak and think more on national matters, privately expressing his distaste for the Democrats and unending New Deal policies he viewed as wasteful. But he found his day-to-day job running the university frustrating, struggling to find understanding with long-term academics and bored of the endless fundraising.[7] As Eisenhower biographer Stephen Ambrose – author of *Band of Brothers* – wrote in 1983, the NATO job offered the ideal platform, moment and opportunity. As a serving officer once again, he would be 'above politics', yet simultaneously meeting frequently with world leaders in a way that would only enhance his reputation.

Few would ever be more genuinely personally committed to the idea of an Atlantic alliance. As he prepared to take up the role, Eisenhower told his son John, 'I consider this to be the most important military job in the world.'[8] Eisenhower's Columbia spell had allowed him to flesh out a public personality. Journalists and pundits talked enthusiastically of his charisma, drive and style, *New York Times* columnist Arthur Krock describing 'physical vigour, ruddy and pleasing countenance, a personal warmth of manner, high intelligence, professional competence and a most infectious grin'.[9] It was this 'star power' on which a young NATO was relying to turn around its fortunes. As Eisenhower's plane flew from capital to capital, his diplomatic aide Doug MacArthur – nephew of that general – was on hand with voluminous briefing materials on every nation. Little was ever read – the staff played bridge on every flight. 'Ike didn't need it,' wrote Achilles, now himself relocating to Paris with the US NATO delegation. 'He charmed everyone.'[10]

On 31 January 1951, Eisenhower returned to the White House and lunched with Truman, before the president ushered him into a top-secret Cabinet briefing. Seating Ike at the head of the table, Truman – who may still have harboured hopes of making him a Democrat – asked the soon-to-be SACEUR to relay what he had found in Europe.

The first thing to understand, Eisenhower said, was that both his appointment and the strategic situation were an indictment of the current state of Europe. Western Europe had a population of around 350 million people, enormous industrial capability and a highly skilled workforce – they simply should not be afraid of 190 million 'backward' Soviets. The reason that they were, he said, was that there was disunity in the West, while the Soviets were united.[11] It was a conviction Eisenhower would hold throughout his presidency and life, noting repeatedly in his diary[12] that it was simply vital for Europe to become politically united, and that nothing else would guarantee its security and way of life. As a political force, Eisenhower said he had concluded Communism was fading in Europe. More dangerous, he believed, was a rise in demand for 'neutralism', the belief – sometimes organic, sometimes deliberately fostered by Soviet-backed Communists – that Western European nations should be neutral. 'This appeals to the timid folks, and the indecisive ones who don't want to have to make up their minds.'

Serious post-war poverty reduced for now what European states could do – and this was why the United States must stay heavily involved for at least a decade. But the will to fight if necessary was clear. 'In Norway, for example, the people live on fish and potatoes and many of them are just scratching out an existence [but] we certainly don't need to have any doubts about Norway. The Norwegians went through one occupation and they aren't going through another one.' 'Gentlemen,' Eisenhower said to the assembled gathering in the White House. 'There is only one thing for us to do and that is to get this combined spiral of strength going up. These people believe in the cause. Now, they have got to believe in themselves.'[13]

The next day, he made the same pitch in a speech to both houses of Congress – again arguing that immediate American support in terms of equipment and personnel was vital, but that in the longer run Europe should be able to defend itself. It would take forty NATO divisions to make the alliance truly credible, he said, but only six needed to be American. 'It was, altogether, a convincing performance,' wrote Ambrose later. 'Reporters concluded that Eisenhower was far more effective in presenting NATO's case than the Truman administration had been.' Within weeks Congress had approved the dispatch of four additional divisions plus supporting air and naval forces for the continent.[14]

In truth, Eisenhower was being a little disingenuous in reporting the positive response he had received in Europe. As he told US Defense Secretary Robert Lovett, 'NATO needs an eloquent and inspired Moses as much as it needs planes, tanks, guns and ships.'[15] If he could be that Moses, he hoped the armaments would follow. On the ground in Europe NATO had only twelve combat divisions; the Russians 175. But Eisenhower still saw the real problem and solution were both political in nature. 'Our problem,' he told Army Chief of Staff Joseph Collins, 'is one of selling and inspiring.' To individual Americans who wrote in wanting him to run for president, he would reply with a rigorous sales pitch for NATO.[16] At his first meeting with staff officers in Paris, US Air Force General Lauris Norstad – now commanding NATO's air forces – watched Eisenhower lose his temper and bang the podium after multiple national representatives complained they did not have enough equipment or personnel. According to Norstad, Eisenhower responded in a voice that 'could be heard two or three floors below', bellowing that while he knew there were weaknesses: 'I myself make up for part of that shortage – what I can do and what I can put into this – and the rest of it has to be made up by you people. Now get at it!' With that, Norstad later recalled, Eisenhower banged the podium again and walked out. 'And believe me there was a great change in the attitude,' remembered Norstad.[17]

*

This was leadership through force of personality. Throughout his little more than one year in command, Eisenhower was almost constantly on the move, cajoling, encouraging and sometimes slightly threatening allied officials to get things moving with the urgency he wanted.

The general was not the only charismatic American touring Europe that winter. John F. Kennedy, thirty-four-year-old congressman for Massachusetts' 11th District, had spent the first five weeks of the year visiting Britain, France, Italy, West Germany, Spain and Yugoslavia, returning to Washington with a somewhat less rosy prognosis of the strategic situation. 'General Eisenhower was not completely frank with the Congress,' Kennedy told the Senate Foreign Relations Committee on 22 February 1951, arguing that accurate figures on European rearmament would show them lagging well behind. Congress should act now to specify a ratio of greater European troops than American to defend the continent, he argued.

It was perhaps the first time that argument had been made on Capitol Hill – that the US needed to add conditions to its defence of Europe, or consider pulling out. From this point forward, it would never be entirely absent from any US discussions over engagement with both NATO and the continent. Kennedy was no isolationist. Stalin was an old man who would likely not risk immediate war, Kennedy told the senators – but every month in which Western forces were weak brought risk. Nor should Americans be in any doubt that the Europeans saw US forces as their only hope and salvation. Kurt Schumacher, the leader of Germany's Socialist party, who Kennedy judged one of the most powerful voices in the country, had told one American visitor that what he wanted to see was 'American hostages' in Germany – US troops that the Soviets would have to kill or capture to take the country.

But genuine isolationist voices were now once again gaining traction. Months earlier, Kennedy's father Joe – the former US ambassador to London who had predicted victory for Hitler in 1940 – had argued in a speech that the US should withdraw from both Korea and Western Europe, warning that the continent would turn 'Communistic', and America's best hope was to keep Russia on the far side of the Atlantic. 'I do not like to speak for my father,' said the younger Kennedy after a senator had raised his father's speech. 'I still feel that we should take the risk to save Western Europe on the assumption that if a war does not take place for at least eighteen months, by that time, by urging and prodding Europeans . . . we will have sufficient forces to deter the Russians.'[18] Then, he and other US officials – including Eisenhower – implied, America might be able to pull back at least some troops, and let the Europeans take the lead.

For the first half of 1951 NATO's home in Paris remained the Hôtel Astoria on the Champs-Élysées, periodically a hotel but also previously the headquarters of US forces after the liberation, and before that of Nazi troops. Bedrooms and bathrooms were again converted into offices, staff perched with typewriters atop washbasins, bidets were used as wastepaper baskets.[19] The Astoria was central and offered a certain faded glamour, but otherwise it was not ideal. Its bar, restaurant and US military-run laundry remained open to outsiders. Security of the entire establishment was threatened by unrestricted traffic on all sides and easy access from nearby buildings to the roof, which housed a supposedly secure facility for military communications. The corridors and atriums were congested, made more so by military policemen and telephone points.[20] Montgomery was particularly unimpressed, describing the Astoria HQ as the most chaotic he had ever witnessed, worse than that of British forces during the Fall of France in 1940.[21]

Headquarters commander Colonel Brown and his French supporting officers threw themselves into the search for a new base with gusto. More than two dozen locations across France were surveyed, before the lack of secure telephone communications restricted the search to land west of Paris. Further problems were identified – local voices expressed opposition to putting the site too close to the Palace of Versailles, lest it be endangered in a war. One location judged ideal was in the possession of a famous racehorse breeder who refused to sell. Another had been previously owned by a vegetarian and anti-militarist, whose will stipulated that the premises could never be used thereafter for slaughterhouses or military activity. Anxious to secure a deal, Chief of Staff Al Gruenther requested a cable from Eisenhower to show French Defence Minister Jules Moch, hinting that it might be necessary to shift the HQ to the UK if matters did not proceed. As he did so, the resourceful Colonel Brown identified what would become the final site at Rocquencourt, in forests 25 kilometres west of Paris on the presidential shooting estate. The deal went through at speed.[22]

SHAPE now had about 150 officers on its staff, one-third of them American. British and French made up the largest other components, but every other country in the alliance was represented except for Luxembourg, whose tiny military was merged with that of Belgium. Small countries were struggling to find suitably qualified personnel – and concerns were soon being expressed that the overall flavour of the headquarters remained more American than was ideal.[23] Eisenhower and Gruenther had also finalised their chain of command. Earlier in the year, Eisenhower had told Montgomery that he wanted him to command NATO's land forces in any battle with the Soviets, not least as he did not know of any Frenchman capable of doing so. Diplomatic niceties forced a different structure: a northern NATO command under British control; the Mediterranean under an admiral from the United States; with Eisenhower retaining overall control of the key battle in the central region, alongside a subordinate French land commander. Montgomery would become Eisenhower's deputy, a key role of influence in forging the new structure and forces.[24] As Eisenhower declared SHAPE operational at the start of April, Monty sat in the front row of senior commanders in his trademark beret, the two military leaders who had liberated Western Europe beside each other once again. 'This is the first time an Allied headquarters has been set up in peacetime to preserve peace and avoid war,' said Eisenhower as the new site at Rocquencourt opened in June. 'We strive to lift from the hearts of men the fear of the prison block and the slave camp. We strive to create a Pax Atlantica.'[25]

In his diaries Eisenhower was at his happiest when visiting NATO troops, but he worried over their 'bewildering assortment' of obsolete weaponry, and what he saw as an absence of true Western leadership. At times, he privately expressed despair. On 5 March, Eisenhower described the role of SACEUR in his diary as 'dismaying and unattractive', and a week later pondered life as 'a slave, with one of the most irksome jobs ever designed by man'. Over the following months he vented over 'fatalistic, if not apathetic' defence leaders on a continent he believed the US could not afford to quit. 'God knows, I personally would like to get out of Europe and I'd like to see the United States able to sit at home and ignore the rest of the world. What a pleasing prospect, until you look at the ultimate consequences: destruction.'[26]

SHAPE's official (and initially classified) history makes clear the range of challenges facing NATO at this point – from whether to use expensive French civilian telephone lines to make calls to Washington; to reconciling pay and accommodation when senior officers in some European armies received less money than US senior NCOs. Money and space were invariably a problem – Paris was experiencing a post-war birthrate boom but had scarcely constructed new housing since 1940.[27] Whether Montgomery was helpful is unclear. 'Eisenhower came over here thinking it would be a very simple matter getting Western Europe and Atlantic Pact affairs moving along smoothly,' he wrote in March. 'I told him it would be difficult and gave him all my experience. He is now learning his lesson! It would not surprise me if he had a nervous breakdown before the year is over.'[28] To outsiders, however, progress remained apparent – and the tone of the official 'SHAPE History', written by officers who were there, suggests that they at least were having fun. 'No window has yet been designed which will let in sufficiently fresh air to please an Englishman, and yet keep a room sufficiently warm to please an American,' they wrote. 'The resulting hardship has been accepted by both nationalities as a sacrifice on the altar of international cooperation.'[29]

In the US, a growing sense of isolationism was now causing genuine concern. Throughout 1951 a string of letters and key figures in the Republican Party made their way to Paris, arguing repeatedly for Eisenhower's return to the US to seek the presidential nomination. Should he not do so, it would almost certainly go to Senator Robert Taft, son of former President William Taft, who had left office in 1913. Eisenhower had made a point of meeting Senator Taft before heading to Europe and had been concerned by his stance on foreign policy, Taft pointedly refusing to commit himself to supporting NATO. The meeting had prompted Eisenhower to tear up a letter ruling himself out of running for the White House, instead preferring to maintain an air of ambiguity.[30] Taft was also now increasingly aligned with former President Herbert Hoover, the last Republican to hold the White House before being ousted by Franklin Roosevelt in 1932. Eisenhower had once venerated Hoover, but utterly rejected his concept of an 'American Gibraltar', in which the US avoided overseas entanglements and relied on its nuclear arsenal to keep it separate from the outside world. A Taft presidency would be catastrophic, he believed, but despite Truman's ongoing outreach – both to himself and other Republicans – Eisenhower felt he did not wish to see another Democratic victory.

His greatest worries were over economics, particularly what he saw as wasteful and addictive New Deal-style spending. Truman had just submitted a budget with a $14 billion deficit to Congress, prompting Eisenhower to write an eight-page protest in his diary – even though he knew his own pronouncements as SACEUR and the war in Korea were pushing US defence spending to levels he increasingly believed were unsustainable.[31] Returning from a visit to the US Mediterranean fleet in autumn 1951, Eisenhower had confided to his diary for the first time his worries over the skyrocketing costs of modern arms.[32] Montgomery's concerns that vast fleets and equipment held ready for war between the Mediterranean and Atlantic were not practicable were being proven prescient. Although Eisenhower did not comment on it in his diaries, the British general's habit of being sometimes right was, along with his arrogance and pettiness, one of the things his contemporaries found most annoying.

How likely a major war with Russia really was, Eisenhower now realised, might be impossible to say. 'There is no greater probability of war today than it was two years ago . . . We can only say that properly balanced strength will promote the possibility of avoiding war. In this sense, we need the strength soon – but it must be balanced between moral power, economic power and pure military power.'[33] To Charlie Wilson, president of General Motors, Eisenhower wrote: 'Any person who doesn't clearly understand that national security and national solvency are mutually dependent, and that permanent maintenance of a crushing weight of military power would eventually produce dictatorship, should not be entrusted with any kind of responsibility in our country.'[34]

The crash militarisation of the United States and its allies that followed Korea was having consequences on the other side of the Iron Curtain. During a January 1951 meeting with party leaders and defence ministers from Poland, Czechoslovakia, Romania, Bulgaria and Hungary, Stalin demanded they begin their own military build-up, with a Military Coordination Committee across the Soviet bloc. By 1953 the Soviet military budget was twice what it had been in 1948.[35] Other shifts were also underway, both within NATO and without. In March 1951 René Pleven's French government collapsed, only to be reconstituted again under his leadership in August. In October,

Churchill returned to power in Britain – although the ageing giant had admitted he was now too deaf to hear a speech made by Eisenhower earlier in the year in which the US general enthusiastically pushed for the creation of a 'United States of Europe'.[36] When the two met later in the year, Eisenhower concluded the prime minister remained stuck in the past, attempting to relive wartime glories and taking on too much work through also being secretary of defence. On the 'European army' which Churchill had himself suggested, Eisenhower now found Britain's leader borderline opposed, apparently irritated that current proposals were too far from his original concepts. He particularly disliked the suggested creation of a European defence minister – a plan that might dilute his own current responsibilities, but which Eisenhower supported.[37]

Within NATO further important moves were underway. The first involved concrete steps towards extending the alliance to include Greece and Turkey, following months of unsuccessful efforts by US diplomats to secure their support against the Soviet Union – most likely through a British-led Middle Eastern military network or alliance. Neither country appeared interested in that – they believed that they must be in NATO to be 'safer', Eisenhower wrote – but like other US and NATO officials he was concerned the alliance might find itself overstretched.[38] Turkish and Greek accession was agreed in October 1951, and would be signed in Lisbon in February 1952.[39] Adding these countries considerably expanded the 'NATO area' eastwards, giving it a border with the Soviet Union for the first time. But it also opened the door to the 1953 and 1954 three-way treaties between the two countries and Marshal Tito's Yugoslavia, formalising the latter's schism from the rest of the Soviet-controlled Eastern bloc.

The shift from the previous year was striking. By March 1951 the US Army had doubled its worldwide strength in the first nine months since Korea to almost three million personnel, albeit spread between commitments in Asia and mainland

Europe. Agreements to create US air bases supporting NATO were made with France, including in Morocco, with Denmark for Greenland, Portugal for the Azores and with Iceland. Canada announced it was sending an army brigade and eleven fighter squadrons across the Atlantic as its contribution to the alliance, with European nations also beginning to significantly increase their efforts.[40]

How sustainable endless rearmament might be, however, was already being questioned. Eisenhower was right: if Western democracy was to be defended but not bankrupted, a balance must be struck. The result was a 'Temporary Council Committee' (TCC), to balance economic, political and military needs, commissioned when NATO ministers met in Ottawa in September 1951. The TCC commissioned what would become the first of several groupings of NATO's 'three wise men' to think the problem through. They were Averell Harriman from the US, legendary former French diplomat Jean Monnet and British industrialist and economic planner Edwin Plowden. They worked fast, supported by a small but effective international secretariat in Paris that delivered its own proposals for improving each country's defence effort, and the financial and economic steps that would be necessary to support that. The decisions of the 'three wise men' would set the tone for NATO's next round of military expansion, as well as its approach to similar problems in future decades. But by the time Eisenhower and other dignitaries filed past the coffin of King George VI in London in February 1952, it was clear the American's time in uniform was ending.

After months of pressure from friends and colleagues opposed to a Taft presidency, in October 1951 Eisenhower had finally secretly conceded his Republican allegiance and pledged to resign his commission if offered the nomination. In January 1952 he said the same in a public statement, his name immediately put forward by supporters for the New Hampshire and other primaries.[41]

7

Massive Retaliation, Massive Divisions (1952–1958)

'Two great powers will be in a position to put an end to civilisation . . . We may be likened to two scorpions in a bottle, each capable of killing the other, but only at the risk of his own life.'

J. Robert Oppenheimer, July 1953[1]

In barely a year, Eisenhower had built a genuine NATO military organisation and command structure – and he had done so at a unique point in its history. Never again would the Cold War see such immediate concern within Western Europe of imminent – and predominantly conventional – Soviet attack, driven simultaneously by the stark imbalance between the forces of East and West and the very real ongoing fighting in Korea. The February 1952 Lisbon summit would mark the high point of NATO's ambitions when it came to conventional military forces. The result was an ambitious commitment to take NATO's total strength to ninety-eight divisions of ground forces by 1954, all capable of mobilising within ninety days – an almost tenfold increase on 1947.[2] But the conflict that those forces were built to fight was already becoming much less likely – and this would become ever harder to ignore as the 1950s progressed.

At Lisbon, it was still possible to imagine a major war in Europe with fighting not unlike that of World War Two, albeit with the added horror of multiple, but perhaps only occasional, Hiroshima-size atomic blasts. That was, after all, the kind of conflict some, including MacArthur, already believed the Korean War could and should turn into, the US using its superior atomic arsenal and larger bomber force to break the conventional deadlock on the ground. It was, arguably, the sort of conflict World War Two could have become if the nuclear bomb had been developed sooner. For now, the number of nuclear devices available to either side remained extremely limited. In one early NATO planning session on the use of atomic weapons, commander of NATO air forces Lauris Norstad later recalled his planners making the assumption that US forces in Europe might only have fifteen atomic bombs available for use, each roughly the size of that dropped on Japan.[3] Such a conflict would be beyond horrific, but not quite unthinkable. Already, NATO planners in Paris were drawing up plans to coordinate civil defence in such a context: from building makeshift shelters in trenches covered with salvaged doors and furniture to coordinating an expected flood of refugees.[4]

By the end of the decade, the increase in numbers, strength and striking power of the Western and Soviet atomic arsenals would render such thoughts almost impossible, particularly following the development of the hydrogen bomb with its enormously greater yield. Nuclear war, national leaders and their populations came to realise, might produce almost instantaneous extinction. By the end of the 1950s, novels and films like *On the Beach* by Neville Shute – which portrayed stoic inhabitants of Australia awaiting the arrival of atomic fallout – would be attempting to imagine that reality.

*

As well as agreeing the massive – still largely unfunded – military build-up, the February 1952 Lisbon summit discussed the further development of the European Defence Community and 'European army'. More importantly still, it agreed that going forward, the North Atlantic Council would move its permanent sessions from London to a new civilian headquarters and beefed-up international secretariat also based in Paris. Even more importantly, given Eisenhower's more imminent departure – he would leave in June – ministers in Lisbon agreed the civilian NATO HQ would be overseen by a new secretary general – a position, it swiftly became clear, that nobody particularly wanted.

British ambassador to Washington Sir Oliver Franks declined the role by telephone during the conference, to the embarrassment of Foreign Secretary Anthony Eden, who had already told other alliance members that he would likely take it. Canadian Foreign Minister Mike Pearson quickly followed suit. Belgian Foreign Minister Paul-Henri Spaak was the next choice of the Americans, but he had already been too outspoken criticising France, which he viewed as an obstacle to European unity. The French delegation now moved to block him, arguing a little disingenuously that since NATO was now based in Paris with an American supreme commander, it was only right that the first secretary general should therefore be British.

This put Britain in a bind, as it still lacked a candidate.[5] One person who was particularly definite that he did not want the position was British junior defence minister Lord Hastings Ismay, acting as a deputy to Churchill who held the formal role. Ismay had complained of feeling like a 'fish out of water' in a seventeen-hour Lisbon committee hearing, telling SHAPE Chief of Staff Al Gruenther: 'This is the first I have seen of NATO, and thank heaven it's the last.'[6] But as Ismay almost certainly already knew, he was not just the frontrunner for the role, but the only name on the shortlist. With Eisenhower clearly on his way out to the presidential race, NATO needed another superstar. Ismay, one of the few senior officers to be able to manage Churchill during World War Two and one of the top 'go-to' guys for the Labour government in its aftermath, was closest to that requirement.

Like Montgomery and Churchill, Ismay – almost universally known as 'Pug' – started his post-Sandhurst military career in

India, followed by the World War One Camel Corps in East Africa. He had served as Churchill's principal staff officer for most of World War Two, handling communication between the prime minister and his service chiefs. After 1945, Attlee and Bevin had sent him to India as chief military adviser to Viceroy Mountbatten to help oversee independence and partition. On his return, the Labour government appointed Ismay to chair the Festival of Britain, a year-long series of events designed to lighten the post-war mood that created London's modern South Bank cultural district.

The Americans now wanted him for NATO – as Achilles put it, time was short and 'nobody could think of anybody else'. US representative to the alliance Charles Spofford told Churchill that if he could not deliver Ismay, Washington would choose a 'continental' for the role. The prime minister protested, describing 'Pug' as his 'good right arm', but Spofford was insistent.[7] A reluctant Ismay was summoned before Foreign Secretary Anthony Eden, who had returned from Lisbon sick and was now working from bed. 'I kept saying "no" as loudly as was permissible in a sick room,' Ismay later wrote, prompting the ailing minister to summon Churchill – now seventy-seven years old and in poor health himself – to the same bedroom to make his instructions even clearer. 'I felt like a defiant little boy who had been told that the head-master was going to deal with him,' said Ismay. When the prime minister arrived, Ismay made his plea for clemency – he was sixty-four years old, had spent much of his life outside Britain on his country's service, and neither he nor his wife wanted him dragged away again. Like all the wartime leadership generation, he was exhausted. But Ismay had also hero-worshiped Churchill since he had read his books as a young officer in India before the First World War, and was not going to turn down his plea to lead an organisation that might save the world. 'There was nothing for it but to surrender,' Ismay later said. 'Was the prime minister prepared, I

asked, to state categorically that it was my duty to accept?'
Churchill said that it was. Ismay acquiesced, and prepared to
move to Paris.[8]

*

By the early 1950s such war fatigue was almost universal. 'The
people of our countries don't want to fight another war,' Truman
told the third anniversary celebrations of NATO in April 1952.
'They want to prevent one.' The alliance's purpose was not 'to
turn the North Atlantic community into one huge garrison,
concerned only with defence,' he wrote. Instead, as it became
effective in deterring war, its members would focus on fighting
poverty, ill-health, disease and ignorance.[9] In Paris, the relocated NAC met frequently from April onwards, reducing the
need for as many meetings of NATO ministers. Ismay and his
team established NATO's International Secretariat, initially
using a prefabricated annexe next to the Palais de Chaillot, originally built for a UN General Assembly meeting in 1951. Soon
known as 'Papa OTAN' ('Father NATO'), Ismay prided himself on keeping the initial structure lean – by July 1954 the total
number of civilian staff, including interpreters and translators,
was still only 189.[10] They included Ève Curie, daughter of scientific pioneers Marie and Pierre Curie, a wartime foreign
correspondent and the first woman to hold a senior position in
NATO as special adviser to the secretary general.[11]

The Ismay era would see NATO take on many of the fea-
tures, functions and activities that would last for generations. They
would include NATO's four-pointed 'star' logo, widespread public
outreach programmes including NATO films, events and travelling exhibitions, as well as national 'NATO associations' at which
Ismay would often speak. As it settled in Paris, the alliance was
also taking on much of its modern character, including the endless backdoor dealmaking. 'Practically everything accomplished
through an international organisation is accomplished not in

meetings but in the delegates' lounge over coffee, tea, martinis, whiskey or vodka,' Achilles later noted.[12]

*

Partly because NATO worked in that idiosyncratic way, many within NATO had hoped Eisenhower's successor as SACEUR would be Chief of Staff Al Gruenther, a known quantity widely respected within both military and civilian circles. But Pentagon and State Department insiders in Washington blocked that appointment, arguing that despite his years at Eisenhower's side, he had never held a command larger than a battalion.[13] It would prove a short-sighted but predictable decision: replacing Eisenhower instead was General Matthew Ridgway, previously the top US and UN commander in Korea, where he had been credited with revitalising demoralised forces and pushing Chinese and Korean forces back. Ridgway would be the first SACEUR explicitly permanently 'double-hatted,' in command of both US and NATO forces, but from the start he faced unflattering comparisons with Eisenhower and struggled to work effectively in the unique SHAPE and NATO structures. Montgomery later described Ridgway as temperamentally unsuited to NATO, surrounding himself with an all-American personal staff. 'Morale began to decline. The crusading spirit disappeared. There was a sensation, difficult to describe, of a machine which was running down.'[14]

Ridgway's priorities, Montgomery believed, were wrong. Like Eisenhower, Monty too now believed the risk of an imminent Soviet offensive had eased – and that Ridgway was focused too much on the immediate 'hot war' danger and not strategies for the long 'Cold War' that was coming.[15] Across the world, from Indochina to the Congo, Europe's fading empires now faced multiple insurgencies, with local liberation movements often Kremlin-backed. Just as during the negotiation of the NATO treaty, the Truman administration remained committed to avoiding the use of US troops to maintain imperial rule – and was now also refusing to help Britain build an atom bomb.

Tired of being patronised by the US, the Attlee government had reluctantly concluded Britain must build its own nuclear device – 'Whatever it costs,' in the words of Ernest Bevin.[16] On 3 October 1952, as Churchill's new Conservative government approached its second year in office, the resulting device was detonated off Australia.[17] Less than a month later, three days before the 1952 presidential election, the first US thermonuclear device – 'Ivy Mike' – detonated off the Marshall Islands in the Pacific. The blast was 10.4 megatons, 750 times that of Hiroshima, creating a fireball two miles wide, a crater 200 metres in diameter and a shockwave and tsunami that swept nearby islands clean of vegetation. Tons of radioactive earth were pumped into the sky.[18] The aircraft and rockets that would deliver these warheads were also now evolving fast. On 15 April 1952 the first prototype B–52 bomber made its maiden flight, the first of more than 700 that would see it become the mainstay of America's airborne nuclear arsenal into the 2020s.[19] The same month, the US Army allocated the codename 'Redstone' to its first nuclear-capable ballistic missile – a direct descendant of Nazi Germany's V2, designed by the same creator, Wernher von Braun. It was set to be operational by 1955.[20]

As the votes were counted on the night of 4 November 1952, Eisenhower's victory became clear, taking 55 per cent of the vote to Adlai Stevenson's 44, the Democrat even losing his own home state of Illinois. At sixty-two, Ike became the oldest man to be elected president since James Buchanan in 1856.[21] Those who would dominate the coming years were itching to get going. Eisenhower's new Secretary of State, John Foster Dulles – whose brother, Allen, would run the CIA – started by advising him to move beyond Truman-era 'containment' to a 'policy of boldness' in world affairs – and, if necessary, to 'liberate' those behind the Iron Curtain.[22]

In his State of the Union address on 2 February 1953, Eisenhower warned the world could not 'indefinitely remain in a posture of paralysed tension, leaving forever to the aggressor the choice of time and place and means to cause great hurt to us at least cost to himself'. Then, unexpectedly, Stalin's death on 3 March opened at least the temporary prospect for rapprochement. The new Soviet leader, Georgy Malenkov, signalled openness. 'There is no disputed or unresolved question that cannot be settled peacefully by mutual agreement of the interested countries,' said Malenkov. Keen to deliver an armistice in the deadlocked Korean conflict, Eisenhower told his cabinet that talking to the Kremlin might be worth it. Simultaneously, the administration planned for a significant escalation in the war if a deal could not be found, threatening the Chinese and North Koreans with a renewed and potentially nuclear-backed US offensive if they could not agree.[23]

*

As NATO made its home in Paris, the French capital remained a febrile place. Radical left-wing anti-NATO demonstrations were an occasional fact of life, often accompanied by suspected Kremlin-backed propaganda campaigns. Ismay was now relishing his role, developing a secondary reputation as an expert on French horse racing, and sometimes giving tips to more junior alliance staff.[24]

As it would throughout the Cold War, the Kremlin was about to demonstrate the limits to its new post-Stalin softness. In June 1953 construction workers in East Berlin downed tools to protest over pay and conditions and call for democratic rights. The result was the first uprising in Soviet-occupied Eastern Europe since 1945, with tens of thousands marching through the city centre on 17 June, ransacking government offices, beating up police and tearing down Soviet flags. Almost immediately, Russian tanks poured into East Berlin. More than 250 men and women were killed, with a further eighteen sentenced to death and executed. More than 1,000 were imprisoned. For West Germans in particular, it was a shocking demonstration of post-Stalin Soviet brutality.[25] For a brief moment, the unrest looked as though it might spark a broader Cold War crisis in Berlin. BBC correspondent Charles Wheeler watched Soviet tanks firing into a crowd near the boundary line with West Berlin, some shots falling into the British sector. Allied troops, however, made no effort to intervene, their commanders too worried about sparking a much wider war.[26]

On 27 July 1953 an armistice ended fighting along the Korean peninsula in positions close to their pre-war starting points. Rightly or wrongly, Eisenhower and those around him concluded that the nuclear threat had been critical to the peace agreement, setting the course for an administration determined to avoid long-running 'quagmire' conflicts and committed to its nuclear 'big stick'.[27] As it conducted its own atomic tests in August, the Soviet Union claimed it now had its own hydrogen device, closing the atomic gap with the United States much faster than anyone had thought possible.[28] The grandiose thoughts of a hundred division-strong NATO force outlined in Lisbon in February 1952 were now unravelling. By mid-1953 member nations had convinced themselves that having met only two-thirds of that, NATO now had all the troops it needed – because any war was likely to be so apocalyptic that numbers of soldiers and equipment might almost be irrelevant.[29] The growing focus on catastrophic nuclear war now highlighted a major transatlantic division, one that would endure to the 1980s and beyond. Within the US, defence and diplomatic voices – and Dulles in particular – now believed that only through explicitly threatening the use of massive nuclear force in the face of even a conventional attack could NATO keep the peace.

Within Europe, however – where such a war might actually be fought – there was much less enthusiasm for talking in such terms. As far back as 1949, Denmark had explicitly requested that references to atomic arms be removed from NATO's strategy documents, largely over fears that they would attract too much comment and left-wing European criticism.[30] By late 1953 wider transatlantic divisions were also becoming clear. At a meeting in Bermuda that December with Churchill, Ismay and French Prime Minister Pierre Mendès France, Eisenhower expressed irritation that Churchill and the British looked on atomic weapons as something 'new and terrible', rather than a potential military necessity in the event of war. Churchill's spontaneous and highly emotional response was redacted from official records until the 2000s. The use of nuclear weapons by America, he said, would lead to Soviet retaliation in Europe and to the 'destruction of all we hold dear, ourselves, our families and our treasures; some of us temporarily surviving in some deep cellar under mounds of flaming and contaminated rubble, there will be nothing to do but take a pill to end it all'.[31]

Behind the scenes, 1953 had seen the transatlantic relationship shift subtly but substantially, driven primarily by the focus on atomic arms. Throughout the year, US State Department and Pentagon officials engaged secretly and separately with several European governments on specific weapons systems, initially particularly new artillery pieces that could fire both nuclear and conventional shells, the first 'battlefield nuclear weapons', that would shape NATO policy and disagreements in the coming decades.[32] 'The military threat may have receded, in part thanks to NATO,' the US delegation noted at the December NATO ministerial meeting, but it warned Soviet propaganda was becoming more sophisticated. In particular, the Kremlin talked of a 'Europe for the Europeans', essentially suggesting the eviction of the US while retaining Moscow influence.[33]

*

NATO now had yet another new military chief. In July 1953, after heavy lobbying from Montgomery,[34] Eisenhower moved

Ridgway from SACEUR to become professional head of the US Army and Al Gruenther, Chief of Staff since Eisenhower had arrived in 1951, became supreme commander. At the age of fifty-three, Gruenther had been the youngest four-star general in the US Army's history, and his reputation within SHAPE and the wider alliance was already a fact of life, as were his endless 'Gruenthergrams' requesting statistics and other facts he demanded for decisions.[35] Even more than Eisenhower, Gruenther had appeared to be going nowhere between the wars, spending seven years teaching mathematics at West Point. His grasp of numbers and detail – as well as the game of bridge – had turned that career around. A *Time* magazine profile would describe him as a 'human IBM machine, the perfect staff officer, the smartest man in the US Army, the most factual man of his times'.[36]

In Moscow, Foreign Minister Vyacheslav Molotov suggested a bold new proposal to Malenkov and Nikita Khrushchev, Stalin's former deputy now making his own bid for power. He suggested the Soviet Union should grab the diplomatic and political initiative by applying for NATO membership. 'Raising the question would make things difficult for the organisers of the North Atlantic bloc,' he noted.[37] It is unclear why Soviet officials dropped this headline-grabbing plan, which would be repeated in a very different era by Boris Yeltsin in 1991. Given the febrile tensions of the 1950s, it is hard to imagine any NATO nations showing appetite – but the move could still have been exploited for propaganda value in the developing world.

Back in Western Europe, the concept of a joint European Defence Community with its own force, which could include West German troops as an alternative to direct West German rearmament, appeared permanently stalled. The problem was relatively simple: while European states might like the concept theoretically, they resisted breaking up their own existing national armies to integrate them into the new force. In Bermuda, Eisenhower had briefly pushed Britain once again to join.

Deterring Armageddon 113

But Churchill, who had first introduced the concept of a European army, had long ago abandoned it.[38] Now, so would everybody else. In August 1954, the French National Assembly – in which the original proposal had been put forward by Schuman and Pleven – finally also rejected it outright. The US and European allies now moved immediately to admit West Germany to NATO, the formal application coming in October 1954. Britain, France and the US would cease their occupation, and Germany would become a sovereign state – one also admitted to the old 1948 Brussels treaty, which was amended to include limitations on the armaments it could build, while Chancellor Adenauer made unilateral pledges including that Germany would never build atomic, biological or chemical weapons.[39]

Getting German membership approved by the French Senate and Assembly was the last remaining hurdle – and it would not prove an easy sell. The US embassy in Paris furiously lobbied the entire French political establishment, particularly Prime Minister Pierre Mendès France. At a lunch with Theodore Achilles – now the Chargé d'Affaires for the US mission – and a *TIME Life* correspondent newly returned from Germany, Mendès France asked, 'If the Assembly refuses, surely the US would not go ahead and rearm Germany unilaterally?' The correspondent was blunt: 'I've just been in Germany and seen the equipment for four German divisions in the US supply depots. You can't put toothpaste back in the tube.' 'It rocked Mendès visibly,' wrote Achilles. Mendès France got the Assembly's approval shortly before his government collapsed. The next French Prime Minister, Edgar Faure, would have to get the treaty through the Senate, and that too was far from guaranteed. Asked by a French colonel at the new NATO Defense College in Paris – another Eisenhower creation – what would happen if the treaty were not ratified, Achilles gave a 'hell and brimstone' reply suggesting that the US might withdraw from Europe, while West Germany could do a deal with Moscow and 'become one of the Soviet republics'. The colonel turned out to be the nephew of the chair of the French Senate Foreign Relations Committee, who began using the same argument himself – a development Achilles judged 'highly satisfactory'.

After the vote was done, the US embassy in Moscow sent Achilles a leading article from a Kremlin-produced newspaper naming him as the key US diplomat exerting 'unconscionable pressure' on the French to accept the remilitarisation of an imperialist, expansionist Germany. Achilles described it as 'the nicest compliment I ever had'.[40]

*

NATO had come a long way from Bevin's late-night suggestion to Marshall in London in December 1947, through the spadework of Hickerson and Achilles, to build the North Atlantic Treaty. As 1955 began, it had acquired not just its essential structures but also its broader aims, pithily summed up in a popular quote ascribed to Ismay, that NATO's purpose was 'to keep the Russians out, the Americans in and the Germans down'. It now had a Soviet-run rival alliance to contend with too. As soon as West Germany was admitted into NATO the Kremlin began efforts to create its own defence structure across Eastern Europe, culminating in its formal creation in May 1955. Clearly inspired by the Atlantic alliance, the 'Warsaw Pact' tied together the Communist governments of the Soviet Union, Romania, Poland, Hungary, Czechoslovakia, Bulgaria, Albania and East Germany, potentially in perpetuity.

Imitation might be flattering, but NATO's ministerial meeting in Paris in December 1955 saw no shortage of concerns. Earlier in the year, Harold Macmillan – British foreign secretary now Eden had replaced Churchill as prime minister – warned the British cabinet that Soviet 'peace propaganda' was becoming 'dangerous'. A new word was now emerging: 'détente', although it would not enter popular usage for another decade. A French term for the loosening of a medieval crossbow more broadly understood as 'relaxation of relations', it had been used to describe the unsuccessful attempts of Germany and France to overcome their differences in the run up to World War One. Now used to refer to Kremlin efforts to improve relations, some Western officials believed its aim was nothing less than to divide NATO nations and unravel the alliance by making it look unnecessary. Russia, they worried, intended to dial back threatening behaviour in Europe until nations no longer felt they needed NATO protection. And then, they feared, the Kremlin might militarily overwhelm a now-divided continent.[41]

As they had since before World War Two, the US and its European allies continued to hold very different views on how to handle the increasing complexities of decolonisation – not to mention the multiple Soviet-backed insurgencies the Kremlin was now openly encouraging. In Kenya, Malaya, Angola, Mozambique and, most importantly, French Indochina (shortly to be known as Vietnam), the European states viewed their battles to retain control and influence as very much part of the wider Cold War struggle – and wanted them discussed by NATO. The Eisenhower administration was much more divided. The CIA under Dulles was not shy in its backing of anti-Soviet forces in multiple proxy wars, but the State Department was also keen to woo post-colonial states directly, whether or not their former imperial masters wanted that to happen. Nowhere was this more complex than in Indochina. In May 1954 the Russian and Chinese-backed Vietcong under Ho Chi Minh inflicted a devastating defeat on French colonial forces, besieging the French garrison at Điên Biên Phủ for fifty-four days before overrunning it completely. More than 2,000 French troops died in the final days of the battle alone; another 10,000 were taken prisoner, many later dying in prison camps or on forced marches.[42]

As the US began its slow but unstoppable journey following France into Vietnam, an even more immediate crisis brewed in the Middle East. The Truman administration had hoped to make Egypt the centre of a NATO-style Middle East Defence Organisation. The new emerging military strongman in Cairo, however, Abdul Gamal Nasser, had very different plans. A perennial contact of both the Soviets and the CIA, Nasser was a hero of the 1948 Arab–Israeli War and a poster child for emerging populist Arab nationalists. It was a world-view that saw both Washington and the Kremlin as allies of convenience, to be played off against each other for arms and investment. Israel, France and Britain, meanwhile, were unquestionably his foes.

By mid-1956, Nasser finally had the presidency and a target he was determined to secure for the Egyptian state: the Anglo-French company that had built the Suez Canal a century earlier and still sent its revenues out of the country to its stockholders. On 26 July, in a violently anti-Israeli, anti-British and anti-French speech, he announced it would be nationalised.[43] The Egyptian government made it clear it intended to keep the canal in full service. International alarm, however, was instant. Traffic through the waterway had been increasing steadily since World War Two – almost 15,000 vessels in 1955 alone, many of them tankers carrying Middle Eastern oil.[44]

Within minutes of Nasser's announcement, frantic diplomatic cables were tearing across the Atlantic. Early on 27 July, British Foreign Secretary Selwyn Lloyd told the US ambassador to London he believed an international military consortium should seize back the canal by force.[45] The French likened the seizure to that of Hitler's occupation of the Rhineland, and also demanded action.[46] At the White House later that day, officials suggested managing statements and discussions through NATO to maintain Western unity. Official transcripts quote Eisenhower saying he 'saw a good deal in this idea'.[47] But it was not to be. Secretary of State Dulles lobbied furiously against using the alliance. Through August, the US focused on finding international consensus, including with the Soviet Union and non-aligned states like India, sidelining France

and Britain. This would be 'jeopardised' by NATO involvement, Dulles wrote, the alliance becoming the 'whipping boy'
for anti-colonial sentiment in the developing world.[48] At the
NAC in September, the US delegation stayed largely silent on
the crisis, while Britain, France and Israel were already plotting
secret military action. Israel would attack, and shortly afterwards London and Paris would use that conflict as a pretext for
their own invasion.

As Britain and France prepared to strike – and the US did
everything it could to stop them – the Kremlin now faced its
own unexpected threat in Eastern Europe. In February 1956
Soviet General Secretary Nikita Khrushchev had given what
became known as his 'secret speech' to Communist Party officials, attacking Stalin for his 'cult of personality' and denouncing
the mass executions and deportations. Segments of the transcript, banned from widespread public consumption within the
Eastern bloc until 1989 were deliberately broadcast into Eastern Europe by the US-run Radio Free Europe with a view to
provoking calls for reform and potentially unrest.[49] In June,
Polish steelworkers in Poznan protested over rising food prices,
sparking a confrontation with Soviet-backed authorities that left
thirty-eight dead and 270 injured – but prompted some concessions from the Polish government, including a 50 per cent
increase in wages.[50]

This sparked calls for change in nearby Hungary. In October, student gatherings and demonstrations intensified rapidly
into major public protests and running battles with Soviet tanks.
The local Hungarian Communist Party found itself divided,
new Prime Minister Imre Nagy attempting to engineer a ceasefire even as new revolutionary committees seized control in
multiple cities and industrial centres. The Hungarian military
was similarly fractured, some units remaining resolutely loyal to
their Soviet masters while others joined the uprising. By the end
of October Nagy's government was on the brink of quitting the
Warsaw Pact. 'People were enormously optimistic that things

had changed,' said BBC correspondent Charles Wheeler. Most Hungarians, he recalled, believed that some form of United Nations or US intervention would keep the Russians from taking back the country.[51]

In Washington, however, the administration remained pre-occupied with Suez. Dulles made a point of showing Eisenhower written records of the Senate Foreign Relations Committee discussing the Atlantic Charter in 1949, highlighting the part in which senators stressed it must not pull the US into the colonial wars of Europe.[52] On 29 October, Israel struck in Egypt, reaching within ten miles of the canal – followed two days later by Anglo-French airstrikes and an airborne assault. Global disruption was enormous. While Nasser had closed the canal to Israel, other shipping had been passing through. Now the Egyptians sank vessels in the channel, blocking it until March 1957. Dulles described it as 'the blackest day which has occurred in many years in relations between England and France and the United States', and the Anglo-French military action as 'nothing but the straight old-fashioned variety of colonialism'.

The consequences for NATO were immediate and serious. Never before in its history had the key members been in such highly public disagreement. Ismay warned the crisis represented the greatest threat to the alliance since the signing of the treaty. German Foreign Minister Heinrich von Brentano pronounced NATO 'dead for the moment' – and with the US threatening to withdraw International Monetary Fund support for Britain if it did not withdraw from Egypt, Dulles wondered whether the US should take the unprecedented step of boycotting the next NATO ministerial meeting in December.[53]

In Hungary, news of the Anglo-French attack on Egypt brought outrage and depression. Charles Wheeler's BBC team were verbally and physically attacked. One Hungarian resistance leader told them angrily the Soviets would now act with impunity because the world's eyes would be on the Middle East and not on Hungary'.[54] The crackdown would indeed be ruthless. Hundreds of Hungarians were killed, and Nagy and other leaders were executed. It would be more than a decade before another significant uprising in Eastern Europe – Czecho-slovakia in 1967 – and another thirty years until it would begin to bring real change. As NATO ministers prepared to meet in December, the alliance found itself effectively a bystander to both Hungary and Suez, a venue for disagreements but not truly a player.

On 10 December, shortly before that meeting, the US sec-retary of state met British Foreign Secretary Lloyd in the US ambassador's residence in Paris. A humiliated Britain was withdrawing from Egypt unconditionally – although Lloyd said there would be an 'awful row' at home. Dulles did not mince his words – although he told the British delegation that 'revulsion' within the US at Britain's actions was easing. No one should think the US had acted because it liked Egypt more than Britain, he continued – Washington's ruthless actions to bring Britain and France in line had been necessary to prevent world war.[55]

The summit itself was more genial. The crushing of semi-independent Hungary and the traumatic divisions wrought by Suez delivered a salutary effect. Belgian Foreign Minister Paul-Henri Spaak described his colleagues as 'more NATO-minded than ever'. Dulles wrote to Eisenhower that there were 'no ser-ious fireworks and there is every evidence ranks will be closed'.[56] The December summit also heard from NATO's second set of 'three wise men', this time tasked to look into deepening non-military cooperation within the alliance. Italian Foreign Minister Gaetano Martino, introducing the report from himself and Norwegian and Canadian counterparts Halvard Lange and Lester Pearson, was blunt: the alliance had nearly fractured because some members had taken action in Suez without con-sulting the remainder. If NATO was to work, nations must agree to a 'considerable degree of pooling of sovereignty'.[57]

While all ministers publicly welcomed the findings, it was

immediately clear the big powers would not really let this happen. France declared the report 'interesting'. British Foreign Secretary Lloyd said the UK could 'broadly accept' it – before noting that Britain had 'worldwide responsibility' and could not consult on every issue. Dulles welcomed the report, before saying that members were not 'committing . . . to every sentence but rather to approval [of] general conclusions'.[58] It was a discussion that would set the tone for the coming decades. Every few years, NATO would discuss how to make itself either more effective at decision-making or more responsive to its smaller members. The real power, however, would remain with the US and the larger states, with the secretary general in the middle.

Events in 1956 would leave another lasting legacy. Every time future secretary generals faced a crisis within NATO, they could always claim it was not as bad as Suez.

8

Sputnik, *Nukes and Charles de Gaulle* *(1957–1960)*

*'I feel at present there are so many points in de Gaulle's thinking
and purposes about which we can only speculate.'*

**US Deputy Under Secretary for Political Affairs Robert
Murphy, handwritten note, 27 May 1958**[1]

In May 1957, Ismay stood down as NATO secretary general
after five years in office, to be replaced by Belgium's Paul-Henri
Spaak, who this time managed to overcome French objections
to finally take the role. At a dinner for his retirement, Churchill
asked Ismay if he had forgiven him for sending him to NATO.
'You were right, sir,' Ismay replied. 'As always.'[2]

Ismay had attended more than 500 Atlantic Council meetings, while the committees beneath the council had come together
no fewer than 7,000 times. NATO was, he said, a success – not an
inch of territory had been lost to Soviet domination, with the alliance achieving a 'degree of unity which would have been thought
impossible a few years ago'.[3] How true that was depended on how
closely you looked. NATO had survived the Suez crisis. Now it
needed to move forwards into a new era characterised by much
more powerful atomic arms and a growing risk of a truly apocalyptic war that must somehow be deterred.

In January 1957, Eisenhower met Harold Macmillan – who
had succeeded a fatally damaged Eden as prime minister – for
another Bermuda conference designed to revitalise the 'special
relationship'. NATO had almost fractured because Britain and

France became too close without consulting the US. Now, largely unintentionally, the two Anglo-Saxon nations were nudging the French out into the cold. That would prove more significant than many appreciated at the time. After the humiliation of defeat in Indochina, the French Fourth Republic was reaching the end of its life. In internal exile in France, Charles de Gaulle quietly plotted his return.

NATO now had its fourth SACEUR, appointed in November 1956 amid the Suez mayhem. Outgoing SACEUR Gruenther – now heading off to run the American Red Cross – was a tough act to follow. He had been in no position to stop Britain and France from acting as they did in Suez, but the alliance he left behind proved resilient enough for NATO's own military activity to continue largely uninterrupted.[4] Like his predecessor, Lauris Norstad had been with SHAPE at its 1951 inception – and before that one of the principal planners of the atomic attacks on Japan. Norstad would be the last of the 'Eisenhower dynasty' of supreme commanders, continuing to enjoy easy access to the president for as long as Ike remained in office. With film-star good looks, he would be the subject of his own fawning media profiles, dubbed NATO's 'Nuclear SACEUR' by his colleagues and the press.[5]

Little more than a decade after Hiroshima, the pace of rocket and atom bomb development remained relentless. By the time Spaak and Norstad took office America's Thor and Jupiter land-based missiles were about to enter service, capable of hurling an atomic warhead up to 1,700 miles. The US Navy also had its first nuclear strike capability at sea, with Regulus cruise missiles carried aboard a pair of World War Two-era submarines.

In October 1957, Russia launched the world's first ever satellite – '*Sputnik*' – from one of its new trial intercontinental ballistic missiles. Circling the world in a way no US space probe had done, the achievement devastated US confidence in its technological superiority over Russia. 'The US couldn't believe someone could be ahead of them in technology,' Sergei

Khrushchev, son of the Soviet general secretary, recalled in 2007. 'It was shock and fear. We were surprised by the reaction.' The Soviet authorities were determined to build on that, he said, grabbing the '*Sputnik* moment' to promote Kremlin achievements at home and abroad. It was a 'soft power' victory to build on the 'hard power' crushing of the Hungarian revolution.[6] The phrase 'missile gap' became ubiquitous, US pundits predicting that by 1960 the Soviets might have intercontinental ballistic rockets capable of bombarding the US, while America itself might still lack its own equivalent land-based missiles.[7]

This was just the sort of challenge that required unity, strength and new ideas for NATO. In Washington, both Eisenhower and Macmillan lobbied Spaak (dubbed 'Spaaknik' in the US press for the perceived visual similarity between the small satellite and his rotund figure) to make the upcoming December ministerial NATO meeting one for heads of government. As the US National Security Council met on 12 December, Secretary of State Dulles outlined Washington's plan. The mere presence of Eisenhower, he suggested, might 'rejuvenate' the alliance. But the meat of the US offer would relate to atomic arms and missiles.[8] Within the alliance, the idea of a jointly owned 'nuclear stockpile' had been around for years, initially proposed by France. US law required US nuclear weapons to remain in US custody during peacetime. Now, Norstad proposed the US transfer rockets to some of its closest NATO allies, co-located with US-controlled atomic warheads that could be fired in time of war.[9] It was, Norstad told the president, just the kind of bold, headline-grabbing plan to make the December summit a success – and potentially make up for less positive news, particularly the suggested withdrawal of thousands of troops from West Germany by a cash-strapped Britain.[10]

The December 1957 leaders' summit, the first in NATO history, would come to represent a significant step towards the modern pattern of NATO life – ministerial meetings leading to a grand summit, with deliberate pronouncements to deliver simultaneous consensus, headlines and deterrence. Together with Eisenhower's presence, the suggestion of 'nuclear sharing' did indeed transform the conference. The president, much weakened by a recent minor stroke and strictly supervised by his doctors, was forced to hand over the second half of his speech to Dulles to finish. Crowds lined the roads in Paris to cheer him, and Macmillan judged the meeting 'a definite plus for the free world'.[11] While the exact details of the nuclear stockpile deal would evolve, it represented the most significant step the alliance had taken since Lisbon in 1952. The alliance would enter the 1960s with US-built missiles deployed in Britain, Italy and Turkey – manned by host nation forces while the warheads were supervised by US personnel. 'Nuclear sharing' would remain a central if rarely discussed aspect of NATO, with twenty-first-century nuclear bombs still in US bunkers in multiple European NATO nations for transfer to respective air forces were atomic war to come.

The deployment of US nuclear missiles in Europe would also have a significant effect on the psyche of the Russian leadership, banishing the brief post-*Sputnik* feeling of superiority and confidence. As Soviet premier Nikita Khrushchev holidayed in the Black Sea, he would brood over the US Jupiter missiles beyond the horizon 'aimed at this, my dacha'.[12]

*

In May 1958, troops and right-wingers acting with the connivance of France's top military commanders seized power in Algiers. The 1950s had seen France humbled in Indochina, and now France's military elite believed Algeria might be about to be surrendered. In language reminiscent of the French Revolution, they formed their own 'Committee of Public Safety' just as new Prime Minister Pierre Pflimlin – seen to favour negotiation with Algerian anti-colonial nationalists – was about to be sworn in. General Salan, the commander in Algiers, was ordered to restore control, but instead backed the coup and – with a little encouragement from the general's supporters – shouted, '*Vive de Gaulle*' from the governor's balcony.

When de Gaulle had resigned as French prime minister in January 1946, unable to control the squabbling parties of his coalition, he expected to return to office within a week to dictate a new constitution. Instead, he had spent twelve years in self-imposed political exile.[13] As two French officers representing the plotters flew from Algiers to Paris to find out his thoughts, de Gaulle gave a press conference in Paris suggesting 'the extremely grave national crisis' might be 'the beginning of some kind of resurrection', explicitly offering himself to be 'useful' to his country once again. British embassy staff in attendance described him as looking older and more frail, but the 'master of the situation', not associating himself directly with the rebels but also failing to condemn them or defend conventional democracy. On 24 May, another Committee of Public Safety seized control in Corsica with the bloodless support of locally-based paratroopers. In Algeria, plans were drawn up to overthrow the government in Paris, with 50,000 airborne troops from Algeria and south-west France. The exercise was dubbed 'Operation RESURRECTION' in a clear reference to de Gaulle's words.[14]

For NATO, this was a new kind of crisis. NATO press officers in Paris refused to comment on the situation – even when French Mediterranean fleet units earmarked for NATO became involved. According to the official SHAPE history, General Norstad – in Malta for a visit – was 'advised' not to return to his HQ in Paris 'as this action might lead to an increase in the general nervousness'.[15] It was not – quite – a military coup. While de Gaulle clearly owed the rebels for his return to power, he never publicly endorsed their actions – and his accession to the premiership was democratically endorsed by the majority of the French Assembly amid fears of civil war.[16] But it was hardly an example of pluralistic democracy either. Secretary of State Dulles told Eisenhower that de Gaulle might still be the only thing standing between France and chaos, or a potentially Communist-backed 'popular front'.[17] By early July, US officials had identified the likely next looming stumbling blocks to their relationship: de Gaulle's wish to make NATO do more globally, coupled with his desire for a French nuclear bomb – and tighter control over any US weapons on French soil. Determined to restore France as a great power, de Gaulle almost immediately suggested to British and French officials that they set up what US officials were already describing as 'a US–UK–France triumvirate to run the world',[18] – something dismissed by Eisenhower as 'completely unrealistic and to be avoided'.[19]

As Dulles met de Gaulle in Paris on 5 July, both knew this might be the opening of a diplomatic marathon. NATO in its current form, the general said, was 'unsatisfactory', although he declared himself personally impressed with Norstad and Spaak. The Frenchman wanted NATO to immediately expand to include operations in the Middle East and Africa. He rejected the concept of 'nuclear sharing', saying that any nuclear weapons on French territory must be under French control.[20]

As de Gaulle prepared for what would be almost a decade of intermittent confrontation with NATO and other allies, the other leaders who had won World War Two were beginning to leave the stage. In September 1958, Montgomery stood down as deputy SACEUR. Described by *Time* magazine as NATO's 'blacksmith', he had flown half a million miles on its behalf, devising its defence plans and cajoling its various commanders and ministers into action. His command post exercises had aimed to 'peer into the future' at a world in which missiles and pilotless aircraft would dominate the battlefield – a world which he felt land commanders were yet to get their heads around. The European war with Russia he had feared imminent in the early 1950s was, he now argued, 'indefinitely postponed' by the strength of the Western alliance and the threat of nuclear armageddon. This 'test match' had instead been replaced with the 'village cricket' of smaller conflicts overseas that 'must be handled firmly so that they do not become the forerunner of a test match'.

Montgomery had made bad calls – including misreading the US approach to Suez and encouraging British commanders and ministers to move against Egypt. His refusals to acknowledge his mistakes were legendary – as he entered his final years in NATO, he was frustrating his publishers by his refusal in his autobiography to treat even the disastrous 1944 airborne landings in Arnhem as an error. Tactless comments concerning a 1956 visit to Eisenhower again irritated the president and the Americans. On 18 September 1958, almost fifty years to the day after he had first been commissioned, and following a dinner for more than 300 guests, Montgomery was presented with a scroll signed by the last four NATO commanders, most of whom somehow professed to regard him with genuine affection. In a rare show of self-awareness, the field marshal thanked the staff at SHAPE 'for having borne with me when I might have appeared to them to have said things rather strongly'. A few weeks later, Montgomery's memoirs – which he had pointedly refused to submit for approval by the War Office – were published. Once again they antagonised almost everyone he had ever worked with, including Eisenhower – to the point that he permanently ended a relationship that in Paris had been close enough for Ike to paint Monty's portrait. Derogatory comments on wartime Italian troops prompted one Italian army officer to challenge him to a duel.[21]

On 17 September, de Gaulle sent his thoughts on the future of NATO to Eisenhower and Macmillan. His missive (of little more than 500 words) was, according to biographer Julian Jackson, 'highly explosive and somewhat vague', describing NATO as 'not in its present form able to meet the conditions of security of the free world'. Again, he pushed for the tripartite alliance. The Italians were said to be 'nearly hysterical' to hear that de Gaulle believed 'only major world powers can define a global policy' and that this just meant the US, France and Britain.

German officials – who believed that only the US and USSR were truly superpowers, and all other Europeans operated on a lower level – were particularly furious, with Adenauer telling Macmillan he felt 'tricked and deceived', as well as concerned over the impact on domestic German support for the alliance.[22] Throughout the autumn, NATO, British, French and American officials tried to defuse the diplomatic consequences, even as a new crisis loomed over the future of Berlin.

As the 1950s ended, Communist East Germany faced a challenge most European nations would not see until the twenty-first century – a declining population. Each year, several hundred thousand quit the Communist area for the democratic West. Even after the closure of the main land border in 1953, the exodus continued through West Berlin, the US-, British- and French-controlled sector, now a thriving capitalist metropolis behind the Iron Curtain. For the Eisenhower and Adenauer administrations, West Berlin's success was a source of pride. For the East German and Kremlin authorities, it was an unambiguous embarrassment – and as Khrushchev cemented his power in Moscow, he was determined to address it. For years, the USSR had repeatedly called for Western forces to withdraw and Berlin to become an 'open city' within an internationally recognised East Germany – a proposal rejected equally repeatedly by Adenauer and West Berlin Mayor Willy Brandt, an anti-Nazi left-wing activist who had changed his name in 1933 to evade the Gestapo.

On 10 November 1958, Khrushchev made a speech including a deadline demanding that all three Western powers quit West Berlin within six months, threatening that the Soviet Union would terminate its post-war agreement and sign a treaty with East Germany, thus handing it control of the autobahn and rail links on which West Berlin depended.[23] On 14 November, Soviet troops stopped US trucks heading along the 110-kilometre autobahn from the West German border to Berlin, holding three American personnel for several hours near the Flatow Tower and Babelsberg checkpoint, demanding to inspect the vehicles before letting them go untouched. Should such an incident happen again, the US embassy warned, the Soviets might not back down even if US troops went in and forced them to release their comrades.[24]

For the first time, NATO nations were now in what could become a direct physical confrontation in the NATO area – and splits within the alliance were emerging. On 17 November US officials reported, following an NAC session, that the 'sense of the meeting was that the West should stand firm against Soviet moves but should use utmost wisdom and soundest deliberation to avoid provocation of incidents'.[25] The Kremlin had chosen its moment well. Some countries, including Norway, pushed publicly for Soviet demands to be considered, while Britain made similar suggestions behind closed doors. US officials expressed concerns over European 'softness'. Normally a hawk himself, Spaak bluntly told US officials that Western public opinion would not support 'a conflict, the sole purpose of which would be to determine who controls the routes of access to Berlin'.[26]

Berlin was not strictly NATO territory – and the US, French and British troops there were not under the direct command of NATO. Under the terms of the Potsdam treaty, West Berlin remained an 'occupied zone' split between the Soviets, British, US and French. While mostly administered by the West German government in Bonn and treated as West German territory, its status as such was disputed by the Kremlin and East German state. But few doubted that any war starting in Berlin would not swiftly escalate to pull in the whole alliance.

Through December, the US encouraged Britain and France to revise their contingency plans for Berlin and agree 'certain actions' to be taken if the route was blocked again. Neither, however, was willing to countenance use of force before a 'mini-airlift' of supplies had been considered or attempted. That irritated the Americans – West Berlin was now too large for its civilian population to be fed and supplied the way it had been in 1948. By early January 1959, the US was asking London and

Paris to consider a more specific course of action once Khrushchev's November deadline for Western forces to quit West Berlin expired in May. If the route was likely to be blocked again, the Western allies should send a military probe up the motorway to Berlin – and then if it was stopped, a reinforced full division of several thousand troops, even at the cost of outright war. This planning would take place outside NATO structures, and without reference to smaller nations.[27]

*

Throughout late 1958 and early 1959, wider strategic conversations between the US, UK, NATO and France continued to frustrate. De Gaulle was clearly angry with the alliance, viewing it as potentially infringing French sovereignty by controlling French forces in time of war – but he also wanted the alliance to do more globally to support French ambitions including in its colonies.

Eisenhower's wartime experiences with the Frenchman left him unsurprised by his intransigence and unpredictability, as well as his preoccupation with his own 'dignity' and that of France. On one occasion during the conflict, Eisenhower told Dulles, the general had threatened, in front of himself and Churchill, to remove all Free French forces from Allied command. The Frenchman had only backed down when Eisenhower told him equally bluntly that if he did so France would not receive a single round more of ammunition – and Britain and the US would defeat Hitler without France. De Gaulle was capable of the most 'extraordinary actions', Eisenhower warned, and the secretary should 'watch out for him'.[28]

In October, Eisenhower wrote what was essentially a personal non-response to the general's letter of the previous month, agreeing that the Western allies faced 'global challenges' but refusing to commit to specifics.[29] In conversations with the French ambassador in Washington, Dulles was blunter – 'expanding' NATO to cover the rest of the world would be difficult or impossible, not least because it would require the consent of governments in Africa and Asia who had only just rid themselves of imperial control.[30] Still, the US and Britain reluctantly agreed to three-way meetings. As trilateral talks began formally in December, de Gaulle told Dulles he was infuriated by the US failure to vote against a UN motion on Algerian independence. The Frenchman proclaimed himself 'not interested' in cooperating with NATO on infrastructure, nuclear weapons or anything else 'when in effect the whole show was being run by the US'.[31]

The NAC ministerial meeting managed a display of unity on Berlin, but only just. Dulles complained getting the communiqué agreed was 'harrowing'.[32] Foreign Secretary Lloyd said he believed the French leader felt 'the present NATO might as well be scrapped and a fresh start be made under triumvirate auspices', while French Foreign Minister Maurice Couve de Murville attempted to reassure the Americans that none of the French leader's advisers truly shared his views, nor necessarily understood them in full.[33] Then, on 6 March 1959, France notified the North Atlantic Council that the French Mediterranean fleet, previously earmarked for NATO command in time of war, would no longer be available to be directly tasked by the alliance. This development that, Secretary General Spaak noted, was 'seriously embarrassing'.[34] Norstad described it as 'psychologically and politically' important, if not militarily, while incoming US Secretary of State Christian Herter worried it would 'give the impression that the alliance was breaking up'.[35]

For now, at least, this did not interfere with contingency planning for Berlin. In March, SACEUR Norstad recommended French and British military specialists – although not those from the rest of NATO – be integrated into the small US team secretly working up Berlin contingencies. Dubbed LIVE OAK and located at the US military's European headquarters outside Paris, it was intended to be a long-term operation. It continued as tensions over Berlin fell off again in late 1958, becoming a UK–US–French permanent military staff preparing plans for future crises involving the city. It was already clear that it would also bring some challenges. In particular, it further muddied the different chains of command atop which Norstad sat. He reported to Washington as the commander of US European Command, as SACEUR to the NAC and now through LIVE OAK separately on Berlin to the US, French and British governments.

LIVE OAK further highlighted the awkward dynamics of that Anglo–French–US partnership. De Gaulle was largely supportive of US policy on Berlin, but wanted the alliance itself upended on a scale no other Western leader wanted. Britain supported the current structures, but the Macmillan government viewed US plans to reinforce West Berlin in a crisis as 'dangerous military nonsense'.[36]

In June, de Gaulle demanded that US nuclear weapons be removed from the soil of France, forcing the US to relocate more than 200 aircraft. Norstad told Eisenhower he hoped growing French intransigence might have the effect of pushing the rest of the alliance back together.[37] As Berlin tensions simmered, fears of imminent conflict were now at the greatest they had been since the early 1950s. When historian Michael Howard visited Washington, he found it a 'military capital . . . almost more uniforms on the street than . . . wartime London'. The United States, he concluded, was already 'a nation that believed itself at war.'[38] Amid the forests and hills of the German Fulda Gap, newly commissioned US infantryman Lieutenant Colin Powell was in no doubt that if the Russians came, he and his troops would 'fight like the devil, fall back and watch the nuclear cataclysm begin'.[39]

*

Despite such underlying tensions, early 1959 proceeded without serious superpower confrontation. Pressured by Macmillan to consider talks with Moscow, Eisenhower invited Khrushchev to the White House. When the invitation hit the headlines in August Eisenhower's approval ratings spiked even higher. As would often be the case when US presidents began talking to the Kremlin, it also prompted nervous twitches from other allies suddenly concerned that they might be abandoned. Eisenhower flew to Europe, making it clear to NATO allies that he did not intend some 'grand bargain' – and reassuring Adenauer that there would be no surrendering of Berlin.[40] Then, days before Khrushchev's arrival in September, the Soviets put a new rocket into space, *Lunik 2*, landing the first manmade object on the moon – and reigniting Western fears about a 'missile gap'. Talks at Camp David were unspectacular but friendly.[41]

As Eisenhower entered his final year in office at the start of 1960, it initially appeared as though it might be an unusually diplomatically successful one. In April, cheering crowds, estimated by Washington DC police at 200,000, welcomed de Gaulle – now French president and with the much-increased executive powers of his new constitution. At the National Press Club, the French leader held what the *New York Times* described as a 'relaxed and informal' press conference that focused heavily on an upcoming Paris 'big four' meeting between himself, Eisenhower, Macmillan and Khrushchev.[42] All four nations expressed their hopes that the meeting – which again largely circumvented NATO – would signal the start of greater cooperation.

Then, on 1 May, a US U2 spy plane operated by the CIA was shot down deep within Russian airspace and pilot Gary Powers was swiftly taken prisoner. Khrushchev kept it secret for several days, before shocking the world with his announcement, proclaiming that he still believed Eisenhower wanted peace. According to Khrushchev's son years later, the Soviet leader genuinely initially believed rogue elements within the US government must have been responsible for sending the plane into Russian territory. But, as Eisenhower was swiftly forced to admit, the flights were definitely authorised, a measure of increasing concern in Washington over Soviet claims to be racing ahead in the building of ballistic missiles. The US again offered an 'open skies' agreement with the Kremlin, ensuring the right to fly reconnaissance over each other's territory. Khrushchev was incandescent. The summit in Paris broke up early, Eisenhower's invitation to visit Russia rudely cancelled.[43]

When NATO ministers met in Istanbul, the NAC expressed its 'regrets that Mr Khrushchev's position has made negotiations in Paris impossible', endorsing the statement by the US, French and British leaders that they remained 'unshaken in their conviction that all outstanding international questions should be settled not by the use of force but by peaceful means'.[44]

Eisenhower's presidency and preceding period of NATO command had been formative for the alliance. Not all his efforts, however, had succeeded. In 1951 he had confidently asserted to Truman in the White House that US forces would be able to pull back from Europe within a decade once it was able to defend itself. Now it was clear that might never happen. 'We sent our divisions there to help them in an emergency,' Eisenhower complained to Norstad in August 1959. 'Now if we talk about taking out one division, they claim we are deserting them.'[45]

Forty-three-year-old John F. Kennedy, now frontrunner in the November 1960 presidential race, swiftly seized on the U2 incident. He argued that he would have managed to salvage the Paris summit, painting the Eisenhower administration as out of its depth and failing to protect America or its allies.[46] But Khrushchev believed the incoming young US president would buckle under pressure. He was prepared to take considerable risks to challenge him, most immediately over West Berlin, a topic on which NATO had already shown divisions.

9

Testing Kennedy in Berlin (1961)

*'I am not suggesting that the blame can all be laid at one door.
But the fabric of the alliance will not stand many more scenes like
that of last Friday.'*

NATO Secretary General Dirk Stikker, December 1961[1]

The Eisenhower–Kennedy transition marked a major shift for
NATO. No future US president would have Eisenhower's
experience of the alliance, nor his emotional attachment to it.
At forty-three, Kennedy would be the first major alliance leader
to be born in the twentieth century. Even before his inauguration,
he was dragged into NATO issues – the State Department
sought his approval for the latest nuclear strategy being presented
to the December 1960 North Atlantic Council, although the
president-elect declined to get involved.[2]

When the US had pledged to defend NATO in 1949, the
risk of an overwhelming atomic attack on the United States was
still distinctly limited. That was changing now – producing
nervousness the US might abandon Europe in a crisis to avoid
nuclear annihilation. As SHAPE official historian Gregory
Pedlow wrote in 1997: 'All over Europe leaders were beginning
to secretly fear . . . de Gaulle might be right in his belief that
"no US president will exchange Chicago for Lyon".'[3] For America's European allies – and indeed NATO itself – the result was
now a complex 'catch-22' situation. On the one hand, they desperately needed the US to stay engaged, fearing outright

annihilation – or perhaps a more subtle Soviet subjugation – should America pull back its troops and warheads. On the other, that dependence left them with only limited influence on events – and in very real danger of being dragged into a catastrophic global war with little agency or warning.

The first two years of the new administration would bring NATO and its members closer to armageddon than at any point in the whole Cold War. First in Berlin, and then over Cuba, US military units would find themselves in direct confrontation with their Soviet counterparts, sometimes seemingly within minutes of outright conflict. NATO would often find itself frozen out of the actual decision-making process, its leaders and other members simply waiting on the US to see what it might do. Already, smaller powers within NATO were complaining at what they saw as the 'hegemony' of the 'big four' – the US, Britain, France and West Germany – now firmly established following its postwar rebuilding as the economic powerhouse of the continent.

In a US bunker outside Paris, the US, British and French LIVE OAK planners continued to work up scenarios for what many believed was a coming crisis in Berlin. For those stationed in Berlin, deep within East German territory and surrounded by overwhelming numbers of Soviet and East German troops, the prospects for survival looked particularly poor. British personnel were issued with aircrew-style escape maps to help them get back to allied lines if the city was overrun. US personnel were told bluntly they would have little chance of rescue or reinforcement, while some officers implied the Berlin area might be swiftly hit by atomic weapons in the event of war. 'If the communists attacked, we knew our chances of survival were slim,' recalled US military policeman Private Tom Ables from West Virginia, posted to Berlin in 1961. 'We partied hard when off duty, as we had this thought that any moment now, World War Three could commence.'[4]

*

As he entered the White House in January 1961 'JFK' and those around him were more acutely aware of the risks of imminent atomic war than any administration before or since. The first US military Single Integrated Operational Plan, SIOP-62, drafted the previous year, allocated 3,200 nuclear warheads to target Russia, China and other Communist nations in the event of war, and was predicted to kill between 360 and 450 million people.[5]

Shortly after Kennedy's inauguration, Secretary General Spaak announced his intention to resign from NATO. Officially, his reason was to return to Belgian politics – he would serve once again as foreign minister from April. But European officials told new US Secretary of State Dean Rusk – a wartime US Army officer who had been Acheson's number three under Truman – that it was a sign of trouble at the heart of the alliance, and a result of frustrations with the situation de Gaulle had produced. German envoys expressed a desire for strong US leadership and even suggested Acheson – who, as with Truman, had a strong personal relationship with the young new president – might succeed Spaak.[6] But with an American already permanently in the top military role as SACEUR, having an American secretary general as well was never truly viable.

Dirk Stikker became the next NATO civilian chief. As Dutch foreign minister, he had signed the North Atlantic Treaty in 1949 and been Holland's permanent representative to NATO from July 1958. Later described by alliance historians as 'business-like' and 'pragmatic', he was reluctant to engage closely with the press but worked fourteen-hour days, seven days a week. Fluent in English, French and German, he would prove popular with Kennedy – but much less so with de Gaulle, who would refuse to meet with Stikker throughout his tenure, and accuse him of taking the US side on all of de Gaulle's sometimes contradictory demands.[7]

Kennedy's term in office was marked by an aggressive Soviet approach from the very start. On 6 January 1961,

Khrushchev gave a bullish speech in which he backed 'wars of liberation' across the world and described the 'occupation' of West Berlin by the 'aggressive-minded imperialists' as 'particularly vulnerable'. Empowered and strengthened in office by the '*Sputnik* moment', the new Kremlin leader was ambitious to secure further propaganda wins. Kennedy remained determined to meet the Soviet leader himself – it was, he said as he entered office, better to 'meet at the summit rather than at the brink'.[8]

Negotiations on arms control – or, at the very least, a ban on atomic testing – had been underway for most of the previous administration, but had resulted in only limited success. De Gaulle had finally detonated the first French atomic device in February 1960, months after the US and the USSR had negotiated an informal moratorium on nuclear tests. His relations with the US and NATO continued to worsen.

Like many within the alliance, Kennedy had already publicly voiced doubts that the Eisenhower-era 'massive retaliation' doctrine was fit for purpose. The risk, he believed, was less from a massive Soviet offensive than from a geographically limited confrontation getting out of hand – and should that happen, the current doctrine could propel Washington and NATO towards a mass nuclear exchange because their conventional forces were too weak for other options. The answer, Kennedy, Rusk and new Defense Secretary Robert McNamara believed, was a more 'flexible response', a much wider menu of conventional and nuclear options – as well as ways of pausing escalation – that might allow a confrontation or initial conflict to be managed. It was a phrase that would come to epitomise the new US doctrine it wanted NATO to adopt – but it worried some member nations who saw it as code for potentially abandoning areas of their territory in the event of war. Some – ironically including France, given its removal of US weapons from its soil – remained happier with Eisenhower-era 'massive retaliation', relying on a potentially overwhelming

US atomic strike to deter even the smallest move against alliance territory.

Visiting Washington on a farewell February visit, Spaak told Kennedy the US needed to give clarity on what 'flexible response' really meant – including US suggestions Kennedy had seen in December to put five new US Polaris missile submarines under NATO control.[9] It was a plan French officials were already sceptical about, suspecting the US would never truly give others power to fire its warheads.[10] Eisenhower had long prioritised strengthening Europe's ability to defend itself, personally briefly favouring giving France atomic bombs – or at least critical information to help them build them – despite opposition from others, including Norstad.[11] Kennedy's White House thought more in terms of stopping 'nuclear proliferation'. That included getting Britain 'out of the nuclear business' – in part to remove the awkwardness of having an ongoing atomic support programme for Britain when it did not want one with France, let alone other US allies it worried might come asking for one after. Instead, the US wanted its European allies to work more closely together to build conventional military capability, ideally leaving nuclear matters either to the US or a NATO structure.[12]

LIVE OAK planning on Berlin continued in the background – some of it now supervised by Dean Acheson, who Kennedy had asked to report on both the city and the wider future of the alliance. When Macmillan and a British delegation visited Washington they were presented with what the British prime minister later described as a 'bloodcurdling' plan to force an entire US division up the autobahn to West Berlin in a crisis, backed up by whatever wider force might be required.[13] US officials gave perhaps deliberately mixed signals over how seriously LIVE OAK's plans should be taken – Norstad acknowledged he had deliberately designed a 'significant amount of bluff', implying that they were intended to reassure European allies and deter the Kremlin.

If the Kennedy administration believed stepping up war planning was likely to deliver more alliance unity, they had misread the European mood. Given the likely damage to Germany of even a very limited atomic war, the West German government was said to be 'very, very anxious not to fight for West Berlin'. British officials talked of an excessive US tendency to 'reach for the sledgehammer' but did not directly oppose the plans for fear of finding themselves in 'bad odour' with the White House. In summer 1961, British Chief of the Defence Staff Air Marshal George Mills warned his government he believed the US administration would try 'everything possible short of large nuclear war' if the Russians moved against Berlin or blocked the access routes again. 'Personally I feel that in the last resort they will fight even at the risk of general war,' he said.[14]

*

By the time the first hundred days of the Kennedy administration were up, it had been humiliated by the failure of the CIA-backed (and originally Eisenhower-administration-planned) Bay of Pigs attempt to overthrow Fidel Castro in Cuba. As Kennedy's friend, special assistant and biographer Arthur Schlesinger noted, the failure brought domestic and international 'astonishment and disillusion'.[15] It was a situation the administration was keen to overturn – and for a while, at least, it saw revitalising NATO as a route to that. On a visit to Ottawa in May, Kennedy pledged five of America's new Polaris ballistic missile submarines to the NATO command area 'subject to any agreed NATO guidelines on their control and use, and responsive to the needs of all members but still credible in an emergency'. This, he suggested, would be the first step on the road to a truly NATO-controlled seaborne missile force, 'truly multilateral in ownership and control'.[16]

Kennedy's summer of 1961 trip to Europe – taking in Germany, Britain, and Ireland, an address to NATO and summits with de Gaulle in Paris and Khrushchev in Vienna – was intended to restore 'Camelot's' sense of purpose. Henry Kissinger – now a part-time adviser to the US National Security Council – suggested Berlin be added to the agenda, but there simply wasn't time.[17]

Even before they met, Kennedy and de Gaulle were fascinated by each other –Jackie Kennedy had translated aloud passages from de Gaulle's memoirs for her future husband in the run-up to their marriage.[18] The meetings of the two men – coupled with the vast crowds and media attention – saw both clearly keen to impress each other. But the Frenchman's antagonism towards NATO had also grown, fuelled by a failed 'generals' putsch' against his government involving several conspirators who had previously served with the alliance, with popular gossip in Paris alleging direct US involvement.

De Gaulle began to outline his complex position. He did not blame Kennedy directly for the attempted coup, he said, but the actions of the plotters showed that they had been corrupted by the 'transnational' nature of working as part of NATO's multinational military structures. Describing NATO as 'first an alliance and second an organisation', the general made it clear that he opposed only the latter, which he believed weakened Europe's own militaries. De Gaulle repeated his belief that only French atomic weapons should be on its soil, while Kennedy rejected the nuclear cooperation France desperately wanted, and avoided commitments on French proposals for tripartite arrangements to coordinate worldwide security policy with the US and UK beyond vague talk of further 'mechanisms'.[19]

On Berlin, however, Kennedy found the French more supportive than the nervous British. To surrender to Russian pressure would be a serious defeat, de Gaulle told him on 31 May – the challenge was to make sure the Kremlin believed in Western firmness.[20] In his speech to the North Atlantic Council, the US president tacitly acknowledged European concerns about the evolving nature of Cold War confrontation, paying tribute to the alliance's success in averting war so far and pledging to deepen the Atlantic community in future. 'We will never acquiesce in the defeat or humiliation of any ally,' he promised. 'And we will resist any aggression, where necessary, with all means at our disposal.'[21]

At their first meeting in Austria on 4 June, Khrushchev threatened Russia might recognise East Germany as a separate state and end the 1945 Potsdam deal that allowed Anglo–French–American occupation of West Berlin. Kennedy replied that if the US were to abandon the West Berliners, 'US commitments would be regarded as a mere scrap of paper.' Khrushchev turned on Kennedy, accusing him of being unwilling to 'normalise the situation in the most dangerous spot in the world'. Working too closely with a rearmed West Germany, the Soviet leader said, left the US dependent on 'Hitler's generals who are now high commanders in NATO'.[22] Kennedy was equally blunt. As the Russians pledged to back East Germany 'to the point of war' if the Communist authorities there closed the Berlin access routes, Kennedy warned, 'If that's to be the case, there will be war, Mr Chairman.'[23]

The next day, US Secretary of State Rusk told the NAC that the US believed the Soviets might force the Berlin issue within the year. Two days after that the US mission to NATO formally informed other members about the previously secret US–French–British LIVE OAK planners, soon to be joined by officials from West Germany, and called for other potential measures, including economic sanctions in the event of a new confrontation.[24] With tensions rising US Defense Secretary McNamara and SACEUR Norstad lobbied Kennedy for an increase of US forces in Europe. In July 1961 the White House asked Congress for the biggest hike in US military spending since Korea, swelling the US Army ranks from 875,000 to a million, with similar increases for the US Navy and Air Force, new conventional weapons and ammunition, and the calling up of some reserves.[25]

Kennedy wanted NATO allies to do the same, but there were disagreements over what to do if the crisis worsened. In May, McNamara had written to Kennedy calling the plans to relieve Berlin 'deficient' lacking enough force even to defeat East German efforts to stop US troops moving up the motorway, let alone a much more powerful Soviet-backed response, while Norstad filed his own similar concerns. In July, Macmillan told French Defence Minister Pierre Messmer the LIVE OAK planning for crises in Berlin 'did not seem very realistic'.[26] On 8 August Rusk again addressed the North Atlantic Council, urging coordination of NATO 'propaganda and political action in support of our position in Berlin . . . If there is any way, short of the actual use of force, by which the Soviets can be made to realise Western determination, it is by making our strength visibly larger.' LIVE OAK, he added, was moving its head-quarters from its US military base outside Paris into NATO's SHAPE HQ, allowing its planners to use the secure communications facilities there should the already mounting crisis became a more serious confrontation.[27]

Within Berlin, there were clear signs trouble was coming. By February 1961, an average of 2,650 people a week were emigrating into the Western sector – increasing to three times that by July. The economic, military and social impact was also growing fast. Within a year East Berlin had lost over half its 700 dentists, and East Germany some 20,000 men of fighting age. On 12 August, East Germany announced it was closing all but thirteen of the 120 Berlin crossing points, simultaneously pledging to respect the borders of West Berlin and keep supply lines open. The next morning, police armoured cars and tanks were deployed along the entire border as workers erected barricades. As the 'Berlin Wall' became a reality, two Soviet divisions surrounded the city in a show of force to deter East Berliners from any kind of insurrection.[28]

Throughout 1961, the two battle groups of the US Army 6th Infantry Division that made up the US garrison in West

Berlin had trained aggressively in public, practising attacks and riot control in the parkland of the city's Grunewald Forest. The assumption, however, had been that any Russian or East German provocation would involve either a foray into West Berlin or a strangling of supply lines.[29] No one in the West had foreseen that the priority for the Soviet and East German authorities would be to stop their own people fleeing – and that they could do so while remaining wholly within their territory.

Until the morning of the wall's erection, East and West Berliners had been able to pass readily between each other's territory. They now looked on aghast at the growing barriers, while the US, British and French troops did nothing. Both East and West Berliners – and even some East German border guards – berated Allied troops for their failure to intervene. 'I'm working as slowly as I can,' one East German building the wall told US Lieutenant Vern Pike a few metres away, daring Allied troops to stop what would become the Berlin Wall.[30]

Arguments over what might have been done would persist for years. That autumn Norstad told Vice President Lyndon B. Johnson that if he had been the commander on the ground, he might have 'slung a hook across the wire when it was erected, attached the hook to a jeep and torn down the wire', or suggested smashing the wall down with a tank. But given the political realities and risk of escalation, he believed US commanders had little choice but to hold back.[31]

Kennedy saw clear propaganda value in the wall, with its obvious implication that only force could keep East German citizens from fleeing for the West.[32] Within Berlin, however, there was outrage – including against the Americans for their perceived inaction. The US diplomatic mission warned the State Department that unless the US responded more robustly to restore morale, the city might collapse. That response, US diplomats said, did not need to be forceful, but a reminder this was not 'Hitler's takeover of the Rhineland'.[33] On 16 August,

US ambassador to Berlin Allen Lightner warned Washington that the wall 'completely tore asunder' the fabric of Berlin's four-power control, and that 'having taken such a big slice of salami and successfully digested it . . . [the Soviets] may be expected to snatch further pieces greedily' perhaps including areas of the Allied sectors.[34] Writing to Kennedy the same day, Mayor Brandt, now contesting elections for the chancellorship of West Germany, demanded the three Western powers recommit themselves to the sovereignty of West Berlin.[35]

The following day the US National Security Council agreed to reinforce the Berlin garrison with a battle group of around 1,500 extra troops. Kennedy explicitly wanted French and British forces to accompany the US unit as it headed up the autobahn, but again that appears to have been too complex and time-consuming. Swift action was what the administration wanted, and that meant it must be unilateral.[36] Later on 17 August, Army Secretary Elvis Stahr announced at least 3,000 troops would leave immediately for Europe. In order to further boost US military readiness, 84,000 enlisted US service personnel about to be discharged would have their service extended and the US National Guard would call up more than 23,000 soldiers.

The next day, the White House announced that Vice President Johnson and retired General Lucius Clay – commandant in Berlin during the original Berlin airlift in 1948, and hugely popular within the city – would fly into Berlin. Just before midnight, Commander of US Army Europe General Bruce Clark activated contingency plans for a single unit – the 1st Battle Group, 18th Infantry Regiment– to conduct a passage to Berlin, bypassing multiple levels in their chain of command to get them on the road within six hours.[37] By the morning of 19 August they were at the border crossing into East Germany in full combat kit – and, beyond some basic checks, Soviet and East German guards allowed them to proceed uninterrupted to Berlin. At one point, the convoy of more than 400 vehicles stretched almost the entire length of the autobahn, watched closely by East German troops along its edge while a Soviet jet flew menacingly overhead. According to US military news-paper the *Berlin Observer*, it was the largest single movement of US troops into Berlin since 1945. That afternoon they paraded through the centre of the city, reviewed by the vice president and General Clay, their presence within the city intended to send its own powerful message of US resolve.[38] Soon, the US troops – together with the pre-existing British and French garrisons – were making their own show of force within the city, establishing checkpoints, with two American tanks guarding the 'Checkpoint Charlie' Friedrichstrasse crossing point. They would patrol throughout September before handing over to West Berlin police.[39]

*

The August US military reinforcement of Berlin had shown speed, determination and the simultaneous use of political power alongside bloodless but blunt military force. But it had also been achieved only by circumventing the standard organs of the US military command chain, with NATO and the LIVE OAK allies either unwilling or unable to do anything but watch.

The consequences were quick to manifest. On 28 August US diplomats warned Washington 'our allies outside the [LIVE OAK] four are becoming increasingly concerned over the dan-gers of the situation and restive under a system which they feel does not respect their desire for adequate consultation'. The LIVE OAK powers themselves also demanded more influence, on 1 September presenting Secretary General Stikker with their own 'Draft Instructions to General Norstad'. This document – a series of guidelines for SACEUR issued in the name of just the US, France, Britain and Germany, without the rest of NATO – immediately caused a further storm. In a memo cir-culated across the alliance, Secretary General Stikker angrily asserted his own authority to 'maintain the unity of the alliance' and 'ensure the proper functioning of the agreed institutions and safeguard the existing chains of command in the political and military fields . . . The dangers which are threatening the alliance did not come only from outside. Problems may arise from inside the alliance.'

Throughout September Stikker and Norstad walked an awkward path, the latter reminding US Defense Secretary McNamara, 'We must keep in mind the fact that NATO strategy must be generally acceptable to our allies if they are to have either the will to face up to possible military operations or the inclination to build up their forces.' North Atlantic Council meetings throughout the month were stormy. Canada argued 'no blank cheque' had been given to the LIVE OAK powers. Belgium complained that while the 'Council received information . . . consultation took place elsewhere . . . Since all members of the Alliance are equally involved in the danger of war, they should all take part in planning.'[40] Divisions were scarcely less stark within the LIVE OAK four. At a meeting on 17 September with Rusk and his French and German counterparts, British Foreign Secretary Alec Douglas-Home questioned what 'purpose' life in West Berlin had now that the city was even more encircled, suggesting the Western powers hand over control of their sectors and that the UN headquarters should move there from New York to establish it as a demilitarised 'free city'. The other three shot down the idea immediately, suggesting it would hand a massive propaganda advantage to the Soviets.[41]

Under the Potsdam Agreement, British, French and US personnel were entitled to enter East Berlin, which officially remained the Soviet-controlled sector. They now continued to assert that right, producing periodic confrontations. On 22 October, a new incident resulted in a face-off at Checkpoint Charlie after East German guards denied the assistant chief of the US mission access to East Berlin, and declined his request to see a Soviet officer. A US tank and infantry team proceeded to the checkpoint, with further tanks and troops deployed after additional US officials were denied access. The tit-for-tat continued for several days, with the US mission using armed troops to assert their right to access East Berlin – and prompting Soviet forces to deploy their own ten tanks on 27 October. That stand-off lasted seventeen hours before the Russian tanks withdrew – and once again NATO had been completely uninvolved.[42] For all their planning, the LIVE OAK team near Paris had also been entirely sidelined. With the exception of two British anti-tank guns moved up to the wall during the Checkpoint Charlie face-off, British and French troops were also largely uninvolved.

While theoretically only in Berlin as in adviser, Clay was sometimes giving direct instructions to US troops, complicating the command chain. During the 27 October confrontation, he coordinated actions on the ground while talking directly to Kennedy in the White House. For young US military police-man Tom Ables and many of his colleagues, Clay was a 'hero' for standing up to Russian pressure. But there was also relief when he departed the city the next year, as: 'I think that he knew about 90% of American officers and men thought what he was doing was on the dangerous side.'[43]

*

Berlin now appeared permanently divided – although following the confrontation, Soviet and East German border guards would continue to allow Allied military personnel into East Berlin for the remainder of the Cold War. No one was happy with the situation. 'It's not a very nice solution,' Kennedy noted privately, 'but a wall is a hell of a lot better than a war.'[44]

Wider Cold War posturing simmered throughout the autumn of 1961. In August the Soviets had announced a resump-tion in nuclear testing, detonating thirty-one devices inside three months, including 'Tsar Bomba' in late October, the larg-est thermonuclear device detonated in human history – at 58 megatons 4,000 times more powerful than that dropped on Hiroshima.[45] In Washington, Defense Secretary McNamara was refining America's atomic war plans. This offered a much more comprehensive 'menu' of options for both nuclear and conventional military action, some designed to allow deliberate pauses for negotiations. It also included a pre-emptive massive US nuclear strike in the event a Russian attack was believed to be imminent.[46]

Within NATO, the cross-alliance planning that might have preceded the Berlin crisis finally began, allowing the alliance to draw up its own plans for NATO-wide action in the event of a further Berlin crisis. Based on October instructions from the North Atlantic Council, SHAPE prepared elaborate Berlin Contingency (BERCON) schemes that included sending up to four NATO divisions, supported by a range of air, land and maritime operations, across Europe, and nuclear tests to demonstrate resolve. Separate Maritime Contingency (MARCON) plans drawn up by NATO's Supreme Allied Commander Atlantic (SACLANT) would follow, again to be presented to the North Atlantic Council in early 1962. Secretary General Stikker and SACEUR Norstad tried to rebuild trust, particularly with smaller NATO allies, hoping that including them more in military planning would lessen their concerns.[47]

Nervousness over Berlin endured. In November Norstad told Kennedy US military teams remained ready to contest any efforts to close remaining crossing points or deny access to allied officials, if necessary being prepared to 'knock down four or five other gates'. LIVE OAK planning to send forces down the autobahn also continued, although with the emphasis back on smaller numbers of troops.[48] These plans – together with suspicions that Clay had deliberately exacerbated the tank face-off at Checkpoint Charlie – unsettled US allies. Rusk and the State Department assured the British that no US tanks would break down barriers without British 'concurrence' – but UK officials worried that the 'American chain of command is so mixed up' that a US commander might think he had the authority to take unilateral action.

They were right to show such concerns. SACEUR Norstad would later say it was a good thing NATO allies did not understand the full extent of US confusion. In a single day of the Berlin crisis, he later recalled, he received multiple conflicting instructions from multiple senior US officials – including three Cabinet members – 'demanding' he take action he 'considered wrong and provocative'.[49] Berlin had tested the relationship between Norstad and the administration – particularly US Defense Secretary McNamara – almost to destruction. McNamara believed major combat operations might be possible across swathes of Germany without a nuclear exchange, while Norstad believed such a conflict would be nuclear almost from the start. Even more inconvenient was SACEUR's belief that his primary loyalty should be to the alliance, while those in Washington were equally definite that it should be to them.[50]

When the foreign ministers of France, Germany, Britain and the US met in Paris on 12 December before the North Atlantic Council meeting, British Foreign Secretary Alec Douglas-Home complained they lacked any truly common position on anything important. German counterpart Gerhard Schröder warned that Russian 'salami tactics' would pick away at Berlin's survival, while Secretary of State Rusk warned that while the US would not make concessions, it 'saw the possibility that the crisis might become so acute as to lead to a nuclear war'.[51] Secretary General Stikker described the NAC meeting as coming 'as near in my memory it ever has to a public breakdown over a major issue', describing 'frank exchanges' but simultaneously 'more of a real discussion . . . than at any ministerial meeting I remember'.[52]

While Stikker warned that the alliance could not survive many more 'scenes like last Friday', his predecessor Spaak was more upbeat, particularly praising a presentation by McNamara that highlighted how far ahead the US remained of the Soviets in the power of its atomic arsenal. That military advantage, Spaak hoped, might open the door to 'a real and rational NATO military policy which thus far has been non-existent'.[53] It was, US officials hoped, another step in guiding NATO policy towards the new US strategy of 'flexible response'. The allies, Rusk wrote to Kennedy, 'now understand . . . our reasons for seeking alternatives between surrender and incineration'.[54]

As a crisis erupted over Cuba the following year, 'incineration' would feel even closer.

10

Cuba (1962)

*'For all the declarations of solidarity made around
the NATO table during that week . . . none of the
Allied governments could claim to have been consulted.'*

Canadian NATO ambassador George Ignatieff[1]

As 1962 began, the chasm with de Gaulle continued to grow
wider. The French 1960 nuclear detonation in the Sahara had
fallen short of a reliable and workable atomic bomb, let alone
one that could be fired by missile – and the US refusal to help
remedy that problem was seen in France as a betrayal.

All the other disagreements with de Gaulle also lingered on,
including his distrust of US and NATO commanders being
able to direct French units and subordinates. 'It is impossible to
go to Paris today . . . without becoming deeply impressed with
their bitterness towards the US government,' Kennedy's military adviser General Maxwell Taylor wrote to the president
after visiting in March. He said France would continue to
pursue its atomic programme regardless of US opposition, and
there was a growing suspicion that West Germany itself might
follow suit. [2]

Talk of a potential German nuclear weapon had started in
the 1950s and gradually increased ever since – particularly
unnerving successive French governments and the Kremlin.
Now, the Berlin crisis unsettled Adenauer's government, to the
point that neither they nor the French proved willing to engage

with the Russians in the talks over the city that ran through the winter. It appeared to be the eternal NATO paradox – the Europeans often claimed to want greater engagement, but did not always want to be implicated in the decision-making or diplomatic fallout, let alone any further military spending. The US and Britain had persisted in talking to the Kremlin, each side still fearing the other might launch a military effort to change the Berlin status quo. Still, in April 1962, US ambassador Lightner told Washington the initial shock and fear generated by the building of the wall was subsiding in West Berlin itself, its population finally reassured that the US would fight if necessary to keep them free. 'I think the immediate crisis in Berlin . . . is over and that we have won this round,' he said, describing economic and cultural vitality returning to West Berlin and supplies continuing through the East German and Soviet cordon.[3]

The US judged the May 1962 NATO ministerial meeting in Athens 'one of the most successful in the history of [the] alliance'. Finally, the allies explicitly agreed to maintain West Berlin as a US–Anglo–French pocket deep within East Germany, rather than negotiate away its existence. The West now called for full German reunification and free elections in the East – something the Kremlin was never likely to agree to, but would provide a solid basis for allied strategy through the coming decades and reach unexpected fruition in 1989. In a closed session of the NAC in Athens, with no notes taken, McNamara outlined the latest nuclear state of play. US intermediate and medium-range ground-based ballistic missiles now ringed the Soviet Union, with the first new Polaris ballistic missile submarines providing a crucial 'second strike' capability. Even if Russia was able to able to mount a surprise attack that devastated the continental United States and Western Europe, America's nuclear forces would retain the ability to respond in kind.

For NATO members, this offered a degree of reassurance. In the Kremlin, it was viewed as catastrophic, shattering the confidence of the '*Sputnik*' era. Soviet scientists had been able to leap ahead of US counterparts on individual rockets, but the USSR lacked the US industrial strength to mass-produce them. That left the USSR with only twenty working long-range land-based Inter-continental Ballistic Missiles (ICBMs) in comparison to the US's 180; six primitive ballistic missile submarines that needed to be within 600 miles of the US coast to launch – much closer than Polaris; and 200 long-range bombers, less than a third of the US total. As 1962 began, the US could strike Russian territory with several hundred missiles, while the Kremlin could reach the continental US with many fewer rockets and would have to rely on aircraft, many likely be shot down before they could drop their bombs.[4] Both sides now knew the 'missile gap' was real – and firmly in favour of the United States. The only other true nuclear power, Britain, lacked missiles of its own and had only the vulnerable aircraft of its V-bomber fleet. The rest of the alliance remained undecided and divided on what to do over Kennedy's Ottawa offer of a NATO-operated 'multilateral' missile force. The US judged this force largely militarily irrelevant – it now had enough missiles to annihilate much of Russia by itself – but was still offering to fund the project as a diplomatic tool for alliance unity.[5]

For their part, at least one European NATO state hoped to receive the latest US atomic rockets: Italy reportedly left space for four Polaris launch tubes on its newly built cruiser *Giuseppe Garibaldi*.[6] As the Kennedy administration pushed Britain and France to abandon their nuclear programmes, SACEUR Norstad felt his own relationship with the White House deteriorating. In July he would finally offer Kennedy his resignation, although he would remain in role throughout the autumn. 'I was a reminder, I think, of the Eisenhower success in NATO, and the new government didn't take kindly to that,' Norstad recalled in 1976. Perhaps more importantly, he believed the Kennedy administration had a fundamentally different understanding of NATO and the role of the SACEUR in particular. 'All too often, they would expect me to be the one who would carry out an American decision independently of the NATO countries,' Norstad said. 'And I couldn't and wouldn't do that.'[7]

To make matters worse, NATO now faced its first major internal spy scandal. At the end of 1961, Anatoliy Golitsyn, a KGB major assigned to the Soviet embassy in Helsinki, defected to the United States. In his debriefing by the CIA, he described multiple spy rings, including a particularly effective one in France, penetrating both de Gaulle's government and NATO HQ. According to French intelligence official Philippe Thyraud de Vosjoli, the defector – codenamed 'Martel' – claimed the KGB access was so good that Moscow could get a copy of any NATO document it wanted within days. Kennedy was sufficiently concerned to write privately to de Gaulle, while US officials began to cut France out of shared intelligence. It would drive worsening US–French relations, as well as US nervousness over sharing information with the alliance.

Throughout the first half of 1962, 'Martel' was debriefed by almost every allied intelligence service, including the French under US supervision. His knowledge of KGB activities was so great that Western governments were able to upend its operations in several allied nations. For the growing number of senior officials in the know, the depth of Soviet penetration into Europe, particularly France, Germany, Britain and Sweden, was acutely embarrassing. It emerged that many of NATO's northern defence plans had been leaked by a British clerk and a Swedish liaison officer with whom they had been shared. But while 'Martel' was able to tell his interrogators that the Soviets had penetrated NATO's Paris HQ itself, he couldn't confirm the identity of the mole or moles.

Behind the scenes, a major but secret spy hunt was now underway – unknown even to the French ambassador to NATO, and perhaps even to the secretary general. Throughout the Cuban crisis, the US government would remain grimly aware that the Kremlin was getting a blow-by-blow account of the alliance's internal workings. But the greatest damage was to mutual trust. 'If NATO does finally break up . . . one of the primary reasons will be the distrust engendered by that damned defector,' one British politician told journalist John Barry after the story finally broke in greater detail in 1968.[8] Nowhere was embarrassment greater than in France, where a humiliated government ordered its intelligence services to attempt to crack down on US and British spying in the country as much as Russian, and where officials were already discussing conducting their own espionage against their allies in order to make the French atomic programme work.

French intelligence did have one advantage the US lacked – sources on the ground in Cuba, where the CIA network had been largely wiped out following the failed 1961 attempt to overthrow Castro at the Bay of Pigs. In the summer of 1962 French intelligence officials began to report new military preparations on the island, including unidentified large missiles, and shared their findings with the Americans.[9]

*

Ever since the Bay of Pigs, US officials had worked to convince sceptical European partners that Cuba represented a real threat and that Castro must be removed.[10] Throughout the first part of 1962, the US administration focused on tightening economic pressure on the island, lobbying European counterparts to impose sanctions of their own.

Berlin might be calmer, but it was still seen as the most likely point for any coming Cold War crisis. Through summer 1962, the East German authorities kept the supply lines to West Berlin open but continued its encirclement, adding barbed wire, tank traps and guard posts. The wall itself was painted white to make potential border-crossers easier to see and shoot. Twelve East Germans had been killed attempting to cross the wall in 1961, and twenty-two more would die in 1962, most as Allied troops stood by desperate to avoid an incident.[11]

*

In July 1962 Kennedy read Barbara Tuchman's newly published *Guns of August*, an account of the missteps that produced global conflict in 1914. Kennedy was appalled at the fatalism of some of those involved and their lack of willingness to compromise or stop the road to war. Shortly afterwards, he installed tape recorders in the White House to record important conversations: if he could not stop another global catastrophe, at the very least he wanted history to recall him trying.[12]

The prospect that Russia might at some point use Cuba as a nuclear launchpad to target the continental United States had been flagged by US officials to Congress midway through 1961.[13] When US U2 spy planes conclusively identified the first ballistic missile sites on the island on 14 October 1962 it was immediately clear to the handful of officials involved that it would precipitate a confrontation of existential danger. 'My instant reaction was dread,' said nuclear weapons analyst William Perry, one of the first to see the photos of several R-12 and R-14 missiles (NATO codename SS-4 and SS-5).[14] By moving the long-range rockets into Cuba, Khrushchev had given himself the ability to strike most of the US – including Washington – almost without warning. Kennedy and those around him believed they must remove that threat – ideally before it was fully ready, or face the possibility of Soviet nuclear blackmail in any future confrontation.

Once the crisis ended, US officials would re-persuade themselves with hindsight that there had, in fact been no Soviet atomic warheads on Cuba in October, and that the nearest atomic warheads had been to the island was on board the Soviet ships already in the North Atlantic – and that the face-off had therefore been less dangerous than feared at the time.[15] Only at a conference for the thirtieth anniversary of the incident in 1992 would Cuban leader Fidel Castro reveal to Robert McNamara just how risky the situation had truly been.

By mid-October 1962 there were, in fact, already 162 Soviet warheads on Cuba, including ninety tactical devices.[16] While the longer-range rockets were indeed not ready, shorter-range tactical weapons, including twenty-five-mile-range Luna rockets and Ilyushin-28 bombers loaded with KSR–2 cruise missiles, were armed and prepped for launch. Russian troops were also – at the start of the crisis, at least – under orders to use the weapons in their own defence in the event of an attack. Soviet Minister of Defence Rodion Malinovsky and Chief of the General Staff Matvei Zakharov had given local commanders the authority 'to make your own decision, and use the nuclear means of the Luna, Il-28 or KSR-2 as instruments of local warfare'.

The US knew of the presence of the bombers, but not the short-range weapons. If the US chose to invade Cuba in the coming days, the attacking US forces were much more likely to be attacked with atomic arms than those in Washington realised at the time. If Kennedy chose airstrikes first as some military advisers wanted, surviving Russian forces would be within their orders to launch the short-range weapons at the nearby US base at Guantánamo Bay, also on the island.[17]

Security was everything in the first week as the Kennedy team argued over the response. NATO's leaders were not the only ones kept outside the loop. Initially, only a handful of individuals were made aware of the missiles. The handful of officials invited to Kennedy's Executive Committee on the crisis left the White House each night packed into an even smaller number of cars with darkened windows, avoiding reporters seeing a string of limousines outside the White House. Keeping the information so secret, senior officials including Attorney General Robert Kennedy would later say, was critical in avoiding the media storm that might have forced faster – and perhaps much worse – decisions.[18]

In truth, the US was only able to approach the Cuban crisis in the way it did because of intelligence from another NATO partner. Technical dossiers provided by Soviet military intelligence official turned British spy Colonel Oleg Penkovsky had delivered final proof of just how weak the Soviet nuclear rocket forces based in Russia and Eastern Europe really were, while the operating manuals for the SS-4 missiles had been critical to identifying those specific types in Cuba.[19] Penkovsky and his British courier Greville Wynne would be arrested during the crisis by the Soviets, the latter held for several months and the former executed – incinerated alive, if rumours almost certainly deliberately spread by Russian intelligence can be believed. Britain was the only ally the president considered alerting to the situation at the start, but Kennedy doubted it was worth it. 'I expect they'll just object,' he said. Macmillan would only be told the night before any US action, such as bombing or invasion.

*

By 18 October, Kennedy had concluded the time had come to tell the other NATO allies, warning it might take 'an awful lot of conditioning' to gain support for US action against Cuba, 'because they think we are slightly demented on this subject'. For now, however, all in Brussels including SACEUR Norstad remained completely in the dark. In Washington, officials suggested a US attack on Cuba might prompt a Russian seizure of West Berlin. Should that happen, General Maxwell Taylor, now chairman of the US Joint Chiefs of Staff, warned the result would be 'general war'. 'You mean nuclear exchange?' asked Kennedy. 'Guess you have to,' replied Taylor, somewhat chillingly. Kennedy bluntly rejected that inevitability, describing such an event as 'the final failure' and asking for further options to reduce that risk.[20]

By the afternoon of 19 October, the president and his civilian advisers – particularly Rusk, McNamara, UN ambassador Adlai Stevenson and former Moscow ambassador Llewellyn

Thompson – concluded that a blockade was the best option on the table, and that it must be briefed to European and Canadian allies. Airstrikes and an invasion would also be prepared.[21]

Late in the afternoon of 20 October those who would brief European leaders – former US Secretary of State Dean Acheson, ambassador to West Germany Walter Dowling (conveniently in Washington) and several CIA officials – gathered at the State Department. The following morning, they boarded a cavernous US Air Force aircraft, then continued to pore over the reconnaissance photos as a trio of armed guards kept the curious flight crew at bay. Landing late at night at the Strategic Air Command base at Greenham Common, west of London, to refuel, they were met by US ambassador David Bruce, carrying his own revolver and a whiskey bottle.[22]

As the envoys flew to Europe, Kennedy met British ambassador David Ormsby-Gore at the White House. The two also discussed US potential military and negotiating options to get Russian missiles out of Cuba. They included invasion, blockade or an eventual deal – including what would become the eventual US offer to withdraw the now obsolete but only recently deployed nuclear-tipped Jupiter missiles from Turkey.[23] Kennedy had faced down many of his own most senior military commanders to push his chosen Cuba option. Now NATO leaders, the Kremlin and the world would be told US naval forces would impose a quarantine around the island, stopping, searching and turning back any Russian ships carrying offensive weapons. Ships attempting to break the blockade would be fired at.

A US invasion would take a week or more to prepare – but Kennedy would make it clear he was keeping that option firmly on the table if the Russians did not withdraw the missiles.

*

After the chaos of Berlin Kennedy was determined to maintain strong command and control – and concerned the Turkey rockets, in particular, might be fired if their crews believed they faced immediate attack. On 21 October, he gave explicit instructions – making a point to ensure the recorders were switched on – that orders be sent to the Jupiter crews there that, no matter what happened in the coming days, no missile was to be unleashed without his personal authorisation.

Why Kennedy was so worried about these specific missiles remains unclear. Around the world, hundreds of US nuclear warheads were under no such tight restrictions.[24] Even before NATO was briefed, all US forces around the world were raised to DEFCON 3, just two steps short of Defence Condition 1, US code for total worldwide war. In the coming days, Strategic Air Command's bombers would fly twenty million miles, while some US armaments factories moved into seven-days-a-week production as troops, planes and ships prepared for action.[25] That included US forces in Europe – the first indication SACEUR Norstad would get of what was going on.

At bases across NATO, crews slept next to aircraft pre-loaded with atomic bombs. Except for the Jupiters in Turkey, which Kennedy had specifically restricted, SAC commanders – including of fast jets based at Incirlik, also within Turkey – had authority to launch their nuclear weapons if they had 'unambiguous' evidence of war. For US missile batteries in Britain and Italy, doing so should theoretically require the acquiescence of local authorities. Whether those governments would be able to stop the multiple US nuclear-armed aircraft on their territory from taking action, however, was much more doubtful. Most were mere minutes away from launch, others already airborne.[26]

*

As Kennedy prepared to address the public on the evening of Monday 22 October, the coordinated international US briefing plan went into action.

US intelligence still did not know about the smaller Russian atomic weapons in Cuba that could devastate a US invasion, but they believed there were now forty of the larger ballistic missile launchers capable of striking the United States. They believed some were perhaps already operational. The ten-minute warning the Cuban crews would likely get of any US airstrikes should not be enough for them to fire their rockets, but the Pentagon doubted it could destroy every missile in its opening attack. Even if it did so, a perhaps devastating Russian response elsewhere in the world was seen as inevitable. Few doubted that striking Cuba could mean immediate and catastrophic war, spreading immediately to Berlin and Western Europe.[27]

Kennedy was aware he had put the NATO leadership – particularly Norstad – in a challenging position. 'As this situation has developed, I have given much thought to the impacts upon NATO and your task as SACEUR,' Kennedy wrote in a cable on 22 October. 'I have regretted the inability to widen the circle of discussion during this period and particularly to enlist the support of NATO governments . . . While I know that our action creates a difficult situation for you . . . I have every confidence in your leadership and experience to help us over this critical period.'[28] The briefing timetable was tight. A telegram from Kennedy to Macmillan in the small hours of 22 October allowed the US to make the claim to Britain that it was being told 'first'[29] – while de Gaulle and Adenauer were told that they, Macmillan and Canadian Prime Minister John Diefenbaker were being briefed almost simultaneously. Acheson's meeting with de Gaulle would be followed almost immediately by one with the North Atlantic Council, although the US delegation did not tell them in advance what it would be about – nor even that Acheson himself was in the country.

The former secretary of state and the CIA's Sherman Kent were ushered into de Gaulle's office just as the clock was striking five – a move Acheson later ascribed to a deliberate French sense of drama. The French president had survived an assassination attempt exactly two months earlier, suspected to have been carried out by the same right-wing elements that had both quietly helped him into office and tried to oust him in the 'putsch'. Now, more than ever, he presented himself as the embodiment of the French state, ready to assist its allies in a time of crisis, whatever their prior disagreements. De Gaulle said he did not need to see the photographs of the rockets – 'I accept what you tell me as a fact without proof of any sort needed' – but pronounced himself fascinated by them, particularly when told they were taken from 60,000 feet. 'We don't have anything . . .' he started to say through his translator, before catching himself and continuing: 'I'm not very familiar with photography, but this seems remarkable to me . . . You may tell your president that France will support him in every way in this crisis.' 'He didn't say "I will" – or "the French government will" – or anything,' Acheson would later recall. 'He was France.'[30] CIA briefer Sherman Kent recalled another lasting impression. 'I was . . . prepared for his vast height but not his bulk,' he later wrote. 'He is surely one of the largest men alive.'[31]

Adenauer was even more supportive than de Gaulle – and similarly intrigued by the exposure to US intelligence, asking the CIA briefer Jack Smith whether that really was his name (it was) or just an alias. Seizing a Russian cargo ship and the weapons on board, he suggested enthusiastically, would be a good next move to bring public opinion further behind Washington's position. 'This comes as no surprise. I have been worried about Cuba,' he said. 'The president is absolutely right. Khrushchev knows the free world rests on American strength, and if it can be eliminated, there will be nothing left.'[32]

The British, as Kennedy had earlier predicted, were less supportive and perhaps more patronising in their response.[33] As CIA briefer Chester Cooper recalled, Macmillan's first comment 'which he addressed more to himself than to the ambassador, was to the effect that the British people, who had been living in the shadow of annihilation for the past many years, had somehow been able to live more or less normal lives and he felt that the Americans, now confronted with a similar situation . . . would make a similar adjustment'. But this was, the prime minister added meanderingly, more of an observation on human nature than a sign that he was not sympathetic to the US.[34]

'Although the British have some concern I am sure you can count on their support,' Norstad cabled Kennedy later that evening after meeting the prime minister, who was hosting him for a retirement dinner. 'As you know, I have not declared a formal NATO alert but have asked all NATO commands and national MoDs to operate in an awareness of the critical international situation.' This, he noted, would be easier diplomatically than announcing a widespread alert.[35] In fact, Norstad had been told by Macmillan that evening that Britain would oppose a NATO-wide alert. Macmillan had served in the trenches of the First World War, and talk of a Royal Proclamation calling up the reserves reminded him too much of the opening stages of that conflict.[36]

The US briefing to the wider North Atlantic Council was broadly well received. Acheson presented the missiles in Cuba as an attempt to shift the global strategic balance to neutralise the US, and therefore a threat to NATO. He outlined what Kennedy was about to tell the world, the blockade of Cuba due to be imposed exactly twenty-four hours after his announcement.[37] As expected, some of America's allies complained at being told of the situation in Cuba mere minutes before the president spoke on television – former Secretary General Spaak suggested they should have been given at least twenty-four hours' notice.[38] By now US and international media had firmly detected that something was underway, although they did not know the details – and radio reports claiming that Norstad had already ordered forces across NATO to alert status also upset several European members. 'When the chips were down and decisions were being made that might plunge the world into a nuclear holocaust, all NATO could do was hold its breath while Washington took whatever steps the president and his military advisers deemed appropriate,' Canadian NATO ambassador George Ignatieff later wrote.[39]

The council meeting broke up quickly. NAC ambassadors whose countries had not already been briefed directly – everyone aside from Germany, France, Britain and Canada – had only twenty minutes in which to inform their governments before Kennedy appeared on television. As the meeting closed the CIA's Kent noted that a map he had passed around was missing. 'Somebody at the NAC has it as a souvenir,' he observed dryly to his superiors, adding that he had removed all codewords and sensitive details from the document beforehand.[40]

*

By Tuesday 23 October, a global media briefing programme was also underway. In London, the CIA's Chester Cooper and the US embassy released reconnaissance photos to the press, partly in response to encouragement by Macmillan – and to the private irritation of the US president.[41] In Paris Sherman Kent briefed sometimes sceptical French journalists, using the same reconnaissance photos US ambassador to the United Nations Adlai Stevenson would present there later that same day. The world watched and waited. In the North Atlantic sixteen Soviet vessels carrying military hardware towards Cuba halted their approach and began to loiter in open sea. Unbeknownst to Kennedy, Khrushchev had also sent new orders to Soviet forces in Cuba, removing their authorisation – although almost certainly not their technical ability – to launch nuclear weapons without direct authority from Moscow.[42] It was the first step towards avoiding an unexpected but cataclysmic conflict, but no one knew that yet. On 23 October, Macmillan returned home late and told his wife, 'I really am most desperately sorry, but we may be at war in the morning.'[43]

Kennedy's own trust and patience with his military

commanders was wearing thin. Ironically, given his past relations with the administration, Norstad would be the only general
in whom the president showed full confidence in that week,
impressed with what historian Max Hastings later termed his
'cool judgement' in not raising NATO's alert status in Europe
and managing alliance tensions.[44] Others were hungrier for a
fight. As the blockade of Cuba began on 24 October, Strategic
Air Command chief General Thomas Power sent a plain-
language message to all his bases worldwide, knowing that the
Russians were listening in. 'We are in a very dangerous situation,' he told his subordinate commanders. 'I know that we are
all ready to do the job that we do, and I want you to know I am
counting on you to do the best you can because we are ready to
go and you are ready to go. We will carry out our mission.'[45]
Even without a formal 'NATO alert', military forces across the
alliance were left in little doubt about what might be coming.
'We were told . . . it was the real thing,' said German air force
NCO Wolfgang Koppenhagen. 'We were told: World War
Three is about to start.'[46] In the Atlantic, no weapons-carrying
Russian ships were yet approaching the US embargo line.
Secretary of State Rusk allowed himself some optimism,
noting that the Soviet authorities had stopped short of telling
their own people they had put missiles in Cuba: 'Our best
judgement is that they are scratching their brains very hard at
the present time and deciding just how exactly they want to
play this.'[47] Kennedy and Khrushchev continued to exchange
letters, both now looking for ways out. Preparations for an
invasion of Cuba continued alongside occasional more hopeful signs – until, on 27 October, a Russian surface-to-air
missile knocked a U2 spy plane from the sky. The same day,
US officials warned NATO counterparts they increasingly
suspected any escalation in Cuba would be followed by an
immediate new flare-up in Berlin.[48]

The news of the U2 shoot-down, Robert Kennedy later said,
felt like the tightening of a noose.[49] Simultaneously, unbeknownst

to senior authorities in either nation, a potentially deadly game of cat and mouse was underway in the waters of the Sargasso Sea off Cuba, as US destroyers and patrol aircraft dropped hand grenades and practice depth charges around the Russian diesel-electric submarine B-59. According to a later account from B-59 hydrophone operator Lieutenant Vadim Orlov, as the explosions mounted the captain ordered its single nuclear torpedo to be prepared for firing, exclaiming: 'Perhaps war has already started up above, and we are going nuts here . . . Now we'll hit them with everything we've got.' According to Orlov, conditions on the sub had become appalling: carbon dioxide levels were rising fast, and one officer collapsed. It took two others to calm the agitated skipper and persuade him to surface the submarine to recharge its batteries, where it continued to be harassed by US naval forces.[50]

Both sides were at their limit, terrified of the consequences of further immediate miscalculation like no leaders before or since in world history. That evening Soviet media reported a new letter from Khrushchev to Kennedy, explicitly now offering the option of withdrawing the Soviet missiles from Cuba in return for the removal of the US Jupiters from Turkey.[51] US officials already knew such an unexpected move would irritate some NATO allies, particularly the Turks. The previous year Rusk had suggested withdrawing the Jupiters to his counterpart in Ankara – such was the pace of technological advance they were already regarded as too vulnerable, particularly to air attack. The Turks, however, had spent months getting parliamentary agreement, and had 'begged' the US not to pull them out so fast as to be a political embarrassment.[52]

No one in Washington at this point, however, appears to have been concerned about such niceties. This was a superpower confrontation, and it would be the superpowers that decided how it ended. Later that night Robert Kennedy met secretly with Russian ambassador Anatoly Dobrynin and reached a deal. The Soviet missiles would be withdrawn from Cuba under

UN supervision in return for a US pledge not to invade – an offer communicated several days earlier by UN Secretary General U Thant. The US would also agree to pull back the Turkey missiles – but Washington's offer to do so must be kept confidential.[53]

As US officials prepared a new raft of signals to other allied capitals, war still looked as likely as peace. In Florida US Marines began boarding assault ships, pilots prepared for air strikes into Cuba and families fled north.[54] Across the alliance and wider world, few were unaffected. Having just turned ten at a convent school in Kent, my mother remembers being told by the nuns to 'pray for peace'. In Canada, one naval officer wrote in his diary of 'anger . . . that our lovely family . . . may be extinguished . . . and for the whole future of mankind'.[55] A twenty-two-year-old Royal Navy officer who had recently joined his submarine recalled primarily excitement.[56] In France, the missile crisis was somewhat overshadowed by the Algerian war and other domestic issues, while some of those who paid attention saw it as an 'education' for the young US president.[57]

In West Germany, likely to be the scene of heavy fighting and atomic warfare from the start, the trauma was very real. 'We didn't know: are we going to wake up tomorrow morning, are we even going to survive today?' recalled Adenauer's secretary Anneliese Poppinga. In Berlin, Willy Brandt's adviser Egon Bahr described feeling the 'completely helpless pawns of larger powers'.[58] British Ministry of Defence official Peter Hudson said he was confident Cuba was by far the closest they came to war. 'The Berlin crisis was familiar pieces being played on the board. Cuba wasn't – it was an entirely different game.'[59]

*

In fact, the danger was already ebbing.

As tensions eased following the announcement Russia would withdraw its missiles, British diplomat Patrick Dean concluded the Kennedy administration judged the role of NATO allies as 'very marginal' in times of trouble, with Berlin and Cuba showing the 'North Atlantic partnership . . . almost completely useless in this context from an American point of view'.[60] From beginning to end, US forces earmarked and assigned to NATO had operated largely or effectively independently under direct US command – indeed, the telegram from the Joint Chiefs of Staff to the US commander in the Atlantic – also NATO's SACLANT – ordering the establishment of the blockade of 22 October made no reference whatsoever to their NATO responsibilities.[61]

When the expected 'NATO-wide alert' proved politically impossible, individual alliance nations took unilateral action, albeit sometimes in loose coordination with US commanders. After US forces cancelled a joint antisubmarine drill with Canada, for example, Canadian officers sent the ships into the Atlantic anyway, where they could help hunt Russian submarines if it came to war.

In other instances, pre-existing military arrangements authorised US commanders to call on specific allies for certain assets without further political approval. When US authorities requested Canadian maritime patrol aircraft at the height of the crisis, for example, they were delivered immediately – to the later surprise and consternation of politicians in Ottawa who might well have vetoed such a move.[62] When de Gaulle discovered something similar had happened with French forces, it would be the start of the process that eventually saw the US and NATO kicked entirely out of France.

The unilateral US offer to pull missiles out from Turkey would also not be unproblematic. At a National Security Council meeting on 27 October, several US officials had voiced concern that taking such a step would infuriate both the government in Ankara and wider NATO allies.[63] And yet they had gone ahead and done it anyway, leaving the US delegation at NATO to sort it out. From Brussels, US ambassador to NATO

Thomas Finletter advised that Turkey set 'great store' by the Jupiters as a 'symbol of [the] alliance's determination to use atomic weapons against [any] Russian attack on Turkey'. He warned against the US making unilateral decisions over their presence without prior discussion with the government in Ankara – and he was comprehensively ignored.[64]

Then there was the larger strategic picture. Both Kennedy and Khrushchev – if not all within their respective militaries – had ultimately been forced to confront the sheer horror of thermonuclear confrontation, and had chosen to back down. Neither they nor those around them would show any appetite to repeat that experience again soon. The December ministerial meeting of the North Atlantic Council took place, one attendee noted, with an atmosphere of 'intolerable serenity'. Rusk wrote to Kennedy that the 'central theme of the meeting has been deep satisfaction [with] your handling of Cuba situation'. French passers-by waved at the US delegation in the streets, and even de Gaulle's esteem for the US president appeared boosted by the crisis. But once again, the US expressed its frustrations over Europe's limited commitment to its own defence. 'My impression is that other [European] ministers are getting seriously concerned, partly because they sense that US patience is running out,' Rusk wrote. 'Whether this will result in effective action [to build Europe's own defences] remains to be seen.'[65]

The signs were far from promising. Just as Norstad was standing down, Secretary General Stikker announced his own ambition to retire after less than two years in role. Once again, Adenauer pushed for an American secretary general, again arguing that only US officials in both military and civilian roles could hold together the alliance.[66]

On 5 November, barely a week after the Cuba crisis ended, Acheson visited the US Military Academy at West Point to talk about the lessons learned for NATO. His speech is best remembered for his assertion that Britain had 'lost an empire, but not yet found a role'. But he had a separate analogy for the alliance he had helped create. NATO, said the man who had once mused with Ted Achilles on making it the basis for a transatlantic union, was approaching the fourteenth anniversary of its birth. 'Like a youth of the same age,' he said, 'it is growing out of its clothes.'[67]

Part 4:
Détente, Disagreements and the Reagan Rollercoaster

11

The Shadow of Vietnam (1963–1974)

'In the 1940s and 1950s, the threats to NATO were really external. In the 1960s and '70s, the threats were all internal.'

**NATO Deputy Assistant
Secretary General Jamie Shea, 2009**[1]

Having ratcheted up tensions between them since 1945, the superpowers had blinked on Cuba. Not until the late 1970s would the dangers truly rise again; not until the eighties would atomic war again feel imminently plausible – and not until Kosovo in 1999 would Russian and NATO forces come so close to combat. As 1963 began US, NATO and Russian leaders alike were determined never to come so close to catastrophe again. Coupled with the equally divisive legacy of Vietnam – in which no NATO member nations would offer significant support to the US – the result would be two decades in which alliance nations would spend much of their time squabbling among themselves. Within NATO itself – as well as within the foreign-policy teams of the successive Kennedy, Johnson, Nixon and Ford administrations – these would often prove frustrating years. 'The secretary general . . . in the 1960s for the first time spent as much of his time keeping the allies together as keeping the Soviets and the communists out,' said NATO Deputy Assistant Secretary General Jamie Shea in a 2009 lecture. 'That is a lesson which has stayed with us today.'[2]

That NATO faced genuine internal threats was also no longer in doubt. In August 1963 NATO deputy press chief Georges Pâques was arrested as he attempted to pass classified documents to Russian handlers in his Paris flat. Initial press reports described him as a 'quiet man' with a glittering career, suggesting he had been passing secrets for the last half-decade. Later estimates would indicate he might have been active as a Soviet source for almost twenty years. Pâques claimed he was neither a Communist sympathiser nor motivated by money, but that by providing the Kremlin with Western military plans he was 'levelling the playing field' and averting conflict. Sentenced to life imprisonment in 1964, he was released after only seven years.[3] Although Pâques was the only one arrested, intelligence insiders suspected other spies remained. 'Manifestly he was not the only one,' wrote French intelligence official Philippe de Vosjoli five years later.[4]

Not until his arrest did many within the alliance become aware the investigation was even underway. A secret and since-declassified report for the NAC indicated Pâques had passed over details of defence plans and NATO's analysis of its own perceived strengths and weaknesses – as well as those of the Warsaw Pact – plus details of recent summits and psychological warfare plans. The documents handed over to the USSR, it said, 'contain most of the essential elements for the enemy fully to appraise, or obtain confirmation of, NATO's basic defence doctrines and policies', as well as 'sufficient information to build up a comprehensive list of existing weaknesses in the NATO force posture'.[5] The damage to alliance credibility would be lasting. Never again would the US feel entirely comfortable it could keep the most sensitive details safe.

From the end of the Cuban missile crisis in October 1962 to his assassination the following November, Kennedy had only thirteen months to digest and react to what had happened. Making the choice between blockade, airstrikes and invasion had taken several days. Even before the Cuban crisis, the

Kennedy administration had believed more forces might be needed to hold back a conventional Russian attack and give Western leaders long enough to decide next steps. Now Kennedy believed that requirement was existential – if forced to act within an hour or two the superpowers might react 'in a spasm' and go nuclear.

Kennedy now intended to push the European states to build their militaries to give NATO more options in another crisis – and he was willing to push much harder than Eisenhower to get it done. 'Why should we have in Europe supplies adequate to fight for ninety days when the European forces around our troops have only enough supplies to fight for two or three?' Kennedy asked his National Security Council in January 1963. 'We should consider very hard the interests of the United States.'[6] Kennedy saw no contradiction between building military strength and pursuing sharply intensified 'détente'. Contact with the Kremlin grew throughout early 1963, and on 10 June, in a commencement address at American University near Washington, Kennedy made a unilateral offer of a test ban treaty as part of a wider pitch for the world to turn away from war. Broadcast uncensored within the Soviet Union, the speech was described by Khrushchev as the best by any president since Roosevelt. Within a month he had refined Kennedy's suggestions to what would become the 'Partial Test Ban Treaty', banning all but underground nuclear tests and signed on 5 August. On 30 August the White House also announced the creation of a hotline with the Kremlin, to 'help reduce the risk of war through miscalculation'.[7]

All of these initiatives were decided without reference to the alliance, yet would have a considerable effect upon it. In policy terms, NATO's focus remained heavily on the alliance nuclear scheme proposed by Kennedy in Ottawa, now known as the Multilateral Force or MLF, which would see mixed-nationality NATO crews at sea carrying US Polaris missiles.

How this would work was far from clear – including whether participating NATO member nations would each have to agree to launch the missiles in a crisis, which might have been impractical. Nor were all nations keen on the idea. 'You don't expect our chaps to share grog [rum] with the Turks,' one British official is reported to have asked a US counterpart.[8] Like the failed European Army and European Defence Community of the 1950s, the MLF would now tie up huge amounts of time with almost no real progress. Other divisions within the alliance were also on the rise.

De Gaulle might have been a supportive ally during Cuba, but the more he found out about that confrontation the angrier he got. According to a story doing the rounds in Paris, he was particularly outraged by a conversation he'd had with Admiral Robert Dennison, US and NATO commander-in-chief North Atlantic. Dennison had apparently told de Gaulle that throughout the crisis he had several French naval vessels under his command, seemingly hopeful this might qualify him for the Légion d'Honneur. Instead, de Gaulle – who had never really grasped the realities of how NATO US commanders asserted control of other national forces, and apparently unaware French forces had been under US command during the crisis – exploded with fury. He was now even more determined to ensure that only the president of France could order French forces into battle.[9] Behind each of the rows between the French leader and the alliance sat a simple constant: he was increasingly convinced that neither the US nor NATO had enough respect for France, and that by cooperating within it militarily his beloved nation lost agency, sovereignty and dignity. In June 1963 de Gaulle removed the French Atlantic fleet from NATO command as he had with the Mediterranean fleet in 1958. Paris was becoming an increasingly uncomfortable home for the alliance, if not outright untenable.

As 1963 progressed, Kennedy's own frustration with his European allies grew. A German delegation visiting the White

House was left in no doubt that if European states made unwelcome comments that made him or the American people feel their troops were no longer needed or welcome, the US would bring its soldiers home.[10] Visiting Europe in June, the president saw US troops in Germany and spoke to cheering crowds in West Berlin. But he avoided Paris, de Gaulle and the alliance it still housed.[11] A 21 November White House memo hints at an imminent presidential rethink on Europe ahead of the December NATO summit, instructing Secretary of State Rusk and Defense Secretary McNamara to avoid extensive discussions with European counterparts while Kennedy reviewed strategy.[12] Two days later, Kennedy was dead, slain in Dallas by Lee Harvey Oswald's bullet.

*

In the years that followed, the transatlantic alliance would be divided on several fundamental issues, not just spending on defence. They would produce multiple 'mini-crises' within NATO, although never any strong enough to threaten its existence. All of that, however, was well in the future as Kennedy's Vice President Lyndon Johnson found himself propelled into the White House. Preoccupied for most of his time in office by domestic concerns including civil rights and the worsening war in Vietnam, he would never see NATO and Europe as his high priorities. After Truman, Eisenhower and Kennedy, this era would feel very different.

After Cuba, Soviet enthusiasm for sparking new crises in Europe was also much reduced. In 1964, Kremlin powerbrokers forced Khrushchev from office, alarmed by his centralisation of power and sometimes erratic decision-making – including over Cuba. Imposed in his place – although without the violence and purges that followed Stalin's death – were a group of senior officials led by Leonid Brezhnev, another party insider from the Ukraine–Russia border. With the Brezhnev regime presenting itself as more predictable than its predecessor, the Johnson administration was quick to reach out and offer trade talks.[13]

How to tackle negotiations with the Kremlin would be another perennial source of division within NATO in the years to come.

NATO's next secretary general – the tall, aristocratic Italian diplomat Manlio Brosio – was appointed in May 1964. His predecessor Stikker had spent much of his time attempting to arbitrate US and European differences, inevitably finding himself accused by Europeans of being excessively pro-American. Brosio intended to avoid that as much as possible, cultivating a reputation for meticulous management and sticking to protocol.[14]

From summer 1964 and throughout 1965 the destroyer USS *Biddle* sailed with a crew that were 40 per cent American, the remainder from other NATO nations, an experiment in multinational crewing intended as a precursor for the nuclear-capable Multilateral Force. The idea of sending mixed NATO crews to sea in Polaris submarines had been abandoned as too complex, but there was still talk of NATO-operated missile-carrying surface ships. But the MLF concept was soon to be abandoned, fatally undermined by the fact that no one truly wanted it or understood its purpose. 'We just let it die,' Secretary of State Rusk said later.[15] De Gaulle, meanwhile, remained angry about US refusals to help France with its atomic programme, or provide it with Polaris missiles. This anger intensified after the US agreed to sell Polaris to the British, one of several reasons the French leader would give for blocking British EC membership.

Brosio's first years in office would see de Gaulle's France continue as a disruptive influence in alliance discussions and decision-making, including repeatedly blocking the adoption of a new strategic concept based on the US 'flexible response'. While Secretary General Brosio usually kept his cool, British officials reported Rusk getting angry, on one occasion telling allies that if France wanted to leave NATO the US too 'could develop alternative defence policies', on one occasion suggesting the US Strategic Air Command could even target Western Europe if relations continued to deteriorate. Some British officials worried that by using increasingly assertive and aggressive language, the US risked 'falling into the trap that General de Gaulle has prepared for them' and might further damage NATO.[16]

European reluctance to join the US in Vietnam also undermined transatlantic trust. Between 1964 and 1967 the number of US troops stationed there rose from 23,000 to almost half a million. Newly arrived soldiers described it as looking as if the US had taken over the entire country.[17] US National Security Adviser McGeorge Bundy told the British that a brigade – or, according to another version of the story, an even smaller battalion-sized force – of UK troops in Vietnam 'would be worth one billion dollars' as Prime Minister Harold Wilson lobbied the US to support the pound. Neither Britain nor any other European state was prepared to get involved, however, even on those terms.[18]

The combination of currency problems and Vietnam would be at the root of some of NATO's deepest coming disagreements. In return for keeping US troops on its soil, the US had negotiated a long-running 'offset' with West Germany in which the Bonn government agreed to buy American weapons. That deal had never been fully implemented, the subject of fraught negotiations with successive German governments throughout the 1960s.[19] Negotiations with Britain and Germany over both their financial and military commitments to the alliance were ill-tempered. In August 1966 US officials warned the strains risked 'the impression NATO is falling apart'.[20]

*

Despite the years of rising tension, de Gaulle's decision to evict US and NATO forces entirely from French soil still came as a shock. On 21 February 1966 the French leader gave a press conference, the contents of which many of his own officials were unaware of beforehand. The conditions under which France had signed the Atlantic Charter in 1949, he said, no longer applied. The Western world was no longer threatened in the same way it had been when the 'American protectorate was organised in Europe under the cover of NATO'. France would not quit the Atlantic Treaty and would keep its troops in Germany to help protect Western Europe, he said, but foreign forces must leave France.[21] Later letters clarified France would quit all of NATO's military structures, no longer allowing its troops to be used at all under direct command of the alliance, nor attending any meetings on NATO's own military matters. France would continue to be a member of the North Atlantic Council and attend political discussions, but the relationship going forward would clearly be much more limited than anything envisaged in 1949. Perhaps most disruptive of all, both SHAPE and NATO's civilian HQ in Paris would now need to find new homes within a year.

'The decision came as a shock to all of us,' wrote Canadian ambassador George Ignatieff. 'Not only did it mean that all the physical facilities of NATO, including the early warning systems and all supply depots, would have to be dismantled; equally important . . . was the symbolic significance of the move.'[22] On 30 June 1966, the withdrawal of the 30,000 US personnel began. US officials pointed journalists towards the French civilians employed at US military bases, now furiously lobbying for jobs elsewhere.[23] De Gaulle, meanwhile, was in Moscow, signing an agreement on scientific cooperation while NATO officials worked furiously to find the alliance a new home outside of France.

The eviction from Paris was unquestionably politically damaging – but the move also offered a new start. In a matter of months Belgian construction crews completed the new Supreme Headquarters Allied Powers Europe in time for its opening on 1 April 1967 in Mons, Belgium. Worried about a nuclear strike in time of war, the Belgian government had refused to allow it to be based close to Brussels, but agreed to build a new motorway to support it.[24]

NATO's new civilian headquarters was welcomed to the Belgian capital, built in twenty-nine weeks on a windswept site near the city's airport and opened in October. Almost half its staff had chosen to stay behind in Paris, while those that relocated complained of a 10 per cent pay cut due to the lower Belgian cost of living. By the end of the year 2,000 people were working at the Brussels site.[25] Designed to last only twenty years, it would be NATO's home until 2017, almost half a century. The new larger Brussels location also allowed the staff of NATO's Military Committee – the descendants of the original UK–US–French Standing Group founded in 1949, extended to include each nation and several hundred personnel – to finally relocate from Washington. Their existence there had remained awkwardly detached from the alliance up to that point, their primary purpose being to arrange the meetings of defence chiefs initially held twice a year.

De Gaulle's departure from NATO's military decision-making also made it easier to replace outdated alliance strategy, still theoretically based around the 1950s-era 'massive retaliation' approach due to French refusal to agree anything new. In its place, the alliance finally adopted the 'flexible response' approach Kennedy had first proposed before Berlin and Cuba, which provided a much wider range of military options short of all-out atomic war. It would provide the basis for NATO planning until the 1990s, and once again from the Ukraine invasion in February 2022.[26] US ambassador to NATO Harlan Cleveland described the strategy discussions as blowing much-needed 'fresh air' through the alliance.[27]

De Gaulle had signalled France would maintain troops in Germany – but for them to fight alongside the US and NATO in any conflict would clearly need a degree of military coordination that would now need to be managed outside NATO. This was negotiated by SACEUR Lyman Lemnitzer, who also agreed that the French would retain access to US tactical nuclear weapons in time of war.[28]

Many within the alliance believed it now faced another growing challenge: the emergence of what US ambassador

Cleveland called a 'generation that does not remember why we got into an Atlantic alliance to begin with'. Neither for the first nor last time, NATO's response was to commission another report, this time from a commission chaired by Belgian Foreign Minister Pierre Harmel to examine the future of the alliance.[29] Through the summer of 1968, that new generation was on the march – from civil rights and anti-war protests in the US to student riots in London, Paris and Berlin. At the beginning of the year, the US had been humiliated by the Tet offensive in Vietnam. No longer able to claim the US was winning the war, a battered Johnson decided not to stand for re-election.

Unrest was not limited to the West. For the first time since Hungary in 1956, it spread behind the Iron Curtain. The 'Prague Spring' saw the government of Czechoslovakia grant unprecedented reform and freedom, sparking a Soviet invasion on 20–21 August, assisted by Warsaw Pact troops from Hungary, Poland, East Germany and Bulgaria. It was a renewed and naked assertion of Soviet willingness to use force to retain control in Eastern Europe – what came to be known as the 'Brezhnev Doctrine'.

This was just the sort of situation NATO's new Situation Centre was designed to track, bringing together news and intelligence feeds to inform alliance leadership and delegations. For the first few hours of the invasion, however, its sole teleprinter was out of action, while NATO radar stations failed to report Soviet planes flying into Czechoslovakia. The German delegation complained that NATO's initial response was 'practically non-existent'.[30] The spectacle of Soviet troops essentially invading a European state inevitably prompted NATO members to re-examine their priorities. A CIA report in November noted that 'for the first time in several years all the allies (save France) accept the necessity of preserving an effective alliance beyond its twentieth anniversary next year'.[31] Having walked out of so many of the alliance structures, even France was now much less disruptive within the NAC. De

Gaulle was now seventy-eight years old, increasingly struggling to assert himself in a very different modern France.

NATO's own efforts to engage a new generation were also yielding mixed results. As NATO ministers met in Brussels in November 1968 the findings of the Harmel Report itself – designed in part to do just that – were described as somewhat 'indigestible'. A Soviet diplomat told a US National Security Council staffer they were baffled as to how such a comprehensive process could yield something so innocuous.[32] The report contained a concept that would underpin NATO's approach to the rest of the Cold War, a commitment to balance the military forces of deterrence with the diplomacy of détente.[33]

*

Newly elected US President Richard Nixon was determined see the Europeans finally pull their weight on defending their own continent. His inaugural speech on 20 January 1969 offered a new era of détente with Brezhnev, and called on other nations of the 'free world' to take on a greater share of the burden of defending it. US ambassador to NATO Harlan Cleveland attempted to manage down his boss's expectations. 'Our main objective is to get the most effective conventional defence effort out of the $90-to-$100 billion the allies (excluding France, and not counting the US contribution) can be expected to put up during the next five years,' he wrote. 'The main objectives of our European allies are to keep the United States physically committed to the defence of Western Europe, so that the engagement of our nuclear power is assured, and to buy a right to be consulted by the United States on anything affecting their security.'[34]

Nixon wanted more than that: a complete enthusiastic rebirth of the Atlantic alliance. It would be one of several points on which his administration would find itself frustrated. At NATO meetings multiple European nations would express the opposition of their populations to the war in Vietnam, as well as the irritation of European defence establishments that the US had removed four billion dollars of military stores from the continent to send to south-east Asia.[35] 'Partners are not expected to agree,' Nixon told the North Atlantic Council in Brussels on 24 February. 'But they are supposed to consult. I know there have been rumblings of discontent in Europe – feeling that too often the United States talked at its partners instead of talking with them.'[36]

Nixon was next to express concerns about the new generation's approach to NATO. Meeting NATO ministers again in March 1969, he described what he called 'a strong, well-intentioned opposition' within each country 'which took the view that NATO was now an anachronism and that the defence posture should be re-examined'. Within the US, he said, major force reductions in Europe would be 'extremely popular' amid 'a growing sense of isolationism'.[37] What NATO now needed, he told them, was a 'political dimension'. Its members should learn from each other, he said in his speech for the twentieth anniversary gathering in Washington, citing 'the care of infant children in West Germany, the "new towns" policy of Great Britain, the development of depressed areas programs in Italy . . . the effectiveness of urban planning by local governments in Norway, the experience of the French in metropolitan planning'.[38]

Not since Dean Acheson at the signing of the treaty itself had a senior US official, let alone a president, voiced such a call for transatlantic political unity and cooperation. Perhaps even more surprisingly, from the perspective of the 2020s, here was a conservative Republican suggesting much could be learned from the social democracies of Europe. Nixon's political advisers were soon explaining to him that their European allies were unlikely to be keen on such a doctrine. Kissinger wrote in June: 'The Allies traditionally are suspicious of plans to create new NATO mechanisms until it is perfectly clear why they are required.'[39] Still, when the newly formed Committee on Challenges for Modern Society met for the first time in December, its chair Pat Moynihan reported to Nixon afterwards that the sessions were 'lively, friendly and intelligent'.[40]

On 29 April 1969 Charles de Gaulle resigned as president of France, having lost a referendum on constitutional reform.[41] Georges Pompidou, previously de Gaulle's prime minister, was the first of several new European leaders. In October 1969 former West Berlin Mayor Willy Brandt became Germany's first left-wing Social Democratic Party chancellor, while in Britain Conservative Edward Heath ousted Wilson in the June 1970 election. Both brought change – Brandt pursuing his own brand of détente with '*Ostpolitik*' outreach to the Kremlin, East Germany and the remainder of the Eastern bloc, while Heath finally brought Britain into the European Economic Community in 1973.

For the Americans, not all were welcome changes. Heath's desperation for European accession was seen as making him too prone to ignore Washington. West German *Ostpolitik* was seen as either dangerous or naïve. Alexander Haig, a former general serving as Nixon's chief of staff, who would later become SACEUR, would in the future allege that Brandt was influenced by the Kremlin directly through an aide – his secretary, Gunter Guillaume, publicly exposed in 1973 as an East German spy.[42] This was the kind of distrust that would bedevil the alliance over the coming decades. But the departure of de Gaulle appeared positive for the transatlantic partnership. By the time Pompidou visited Washington in February 1970, the US and French militaries were already in quiet negotiation over US support for the French ballistic missile programme. Even today, many of the details of what support the US provided remain classified.[43]

Bolstering the French nuclear deterrent was a canny move ahead of arms negotiations with the Kremlin – Nixon was willing to cut the number of US warheads, but some of those reductions could be offset by the new French weapons that would not be covered in the negotiations. American ground troops were by this point largely out of Vietnam, but relentless

US bombing there, and across the border in Cambodia and Laos, was turning European sentiment not just against the US but also the alliance. In Norway hordes of young activists – including a teenage Jens Stoltenberg – sang songs calling for the country to leave NATO.[44] In West Germany an opinion poll showed 50 per cent of the population favouring a neutral position between East and West.[45]

American isolationism looked quite different. Senator Mike Mansfield put forward a resolution to withdraw US troops from Europe, prompting a massive bipartisan effort from current and former officials to block it. European confidence in the US commitment to Europe was now deteriorating. US Assistant Secretary of State for European Affairs Martin Hillenbrand quoted some Europeans as talking of US 'negotiation with the Soviets and confrontation with our allies'. The *Economist* reported 'evidence of the apparent withdrawal of the United States into a querulous and indiscriminate rejection of the world'.[46]

US military confidence was also somewhat diminished. The first REFORGER exercises – conducted annually from 1969 – showed US equipment in Europe was not always maintained well enough for use. Kissinger fumed that Pentagon estimates of working US tank numbers in Europe fluctuated so widely, he hoped US intelligence on the Russians was better than on its own forces.[47] Arms control, however, continued to push ahead in earnest. Both the US and Soviets were now developing their first generation of anti-ballistic missile (ABM) systems: rockets that aimed to shoot down incoming missiles at many times the speed of sound. The technology would prove challenging well into the twenty-first century – and hugely pricey. An agreement to limit ABM deployment was a natural place to start the US–Soviet Strategic Arms Limitation Talks (SALT), which aimed to permanently halt the race for the largest rockets and warheads.

*

As North Vietnamese forces went on the attack again and US
bombing continued at the start of 1972, Nixon headed for Beijing to meet with Mao Zedong. The trip was also, quite
deliberately, intended to shape conditions for the president's first
meeting with Brezhnev that May. 'It set up a triangular relationship between Russia, the United States and China, in which
we attempted to be closer to each of them than they were to
each other so we could calibrate our policy,' Kissinger later
said.[48]

Nixon wanted the US to be seen to be consulting NATO
allies before his Moscow visit, sending senior officials from both
Pentagon and State Department to the North Atlantic Council.[49] But a mounting US tone-deafness to its European partners
was now becoming clear. European nations were increasingly
concerned that US–Kremlin direct talks might deliver concessions European capitals did not want, including perhaps the
partial withdrawal of US troops or atomic arms. It was a tension
that would endure through to the 1980s. Most European leaders understood intellectually that bilateral talks between the
superpowers could be the best and fastest way of reducing tension. But both they and their electorates disliked feeling their
destiny was being discussed without them. At worst, they feared
either the current or a future US administration might strike a
'grand bargain' with the Kremlin that not only acknowledged
its dominance in Eastern Europe but also left Western European states more vulnerable and less defended.

According to the *New York Times* later in the year, NATO's
European members extracted pledges from Hillenbrand and
Secretary of State William P. Rogers not to discuss wider
aspects of East–West cooperation beyond strategic arms and
other specified topics when Nixon went to Moscow. In particular, they believed they had a NATO-wide agreement to avoid
the Kremlin phrase 'peaceful coexistence', which they feared
risked endorsing the Brezhnev Doctrine asserting the Soviet
right to interfere in Eastern Europe.[50] European officials were

therefore furious to see 'peaceful coexistence' at the top of the resulting twelve-point memorandum from the May 1972 Nixon–Brezhnev meeting. Their fury deepened when Kissinger told the press the wording had been secretly negotiated with the Russians even as other US officials made promises to the contrary in Brussels.[51]

The Europeans kept their concerns quiet as the Strategic Arms Limitation Treaty (SALT 1), signed by both leaders on 27 May 1972, limited each country to only two ABM sites and froze the number of land-and submarine-based long-range ballistic missiles at current levels. Only in July 1972 did European NATO representatives finally break their silence – albeit anonymously – pouring out their complaints to Flora Lewis of the *New York Times*. Her 26 July report described them as 'baffled and bitter' over their treatment by the US and Kissinger in particular.[52] European states got their revenge by opening their own negotiations with the Kremlin. For several years Soviet officials had suggested a 'European security conference' – which, they suggested, might exclude the United States. It was a proposal successive US administrations had bitterly opposed. Now, Germany agreed for discussions on this to go ahead. Kissinger was scathing. 'The Germans are really insane,' he said. 'They have nothing to offer the Russians. The only thing they have left for the Russians is to wreck NATO.'[53]

US nervousness over European negotiations with Moscow continued throughout the 1970s. The first ambassador-level meetings of what became the Conference on Security and Cooperation in Europe – known as the 'Helsinki Process' began in 1972, with thirty foreign ministers meeting the following July. These included both every participant in the Warsaw Pact as well as every NATO nation – for all their irritation with Washington, European leaders had no appetite to play the Kremlin's game by freezing the US out.

The Russians, the *New York Times* suggested, hoped the 'Helsinki' negotiations – actually conducted in multiple locations – would deliver a binding agreement that would 'seal the division of Europe and . . . pronounce the formal end of the Cold War'. Western participants were less ambitious, it suggested, but 'would like to use the Soviet enthusiasm . . . to get major and specific concessions from the Eastern bloc including on arms control and human rights'.[54] Throughout the next three years, NATO's structures including NAC ministerial meetings would be used to build a coordinated Western position for these negotiations.

From October 1971, NATO had another new secretary general: Joseph Luns, a former Dutch foreign minister who had been at the top table of NATO diplomacy for almost its entire history. He would become the longest-serving holder of that role in alliance history, remaining in post until 1984. His tenure would see a return of worries that the Soviet military machine was again becoming stronger than Western forces in Europe, and initial serious divisions within NATO over where the responsibility for defending the continent truly lay. It would also see the US and Europe increasingly at loggerheads economically, further adding to the strains.

As US troops scaled back in Vietnam, their numbers in Europe increased slightly to 320,000 by 1972. In the presidential election that year, Democratic candidate George McGovern suggested halving them as part of a wider package of military cuts. Nixon readily defeated him – once again, the alliance had dodged the bullet of an isolationist becoming president, while Nixon once again demonstrated the post-war US electoral value of looking strong on defence. Amid the genuine relief in Europe, few noted the arrest of five burglars in the run-up to the election in the Democratic Party HQ in the Watergate building.

As it entered its second term, the Nixon administration decided to declare 1973 'the Year of Europe', putting the continent explicitly centre stage after the focus on Russia and China in 1972. It was a move partly provoked by irritation – both Kissinger and Nixon were particularly angry at what Kissinger called 'vicious' European criticism of US actions in Vietnam, Cambodia and Laos.[55] Ever since Eisenhower, US presidents had encouraged Europe towards ever greater integration. Nixon decided this had been an error. In a March memo to Kissinger, he warned that Europe would be increasingly dominated by the left and 'European unity will not be in our interest, certainly not from a political viewpoint or from an economic viewpoint'.[56] In a 23 April speech announcing the 'Year of Europe' Kissinger warned that the Atlantic alliance 'cannot hold together if each country or region asserts its autonomy whenever it is to its benefit and invokes unity to curtail the independence of others'. He called on the NATO allies – together with Japan – to create a 'new Atlantic Charter setting the goals for the future', explicitly linking trade, finance and defence.[57]

Neither US embassies nor State Department officials in Washington had been properly consulted.[58] Kissinger would later tell the British that the speech had been 'one of the worst mistakes that he had made'.[59] Initially, the administration was slow to notice it had blundered, but Kissinger described the June NATO meeting as a 'disaster'. European capitals and Washington were already at loggerheads on a host of economic issues, and had no appetite to use NATO as a venue to discuss them.[60] Once again, relations with Moscow appeared easier than with America's European allies. Later that month Nixon welcomed Brezhnev to the White House with full military honours, presenting him with a brand-new Lincoln Continental car – which the Soviet leader drove erratically through the narrow winding roads around Camp David, to the horror of the Secret Service.[61]

The US now attempted to make good its pledge to talk to European nations ahead of the next round of direct US–Russia talks, taking place in parallel but separate to the 'Helsinki' multination negotiations. Kissinger planned to have his own meetings with each European leader to gain input for what Washington called a 'New Atlantic Charter' defining their relationship – and then, presumably, to tell European nations what he had decided. But rather than giving the US any chance to set European states against each other, European governments announced their talks with Kissinger would be conducted through a single European negotiator, Danish Foreign Minister Knud Børge Andersen. Kissinger found this demeaning. He described the Dane – whom he had barely met – as 'a messenger boy'. Nixon's next trip to Europe, he said, might well be cancelled.[62]

For years, successive US governments had called for their European counterparts to work more closely together. Now that they were doing so, the Nixon administration hated it. Nor was this the only area of irritation. More nakedly than any previous administration, Nixon and Kissinger were telling the Europeans that unless they increased military spending, Congress might pull out US troops – but the Europeans did not believe them. In the White House anger was now the order of the day. In August, Kissinger angrily promised Nixon 'the Europeans will be on their knees by the end of this year'. In language reminiscent of a disappointed lover, Nixon told Kissinger, 'We don't have to stay, Henry.'[63]

A new Middle East crisis complicated matters further. In October, Egypt and Syria – now heavily armed by the Soviets – launched a surprise attack on Israel. As the US rushed arms to Israel, European nations – with the exceptions of Portugal and the Netherlands – refused to allow Washington to use US bases on their territories. The war prompted further divisions within NATO. A suggestion from Donald Rumsfeld, the new US representative to NATO, that the alliance should 'coordinate or harmonise' policies on the Middle East irritated some Europeans – and they became even angrier on 25 October when the US military went to DEFCON 3 without notifying NATO. Nixon was sufficiently upset that he told Kissinger one more vote from a NATO ally against an American resolution in the United Nations 'would be the end of our NATO relationship', threatening to 'get our boys back home'.[64] Rumsfeld noted that some of the allies appeared 'somewhat embarrassed' at being blindsided by events in the Middle East. He wrote, 'It makes them feel that they are next to irrelevant in the truly important matters.'[65]

By the start of 1974 the Watergate scandal was beginning to seriously hurt the US administration. The president, however, was determined to keep up pressure on America's European allies. In a Q&A session at the Executives' Club of Chicago on 15 March Nixon deliberately concluded an answer with 'an observation for our European friends'. 'The Europeans cannot have it both ways,' he said. 'They cannot have the United States' participation and cooperation on the security front and then proceed to have confrontation and even hostility on the economic and political front.' If the Europeans were not willing to sit down and discuss the necessary cooperation, he said, there could be no meetings of the heads of government of the West.[66] When Kissinger's deputy Brent Scowcroft visited West Germany later in the month, he reported that Nixon's words had had 'a major impact', finally worrying that the US might be serious about pulling back its forces if it did not get its way.[67]

In Britain, Harold Wilson was now back in Downing Street, keen to signal to Washington that the UK would be less susceptible to European pressure, particularly from the French. As the 'Year of Europe' approached the first anniversary of its announcement, US officials began to draft a new 'Atlantic declaration'. Finally agreed at a NATO foreign ministers' meeting in Ottawa in May, it was described by the British as a 'mixture of euphemism, cliché, half-truths and of empty promise . . . more reminiscent of a Warsaw Pact Declaration than of a statement by the members of the alliance'.[68] But it was done, ready to be signed by Nixon in Brussels to celebrate NATO's twenty-fifth anniversary before the president flew to Moscow for his final meeting with Brezhnev. 'Without the alliance,' Nixon told reporters, 'it is doubtful that détente would have begun. Without a continuing strong alliance, it is doubtful détente would continue.' By now impeachment proceedings were underway, and some questioned whether he should even have attended.[69] Still, NATO had survived – and as Wilson told Nixon, the painful process following the 'Year of Europe' had 'made people concentrate their thoughts on the importance of NATO'.[70]

*

As Nixon resigned and Gerald Ford was sworn in as president on 9 August 1974, Kissinger summoned NATO ambassadors to the White House. The new president asked Donald Rumsfeld to leave his role as representative to NATO and lead the transition from what was now seen a catastrophically tainted Nixon administration, later appointing him secretary of defense.[71] Since 1973, Kissinger had also been secretary of state alongside his national security adviser role. For months he had been watching power leak away from Nixon. Now he told the NATO ambassadors that despite the change of government, business would continue as usual under Gerald Ford, joking that 'even our quarrels can continue with the usual vigour'.[72]

Ford was determined to continue negotiations with Brezhnev, whom he would meet in November in Vladivostok to pursue further strategic arms reduction talks. His arrival in the White House, however, coincided with mounting US and European worries that the Soviet Union was again closing the military gap. Maintaining US dominance, some in Washington now argued, would require a whole new military technological revolution. As secretary of defense, Rumsfeld would hold frequent congressional briefings on Russian military capability in the Roosevelt Room, the president himself often dropping by.[73] On being appointed supreme allied commander Europe in December, General Alexander Haig warned of what he called 'the more sophisticated' Soviet military position, describing the present as 'a time of great danger and great challenge'. Haig was a controversial choice as SACEUR, having left the army in 1973 to become Nixon's chief of staff. Ford's team viewed him as far too closely linked to the scandals of his predecessor, and were determined to get him out of town. Some questioned whether he truly had the military experience for the top job at NATO. 'I've seen much battle and I've been shot at,' he told reporters, pointing to his time as a battalion and brigade commander in Korea and Vietnam.[74] Arriving in Brussels, Haig pronounced himself deeply dissatisfied with the preparations made by his predecessor, General Andrew Goodpaster. 'There was no integration of command, control, communications, intelligence or coordinated fire support, air or ground. It was a disaster, a gaggle of national enclaves across the front from Norway to Turkey,' he later told a Pentagon historian. 'We could not fight our way out of a paper bag.'[75]

12

Back to the Brink (1975–1980)

*'NATO is saved every ten years or so by
a Soviet flare-up which scares them.'*

**White House Chief of Staff Donald Rumsfeld to
Joseph Luns and Gerald Ford, 27 March 1975**[1]

In Vietnam, the US was finally out of time and luck. Nixon had
successfully extracted US troops, but through the first four months
of 1975 North Vietnamese forces advanced relentlessly towards
Saigon. Meanwhile, in Europe, the US and its NATO allies worried they might be about to lose southern Europe to Communist
control in a way they had not feared since the early 1950s. In
Greece the right-wing pro-US 'Rule of the Colonels' collapsed
following the Turkish invasion of Cyprus in 1974, with anti-NATO
protests and talk of a Communist takeover.[2] In the aftermath of
the invasion, both Greece and Turkey pulled back their direct
military involvement in the alliance. Like France after de Gaulle's
withdrawal from NATO's military structures, they remained
members of the treaty and the North Atlantic Council, but would
take much less part in military planning and activities.

Portugal now provided the greatest worry in Washington
and Brussels. Salazar had died in 1970, his successors ousted by
left-leaning military officers in April 1974. 'We are worried about
Portugal,' Secretary General Luns told Kissinger and Nixon in
early 1975, warning that it could soon become the first NATO
nation controlled by explicitly Kremlin-leaning leaders. 'Two

hundred faceless officers want to retain power. There are seven top leaders, four of whom are very left-wing.'[3] In January 1975 Ford and Kissinger discussed whether the US should conduct covert activity within Portugal.[4] Throughout the Cold War the US had run clandestine operations in several NATO nations, particularly in Italy. But overthrowing the government of a NATO member in its entirety would be a dramatic escalation. Communist or openly anti-US and anti-NATO Socialist parties were also gaining ground in Italy and France. The Atlantic Treaty contained no provision for kicking members out – creating the risk that any member state turning Communist could leave the alliance deadlocked.

On 11 March right-wing elements within the Portuguese military attempted an unsuccessful coup. According to the Associated Press, the Portuguese security forces chief 'hinted that he believed the United States was involved', and that the US ambassador 'had better leave after what happened today' as his security could not be guaranteed.[5] In 1973 Kissinger and Nixon had dismissed West German Chancellor Brandt as a 'dolt' for what they viewed as his naïvety in negotiations with the Eastern bloc.[6] Now replaced as chancellor by Helmut Schmidt in 1974 after his aide was exposed as a Stasi spy, the White House suddenly and unexpectedly found Brandt a useful intermediary and guide to both Portugal and other leftist parties. He encouraged the US not to overplay its hand too soon, and to see how the forthcoming Portuguese election went.[7] Portugal's first free national vote in almost half a century saw a 'massive, orderly turnout' with the vote largely split between the Socialists and more centrist Popular Democrats, with the Communists coming third with 13 per cent, a 'disappointing' result for them.[8] In the decades that would follow, Portugal would become one of the most reliable members of the alliance. Polling conducted by NATO in 2023 indicated 87 per cent of Portuguese would vote to remain within the alliance in a referendum, more than in any country aside from Poland and Lithuania.[9] In the short term, however, worries would remain, and US and NATO officials would periodically discuss how Portugal might need to be evicted from the alliance.

Policy on Portugal inevitably proved evolutionary. While Kissinger still wanted a coup, the US embassy in Lisbon reported leftist moderates strengthening their hand, supported by European aid.[10] From August 1975 the US reached out to Foreign Minister Ernesto de Melo Antunes, assuring him of backing if civil war came to Portugal.[11] When Communist-backed paratroopers and other units rebelled in November and attempted to take control, the government – buoyed by the knowledge of US support – was able to survive.[12] As nervousness over Portugal eased, worries over Italy increased. In local elections in 1975 the Italian Communist Party had taken almost a third of the vote and now seemed poised on the brink of national power. This resulted in another flurry of Western covert activity, including secret discussions of a Western-backed coup if the Communists took power.[13]

As the US pondered its engagement in Portugal in the last days of April 1975 US-backed South Vietnam finally collapsed. South Vietnamese troops abandoned their uniforms and melted away as an armada of refugees fled the country in tiny boats. US helicopters airlifted the lucky from the US embassy in Saigon.[14] It was the kind of scene to alarm any US ally. When Ford met European and US journalists before flying to Brussels for the NATO summit the following month, he acknowledged a resurgent isolationist mood within the US. But he presented the fall of Saigon as the start of a new era, claiming, 'The American people are getting out from under the trauma of our problems in Vietnam.'[15]

*

In July 1975 Ford, Brezhnev and delegations from thirty-four other nations descended on Finland for the largest treaty-signing of the Cold War to date: the Helsinki 'Final Act', negotiated over multiple diplomatic meetings since 1972. Viewed by some at the time as perhaps even 'ending' the Cold War, in fact, it would mark the start of a new decade of rising tensions that would take NATO and the Warsaw Pact back to the brink of conflict.

Despite its name, it was very much the middle of a process, spawning its own series of arms control and other talks that would last for years to come. Some of the elements of the hundred-page agreement negotiated since 1972 were relatively uncontroversial, including measures to boost trade and scientific cooperation, and 'confidence building' measures between Warsaw Pact militaries and the West. Each agreed in principle to observe each other's exercises and set up further arms-control negotiations. Others were already prompting angry arguments, including the official recognition of each other's territorial integrity as 'inviolable' – a move some Western critics felt was a tacit endorsement of Soviet dominance of Eastern Europe and annexation of the Baltic states. Only furious lobbying by Estonian, Latvian and Lithuanian expat groups forced US assertions that Washington still regarded those countries as illegally annexed, leaving the door open to their independence in 1991.[16]

Helsinki also committed its signatories to multiple improvements in human rights, including open migration and free speech. With hindsight, most historians agree the Kremlin never truly intended to abide by many of those points, including 'freedom of thought, conscience, religion or belief'. But they received news coverage within the Warsaw Pact, particularly attracting the attention of a new dissident generation. Ford would later describe Helsinki's human rights provisions as among his most significant achievements, crediting them with helping inspire the 1980s uprisings that later overthrew Communism. 'The Soviet Union and the Warsaw Pact nations did not recognise that the human rights provision was a time bomb,' he told an interviewer in the 1990s.[17]

In its first year, the Helsinki deal would prove a disappointment. Despite its pledges on freedom of movement, the Soviet

Union allowed fewer people to emigrate in 1975 than in the previous year. Cultural exchanges remained limited, and while representatives of NATO nations began to attend Soviet military drills, Eastern European nations refused to visit NATO's.[18]

Helsinki was supposed to slow the conventional and atomic arms race between East and West. In fact, the opposite was already happening.

As part of its 'Flexible Response' defence strategy from the late 1960s onwards, NATO had committed itself to what it called 'Forward Defence'. The result particularly of West German pressure, it committed allied forces to defending all areas of its territory. The US National Intelligence Estimate suggested that would almost certainly prove unachievable. The sheer strain of maintaining that military machine, however, was now threatening the Soviet economy. Amid reports of Russians in civilian clothes using European trucking routes to conduct reconnaissance of potential invasion options, SACEUR Haig pursued his own reforms. A US brigade was moved to bolster the British sector of the Rhineland front, and the US Marine Corps assigned to help Norway strengthened its defences. But the US Army after Vietnam was still traumatised and weakened. Haig would spend a year fighting for the Pentagon to begin drug tests of US personnel, tackling a drug addiction rate he believed was as high as 30 per cent among US troops in Europe. Once testing was underway, reports of drug use gradually began to fall, he later said.[19]

*

Ford was preoccupied at home, as the 1976 election saw both Republican and Democratic challengers criticise his record on détente. Former California Governor Ronald Reagan accused him of acquiescing to the 'enslavement' of Eastern Europe, forcing a brutal battle in the primaries that Ford was lucky to eventually win.[20] Democrat Jimmy Carter was also on the offensive, increasingly echoing Reagan's criticisms of the administration over its failure to push the Communist bloc to deliver the human rights reform it had theoretically signed up to in Helsinki.[21]

On defence, Carter promised up to seven billion dollars in cuts, which alarmed Europeans. According to a UK Foreign Office dispatch, Chancellor Schmidt went so far as to privately express a preference for a Ford victory. On election day itself SACEUR Haig told NATO's Military Committee the alliance was at a 'watershed': Soviet forces now represented an 'unpreced-ented threat', with enough combat power to support an 'imperialist phase in Soviet foreign policy'.[22] The new Carter administration had no illusions over how it was perceived in Europe. Almost as soon as the new president completed his inaugural address in January 1977, Vice President Walter Mondale flew to Brussels to reassure the NATO allies of US commitment. Carter's election pledges on defence spending had left many expecting the imme-diate withdrawal of troops. Now, Mondale stated that any reduction in the 300,000 personnel in Europe would only come as part of an arms control deal negotiated with the Warsaw Pact.[23] A NATO spokesman spoke afterwards of a 'noticeable sigh of relief'.[24] The administration was keen to push ahead with the next round of Strategic Arms Limitation Talks, SALT 2, which required good relations with the Kremlin.

In early 1977 the first mutterings of post-Helsinki unrest began in Eastern Europe. In January Czech dissidents, includ-ing future president Václav Havel, circulated a document known as 'Charter 77', highlighting the failure of Communist Czecho-slovakia to live up to promised reforms. As if to prove its point, the government in Prague swiftly banned the group, arresting several of its founders.[25] The Soviet Union also clamped down on its own domestic criticism, jailing several dissidents. The view that the Soviet Union was much weaker than it portrayed itself was gaining traction within Washington, Whitehall and beyond. 'It became increasingly obvious . . . in the late seventies that serious people in Russia knew they had lost . . . that the state Socialist system simply could not compete with democratic capitalism,' said British diplomat Michael Alexander in 1998.[26] Carter's administration was determined to exploit that, asking Congress for an additional $45 million to double the power of transmitters used by Radio Free Europe and Radio Liberty.[27] 'Our commitment to the concept of human rights is permanent,' Carter announced in January 1977. 'I don't intend to be timid in my public statements and positions.' The Kremlin was furious, Brezhnev telling Carter he would not tolerate 'interference in our internal affairs, whatever pseudo-humanitarian slogans are used to present it'.[28]

At his first major NATO summit in May 1977, Carter complained of an 'enormous amount of waste', non-standardisation of weapons and equipment and competitive arms sales. Now twenty-eight years old, NATO was a 'middle-aged alliance', he said, calling on its members to undertake a major study of East–West relations and its future. *New York Times* reporter R.W. Apple felt Carter had 'convinced many previously sceptical Europeans of his competence'. British Prime Minister James Callaghan described the president as 'a breath of fresh air in the Western world'.[29]

A follow-on meeting of NATO defence ministers in Brussels set up a host of committees to look at NATO and consider longer-term reform. Alliance members also made a non-binding commitment to pledge 3 per cent of GDP to defence, the first time such a target had been set.[30] The challenges of defending Europe were laid bare in leaks of a secret US war plan reported to advocate abandoning whole swathes of West Germany to more defensive positions around the Rhine.[31] The result was an immediate protest from the German government, further damaging already fraught relations between Carter and Chancellor Helmut Schmidt.

To counter that and reassure the Europeans, the US had its own new intermediate-range missiles intended for set-up in Europe. The Cruise and Pershing 2 rockets would allow the US to strike much faster and deeper into Russian territory without

warning, reaching Moscow within six minutes. The US and
NATO regarded these as a direct response to Russia's SS-20,
in line with the Harmel Report's approach of matching détente
with military deterrence.[32] 'We very much believed that we had
the moral high ground,' said Jamie Shea, who joined NATO as
a junior official shortly after.[33] The Russians, however, would
not see things that way.

In January 1979, French, German, US and British leaders
met in Guadeloupe without the smaller powers and agreed what
would be known as NATO's 'dual track' approach: the US
would deploy Cruise and Pershing 2 missiles into Western
Europe from 1983, but simultaneously pursue an arms deal
with the Kremlin that would cut back or eliminate both new
US missiles if the USSR abandoned SS-20.[34] The announcement that Cruise and Pershing 2 would be deployed appeared
to further upset those in Moscow, with hardliners arguing the
West now might genuinely be planning war. Not until Gorbachev
in the mid-1980s would the Russian leadership be prepared to
pull back its SS-20s, paving the way for an East–West deal on
intermediate missiles that would help bring the Cold War to its
conclusion. Fiendishly complex arms negotiations, both conventional and nuclear, would now dominate the years to come,
understood by few and ultimately going nowhere until *perestroika*
in the late 1980s. By the time the Carter administration entered
the White House, NATO and Warsaw Pact negotiators had
drawn up rival proposals to cut back conventional forces on the
continent. But none of these had been agreed, and by 1977 the
process appeared stalled.[35]

The US had a new secret up its sleeve: the 'Enhanced Radiation Weapon' (ERW) or 'neutron bomb', designed to deliver a
relatively small physical blast but enough radiation to kill soldiers and tank crews while leaving equipment and buildings
much less damaged. On 6 June 1977 its existence was unexpectedly revealed to the world by the *Washington Post*.[36] The story
played appallingly in Europe, particularly in West Germany,

the country it was most likely to be used in. NATO had quietly discussed the deployment of these warheads since 1976, but there had been a tacit acceptance this would be done without publicity. The new weapon was intended to allow more precision strikes and avoid catastrophic damage to civilian infrastructure. But Soviet propagandists and anti-war campaigners portrayed it as the ultimate capitalist device, killing humans but leaving property intact.[37]

Various proposals followed, including the suggestion that the US might build the devices for leverage in arms control, then destroy them if the Soviets made concessions. Then, a month before a major NATO summit in Washington in May 1978, US newspapers reported Carter was cancelling the project in its entirety – infuriating European allies who had just spent ten months planning for its deployment.[38]

Unknown to those within the alliance, the Warsaw Pact was now pulling off one of the intelligence coups of the Cold War within NATO's own Brussels HQ. Rainer Rupp, a West German national recruited by the East German Stasi after a student demonstration in 1968, was deeply committed to his Socialist beliefs, and easily persuaded to progress from investigating neo-Nazi groups to acting as a 'sleeper agent' in Brussels. Dating a young British secretary working for the alliance, he broke all intelligence protocols by revealing himself to her as a Stasi spy, then persuading her to marry him and give him documents. When a job appeared at NATO headquarters, his handlers encouraged him to apply, beating seventy other candidates for the role. As 1977 ended, agent 'Topaz' – as the East Germans dubbed him – was establishing himself as a cheerful, committed and intelligent analyst at the heart of the alliance, gaining repeated promotions and smuggling documents home to photograph. As he told a British TV crew thirty years later, 'NATO was my enemy, and I went into it to destroy it.'[39]

Exactly how well-prepared NATO was for war remained itself in dispute. During the REFORGER 77 military drills one

US mechanised brigade was deployed by air and sea to Germany while another flew its troops across to pick up the vehicles already pre-positioned in Europe for their use. After maintenance failures earlier in the decade, 97 per cent of the equipment stored in climate-controlled hangars proved immediately operational this time around. Pentagon planners, however, doubted the exercise was realistic enough. Three further US tabletop drills in October 1978 – 'NIFTY NUGGET, PETIT NUGGET and REX '78 – proved much less positive, highlighting massive issues with communications and logistics. 'We couldn't go to war if we had to,' complained a three-star general. Again, Pentagon and NATO planners engaged furiously to fix those problems.[40]

In the run-up to the 1980s, a new generation of high-tech military equipment would be commissioned and start to enter service. Incoming US weapons would include the new Apache attack helicopter, US M1 Abrams tank, the Humvee utility vehicle, F-15, F-16 and F/A-18 jets. The Pentagon and then NATO also introduced a new approach to combat, dubbed 'Air-Land Battle', utilising the networked communications that would let them fight together, later to be showcased in the first Gulf War in 1991. The Soviet Union would embark on its own arms spending spree, pushing it towards bankruptcy.

*

Around the world, the Cold War was again getting hotter. Across southern and eastern Africa, Soviet–Western proxy wars became bloodier. In April 1978 Communist revolutionaries seized control in Afghanistan, killing the Afghan president and installing a People's Republic that immediately began savage executions and repression of its rivals. 1979 would prove another violent year. On 17 January Iran's shah fled after months of unrest, opening the door to the Iranian Revolution. Later that month, China invaded Vietnam, a major Soviet ally, deepening already serious divisions between Moscow and Beijing.

SALT 2 negotiations between the US and Kremlin delivered a June deal to limit long-range missiles to 2,400 on either
side, but Carter found himself struggling to persuade US and
European critics that the deal was wise. NATO Military
Committee Chairman General Herman Fredrik Zeiner-Gundersen
told NATO ministers that Europe was much more threatened
by shorter-range Soviet intermediate and medium-range
weapons, particularly the SS-20, than by the ICBMs covered
by SALT 2.[41]

In April 1979 Brezhnev's advisers warned him that
Afghanistan's new supposedly Russian-backed leader Hafizul-
lah Amin – who, declassified documents later revealed, was
already meeting secretly with US officials – was no longer
under Soviet control. Kremlin leaders decided to move against
him with plans for an invasion.[42] As they did so, the US suffered the first of what would become a series of 'war alerts'. On
9 November 1979, US National Security Advisor Zbigniew
Brzezinski was awakened by a telephone call reporting a Soviet
missile attack, only to be told minutes later it appeared to be a
false alarm. After the incident was reported in the US press,
Soviet leader Brezhnev told Carter that the scare – traced to a
malfunctioning computer chip – was 'fraught with tremendous
danger'. For the first time in almost twenty years atomic war felt
both imminent and plausible. For a few moments in the darkness,
Brzezinski had believed Soviet warheads were on their way. He
had decided not to wake his wife, concluding there would be no
point and it would be best for her to be asleep when the first
warheads hit.[43]

On Christmas Day 1979 the USSR invaded Afghanistan.
Heavy transport planes landed almost continuously in Kabul,
while fighter jets roared overhead and Soviet armoured vehicles
secured the city. 'Any semblance of Afghan civil independence
has virtually been eliminated,' the US embassy told Washington on 27 December, reporting 'despair' among the Afghan
population. Soviet troops would likely remain in place for years,

US diplomats predicted.[44] On 15 January the North Atlantic Council denounced the Soviet invasion, but could not agree united action.[45] The Carter administration was not going to wait. It banned grain exports to the Soviet Union and announced a boycott of the Moscow Olympics – a suggestion first made by West Germany at the NATO meeting. The US ambassador to Moscow was recalled and Carter pledged to increase defence spending by 5 per cent for the next five years, reinstating registration for the US draft. SALT 2 was withdrawn from consideration by the Senate.[46]

The Russians were surprised by the scale of the response. 'From all my experience of anti-Soviet campaigns in the United States, I have never encountered anything like the intensity and scale of this one,' Kremlin ambassador Anatoly Dobrynin, who had now endured twenty-four years and six presidencies in Washington, recalled years later. Before leaving Moscow for Washington, his US counterpart, Thomas Watson, received a barrage of shouted insults from Foreign Minister Andrei Gromyko. Walking away from the meeting, Watson told Gromyko bluntly, 'The Cold War has resumed.'[47]

*

In June 1980 the joint US–Canadian North American Air Defense Command (NORAD) inadvertently issued three more accidental attack alerts, again traced to technical or human error. In at least one case the National Emergency Airborne Command Post (NEACP) – the 747 from which the US president could control a nuclear war – taxied into position at Andrews Air Force Base and readied for launch. While the 1979 alert had been reported by the press, these were kept secret from the public, and almost certainly from NATO.[48]

Meeting in Ankara later that month, alliance foreign ministers called again for the 'immediate, unconditional and total withdrawal of foreign troops from Afghanistan'. The invasion, they said, had done 'serious damage to détente', but they wished 'to keep open channels of communication between the countries of East and West'.[49]

June brought further drama as a remote-controlled bomb exploded underneath a Belgian road as SACEUR Haig drove overhead. The general escaped unharmed, but the blast injured three security guards in his escort vehicle and blew a five-metre hole in the highway.[50] By now Ronald Reagan was well on the way to securing the Republican nomination, attacking what he called an 'amateurish and confused administration' that had lost the respect of US allies. Before they voted, he said, Americans should ask themselves, 'Is the United States stronger and more respected now than it was three-and-a-half years ago? Is the world today a safer place?'[51]

As Reagan spoke, Carter signed Presidential Directive 59 (PD–59), an ambitious and aggressive doctrine for nuclear war that explicitly widened US targeting to include Soviet command facilities.[52] It was a document the White House hoped would push back against its critics, but it was also designed – and deliberately briefed – to grab the attention of the Kremlin. The *Washington Post* described it as 'placing less emphasis on all-out retaliation against Soviet cities . . . Instead, there will be a greater emphasis on destroying Soviet forces and both political and military command centres early in a conflict in the hopes of convincing Moscow that it could not ultimately "win" a war.'[53] Both sides were now planning again for conflict with a realism not seen since before the Cuba crisis.

What should have worried Moscow just as much was the risk of unrest in Eastern Europe. In October 1978 Poland's Cardinal Karol Wojtyła was elected pope, visiting the country of his birth the following summer and drawing enormous crowds. Shortly afterwards Polish dockworkers and shipbuilders in Gdańsk went out on strike, demanding economic and political rights and erecting a giant image of the pope outside the gates of the shipyard.[54] Protests in Poland escalated through autumn 1979, making new independent Polish trade union

Solidarity and its leader, Lech Wałęsa, household names across the West.

Shortly after Reagan's victory over Carter in the November 1980 presidential vote, the Kremlin mobilised troops along the Polish border in what appeared to be a precursor to military intervention in the country. NATO was determined to show a more united front than it had following the invasion of Afghanistan. New SACEUR Bernard Rogers asked the Pentagon for four additional AWACS airborne early warning aircraft to track European airspace, reportedly to counter the risk of a surprise Russian air attack 'growing out of' any Soviet move on Poland. NATO's Atlantic maritime forces were ordered to remain at readiness rather than standing down for Christmas leave, while officials described the situation as 'sobering'.[55] On 12 December NATO ministers published a communiqué explicitly informing the Soviet Union that intervention in Poland would 'alter the entire international situation', effectively destroying workable East–West relations. This placed NATO firmly in unprecedented territory, using its diplomatic, economic and everything short of direct military power to deter Soviet action within a nation of the Warsaw Pact. These were actions it had very deliberately chosen to avoid during previous crackdowns in Hungary in 1956 and Czechoslovakia a decade later.[56]

As the year drew to a close the Soviet armed forces newspaper *Krasnaya Zvezda* accused NATO of being part of a 'broadly conceived and extensively implemented programme of subversion' in Poland that was attempting to 'blackmail' the government in Warsaw. Western leaders, it claimed, 'want the winds over Europe to blow even colder, the political atmosphere to become even worse'.[57]

13

The Gloves Come Off (1981–1982)

'Never, perhaps, in the post-war decades has the situation in the world been as explosive as in the first half of the 1980s.'

Mikhail Gorbachev, February 1986[1]

From Truman in 1945 to Carter in 1979, US administrations had viewed their confrontation with the Soviets as something to be managed rather than a competition that might end in outright victory for either side. Reagan was more ambitious from the start. 'A lot of complex things are really simple if you think them through,' Reagan told Republican foreign policy expert and future National Security Adviser Richard Allen in 1977. 'My theory on the Cold War is that we win and they lose.'[2] As head of the Screen Actors' Guild in Hollywood in the 1950s, Reagan had long been a devoted anti-Communist. Entering office in January 1981, he described détente as 'a one-way street that the Soviet Union has used to pursue its own aims'.[3]

To the Pentagon Reagan appointed Caspar Weinberger, a former World War Two soldier, lawyer and fellow California politician determined to revitalise America's friendships overseas. 'It was the most important alliance we had,' Weinberger said later of NATO. 'Yet it was not in very good shape because they didn't regard us as a very reliable ally.'[4] By February 1981 NATO Secretary General Luns was joining Reagan in his dismissal of détente, telling a West German annual military conference that the negotiating process had weakened the alliance.[5] Already, however, the new administration was showing an appetite for risk not shared by many Europeans.

Behind the scenes, with the knowledge of only a few within the White House and Pentagon, the president ordered a dramatic increase in covert action around the world. According to several sources, including once-classified official US histories, this involved a succession of military activities along the Soviet border designed as a deliberate 'psychological operation' to destabilise and confuse Soviet decision-making, commencing in February 1981. Details remain deliberately clouded. 'It was very sensitive,' a CIA report quotes former US Undersecretary of Defense Fred Iklé saying. 'Nothing was written down about it . . . no paper trail.' But both the CIA report and a 1999 National Security Agency (NSA) history make it clear the operation included multiple US Air Force sorties towards Soviet airspace in the Arctic, Europe and Asia. 'These actions were calculated to induce paranoia, and they did,' wrote NSA historian Thomas Johnson.[6]

By 1984 the Reagan administration wanted to be spending $256 billion annually on defence, up from $163 billion in 1981.[7] Reagan wanted a 600-ship navy, and he wanted it pushing into regions that would alarm the Soviets. Within weeks a specially outfitted US reconnaissance vessel, USS *Fairfax County* probed deep into waters off the Russian naval stronghold of Murmansk, attempting to retrieve a torpedo during a Soviet exercise while a Russian warship trained her guns. A few weeks later a US destroyer disrupted a Soviet anti-submarine exercise in the North Atlantic, prompting several smaller ships to scatter.[8]

Such actions sent Soviet worries skyrocketing. On 25 March KGB chief Yuri Andropov addressed the agency's senior spies. 'The imperialists are waging an arms race on an unprecedented scale, and are expediting the preparations for war,' he told them. The most important task now for the KGB, he instructed, was to detect any US and allied preparations for such a pre-emptive strike.[9]

Allied officials had their own worries over a surprise Soviet attack. A CIA report in February 1977 declared the Warsaw Pact had increased its forces in Central Europe to the extent that the fifty-eight divisions based in East Germany, Poland and Czechoslovakia could be put on the offensive without needing any reinforcements, denying NATO any warning.[10] Behind the Iron Curtain, some appeared to advocate exactly that. Future Hungarian Prime Minister Gyula Horn – at the time an official in the Communist-run foreign ministry – wrote in his memoirs that, after a little vodka, Soviet marshals would openly advocate an attack on the West 'before the imperialists gain superiority in every sphere'.[11]

On 30 March 1981, US officials briefly believed a Soviet effort to decapitate the United States was happening for real. As President Reagan stepped from the VIP entrance to the Washington Hilton in the early afternoon, a US reporter asked, 'What's the latest on Poland, Mr President?' Suddenly, a young man stepped forward carrying a handgun, and fired several times. As a Secret Service agent, policeman and White House aide fell wounded, the president was whisked to the nearby George Washington Hospital emergency room, his lung collapsing from a bullet ricochet.

Senior officials gathered in a chaotic White House situation room, National Security Adviser Dick Allen slapping down a tape recorder to capture their conversations. Vice President George Bush was in Texas, racing back to Washington on Air Force Two but without secure communications. Secretary of State Al Haig incorrectly told reporters at a press conference during the pandemonium that he was the next in line to succeed the president.[12] As he did so, word came in from the Pentagon that several Soviet submarines had moved closer to the eastern seaboard from their normal patrol positions, reducing their missile flight time to Washington by two minutes. Unclear as to who was actually in charge, Allen and Caspar Weinberger instructed Strategic Air Command to heightened alert, sending bomber crews to ready rooms and saving three minutes in the event of a launch. Once again, command authority in a crisis had proved chaotic, with Haig openly disputing Weinberger's authority to give the order. Not until almost 7 p.m., almost four and a half hours after the shooting, did Vice President Bush enter the situation room and assert control.'[13]

By then it was clear that Reagan was likely to survive, that the gunman was a young American with severe mental issues, and concerns over a surprise Soviet strike were groundless. It is unclear – and, perhaps, unlikely – that US officials ever discussed the details of the scare with NATO counterparts.

*

As April 1981 began, the Soviet military build-up around Poland continued. Flying to West Germany for a NATO defence ministers' meeting Weinberger warned any invasion would prompt not just much tougher sanctions, but also potentially US arms sales to China, now unquestionably Russia's foe.[14] Outside the NATO meeting 15,000 anti-nuclear activists protested over the proposed Pershing and Cruise deployment, a sign of things to come.[15] Weinberger showed the NAC more satellite photos of the Soviet formations menacing Poland, new SS-20 deployments and the vast new Soviet 'Typhoon' class ballistic missile submarine.[16] The NATO ministers pledged to go ahead with the Cruise and Pershing deployment in principle, again also asserting unity on Poland.[17]

So far, however, only West Germany and Italy had agreed to take the short-range Pershings, and European governments argued that the second element of the 'dual track' approach – arms control negotiations – was particularly vital to maintaining any public support. 'There is a sharp disagreement on this between the Europeans and the Americans,' said one Italian official. 'Public opinion, particularly young people, are against the deployment of nuclear weapons.' Without negotiations with the Russians, he said, European electorates would simply not accept the deployment of the new missiles.'[18] When NATO foreign ministers met in March, Haig agreed to reach out to the Kremlin. In return, the communiqué hardened NATO rhetoric on détente, which it said it would only pursue 'where Soviet behaviour makes this possible'.[19]

Less than a week later Socialist François Mitterrand took the presidency in France, promising to nationalise some French industry but not to 'collectivise' the French economy. It was a very different vision to that of the Reagan administration, but the new French leader swiftly presented himself as a strong opponent of the Kremlin, and particularly opposed to the SS-20 deployment.[20] Behind the scenes, he was even more supportive, handing US officials access to French intelligence on Russia. US officials described some other European nations, however, as outright 'Vichyite'. At a NATO meeting in Ottawa, Reagan unsuccessfully lobbied Chancellor Schmidt to abandon a multibillion-dollar gas pipeline bringing Soviet gas from Siberia to the heart of the continent, particularly West Germany. Washington offered a host of alternatives, including coal, oil and uranium, but its suggestions were rejected.[21]

American personnel in Europe were now under mounting threat, too, while Schmidt's government was also under domestic pressure for its support of the US administration. On 31 August a bomb at the US Central European Air Force HQ in Ramstein injured twenty, followed the next day by arson attacks on seven cars at a US Air Force housing compound. The same day, Egon Bahr, SDP spokesman on disarmament, accused the US of behaving as if Western Europe was 'its protectorate'; SDP youth chairman Willy Pieczyk called Reagan 'a terrifying president'.[22]

The gap between the anti-war movement and those at the top of NATO could hardly be more obvious. On 4 September Secretary General Luns praised the US administration for its decision to resume production of neutron bombs. When Secretary of State Haig visited West Berlin later in the month he was met with its largest demonstration since Vietnam. Protester Jochen Hellmann told US reporter John Vinocur that West Germany should become neutral as soon as possible, 'like Austria or Finland . . . otherwise we are not going to survive Reagan'. With West Berliners exempt from conscription, the city was now home to thousands of mostly left-wing 'refuseniks' from across West Germany. While many were peaceful, violence surged around the fringes of the protest. US Army helicopters clattered overhead as marchers knelt and directed mock anti-aircraft fire against them. One poster referenced a bomb attack on Haig's car in Brussels in 1979, showing a destroyed motor vehicle and the words '2.7 seconds too late'. Others read: 'Haig the vulture, hang him higher!'

Haig publicly defended the right to protest in the shadow of the Berlin Wall, calling it 'the warmest reception I've received since I returned to Washington'. But talking to West Berlin Mayor Richard von Weizsacker, he called it 'a discomforting visit, or at least a dislocating one'.[23]

On 15 September attackers fired rocket-propelled grenades and gunshots at the commander of the US Army in Europe, General Frederick Kroesen, although he and his wife escaped with minor cuts. The attack, claimed by the Red Army Faction, was the fourth on US personnel and installations in the country in three weeks, and the tenth in 1981.[24] On 17 December gunmen broke into the apartment of US Brigadier General James L. Dozier, Deputy Chief of Staff for Logistics and Administration at the NATO Land Forces Southern Command in Verona. Holding a gun to his wife's head to force cooperation, they dragged him away, the first time a US general had ever been taken prisoner by a non-state group.[25] He would be rescued a month later, only the second ever hostage recovered alive from Italy's Red Brigades.

NATO's exercise season in the late summer and early autumn of 1981 was once again the largest and most sophisticated in recent history. Exercise OCEAN VENTURE contained elements deliberately designed to be provocative, involving 250 ships and 1,000 aircraft from fifteen nations, making up perhaps the strongest NATO naval force ever assembled, and with activity ranging from the Mediterranean to the Baltic and Arctic. Using US intelligence on Soviet satellite operations, a substantial force, including US and British carriers, switched off its radio and radar to penetrate within striking distance of Russia's main naval station at Murmansk. Russian commanders were left unaware until carrier-borne aircraft began operating near their bases.[26] The message of such activity, US Navy Secretary John Lehman later wrote, was intended to be simple: *'attack NATO and you will lose.'*

With hindsight, US and NATO commanders concluded they had been helped in maintaining an element of surprise by two unexpected factors: bad weather in the North Atlantic, and the fact that Soviet naval intelligence had been handed an outdated set of orders for the exercise that did not include the northern thrust.[27] While such details remained classified for years, the fact that the new administration was taking a much more aggressive approach was widespread public knowledge. A poll of 1,000 Britons for the *Observer* newspaper found only 5 per cent wanting British neutrality, unilateral disarmament and withdrawal from NATO – compared to 67 per cent wanting the UK to keep its own atomic weapons. But 53 per cent said they believed US warheads should be removed from Britain, and 57 per cent said they thought Reagan was making nuclear war more likely.[28]

As November began, the Associated Press reported more than 300,000 Italians marching in Rome, Verona and Sicily against the deployment of Cruise and Pershing 2.[29] On 3 November Brezhnev gave a news conference aimed firmly at Western Europe, asserting that Russia would never use its weapons first, and claiming that the SS-20 posed little more threat than its immediate predecessors. Several West German newspapers carried the story on their front pages.[30] The next week, the new left-wing government in Greece said it wanted to ban US nuclear weapons from its soil.[31] In newly democratic Spain tens of thousands marched in Madrid in the largest demonstration since the death of Franco, demanding a referendum on their upcoming NATO membership.[32]

In August US naval vessels had breached Muammar Gaddafi's self-declared 'line of death' off the Libyan coast, US jets shooting down two Libyan aircraft that engaged them – a move that may also have been intended to also show the Russians the new administration would pull no punches.

On atomic arms, Reagan wanted to take back the initiative with a speech publicly asserting that the US would halt its Cruise and Pershing deployment providing the Russians withdrew SS-20, an offer secretly agreed by NATO defence ministers the previous month.[33] US officials believed Gaddafi might try to assassinate the president, and warned him not to make his nuclear weapons address in public. But Reagan was determined to go ahead, wearing a bullet proof vest underneath his shirt.[34] It was broadcast live across Europe and the world, reportedly drawing the largest ever audience for a presidential speech. Chancellor Schmidt said its content confirmed Reagan was a man of peace 'who deep in his heart is searching for peace and is willing to negotiate, negotiate and negotiate. The president,' he continued, 'shows a specific consideration for the political, strategic and even psychological needs of Europe.' British Prime Minister Margaret Thatcher praised it as 'hugely significant', and it was even welcomed by the staunchly anti-nuclear opposition Labour party leader Michael Foot.[35]

Arriving in Bonn to meet Schmidt shortly afterwards, Brezhnev offered once again to halt the new rollout of SS-20s, a demand the West German leader immediately dismissed as unacceptable providing the current missiles were not also withdrawn.[36] Still, the Kremlin was able to sign gas contracts with firms from Belgium, Italy, the Netherlands, Austria, France and West Germany, all but one of them NATO members. The deal would leave Moscow supplying 20 per cent of those nations' gas needs, much to US irritation. By the end of the year America had imposed sanctions on the pipeline, but the construction continued.[37]

In Poland unrest barely held in check all year was ready to explode. As Solidarity leaders met in Gdańsk to discuss a national referendum of no confidence on 12 December, the government imposed martial law. Troops and militia seized control of communication hubs and radio and television centres at midnight, effectively taking all telephones in Poland out of action for a month.[38]

As 1981 ended Reagan told his National Security Council this might be the last chance in their lifetime to change what he called 'the Soviet Empire's colonial policy regarding Eastern Europe': 'We should take a stand and tell them that until martial law is lifted in Poland, the prisoners released and negotiations resumed between [Solidarity] and the Polish government, we will quarantine the Soviets and Poland with no trade or communications across their borders.' NATO allies should do the same, he said.[39] Most NATO states, however, were not interested. 'The assumptions on both sides of the Atlantic aren't quite the same anymore,' wrote Flora Lewis, now a *New York Times* columnist, noting a growing feeling that West Germany could and should act independently as an 'interpreter' between East and West. 'Mr Reagan's forceful rhetoric was not seen as a corrective to President Carter's indecision, but as yet another example of American excess and unpredictability.'[40]

In mid-January 1982 NATO foreign ministers met for the first emergency summit in its history, with Poland top of the agenda. The resulting communiqué on Poland proved to be tougher than many had expected. As well as condemning martial law and a 'sustained' Soviet campaign against reform in Poland, it warned the situation threatened economic relations with the West and suggested a range of potential sanctions, including withholding credit.[41] Only Greece abstained.[42] As February began, protests in Gdańsk turned violent, and state Polish media accused the US of instigating bloodshed.[43] General Wojciech Jaruzelski's government now faced rising food prices, unsustainable foreign debt and collapsing economic output.[44]

Soviet expenditure on defence, meanwhile, continued to ramp up. The CIA believed the Kremlin was now spending as much as 17 per cent of its gross domestic product on the military. One declassified Soviet document found in the early 2000s put the figure even higher, at around a fifth, almost unprecedented for any economy during peacetime – and also unsustainable.[45] Briefed on Soviet armaments manufacturing in mid-February, Reagan judged it 'sobering', more than justifying his administration's own spending spree.[46] In Brussels SACEUR Rogers wanted NATO nations to up their commitment to 4 per cent of GDP. 'We have to make sacrifices today,' he said, noting that this would be painful for Western nations facing economic troubles.[47] By late March Reagan believed the US too needed to find budget cuts – but he was determined to cut social spending rather than the military. As for the Soviet economy, he suggested in his diary that he believed it could be leveraged to Western advantage if the US cut back trade and credit. 'They are in very bad shape and if we can cut off their credit they'll have to yell "Uncle [Sam]" or starve.'[48]

In early April 1982 Argentina invaded the Falklands. That NATO might become involved in the conflict was never seriously discussed – the 1949 treaty had clearly defined the southern limit of the NATO area above the Caribbean, specifically to avoid such fights. For the United States, however, allied to both Argentina and to Britain, it was an immediate diplomatic challenge. While Reagan himself hoped for a peaceful solution, his administration was divided. Defense Secretary Weinberger, an unabashed Churchill fan only prevented from fighting for the RAF in World War Two by poor eyesight, was determined to support Britain. Secretary of State Haig favoured the Argentines retaining the islands, but allowing the British occupants to remain.[49] As the British task force sailed south, NATO leaders looked on nervously. While hugely diminished from its mid-twentieth-century peak, the Royal Navy remained a substantial part of NATO's maritime combat power. Now, two-thirds of its surface fleet, 4,000 of its best-trained troops, more than half of its Harrier vertical take-off fighters, and several modern submarines were heading to potential destruction 8,000 miles away.[50]

In mid-April there was brief media speculation – attributed to 'NATO sources' – that two Russian Echo II nuclear-powered submarines might join the fray, or at least help the Argentines track the British task force. Other reports suggested Soviet satellites had been re-tasked to help the Argentines.[51] At the start of May fighting began in the South Atlantic and the US announced logistics support for Britain.[52] As Weinberger headed to a NATO summit in Brussels, the British nuclear submarine HMS *Conqueror* sank the US-built Argentine cruiser *General Belgrano*. Two days later a French-manufactured Exocet missile struck the destroyer HMS *Sheffield*, leaving her ablaze. Weinberger said there was 'great regret' over the *Sheffield* but said he did not sense any 'lessening of support' for Britain.[53]

The US was now determined Britain must not lose. Worried a British aircraft carrier might be sunk, US officials prepared secretly to loan the Royal Navy the assault ship USS *Iwo Jima*, capable of carrying the British Harriers. Whether the British would be able to completely crew the vessel was unclear, with US officials considering the option of using contractors instead if necessary.[54]

As Reagan prepared to fly to Europe at the start of June British troops slogged their way across the Falklands, and bombings again hit US bases across West Germany.[55] 'Our fate is tied to Europe,' Reagan told European journalists before departing. Behind the scenes, however, economic differences still rankled – and the 'Kremlin pipeline' continued to be built.

Unemployment in Western Europe was now five million

higher than in mid-1981. European nations blamed higher US interest rates for sucking up investment, reducing appetite for Reagan's plans to cut the Kremlin off from foreign credit.[56] As anti-nuclear campaigners prepared to rally in Bonn, West Germany's centre-right Christian Democrat party organised pro-US demonstrations, allowing what they called the 'silent majority' to show its gratitude. Posters carried in the crowd read 'Rather Dead Than Red' and 'Say Something Good About America'. Reporters estimated the crowd at about half the size of a 1981 anti-nuclear demonstration at the same location. Schmidt – whose SDP was now violently split over Cruise and Pershing – dismissed the rallies as a political gimmick. But Christian Democrat leader Helmut Kohl was already drawing ahead in German polls, and would replace Schmidt as chancellor in October.

In his London address to both houses of Parliament, Reagan expressed unambiguous support for Britain's Falklands fight, framing it in the context of a wider battle to entrench democracy and 'leave Marxist-Leninism on the ash heap of history'. Reagan's words were firmly rejected by Michael Foot's opposition Labour Party, accusing the administration of seeing the world 'as a simple black and white struggle against the Soviet Union'.[57] At a speech the next day, Reagan pledged US support for Europe and expressed his sympathy with the peace protesters, saying they only disagreed on the tactics to deliver a safer world. He suggested NATO and the Warsaw Pact should both limit military personnel to 700,000 – a modest reduction for NATO from the current 790,000, but a significant drawdown from Western estimates of Warsaw Pact forces at almost a million troops.[58] Within the building Reagan felt his words were well received.[59] Outside, estimates of the anti-war protesters ran to above 200,000.[60]

Spain was now joining the alliance, despite ongoing calls at home for a referendum on that choice. Minutes after its flag was ceremonially added to those of the fifteen other NATO allies,

Prime Minister Leopoldo Calvo-Sotelo expressed his country's 'Latin American calling' and warned Britain's actions in the Falklands risked 'tearing the Western world apart'.[61] By now, however, British troops were approaching Port Stanley, and the war would soon be over.

*

At the end of July 1982, US efforts to tighten an embargo on industrial supplies to the 'Kremlin pipeline' caused relations between Washington and Europe to again deteriorate. US officials complained of 'yearnings for détente' in Europe, while their European counterparts returned to their age-old complaint that the US believed it could dictate global events.[62] Within US forces based in Europe, there was a new controversy. American forces newspaper *Stars and Stripes* quoted US officials as listing more than a hundred bars, restaurants and entertainment venues discriminating against ethnic minority US personnel. When a West German newspaper sent a reporter out with two African-American soldiers, they were kicked out of a pizzeria. The reporter noted multiple instances of racist abuse, including shouts of 'Give some bananas to our guests'.[63] In August the US pointedly appointed Lieutenant General Roscoe Robinson as the new US representative to the NATO Military Committee, the first African-American to hold that rank in the army and only the second to hold it in any US service.[64] Within the alliance he would now be the one briefing his European counterparts on the fast-growing US military activity in Europe.

As part of the autumn REFORGER 82 exercise, US aircraft carried a parachute brigade of the 82nd Airborne Division for ten hours across the North Atlantic to drop them directly into Europe, the first time such an operation had been attempted.[65] The equivalent US and NATO drills in 1983 would be larger and even more aggressive, and they would inadvertently bring the alliance closer to atomic war than at any point since 1962.

14

Dancing Blindly on the Edge (1983)

*'In 1983 we may have inadvertently placed our
relations with the Soviet Union on a hair trigger.'*

**President's Foreign Intelligence
Advisory Board, 15 February 1990**[1]

Decision-makers, spies, researchers and historians will always
disagree on how close the world came to catastrophe in the final
months of 1983.

On taking office in 1989, the older George Bush was concerned enough by what he already knew to order his President's
Foreign Intelligence Advisory Board to investigate hundreds of
often still-classified documents and interview seventy-five officials from both sides of the Atlantic. Their report – declassified
a quarter of a century later – described a more than a year-long
period in which the US and its allies unwittingly fed Kremlin
fears of imminent attack. 'We believe that the Soviets perceived
the correlation of forces had turned against the USSR, that the
US was seeking military superiority, and that the chances of the
US launching a nuclear first strike – perhaps under cover of a
routine training exercise – were growing,' they wrote.

Those advising Reagan and other top officials, however,
were unaware of this throughout most of 1983 – as were most
US and NATO commanders planning the alliance's largest
ever drills.[2] Largely sidelined in the face-offs over Berlin in 1961
and Cuba the following year, NATO was much more at the

heart of the '1983 war scare'. Two key exercises – the US-led REFORGER and NATO SHAPE nuclear command drill ABLE ARCHER – would be particularly critical. So, in the background, would be the febrile political environment produced by SS-20, Cruise and Pershing 2.

As 1983 began, Warsaw Pact leaders met in a medieval fortress in Prague. The Czechoslovakian press agency described their priority as 'the struggle for the preservation of peace'. Western diplomats believed it was to sign off a PR offensive to block the European rollout of the US rockets.

In late December, Kremlin leader Yuri Andropov had offered to reduce the number of Soviet medium-range missiles in Europe from more than 600 to 162, the same number currently held by Britain and France together – providing the US dropped its plans to deploy its 572 missiles altogether. The proposal had been immediately rejected by all three allies, who said it would leave the Soviets with a larger force.[3] In Moscow, Andropov and those around him were moving fast to entrench his rule. His first weeks in office saw shelves in Soviet stores noticeably fuller, although the effect did not last. The large portraits of Brezhnev that had featured in town and city centres were not replaced, while the Kremlin launched a heavily publicised crackdown against corruption.[4] But soon the new Kremlin's chief's mental and physical health was clearly in decline. Despite it all, he retained the loyalty of Russia's spies. Andropov's 1981 instruction to the KGB to track potential warning signs of Western military preparations had, by 1983, led to a major operation dubbed RYAN, the Russian acronym for the words 'Nuclear Missile Attack'. Even before Reagan took the White House, Andropov told East German spymaster Markus Wolf his fears that a rearming US could soon overwhelm the Soviet Union. As the 1980s progressed, Wolf wrote later, the Kremlin became 'obsessed'; its preoccupation with warnings of war became the primary task – beyond domestic dissent – of the KGB and its Warsaw Pact spy services.[5]

Having pledged to deploy its Pershing 2 and Cruise missiles by the end of 1983, the US military was now in a race against time to make good on its promise. Five countries had agreed to take the rockets – Britain, Germany, Italy, Belgium and the Netherlands – although parliamentary opposition in the latter two nations now left those deployments deadlocked. In Britain and Germany general elections were underway, with nuclear weapons policy arguably the defining issue. At Greenham Common, west of London, the women's peace camp – any remaining men had been evicted in early 1982 – was now globally renowned. Dozens of women lived in a tented camp outside the wire, periodically joined by hundreds, sometimes thousands more who surrounded the perimeter to 'embrace the base' and occasionally break inside.[6]

Visiting Europe in early February, Vice President Bush was keen to assert that the US too wanted all intermediate-range missiles banned from Europe, and that the new US missiles were only a response to the Soviet SS-20s.[7] Confronted by a senior member of the UK Campaign for Nuclear Disarmament at a speech in London, Bush told him nothing had stopped war in Europe in the way NATO's deterrence policy had for thirty years. 'Don't you think we don't want peace?' Bush asserted angrily, his voice rising. 'Do you think we care less than others about a nuclear war?'

A Gallup opinion poll showed that while most Britons wanted US bases to stay, they opposed the Cruise deployment.[8] Even among Conservatives and pro-nuclear Labour and Social Democrat politicians, there were calls to ensure the missiles could not be fired without UK political approval – a promise US officials were pointedly unwilling to make.[9] Beyond the headlines, however, both Thatcher and Kohl were quietly reaping the political benefits of appealing to those at least equally strongly opposed to giving up atomic arms (not all were quiet about it – my maternal grandmother is reputed to have chased away Labour doorstep campaigners in 1983 with the words 'I'm all for the bomb' ringing in their ears).

The most important political battleground was West Germany, where Kohl had quite deliberately put the deployment of Cruise and Pershing at the core of his manifesto. Compared to the Labour Party in Britain, the SDP opposition in Germany was much less clear on where it truly stood – but the chancellor pounded them regardless for their 'unwise anti-Americanism'. 'Without the protection and shield of the United States, there would be no free election here,' he said. 'Those who want to leave NATO must say so. The first stage is neutralism, and the second stage is to fall under Soviet hegemony.'[10] On 6 March Kohl's Christian Democrats took 48.8 per cent of the vote in national elections. The SDP suffered their worst defeat since 1961.[11] In June Thatcher too would win a resounding election victory, although neither would stop the anti-nuclear protests spreading.

NATO leaders felt more confident following Kohl's election win. On 19 March SACEUR Rogers described the alliance as possessing the 'moral high ground' by having nuclear weapons to deter the Soviets, and that it would be 'immoral' not to try to deter a devastating atomic war. 'We have to deal with the world as we find it,' he said. 'And there is a Russian deployment of a massive number of warheads, and they are aimed at us.'[12]

Reagan now had a new plan to reduce the risk of atomic war, one that would significantly complicate relations. In February an expert told him high-energy lasers and particle beams could be used to bring down oncoming missiles. The president judged it a 'super idea'. 'What if we tell the world we want to protect our people, not avenge them?' he wrote.[13] In the run-up to Reagan's major speech on arms control on 23 March, US newspapers reported that the administration might be about to soften its negotiating position. Instead, Reagan announced the 'Strategic Defence Initiative' – immediately dubbed 'Star Wars' – which would destroy Soviet missiles before they touched US soil. This not only blindsided NATO defence ministers meeting in Portugal to discuss nuclear planning, but also both

Secretary of State George Shultz and Weinberger, both of whom objected when they heard about it with only two days' warning.[14]

Hours earlier NATO ministers had endorsed the US nuclear position, Secretary General Luns declaring that any substantial change must be agreed by the alliance. Weinberger had expressed himself delighted at the show of unity, which included a communiqué pledge that 'for arms control to be successful, the Soviets must be convinced that NATO is determined to deploy its missiles as planned'.[15] Now, the US was unveiling what appeared to be a completely new class of weapons: a technology that could render the US invulnerable to attack – but might not cover Europe.

Two weeks earlier Reagan had described the Soviet Union as an 'evil empire' in a speech to evangelical Christians – another speech that senior foreign policy officials were unaware of in advance. As with the Strategic Defence Initiative, the *Star Wars* parallels were enough to guarantee massive media coverage, and the attention of the Kremlin. Soviet leaders were appalled and furious. 'All attempts at achieving military superiority over the USSR are futile,' Andropov responded in a speech four days later. 'Engaging in this is not just irresponsible. It is insane.'[16] A few days later the US finally came forward with an interim negotiating plan, one that suggested both sides reduce numbers of intermediate missiles as a first step – it was endorsed publicly by NATO.[17] By then, however, US naval forces in the Pacific were on the brink of one of their riskiest moves in years.

According to declassified accounts of FLEET-EX 83, forty US warships, including three aircraft-carrier battle groups accompanied by B-52 bombers, sailed within striking distance of Soviet territory, their jets carrying out simulated bombing attacks on the Soviet-occupied islet of Zelyony in the Kuril Islands. Simultaneously, warships moved into the Baltic and Black seas while an additional US-carrier battle group positioned itself off

Norway and US attack submarines simulated attacks on Soviet ballistic-missile submarines beneath the polar ice cap. 'These US demonstrations of military might were aimed at deterring the Soviets from provocative actions and displaying US determination to respond in kind to Soviet, regional and global exercises that had become larger, more sophisticated and more menacing in preceding years,' the CIA's Ben Fischer wrote.[18] As the carriers sailed towards the Russian coast, Warsaw Pact military chief Marshal Viktor Kulikov spoke to a Soviet army newspaper of 'clouds of a threat of war thickening on the horizon', and viewed the US military build-up as a potential 'detonator in the present explosive situation'.

By now the Soviets had rejected the latest US missile offer, although a new Warsaw Pact summit pushed NATO to again examine its proposals for a non-aggression agreement between the groups.[19] On 3 April the Soviet embassy issued an official protest on the overflights, rejected by the US which said it did not view the island – also claimed by Japan – as Russian territory. Three days later a State Department cable reported that two Soviet aircraft had breached US airspace over an island off Alaska, 'the first overflights of US airspace by a Soviet bomber since March 1969'.[20] Neither for the first nor last time, events in the Middle East now distracted Washington. On 18 April a suicide truck bomber at the US embassy in Beirut killed sixty-three people including seventeen Americans. It all piled up the pressure on Washington foreign policy and defence officials, while the flurry of US military activity it produced was almost certainly monitored by the KGB, all adding to the Kremlin's nerves.

In Russia KGB officials were now feeding data into the RYAN programme, rumoured to be collated by a primitive supercomputer attempting to calculate when the West might have sufficient 'superiority' to launch a surprise attack. Its sources of data, however, were likely almost useless. For all its fearsome reputation, the KGB of the early 1980s was as rickety as the Soviet state it was trying to protect. Before being posted to London in 1982, secret British double agent Oleg Gordievsky was briefed by a KGB expert on NATO who made it clear that the agency was now struggling to recruit sources who knew what was going on in Western governments. Instead, Russian agents overseas were encouraged to look for much more basic details, often meaningless in hindsight. Indicators sought by RYAN included lights burning in government offices late at night, VIP movements and high-level committee meetings. It was a risky stratagem. 'Lurking around well-guarded official installations seemed almost certain to attract the attention of host-country security services,' noted CIA writer Fischer.

Certainly, 1983 saw a record 147 KGB expulsions from Western and other countries, including forty-one from France alone. According to the CIA history, most were part of a coordinated crackdown on a concerted Soviet campaign to extract cutting-edge Western science and technology, revealed by intelligence provided by Mitterrand to other NATO allies.[21] It all added to the tension. According to the later Bush-era review, Soviet military intelligence – the GRU, long-term rival to the KGB – expected its officers to work under wartime conditions 'because they believed war could break out at any moment'.[22]

Rainer Rupp, the Stasi spy in NATO headquarters, was now likely the best-placed operative the Eastern bloc had within the West. Rapidly promoted and appointed head of NATO's Current Intelligence Group, he had access to almost every item of sensitive material member states were prepared to share with the alliance. According to his later interviews, in March 1983 Rupp gave his handlers a copy of NATO's 'MC-161' report, a line-by-line survey of the strengths and capabilities of Warsaw Pact and NATO nations. The document accurately revealed the Eastern bloc's shortcomings, and suggested Communist nations were 'locked in a precipitous spiral of decline'. Now, the Stasi's foreign wing, the HVA, wanted Rupp to probe the Strategic Defence Initiative. Asked to join a working group to assess the NATO response to 'Star Wars', Rupp initially put on a show that he was too busy, desperate to avoid arousing suspicion. Ultimately, however, he worked his way on to a two-week briefing in Washington that convinced him the entire SDI project was unfeasible.

From Brussels, Rupp fed back the growing European concerns on 'Star Wars'. Thatcher, he told the Stasi, was particularly opposed, worrying that a US shielded from incoming missiles might leave Europe at higher risk – but she also doubted it would work.[23] Later declassified British documents would confirm that was indeed her view, supported by similarly high levels of scepticism among British scientists.[24]

Summer 1983 saw Mikhail Gorbachev visit Canada and the final official lifting of Polish martial law. One of the youngest Politburo members at fifty-two and theoretically responsible for agriculture, Gorbachev was both trusted by Andropov and increasingly talked of as a future leader – and this would be his first trip to a capitalist country or NATO state. Canadian Prime Minister Pierre Trudeau was keen to show him real life in the West, so Minister of Agriculture Eugene Whelan invited him to his home farm in small-town Ontario. The contrast with the Soviet Union was unmistakable. Walking in the fields with Soviet ambassador to Ottawa Alexander Yakovlev, the two privately discussed the true scale of the USSR's political and economic challenge in a way they could never have done in Moscow.[25]

Through May and June three separate NATO public statements asserted the missile deployment would go ahead unless Russia pulled back their SS-20s. 'At this point, there's absolutely no question about it,' the US Secretary of State told reporters following one meeting. Socialist Greece again refused to put its name to the missiles motion, while the Danish Parliament's reservations were also noted.[26]

Meeting Chancellor Kohl in Moscow for the first time, a visibly sickening and weakened Andropov warned the German it

was a 'profound and dangerous delusion' to think the new missiles would make Moscow more liable to concessions. 'The
military threat will grow manifold,' he said.[27] Looking back the
following year, US intelligence would find further signs of unusual
Soviet activity in summer 1983, unnoticed at the time. That
included increased civil defence activities and broadcasts,
improvements to military logistics, extended reservist call-ups,
and the repurposing of civilian tractor and commercial airline
factories to build tanks and military planes.[28] By summer 1983
some Westerners living in the Soviet Union told US officials they
believed coverage of looming nuclear war was designed to prepare the Soviet population for its 'inevitability'.[29]

At the start of June, Averell Harriman – the veteran diplomat, politician and all-round Washington insider who Truman
and Theodore Achilles had once hoped would be the first US
envoy to NATO , now ninety-one years old – visited Moscow
and met Andropov as a 'private citizen'. With him were his
wife – he had married Churchill's daughter-in-law, Pamela, after
her husband's death – and a translator provided by the State
Department.[30] Harriman was not to negotiate, Secretary of
State George Shultz told him before he left, but he should gauge
Andropov's attitude, health and potential areas in which the
two nations might begin to compromise. The US–Soviet relationship was 'lousy', Shultz confided, but the president wanted it
to recover and viewed the unofficial visit of the aged diplomat –
who had known Andropov since Stalin's time – as the best
chance so far to start that process.[31]

Andropov's hands occasionally shook, Harriman noted in
his report back to Washington, and he had a 'rather rigid walk',
but he seemed in command of himself, the Kremlin and the
meeting – and both keen for relations to improve and worried
about their current state. 'He seemed to have a real worry that
we could come into conflict through miscalculation,' wrote
Harriman.[32]

In July, the nations that had signed the Helsinki agreement in

1975 began a new series of meetings in Madrid aimed at finding further areas of cooperation. Expectations of progress were relatively low, but NATO members agreed between themselves to scale back their demands for human rights reform in Eastern Europe in the hope of agreeing a communiqué. The resulting agreement included movement towards greater trade with the Eastern bloc, something the Kremlin now desperately needed.[33] By now, however, NATO's autumn exercise season was commencing, delivering many of the indicators the KGB was looking for to signal war was imminent.

*

On 25 August the first phase of REFORGER 83 began, the movement of almost 800 vehicles by sea from the US and the airlift of 16,000 troops, most of them flying the Atlantic under radio silence on civilian and military planes.[34]

A week later, on 1 September, a Soviet SU-15 blasted Korean Airlines Flight 007 from the sky after it strayed into Russian Pacific airspace, killing all 169 aboard.[35] US intelligence quickly concluded the shootdown was the result of the aircraft being misidentified as a US military reconnaissance plane – but that did not stop the Reagan administration presenting it as a deliberate act.[36] For the Kremlin, the shootdown was a political disaster. The outcry against it across NATO and beyond was furious and immediate, with even Italian Communists, West German Greens and neutral Sweden joining in.[37]

Foreign ministers from the thirty-five Helsinki nations were now meeting for their final Madrid session – but US Secretary of State George Shultz made it clear the downed plane was the only thing he was interested in discussing. NATO ministers met separately on the sidelines, discussing a suspension of commercial flights to Russia.[38]

US cargo ships now disembarked tanks and trucks in Dutch and Belgian ports, picked up by the troops that had just flown the Atlantic. Some headed to Germany to take part in a NATO exercise, CONFIDENT ENTERPRISE, others to the Dutch-led ATLANTIC LION. An additional US company flew to West Berlin to take part in urban combat training.[39] Then, at a quarter past midnight on 26 September, the alarms at Soviet satellite monitoring station Serpukhov–15 outside Moscow began to sound. Soviet satellites observing US Minuteman silos in the US Midwest had detected flashes, and the base computer identified them as rockets blasting from the earth.

Lieutenant Colonel Stanislav Petrov, duty officer that night, was forty-four years old and the deputy chief of the military's Department of Military Algorithmics. As such, he knew the inherent glitches within the primitive supercomputers on which his political and military masters increasingly relied. Desperately, he told the team to check more closely – to him, none of the flashes looked like genuine launch plumes. Petrov reported it appeared to be a false alarm. As he was on the phone, however, the sirens sounded again.

Petrov later told a British TV crew he felt 'terrified', hot and sweaty 'as though I was sitting in a hot frying pan'. His imagery analysts believed there had not been a launch, but his other computer specialists trusted their machines. By now, he suspected the Soviet Union's top military commanders had been told of the alert, perhaps even Andropov. Shaking with fear, Petrov asked himself why the US might launch so few missiles if it intended to overwhelm the Soviets. Perhaps, he thought, a rogue individual might have launched despite the safeguards. 'It is 1983 and our relations with the United States are very tense,' he later recalled. As he considered all this, the satellite detected two more potential launches. The window of danger was mercifully brief. Within minutes, additional senior officers poured into the control station, and all realised that if the launches were real other stations would now be seeing them as well. Those clamouring for information in Moscow could be told it was a false alarm.

Later investigation would reveal the flashes were in fact

reflections of the sun on freak high-altitude autumn equinox clouds. Aware the first Carter-era alert had become global news, the Soviet authorities chose to keep the incident entirely secret. Petrov was charged for failing to keep a proper log during the incident, discharged from the military the following year and left living in a dilapidated apartment.[40] The 26 September incident may have been the most dangerous single point of 1983 – although, as with events aboard the Soviet submarine B-59 during the Cuban missile crisis, much rests on an account from a single Russian witness.

In a 1990 interview Marshal Sergei Akhromeyev, deputy chief of the Soviet General Staff in 1983, played down talk of a genuine war scare that year, but acknowledged Soviet leaders were worried. 'There was the opinion that the tension between the two countries had reached a very high level, that the confrontation had reached its peak and that we should find a solution out of this situation,' he said. Akhromeyev – who would commit suicide after the failed coup against Gorbachev – was not necessarily a good witness. Among the most committed Soviet 'true believers', he maintained until the end that the Korean Airlines shootdown was a US orchestration. But on one thing he was very clear – the most dangerous military exercises, he said, were REFORGER and AUTUMN FORGE.[41] Those exercises had already moved tens of thousands of US troops across the Atlantic, while NATO forces along their border with the Warsaw Pact were now also on manoeuvres.

*

Most of NATO's autumn 1983 military drills were built around fictitious narratives of escalating conflict, culminating in the nuclear exercise ABLE ARCHER in November, which would train NATO's SHAPE HQ and various forces in the field in the processes they would use to launch an atomic strike. These drills appear to have been initally intended to be so realistic they would involve Western political leaders including Thatcher and Reagan. How much of this the KGB, Kremlin and Russia's military leadership really understood has never been disclosed. When US intelligence officials looked back from the late 1980s and early 1990s, however, they noted multiple indications the Soviets believed war might genuinely be imminent.

From late summer 1983, air-raid shelter notices appeared in Moscow, US intelligence would later report, with factories told to include attack drills in their normal work plans. Andropov was reported to have sent a letter to be read at secret party meetings, declaring the motherland 'truly endangered'. New Soviet missile deployments were announced to Czechoslovakia and East Germany. In October, Soviet air forces in Poland were told to reduce arming times and to ready aircraft with nuclear munitions. Little of this, however, was put together by US analysts at the time. Even less was noted by NATO – if it had been, it would have been sent to the Stasi by their agent in its headquarters.[42]

After Reagan was shot in 1981, US officials had briefly believed the US might be about to be under Soviet attack. In Russia, Premier Andropov was dying, the fragility observed by Harriman in Moscow worsening by the week throughout the second half of 1983. As September ended, he received dialysis each day as he attempted to recuperate by the Black Sea, remaining in touch with his deputy Konstantin Chernenko and rising protégé Gorbachev.[43] For the more paranoid forces in Moscow, that weakened leadership may have increased speculation of a surprise attack. By the same token, however, others may have wondered why the US and its allies might attack in 1983 when they needed to wait only a few weeks before the new short-range Cruise and Pershing rockets the Kremlin feared so much were ready for deployment.

*

As October drew to a close, hundreds of thousands marched across Europe against the US missiles, joined by tens of thousands at more than 140 locations across the United States.[44] Then, for the second time that year, US decision-makers found themselves savagely distracted by a bombing in Beirut. Early on a Sunday morning, 23 October, two truck bombs slammed into the barracks housing US and French peacekeepers, killing 307, including 241 US military personnel. Two days later the US and a coalition of six Caribbean nations invaded the island nation of Grenada, responding to a Communist takeover that had seen the execution of Prime Minister Maurice Bishop. That resulted in another blizzard of communications between Washington and London, again many likely tracked by RYAN.

While historians often talk of ABLE ARCHER as causing the 'war scare' itself, the nuclear planning exercise of that name began on 7 November, well after many of the events that had already panicked the Kremlin. What ABLE ARCHER did, some sources suggest, was provide pointers that the final attack might now be being launched. Whether the Russians were aware of it by name remains unclear – deputy army chief Marshal Akhromeyev said he had no memory of it when interviewed by *Washington Post* journalist Don Oberdorfer in 1990.[45]

The hypothetical situation for ABLE ARCHER was that the early months of 1983 had seen mounting unrest in Eastern Europe and increasing 'ORANGE' – clearly code for 'Soviet' – support to Iran, Syria and South Yemen. In addition, this training scenario added growing conflict in Yugoslavia, with pro-'ORANGE' elements challenging the government in Belgrade and Albanian-backed unrest in Kosovo. In a mirror image of what would take place in 1999, the Yugoslav government was said to have asked for NATO support to defend Kosovo against ORANGE intervention.

In the scenario, this then sparked a global conflict. In late October ORANGE and 'ORANGE Bloc' forces were imagined to have invaded Yugoslavia, also crossing into Finland on 3 November as a precursor to a much wider assault against the West. On 4 November, three days before the start of ABLE

ARCHER, ORANGE was said to have launched massive air
and naval conventional attacks against BLUE (NATO) across
Europe and the North Atlantic and invaded Norway. In the
SHAPE bunker in Mons, participants sat arrayed around a
giant map table, receiving teletype messages from other
involved headquarters, including reports of ORANGE chemical attacks.[46] At one point in the game, some US Air Force
players were instructed to evacuate to another NATO base in
West Germany and put on gas masks and protection suits for
several hours.[47]

US Air Force Master Sergeant Todd Jennings, taking part
from Norway, later said, 'We began doing the "what if?" questions. "What if the Soviets actually think we're going to launch
nuclear weapons and we are disguising it as an exercise? What
if they launched against us? . . . It was a pretty crazy time."' In
West Germany, another US serviceman recalled setting up
command centres and aerials in forests, sending messages very
similar to those that would have been sent in the early stages of
an actual war. This 'must have caused [Russian] paranoia to a
greater degree than in other situations', the anonymous serviceman said.[48]

When President Bush's intelligence experts looked back from
1990, they concluded this was exactly what had happened.
Their findings remain partly classified, but they note a tip-off
from the KGB Moscow Centre to missions across Western
Europe from 8 or 9 November ordering them to report on the
alert status of US military bases. One source – likely double
agent Gordievsky, who later made similar comments publicly –
told the US review in 1990 that he had been 'particularly
occupied trying to obtain information on a major NATO exercise' in early November, and specifically to 'look' for any
indication that the United States was about to launch a pre-
emptive missile strike against the countries of the Warsaw Pact'.

Soviet aircraft conducted thirty-six intelligence-gathering
patrols during ABLE ARCHER 83, more than during the

equivalent period in any previous year. Other steps, the review notes, were 'highly unusual', including the pre-positioning of some nuclear warheads by helicopter. Some Soviet air force units were put on a thirty-minute around-the-clock alert – then stood down as the exercise concluded on 11 November. The same day, Defence Minister Dmitry Ustinov told high-ranking officers that recent US military actions had been judged 'sufficiently real' to order an increase in Soviet combat readiness.[49]

A series of UK television interviews conducted in the early 2000s with Soviet officials suggest matters went even further. On 8 November, as part of the ABLE ARCHER scenario, NATO personnel changed the top-secret codes they were using, seen as a signal by some in Moscow that this was no longer a drill. Andropov was in hospital, having missed the previous day's anniversary of the Bolshevik Revolution. According to some Soviet sources, that night either Andropov or Ustinov – or both – ordered the entire Soviet arsenal of 11,000 warheads to maximum combat alert. According to Soviet missile battery officer Captain Viktor Tkachenko, his crew in the command bunker were then joined by a 'third man' who said he was there to ensure there was no breakdown in communication with Moscow – almost certainly from the KGB. 'We were ready for the Third World War but only if it had been started by the Americans,' Tkachenko later said.[50]

At the top levels of the US and British governments, and possibly within the US Strategic Air Command, there are some indications that reservations had been noted in advance about ABLE ARCHER. US Air Force documents show a last-minute change: 'nuclear play' would be downgraded to 'low spectrum', with more 'conventional play' in the exercise. But they made it clear nuclear strikes would be involved.[51]

The political leaders who were to have played a part on the fringes of ABLE ARCHER also now pulled out. Shortly before the exercise, Reagan's National Security Adviser Robert 'Bud' McFarlane decided the international situation was too tense and there were too many demands on Reagan's time, and he should not be involved. The president agreed, reportedly noting, 'However misguided Soviet perceptions might be we shouldn't add to them by having the principals involved.' In London, Thatcher and Defence Secretary Michael Heseltine decided to follow suit, standing down their own personal involvement.[52] Within NATO and SHAPE headquarters, however, there appears to have been no such talk of 'war scares'. Indeed, many there would have been unaware even of ABLE ARCHER or other major drills.

The first to become aware within NATO HQ of just how worried the Russians were, ironically, was almost certainly East German spy Rainer Rupp, contacted by his handler on 9 November with an urgent query as to whether a NATO attack was imminent. He was not involved in ABLE ARCHER or AUTUMN FORGE, and as far as he was concerned everything was normal. Using an encryption device disguised as a pocket calculator, Rupp entered a message to that effect, went to a payphone, called a prearranged number and held the device to the receiver. The 'pocket calculator' transmitted the message as a series of beeps and clicks – presumably similar to an early modem sound.[53]

Not until newspaper reports linked ABLE ARCHER to a war scare in the 1990s would most in NATO and the majority of its member states begin to understand what might have happened. In 2006 official SHAPE historian Gregory Pedlow interviewed a number of senior participants in the exercise, none of whom recalled any 'war scare' at all.[54]

Senior American officials in Europe had access to more secret information. US Air Force Europe intelligence chief Lieutenant General Leonard Perroots was receiving highly classified US satellite and National Security Agency reports, many of which were almost certainly never declassified to most other NATO allies. They told him of significantly increased Soviet intelligence flights, then fighter jets on runway alert, and SS-20s deployed into the field.[55] Most alarmingly of all, in his opinion, one decrypted communications fragment described the necessity of removing an electronic jamming pod from a Soviet jet, which led him to suspect it was being loaded with something it had never carried before: an actual atomic warhead. Asked by the head of the US Air Force in Europe – also NATO's air commander – whether US and allied forces should change their alert posture, Perroots recommended strongly they did not. Western intelligence collectors, he later argued in 1989, might well have missed critical clues – they believed it was 'peace time without even the most basic ripples of a crisis'.[56]

To use such words to describe 1983 points to a wider truth about the year. For those who truly focused on the prospect of upcoming Doomsday – Reagan; the more paranoid elements of Soviet leadership and military intelligence; the anti-nuclear protesters – the year had felt pregnant with danger, worries that with hindsight might have become self-fulfilling. For millions just getting on with life, however – particularly within the Western alliance – all these tensions were merely background noise. The contrast with the Cuban missile crisis, when all feared imminent catastrophe, was remarkable in the extreme. Even now, many who paid relatively close attention to daily news through 1983 remain unaware the 'war scare' ever happened.

They do, however, remember the broader atomic tensions. On 14 November, three days after the conclusion of ABLE ARCHER, the first US Cruise missiles arrived by plane at Greenham Common, announced by Michael Heseltine to howls of outrage by anti-nuclear Labour parliamentarians in a packed House of Commons. In a speech that night Thatcher stuck solidly to US talking points, suggesting that the Pershing 2 deployment to West Germany and Italy could still be halted if the Soviets pulled back their missiles.[57] As the first Pershings arrived in West Germany the following week, Kremlin negotiators walked out of arms talks in Geneva.[58] As further rockets arrived in Sicily, NATO defence ministers asserted their commitment to the rollout. Once again, Greece and Denmark held back.[59]

Only at the start of December, according to Perroots, did a National Security Agency intercept connect the recent Soviet and Eastern bloc activity to NATO drills, including ABLE ARCHER. Across the six months that followed he described himself as being 'on a soapbox' to lobby senior leaders on the subject, advising that future NATO drills at the very least be moved away from major Soviet holidays so they were less likely to be confused with a surprise attack.[60] Over time, these and other fragments – and particularly the revelations from Gordievsky – prompted more and more investigation, gradually rewriting history. When the ninety-four-page 'above top secret' report commissioned by Bush in 1990 was finally published in 2015 a member of the US Information Security Oversight Office – the arbiter of classification in the US government – described it as 'probably the most interesting document ever to have come across our desks'.[61]

For those directly involved in the drill, like SHAPE military planner Spike Callender, it was a particular revelation. 'We felt that this exercise was no more provocative in 1983 than it would have been in 1981 or 1982,' he told a researcher later. Robert Gates, deputy director of the CIA and later secretary of defense for George W. Bush and Barack Obama, described the entire affair as an immense intelligence failure. 'We may have been at the brink of nuclear war and not even known it,' he later said.[62]

*

On 8 December US military planners disseminated the orders for another nuclear command drill – NIGHT TRAIN 84 – that would commence the following April, and involve US and Canadian personnel only. The scenario envisaged a conflict along the Soviet–Turkish border escalating to a full strategic exchange, and the efforts at reconstruction that would follow. For perhaps the first time, the planning considerations – written by Colin Powell, now a senior military aide to Weinberger – explicitly acknowledged the danger that the exercise might be misinterpreted, and included public notes on managing that risk.[63]

Powell's first duty overseas had been to guard a nuclear artillery piece in West Germany in 1958. He would end the Reagan era as national security adviser, then oversee the Gulf War and early talk of NATO expansion as Chairman of the Joint Chiefs – proof to any remaining German racists that African-American GIs knew what they were doing.

First, though, NATO and its members would have to navigate some very new dynamics. The 'war scare' of 1983 might or might not have nearly ended the world, but the second half of the 1980s would serve up a very different drama.

15

Endgame (1984–89)

*'Eventually, the German nation will be reunified within a
very different Europe. But whether that will take place
twenty years from now or 200 . . . I don't pretend to know.'*

**US ambassador to West Germany
Arthur Burns, January 1984**[1]

As 1984 began, Britain announced the first Cruise missiles at
Greenham Common were operational,[2] the first natural gas
flowed down pipes from Siberia to Western Europe and *Time*
magazine named Reagan and Andropov their 'men of the
year'.[3] Andropov, though, was on his deathbed – if not already
gone. It would be Reagan and Thatcher who would call the
shots in 1984, before Gorbachev came to power and the Cold
War came to an end faster than anyone had predicted.

From February 1984, agent reports from KGB mole Oleg
Gordievsky to his British handlers were being shared directly
with the White House, alerting both British and French leadership to the scale of Russian worries over war. Reagan's diaries,
for his part, identified November 1983 as the moment he grasped
'something surprising about the Russians . . . I feel the Soviets
are . . . so paranoid about being attacked that without in any
way being soft . . . we ought to tell them no one here has any
intention of doing anything like that.'[4] Asked by *Time* about his
'evil empire' comments, Reagan replied, 'I would not say things
like that again. I would like to convince the Soviets that no one in

the world has aggressive intentions towards them.' Warming to his theme, Reagan went so far as to publicly suggest ridding the world of atomic arms. 'Why do we keep them?' he said. 'Let's get back to being civilised.'[5]

Talk of renewed arms control came against the backdrop of still frenetic military activity. January saw the announcement of large Arctic drills later in the year, with 25,000 alliance troops scheduled to head to Norway.[6] April would see what US and British officials described as the largest Soviet naval exercises ever – more than one hundred vessels and submarines pushing into the North Atlantic with simultaneous manoeuvres in the Indian Ocean, Mediterranean and Caribbean.[7] Arriving in West Germany as a new qualified RAF Jaguar pilot, twenty-one-year-old Bob Judson found himself almost immediately flying simulated strike missions against advancing Soviet troops. The multiday NATO exercises that ran day and night throughout the year all followed the same scenario: a conventional Warsaw Pact offensive that led to nuclear war within a week.[8]

All sides, however, were beginning to refocus on avoiding that. In January 1984, at a disarmament conference in Stockholm, NATO states formally presented a six-point proposal on preventing an accidental war. It included exchange of information on the locations of military forces, advance warning of military drills, exchange of observers, and improvements in communications.[9] In February, Canadian Prime Minister Pierre Trudeau and Margaret Thatcher began their own diplomatic forays into Eastern Europe. Trudeau's mission, described as a personal 'crusade' to limit nuclear arms, saw him visit Romania and become the first NATO leader to visit East Berlin.[10] Thatcher's visit to Hungary, following on the heels of Vice President Bush in September 1983, was believed the first by a British prime minister – it was telling that no one knew for sure. Hungary was becoming the most economically liberal of the Warsaw Pact members, and desperate for international trade and credit.[11]

Andropov's death was announced on 9 February. Reagan sent

Bush to meet new – and not much healthier – leader Konstantin Chernenko, who agreed on the need 'to place our relationship on a more constructive path'. Thatcher and Kohl also decided to attend, despite missing the funeral of Brezhnev a year earlier.[12] Initially, though, relations remained tense. In March, Chernenko told *Pravda* that despite occasional 'peace-loving rhetoric' from the United States, the world situation remained 'not improving [and] very dangerous'.[13] Soviet air force leaders warned any breaches of Soviet airspace would lead to aircraft being shot down, and continued to describe the Korean Airlines shootdown as a Western 'provocation'.[14] As Soviet warships headed into the Atlantic and NATO and Warsaw Pact delegates met in Vienna to discuss troop levels, a Soviet-built jet fired at a US Army helicopter near the West German–Czechoslovak border. It was the first such aerial incident since 1964.[15]

Behind the scenes several European nations were quietly discussing taking a larger stake in their own defence, a process they dubbed 'Europisation'; a tacit acknowledgement of transatlantic differences. French officials wanted to revitalise the Western European Union, largely ignored since the growth of NATO in the 1950s.[16] Foreign ministers from Britain, France, West Germany, Italy, Belgium, the Netherlands and Luxembourg attended the first meeting of the Western European Union in almost thirty years, and pointedly avoided any discussion of nuclear weapons while stressing the Western European Union's (WEU) intention was not to act as a rival to NATO. 'It is not that the United States is too strong in the alliance, but that Europe is too weak,' argued West German Foreign Minister Hans-Dietrich Genscher.[17]

In part, the WEU's purpose was to reassure congressional voices in the US that European states were willing to do more for their own defence. As they met, European and British officials – encouraged by the Reagan administration – were furiously lobbying senators to reject a motion to cut back US troops in Europe. Senator Sam Nunn, its author, described it as 'not a petition for divorce [but] a petition for the alliance to carry out its vows'.[18] In the run-up to his June visit to Europe, Reagan met with both Mitterrand and Kohl. All were now convinced the Communist bloc was in terminal decline, but Mitterrand warned a failing Soviet Union might yet become more dangerous.[19]

NATO's new incoming secretary general, former British Foreign Secretary Lord Peter Carrington, had already politely criticised the more strident nature of Reaganite diplomacy. Now, months away from taking office, he publicly disputed US suggestions that Europe might be 'more interested in material prosperity than their own defence'. European nations, he said, worried about losing the social and economic gains made since 1945, as well as the risk of atomic war upon their territory.[20] Efforts to simulate and prepare for potential conflict continued through 1984. As well as another large REFORGER, the autumn exercise season included LIONHEART, the largest British exercise of the entire Cold War.[21]

As tens of thousands of British troops went through the motions they would take in an actual war, the BBC broadcast a drama entitled *Threads* that attempted to portray the reality of a major nuclear exchange. Focusing principally on the British city of Sheffield, its portrayal of firestorms, fallout, looting and complete collapse went beyond that seen in other portrayals of atomic warfare. Widely watched across Britain, few who saw it would ever forget its scenes. 'Everyone at school was traumatised the following day,' recalled Keelin McCarthy, a schoolgirl in Nottingham at the time. 'People really thought that was how we were going to die.'[22] Such worries fed a wider trend – US officials worried about an 'unravelling' of European support for nuclear weapons that might undo the alliance altogether.[23]

Carrington was determined to maintain or arguably restore the balance between deterrence and détente and support the US as it attempted to do a deal on atomic arms. A December 1984 NATO ministerial meeting again blamed the Kremlin for exacerbating the arms race with ongoing missile deployments. Carrington said NATO had 'to make the Soviet government understand that the West is serious about these negotiations'.

Much more dramatic change, however, was now coming. As the NATO summit closed, Mikhail Gorbachev landed at RAF Brize Norton in Oxfordshire to visit Margaret Thatcher. Having been to Italy earlier in the year, it was his third visit to the West – Chernenko was now sickening fast – and Gorbachev was suddenly the favourite to succeed him.[24] His talking points over lunch and drinks at Chequers, Thatcher later noted in her memoirs, were largely the same as other senior Soviet officials – but his style was very different. As Thatcher told reporters afterwards, Gorbachev appeared a man the West could do business with.[25]

*

As Reagan was sworn in for his second term as president at the end of January 1985, transatlantic divisions simmered over the 'Star Wars' Strategic Defence Initiative. While privately opposed, Thatcher and Kohl were prepared to endorse research in the interests of maintaining good relations. Other European leaders and officials, however, were sceptical at best, doubting it would work but fearing if it did it would only protect the US mainland and risk Europe being sacrificed.[26]

Examples of Reaganite tone-deafness continued. Publication of new US contingency plans to station further nuclear weapons in NATO nations including Canada, Iceland and Spain caused further embarrassment after it emerged those countries had not been consulted. Spain, already planning a referendum on NATO membership for 1986, said bluntly that it would block such plans, and the US administration was forced into awkwardly conceding it would not deploy the weapons without host government consent.[27]

Despite anti-nuclear feeling remaining high, at the end of March the Belgian Parliament finally backed the deployment of

US Cruise missiles.[28] Shortly afterwards Gorbachev's appointment as general secretary of the Communist Party of the Soviet Union appeared to open the door to more serious renewed détente. As the world stood on the brink of change, one last incident threatened to disrupt it. On 24 March 1985 US Major Arthur Nicholson, a liaison officer on the East–West German border, was shot dead by a Soviet soldier. Soviet and East German officials offered 'regret', but claimed he had entered a prohibited area and ignored warning shots.[29]

Events were moving fast. At Chernenko's funeral Vice President Bush handed Gorbachev a handwritten letter from Reagan inviting him to a summit. In his first foreign policy speech, on 7 April, Gorbachev accepted, simultaneously announcing a unilateral freeze of Soviet SS-20 deployment ahead of the resumption of arms talks in Geneva.[30] On 15 April, the chief Soviet and US army commanders in Germany met to discuss the killing of Major Nicholson, drawing up rules avoid any repetition of the event.[31] The process of de-escalating tensions in Europe had begun – driven firmly by bilateral US–Soviet discussions, with NATO structures and processes often initially on the sidelines.

By mid-1985 it was becoming increasingly apparent that Gorbachev intended to take the Soviet Union down the reformist path of what he called *glasnost* (transparency) and *perestroika* (restructuring). Not everyone, however, found that reassuring. Until the very end of 1989, Europeans remained nervous that the US might cut a deal with the Kremlin to abandon them to their fate.

Gorbachev's diplomatic offensive, some US hawks believed, was designed to trick and divide the US and its European allies, potentially leaving the continent ripe for conquest by the Kremlin. Visiting Paris in October, Gorbachev floated the idea of a separate arms agreements with Britain and France, which looked like an even more explicit attempt to split the allies.[32] The initial Soviet offer to the US – to reduce strategic long-range atomic rockets that could reach each other's territory by 50 per cent – was swiftly rejected by the Reagan administration, which argued it would force the US to cut back its nuclear forces in Europe while the SS-20s – which could devastate Western Europe – were 'tactical' medium-range weapons not covered by the deal. But while some viewed the Kremlin offer as disingenuous, Carrington described the fact that it had been proposed at all as 'welcome', predicting more negotiation.[33] He was determined to maintain as much unity as possible, particularly on arms talks. That meant diplomatically taking the European side in arguments with Washington, yet aiming to quietly pressure the Reagan administration while still maintaining a unified – and optimistic – front. When Gorbachev made an offer, Carrington was determined that the West made just one response.

As 1986 began, more aggressive US voices accused Reagan of 'surrendering' to America's NATO allies and 'Europeanising' US policy to re-embrace détente.[34] As it became apparent the Reagan administration might scale back or withdraw the Cruises and Pershings as part of a bilateral deal with the Kremlin, some of the European nations also got more nervous, returning to the worries that had prompted West German Chancellor Schmidt to ask for those missiles in the first place. Even if the SS-20s also left, some in the West German government worried it would leave them too vulnerable to a Soviet conventional assault. French officials, ironically given their earlier eviction of US atomic arms from their soil, were now among the most vehement that the US must not abandon the right to station its nuclear weapons in European territories.[35] Meanwhile, Spain's referendum saw almost 57 per cent of respondents choose to remain within the alliance. It was an unexpected victory for Prime Minister Felipe González, who had argued membership was critical to integrating post-fascist Spain back into mainland Europe. For the alliance, it was a spectacular relief.[36]

*

Disagreements with the Kremlin did not disappear with Gorbachev. Throughout March and early April 1986 tensions rose again between the US and Muammar Gaddafi's Libya, already blamed for a string of attacks on US targets in Europe. On 14 April an aircraft carrier and US jets flying from England struck the Libyan capital Tripoli, while France refused overflight rights. The strike – immediately condemned by Gorbachev as 'militaristic' – highlighted once again divisions within Europe, and might have given an opening to the Kremlin.[37] Then, on 26 April, the Chernobyl nuclear power station went into meltdown. On both sides of the Iron Curtain anxious populations awaited news on the realities of fallout. In Hungary the initially incompetent Soviet response was publicly and officially criticised. In Western Europe leaders rapidly dropped plans for new atomic power plants following Chernobyl and became even less keen to publicly discuss atomic arms.[38]

On 21 September 1986, as NATO's AUTUMN FORGE and associated drills began, the Stockholm disarmament conference that had grown out of the Helsinki process finally reached an agreement between NATO and Warsaw Pact states designed to increase military transparency on both sides and reduce the risk of war. For the first time NATO and the Warsaw Pact agreed to give each other advance knowledge of significant military exercises, as well as allowing inspections by the other side to provide reassurance they were not cover for a surprise attack. 'No one can get everything they want from this kind of agreement,' said Robert Barry, the head of the US delegation, but argued it was a good first step that showed 'East and West can say yes to each other for a change'.[39] As the two-day Reagan–Gorbachev summit in Reykjavík ended in October 1986 with a firm commitment to more talks, Carrington said 'possibilities for significant progress had emerged' and should be followed up 'energetically'.[40] It was now Western European countries that were expressing concern over what they believed was a real danger Reagan would give too much away, cutting back the US atomic arsenal to the extent that it could no longer defend Europe. In November, West German military intelligence briefed journalists that Soviet and Warsaw Pact commando forces were continuing to routinely enter Western Europe – sometimes on Soviet civilian trucks – to reconnoitre potential invasion routes.[41] Still, the December 1986 NATO summit endorsed the US–Soviet suggestions of reducing atomic forces on both sides by 50 per cent, arguing that nuclear reductions would require the alliance to spend more on conventional forces.[42]

As he prepared to receive Thatcher in Moscow in March 1987, Gorbachev offered a unilateral deal to eradicate intermediate-range atomic arms in Europe – specifically SS-20, Cruise and Pershing – which Carrington's official spokesman called a 'welcome development', even as French and West German officials signalled caution.[43] Three days later, Reagan announced the US would 'seize this new opportunity', and sent his own arms negotiators to Moscow too.[44] French officials talked darkly of the 'denuclearisation' of Europe, leaving it undefended and at the mercy of the Soviets.[45] Other leaders were less sure of their position. 'NATO leaders are not going to stand up in front of the public and say a Europe free of nuclear missiles is a bad idea, because they will have orange peels thrown at them if they do,' said one Western diplomat. 'It may take a while for consensus to form.'[46]

In fact, the Reagan administration was determined to push ahead regardless of consensus. Thatcher and Kohl agreed to support the Cruise and Pershing removal, but others in the alliance were openly reluctant. Leaked secret NATO analysis from SACEUR Rogers warned removing the missiles increased the danger Europe might be overrun by a Soviet attack.[47] Rogers – now on the brink of retirement – would continue to accuse the administration of being too keen to conclude an agreement before Reagan left office at the end of 1988.[48] Attempting to walk a middle line, Carrington warned NATO nations not to get carried away in the 'euphoria' on arms control but not to make themselves 'fearful' either over US missile withdrawals.[49]

On 19 September 1987, US and Soviet negotiators announced a preliminary deal to ban medium-and short-range missiles from Europe, hailed by Britain as a 'profound development . . . a formidable achievement' and West Germany as the 'first major disarmament achievement'. NATO's official statement was more cautious, saying the alliance hoped 'an agreement will be the beginning of a process in which we can live at a much lower level of armaments for the same security'.[50] As Reagan and Gorbachev signed the intermediate missile treaty in December, the first sparks of a new round of unrest were about to spread across Eastern Europe.

As Reagan flew to Moscow at the end of May 1988 the first Hollywood blockbuster filmed on Soviet soil – *Red Heat*, starring Arnold Schwarzenegger as a Russian cop – prepared to open in America. The intermediate missile treaty had been ratified by the Senate days before the visit, and by mid-May military observers and journalists from both sides of the Iron Curtain were at missile bases to scrutinise the weapons shortly to be destroyed. First was a Soviet installation in Ukraine, followed by a US air base at Gosselies in Belgium. The Cruise missiles there, the visitors were told, would be shipped to Arizona for destruction by early 1989, as would those in England and Italy. Similar displays were held at the British base at Greenham Common, plus a Pershing site in Germany.[51] Foreign ministers urged that wider NATO military spending remain constant, though. 'Whatever else may have changed in the Soviet Union, the military machine is still, so far, operating at exactly the same level as it was in the days before *perestroika* and *glasnost*,' said Carrington, now in his final days before retirement.[52]

On 8 July 1988, Soviet Prime Minister Nikolai Ryzhkov said the Kremlin was willing to pull all Soviet troops from foreign territory by the year 2000 – but only if the US and Britain did the same. US officials, however, suggested a more dramatic unilateral move might be imminent, with the Kremlin said to be considering removing all its 65,000 troops from increasingly independent Hungary.[53] In Soviet-controlled Estonia, what had started as a relatively subtle protest movement of music and environmental activism was now turning into a clear opposition party and independence movement, something Gorbachev had specifically stated would not be tolerated. Strikes in Poland also escalated through the summer, with the government offering pay increases and suggesting it might give in to public demands to legalise Solidarity. Arrests and crackdowns rose, and as the government threatened to close the Gdańsk shipyards in November – birthplace of Solidarity – the Communist leadership claimed they were inspired by Margaret Thatcher's ruthlessness in taking on trade unions and closing industries.[54]

Speaking to the UN General Assembly in December 1988, Gorbachev attacked the West for efforts to impoverish countries through Third World debt, but made it clear *perestroika* and *glasnost* would continue. Then, he shocked the world with a unilateral pledge – explicitly independent of any arms control agreement – to cut the Soviet military by 500,000 personnel, approximately a tenth. The implications for NATO were profound. Gorbachev pledged to withdraw and disband six tank divisions from East Germany, Czechoslovakia and Hungary by 1991 – a total of 50,000 men and 5,000 tanks. Forces within both European and Asian parts of Russia would also be reduced, he said, and the structure of remaining forces in Eastern Europe would be purely defensive.[55] Those who had helped shape NATO policy for years were simply astonished. 'My mouth fell again,' said one Pentagon consultant. Some alliance diplomats and officials viewed it as a deliberate gambit to seize the agenda in arms negotiations. But if the proposed cuts were made, incoming NATO Secretary General and former German Defence Minister Manfred Wörner said, 'It is a very significant step that we emphatically welcome.'[56]

Meeting over the following two days in Brussels, NATO ministers cautiously praised what they described as 'clear signs of change in the internal and external policies of the Soviet Union and some of its allies', pledging to 'seize every opportunity' for cooperation, and calling for even larger arms cuts.[57] Amid all the focus on arms control, however, many commentators missed one crucial detail. In pulling back troops from Eastern Europe, pledging to respect political and economic 'diversity' and refusing to be 'hemmed in' by ideology, Gorbachev was explicitly disavowing the Brezhnev Doctrine that the Kremlin would intervene to keep its fellow Communist governments in power. If revolutions like that in Hungary in 1956 or the 'Prague Spring' occurred again, the Soviet Union would stand by and let them happen.[58]

*

By the time George Bush senior entered office in January 1989, it was clear the face of Europe would be changing – but not how quickly. Secretary of State James Baker told the *New York Times* the US State Department had been discussing a plan initially suggested by Kissinger, in which the Kremlin would be called on to reduce its control over Eastern Europe so that countries could run their own affairs. In exchange, the West would provide 'some type of promise' that NATO would not exploit that by moving into Eastern Europe or undermining Soviet interests. It was important to get it right, he said, and the US would give itself time to do so.[59]

In fact, time was already up. Gorbachev's commitment not to intervene in Eastern Europe was a death sentence to the Kremlin's allies, who could not keep pace with the calls for change. Hungary's Communist Party was the first to embrace economic and then political reform – and was soon divided between the hardliners who wished to regain control and those who saw democracy as the way forward. 'A Hungarian soldier ordered to shoot his own people would either shoot his

commander or go home,' senior party official Imre Pozsgay told
the hardliners in April 1989. They agreed to multiparty elections and dismantling the 'Iron Curtain' along their borders and
opening travel to the West. The first sections were taken down in
May to gauge the Soviet response. When none came, the rest
quickly followed. As East Germans flocked into Hungary for
their traditional summer holidays, crossing remained technically
illegal – but there would be little to stop them.[60] For decades
officials and pundits within NATO nations had worried their
own side would collapse, whether overwhelmed by Soviet force
or undermined by internal divisions and a reluctance to fight or
face atomic war. Now, it was their adversary that unravelled.

As NATO turned forty on 4 April, new Secretary General
Manfred Wörner said the alliance had given Europe its longest
period of peace since the Roman Empire. But whatever hap-
pened next in Eastern Europe, Wörner predicted the Soviet
Union would remain a major force.[61] Not everyone was so sure.
'The unity of the Eastern Bloc is gone,' said one French official.
'We are entering a period of turbulence in a historically turbu-
lent area that has been kept artificially stable by the presence of
Soviet troops.'

In Romania, Nicolae Ceauşescu's doubling down on repression raised fears of a bloody civil war. Czechoslovakia was
similarly refusing to reform. Poland had legalised Solidarity and
set democratic elections for June, their first since 1945, but no one
knew how they would go. In West Germany officials increasingly
questioned if East Germany could survive at all. 'What you're
really dealing with is German nationalism,' said one senior
American official. In London and Paris such worries ran even
deeper. Ever since the 1960s, all the NATO allies had committed on paper to supporting German reunification – but none
expected it to happen. Now, both Mitterrand and Thatcher felt it
was occurring much too quickly, and that a unified and powerful
Germany might again prove a threat to its neighbours – or at the
very least too powerful to be controlled.

Talks on conventional force reductions in Europe were now accelerating further. In mid-May the Bush administration regained some of the initiative by revitalising the Eisenhower-era 'open skies' offer, allowing US and Soviet planes to overfly each other's territory as a tool for arms control. The second NATO leaders' summit in two years at the end of May 1989 in Brussels delivered a remarkably united front. The communiqué pledged further arms control – but it also echoed Reagan's rhetoric by pledging to 'tear down the walls that separate us physically and politically . . . [and to] simplify the crossing of borders'. In what appeared to be a veiled and vague warning to the Eastern bloc, it also committed to ensuring people were not 'prevented by armed force from crossing the frontiers and boundaries which we share with Eastern countries' – although what action NATO might take remained extremely vague.[62]

The worst bloodshed of the year, however, would happen far from Europe. As Gorbachev visited China in mid-May, tens of thousands of protesters took to Beijing's Tiananmen Square, demanding similar change in China to that the world was witnessing in Europe. Some of the Chinese protesters even wrote to the Soviet embassy to invite the Soviet leader to their tented camps. As Gorbachev and his delegation watched the crowds grow, they felt the scenes justified the steps they had taken, wondering if the Chinese Communist officials they were meeting would be 'dead men' in the weeks to come.[63] Instead, in the first days of June 1989, Chinese leader Deng Xiaoping sent in tanks and troops. Authorities put the death toll at 200, but the Chinese Red Cross told foreign diplomats Beijing's hospitals had received 2,600 bodies.[64]

In Central and Eastern Europe, however, it was now too late to do the same. Through the first two weeks of June, Poland held its first democratic elections since the 1920s, and the newly legalised Solidarity – now established as a political party – swept almost all the seats. Polish General Czesław Kiszczak, the Communist interior minister who had signed the arrest order for

Lech Wałęsa in 1981, now shook the Solidarity leader's hand and offered his 'hearty congratulations'. The government itself remained in Communist hands, but that looked unsustainable.[65] On 16 June a quarter of a million Hungarians witnessed the reburial of Imre Nagy and other executed leaders of the 1956 Hungarian Revolution. Speaker after speaker, including a young Viktor Orbán, demanded the withdrawal of Soviet troops. By early July, Solidarity parliamentarians were negotiating publicly for a managed transition of power in Poland. As Bush prepared to visit Warsaw he told Polish journalists the time had come for the Soviet Union to withdraw its forces from that country and the rest of Eastern Europe.[66] Speaking before the Council of Europe in Paris a few days later, Gorbachev implicitly ruled out the use of force against Eastern bloc nations and told NATO the Kremlin would reduce its shortest-range atomic arms including artillery and smaller rockets 'without delay' if NATO was willing to talk about doing the same. 'Any interference in domestic affairs and any attempts to restrict the sovereignty of states – friends, allies or any others – are inadmissible,' he said, referring once again to a 'common European home' stretching from the Atlantic to the Urals.[67]

In mid-July, NATO announced they wanted to limit combat aircraft in Europe to 5,700 on either side.[68] Given their numerical superiority but poorer aircraft, the Soviets were unsurprisingly unimpressed.[69] As the G7 met in Paris, Gorbachev surprised Bush and other leaders by calling for expanded economic cooperation involving the Kremlin. The summit approved a major financial assistance package for Poland and Hungary, including emergency food supplies.[70]

August saw unprecedented events once again in the Baltic states, still theoretically Soviet republics. At 7 p.m. on 23 August approximately two million Baltic citizens joined hands from Tallinn through Riga to Vilnius, joining the three capitals in the longest unbroken line of interlinked human beings in history. Soviet television claimed the chain should not be regarded as a 'manifestation of a separatist mood'. On the streets, however, the talk was of independence, while the leadership of each republic pledged 'self-determination' and 'sovereignty'.[71]As late as September 1989, what was about to happen still seemed unthinkable to many within NATO. At an alliance conference that month, a British MP asked a German general from SHAPE what planning he and colleagues were doing about potential reunification. The general replied with a grin, saying they were doing as little thinking as possible as the prospect was too far-fetched. The major issue for 1990, officials confidently predicted, was the potential modernisation of the US Lance short-range atomic rocket in West Germany.[72]

Others already worried chaos might be coming. The same month, Deputy Secretary of State Lawrence Eagleburger told Georgetown University students: 'For all its risks and uncertainties, the Cold War was characterised by a remarkably stable and predictable set of relations among the great powers.' Eagleburger warned that relaxed Soviet control over Eastern Europe was 'bringing long suppressed ethnic antagonisms and national rivalries to the surface, and putting the German question back on the international agenda'.[73] The 'German question' would now answer itself at speed. With the Hungarian border open, tens of thousands of East Germans flooded into Western Europe, the exodus Erich Honecker's 'socialist paradise' had held back for a generation. Czechoslovakia followed suit, prompting East Germany to block its own borders to both countries.

The alliance now realised it might need to work to maintain relevance. On 12 October, Secretary General Wörner told the NAC he expected both NATO and the Warsaw Pact would 'play a very important role in the next decade and will not disappear', describing them as a 'useful framework for the necessary political change'. The fact he felt the need to reassure them on this point, Council of Foreign Relations expert Michael Mandelbaum told journalists, 'tells you what a revolutionary international environment we are now in'.[74]

As Moscow did not intervene, protests spread across East Germany. Honecker resigned on 18 October. The new East German leadership tried to save itself by liberalising border controls, but had no idea how to do so without sparking an enormous movement of population. On 9 November, a Communist Party spokesman announced incorrectly that East German citizens could cross the border that night. In the hours that followed, citizens from both sides of the city tore down barricades and checkpoints. In the days that followed, more than two million people crossed into West Berlin. At NATO and military headquarters across Western Europe those who had prepared to defend the continent against the Warsaw Pact now watched as it unravelled. RAF pilot Bob Judson was on exchange with the West German Luftwaffe, who were equally astounded: 'Everyone was glued to the television . . . their jaws just dropped.'[75]

As the wall came down on the night of 9 November, Secretary of State Baker told ABC, 'It has been the policy of the NATO alliance and it has been the policy of the United States of America to support reunification for over forty years.' 'That sounds like boilerplate,' said news anchor Chris Wallace. 'That is our policy,' replied Baker.[76] For a brief moment almost anything seemed possible. On 10 November, East German ambassador to Washington Gerhard Herder warned that a 'miscalculation' in Berlin could lead to conflict between East German and nearby American, British or French troops. Almost simultaneously, however, US Defense Secretary Dick Cheney told reporters the risk of conflict in Europe was falling fast to the lowest point since 1945. Others still feared a secret Soviet agenda: one senior US defence official warned that the Kremlin might still be 'very much playing the game of trying to drive us out of Europe'.[77] Wörner was determined that should not happen. 'Take away the United States and a decisive factor of stability in Europe has gone,' he said. Others talked of a role for the alliance as a 'counterbalance to German might'.[78]

Thatcher, Mitterrand and Gorbachev worried about German reunification, as Bonn wondered how fast to go. As the wall came down US TV aired footage of the British prime minister saying 'much too fast, much too fast'. Thatcher believed European borders should not be redrawn until 'genuine democracy [had been] established throughout Eastern Europe and eventually the Soviet Union'.[79] One thing was clear: the West German government now had no intention of renewing the smallest nuclear weapons on its territory such as the very short-range Lance. 'The question of nuclear modernisation makes us laugh,' said one West German official visiting Washington. 'I don't think there is any possibility of it being implemented.'[80]

On 2 December, Gorbachev and Bush met in Malta, hoping to mark the end of the Cold War – whatever that might mean. In much of Eastern Europe chaos still reigned; euphoria was mixed with both relief and trepidation. The Czechoslovakian and Bulgarian governments had fallen; only Nicolae Ceauşescu in Romania clung on. At a joint news conference, the Soviet leader announced: 'The world is leaving one epoch and entering another. We are at the beginning of a long road to a lasting, peaceful era.' Then he pledged not to start a 'hot war' with the United States. Bush was more circumspect, pledging to 'transform the East–West relationship into one of enduring cooperation'.

Addressing NATO leaders on 5 December, Bush described Europe as standing on the 'threshold of a new era' – but pledged to keep a significant number of US troops on the continent. Both Bush and Gorbachev had stopped short of pledging to abolish either the alliance or the Warsaw Pact, but in truth neither now knew what its role would really be. At the Brussels summit Bush, for the first time, voiced his own full-throated support for German reunification. In what was left of East Germany crowds were now overrunning and torching Stasi offices. On the night of 5 December, hours after Bush addressed the NATO summit, the mob came for the KGB in Dresden. Inside

the building, thirty-seven-year-old KGB Lieutenant Colonel
Vladimir Putin would later recount how he phoned a nearby
Soviet army tank unit to ask for protection. 'We cannot do anything without orders from Moscow,' an army officer told him.
'And Moscow is silent.' The protesters continued to push forward, the gate guard fleeing. Witness and protester Siegfried
Dannath later recalled a more senior officer – 'quite small, agitated' – emerge. His message was very clear: if the protesters
came any further into the compound, the man Dannath would
later identify as Putin warned, they would all be shot.[81]

Part 5:
The Era of Intervention

16

Driving Fast through Fog (1990–1991)

> *'The threat is no longer Russia. The threat is uncertainty.'*
>
> **Captain John Heidt,**
> **US Naval War College, January 1990**[1]

The Berlin Wall was gone, but the Soviet Union remained. In January 1990 the smallest REFORGER drills yet began in West Germany, postponed amid the chaos of the previous year and now involving far fewer troops and no tanks at all. All were still reeling from the events of 1989. After the deaths of several thousand protesters in mid- to late December, Romania's Nicolae Ceauşescu had finally been forced from office, hunted down, subjected to a summary trial and shot on 25 December. In Poland, Hungary, Czechoslovakia and Bulgaria, new governments were still finding their feet.

Across much of the rest of NATO the mood was one of shock. When fifty generals and admirals from across the alliance assembled for tabletop war games at the US Naval War College, there was a tacit acknowledgement that the scenario – a Soviet attack on Norway – now seemed implausible. 'When military men don't know what to do, they do what they know,' said one British officer. 'It's like driving in a fog,' said academic dean Captain Betsy Wylie, arguing the future was now too unpredictable to plan in detail – but that driving too fast was inadvisable.[2]

Going slowly, however, would not prove an option either.

On 15 January 1990 the professional heads of every military in Europe except Albania and Vatican City – thirty-five nations in total, including the US – met for the first time. It 'must not be a routine conference', General Colin Powell, US Chairman of the Joint Chiefs of Staff, told them, arguing that 'the era of confrontation in Europe must end'.[3] Since 1945, Western nations had always known they would be outgunned by the Soviets in terms of troops and tanks in Europe. Now, US delegates at disarmament talks in Geneva pushed for parity. On 26 January, Bush told Kohl the US expected to call for an upper limit of 275,000 troops by the mid-1990s, requiring small US force reductions but more than 100,000 Soviet withdrawals. Poland, Czechoslovakia and Hungary, however, were already demanding Soviet troops quit their territories completely.

Bush was determined to retain significant troops in Europe. The German chancellor agreed, praising Bush for 'taking the offensive' to keep NATO together. The most immediate problem, he said, was keeping Eastern Europe from outright collapse. Even in Moscow there were growing problems with the supply of food. East Germany, meanwhile, was in abject crisis. 'Confidence in the administration is catastrophic,' Kohl said. 'People are leaving in the thousands, and the rest are sitting on packed suitcases.' Kohl told Bush his job now was stopping further destabilisation in Eastern Europe, implicitly asserting that Germany would reunite and lead the continent.[4] Bush made no objection. The first six months of 1990 saw the West German chancellor ruthlessly pursue reunification with the support of both the US and NATO Secretary General Manfred Wörner. That meant ignoring concerns and sometimes outright opposition from Mitterrand and Thatcher, who would continue to publicly worry a reunified Germany would be just too powerful.

As West German defence minister, Wörner had backed Kohl to the hilt. Now, the former lawyer and reserve fighter pilot was determined to keep the alliance relevant, while backing West German efforts to reunify at speed. Wörner told Bush that whether

Germany became 'neutral' or a NATO member 'would decide future decades of European history'. If it did not join the alliance, he predicted 'the old Pandora's box of competition and rivalry in Europe would be reopened'. 'An American president who wants a Europe whole and free cannot accept neutralisation of a united Germany,' he told Bush, repeating a phrase the president had first used in a speech the previous year. 'There can be no ambiguity.'[5]

At the start of February the Bush administration and German Foreign Minister Hans-Dietrich Genscher announced a critical decision – a united Germany would remain within NATO, but without alliance troops and weapons being based in the former East.[6] The US and Kohl would now need to sell this idea to both the Kremlin and soon-to-be German electorate, including those in the East who had been told for decades to view NATO as an enemy. Meeting Gorbachev in Moscow on 9 February, Secretary of State James Baker told him that German reunification was unstoppable and imminent, and that Western European governments including Germany were keen for US troops to stay and NATO to endure. 'We understand that not only for the Soviet Union but for other European countries as well it is important to have guarantees that if the United States keeps its presence in Germany within the framework of NATO, not an inch of NATO's present military jurisdiction will spread in an eastern direction,' he said according to the official conversation notes.[7] Gorbachev said that any expansion of the 'zone of NATO' was unacceptable, and later claimed that US Secretary of State Baker had replied, 'We agree with that.'[8] Never again would US or NATO officials explicitly make that promise to the Kremlin – and the expansion of the alliance over the years that followed would yield resentment in Moscow that would last for decades.

Already, however, the new democracies of Eastern and Central Europe were making their voices heard, some within them already hoping NATO membership could be achieved. New Polish Foreign Minister Krzysztof Skubiszewski was first to break with the official Soviet and Warsaw Pact position that a reunited Germany must be 'neutral', saying Warsaw would much rather it remained in the NATO alliance. Should it not, he warned, it might otherwise become an isolated 'power or superpower on the European stage'. Shortly afterwards, Czechoslovakia and Hungary said the same.[9] Hungary then rejected Soviet suggestions the Warsaw Pact and NATO should be simultaneously abolished, announcing it wanted closer ties to the alliance. Within three weeks the Soviets agreed to a full withdrawal from Hungary.[10]

Moscow felt it had little choice but to let Central and Eastern Europe go, but the Baltic states would prove a very different matter. On 10 March, Lithuania declared its intent to restore independence, its pre-USSR flag emblazoned on the wall as parliamentarians joined hands and sang the national anthem. The Bush administration urged Gorbachev to respect the move, reminding the Kremlin it had never recognised Soviet annexation of the Baltic states.[11] But neither the US nor any European nation was prepared to offer outright recognition.

As Soviet leaders pondered their reaction, Kohl was rapidly reunifying the German nation. On 18 March, East Germany held democratic elections, the only ones in its history. The West German leader addressed enormous crowds across the East, seeking to persuade them that the reconstituted country should have membership of NATO. Kohl and his Christian Democrats led a multiparty group running on a strategy of imminent reunification, and won the election. Within little over four months of the wall coming down – despite mutterings from France, Britain and the Kremlin – Kohl had achieved an indisputable democratic mandate for a united Germany. 'You're a hell of a campaigner,' Bush told him.[12]

April 1990 brought agreement that a united Germany would simply inherit West Germany's membership of the twelve-nation European Community. Germany's embrace of French plans for European integration – essentially signing off the creation of the modern European Union – persuaded Mitterrand to drop his opposition to a united Deutschland. 'We don't want to be the Fourth Reich,' Kohl told reporters. 'We want to be European Germans and German Europeans.' In an implicit criticism of Thatcher's opposition – she was no more a fan of greater European integration than she was of German reunification – he warned a move for European unity was similarly unstoppable.[13]

The US expected to close at least eighty military bases in West Germany, a tenth of the number across the country.[14] As it did so Soviet officials told reporters they were launching the kind of military intervention seen in Hungary and Czechoslovakia in 1956 and 1967 in the Baltic states. As he met Soviet Foreign Minister Eduard Shevardnadze in April, Bush said: 'We don't have a desire to interfere in your affairs, but the . . . crushing of Lithuania would be a problem.'[15] Mitterrand thought Lithuania had 'jumped the gun' with its March declaration of independence, making it harder for Gorbachev to handle similar demands from other Soviet states. Baker suggested France quietly pressure the Lithuanian authorities to revoke their declaration. As with German rearmament thirty-five years earlier, however, the toothpaste was firmly out of the tube. With the Nordic states now actively encouraging the rebel administrations in the Baltics, NATO member Norway now offered petrochemicals to sustain Lithuanian independence.[16]

Soviet officials now suggested the new unified Germany should retain its membership of both NATO and the Warsaw Pact, a slight tweak on their previous position that it should be neutral and a member of neither.[17] In reality, however, the Kremlin's influence was already gone. Kohl's government was effectively already in charge in the old East Germany, while the other three occupying powers – the US, France and Britain – were unified and left the Kremlin little room to shape events.

Post-war Germany, the allies offered, would never develop nuclear, chemical or biological weapons, while the remaining short-range atomic arms stationed there would be removed entirely. Soviet troops would remain for a limited period in East Germany, just as the Western allies would within Berlin, and a united Germany would help fund Soviet troops throughout that time. Already some expressed concerns over treating Russia like a 'defeated nation'. 'The Soviets . . . will find it hard to accept the notion of NATO emerging as the sole, dominating security structure in Europe,' wrote Thomas Friedman in the *New York Times*. As NATO foreign ministers met on 3 May, Baker and Wörner asserted there would be no 'winners or losers' in Europe. Wörner said NATO had 'no intention of shifting the balance in Europe to the detriment of the Soviet Union'.[18] In a speech at Oklahoma State University the next day, Bush pledged that NATO would remain 'the foundation for America's engagement in Europe', with the US remaining firmly a 'European power . . . politically, militarily and economically'.[19] Wörner said the leaders' meeting scheduled for the summer must also transmit a new message to the Kremlin: 'NATO is a force for peace and European security, in cooperation with the Soviet Union.' Bush agreed. 'President Gorbachev needs to be convinced NATO isn't dangerous in the new era,' he said. 'That is a big assignment, especially among his military.'[20]

As NATO's heads of government came together in London on 5 July 1990, newspapers referred to it as the most important alliance gathering since 1949. Bush suggested the time had come to allow the Kremlin to open a liaison mission at NATO HQ.[21] Bush had phoned the potentially difficult Dutch, Belgian and Danish prime ministers directly to ensure they would agree to the communiqué. 'It's an old dilemma,' mused Wörner. 'Everybody wants US leadership, but they do not want to admit it.'[22] Baker had noted that the primary value of NATO to many Europeans was that it kept America engaged in Europe: 'They are beginning to realise that there could be no US presence in Europe outside of NATO.'[23]

Whether the Soviet Union remained a threat to NATO was

now a substantive question – one with hefty implications for alliance defence and particularly nuclear thinking. 'The point of nuclear weapons in particular is to deter, and indeed they have been very satisfactory in that respect,' Thatcher told the conference, repeating previous comments that as long as Gorbachev remained in power, the Cold War was over – but things could change extremely rapidly.[24] To placate the British and French, the eventual communiqué hedged its bets, stating: 'There are no circumstances in which nuclear retaliation in response to military action might be discounted.'[25] Also left vague were the longer-term aspirations for the alliance, with some arguing its supreme purpose remained protecting against an 'act of madness' by a future Russian leader, while others saw it as a broader security framework into which a democratic Kremlin might one day be integrated. In Moscow, Soviet Foreign Ministry spokesman Gennadi Gerasimov said the NATO statement would help Gorbachev rebut hardliners who had opposed concessions to the West. 'Now we can show them [the hardliners] they are wrong,' he said, as a G7 meeting prepared to discuss further Western economic aid for Russia.[26]

*

For a brief moment following the July summit, some pondered whether military confrontation might be a thing of the past. Then, on 2 August 1990, Saddam Hussein invaded Kuwait.[27] Initially, NATO and US officials talked up the prospect of the alliance having a direct role in the military response.[28] In early August NATO launched its first-ever military operation, ANCHOR GUARD, deploying two NATO-owned and operated E-3 AWACS airborne early warning planes to Turkey at its request. Soon they were flying ten- to twelve-hour patrols every day, albeit with tight rules of engagement that prevented them from approaching Iraqi airspace.[29]

In fact, NATO's involvement in the war in the desert would be minimal. But without decades of NATO planning, little of the upcoming Operation DESERT STORM would have been possible. US forces in Europe earmarked for the Gulf were engaged in what some termed a 'REFORGER in reverse', moving tens of thousands of troops and equipment out of the continent to the Saudi desert. West German authorities allowed US military movement at weekends, something almost unheard of during the Cold War when NATO commanders were nervous of inconveniencing German citizens.[30]

On 12 September the victors of World War Two – Britain, France, the US and the Soviet Union – signed away their rights in Germany, first established at the Potsdam Conference in July 1945. The 'final settlement' would end the division of Berlin, and open the way for reunification.

In the Baltics, this stoked fears that their struggle for independence might be ignored for ever. Soviet Foreign Minister Shevardnadze dismissed the Baltic issue as 'an internal matter'. Secretary of State Baker repeated that the US had never recognised the annexation of the three countries, but that their fate would have to be decided later and elsewhere.[31] Eastern European nations were also forced to accept that their integration into Western Europe would take longer than they hoped. The European Community had pledged to take no new members from Eastern Europe until the mid-1990s, with NATO officials talking of similar reticence. 'If we accepted, say, Hungary and Czechoslovakia, Moscow could be pardoned for feeling paranoid,' one senior Western official told the *New York Times*. 'What we all want now,' Wörner said, 'is to establish a basis on which to stabilise Europe without changing the military and strategic equilibrium.'[32]

While the Soviet Union remained firmly in existence, the Warsaw Pact was fading fast. As its members and NATO signed the Conventional Forces in Europe agreement on 3 October the Soviet-led alliance was said to be in 'disarray'. The countries of Eastern Europe had no appetite whatsoever to take direction from Moscow, and the Western journalists and inspectors visiting their forces found them desperate to demobilise and get out of uniform.[33] 'As a threat, you can forget it,' Secretary General Wörner said in late November. 'As a military structure, it has ceased to exist. There's nothing, or practically nothing, left of it.'[34] Some argued that if it was not careful NATO could yet follow. 'The role of NATO will have to change,' said Sir James Eberle, a former senior Royal Naval officer now running London's Royal Institute of International Affairs. 'Unless it makes itself useful, it will wither and die.'[35]

*

On 2 January 1991, thirteen days before a UN deadline for Saddam Hussein to leave Kuwait, NATO announced it would send three squadrons of German, Italian and Belgian jet fighters to Turkey. The Ankara government was not participating in the liberation of Kuwait, but it feared being caught in any backlash and was therefore appealing for alliance help. The fact that the aircraft would be based nearly 240 miles from the Iraqi border, not far off their maximum flying range without refuelling, did not deter the critics.

German opposition politicians warned Kohl was 'dragging us or letting us slide into war'.[36] Even within the German military, some pilots blamed the war on oil and bluntly told commanders they would not go to fight if asked.[37] A NATO statement said the deployment would 'demonstrate the collective solidarity and determination of the alliance in the face of any potential threat to Allied territory'. But, as both Belgium and Germany stressed, the aircraft were restricted to patrols in Turkish airspace, with no change to their mission possible without the agreement of NATO's Defence Planning Committee.[38] As the UN Iraq deadline neared, what had once been the European anti-nuclear peace movement turned against US involvement in the Middle East. On 12 January vast crowds gathered in multiple European cities.[39]

As they did so, Mikhail Gorbachev's Soviet Union launched its last-ditch attempt to strangle the fragile de facto independence of the Baltic states. Within the Soviet Union, the Baltics were no longer the only republics pushing for outright independence. In Georgia, a separatist administration was on the brink of just that step, also sending troops to the border region of South Ossetia and risking outright conflict. The Kremlin was determined to make an example of Lithuania and hold the USSR together. With Washington and the West distracted, black-clad Soviet Interior Ministry troops poured into the Baltic states, while Lithuania's new 'border posts' were increasingly attacked and smashed. In Vilnius itself thousands demonstrated mostly peacefully, sometimes pushed back by water cannon.[40] On 12 January, three days before the UN deadline for Saddam to withdraw from Kuwait, a column of Soviet tanks smashed through a crowd and parked cars to seize the main Lithuanian TV station. At least eleven civilians were killed and a hundred or more wounded amid bursts of gunfire. That their reformist hero Gorbachev could apparently unleash such force left many shocked. 'Until the last minute, nobody believed they would let tanks roll through people,' said one witness in horror. Crowds of Lithuanian activists formed around the Parliament building, preparing to face a similarly brutal Soviet assault.

Lithuania's pro-independence government found an unexpected ally: Boris Yeltsin, the most powerful politician in the Russian Federation, the core Russian state that had long dominated the rest of the Soviet Union, but was increasingly functioning independently. He was determined to dismantle the USSR and get rid of Gorbachev, placing himself in the Kremlin as the Soviet state unravelled. Yeltsin's first step towards this was to announce that he was backing Lithuania, warning that Gorbachev's use of force could 'unleash large-scale civil conflict' across the nation.[41]

In the early hours of 17 January coalition forces launched Operation DESERT STORM; the military machine built up under Carter and Reagan to fight NATO's war in Europe unleashed for the first time in anger. The opening hours would set the pattern for future Western military interventions, including

NATO's campaigns in Yugoslavia. The US had anticipated losing as many as seventy-five aircraft during its first day of strikes, more than one in ten of the aircraft committed. In fact, it only lost two.[42]

Meanwhile, on 20 January Soviet troops smashed their way into a Latvian government ministry, killing at least five. The building was then surrounded by police loyal to the pro-independence Latvian government. Further violence seemed inevitable.[43] As Iraqi Scud missiles hit Israel and sparked panic in Turkey, NATO faced simultaneous crises in the Gulf and Eastern Europe. NATO and European Community nations condemned the Russian crackdown, and were joined by Czechoslovakia, Poland and Hungary – all still theoretically members of the Warsaw Pact. Unless the Kremlin pulled back, Western officials warned, it would face economic sanctions.

Both the Iraqi and the Baltic situation were driving new East–West disagreements. Visiting the US for the first time at the end of January, new Soviet Foreign Minister Aleksander Bessmertnykh criticised the scale of US military action in Iraq, accusing the Bush administration of risking the 'destruction' of the country,[44] while Scandinavian governments doubled down in their support of the Baltic states. On 11 February Iceland – NATO's smallest member, and the one place that had seen protests against joining in 1949 – became the first country to publicly recognise Lithuania. Although few realised it at the time, the battle lines of future twenty-first-century NATO–Russian confrontations were being drawn. In the British Cotswold town of Fairford, the US air base had been mothballed in 1990 with the assumption it might soon be permanently closed. Suddenly US B-52s were flying again from it every night against Iraq, as they would to Kosovo in 1999, Iraq in 2003 – and to patrol over Ukraine and Eastern Europe throughout the 2020s.[45]

The author was nine years old, just discovering how to listen to the BBC World Service on a radio in his bedroom, and slightly awed by how much history could happen in a single day.

On 24 February 1991, coalition troops moved forward into Iraq and Kuwait to launch their long-awaited ground offensive. The same day, Warsaw Pact states agreed to dissolve their thirty-six-year-old military alliance by 31 March. Its political structures would linger on for several months before their formal abolition, but Eastern European states judged it dead. 'When you deprive the Warsaw treaty of its military essence, it becomes more or less an empty shell,' declared Polish Foreign Minister Krzysztof Skubiszewski at a press conference, not a single representative of the Soviet Union in attendance.[46] On 25 February the *New York Times* quoted US officials saying for the first time that NATO might indeed expand to the former Eastern bloc.[47]

In the Gulf, US forces advanced faster than anyone thought possible. Within two days the US Marine Corps was fighting in Kuwait City. Within five – barely one hundred hours – the war was over, Iraqi troops evicted from Kuwait and US-led forces preparing to withdraw from locations they had fought to within Iraq itself. Coalition losses stood at just 300, compared to thousands of Iraqi dead.[48] The high-tech military machine the Pentagon and its NATO allies had built to fight Russia in Europe had triumphed in the desert – and while the alliance itself had not been directly involved, those fighting there acknowledged that years of NATO drills in German plains and forests had achieved their goal. But the unexpected ease of victory – together with the visible unravelling of the Soviet state – deepened calls for new defence cuts. Some British Army units returned from the desert in 1991 to find themselves abolished. US officials briefed that the number of Soviet and Eastern bloc troops facing the alliance could soon be a million less than in the 1980s, justifying Pentagon plans to bring home roughly half its 320,000 troops in Europe.[49]

French officials suggested that what had been NATO's role of providing high-readiness forces for the defence of Europe might be passed to the European Community, a move which would allow them to be French-led without Paris rejoining NATO's military structure. But that proposal found little support elsewhere. US ambassador to NATO William Taft – another descendant of the US president of the same name – made it clear Washington was wary of diluting NATO, arguing the alliance 'must remain the principal venue of consultation'.[50] Germany and France were preparing the 1992 Maastricht Treaty that would turn the European Community into the modern European Union. Their wider efforts at integration included the creation of a joint Franco-German 'European army corps' – something US officials warned should not disrupt NATO.[51]

NATO had its own new planned force structure for any future interventions – the Allied Rapid Reaction Corps (ARRC), built from what had been the British Army of the Rhine's 1 Corps tasked with defending northern Germany. Troops that might support this during any future conflict would be drawn from member states, but the headquarters itself would function permanently with a UK-led international NATO staff.[52] It would prove a prescient move. The ARRC headquarters would deploy to both Bosnia and Kosovo to command NATO missions there, as well as later to Afghanistan. As tensions rose again in the 2020s, it would be frequently mentioned by European nations as one of the most useful tools in time of war.

Gorbachev's rule was now unravelling. On 29 April 1991, the CIA reported 'all ingredients are now present' for a Kremlin regime change that could 'quickly sweep away the current . . . system'. Wörner told US officials the Soviet leader was a 'drowning man', quietly advising Central and Eastern European countries not to provoke the Soviet military in the coming months given the unpredictability of who might be in charge.[53] With talk that hardliners might return to power in Moscow, in the first six months of 1991 delegations from Hungary, Czechoslovakia and Bulgaria visited NATO headquarters and publicly expressed hopes of joining the alliance. NATO officials were cautious, but the June foreign ministerial meeting saw the alliance declare any 'coercion or intimidation' of these countries would be a matter of 'direct and material concern' to NATO.[54]

It was an important moment. For the first time, NATO was not just extending a degree of protection to the new democracies of Eastern Europe, but declaring a potential willingness to intervene outside its immediate area of membership in Europe. In late June, Slovenia and Croatia declared independence, and US officials suggested for the first time that NATO might need to involve itself in the Balkans.[55] As the Yugoslav army moved to use force in both locations, the NAC met in emergency session, a NATO spokesman calling for the violence to stop and all sides to embrace human rights, and a peaceful and democratic solution.[56] A deal brokered by the increasingly active European Commission halted fighting in Slovenia within two weeks, but violence escalated across Croatia.[57]

On 17 July, as hardliners prepared to move against him in Moscow, Gorbachev met with the leaders of the G7.[58] On 31 July, Bush and Gorbachev signed the bilateral Strategic Arms Reduction Treaty, START 1, pledging both powers to reduce their strategic nuclear weapons stockpile. It was the last time they would meet as leaders.[59] On 19 August, as Gorbachev prepared to sign a 'New Union Treaty' that significantly increased the powers of the former Soviet republics, Communist and military officials determined to maintain the USSR launched a coup. In Crimea on vacation, Gorbachev found himself under house arrest. The public and US officials were told that he was ill, prompting Bush to wonder aloud whether that was a euphemism for being tortured. In Moscow, ordinary Russians opposed to the coup poured towards the parliament building, where Boris Yeltsin addressed them from a tank. Privately, Yeltsin warned Bush that Soviet special forces were not under his control and might seize key sites in the Baltic and beyond. But the surviving Soviet security state could barely control Russia, let alone the outlying republics or Eastern Europe. In the days and weeks that followed, multiple Soviet republics, including Ukraine and Georgia, declared independence. Kazakhstan asserted it was breaking free by simply announcing the closure of the Soviet nuclear test facility on its territory without consulting Moscow. By 22 August, Yeltsin had persuaded troops and tanks to withdraw to the outskirts of Moscow, also sending an aircraft to rescue Gorbachev and arresting many of the coup plotters.[60]

The unravelling of the USSR had taken the United States and its allies almost entirely by surprise. On 1 August, Bush had been in Kyiv meeting pro-democracy and independence activists, disappointing them with a speech so negative to the idea of Ukrainian independence that it was dubbed the 'Chicken Kyiv'. By the end of August, the Baltic states had all won official recognition as independent states from the twelve nations of the European Community, with the US following days behind. 'The old system in the Soviet Union is smashed beyond putting together,' said British Foreign Secretary Douglas Hurd.[61] Once again NATO looked outpaced by events it had no particular means of shaping. 'Europe has security problems which no organisation is addressing effectively,' Robert O'Neill wrote in the *International Herald Tribune*, pointing to events in Moscow and Yugoslavia. 'NATO still has basic relevance to the old East–West military balance but is unable to tackle the new problems of Central and Eastern Europe and the Soviet Union.'[62]

By October, Latvian, Lithuanian and Estonian delegations were visiting Wörner at NATO headquarters, even as the US warned it did not feel it was the 'right time to extend NATO's security guarantees eastwards'.[63] Ukraine, meanwhile, was struggling to establish an independent government as its economy imploded. As its new defence chiefs attempted to assert military control after the declaration of independence, they lacked even an office. It was suggested they take over the former Communist Party headquarters, as 'no one else was using it'. Yeltsin had been happy to let the Baltics go, but was less willing to abandon Ukraine's vast territory, particularly predominantly Russian-speaking Crimea and the Donbass. Shortly after the coup, his press secretary issued a statement asserting Russia's right to challenge its border with Ukraine, especially in those areas. The response from Ukraine was furious.[64] Ukraine held one card above all others – it still housed thousands of atomic warheads and the missiles that could hurl them all the way to the US heartland.

At the end of September Bush invited new Ukrainian Supreme Soviet Chairman Leonid Kravchuk – a former Communist Party apparatchik who, like many politicians in Kyiv, had suddenly discovered an appetite for independence – to the White House. Offers of Western support were dependent on Ukraine giving gave up its atomic arms, something Kravchuk pledged to do as soon as possible.[65] Bush announced the US would destroy its entire short-range ground-based nuclear arsenal – a deliberate step to encourage the USSR to do the same.[66] Up to 27,000 nuclear weapons were believed to be within the collapsed Soviet Union. According to a Harvard study, the phrase 'everything is for sale' was increasingly popular in Moscow, with talk of nuclear weapons available to the highest bidder.[67]

On 6 October, Polish, Hungarian and Czechoslovakian foreign ministers called to be included in NATO activities. Less than two weeks later NATO defence ministers announced the alliance's stockpile of sub-strategic nuclear weapons in Europe would be cut by 80 per cent.[68] NATO's heads of government summit in early November opened with Bush telling the alliance it needed to build links to Eastern European members. News coverage, however, focused on warnings to former Soviet states to give up their atomic arms, as well as ongoing discussion – for the first time since the 1950s – over whether a 'European army' was something nations there should pursue in earnest.[69]

As December 1991 began, 84 per cent of Ukrainians voted for nationhood. Even in Crimea the pro-independence vote was logged at 54 per cent, and more than 80 per cent in heavily Russian-speaking Donetsk and Luhansk. Yeltsin was in a hurry to get the USSR consigned to history – and Gorbachev out of the Kremlin – by abolishing the USSR and creating the new Commonwealth of Independent States.[70] On 8 December NATO hosted the inaugural meeting of the North Atlantic Cooperation Council, attended by the foreign ministers of sixteen NATO countries and nine Eastern and Central European nations, as well as Soviet ambassador to Belgium Nikolai Afansyevsky.[71] A letter from Boris Yeltsin read aloud expressed the Kremlin's 'long-term aim' of joining NATO. 'I have seen the letter,' Wörner said, following the meeting. 'He did not apply for membership, he just raises the question, and then says he regards this as a long-term political aim.' Other European officials were already urging caution, warning such a step might give the Kremlin the ability to block NAC decisions.[72]

Yeltsin's letter had not been the most dramatic moment of the meeting. Roughly four hours in, Kremlin ambassador Afansyevsky had returned from taking a telephone call from Moscow to tell the foreign ministers that the Soviet Union would cease to exist entirely before the year was out, and that references to it should be struck entirely from the communiqué. 'We got to see the Soviet Union disappear right before our eyes,' said an American official. 'It was a dramatic moment,' said Dutch Foreign Minister Hans van den Broek. 'It shows really what a whirlwind we are in.'[73]

17

Into the Balkans (1992–1994)

*'The collapse of Soviet Communism has left us with
a paradox: there is less threat, but also less peace.'*

**NATO Secretary General Manfred Wörner,
10 September 1993**[1]

During the Cold War, few had ever seriously suggested NATO
might have a purpose beyond protecting the territory of its own
members from a Soviet attack. From 1945 to 1990, Europe saw
not a single serious conflict. But by the end of 1991, war was
spreading in the Balkans and some were already murmuring
that if the United Nations failed to stem the bloodshed, NATO
might find itself called in.

Throughout the 1980s, millions had feared catastrophic
nuclear war that might destroy everything they knew. Now, their
TV screens showed just how horrific even a much smaller European conflict could really be. In March 1992 the largest UN
peacekeeping force since the Congo in the 1970s was deployed
across Bosnia and Croatia, entering a newly war-scarred land-
scape of bullet-pockmarked villages and burnt-out homes. The
UN Protection Force – UNPROFOR – would be made up of an
initial 14,400 troops, including those from multiple NATO members plus 900 Russian airborne soldiers. It was the first significant
Russian contribution to UN peacekeeping, and the closest Russian and Western forces had worked in concert since 1945.[2]

Secretary General Wörner was extremely keen the alliance

should have a central Balkans role, but lacked any kind of mandate. At the start of 1992, he offered NATO's resources to the UN for a no-fly zone over Bosnia – more than the international organisation had requested – should the Security Council authorise the use of force.[3] In fact, it would be two years before NATO would fire its first shots in anger, and another two before it would decisively intervene.

Western officials, meanwhile, were still absorbing the USSR's unexpected death. In the Baltic, Scandinavian military officers told reporters the Soviet submarines that had prowled for years around their waters had vanished abruptly in the last weeks of 1991.[4] In Russia and multiple other Soviet states, the economy was collapsing, raising Western fears over the vast atomic arsenal. Visiting Camp David, Yeltsin told the White House team that the smallest tactical devices were already being removed from the newly independent republics, particularly Kazakhstan, where there were fears of them falling into the hands of Islamists. Only Yeltsin and his military chief had the ability to launch the remainder of the weapons, he said, even those outside Russia. Kremlin desperation for economic assistance and cash was obvious. Yeltsin suggested selling Russian uranium to the US, requested expertise to build a space station, and asked the US to join British and Japanese experts to retool Soviet arms factories to build modern Western-style tractors.[5]

US officials, meanwhile, were now under mounting pressure from Eastern and Central European states to get NATO expansion started – but they could scarcely have been less enthusiastic. 'We see no politically sustainable way to stop it [enlargement] once we start,' worried Assistant Secretary of State Thomas Niles, noting multiple potential diplomatic problems. Excluding Russia from future NATO membership, he warned, 'would in effect tell Moscow that the end result of . . . forsaking its Soviet/Warsaw Pact empire is the expansion of NATO to its border'.[6] Worried that they and other former Warsaw Pact nations might be permanently blocked from NATO membership, Polish officers warned that without it they might develop their own nuclear weapons. The NATO secretary general was concerned. 'If you look back ten years from now, most likely we will come to the conclusion that we did not live up to the challenge of helping the East in this very critical phase,' Wörner said.[7]

At the start of April 1992 Serb forces closed supply routes into Sarajevo and began the longest siege in modern warfare, repeatedly shelling the city that housed UNPROFOR's HQ. From July, NATO warships in the Adriatic began monitoring shipping into the conflict area. November UN Security Council Resolution 787 called on member states to enforce an arms embargo, and the NATO operation – renamed from MARITIME MONITOR to MARITIME GUARD – received authorisation to fire warning shots and board non-compliant ships. NATO forces had never been authorised to take such action before, and not all countries were happy with the concept. German warships were specifically banned from taking such action, the government in Berlin limiting its vessels to questioning potential blockade-running ships by radio.[8]

Despite such issues, some were already suggesting NATO might be a more credible alternative to the UN, which had so far failed to stem the fighting.[9] It was a suggestion that US officials openly disliked. Bush was already struggling against Bill Clinton in the presidential election, and the prospect of deploying US troops into the unravelling Balkans was regarded as politically untenable. 'There is no appetite anywhere to send ground troops over to do this,' said a senior administration official. 'That is a real problem.' The only country reported willing to send a significant force was Turkey, openly committed to helping Bosnia's increasingly embattled Muslim population.[10]

Still, following Clinton's election win in November 1992, new UN Secretary General Boutros Boutros-Ghali asked NATO to conduct military planning for three possible new UN resolutions: on a more tightly enforced 'no-fly zone', a ground intervention to protect humanitarian 'safe areas', and a wider regional mission designed to stop conflict spreading geographically.[11] US, UN, British and French negotiators intended to use that implicit threat to push the Bosnian Serb leadership and Yugoslav President Slobodan Milošević towards a deal. The territory the government in Belgrade directly controlled was now largely limited to Serbia, Kosovo and Montenegro, but Milošević was still believed to exert considerable control over Serb leaders elsewhere in the still-fragmenting nation.[12] In the months that followed, however, repeated rounds of peace talks appeared to be going nowhere.

In February 1993 the new Clinton administration began publicly considering humanitarian aid drops. It was a move opposed by Britain and France, nervous that US aircraft would be shot down and that any resulting US military action could prompt Serb reprisals against their UN peacekeepers on the ground. It was to become a familiar Anglo-French refrain over the next two years, but the first relief-flight mission launched in March regardless.[13] US officials called for NATO to prepare up to 50,000 peacekeepers, including up to 20,000 US troops, but were rebuffed by France. The government in Paris was said to be reluctant to let the UN force be shifted to a NATO structure, likely costing senior French officers their current leadership positions.[14]

On 2 April 1993, two days after the UN authorised the enforcement of a no-fly zone, NATO ambassadors voted unanimously to commence a military operation to enforce it. More than 500 aircraft had breached the previous no-fly zone resolution, international monitors said, many of them suspected of carrying arms. The main violators of the no-fly zone were Serbian military helicopters, ferrying supplies and men.[15] NATO was once again in uncharted waters. 'It is the first time this alliance will run a military operation in practice, not an exercise,' said Wörner. 'It is the first time this will take place "out of area" and the first time in support of the United Nations.' The

no-fly zone mission immediately proved even more contentious
than the arms embargo. Italy, Greece and Turkey were now
proclaimed 'too close to the conflict' to take part.[16] German
planes and personnel were unable to deploy until its Constitutional Court agreed that post-war legislation banning its troops
fighting outside its own and NATO's borders should not stop it
fulfilling obligations to the alliance.

The rules of engagement for NATO planes patrolling Bosnia
were soon criticised as overly restrictive, with multiple warnings
required before military jets could be attacked. Civilian aircraft –
including those believed smuggling arms – could not be shot
down under any circumstance. The result was predictable:
NATO aircraft now overflew Bosnia every day, but did nothing
to significantly affect the situation on the ground.[17] At SHAPE
in Mons, morale slumped. 'We are in the woods,' a US official
said on condition of anonymity. 'I hope we'll get out soon.'[18]

More than a million Bosnian Muslims were now living in six
UN-defined 'safe havens', many under almost constant fire. On
3 June the UN Security Council authorised use of airstrikes to
defend those areas, but the US wanted to use strikes only to
specifically protect UN peacekeepers.[19] A month later, no action
had been taken. In the ruins of Sarajevo, the phrase 'safe area'
became a joke.[20] Among NATO pilots supposedly enforcing
the no-fly zone, the mood was jaded. 'The people who drew up
the rules of engagement have granted the Serbs every kind of
flexibility to operate anytime they want,' said one NATO official.[21] On 25 July, Serb tanks and mortars bombarded French
peacekeepers near the wrecked Sarajevo Olympic Stadium,
destroying ten French military vehicles and lightly injuring several troops. There was no military response.[22]

At the start of August 1993, as alliance ministers prepare to
meet in Brussels, the State Department warned that US forces
might carry out strikes without NATO agreement if necessary.[23] After twelve hours of meetings the next day, NATO
states reluctantly agreed to join the US in bombing individual

Serb targets, but only if asked directly to do so by UN Secretary General Boutros Boutros-Ghali.[24] Serb forces seized key hills overlooking the city even as the NATO ministers met, a move that both embarrassed the alliance and entrenched Serb positions in the event NATO did eventually intervene.[25]

*

As it struggled to find a way forwards in Bosnia, the Clinton administration was as conflicted as its predecessor over what do regarding Russia and potential NATO expansion. Visiting Clinton for the first time in April 1993, Boris Yeltsin took home a $1.6 billion financial US aid package. While US officials expressed amazement at Yeltsin's prodigious alcohol consumption, the US president – who had grown up with an alcoholic stepfather – reassured them by noting 'at least Yeltsin is not a mean drunk'. What that really meant, historian M.E. Sarotte later wrote, was that 'Clinton sensed that Yeltsin drunk was better for the United States than most Russian leaders sober'.[26]

As Hungarian, Polish and Czech leaders attended the opening of the United States Holocaust Memorial Museum, they doubled down on their calls for NATO membership. 'If Russia again adopts an aggressive foreign policy, that aggression will be directed towards Ukraine and Poland,' said Lech Wałęsa. Estonian President Lennart Meri told visiting US officials that NATO membership was the only answer to what he called a 'security vacuum in this part of the world'.[27]

Clinton was instinctively supportive. Others were more cautious. General Colin Powell said he was 'personally reluctant to cross the bridge of Eastern European membership of NATO' given that he was 'not sure what it would mean'. Secretary of State Warren Christopher told NATO foreign ministers in June the time was 'not yet appropriate' for Eastern and Central European membership, also worrying that expansion would leave Ukraine 'the buffer between NATO, Europe and Russia'.[28] Meeting at the G7 in Tokyo in July, Yeltsin and Clinton bonded over the difficulties of dealing with Ukraine and pressing it to give up its atomic weapons. A State Department memo suggested NATO membership as 'the ultimate carrot' to promote democracy and reform in Ukraine, and specifically 'ensure Ukrainian denuclearisation'.[29]

To sidestep US and Western intransigence, Poland now made its pitch for NATO membership direct to Russia. If the Warsaw government could persuade the Kremlin to drop its objections to Poland joining the alliance, if only for a moment, it would be a lot harder for the US to keep turning the option down. It was an audacious step, and proved remarkably successful – as well as revealing of the chaos at the heart of the Yeltsin administration. Over dinner – and presumably drinks – on 24 August 1993, Wałęsa persuaded Yeltsin to agree a statement that Polish NATO membership was 'not contrary to the interest of any state, also including Russia'. When Yeltsin tried to backtrack the next day, the Polish president asked the Russian leader if he believed Poland was a 'sovereign country'. When Yeltsin said it was, Walesa announced that 'as a sovereign country' Poland would join NATO.[30]

Elsewhere across Eastern and Central Europe, frustration with the slow rate of progress towards NATO and European Community membership was growing. Václav Havel described Western Europe as having a 'do not disturb' sign on its door. Hungary, now hosting NATO aircraft that might strike targets in Bosnia, was particularly underwhelmed not to receive binding security guarantees in return.[31] 'NATO is not ready to take new members in,' one US official told the *New York Times*. 'The Clinton administration has not decided yet what role it thinks the NATO alliance should play, let alone who should join.'[32]

In a 10 September speech in Brussels, Wörner pushed back against those views. 'NATO is not a closed shop,' he said. 'Even if there are no IMMEDIATE [capitalisation in original speech] plans to enlarge NATO, such a move would increase the stability of the whole of Europe.' Wörner avoided referencing Yeltsin's suggestion directly that Russia might one day join itself. But he said he was glad the Russian president had stated that an enlarged NATO was not a threat.[33]

In reality, of course, Yeltsin and his government were now trying to pull back from the comments made to Wałęsa. In October a secret Yeltsin letter to Clinton, new British Prime Minister John Major, Mitterrand and Kohl became public knowledge, expressing diplomatic but firm Russian opposition to any eastward NATO moves. If Eastern European nations were able to join the alliance before Russia, Yeltsin wrote, the effect on Russian public and elite opinion would be serious: 'Not only the opposition, but moderate circles as well, would no doubt perceive this as a sort of neo-isolation of our country.'[34]

US officials now wanted NATO to lead the scaled-up peace-keeping mission in Bosnia, while Britain and France believed it should remain with the UN force they were already supplying troops and senior leaders for.[35] Then, on the night of 3 October, a US military operation to capture Somali warlord Mohamed Farrah Aidid failed catastrophically, leading to the deaths of eighteen US personnel in Mogadishu. It was enough to ultimately collapse the entire US mission in Somalia, and significantly reduce appetite for interventions overseas.[36] 'Have no doubt about this,' Bosnian President Alija Izetbegović told his MPs shortly afterwards. 'There will be no American intervention. We are on our own.'[37]

Russia faced its own constitutional crisis: a fight between Yeltsin and the parliament he wanted to dissolve that ultimately saw his own troops shell the Russian parliamentary 'White House'. The post-Cold War world was feeling much more dangerous, enough so to prompt a shift from Germany on expansion. On 9 October, German Defence Minister Volker Rühe expressed support for Eastern NATO and EU membership, providing the alliance not be seen as anti-Russian. 'We expect a clear signal from the January 1994 NATO summit,' he said.[38] Having moved its capital to Berlin, Germany felt exposed – and keen to have further NATO nations on its eastern flank. As senior defence ministry adviser Vice Admiral Ulrich Weisser put it: better 'to defend Germany in Poland than in Germany'.[39]

The Clinton administration now put forward a new suggested framework for NATO to engage with other nations: 'Partnership for Peace'. It was less a membership scheme, more a broad framework that included Poland, the Czech Republic, Slovakia and Hungary – and others perceived much further from NATO membership, including those in the Balkans and Baltics, Russia and Ukraine. Meeting Yeltsin in October, US Secretary of State Warren Christopher appears to have presented the 'partnership' as a potential means of avoiding NATO expansion: 'Partnership for all, not NATO for some.' Yeltsin responded positively, though Russia held back from joining the scheme itself for several months. Simultaneously, however, the US seemingly described it to Eastern and Central European nations as a step towards the membership they craved, albeit without a timetable.[40]

*

NATO's forty-fifth year of existence, 1994, would be a defining one for the alliance. For the first time it would fire shots in anger over the former Yugoslavia, albeit less decisively than many hoped.

Secondly, it would finally set a course firmly towards expansion to the east, a move that would infuriate the Russian security establishment. '[NATO] expansion would bring the biggest military grouping in the world, with its colossal offensive potential, directly to the borders of Russia,' Russian intelligence chief Yevgeny Primakov had told reporters in Moscow in late 1993. 'If this happens, the need will arise for a fundamental reappraisal of all defence concepts on our side, a redeployment of armed forces and changes in operational plans.'[41] Partnership for Peace was already proving too anaemic to satisfy anxious nations of the former Warsaw Pact, and the Clinton administration's language on the topic would shift throughout the year. When Clinton went to Moscow in January 1994, he said that while NATO 'plainly contemplated an expansion' the Partnership was 'the real thing now'. Only days later in Prague, however, he said 'the question is no longer whether NATO will take on new members, but when and how'.[42]

Such shifts would help fuel the growing narrative in Moscow of Western diplomatic and economic betrayal, intensified further by the collapse of the rouble that wiped out many savings. A backlash was emerging among the Russian elite, just as Yeltsin's backers passed a new constitution giving the executive president potentially massive powers. In early 1994 Russian conservative politicians began calling for the restoration of 'Russian statehood', the protection of national markets and wealth, the fixing of unemployment and hunger, and an assertive foreign policy.[43] Mutual distrust was growing once again. By 1994, US and British officials were convinced Russia had resumed its Cold War-era biological weapons programme even as Yeltsin promised Western leaders it had not.[44] They would later conclude Russia's chemical weapons programme also remained active, including refining the 'Novichok' types later used in Putin-era assassination attempts.[45]

As late as September 1994, US Defense Secretary William Perry refused to rule out that Russia might one day join the alliance as a full member. Speaking at the same meeting, however, German Defence Minister Volker Rühe laid down a much starker position: Poland, Hungary, the Czech Republic and Slovakia, he outlined, deserved to become NATO nations because 'they belong to the European system and they were artificially separated from it'. As the country that had occupied those nations and denied them freedom, Russia was in a very different category. 'If Russia were to become a member of NATO, it would blow NATO apart,' he said. 'This isn't going to work, and why should we lie about it or be ambiguous about it?'[46]

*

Sarajevo had been under since April 1992, its 280,000 residents entering 1994 without electricity or heat, and only sporadic food and water. On a single day, 6 January 1994, UN officials counted 752 Serbian shells striking government-held neighbourhoods. One decapitated a woman in a once-busy shopping street. Another struck the Holiday Inn where diplomats and foreign journalists discussed, over endless drinks, whether NATO might finally intervene.[47] Conditions in Bosnia were worse than anything seen in Europe since 1945. At the end of January UNPROFOR commander, French General Jean Cot, described the force as 'goats tethered to a fence'. His requests to Boutros Boutros-Ghali for authority to call in the NATO airstrikes, he said, were regularly rebuffed.[48]

On 5 February a strike on a Sarajevo market killed at least sixty-six and wounded around 200. The UN officials denied they could determine who was responsible, but the international mood was shifting.[49] Following a twelve-hour meeting on 9 February, NATO demanded both Serbs and Bosnian Muslims pull back their heavy weapons from around Sarajevo by 21 February or face airstrikes. 'No one should doubt NATO's resolve,' said Clinton in Washington, his most substantial remarks on Bosnia in months. 'NATO is now ready to act.'[50]

By 20 February the Serbs reported they had pulled back as requested, with a detachment of Russian peacekeepers taking up positions in the Bosnian Serb capital Pale as part of a deal intended to reduce the risk of airstrikes.[51] Then, on 28 February, the Bosnian Serbs finally tested alliance and Western patience beyond its breaking point as six J-21 Jastreb and two J-22 Orao ground attack aircraft launched a bombing raid in a flagrant challenge to the UN and NATO no-fly zone. They were swiftly tracked and warned by a NATO AWACS aircraft. A second warning followed from two US F-16s. A minute later US Air Force Lieutenant General James Chambers, heading up the NATO air command centre in Italy, authorised them to fire. Four Serb aircraft were destroyed almost immediately with air-to-air missiles, with another reportedly also lost. 'It wasn't much of a contest,' a US pilot told reporters. 'We just ran them down from behind.' The US crews saw no parachutes, but there was little sympathy. 'As far as being "fish in a barrel" it's a matter of perspective,' said one of the US pilots. 'You could say the same for the people on the ground that they were dropping bombs on.'[52]

As late as January 1994, NATO Secretary General Wörner had been telling colleagues he had beaten the cancer that had dogged him since 1992, joking about his new vegetable-based diet and describing himself as 'leaner and meaner', like the alliance he still led. That same month, however, he was hospitalised again. The shaking of his hands and the pallor of his skin were impossible to conceal, but the former part-time reservist fighter pilot was determined to lead the alliance until the last moment that he could.[53] Now, he pronounced himself happy with the shootdown over Bosnia. 'We have to make clear that NATO has a new task of ensuring stability and peacekeeping within the United Nations framework,' he said.[54]

For a few weeks the Serb heavy weapons withdrawal allowed a sense of calm and normality to return to Sarajevo.[55] But around the Bosnian Muslim enclave of Goražde, Serb troops still pushed forward under heavy shellfire. On 10 April new UN Bosnia commander Lieutenant General Michael Rose – who had previously commanded Britain's SAS – requested NATO airstrikes. Two US F-16s dropped three 500-pound bombs on Serb positions. In response the Bosnian Serbs threatened to suspend cooperation with UN forces, and accused NATO of inflicting civilian casualties – although no evidence was ever shown. In the aftermath of the first NATO strikes, sources in Goražde reported much-reduced shelling and a local feeling of jubilation.[56]

The airstrike crossed a major line. On the ground the relationship between the UN and NATO had until then proven complex, with a messy chain of command that could take hours to make a decision. In March, a request from the UN's Rose for airstrikes to protect French peacekeepers near Bihać had taken so long to get through, the Serbs had withdrawn by the time approval was given. On this occasion, it had taken less than an hour.[57] The next day, 11 April, Rose told Bosnian Serb commander Ratko Mladić he had ten minutes to stop shelling. When he failed to do so, two US Marine Corps F/A-18s attacked further targets, prompting immediate Bosnian Serb threats to bring down planes.[58]

By 14 April Serbian forces were stepping up harassment of UN troops, trapping some behind new minefields and bringing a tank up into the exclusion zone around Sarajevo.[59] Two days later NATO attempted to strike Serb positions around Goražde, but failed to drop bombs due to cloud and fog – and lost a British Sea Harrier to a Serb anti-aircraft missile.[60] It was NATO's first ever combat loss – although the pilot, Royal Navy Lieutenant Neil Richardson, ejected to safety behind Muslim lines where he linked up with a British SAS patrol already in the city before being picked up by a French Puma helicopter.[61] Wörner warned of 'serious consequences' if the Bosnian Serbs did not pull back.[62] They did so, burning and destroying Muslim homes as they retreated.

Elsewhere, the war continued. An observation post run by the Nordic UN battle group outside Tuzla came under heavy Serb fire, prompting the deployment of seven Danish Leopard 2 main battle tanks. In a ninety-minute battle, the Danish crews fired seventy-two 120mm tank rounds, striking a Serb ammunition dump and killing at least nine (some estimates put the figure much higher still). It was the first major military action involving modern Western battle tanks in Europe since World War Two.[63]

To lead its Bosnia policy, the Clinton administration now turned to foreign policy heavyweight and US ambassador to Germany Richard Holbrooke. He was anything but optimistic. 'The Europeans will not use NATO force to help the Muslims, and the United States will not put ground troops in the region,' he told his audio journal, shortly after being appointed assistant secretary of state for European affairs. 'I feel sick about being part of such a policy. I don't feel responsible, however, as I inherited a terrible hand.'[64] In the first days of August UN observers chalked up 3,000 ceasefire violations in less than a week, both before and after NATO airstrikes. UN patrols fired at Serb snipers when they could.[65]

Secretary General Wörner's death in mid-August reopened the usual parlour game of guesswork and negotiations before his successor, former Belgian Defence Minister Willy Claes, was appointed in October 1994. By then, the situation in Bosnia had deteriorated further, and NATO was moving ever closer to more serious military action, while UNPROFOR was publicly considering pulling out entirely. If the UN arms embargo was lifted to help arm the Bosnians – as many in the US and elsewhere now demanded – the UN troops felt they might be caught in the middle.[66] On 9 November, aircraft flying from a Serb-held base struck the Bosnian town of Bihać, killing ten. UN observers said the planes appeared to have fired from across the border in Croatian airspace, leaving it unclear whether they had technically violated the Bosnian no-fly zone.[67] The next day, Clinton announced the US would no longer enforce the UN arms embargo against Bosnia, effectively allowing arms shipments to the Muslim government. 'The US has just taken sides,' one NATO official said.[68]

NATO's mission in the Adriatic, meanwhile, was still trying to enforce that same embargo – although US officials made it clear US units would no longer take part.[69] On 21 November 1994, after several more Serb air raids, NATO launched the largest military strike in its history: thirty-nine attack and reconnaissance planes struck the Udbina airstrip in Serb-held Croatia. Damage, however, appeared deliberately limited – the concrete runways could be fixed in days, while the control tower and fifteen Soviet-built Serb aircraft appeared to have been deliberately spared following negotiations between UN and NATO teams.

When Bosnian Serb missiles targeted two British aircraft, NATO launched further strikes against Serb anti-aircraft sites on 23 November, this time involving more than fifty American, British, French and Dutch aircraft – and prompting further Bosnian Serb threats of outright war on UN troops.[70] After dozens of UN peacekeepers were taken hostage then released, NATO jets remained over Bosnia in case of any further incidents. The Clinton administration, however, said further strikes would accomplish nothing. 'What we want to see here is peace, not the reign of terror that would come from carpet bombing,' said US Secretary of State Warren Christopher in December.[71] NATO would take no further military action in Bosnia until May 1995. In the meantime, as successive peace plans unravelled, the conflict raged unchecked.

On 5 December 1994, Ukraine gave up its nuclear weapons in the Bucharest agreement also signed by Russia, Britain, France and Germany. After the invasion of Ukraine in 2022, Clinton would tell an interviewer he felt 'terrible' for his role in persuading Ukraine to take the deal. Despite their security guarantees, Ukrainian President Leonid Kravchuk reportedly complained: 'If tomorrow Russia goes into Crimea, no one will raise an eyebrow.'[72] Less than a week later Russia's military began its first offensive against separatists in Chechnya. Until the Yugoslav war began in Croatia in 1991, not a single city in Europe had been shelled with heavy artillery since 1945. Now, as the end of World War Two approached its fiftieth anniversary, such scenes had become an omnipresent feature of the nightly news.

18
'Where Angels Fear to Tread' (1995–1998)

> *'I suppose we are going to have to go on putting ourselves in places where angels used to fear to tread.'*
>
> **Anonymous NATO ambassador to the *New York Times*, June 1998**[1]

By 1995, Europe's political and security environment had developed hugely since the beginning of the decade. From 1991, the Maastricht Treaty and its successor agreements rapidly built the modern European Union, setting the stage for the European single currency and what many increasingly referred to as a 'superstate'.

The Committee for Security and Cooperation in Europe that had grown out of the Helsinki agreement in 1975 also continued to evolve, the most significant diplomatic structure that included members of both NATO and the former USSR and Warsaw Pact. From 1995, it would become the Organisation for Security and Cooperation in Europe (OSCE), which provided election and sometimes ceasefire monitors in Central Asia, Eastern Europe and the Balkans. A few years earlier, the emergence of the OSCE might have threatened NATO's very being. Instead, largely thanks to Wörner, its major member nations – even including France – were agreed not only that NATO should endure but also that it offered the best vehicle for any intervention in conflicts in the region. On the ground in Bosnia, however, it was the UN that remained theoretically in control of all international action. For NATO to act unilaterally without its permission would be hugely controversial – as would later be shown in Kosovo and Libya. Up to now Western states had showed little appetite to act substantively in Bosnia – as foreign policy commentator Lawrence Kaplan put it, they were content to use the UN as a 'cover for their own inaction'.[2]

From 1995, this began to shift as relations between NATO and the UN in Bosnia worsened once again. According to officials, NATO's southern commander US Admiral Leighton Smith now refused to share NATO's plans with UNPROFOR, ostensibly over concerns UN officials would share them with the Serbs. The result was a shouting match with UN Bosnia commander Michael Rose, and what appeared to be a temporary cessation in UN requests for NATO air support.[3] The arms embargo was another subject of dispute – perhaps unsurprisingly given that the US was now abandoning its enforcement. UN officials reported unmarked US-made C-130 transport aircraft, sometimes escorted by jet fighters, flying into Bosnian Muslim territory.

NATO denied deliberately turning a blind eye,[4] but later-declassified Dutch reports claimed the flights were conducted by Turkey with US acquiescence. Arms were also said to be coming in from Iran and Saudi Arabia.[5] By late March the weapons had helped the Bosnian Muslims to reclaim some territory, but Serb forces advanced in other areas.[6] As shelling of Sarajevo increased in early May, new UN Bosnia commander Rupert Smith finally asked again for NATO airstrikes – only to be overruled by his civilian boss, Yasushi Akashi.[7]

At the fiftieth anniversary of VE Day celebrations in Moscow in May 1995, and in the weeks that followed, the US administration lobbied Western allies for further military action. On 25 May NATO jets finally made their first strikes of the year, hitting an ammunition dump near the Bosnian Serb capital of Pale. When the Bosnian Serbs retaliated by intensifying shelling around the UN-protected safe havens, US officials predicted more NATO action might become inevitable.[8] Two days later, the NAC demanded that the Serbs stop such attacks and comply with a UN ultimatum to remove all heavy weapons from the exclusion zone around Sarajevo or place them under UN control.[9]

The situation on the ground was now much tougher, with UN troops increasingly facing threats and kidnap. By late May the Bosnian Serbs held 220 peacekeepers as hostages, including French, Canadians and Russians. While troop-contributing countries pledged to 'stand firm', most now opposed what they called 'generalised airstrikes' for fear their soldiers would be harmed.[10] Many believed the Bosnian Serbs were now beyond the control even of Slobodan Milošević. On 28 May they shot down a Bosnian helicopter, killing Bosnian Muslim Foreign Minister Irfan Ljubijankić, and took a further thirty-three British soldiers and eight Canadians prisoner. NATO jets flew low overhead, but took no action. There were reports that more than a hundred of the captured UN troops had been positioned as human shields in places likely to be airstrike targets.[11] Even a 'limited' US or NATO mission to extract the UN peacekeepers, officials now warned, would be fraught with danger.[12]

On 2 June 1995 the Bosnian Serbs freed most of their UN hostages amid hopes of a de-escalation. Hours later a Serb missile blasted a US F-16 from the sky. As Clinton described the Bosnian Serbs as 'outcasts and pariahs', officials told reporters they believed the pilot might have been killed or captured.[13]

In fact, US Air Force Captain Scott O'Grady was hiding on the ground. After six days of living off the land, one of his short-range radio transmissions was finally received by a fellow US flyer overhead.[14] O'Grady described the rescue team that reached him the next day as 'like the air force of a small country'. Two US Cobra gunships escorted two giant Super Stallion transport helicopters carrying forty-two US Marines. Providing additional protection were US F-15, F-16 and F-18 fighters, A-10 tank busters, British Harrier jump jets and US electronic warfare aircraft.[15] Simultaneously, the UN moved heavy French artillery into positions around Sarajevo, while new French President Jacques Chirac made it clear he expected French troops to return fire if attacked again.[16] Shortly afterwards Bosnian forces went on the offensive.[17]

In response Bosnian Serb forces moved savagely against the most vulnerable safe area, Srebrenica. With their peacekeepers now in even greater danger, European officials increasingly blamed the US for arming the Bosnian Muslims and putting everyone in peril. The official Pentagon plan was now for an additional 60,000 European and US troops – supported by tanks, gunships and artillery – to help UN troops fight their way out of Bosnia if necessary; a prospect the Europeans openly disliked. 'The goal is to give the peacekeepers the means to stay,' said Dutch Defence Minister Joris Voorhoeve. 'It is not to prepare for their withdrawal.'[18] With fuel supplies in Srebrenica now exhausted, Dutch peacekeepers were only able to patrol by foot, using borrowed starving horses to reinforce vulnerable observation posts. Beyond that, there was little they could do for those they were intended to protect. 'There was starvation for the refugees,' Colonel Thomas Karremans told the International Criminal Tribunal for the Former Yugoslavia almost exactly twelve months later. 'There was no medical treatment at all for the population . . . The situation was hopeless, inhuman, [there was] a lot of suffering.'[19]

On 6 July the Bosnian Serbs began their assault on Srebrenica.[20] 'There was panic, chaos,' reported Karremans. Thousands now fled to the UN compound, where Bosnian Serb shells began to fall, prompting the Dutch peacekeepers to call once again for NATO airstrikes.[21] From 9 July NATO jets flew overhead, but launched no strikes. The UN deployed a seventy-soldier 'blocking unit' to protect the town, and warned crossing it would lead to NATO bombing. Then, UN commander French Lieutenant General Bernard Janvier – commanding UN forces across the whole former Yugoslavia – vetoed that request. European Union mediator Carl Bildt was in Belgrade pushing Milošević to recognise Bosnia and Herzegovina as an independent state, and Janvier worried that could be jeopardised by military action. By the morning of 10 July the town's hospital was also being shelled.[22] Late that day Karremans told the townspeople he expected imminent heavy NATO airstrikes – but as Bosnian Serb forces pushed forward on the morning of the 11th there was no sign of them. Only at 2 p.m., with the town already falling, did four US F-16 jets finally strike the outskirts, destroying one Serb tank.[23] It was, Karremans said, 'too little too late'. Soon he and his troops were being rounded up, blamed for killing Serb forces with NATO strikes and forced to drink water 'toasts' with their Bosnian Serb captors. 'This is the worst day of the war,' one Western diplomat said as both the UN and NATO met in emergency session.[24]

If further airstrikes took place, Ratko Mladić said, he would shell the UN compound and the refugees around. Having pledged to protect civilians, he now wanted to collect all men aged between seventeen and sixty, telling the Dutch he believed there were 'a lot of war criminals amongst them'. Over the coming days, as women and children were bussed out of the enclave, the majority of the men – more than 8,000 by a later estimate – were executed and thrown into mass graves.[25]

*

As the scale of the massacre became clear, calls for NATO intervention mounted. On 21 July, Western states threatened further airstrikes if the enclave at Goražde was attacked – but diplomats at NATO HQ questioned whether they would follow through. The chain of command between the UN and NATO was now unclear and sometimes openly disputed. US officials told journalists the decision to launch airstrikes would be made jointly between new UN Bosnia commander Major General Rupert Smith and NATO commander Admiral Leighton

Smith, effectively ignoring the British general's civilian and military UN superiors. 'I'm not sure what that means for the integrity of UN operations there,' said one NATO military officer.[26]

In reality, the UN was all but shut out of the loop as Western intervention neared. On 22 July, after the death of two French peacekeepers, the US, Britain and France sent three generals to Belgrade to warn that attacks on Goražde would result in NATO airstrikes 'at unprecedented levels'.[27] The next day, US officials told the *New York Times* that three French Mirage jets had bombed the house of an aide to the Bosnian Serb leadership in Pale without telling NATO allies.[28] For years to come, critics from other Western nations would complain France had been too pro-Serb throughout the Balkan wars – but when the Chirac government decided to play tough, it rarely pulled its punches.

The 21 July NATO ultimatum had indeed halted Bosnian Serb advances around Goražde. On 1 August the allies extended that protection to all remaining safe areas, warning that any further attacks or advances would prompt 'firm and rapid' bombing.[29] On 19 August a French armoured personnel carrier transporting senior US officials plunged into a ravine on its way from Sarajevo Airport. The dead included Deputy Assistant Defense Secretary Joseph Kruzel, US special envoy to the former Yugoslavia Robert Frasure and US Air Force Colonel Sam Drew of the US National Security Council.[30] For the Clinton administration it was a traumatising moment – and one that made them more determined to intervene. By 28 August chief US negotiator Holbrooke – who along with US General Wesley Clark had been in the vehicle ahead of the destroyed APC – said that unless the Bosnian Serbs pushed forward in negotiations, NATO airstrikes might 'level the playing field'.[31]

The next day, five shells hit the Markale marketplace in Sarajevo, scene of the February 1994 attack that killed sixty-eight. This time the death toll was forty-three with seventy-five injured.[32]

For years, rumours would circulate that the strike was conducted by someone else – perhaps the Bosnian Muslims, Russian and Bosnian Serb pundits and media said.[33] But on 29 August, the UN announced its radar tracking teams had proved 'beyond all reasonable doubt' the attack came from Bosnian Serb territory. The UN and NATO finally decided it was time to act.

For months, US and NATO planners had been working up target lists. Now, the US aircraft carrier *Theodore Roosevelt* steamed more than 900 miles in twenty-four hours, joining the French carrier *Foch* and aircraft from across the alliance in NATO's first true shot at coordinated military action.[34] In the early hours of 30 August jets and US missiles struck Bosnian Serb targets around Pale, albeit less heavily than some expected. Within twenty-four hours the Pentagon said one hundred aircraft – from the US, Britain, France, Spain and the Netherlands – hit twenty-four targets. After two days of bombing the allies called a temporary halt, ostensibly to let the Bosnian Serb leadership review the damage and allow Holbrooke to push Milošević into forcing his Bosnian Serb allies to negotiate.

The pause prompted some US and NATO leaders to question the value of the bombing. Holbrooke described 'great ambivalence in Washington'. The military personnel planning the campaign were divided over it, Holbrooke noted, in part because of the absence of clear military objectives. The diplomats had no such doubts – they could already see the Serbs being bombed to the negotiating table.[35] After the Serbs again failed to pull back artillery from Sarajevo, NATO airstrikes resumed on 5 September – a NATO statement described the attacks as 'punitive'.[36] On 14 September Mladić grudgingly agreed to withdraw artillery, prompting a NATO pledge to suspend strikes for seventy-two hours. This was followed by another similar pause, then a UN and NATO announcement on 20 September that a 'resumption of airstrikes is currently not necessary'.[37]

At NATO HQ, new Secretary General Willy Claes had

spent the year facing a scandal of his own: allegations that he had knowledge of backhanders paid by defence firms to the Belgian government in the 1980s. Initially he denied being present in the meetings – but then changed his story and said he had no memory of the discussions. The resulting row finally forced his resignation in October 1995.[38]

*

On 1 November, all the major players in Bosnia gathered at the massive Wright-Patterson Air Force Base at Dayton, Ohio, the location serving as an unambiguous reminder of US military power. If the warring parties were not ready to sign after two or three weeks, the Clinton administration made it clear the international community would walk away and let the Balkans burn. Between them, the warring parties and Western negotiators carved out ethnic enclaves that would shape the post-war Bosnia-Herzegovina. The Bosnian Muslims were unhappy that Republika Srpska – the separatist Bosnian Serb entity that had been their mortal enemy – would endure as a quasi-independent state alongside the Muslim-Croat Bosnian Federation. The US, however, was in no mood for further discussion.[39]

How well the deal would hold, no one yet knew. Dayton marked the end for UNPROFOR, the UN's toughest mission in decades, which had suffered more than 200 fatalities. Enforcing the Dayton Agreement would be down to a new Implementation Force: IFOR, NATO's first-ever operational ground mission, 60,000 strong and scheduled to be deployed by Christmas. For more than three years, NATO planners in SHAPE, Naples and elsewhere had drawn up plans for such a mission. But the task facing the handful of British and French troops that would transition from UNPROFOR to IFOR was still extremely daunting. Under Dayton, huge swathes of territory were to be transferred, including the Serb suburbs surrounding Sarajevo from which artillery had pounded the city for three years. In a letter home, Lieutenant Colonel Ben

Barry of the British Light Infantry described a destroyed land-scape: 'Bare, burned-out timbers, skeletal frames against the dull, leaden sky. Gardens are overgrown and few trees have sur-vived the storm of fire or the population's foraging for firewood.' Soon, Bosnian Serbs were torching more houses before handing them to the Muslim-Croat Federation.[40]

NATO had a 1,100-page strategy, its overarching aim relatively simple: 60,000 troops, comprising three US, British and French-led divisions, deployed for a year to deliver peace and 'breathing space' to build a lasting settlement.[41] An additional fourteen non-NATO countries would join the mission – including Russia and Ukraine. Iceland, with no military forces of its own, would send medics.[42] For many of these nations it was a chance to bolster their case for NATO membership. The Polish government demanded a reluctant finance ministry find the cash to send 660 Polish paratroop-ers, which Prime Minister Józef Oleksy said would prove: 'We are determined to join NATO, and nothing can change our minds.'[43]

On 20 January, the UN ceded command to NATO. Troops on the ground in Bosnia removed their blue berets and unveiled the letters IFOR on their armoured vehicles, no longer painted UN white but back in combat-ready camouflage. 'EXHIL-ARATING!' Lieutenant Colonel Barry wrote in his diary. One of his soldiers described the responsibility as 'fucking awe-some'. Within hours they were advancing into areas of Bosnia that had seen no peacekeepers for years, with rules of engage-ment that allowed – perhaps even required – them to use lethal force if necessary.[44] Over the weeks that followed, IFOR arranged massive firepower demonstrations for local leaders – a not-so-subtle display of what they could expect should they push their luck.[45] Muslim residents returned to their homes in areas they had fled in 1992 as NATO engineers made safe booby-traps and buildings torched by withdrawing Serbs and Croats still smouldered. 'I can't explain how much this means to me,' said twenty-nine year old former resident Suada Omerivic.[46] During what Britain's Major General Mike Jackson described as 'long, large and liquid Balkan lunches' with local faction leaders, NATO commanders pondered what crimes those sitting across the table might have overseen. The lunches allowed the warring parties to frankly discuss their worries and priorities, gradually stitching the truce together.[47] In February, NATO troops detained two Bosnian Serb officers indicted for war crimes, flying them to The Hague and sparking immediate outrage from the Bosnian Serbs.[48]

Meanwhile, at bases across Bosnia, Russian peacekeepers engaged in a furious trade for belt buckles, badges and other military memorabilia with their US counterparts, who told reporters many of the Russians had not been paid for at least two months.[49] The parlous state of Russian forces in Bosnia pointed to a similarly complex position within Russia itself, where the rapid transition to capitalism brought economic disruption and mounting dependence on the West. Nationalist forces, however, continued to dream of the day when they could better confront the US, the West and NATO.

NATO itself had a new civilian leader. Claes was the first secretary general to be forced out, prompting an inevitable round of posturing and horsetrading until Spanish Foreign Minister and former physicist Javier Solana proved acceptable to all, his appointment signed off by the NAC in December 1996.[50] 'He is off to a flying start,' said US representative to NATO Robert Hunter. 'It is striking how fast he has gained the unanimous respect of the people round the table.' Another described Solana as a 'straight, direct, political figure'. His arrival was accompanied by another positive development: France was expressing enthusiasm to play a full part in NATO once again.[51]

As so often, however, this was the precursor to another row about which nationalities should hold particular appointments. As a condition of rejoining NATO's military structures, France demanded that NATO's Southern Command in Naples no longer be held by a US officer but be rotated among France, Italy and Spain – a concession the US refused to make.[52] It was enough to block the rapprochement with Paris, France remaining part in, part out of the NATO command structure, only willing to cooperate on specific missions such as Bosnia, until its full return in 2009.[53]

Eastern expansion was also now firmly and finally on the table. In December 1995 the Clinton administration had denied doing a deal to delay NATO expansion in exchange for Yeltsin's support for Dayton. By February 1996, US Defense Secretary William Perry described growth as 'inevitable'. 'If NATO enlargement is the carrot encouraging reforms [in Eastern and Central Europe], then we cannot keep that carrot continually out of reach,' he said.[54]

As NATO ministers met in a reunited Berlin in June 1996 the alliance was in a self-congratulatory mood. 'IFOR has been a resounding success,' Solana told the opening session, describing it as a 'vivid demonstration of what can be achieved if the European and North American allies act resolutely to pursue shared objectives'.[55] Bosnia's September 1996 election passed largely peacefully, further entrenching the country into separate ethnic entities as Dayton had intended.[56] Then, as Clinton won re-election in November, Bosnian Serb fighters attacked Muslims attempting to return to their homes under the peace agreement. NATO officials warned that if the US refused to join an extended NATO mission for at least another year, the entire force would pull out, producing a new crisis in the alliance, just as peace was in the balance.[57]

On the ground, IFOR troops were discovering the challenges of appearing neutral and unbiased between the former warring parties. On 14 November, US troops under NATO command raided a Bosnian government army camp and confiscated tons of weapons and ammunition scheduled to be destroyed under the Dayton agreement. They found themselves

surrounded by unarmed Muslim civilians who punched them
and hit them with bottles. The US commander said his troops
were in enough danger several times to be justified in firing,
although they avoided doing so.[58] In December 1996 an extension of the NATO mission was announced as IFOR was
trimmed and renamed the Stabilisation Force – SFOR. For all
the ongoing issues, the overall Bosnia mission was judged a substantial success.[59]

*

In early September 1996, US Secretary of State Warren Christopher announced what many had suspected: that an initial
round of NATO expansion would go ahead, with the first new
members likely to join in 1999. In parallel, he called for Russia
to become 'our full partner in building a new Europe free of
tyranny, division and war'.[60] As it became clear the first admis-
sions would be limited to potentially Poland, Hungary and the
Czech Republic, others – particularly the Baltic states and
Ukraine – began protesting loudly. 'The problem was never
defining how to enlarge NATO, but what you do with the
countries left out of it,' one Western official said.[61]

In Moscow Yeltsin was becoming sicker, only able to meet
Clinton in Finland in March 1997 rather than journeying to
Washington. Russian officials acknowledged they could do little
to stop the first three nations joining the alliance, but were still
keen to prevent the Baltic states' admission. US counterparts
made it clear the Kremlin would not be allowed to stop them.[62]
Returning from Helsinki, Yeltsin told critics that delivering 'a
new isolation for Russia' through being too obstructive on
NATO expansion was simply not an option. Instead, he said he
had achieved significant concessions from the US, including the
admission of Russia to the G7 – making it the G8 – and a mutual
commitment not to develop anti-ballistic missile weapons that
could negate each other's atomic arsenals.[63]

In May 1997 the Kremlin made a further move, agreeing to

drop demands that NATO conventional forces in Europe be limited to set numbers of tanks and aircraft.[64] A formal agreement – the 'NATO–Russia Founding Act' – followed later in the month, establishing the NATO–Russia Council that would meet at least monthly to give the Kremlin what NATO called a 'voice but not a veto' on key NATO decisions. Finally, Russia now also had a written pledge that NATO would not base permanent combat forces in the eastern part of the alliance.[65]

As it prepared to put NATO expansion to a Senate vote, the Clinton administration now faced an unexpected US grassroots campaign against it whose supporters ranged from diehard right-wing Republicans to liberal left-wingers such as Ben Cohen, co-founder of ice cream chain Ben and Jerry's. It included some who would later back Donald Trump, and others who would march against the 2003 invasion of Iraq. 'Ben's belief is that NATO's expansion will soak up millions of tax-payer dollars that could be better spent on our domestic agenda, such as education,' said Gary Ferdman, executive director of a lobby group funding anti-NATO expansion adverts. 'It would oblige us to go to war to defend the borders in Eastern Europe,' said conservative activist Phyllis Schlafly. 'We don't think that's an American responsibility. We see this as one Bosnia after another.'[66] Ahead of the Senate vote, divisions between the US and France broke into plain sight after US officials accused a French officer of secretly tipping off the Bosnian Serbs over a coming NATO operation to capture Radovan Karadžić, allowing the Bosnian Serb leader to escape.[67] On 30 April, however, the Senate approved NATO expansion by eighty votes to nineteen.[68]

The July 1997 Madrid summit, proclaimed Secretary General Solana – with its formal issuing of invitations to Poland, Hungary and the Czech Republic to join – was to be the most important since 1990.[69] Projecting unity was the order of the day. French officials said it would be 'inconceivable' for divisions over the Naples command and the immediate entry of Romania and Slovenia – favoured by France, blocked by the US – to slow the initial expansion. Only one issue prompted significant controversy: the failure of the remaining 33,000 troops in Bosnia to detain the highest-profile war crimes suspects, particularly former Bosnian Serb leaders Karadžić and Mladić.[70]

Of some seventy-five suspects indicted by the International Criminal Tribunal for the Former Yugoslavia, only eight were in custody. On 10 July, British NATO troops captured a ninth and killed another in a shootout.[71] The arrests were followed by a series of explosions at a NATO base in the town of Banja Luka, and by the end of the month Western officials were blaming top Bosnian Serb leaders – both elected officials and war criminals in hiding – of coordinating multiple incidents attacking NATO.[72]

On 9 August, NATO officials announced all paramilitary forces in Bosnia were to disarm or face arrest.[73] Later that month British NATO troops, backed by US Apache gunships, seized six sites, significantly reducing Karadžić's remaining armed power base.[74] US troops found themselves doused with water and beer, and facing shouts of 'Somalia!' and 'Vietnam!'. 'We try not to take it personally,' one US commander said.[75] Tensions simmered throughout the autumn, but with fewer substantial incidents. By the time NATO defence ministers met in December 1997 the plan had shifted from withdrawal from Bosnia to maintaining the current force level of 34,000 – including 8,000 US troops. Exiting now, NATO intelligence assessments warned, could lead to the country collapsing altogether.[76]

While US officials continued to make pointed comments about the need for Europe to contribute more money and resources for the Balkans, the Pentagon discovered its troops were finding the experience rewarding. Psychological screening of US troops returning from Bosnia found them feeling better about themselves than the average American, while re-enlistment rates rose for units recently returned from NATO duties. 'We are really helping people,' said Lieutenant Daniel Finkel of Miami. 'You can't send soldiers halfway around the world to save a country and then say, "Don't get emotionally involved."[77]

*

On 16 January 1998 the Clinton administration and three Baltic states finally signed a formal charter explicitly supporting Estonian, Latvian and Lithuanian membership of NATO, although without any formal timeframe. The Russian response, Western officials said, was surprisingly subdued.[78]

Much more worrying were events in Kosovo, Serbia's majority Albanian-populated province. Yugoslav President Slobodan Milošević had begun his rise to power in the late 1980s by exacerbating Kosovo's ethnic tensions, vowing to its Serb minority that no one would ever 'beat them' again. By the end of 1996 the Yugoslav state's repression of the Kosovan Albanian majority was fuelling a growing armed insurgency. Through early 1997 the Kosovan Liberation Front killed Serb officials and 'collaborators' in occasional gun battles with Yugoslav forces.[79] After the killing of two Serb policemen in February 1998, Milošević ordered a police crackdown.

The temporary international respectability Slobodan Milošević had obtained with his engagement with the Dayton process was already gone. 'We are not going to stand by and watch the Serbian authorities do in Kosovo what they can no longer get away with in Bosnia,' Secretary of State Madeleine Albright said in March 1998 as the US and Europe imposed economic sanctions.[80] In late May, NATO ministers agreed to police the Yugoslav border with Albania – although officials warned it could take 20,000 troops, more than they believed member states were likely to offer. As the Yugoslav army launched a new offensive into Kosovo, SACEUR Wesley Clark described NATO as 'watching the evolving situation in Kosovo with increasing concern'. More than 40 per cent of the province was now in separatist hands, with at least 200 dead in March, including multiple Serb soldiers.[81]

The mood music on intervention was changing. US Balkan envoy Richard Holbrooke was back in action, attempting to build dialogue between the Kosovan separatists and Milošević, backed implicitly once again by the threat of NATO action. 'Has Slobodan Milošević learned anything?' Holbrooke asked rhetorically. 'That remains to be seen.'[82] On 15 June 1998 more than eighty NATO warplanes conducted a show of force through Adriatic, Albanian and Macedonian airspace the day before the Yugoslav leader met Yeltsin in Moscow.[83] Milošević agreed to allowing monitors from the Organisation for Security and Cooperation in Europe and humanitarian aid to enter Kosovo, as well as committing to allowing refugees to return and the resumption of talks. But he did not pull his security forces back.[84]

On 23 September, with hundreds dead and almost a quarter of a million Kosovans displaced, the UN Security Council passed resolution 1199, condemning Yugoslavia's actions in Kosovo and calling on Belgrade 'to order the withdrawal of security units used for civilian repression'. Ultimately, this resolution would be used to justify NATO's airstrikes the following year – but it included no reference to potential use of force. Had it done so, Russia would not have signed. China took a tougher line, abstaining altogether and arguing that the Belgrade government had the right to do whatever it wished within its territory.[85] US officials pressured their European counterparts to ready forces for attack plans that were now written. Defense Secretary William Cohen told reporters that NATO 'must go forward with this, or it will simply be seen as a hollow warning'.[86] As defence ministers met they stopped just short of readying forces but called for further planning. 'Something has to happen soon; we can't just sit back now,' said German Defence Minister Volker Rühe, pledging fourteen German Tornado fighter bombers and calling for an ultimatum within the next ten days if Serb attacks continued.[87]

On 13 October, Holbrooke announced a deal: 2,000 international observers from the OSCE would enter Kosovo, supported by NATO reconnaissance flights, to monitor the promised withdrawal of Yugoslav police and troops.[88] European states complained the US was barely consulting them. 'It was almost funny, if not so worrying,' a senior German official said. 'There seems to be very little willingness to treat Europeans on an equal footing. Our impression is sometimes that the Americans prefer to cut us out and that they are no longer capable, intellectually speaking, of being part of a team.' Holbrooke complained that going back and forth was damaging their ability to negotiate. 'The fact is that Europeans are not going to have a common security policy for the foreseeable future,' he said. 'We have done our best to keep them involved.'[89]

In Moscow, meanwhile, November 1998 saw a Federal Security Bureau (FSB) employee named Alexander Litvinenko unexpectedly call a press conference, claiming the agency was infested with a 'criminal group' that planned to kill oligarch Boris Berezovsky. Thinly disguised behind dark glasses, Litvinenko and several colleagues believed the problems predated the agency's new chief, who had taken office in August – but they were clearly also critical of the new man in charge. A furious Kremlin ordered an investigation, and Moscow talked of little else for several days.

The new FSB chief, a relative unknown named Vladimir Putin, responded furiously too, saying these officers 'will be dismissed in strict accordance with the law'.[90] As NATO began its air campaign against Yugoslavia in March 1999, Putin would be sworn in as Yeltsin's security council director. Soon after he would become prime minister, then succeed Yeltsin as president on the stroke of the millennium. Six years later FSB whistleblower Litvinenko would be dead, poisoned in a London hotel – an unambiguous sign of just how audacious Russia's twenty-first-century leader would prove in challenging everything NATO had achieved since the Berlin Wall came down.

19

Kosovo (1999)

*'I still think it was worth . . . it. The alternative
would have been to tolerate ethnic cleansing in Europe.
And I think that's no alternative you can accept.'*

**General Klaus Naumann,
NATO Military Committee Chairman, 2000**[1]

For the first two weeks of 1999 it looked like Holbrooke's diplomacy might just hold. Then a new massacre in Kosovo changed the game. Later investigations put the death toll at forty-five, an apparent retaliation for a Kosovo Liberation Army (KLA) attack on four Serb policeman. It was the brutality of the murders at Račak, however, that was truly shocking.

The first body encountered by US ambassador William Walker was of an old man who had been decapitated. 'They were killed where they lay,' he said, recounting finding a pile of almost twenty bodies.[2] Milošević accused Walker of bias, threatening to evict the entire OSCE mission – the one major concession Holbrooke had won the previous year with the threat of NATO bombing. After Bosnia, Western governments worried the 500 unarmed monitors might become hostages to the Serbs against bombing. Now they were keen to get them out of the way before any action started.[3]

Negotiations would go nowhere. Milošević refused to leave Belgrade for talks in the French château at Rambouillet, wary of being arrested and dragged to the International Criminal

Tribunal. Those he sent in his place, the US and NATO delegation quickly realised, lacked the authority to make decisions. On the Kosovo Albanian side there was disunity, what Holbrooke would later describe as 'eighteen different people who spend most of their time arguing with each other'.[4] At NATO, planning accelerated not just for airstrikes but the use of troops – even if, for now, no one was truly willing to countenance a full-scale invasion, least of all the United States. Clinton was under pressure from fellow Democrats – particularly Joe Biden, ranking member on the Senate Foreign Relations Committee. Wary of US overstretch, Biden said he would only support a NATO mission in Kosovo if the US was the smallest contingent.[5]

As March 1999 began it felt as though NATO's history in Bosnia was repeating itself in Kosovo. NATO had 430 planes ready to strike – but no agreement on what to do with them. 'We are back to square one again,' said one Pentagon official. 'NATO has pulled out the "we are ready to act" way too many times.' As Holbrooke headed back to Belgrade on 9 March the Yugoslav government announced new terrorism charges against several members of the Kosovan delegation taking part in peace talks. Compromise on either side was now all but impossible. Holbrooke warned that Yugoslavia and the West were on a 'collision course'.[6]

On 12 March, Poland, the Czech Republic and Hungary signed their accession to the North Atlantic Treaty. Polish President Aleksander Kwaśniewski described it as 'the most important moment in our history'. Czech President Václav Havel, jailed by the Communist regime, said membership meant that 'we will have a solid security anchoring for the first time in our history'. Already, however, potential war in Kosovo was undermining enthusiasm for the alliance. In Poland and Hungary opinion polls showed around 60 per cent favouring membership, down from 80 per cent a year earlier. In the Czech Republic, support was down to 50 per cent from 55 per cent. Neither of the three militaries was truly up to NATO standard, officials quietly conceded. Hungarian, Polish and Czech pilots lacked the flying hours to operate effectively – forty Polish pilots had quit the previous November over poor training. Still worried over leaks from France, other NATO nations also expressed concerns over sharing intelligence with former Communist militaries.[7]

Still, the alliance was already extending offers of protection to new territories. As it prepared for the largest air war in its history, NATO officials promised several other nations, including Albania, Bulgaria, Macedonia, Slovenia and Romania, that NATO would consider any military action against them 'unacceptable', and would treat any such action 'with the utmost seriousness'. Macedonia, now home to 12,000 allied troops, got an additional if euphemistic pledge that any attack on those forces would meet with 'an appropriate response'.[8]

On 20 March the OSCE withdrew from Kosovo. Two days later, Holbrooke made one final visit to Belgrade. 'You understand that if I leave here without an agreement today, bombing will start almost immediately,' he said. The Yugoslav leader replied that he did. 'You understand it will be swift, severe and sustained,' said Holbrooke, words he had discussed with the Pentagon – although not, it seems, with NATO. Milošević replied: 'You're a great country, a powerful country. You'll do anything you want. We can't stop you.'[9]

*

In the early hours of 24 March the largest aerial assault since DESERT STORM began – albeit much smaller than some US planners had wanted. As most had expected – and as in the Gulf in 1991 – the initial salvos included multiple Tomahawk cruise missiles launched from ships and B-52 bombers flying from England, mainly targeting air defences. Both F-117 and B-2 stealth jets joined the raid, the latter going into combat for the first time in thirty-hour round-trip missions from their continental US home.[10] F-16s of the Dutch Air Force scored their first to-air kill since World War Two after intercepting three Yugo-slav MiG–29s. They shot down at least one of the MiGs almost immediately, while two US F–15s brought down two more.[11] Explosions rang out in both Belgrade and Pristina, where the airport was also hit. 'Clear responsibility for the airstrikes lies with President Milošević, who has refused to stop his violent action in Kosovo and has refused to negotiate in good faith,' said Secretary General Solana. Clinton said the strikes were neces-sary to 'defuse a powder keg' at the heart of Europe – before ruling out ground troops. 'I don't intend to put our troops in Kosovo to fight a war,' he said.[12]

In Bosnia, NATO had effectively struck as a 'subcontractor' of the United Nations to enforce a Security Council resolution. In Kosovo, Russian opposition in the Security Council made that impossible. Russia's UN ambassador Sergey Lavrov demanded the bombing cease immediately, announcing that Russia would recall its military representative to NATO, sus-pend Partnership for Peace participation and postpone talks on the opening of a NATO liaison office in Moscow.[13] Three years earlier some in Russia had viewed Yeltsin's acquiescence to NATO strikes in Bosnia as a betrayal of Russia's Bosnian Serb ethnic brethren. On Kosovo the failure to prevent NATO bombing would infuriate hardliners in Moscow's military and political elite, while some would prove willing to take much greater risks to influence the closing stages of the war.

From the start, it was clear that there were different cam-paign visions. Pentagon spokesman Kenneth Bacon described a 'swift and severe air campaign' designed to push Milošević back to negotiations. In a simultaneous but apparent contra-dictory statement, SACEUR Clark publicly outlined a much longer-term plan to 'systematically and progressively attack, disrupt, degrade, devastate and ultimately . . . destroy Serb forces if they did not withdraw'. That an immediate Serb with-drawal was not on the table swiftly became apparent. Instead, the Serbs accelerated ethnic cleansing, clearly hoping to evict

Kosovo-Albanian-speaking inhabitants while outlasting the bombing.[14] On 26 March, US jets shot down another two Serb MiG–29s over Bosnia, rumoured to have been about to strike NATO forces there.[15] The next day, the loss of a US F–117 stealth fighter was kept secret until the pilot was safely rescued. NATO was under mounting pressure to strike at army units within Kosovo, but it was proving difficult.[16] Worried by Yugoslavia's Russian-made air defences – much more sophisticated than anything seen in Saddam Hussein's Iraq – the US and NATO wanted to keep jets above 15,000 feet. Western air planners had expected to destroy the missiles early, but instead the Serb air defence operators were largely keeping themselves hidden, rarely turning on their radars or firing missiles for fear of being struck.[17]

Near the Kosovo border in Albania, the 7,500 personnel of the NATO Allied Rapid Reaction Corps now waited, headquartered in an abandoned shoe factory and commanded by Britain's Lieutenant General Mike Jackson, previously responsible for the UK-led division within IFOR in 1996. Lacking the combat power to fight their way into Kosovo, their responsibility was largely dealing with the refugees and deterring Serb attacks, while preparing for any eventual long-term assault. Already dubbed KFOR – Kosovo Force – they would provide the nucleus of any ground invasion, or the first troops across the border if a peace deal could be agreed.

As April began, NATO was three weeks away from its landmark fiftieth anniversary – meanwhile TV screens across the world were full of the ethnic cleansing it was failing to stop in Kosovo. In Brussels, Secretary General Solana now lived largely in his office, the alliance relying on his charm and relationships to maintain what consensus still remained.[18] 'It's clear we will need to roll back the Serbian offensive,' said another NATO official. 'We can't stay in Albania or Macedonia very long, or those states will collapse.'[19]

The risk of maintaining Western forces on the edge of the

conflict zone was also becoming clear. At the start of April, Serb officials announced the capture of three US soldiers near the border.[20] According to British ground force commander Jackson, Clark initially believed the three US personnel had been kidnapped by Serb special forces from inside Macedonia – but it later transpired that the US soldiers had got lost and inadvertently crossed into Serb-held Kosovo where they had been detained.[21]

In Washington the use of ground forces for an outright invasion remained off the table – while in Brussels multiple member states were insisting the air war be taken deeper into Kosovo, to attack the Serb units that had driven the Kosovans from their homes. NATO air commander USAF Lieutenant General Michael Short viewed that as a bad idea. 'We feared that we would kill refugees,' he said. 'My advice was to go after the head of the snake, go after the centre of gravity.' That, he said, meant striking in Belgrade in preference to Kosovo itself.[22]

NATO was also in an information war. In Bosnia in 1996, SFOR had experimented successfully with daily press briefings to the international media. Now NATO spokesman Jamie Shea gave televised briefings at 3 p.m. each day. The *Washington Post*'s Steven Pearlstein described Shea's performances as 'an idiosyncratic blend of press briefing, homily, university lecture and theatrical performance, delivered in an east London Cockney accent that gave little hint of the Oxford Ph.D on his résumé'. Over the course of the war, the spokesman would compare Milošević to Harry Houdini, Louis XIV of France, Al Capone and Saddam Hussein.[23] NATO's rudimentary website was also gaining more attention, its number of daily hits rising to 90,000 by early April, three times its pre-war average. It was out of action for several days as unidentified attackers flooded it with emails and a Directed Denial of Service (DDoS) attack, perhaps the first 'cyber attack' of its kind in modern warfare.[24]

Early April saw the creation of two new NATO target lists: one covering critical strategic infrastructure within Yugoslavia;

the second tactical targets in the field.[25] On 2 April, NATO struck its first bridge over the Danube in the Serbian town of Novi Sad – also the first attack that significantly affected the civilian population. It also broke new ground in striking an armoured column within Kosovo.[26] Each such target, however, had to be reviewed by not just NATO commanders but also each major NATO capital. It was a hugely frustrating process. 'Airpower works best when it is used decisively,' USAF General Richard Hawley said. 'Clearly, because of the constraints in this operation, we haven't seen that at this point.' Poor spring weather was another complicating factor. On one night, NATO commanders said the weather forced the entire war 'cancelled', the long-range B-2 bombers turned back in mid-Atlantic.[27]

US and NATO commanders wanted to wage the war from altitude with precision-guided weapons, while staying out of the range of small-arms fire from the ground. Western pilots, however, lobbied their commanders to come down to 12,000 feet to identify targets. As April progressed they were finally granted more permission.[28] But divisions were becoming ever more apparent. Some senior US military leaders told journalists that they had opposed the Kosovo intervention all along. 'I don't think anybody felt like there had been a compelling argument made that all of this was in the national interest,' one senior officer told the *Washington Post*. 'I think it's safe to say the Joint Chiefs had reservations,' said another. Now they were enmeshed in the war, however, some senior US officials briefed the press that NATO were being too cautious. 'If you're going to go to the ground option, let's not screw around,' one general was quoted as saying.[29]

On the morning of 12 April two missiles fired by a US F–15E Strike Eagle hit a passenger train crossing a bridge in the Grdelica Gorge, some 190 miles south of Belgrade. According to Human Rights Watch, at least twenty were killed. Serbian government estimates were as high as fifty. In an attempt to show that the aircrew had no chance to abort the attack, NATO released the footage of the first bomb falling, the train coming into view at the very last second before impact. Wesley Clark, however, had difficulty explaining why the US pilot then struck the bridge a second time.[30]

The problem of civilian casualties kept growing. On 14 April, Serb officials announced NATO had bombed several groups of Albanian refugees, killing at least sixty-four. Yugoslav state TV showed footage of mutilated bodies, destroyed tractors and stunned civilians. The official response was again confused. Clark initially claimed there was evidence the Serbs had shot the refugees following a NATO air attack, before the Pentagon announced later in the day that neither it nor Clark believed this to be true.[31] 'Under the limitations I had placed on the crews . . . it was inevitable we were going to drop a bad bomb,' said NATO air commander Michael Short after the war. Effective immediately, NATO reconnaissance jets were authorised to drop down to 5,000 feet to identify targets, with attacking aircraft allowed to come down to 8,000 feet. 'We acknowledged that this increased the risk significantly, but none of us wanted to hit a tractor full of refugees again,' Short said.[32] By now hundreds of thousands of Kosovans were living in tent cities in Macedonia and Albania, with an estimated 260,000 displaced within Kosovo itself. NATO was meanwhile refusing to risk its cargo planes to drop aid.[33] Clark described April as a 'very painful period'. If NATO were to prepare a ground assault, SACEUR warned, it would have to decide as soon as possible if forces were to be ready before the autumn.[34] Senator Biden – who had placed major limitations on a NATO force barely a month earlier – was now blunt in assessing the risks. 'If we do not achieve our goals in Kosovo,' he told the Senate Foreign Relations Committee, 'NATO is finished as an alliance.'[35]

On 22 April twenty-two delegations and twenty-three national leaders touched down in Washington for the NATO fiftieth-anniversary celebrations, the largest in the city's history. Streets were closed, Washington florists reported record demand for multiple embassies and events, and as many as 90,000 federal workers were told to take the day off from downtown offices.[36]

As they did so the first US Apache gunships of a proposed twenty-four-helicopter formation were arriving in Albania, part of a deployment long sought by Clark that had required a massive logistical effort by the US Air Force. 'The Serbs have been successful in defeating women and children that are unarmed,' one pilot told reporters, promising that his 'fired up' comrades would ensure 'the tables are about to be turned'.[37] In fact, the Apaches would never see action, even as the war dragged into June – although two would be lost in accidents, with the death of two crew members. Sending them into Kosovo against Serb small arms fire and missiles was regarded as simply too dangerous.[38]

NATO was more confident taking risks with its strikes against Belgrade. On 21 April, cruise missiles hit downtown Belgrade, knocked three TV stations off air and destroyed the Yugoslav leader's party offices. Other attacks damaged the last of the three Danube river crossings in Novi Sad.[39] At the summit in Washington, officials briefed that deploying ground troops would be a major subject of discussion in closed sessions at the conference. British Defence Secretary George Robertson described a need to 'go in quickly when the circumstances are ripe', but declined to elaborate as to whether that included fighting their way in if the Serbs resisted. Asked whether he could envision sending in troops without the agreement of the Belgrade government and Milošević, Clinton was even less forthcoming. 'Well, that's a hypothetical question,' he said. 'But of course there are scenarios under which that could occur.'[40]

During the conference, Clinton and British Prime Minister Tony Blair met privately face to face. It was, some US officials later said, a pivotal meeting. 'They took a kind of metaphorical blood oath, which I think sealed the unity of the alliance,' US National Security Adviser Sandy Berger said later. 'They looked each other in the eye and they said, "Whatever it takes" . . . We agreed that we needed to do more quiet planning for a ground campaign.[41] But it would not be the end of tensions between the two men, with Blair later reportedly worrying he might have upstaged Clinton at the summit and made him look 'weak' following British demands for troops and action.[42]

Over its three days, the summit obtained the agreement NATO needed for members to enlarge the air campaign, and also established that the alliance might again operate outside its borders – helping authorise its future actions in Afghanistan – while approving a major post-war rebuilding effort for the Balkans. But it also continued to showcase its divisions. Italy opposed both an oil boycott against Serbia and the bombing of the TV stations. Chirac exerted considerable diplomatic effort to ensure that the communiqué stated that the allies 'recognise the primary responsibility of the United Nations' Security Council for the maintenance of international peace and security', only for US officials to dismiss the wording as 'virtually meaningless' because it did not explicitly require the alliance to obtain UN approval for its future actions.[43]

As the summit concluded, the White House announced an hour-long telephone call between Clinton and Yeltsin, who had now appointed former Russian Prime Minister Viktor Chernomyrdin his peace envoy to the Balkans and sent him to Belgrade.[44] Soon the Russian had persuaded the US to allow him to work alongside Finnish President Martti Ahtisaari as a fellow envoy.[45] By the end of April the factors that would ultimately end the war – the intensifying NATO bombardment, growing economic pressure, mounting threat of ground troops and simultaneous Russian-backed negotiations – were all in place. But it would take another five weeks to finally bring Milošević to the point where he would withdraw his troops.

On 2 May civil rights campaigner Jesse Jackson secured the release of the three US soldiers captured near Macedonia. Later that night NATO 'graphite bombs' temporarily short-circuited much of Serbia's electricity supply; a US F–16 was lost in action the same night. The next day, NATO killed at least seventeen civilians in another attack, followed by another disaster on 14 May in which it killed as many as eighty-seven Kosovan Albanians allegedly being used as human shields.

But the most embarrassing and diplomatically damaging incident – with geopolitical consequences extending well beyond the Kosovo war – had occurred on 7 May, when US bombs struck the Chinese embassy in downtown Belgrade, killing three Chinese staff. Whether that particular location – misidentified by US intelligence planners due to outdated maps – was included in the NATO targeting process remains unclear. An official French report published later in the year alleged the building was targeted through a separate US targeting process outside NATO command, something a French official said should not happen again in a NATO-run operation.[46]

In Brussels, Mons and Italy, NATO planners were starkly aware of the dangers on all sides. Working to approve one particularly sensitive target in Belgrade, NATO Military Committee chairman General Klaus Naumann noted it was near a hospital. 'I said to Solana, "If we by sheer accident hit this hospital, then the war is over."' It is not clear from his account whether that target was struck.[47] Most contentious, with hindsight, were cluster-bomb attacks on the Serb city of Niš on 7 and 12 May. Researchers from Human Rights Watch would later judge these as among seven confirmed uses of such munitions, killing at least ninety to 150 of the at least 500 civilians it believed to have died from NATO bombs in total. They reported sources within the Pentagon telling them that the White House ordered cluster munition use to cease following the Niš attack, something not publicly confirmed.[48]

For the hundreds of thousands of Kosovan refugees now in tent cities in Albania and Macedonia – or those trapped within the province itself – life was becoming increasingly miserable. At the start of May, Norway became the first NATO nation to call for plans to house and feed the refugees through the winter if the bombing campaign was forced to continue into the new millennium.[49] Tempers were becoming frayed. On 18 May, Clinton read a *New York Times* article on mounting pressure from Downing Street for a troop deployment. 'Get your people under control!' he is said to have shouted at Blair on a telephone call, demanding that the briefing stop.[50] Those around Blair and Clinton were increasingly realising just how far the two leaders had staked their personal credibility on a successful outcome in Kosovo. Whitehall officials, used to British leaders failing to get their way with Washington and NATO, encouraged Blair to build potential 'exit strategies' – but he refused. 'This is shit or bust,' he told them.[51]

On 27 May, US Defense Secretary William Cohen met secretly with his British, French, German and Italian counterparts for six and a half hours in Cologne, concluding they must decide within days whether to assemble ground troops. Relations between Cohen – who still opposed an invasion – and SACEUR Clark, who favoured it, were now also deteriorating. According to the *Washington Post*, British officials deliberately fed Clark direct notes on Blair's conversations with Clinton, partly out of a concern the US chain of command would be unwilling to brief SACEUR on them directly.[52]

US planners had hoped such an assault could be prepared in ninety days – but now realised the road network around Kosovo would need to be improved to take US tanks. Clark's full invasion plan was said to call for 175,000 troops, potentially simultaneous assaults from Albania, Macedonia and Hungary, and an air assault from Italy. In the first three days of June senior White House officials finally began considering authorising such a build-up. By now Milošević and those around him were signalling through the Russian and Finnish peace envoys that they were finally ready for a compromise – but NATO states simply did not believe them. 'We knew he [Milošević] would have to capitulate some time,' said one Western official. 'The only question was when. And no one expected him to cave in so soon.'[53]

On 26 May the KLA had launched their own major offensive – but soon found 250 of their best fighters pinned down by more than 700 members of the Yugoslav Third Army on Mount Pastrik near the Macedonian border. 'That mountain is not going to get lost,' Clark is said to have told his subordinates on a video conference. If the Serbs took the heavily defended location, he warned, 'We'll pay for that hill with American blood [to take it back in any ground offensive].'

Through the first week of June, US and NATO officials began their preliminary talks with the Serbs on stopping the air campaign and allowing a NATO force – KFOR – to enter the province while the Yugoslav Army withdrew. By the end of the week that included direct force-to-force negotiations between KFOR commander Jackson at the 'shoe factory' and his Serb counterparts on the ground. Throughout that week NATO kept up its bombing – and as the talks appeared to be breaking down on 7 June two US B–52s pulverised what they believed to be Serb positions on Mount Pastrik, although later assessment showed less damage than expected.[54] By 10 June the Serbs finally signed an agreement to withdraw their forces, bombing permanently ceased and the UN had cleared NATO troops to enter Kosovo through Security Council Resolution 1244, passed with Chinese abstention but Russian support.[55]

In Western capitals, Serbian withdrawal from Kosovo after seventy-nine days of strikes brought relief. 'We have achieved a victory for a safer world, for our democratic values and for a stronger America,' Clinton told the US in a public address.[56] In Brussels, Solana warned that all violence must 'cease immediately'. Whether that could be policed by the forces immediately available, however, was desperately unclear – less than half the 50,000 troops allocated to KFOR were on the ground. Russia's intentions were also a mystery – Russian officials said they would join the Kosovo mission, but not under NATO command. NATO had ruled out a 'separate sector' for Russian forces. Most expected further negotiations to resolve the issue.[57]

Just 15,000 troops in six brigades, two of them British, equipped with only forty tanks, were now ready to enter Kosovo. Should Serb units decide to stay and fight unexpectedly, NATO risked being overmatched. The Serbs, however, appeared to be cooperating. A request from them to delay D-Day by twenty-four hours was readily accepted by General Jackson's KFOR on the ground.

Then, in the early hours of 11 June, a Russian light armoured column, comprised of peacekeepers theoretically attached to the NATO-run SFOR in Bosnia, crossed into Serbia, images of it appearing almost immediately on Yugoslav TV. 'I thought back to that Serb request to delay the D-Day,' said Jackson. 'At the time, the request seemed to be nothing more than practicality. Now . . . it could be seen in a more conspiratorial light.'[58]

SACEUR Clark suspected 'some kind of Russian double-game to double-cross our plans'. He ordered the preparation of a helicopter-borne occupation of Pristna airport. 'What followed was a crazy seventy-two hours of zigzags, lies, high-level confusion and confrontation,' he later wrote.[59] As the Russian column headed through Serbia towards Kosovo, NATO commanders considered their options. US Secretary of State Madeleine Albright was in contact with Russian Foreign Minister Igor Ivanov, who assured her that there was nothing significant to the troop movements. Jackson suspected 'perhaps he didn't know what the hell was going on either'. Next, a Russian news agency reported that at least six heavy transport aircraft were airborne, preparing to deliver reinforcements. Jackson's orders were still unclear on how and if his troops were supposed to block the airfield, or if they should open fire on incoming Russian aircraft. To make the decision more personal, his son was likely to be among the first on the ground in the event of any trouble.[60]

Others were scrutinising Security Council Resolution 1244, the agreement the Russians had signed that Western nations had believed put them in charge of forces moving into Kosovo.

On closer examination they realised it had undergone last-minute amendments before the Russians signed.[61] In particular, any direct reference to NATO had vanished. A footnote in an earlier draft that described the security force having 'NATO at the core' was gone, as well as another key sentence describing a 'unified NATO chain of command'.[62]

Amid this mayhem General Jackson received a written order from Clark to 'move and occupy Pristina airfield' once Clark approved the precise plan. Jackson complained of micromanagement and believed the operation was not supported by the UN resolution, giving each nation taking part the clear option of declining. The French shared Jackson's worries, pulling their troops from the operation. Jackson called British General Rupert Smith – now Deputy SACEUR – and outlined his 'very serious reservations'. The feeling in KFOR HQ, he later said, was that 'the US wanted to seize the airport – but was not prepared to risk American lives to do so'. As Jackson entered a video conference with Clark at 3 p.m., the British general believed he might have to resign to make his point. Clark, however, surprised all by announcing that the plan would not be put into effect, at least not immediately. 'We will now wait to see if Yeltsin has lied to the president,' he said.

NATO troops would enter Kosovo in the early hours of 12 June – meaning that by the time they got to Pristina the Russians would be there.[63] A declassified Canadian account published a decade later reports one theory popular among NATO staff officers at the time: Pristina airport contained a highly sensitive military bunker operated by the Serbs. Its contents were unknown. On arriving at the airport on the evening of 11 June the bunker was the first thing Russian troops secured.[64] Remaining Serbs greeted them as liberators, but even within Moscow there remained abject confusion over what was going on. 'Today's commotion in Western capitals is quite justified,' said Russian MP Vladimir Averchev, 'because it is not clear who makes decisions in Moscow.'[65] Across the world TV coverage of Kosovo was dominated by the arrival of the Russians – although reports of inbound transport aircraft turned out to be untrue. For a few hours Jackson's command team were told their entry into Kosovo was to be delayed – although no reasons were given. Then, at 5 a.m., Clark ordered Jackson to reach the airport as quickly as possible and 'co-occupy' it with the Russians.[66]

For all the focus on the Russians, it was the Serbs – and to a lesser extent the still heavily armed KLA – that really worried the troops and their commanders. Houses once owned by Kosovo Albanians were being torched, and it still remained plausible that the Serbs might fight.[67] The narrow Kaçanik valley, through which the vast majority of KFOR would advance, was perfect for an ambush. Driving to the border through Albanian neighbourhoods of Macedonia, civilians and refugees were cheering and holding up signs, but the more populous towns within Kosovo contained Serbs and increasingly sullen troops of the Yugoslav army.[68] The advance was slower than expected – the removal of landmines causing the first of multiple delays as the lead NATO elements moved into Kosovo itself past shattered and still burning villages and towns. Many NATO troops were struck by how much of the Serb military had survived. 'Before we went in, we hoped that the air campaign had destroyed 80 per cent of Milošević's armour,' said Canadian troop leader Lieutenant Derek Chenette. 'This was untrue.' 'They were by no means a defeated army,' said Captain Trevor Gosselin. 'They were quite happy to be going home, on the other hand.'[69]

General Jackson was determined to make sure the Russians were not potential 'enemy'. By early evening he was making contact with his Russian counterpart, who informed him that 'the leading element of the Russian KFOR contingent' now control the airport in Pristina. The formal letter to Jackson addressed him as KFOR's commander – a sign, he hoped, that they would be willing to work together. But Clark was still concerned about Russian aircraft delivering reinforcements, and wanted the runway blocked. On the morning of Sunday 13 June, Clark and Jackson had what was arguably the most serious command row in all of NATO's history.

Clark has always claimed this was overblown.[70] Jackson, meanwhile, has repeatedly described a blazing argument in which he refused to follow SACEUR's orders, including telling Clark: 'Sir, I'm not going to start World War Three for you.' 'I made it clear to Clark that I was fed up with taking orders from Washington, from people who seem to have no appreciation of the problems on the ground,' Jackson said. Jackson called British Chief of the Defence Staff General Sir Charles Guthrie, who supported his decision not to block Pristina airport – and who, without Clark's knowledge, was now also talking directly to the US Chairman of the Joint Chiefs General Hugh Shelton. 'Mike, do you understand that as a NATO commander I'm giving you a legal order, and if you don't accept that you will have to resign your position and get out of the chain of command?' asked Clark. Jackson replied that he did. 'OK, I'm giving you an order to block the runways at Pristina airport,' said Clark. 'I want it done. Is that clear?' Jackson ordered British vehicles onto the runway – but he knew the UK contingent on the ground would have to escalate the request to Whitehall, where Guthrie and Blair would exercise their national veto.[71]

Exactly how close confrontation came remains unclear. Singer James Blunt, one of the most successful musical artists of the 2000s, was a second lieutenant with the Household Cavalry approaching Pristina airport. He later told an interviewer, 'The direct command [that] came in from General Wesley Clark was to overpower them. Various words were used that seemed unusual to us. Words such as "destroy" came down the radio.' Instead, Jackson told the vehicles to encircle the base.[72] In fact, the risk of Russian aircraft landing was already fast reducing. In response to US pressure, Hungary, Romania and Bulgaria agreed to close their airspace to the Russian transports. Whether those nations would have proved willing to shoot down Russian aircraft remains a very different question.[73]

It would never be truly clear whether the Russians at the airport were simply posturing or would have fought back if NATO troops had tried to clear them. Within a few days the relatively weak position of the Russian forces became clear as British personnel shared food and water with them in the absence of Russian reinforcements and resupply. Less than a year later Jackson was promoted to chief of the UK General Staff, the professional head of the British Army. Clark, in contrast, found himself relieved as SACEUR several months early in June 2000. He wrote, 'The Europeans were mystified, and they asked why a victorious general would be ordered to early retirement. But I knew. I had pushed hard to do what I believed was necessary, and I had apparently pushed too hard.' [74]

Barely a week after the near-confrontation at the airport, and with Clinton and Yeltsin shortly to meet for the first time since the war, US and Russian officials agreed on what Russian troops would do as part of the KFOR force – including acknowledging NATO leadership.[75] Russia's military, however, may have been determined to make one final show of force. In the early hours of 20 June two Russian Bear–H bombers and two Tu–160 bombers flew towards North America. It was the first such flight in eight or nine years. 'It is impossible to interpret this deployment as anything other than an attempt to intimidate NATO with a nuclear threat,' wrote Sean Maloney, author of a Canadian history of the war.

The next day, a Russian transport aircraft was permitted by NATO to fly into Pristina airport and offload Russian personnel to 'repair' the airfield. Tense negotiations would continue until July, when a deal allowed the first of 3,000 incoming Russian troops to arrive by air.[76] The Russian contingent would remain part of KFOR, at least on paper, until 2003, when the Kremlin simultaneously withdrew its forces from Kosovo and Bosnia. Over that time they would comprehensively clear out the secret bunker they had seized as soon as they took the base – and to which they denied NATO personnel access. Rumours among allied forces suggest the contents ranged from nuclear or chemical weapons to secret torture chambers. Canadian military historian Sean Maloney believed the answer was likely that it contained Russian radar domes and aerials that had been shared with the Serbs – and which potentially helped bring down the US F–117 Nighthawk. 'Given the extremely tense relationship between Russia and NATO . . . explicit proof of Russian military support to Belgrade – support that posed a direct threat to the lives of NATO pilots – could not have been allowed to fall into NATO hands,' he wrote. 'The political repercussions would have been enormous.'[77]

The years since have brought only limited clarity. Many of the archives remain classified and, in particular, it remains unclear who in Russia ordered the 200 troops in Bosnia to move, or the hundreds more elite paratroopers said to have been ready to support them. In his autobiography Boris Yeltsin claimed to have ordered the deployment, although many have questioned this claim. US officials simply did not know. Russian sources told the *Washington Post* it was agreed between Yeltsin and Russia's top military commander, General Anatoly Kvashnin.

What we do know is that, in March 1999, Vladimir Putin was appointed chair of Russia's National Security Council.[78] As the Kosovo war came to its conclusion, Putin was fast becoming the most powerful man in Russia's national security establishment, and was eyeing up the Kremlin. He was also, like many Russians, furious over what he regarded as the humiliating failure to stop NATO in Kosovo.[79] In August 1999, Putin, a complete unknown barely a year earlier when appointed to lead the FSB, was appointed one of three prime ministers, explicitly presented as Yeltsin's chosen successor to be sworn into the presidency as the new millennium began.

20

Into a New Century (1999–2001)

*'A triumph of preventative diplomacy which went largely
unsung . . . defusing a crisis which could so easily
have led to another Balkan war.'*

**Tony Blair in a letter to Lord Robertson
on NATO's 2001 Macedonia intervention**[1]

The immediate face-off with the Russians looked to be over, but
Kosovo was still in chaos. By 20 June 1999, NATO forces had
control of every major city in the province and the withdrawal
of Serb police and military units was supposed to be complete.
With them, up to 60,000 Serb civilians also left the province –
nearly 30 per cent of the pre-war population. 'What we need
now is cool heads,' said a NATO spokesman. The refugee
camps in Macedonia and Albania emptied as ethnic Albanians
poured back into Kosovo – despite warnings it remained full of
landmines and lawlessness. The alliance, UN and aid agencies
needed to provide almost everything for them in the short term.[2]

Moving military material from nearby Greece also continued
to be a challenge. US Marines were met with an enormous
banner reading 'US killers go home'. In Kosovo itself things
were more complex still. For several days Serbs in civilian dress
calling themselves 'warrior citizens' prevented Albanians entering the town of Mitrovica, in southern Kosovo, declaring their
neighbourhood a 'Serbian zone'. With its population of 9,000
Serbs – and soon as many as 1,500 returning Albanians – and

key supply routes running through it, Mitrovica had the largest remaining Serb population in Kosovo, remaining effectively a partitioned and significant point of tension two decades later.

The Serbs continued to view the Russians as liberators and protectors. Kosovo Albanians warned they were vulnerable to attack from them. 'The Russians are here against our wishes, and we will continue to be against that,' said one KLA commander – although he pledged to 'be against that' in a 'peaceful way'. 'We do not sleep all night,' countered one Russian paratrooper officer.[3] Whether they knew it or not, this was not the only risk Russian forces were running. Flying from Pristina airport, Russia's Hind helicopter gunships reminded the Kosovo Albanians of the almost identical models used by the Serbs. Those same Serb gunships were believed to be periodically probing Kosovo airspace themselves – and while NATO would have been within its rules of engagement to shoot them down, any incident with the similar Russians gunships could have sparked a diplomatic nightmare.[4]

The purging of Serbs from many parts of Kosovo continued. 'It felt like a defeat,' US First Lieutenant Ryan Leigh told journalists as 350 Serb villagers quit his sector to move across the border. 'We did everything we could to get Serbs to stay, but they really wanted to go.' There was little sympathy from the returning Albanians. 'When we watched them go, I was thinking of how we were thrown out by them,' said Nevrete Emini, describing how Serb paramilitaries threatened to cut her son's throat. 'We left through clouds of bullets, while they got to go with an escort from the Americans.'[5]

In June 1999 Solana was appointed as the next secretary general of the EU council, with the announcement he would simultaneously be responsible for heading up bloc-wide foreign policy. Taking his place at NATO would be British Defence Secretary George Robertson. Robertson's first priority, he said, would be to attempt to streamline European defence spending to maximise its effect. 'We spend two-thirds of what the United States spends on defence, but we don't have anything like two-thirds of the capability,' Robertson said of Europe. 'That is because we compete with each other, we duplicate each other and that era is now over.'[6]

Jackson's successor as commander KFOR was also a popular choice: German General Klaus Reinhardt. As 1999 drew to a close, Reinhardt's KFOR peacekeepers were increasingly drawn into policing, the 1,800-member UN police force unable to cope. That meant roadblocks to check cars for weapons, high-profile patrolling and, at times, basic detective work to catch criminals. In Pristina, British commanders recruited former members of the KLA to act as law enforcement. With five brigades in Kosovo, Reinhardt now had 120 patrols out on the streets every day, he said, with a thousand troops committed to guarding Serb families in their homes.[7] Among NATO forces on the ground, distrust of the Russians remained significant. Canadian Kosovo veterans recount claims that Russian peacekeepers were kidnapping Albanians and holding them for ransom. NATO troops suspected Russian forces of colluding with the Serbs to smuggle materials in and out of Kosovo, perhaps including weapons. There were reports of Russian efforts to get inside Canadian vehicles, and at least one instance in which a Russian soldier raised his weapon to threaten a Canadian.[8]

Russia was also on the offensive again in Chechnya – with Russia's generals saying they were taking cues from NATO's Kosovo campaign. Russian Air Force commander Colonel General Anatoly Kornukov gave briefings in a similar style to SACEUR Clark, narrating combat videos of airstrikes and claiming 'certain parallels' with NATO's actions.[9]

As the new millennium began, the International Criminal Tribunal for the Former Yugoslavia considered whether NATO and the US had committed war crimes with the Kosovo intervention. The tribunal had spent several weeks in late 1999 collating evidence on NATO's actions during the war, but chief prosecutor Carla Del Ponte stressed that this was not the same as a 'formal inquiry'.[10] NATO claimed only twenty or thirty civilians had been killed by its bombings, in comparison to the approximately 500 documented by Human Rights Watch.[11] The discussion of war crimes was accompanied by an actual murder. In mid-January the US military arrested one of its own soldiers for the killing of an eleven-year-old Albanian girl. He had, investigators concluded, hoped to blame the murder on the Serbs.[12] Parts of southern Kosovo erupted in protest, with US troops in the firing line. Their attempts to clamp down on local crime were provoking a much greater backlash. When several local men were arrested for unrelated offences, crowds of 500 protested for two days.[13] But while few Albanians wanted NATO forces to leave, the alliance was struggling to win the confidence of Serbs. At the start of February two Serb civilians were killed in a gun and rocket attack on a UN bus outside Mitrovica, witnesses complaining that escorting NATO troops did not fire on the attackers or pursue them.[14]

The next day, Mitrovica itself erupted into violence, with seven Albanians killed and at least nine wounded as angry crowds rampaged through the city. On Mitrovica Bridge itself French peacekeepers fired teargas to disperse around 500 clashing rioters.[15] A week later British troops arrived to guard the bridge, but not for the first time in the Balkans French troops were accused of favouring the Serbs. Officials in Paris were predictably defensive. 'Our troops acted scrupulously according to NATO guidelines,' said a French military spokesman. The days that followed were the most violent since the war: explosions and gunfire rang out in multiple parts of Mitrovica as French, British and Italian peacekeepers alike struggled to control the violence. The now-outlawed KLA told journalists it had been forced to protect Albanian areas. Many of the Albanians still living in Serb areas fled across the bridge, sometimes under gunfire.[16]

For months Slobodan Milošević had been facing mounting domestic unrest: his defence minister was killed, and people turned against him. Now NATO reported his troops were massing in areas around Kosovo. NATO and the US accused Milošević directly of exacerbating the situation inside Mitrovica with 'guidance, men and arms' as well as radio broadcasts. One Western official warned that NATO was in a potentially 'lose-lose' position. 'If NATO gets tough, then Milošević can say the Serbs are victims,' he said. 'If NATO shrinks from doing anything, the situation gets worse.'[17] NATO was already under-strength in Kosovo, 12,000 short of the original 49,000 troops planned for KFOR. It requested another two battalions, some 1,200 soldiers, to make up for recent reductions by both France and Britain.[18]

Some in the UN warned Kosovo's real problem was even broader: the failure of NATO and the international authorities to 'read the riot act' to the KLA and safeguard the non-Albanian minority.[19] Divisions between the US and its European allies were in plain sight once again too. The administration wanted Europe to send in more troops and get Kosovo 'off the front page'. The violence, however, continued to rage relatively unabated. In Congress, Republicans asked what the intervention had achieved and whether there was any point in American troops remaining.[20] As George W. Bush and Vice President Al Gore faced off in a US election too close to call, pollsters noted a growing divide between US and European opinion on a range of topics, apparently exacerbated by the war in Kosovo. 'What they see is an America that has the ability to impose its values and they are not values that the Europeans believe in,' said Stéphane Rozès, director general of pollster CSA Opinion. 'There's a great deal of fear out there that the strength of America's economy will impose not only economic changes but social changes as well.'[21]

In Russia, Putin was beginning to revolutionise society and the military, simultaneously renegotiating relations with the West. By the Russian presidential election in March 2000 the renewed war in Chechnya was eight months old, with several thousand dead and 300,000 refugees. In many respects this *was* Putin's election campaign – he avoided debates with other candidates, gave only a handful of interviews, and relied on largely positive TV coverage. His closest rival was Communist Party leader Gennady Zyuganov, who favoured an even tougher approach to the West. Putin claimed he would end the chaos of the Yeltsin years and give Russia back its self-respect.[22] For the West, the signs were mixed. After years of Yeltsin being unable to push the START 2 nuclear arms control treaty through the Russian parliament, Putin delivered it within weeks of the election. The thorny issue of missile defence, however, was back on the table for the first time since Reagan. The Clinton administration believed a missile-defence shield for the US was both achievable and vital. For Russia and Putin this threw into doubt the entire post-Cold War settlement, potentially undermining the Kremlin's capability to make nuclear threats against the US in any crisis. For the US to deploy serious antiballistic missile capability would mean throwing out the Anti-Ballistic Missile Treaty negotiated as part of the Strategic Arms Limitation Talks (SALT 1) in 1972. Should that happen, Foreign Minister Igor Ivanov told reporters, it would cast the world into 'a new confrontation'.[23] It was one of several issues that would grow and metastasise in the years to come.

At the start of April 2000 French SFOR troops in Bosnia – perhaps stung by the unending criticism that they were soft on Serbs – seized Bosnian Serb nationalist politician Momcilo Krajisnik. Days later, he appeared at the International Criminal Tribunal in The Hague to be charged with genocide, crimes against humanity and violations of the laws of war. NATO forces were under heavy pressure to deliver Radovan Karadžić and Ratko Mladić – although it later emerged that the pair were living separately in Serbia under Milošević's protection.[24]

That tribunal was also still considering whether NATO itself might have committed war crimes during the Kosovo intervention. In June 2000 the prosecutor announced that it had not. 'Although some mistakes were made by NATO, I am very satisfied that there was no deliberate targeting of civilians or unlawful military targets by NATO during the bombing campaign,' Carla Del Ponte told the UN Security Council.[25]

The confrontation over Mitrovica continued through the summer 2000, as it became almost impossible for Albanians to keep living on the predominantly Serbian southern side of the city. Serbs, meanwhile, continued to flee the rest of Kosovo. Then, in October, following a disputed election, Milošević became the first twenty-first-century leader forced from power in a popular revolution. In his place came Vojislav Koštunica, the opposition leader widely agreed to have actually won the vote. The removal of Milošević did not mark the end of problems in Kosovo, but it did remove one of the causal factors – as well as marking the end of Yugoslavia, with future NATO member Montenegro seceding as an independent nation.

Serbian nationalism and anger over Kosovo remained. But Koštunica was much better able to negotiate with the alliance. When violence flared in early 2001 in the 'buffer zone' along the Serbian border from which Yugoslav forces had retreated in 1999, NATO powers agreed within six months to allow Serb forces to return to avoid the area being used by Albanian militants to mount attacks.[26] By then, however, a new crisis was underway in the Former Yugoslav Republic of Macedonia, and a tiny NATO team there was attempting to avert catastrophe.

*

As 2001 began and President-Elect George W. Bush awaited his inauguration, NATO and UN officials worried the new administration might pull its forces from the Balkans, where they made up 15 per cent of KFOR. 'We don't need the 82nd Airborne escorting kids to kindergarten,' future US national security advisor Condoleezza Rice had been quoted as saying during the campaign.[27] The incoming president played down such suggestions, pledging to 'honour the agreements' Clinton had made. A US departure, diplomats warned, would lead to a resurgence of the KLA and Albanian hardliners in Kosovo, and potential further regional escalation.[28]

In fact, it was already happening. On 22 January, Albanian militants attacked a police station near Macedonia's second largest city, Tetovo, killing one policeman and injuring two others. Soon an insurgency spread across the region, fuelled by Albanian and Macedonian media that demonised each other. A government counteroffensive forced the rebels into retreat, but tensions remained high, Albanians complaining that they were treated like second-class citizens, the government denouncing them as terrorists.[29] On 16 March, German troops guarding NATO supply lines in Macedonia came briefly under attack from the rebels, possibly inadvertently. Many Macedonian Slavs were now uncompromising, calling for the rebels to be disarmed or killed. Carl Bildt, UN envoy for the Balkans, described the crisis as 'one of the worst pieces of news to come out of the Balkans for many years', warning that it could also upset and destabilise Greece, Bulgaria and Albania.

That such a conflict would be avoided would be largely down to a small number of NATO officials on the ground, later backed up by an extremely limited military intervention. British politician and later UN Bosnia administrator Paddy Ashdown described it as the 'best example of a successful act of prevention [which] probably saved tens of thousands of lives'.[30] Secretary General Robertson told reporters a 'small number of extremists' should not be allowed to destabilise the region. But NATO did not have a military mandate in Macedonia nor had it been invited in by the government.[31]

Two years after NATO bombed Serbia to protect Kosovo Albanians, Albanian hardliners were now the problem. The attacks in both southern Serbia and northern Macedonia appeared part of a deliberate strategy to carve out a larger Kosovo at the expense of its immediate neighbours.[32] KFOR commander Lieutenant General Carlo Cabigiosu called for more highly mobile troops to patrol the borders. As the security situation stabilised in southern Serbia, it deteriorated in Macedonia – likely due to some Albanian hardliners relocating from one to the other. NATO now wanted to support the Macedonian government against the rebels while restraining it from making the situation worse. Both Robertson and predecessor Solana – as EU foreign policy supremo – made their own personal interventions, the two individuals and institutions cooperating with unprecedented closeness. In May they visited Skopje together. By now, violence was more or less continuous, government forces hitting rebel positions with artillery and gunships. 'This country may well be on the brink of an abyss, but I believe there is enough common sense and political courage to step back,' said Robertson, persuading the government to postpone a parliamentary vote on whether to declare a state of war. Robertson described the rebels as a 'bunch of murderous thugs' determined to destroy the country and deliver 'a downward spiral of violence into another Balkans bloodbath'.[33]

In June the Macedonian government allowed a small NATO team into the country. It was led by Pieter Feith, director of NATO's Balkans Task Force, who had also led on resolving the situation in southern Serbia earlier in the year. Robertson appointed him as a personal special envoy of the secretary general. It meant every action did not have to be referred to the NAC, although NATO ambassadors would still be required to agree any particularly major alliance moves to intervene.[34]

*

As the Bush administration bedded in, it became increasingly clear that they were even keener than their Clinton-era predecessors on building a missile-defence system for the United

States, immediately antagonising both European allies and the Kremlin. New US Secretary of State Colin Powell failed to persuade members that missile attacks were a major threat to the alliance. Defense Secretary Donald Rumsfeld returned to the time-honoured US tactic of briefing classified intelligence to alliance members, covering missile developments in Iran, Iraq, Libya and North Korea. Not all member nations found the briefing conclusive. 'The information was not new to us,' said a German defence official. 'We knew there were bad guys out there.' Others said the administration might get its way through sheer refusal to consider compromise. 'When you know they are going to build it no matter what, is it really worth the fight?' asked one NATO official.[35] As Bush himself prepared for a trip to Europe, his own administration acknowledged a charm offensive would be necessary. 'The common European perception is of a shallow, arrogant, government-loving, abortion-hating Christian fundamentalist Texan buffoon,' said a senior administration official.[36] The visit highlighted other divisions as well – particularly on climate change. European nation after European nation lined up to criticise the Bush administration for its rejection of the 1998 Kyoto Protocol, while divisions over the missile proposal continued unabated.[37]

The Baltic states continued to push for rapid NATO membership, with the Bush administration openly supportive. When Bush met Putin for the first time in Slovenia in June 2001 the Russian leader warned him not to act unilaterally on missile defence or NATO expansion. Overall, however, the meeting was claimed by both sides as a success. 'I am convinced that he and I can build a relationship of mutual respect and candour,' said Bush, adding later, 'I looked the man in the eye. I was able to get a sense of his soul . . . a man deeply committed to his country.'[38]

In Macedonia rebels seized villages on the outskirts of the capital. Despite talking of a peace plan, the government launched a renewed offensive.[39] By now the NATO team was heavily engaged within the country, driving deep into the hills to talk to the militant Albanian minority political leader Ali Ahmeti – and, shortly afterwards, embedding Robertson's special adviser and former BBC correspondent Mark Laity directly in the office of Macedonian President Boris Trajkovski. In Kosovo, meanwhile, KFOR moved to arrest rebels attempting to cross the border.[40]

On 14 June, Macedonia formally requested NATO troops to help disarm the rebels. Critically, the main Albanian-speaking militant group the National Liberation Army (NLA) – closely affiliated with the KLA across the border – agreed that they would accept the plan if demands for greater autonomy were granted and the deal was guaranteed by the US, NATO and European Union.[41] At the end of June the NATO and EU delegation brokered an Albanian rebel withdrawal from Aracinovo, the militants allowed to keep their guns for now. The evacuation was escorted by NATO military advisers, civilians, OSCE, Red Cross and EU personnel. The entire operation had almost collapsed immediately, however, due to a lack of buses, the secretary general forced to broker an arrangement himself for the US military to provide them.

When the news broke of the deal, many in Macedonia furiously dismissed it as a humiliation for the government, allowing the rebels to keep their weapons rather than defeating them entirely. Angry crowds, fanned by ethnic propaganda, besieged Parliament and government offices, with the president forced to flee. Suddenly, conflict looked even closer than before.[42] On 26 June President Trajkovski addressed the Macedonian people, telling them bluntly that the supposedly successful offensive against the militants had failed after all, and he had been forced to find another way. The ceasefire that allowed the evacuation only covered the area around the capital. Further towards the border, fighting continued, filling Skopje with ethnic Slav Macedonian refugees and deepening the pressure on the government.

The NATO team – again, operating in conjunction with the EU and other partners, and supported by Robertson and Solana's personal intervention – was pushing for a wider deal that would disarm the rebels, so reducing the risk of outright war. By late July the ceasefire was in tatters once again.

Talks were to be held in Tetovo, but Macedonia's north-west remained too volatile, prompting their relocation to the resort town of Ohrid.[43] Between the initialling of the agreement on 8 August and its formal signing on 13 August, Macedonian troops suffered some of the heaviest losses of the conflict, eighteen soldiers dying in separate ambushes. Following that, Macedonian troops attacked the ethnic Albanian strongpoint of Ljuboten, with eight local men killed in what appeared to be executions by government forces. Once again, Macedonia seemed on the brink of much worse conflict, the government at one stage considering airstrikes with newly purchased Ukrainian Su–25 jets. Through serious diplomatic effort and no small amount of Western pressure, the deal was saved. Robertson flew back to Brussels for a meeting of the North Atlantic Council to authorise Operation ESSENTIAL HARVEST, a one-month British-led mission to disarm the militants.

Negotiating how many weapons ESSENTIAL HARVEST was to recover was inevitably a complex process – the rebels provided unrealistically low estimates, while the government numbers were ludicrously inflated. Eventually, a total of 3,300 was agreed on – including the heaviest rebel weapons – to be collected by 3,500 NATO troops over thirty days. This was not a UN-mandated mission – NATO was only there at the invitation of the Macedonian government, and it could only work if the rebels acquiesced.[44] Scepticism was widespread, both within the country and in Western capitals – and the US was notable by its absence. 'It was undoubtedly one of NATO's finest hours since the end of the Cold War,' Laity said. 'For all the problems, no other international organisation could have done so much, so quickly.'[45]

The deployment began with tragedy. On 26 August, Macedonian youths near the airport hurled a concrete block through the windscreen of a British Land Rover, killing Royal Engineer Ian Collins. A hostile crowd gathered around the wreckage, frustrating the recovery operation. The *Wall Street Journal* asked, 'Does the Western alliance know what it's in for?' Even Macedonian government spokesmen, who were supposed to be supporting the deal, predicted failure.[46] In Kosovo, NATO had nearly lost the information war – and now it looked like happening again. Robertson pulled his adviser Laity from the presidential office to act as civilian spokesman for ESSENTIAL HARVEST. From Brussels and on the ground within the country, NATO officials now pushed a coordinated line relentlessly, to both local and international media.[47] The initial weapons handed over were old and rusted – but even more worrying were what appeared to be night-time shootings by government-backed paramilitaries known as the 'Lions'. After a Canadian reconnaissance vehicle caught them in action on video, the NATO liaison team – comprising mainly special forces – visited the Lions and 'suggested' they pull back.

By the end of the first week in September the alliance believed it was most of the way to success in Macedonia. While the disarmament operation still had almost three weeks to run, it appeared the alliance might emerge the hero of the main foreign and security policy story of the year.[48] For the Bush administration this was a vindication of their decision to hold back forces. 'Bush said we should transfer more peacekeeping responsibilities over to Europeans,' said a senior US administration official. 'Here is a situation where the Europeans have the will and the capability.'

In truth, that was an oversimplification – US drones remained key to surveillance, while casualties including the slain UK soldier were evacuated by US helicopters attached to KFOR. Nor could the operation have taken place without US troops patrolling the border in nearby Kosovo.[49] It did, however, point to where most believed the US–NATO relationship might be heading. With the Bush administration focused on homeland defence, European NATO states were increasingly expected to pick up the slack.

All of those assumptions were about to be overturned. In the hours after the attacks of 11 September 2001 the US and British special forces that had been supporting ESSENTIAL HARVEST quite literally vanished overnight. The news crews were gone shortly afterwards. The remainder of the weapons collection passed largely without incident – in the new post-9/11 era no one in the Balkans wanted to risk being labelled Islamist militants by a vengeful United States.

21

9/11 and its Aftermath (2001)

*'We knew that something fundamental had happened
and that for the world a new chapter had opened.'*

**Former NATO Secretary General
George Robertson, 2011**[1]

It was 3.03 p.m. in Brussels when the second plane hit the World
Trade Center. NATO Secretary General George Robertson was
just concluding his weekly lunch meeting with the permanent
representatives. These meetings – private and off the record –
would diminish in importance throughout the coming years as
the alliance got busier and the pace of life more frenetic. In 2001,
however, they were still considered 'sacrosanct', described by
Robertson as 'no interruptions, no notes, no holds barred.'

The alliance and its secretary general had something to
celebrate that Tuesday. The new government in Belgrade had
just communicated to NATO that a criminal case against the
alliance and its senior leadership in the Serbian courts had
finally been thrown out. Robertson, who as UK defence secretary had been intimately involved in bombing Yugoslavia over
Kosovo, would no longer face twenty-five years in prison if he
visited.

When one of Robertson's bodyguards entered the room to
say that a plane had hit the World Trade Center, the assumption was that it must have been an accident.[2] When the guard
returned minutes later to announce a second plane had also

hit, a stunned silence fell across the table.[3] Soon Robertson was racing back to NATO's ageing headquarters in his armour-plated car. In his office, surrounded by NATO's senior diplomatic and military staff, he watched the footage – suddenly grimly aware of planes passing overhead into Brussels airport. Robertson ordered that all non-essential personnel leave the building immediately.[4]

In Lima for a visit, US Secretary of State Colin Powell decided immediately that he must return to Washington. As he began the journey back, the former soldier began scribbling notes. One of them read simply: 'What about NATO?'[5] In Brussels, Robertson was being briefed repeatedly by US ambassador to NATO Nicholas Burns. The US administration was temporarily in chaos.[6] President Bush was reading to second graders at an elementary school in Florida when White House Chief of Staff Andrew Card told him about the second plane. 'They have declared war on us,' Bush later remembered thinking. 'I made up my mind in that moment that we were going to war.'[7]

But war against whom? In Brussels, Robertson was determined that if the US was going to fight, NATO should do so too. Throughout the afternoon and evening, US ambassador Burns was swamped with expressions of condolence and offers of support from the seventeen other NATO nations.[8] One European diplomat remembers a sense of anger, sadness 'and also urgency in tackling this – huge sympathy for the US and a huge willingness to be part of and contribute to whatever happened next'.[9] An emergency meeting of NAC ambassadors agreed a statement unanimously condemning what it called 'barbaric acts' and 'mindless slaughter', describing the battle against terrorism as one that NATO nations – 'indeed, all civilised nations' – must win. Robertson read the statement to the waiting TV cameras: 'NATO solidarity remains the essence of the alliance . . . Our message to those who perpetrated these unspeakable crimes is equally clear: you will not get away with it.'[10]

On the other side of the Atlantic, Secretary of State Powell was tasked with building an international coalition. Bush had already spoken to Blair in London, saying he wanted military action that would seriously hurt the attackers, already believed to be Osama bin Laden and his Afghan-headquartered Al Qaeda network.[11] When Robertson first spoke to Powell in the early hours of the morning of 12 September, Brussels time, his first question was: 'What about Article 5?' 'What about Article 5?' responded Powell. 'An attack on one is an attack on all,' said Robertson. 'I know what Article 5 is, but why are you raising it?' responded the secretary of state. 'Well,' said Robertson, 'you've been attacked.' 'Ah,' replied Powell. 'There's a thought. I'm going to have to get back to you on that.'[12]

In fact, a row was raging in Washington over just that option. 'The allies were desperately trying to give us political cover, and the Pentagon was resisting it,' one senior US official said. 'It was insane. Eventually Rumsfeld understood it was a plus, not a minus, and was able to accept it.'[13] This was scarcely an enthusiastic US endorsement of NATO action, and certainly well short of a US request to trigger Article 5. Nor did any European nation mention Article 5 when Robertson attended an unprecedented EU meeting on the attacks – despite Robertson directly asking British Foreign Secretary Jack Straw and Belgian counterpart Louis Michel to raise it as a question. The fact the European Union had not been told NATO would push ahead with an Article 5 motion, Robertson conceded, caused some 'bad blood' between the two organisations.[14] But he was determined to push ahead, for the first and only time ignoring his predecessor's advice never to put a motion before the NAC without knowing whether it would pass.

It was a risky gambit. On the surface, the vote to trigger Article 5 required a simple reaffirmation of an equally simple statement in the North Atlantic Treaty. If the NAC failed to agree it, however, it might throw the entire existence of the alliance into doubt. Robertson's team believed time was of the essence. 'It was critical,' said one NATO official of the time. 'Otherwise once the Americans were getting underway, NATO would have been left behind. But he [Robertson] didn't force it through – it's worth emphasising that. He made it an opportunity for solidarity, and sold it that way.'[15] Robertson described the more than five hours of conversations with nineteen NATO capitals as 'fraught' and 'nerve-racking'. On one occasion he found himself addressing an entire national Cabinet meeting through the foreign minister's mobile phone. By 9.20 p.m. he had unanimous support. 'I was drained but enormously relieved,' he later wrote.[16]

More than two decades later NATO's decision to trigger Article 5 is frequently portrayed as a critical point in both its history, and in the relationship between Europe and the United States. In the years since, it has been used ruthlessly by NATO and European leaders, particularly during the Trump administration, to remind Americans – and their president – of prior allied resolve. In 2001 it captured the mood of a very specific moment – the outpouring of global sympathy and shock in the days after the attack, when French newspaper *Le Monde* proclaimed, 'We are all Americans.'[17] As that mood dwindled in the era of Guantánamo and Iraq, the fact Article 5 had been declared became all the more important, just as Robertson had hoped. 'Do not underestimate the importance of that first, great act of solidarity and alliance to the American people,' US ambassador Burns told the alliance a year later. 'No American will ever forget the messages of solidarity and comfort uttered by our allies in those bleak hours.'[18]

That moment, however, was never set to last. Donald Rumsfeld was already talking in terms of a much broader war against terrorism that would go beyond Al Qaeda to include enemies like Iraq. Powell warned that such a coalition would be much harder to hold together.[19] From the very start Bush didn't want other countries dictating terms or conditions in the US response. Defeating America's enemies now, he told his national security team on 13 September, would set the tone for future presidents – but it might cost Washington its allies. 'Two years from now, only the Brits may be with us,' he said. A few days later Bush speculated that, further down the line, the US might need to fight alone.[20] Within a week of the attack some of NATO's European members were indeed becoming lukewarm at the prospect of supporting Washington in a conflict yet to be defined. Belgian Foreign Minister Louis Michel described the EU as 'on watch' and 'mobilised', but 'not at war'. French Prime Minister Lionel Jospin warned that there was 'no war against Islam or the Arab-Muslim world', and appeared to question whether France would automatically support military action.[21]

The *New York Times*, meanwhile, suggested dismissively that, while the US was glad to have the 'political consensus' of the Article 5 declaration, the alliance 'offers little militarily'. 'The US does not really need NATO,' said British analyst Jonathan Eyal. Rob de Wijk, a military analyst with the Dutch Institute of International Relations, said the number of European military personnel suitable to support the US in Afghanistan likely numbered only in the thousands – almost all British and French special forces, with a few hundred from other countries.[22] For now, a loose calm prevailed within the alliance, as the world cautiously awaited the US military response. 'The Americans are behaving responsibly, taking their time to mobilise military instruments and to plan for an effective action, while at the same time building up an international coalition,' said one French official. The major issues that divided European and US policymakers before – missile defence, Macedonia, NATO enlargement – now seemed 'less urgent and important', it was said. A British official was more cautious. 'Solidarity is holding,' he said. 'But . . . the Americans haven't done anything yet.'[23]

In late September, US Deputy Defense Secretary Paul Wolfowitz suggested it was unlikely Washington would need NATO in the immediate future. 'If we need collective action, we will ask for it,' he told reporters. The following week US ambassador at large, and former counterterrorism chief, Frank Taylor briefed the NAC, before heading on to Moscow to do the same for Putin. One senior diplomat described the briefing – which included no slides, images or handouts – as 'nothing particularly new or surprising . . . no attempt to build a legal case'. Secretary General Robertson described the evidence presented as 'classified', but 'clear and compelling'. 'We know that the individuals who carried out these attacks were part of the worldwide terrorist network of Al Qaeda, headed by Osama bin Laden and his key lieutenants and protected by the Taliban,' he said.[24]

The US was not simply focused on Afghanistan. By now the CIA had generated a 'worldwide attack matrix' detailing covert operations in eighty countries, either underway or recommended. But this was the kind of detail that would be briefed to US journalists three years later, not to NATO now.[25] In one single day following 9/11 Powell claimed to have called fortyseven world leaders. 'I've been so multilateral . . . I'm getting seasick,' he joked.[26] As Robertson worked to keep the alliance relevant, two leaders in particular – Blair and Putin – were embracing Bush. In September, Blair embarked on a whirlwind tour of European capitals largely on behalf of the US before heading over the Atlantic to become Bush's first foreign visitor following the attacks.[27]

Putin's charm offensive appeared equally deliberate. US officials flew to Moscow in mid-September. 'We are in a war,' counterterror chief Cofer Black informed Russian officials, telling them that the US knew that Afghanistan was in their 'sphere of influence' but 'at the very least, we want you to look away'. The Russians told him the US would get the 'hell kicked out of it' in Afghanistan, but they would provide imagery and intelligence.[28] 'We are going to support you in the war on terror,' Putin told Bush, although he said the US would only receive overflight rights across Russia for humanitarian purposes, and Russia would not put its own troops in Afghanistan. Russian forces would, however, provide search and rescue support for US pilots in northern Afghanistan if necessary – it never was. Putin offered to use the Kremlin's influence in Central Asia to get the US basing rights, something that would eventually give the Pentagon access to a major Uzbek airbase.[29]

Unlike some of America's NATO allies, Putin stressed that the Kremlin needed no encouragement to clamp down on Islamic terrorism. Criticism of Putin's actions in Chechnya had all but ceased, although some in Russia criticised him for following his predecessor in getting too friendly with the West. Putin also spoke repeatedly to NATO Secretary General Robertson, who reported that they had developed a 'habit of straight talk' that was transforming the relationship. 'For some forty years, NATO and Russia . . . glowered at one another,' Robertson said. 'For ten years, we tiptoed around each other. Now, I believe we are entering an era of substantial and practical cooperation.' Less than a year earlier Putin had warned that NATO expansion into the Baltic states would be a 'serious matter'. Now he appeared to be softening that stance. 'If NATO takes on a different shape and is becoming a political organisation, of course we would reconsider our position,' Putin said.[30]

For Eastern European states this was a game-changer. Behind the scenes the US administration was already deciding that, as well as 9/11 ushering in a new era of US intervention across the Middle East, NATO would expand to encompass most of Central and Eastern Europe. For the countries there, it was everything they had hoped for – and they would prove more than willing to support the US in its coming wars if that was the price of permanent NATO membership and protection.

The initial US strategy in Afghanistan could hardly have been more different to the troop-heavy NATO intervention it eventually became. Clandestine CIA operators and a handful of special forces would supercharge the estimated 20,000 irregular Afghan fighters of the anti-Taliban 'Northern Alliance'.[31]

At the end of September the CIA team on the ground – code-named JAWBREAKER – showed the Northern Alliance classified maps and gave them $1 million in cash.[32] NATO now had its first request for direct support for US military activity – an eight-point list of requests for access to bases and airspace, airborne early warning aircraft and replacement forces for any US troops and ships removed from NATO tasks in Europe. The alliance, Robertson said, would not be directly involved in the military action – but within days every item on the list had been provided.[33]

A senior US administration official bluntly explained why America was going it alone, supported only by a few British forces: 'The fewer people you have to rely on, the fewer permissions you have to get.' It was an overstatement – without multiple bilateral agreements, particularly with nearby states, the US would not have been able to mount the campaign at all. But it was also a sign of things to come.[34]

In the dying hours of 8 October – mid-afternoon, Washington time – US and British forces finally struck with Tomahawk cruise missiles and jets. Explosions were reported in multiple Afghan cities, with the power failing in Kabul almost immediately. 'The battle is now joined on many fronts,' Bush told the world in a TV announcement. 'Now the Taliban will pay a price.'[35]

Shortly before the strikes began, Robertson had been told by Vice President Dick Cheney they were imminent. Now Robertson assembled the NAC once more to pass another motion endorsing US action. NATO also approved the deployment of five NATO early warning AWACS aircraft to the US, the first time its forces had been sent to North America.[36] As Robertson visited the White House on 10 October, Bush stood by him in the Rose Garden praising his leadership and the triggering of Article 5 as an 'act of great friendship in a time of great need'. The US president described NATO as 'the cornerstone' of a global 'coalition against terror' – but there was still little clarity on what it might actually end up doing.[37]

By early November the international and US press were full of questions as to why Kabul and other major cities were taking so long to fall. US air power, however, was proving a decisive factor, as was the support and guidance of US and British special forces with their bags of cash – when suddenly, almost without warning, the Bush administration realised the capital might fall at any time. The shift was so dramatic and the US so unprepared even Rumsfeld changed his tune. 'We want to get a multilateral force into Kabul soon,' he told a meeting at the White House, keen to avoid US forces being used for nation-building. Events, however, were moving too fast. Within days US special forces were on the outskirts of the capital, calling in dozens of airstrikes, killing hundreds of Taliban and opening Kabul to capture.[38]

Germany now pledged 3,900 troops, including medics and special forces – the first German troops to be deployed outside Europe since their eviction from North Africa in 1943. There was talk of NATO itself also taking action in Afghanistan, delivering food throughout the winter – although such suggestions would come to nothing. Italy offered another thousand troops, while Chirac, who so far had his offer of special forces rejected, said Washington was now showing more openness to their use. Few were more enthusiastic to send troops than those in Eastern Europe. Poland had already offered special forces; the Czech Republic a chemical warfare protection unit.[39] Turkey announced it would be the first muslim US ally to send its special forces to Afghanistan, although Foreign Minister Ismail Cem pledged to keep the risk of actual combat to a minimum.[40] All of this, however, was coordinated outside NATO.

At the start of November, before the fall of the capital, many still predicted the war could last throughout the winter. But by 13 November, exactly nine weeks after 9/11, Taliban fighters appeared to abandon Kabul altogether, a BBC team finding itself able to enter the city surrounded by cheering fighters.[41] Within a month Taliban forces also fled Kandahar, in the south, defeated by a combination of US airstrikes and ethnic Pashtuns led by the man the US would shortly appoint as Afghan president, Hamid Karzai. According to accounts by the Northern Alliance and others around Karzai, Rumsfeld deliberately blocked a potential peace deal with the Taliban that would have allowed their leader Mullah Omar to escape. Whether that is true remains hotly contested. 'If true, the United States purposefully scuttled a chance for peace at its moment of peak bargaining power and set Afghanistan back down the road to war,' wrote Carter Malkasian in his 2021 history of the Afghan war.[42]

On 10 November, shortly before the fall of Kabul, US ambassador to NATO Nicholas Burns outlined Washington's priorities for the alliance. The top priority, he said, remained the Balkans – with the US committed to keeping its forces in Bosnia, Kosovo and Macedonia 'to staunch the kind of instability that let terrorists take root in Afghanistan'. The second was a 'new relationship' with Russia, including deeper direct cooperation with the alliance. Certainly, he believed, it was 'necessary to strengthen NATO's capabilities to meet new challenges' – with the US now even more committed to missile defence following the attacks. 'Finally,' he wrote, 'September 11 also demands that we expand NATO to consolidate democracy eastward and southward. The United States will support a vigorous round of enlargement next year.'[43]

On 15 November, 160 British and American military personnel flew to Bagram air base to secure it for a much larger peacekeeping force, while a detachment of French troops prepared to perform a similar operation in the northern city of Mazar-e-Sharif.[44] It was the beginning of what would become the multinational International Security Assistance Force that would eventually be run by NATO – but for now, the deployment remained independent of the alliance.

On 5 December the Bonn agreement – partially shepherded by the US, but also Germany – finally delivered an Afghan government under Karzai, as well as a mandate for the

ISAF, which was also endorsed by a UN Security Council resolution. The UK got its wish to be the leading nation – but the remit of that force was limited to Kabul and its immediate surrounding area. For now, however, there was no role defined for NATO.[45] This was becoming embarrassing for the alliance, newspapers quoting anonymous US officials as dismissing it as 'not relevant'. French security expert François Heisbourg talked once again of the 'death of NATO', while others contrasted the multilateral chaos of Kosovo's war planning with the effectiveness of America's post-9/11 actions. Charles Grant, director of the London-based Centre for European Reform, predicted NATO might 'get squeezed" between a European Union that increasingly ran its own military operations and a post-Kosovo United States 'that's learned it doesn't ever want to run a shooting war via NATO [again]'.[46]

December 2001 ended with highly public disagreements at the meeting of foreign ministers over how to handle Russia – with the US and NATO's leadership determined to bring the Kremlin much more closely into the decision-making of the alliance and what would become the NATO–Russia Council. That alarmed Eastern and Central European and Nordic members, with Danish Foreign Minister Per Stig Møller warning that Russia could not be given a veto on NATO expansion.

The foreign ministers' meeting gave an unusually detailed insight into the growing clash between Rumsfeld and Powell over how to handle US foreign policy. For almost half a day agreement of the communiqué was held up after US ambassador Burns told the NAC he had received competing signed instructions from the two Cabinet members. Officials told the *New York Times* that the disagreement related specifically to the phrase 'NATO at twenty', which referred to the members plus Russia. Rumsfeld wanted the terminology removed; Powell felt it should be kept. Ultimately, the latter prevailed – reportedly because the terminology had been personally agreed between the president and Putin. This did not reduce the worries of

Eastern Europe. 'Some of these countries were saying that they just got into NATO a few years ago to get security from Russia – and now look who is seated at the table,' said one Western diplomat.[47]

In a much larger spat with Rumsfeld, Powell was comprehensively defeated. In the coming year it would become apparent the US was going to invade Iraq, even if the cost was damage to its relations with almost every major partner. Nor was the US prepared to let its new friend in the Kremlin hold any significant veto over US or allied actions. On 14 December, Bush announced the US would withdraw from the Anti-Ballistic Missile Treaty to pursue more sophisticated anti-missile systems. Condemnation from the Kremlin was relatively light, but even moderate voices in the Russian parliament warned of lasting damage to relations and goodwill. 'After the tragedy of September 11, Russia extended its hand full-length to meet the United States,' said Alexei Arbatov, a moderate MP and military expert. 'The United States has spat on that extended hand.'[48]

This unilateral approach would only become more controversial in 2002 and 2003. At the end of December 2001 the Bush administration took another action that would permanently influence how some viewed the United States – it opened a prison camp at its military base at Cuba's Guantánamo Bay, to hold individuals that it did not wish to be processed under US or perhaps even international law. 'That was already starting to make some people feel uneasy,' said a European diplomat. 'But nobody here wants to go directly against the United States.'[49]

22

The Schisms of Iraq (2002–2005)

'The thing about Iraq is that NATO was not directly particularly involved – but it had an impact on almost everything.'

Former NATO official, 2023[1]

In Afghanistan an uneasy calm prevailed as 2002 began. As Brigadier General Stanley McChrystal, NATO's future commander in the country, later noted: 'It wasn't clear whether there was "any war" left. The hunt for Al Qaeda continued, but the Taliban seemed to be decisively defeated. Most had essentially melted away, and we weren't sure where they'd gone.'[2] While the British-led International Security Assistance Force (ISAF) patrolled Kabul, the US remained firmly in charge of operations elsewhere in the country. Its 8,000 personnel on its ENDURING FREEDOM counterterrorism operation outnumbered the anticipated 5,000 international troops, outstripping them even more comprehensively when it came to military capability.[3]

NATO was still not doing anything in Afghanistan, and its post-9/11 unity was fading. Europeans had their own success to tout: the launch of the European single currency. Now they resumed criticism of how the Bush administration handled the world on everything from trade to terror. 'The Europeans think the United States is so powerful it can't be constrained,' one US official noted.[4] That impression deepened as it became apparent just how determined the US truly was to now invade Iraq.

As the Bush administration became increasingly frustrated with its Western European allies, the US relationship with Central and Eastern Europe became ever more important. Responding to a reporter's question in January 2003 on 'European' attitudes on Iraq, Donald Rumsfeld dismissed those opposed as 'old Europe'. 'If you look at the entire "NATO Europe" today, the centre of gravity is shifting to the east,' he said.[5] For the Baltic states and several others in Eastern Europe, this was an opportunity to finally lock in the NATO membership they had always hoped for. While that might upset the Kremlin, many now believed Russia judged its own relationship with Washington was too valuable to lose. 'Putin has ended centuries of Russian wavering between East and West and made a strategic choice,' wrote former senior US official Philip Gordon, adding that that the only way to restore Russia's economy was with Western cooperation. It was, he said, working: Russia had returned to growth, supported by high oil prices after 9/11, taking Putin's approval ratings to above 80 per cent. For all that, Russia's GDP remained the size of Belgium's while its entire defence budget, some $50 billion, was roughly equal to the amount by which the US planned to increase its military spending in the coming year.[6]

In Iceland in mid-May 2002, NATO foreign ministers agreed to expand the alliance, but did not specify individual nations. The communiqué expressed concerns over 'WMD' – the increasingly ubiquitous acronym for 'weapons of mass destruction' – but did not name Iraq. With Foreign Minister Igor Ivanov in attendance, considerable effort was put into keeping Russia happy, including recognising its right to protect its territorial integrity in Chechnya. The Iceland meeting signed off the creation of the NATO–Russia Council, to meet at ministerial level at least twice a year.[7] British Foreign Secretary Jack Straw described it as the 'funeral of the Cold War'.[8] Two weeks later a presidential tour of Europe took Bush to

Moscow and Putin's hometown of Saint Petersburg, after which the two leaders headed to Rome to meet their NATO counterparts.

As Russia and NATO moved closer together, Ukraine was thrown into the diplomatic darkness after leaked phone recordings appeared to link the Kyiv government to the secret sale of a radar system to Saddam Hussein. By September 2002, US officials were briefing that they believed the recordings to be genuine, with 'some indications' the radar was already in Iraq. A furious Washington suspended a $55 million-a-year aid programme amid talk of sanctions and prosecution.[9] Ukrainian officials described the allegations as groundless, but US counterparts did not believe them.[10]

The November 2002 NATO leaders summit in Prague would be used to showcase both NATO expansion and Ukraine's new isolation. Ukraine's President Leonid Kuchma was encouraged not to attend the Prague session for countries in the Partnership for Peace. When he turned up uninvited, he found nations were no longer in alphabetical order around the table in English but in French. It was a canny diplomatic fix by NATO staff. Ukraine was no longer next to the United Kingdom and United States, now moved safely away by the French spellings of 'Grande Bretagne' and 'Étas-Unis'. Instead, Ukraine was now its own at the end of the table next to Turkey and, with no one on the other side, unambiguously in a state of isolation. Officials made it clear to journalists that this was not an accident.[11]

For most attendees in Prague, Ukraine's humiliation was a footnote amid the preparations for the coming war. But for NATO's new additions – now confirmed as the Baltic three, Bulgaria, Romania, Slovakia and Slovenia – the summit brought the life-altering binding promise of full membership and protection. For Robertson, it was also about making the alliance more 'relevant', including building forces that could operate 'out of area' – which increasingly felt like code for the Middle East. The result was the NATO Response Force, a rotating collection of several thousand troops able to be deployed at short notice wherever the alliance needed them.

From the US delegation the words 'weapons of mass destruction' now featured in almost every statement, with those nations that wanted to keep Washington on side following suit.[12] Putin had stayed away from the summit, despite receiving an invitation, but Foreign Minister Igor Ivanov told reporters Russia expected to 'intensify' its cooperation with the alliance. Afterwards he joined Bush on Air Force One as the US president flew from Prague to Moscow to meet the Russian leader.[13] At the Kremlin, Putin described NATO expansion as a 'problem'. But, he said, 'We take note of the position taken by the president of the United States, and we hope to have positive development of our relations with all NATO countries.'[14] From the perspective of the 2020s, the 2002 Prague summit would be viewed as one of the more successful in alliance history, delivering the expansion into the Baltic states that should protect them in perpetuity. At the time, however, attention remained almost exclusively on the coming battle for Iraq. Even Afghanistan – where NATO still had no formal role – was scarcely mentioned.

When US Deputy Defense Secretary Paul Wolfowitz visited NATO HQ in early December 2002, he suggested actual NATO military assets – including its airborne early warning planes – might yet play a part in any Iraq invasion. More than ever before, he was clear that the US was asking other NATO members to commit their own troops to the battle.[15] Robertson said NATO's role itself in any conflict was yet to be defined. The alliance, he added, was 'very, very supportive of the United Nations process and if that breaks down then clearly there is a moral obligation by NATO to give whatever support is required'.[16] In reality, the US failure to secure UN backing for its actions in Iraq would leave the alliance at perhaps its most divided since Suez.

US conversations with individual NATO nations were increasingly transactional and awkward. 'The level of anti-Americanism is extremely high,' Polish President Aleksander Kwaśniewski said in a private conversation with Bush on 14 January 2003. 'Success helps to change public opinion,' said Bush, predicting a US victory.[17] Other NATO allies publicly refused to send troops and expressed outright opposition. On 21 January, a French, German and Belgian veto saw the NAC fail to agree military assistance for the protection of Turkey, now expected to host both US troops and planes for the attack on Iraq. 'It was a pretty tough discussion,' one diplomat said afterwards. 'The arguments were flying.'[18] The diplomatic strain was also showing. At the end of January 2003, Secretary General Robertson surprised many by announcing he would stand down by the end of the year. His term had already been extended for one year, and the most important nations wished him to continue. He did not explain his reasons.[19]

*

In January 2003 the Baltic nations found their gas and oil supplies through pipelines from Russia unexpectedly suspended. With Russia's state gas firm Gazprom already a major player in Latvia and Lithuania, it was a sign that Putin had no intention of readily abandoning Moscow's influence in Eastern Europe.[20] The countries of the former Eastern bloc, however, had no doubt that their long-term security lay with the US, NATO and the West. Seeing the prospects fade for a second UN resolution on Iraq, 'new Europe' states fell over themselves to assert their support for invading Iraq without one. 'Our countries understand the dangers posed by tyranny and the special responsibility of democracies to defend our shared values,' said a strongly worded statement from ten nations, including the seven new NATO entrants.[21]

The prospect that war could genuinely be avoided was diminishing by the day. As Rumsfeld visited Munich in February, thousands demonstrated in the streets. With NATO still deadlocked over providing support to Turkey, Rumsfeld criticised the alliance directly. Delays to aid to Turkey, he said, were 'inexcusable . . . The United States and the countries in NATO will go right ahead and do it . . . What will be hurt will be NATO, not Turkey.' At the NAC, US officials again pushed for Article 4 'consultation' over the supposed Iraqi threat to Turkey, invoking the clause of the North Atlantic Treaty that allowed any nation feeling itself in danger to consult with the remainder. Amid newspaper headlines talking of the worst internal row in NATO's history, US ambassador Nicholas Burns warned the alliance faced a 'crisis of credibility' if it was not prepared to provide defensive missile systems to the Turks.

Even the normally diplomatic Robertson described the discussions as 'very heated'. French and Belgian officials doubled down on their position. This was not about mutual self-defence, they said, it was about avoiding further inflaming regional tensions and stopping an unnecessary war. 'If Turkey is ever attacked, we will stand on its side, that is not an issue here,' said Belgian Prime Minister Guy Verhofstadt. 'A peaceful solution is still possible, if we give more equipment, more possibilities to the UN weapons inspectors.' French Defence Minister Michèle Alliot-Marie argued similarly. 'If Turkey was really under threat, France would be one of the first at its side,' she said.[22]

US appreciation for those that held the line would be considerable. NATO's next two secretary generals, former Dutch Foreign Minister Jaap de Hoop Scheffer and Danish Prime Minister Anders Fogh Rasmussen, would both notch up significant political capital with Washington for maintaining support in the face of mounting public pressure. Shortly after the NAC meeting closed, Germany, France and Belgium joined with

Russia in issuing a statement calling to intensify weapons inspections as an alternative to war. Between them, Putin and Chirac
were now explicit that the Security Council would block any
US move. US officials avoided commenting on the emergence
of a Moscow–Paris–Berlin diplomatic axis – a moment Putin
would repeatedly try to recreate in the decades to come.
NATO's new members, meanwhile, were getting an early taste
of the challenges of the NAC in a time of crisis, and they did not
like it. 'Not to take Turkish worries very seriously raises important questions about the fundamental purpose of the alliance,'
said Czech ambassador Karel Kovanda.[23]

The US put forward a compromise motion, more tightly
worded around the defence of Turkey, this time working even
harder with other European nations to ensure that it got
through. 'You cannot say Turkey doesn't feel threatened,' said
Dutch Foreign Minister de Hoop Scheffer.[24] Once again, it was
down to NATO officials to find a procedural way forward.
The decision to support Turkey was moved to NATO's Defence
Planning Committee – on which France did not sit – while Germany and Belgium were persuaded not to oppose the newly
worded motion. Nor, quite, did the agreement deliver immediate support. Instead, it committed NATO's military authorities
to 'provide military advice . . . on the feasibility, implications and
timelines' of deploying airborne early warning aircraft, air-
defence missiles and chemical and biological defence capabilities
to Turkey.[25] But it was just enough for Robertson to claim initial
victory. 'Alliance solidarity has prevailed,' the secretary general
told a press conference.[26]

Three days later NATO announced it was indeed sending
the aircraft, missiles and support troops to Turkey.[27] Robertson
flew to Washington where Bush told him NATO represented
'our nation's most important alliance' and congratulated him
on his 'great leadership'.[28] 'Nobody can write off this alliance on
the basis of this one argument,' Robertson told the European
Institute in Washington. 'We've been through arguments in the

past, will undoubtedly have arguments in the future. But ultimately, we make the decision.'[29]

*

Robertson had already concluded that while Iraq had almost broken NATO, it could find unity on Afghanistan – and there was now an opportunity to get the alliance much more seriously involved in those operations.

In mid-2002 Turkish troops and commanders had taken over from the British in leading ISAF in the Afghan capital. They were in turn replaced by a German–Dutch headquarters and a predominantly German force which had only limited capability to provide its own supplies, prompting Berlin to request NATO to support the mission with logistics. Robertson and his team spotted opportunities for the alliance to do even more – European nations that had opposed Iraq appeared much keener to work under NATO in Afghanistan than direct US command. German Defence Minister Peter Struck was particularly forthright in calling for greater NATO involvement, now supported by Robertson as he lobbied US officials. 'There is a general feeling that this is an interesting idea,' said a US official of a greater NATO Afghan role.'[30]

The popular anti-US backlash against the Iraq invasion continued to spread across Europe and the Middle East on a scale not seen since Vietnam. On 1 March the Turkish parliament voted against allowing US troops to use the country to attack Iraq, forcing the Pentagon to abandon its plans to invade simultaneously from north and south. Within a growing number of European capitals, the idea of using NATO to coordinate their activities in Afghanistan offered a way of keeping their operations there visibly separate to the increasingly unpopular actions of the United States.

The US launched its first strikes against Iraq in the early hours of 19 March, an attempt to kill Saddam Hussein based on last-minute intelligence that – like so much else in the lead-up to the war – would turn out to be wrong. Hours later Polish special forces were among the first into action, seizing key oil platforms in the Persian Gulf alongside US Navy SEALs.[31] Less than a decade and a half after the unravelling of the Warsaw Pact, NATO's new and incoming members viewed fighting in America's new wars as central to ensuring their security in the future. For them, that gamble was already paying off, securing membership for most of Central and Eastern Europe – less Ukraine, Georgia and Moldova – within NATO. Across much of the rest of the alliance, however, the Iraq invasion would soon come to be regarded as a disaster.

Still, in the short term, the rapid fall of Baghdad made it look as though the US had won, and NATO officials believed the time had come to reignite the alliance and pull the US back to a more multilateral approach with allies. As Powell and NATO foreign ministers met in early April, Secretary General Robertson announced a 'consensus' that the United Nations – sidelined by the US in the run-up to the invasion – would be encouraged to take a 'central role' in the post-war rebuilding of Iraq. What that role might be remained unclear, but the basic agreement was important. In the run-up to the invasion, even America's closest European allies worried the Bush administration might be about to tear up relations with both the UN and the alliance, abandoning any efforts at global and regional governance and structures in favour of unilateral action. By re-embracing the UN, the Bush administration too hoped it could re-engage with European nations opposed to the original invasion.[32]

Robertson and the US now hoped to make NATO not just the mainstay of operations in Afghanistan, but ideally to integrate it into post-war military activities in Iraq, using both to rebuild the damaged spirit of allied cooperation. Anti-Americanism in Europe remained widespread. In Greece – always sceptical of US military activity – 94 per cent opposed the war, with another poll showing Greeks held more positive views of Saddam Hussein than of Bush.[33] Relations with France also remained tense. Even arranging a simple telephone call between Chirac and Bush took hefty diplomatic negotiations. Still, on 16 April, the two men finally spoke in a 'businesslike' call. Back in October 2002, France had opposed any efforts to engage NATO directly in Afghanistan, arguing – in a reversal of de Gaulle's calls for worldwide intervention – that the alliance should not stray so far from Europe. Following the Bush–Chirac call, the French dropped their opposition.[34]

Hours later the NAC signed off a request from Germany, the Netherlands and Canada to enhance support to ISAF, agreeing NATO would take command of international forces in Kabul from summer 2003.[35] Keen to rebuild relations with the Americans, French officials now described it as a 'pragmatic' step. German counterparts were particularly relieved. Had NATO not agreed to step up and take over ISAF, German commanders would have had no one to hand their Afghan mission over to when they left aside from the US, a controversial move amid the anti-Americanism of Europe in summer 2003.

The US Afghan operation ENDURING FREEDOM would remain a separate US command even as NATO took over ISAF in Kabul. It was still very much a counterterrorism mission, lumping together Al Qaeda and the Taliban into a single group of 'targets'. Intelligence failures were frequent, as were collateral deaths. In total, six US special forces raids in Uruzgan killed at least eighty Afghans in the summer of 2002, alongside an accidental bombing of a wedding party by US military aircraft. Lacking solid insights on where Al Qaeda's leaders really were, US forces found themselves locking up low-level Taliban in Afghanistan's overcrowded jails, further radicalising those that Karzai hoped to bring into the political process to de-escalate the conflict.[36]

*

In Brussels and beyond, there was optimism NATO could 'do' Afghanistan better than the US, building on success in the

Balkans where its Bosnia peacekeeping duties would shortly be handed to the European Union. In contrast to the US approach of seeking out and attacking militants, the German-led ISAF mission in Kabul was much more focused on rebuilding. For many of those involved, this was ideological, a chance for the reunited Germany to rebuild another nation. German military nurse Dunja Neukam described German troops delivering medical relief. 'We always pointed to the German flag on our uniform jackets,' she said.[37]

The risks of that approach now became apparent. On 7 June 2003, barely two months before the NATO takeover, a taxi packed with explosives ploughed into a bus carrying German ISAF troops to Kabul airport for their final trip home after months in the Afghan capital. Four were killed, twenty-nine wounded. The suicide attack was almost as shocking to Afghans as the peacekeeping contingent in Kabul. Even in their long war against the Russians, Afghan fighters had never used such tactics. The only previous suicide attack in Afghan history, which killed Afghan resistance leader Ahmad Shah Massoud two days before the September 11 attacks, had been conducted by Arabs working for Al Qaeda. While no group ever claimed responsibility for the strike against the Germans, the effect was clear: foreign troops attempting to stabilise Afghanistan would be forced to separate themselves from the population, and travel in heavily armed convoys – which became an increasingly frequent target.[38]

NATO's formal assumption of the ISAF mission on 11 August 2003 took place behind dramatically increased security, with bomb-sniffing dogs and troops in heavy body armour. NATO's first commander there, Lieutenant General Götz Gliemeroth, was another German.[39] His 5,000 ISAF troops remained significantly outnumbered by the 9,000 US troops of ENDURING FREEDOM, their operations initially still limited to Kabul and its surroundings. Outside Kabul, the first international Provincial Reconstruction Teams (PRTs) were fanning out across the country, groups of seventy to 300 person-nel engaged in building government and military capacity.[40] German officials sought NATO agreement for the alliance to take over management of their PRT in Kunduz from mid-2003, with other member nations keen to follow suit. 'NATO found itself pulled into Afghanistan because no one else was able to take charge in Kabul,' said Mark Laity, at the time NATO spokes-man in the country. 'It ended up taking over the PRTs because the Germans didn't want the Americans in charge of them.'[41]

*

This increasingly central Afghan role was exactly what Rob-ertson had wanted. But the limits of member enthusiasm for sending forces were fast becoming clear. Robertson's final weeks in office were spent sourcing a handful of helicopters needed in Kabul from Turkey and the Netherlands.[42] Even that simple-sounding deal proved complex, requiring weeks of negotiations. Nevertheless, Robertson viewed his tenure as NATO's civilian chief as broadly a success – particularly the improved relations with the Kremlin. 'We will not always agree with Russia politically,' he said in his final speech, '[but] not even the most imaginative Hollywood screenwriter can day-dream up a scenario which would plausibly pit NATO and Russia at each other's throats in the old-fashioned Cold War style.'[43]

As NATO's new Secretary General Jaap de Hoop Scheffer took the reins in January 2004, further expansion of alliance activity in Afghanistan was his top priority.[44] 'If we want to win the war on terrorism, we must win the peace in Afghanistan,' he said.[45] Violence was now visibly rising. As SACEUR James Jones made the first of many calls for further NATO troops, another suicide attack in Kabul killed a Canadian peacekeeper and an Afghan civilian, followed by another that left a British soldier dead.[46] At NATO HQ and SHAPE, keeping even the Kabul mission up and running was an effort, and there were endless battles to persuade nations to offer troops and other resources. As defence ministers met in February, the airport still lacked enough air traffic controllers and ISAF was short of frontline combat troops. More nations, however, were volunteering to lead the smaller PRTs, believed less likely to be involved in heavy fighting. Britain, Italy, Turkey and Norway would lead four out of the five upcoming PRTs now to be NATO-managed. The Netherlands, Romania and Lithuania would also contribute forces.[47] Some saw the alliance expanding its role still further. In February 2004, NATO agreed to support Greece with security arrangements for the Olympic Games, in part intended to help restore relations after tensions over Iraq and Kosovo. The following month, the US and Norwegian NATO delegations agreed to host their first ever summit on human trafficking, suggesting the alliance might develop some vaguely defined role in combating cross-border criminality.[48]

More conventional European security worries now briefly grabbed centre stage, intersecting savagely with the post-9/11 politics of Europe. On 11 March, days before Spain's general election, bombs ripped through crowded commuter trains in Madrid, killing 191 and wounding more than 1,800.[49] Spanish Prime Minister José María Aznar was ousted in the post-bombing election backlash, his successor pledging to withdraw Spain's 1,300 troops from Iraq – but suggesting they might be sent to Afghanistan instead.[50] Barely a week later, at least eight people were killed and hundreds injured in ethnic clashes in Mitrovica, southern Kosovo, in the worst violence seen there since 1999. The injured included twelve French soldiers and one Danish, as well as seven UN policemen.[51] More than 2,000 NATO troops found themselves on their way to Kosovo, the total death toll there now approaching thirty.[52] March 2004 would prove a busy month. De Hoop Scheffer made unscheduled trips to both Spain and Kosovo, attended the accession ceremony of NATO's newly incoming members, and told

Russia's newly appointed Foreign Minister Sergey Lavrov that NATO was sending fighter jets to the Baltic states.[53]

As Bush welcomed the leaders of Estonia, Latvia, Lithuania, Bulgaria, Romania, Slovakia and Slovenia to Washington on 29 March 2004, his speechwriters could not resist a touch of Reaganite rhetoric. 'When NATO was founded, the people of these seven nations were captives to an empire,' he said. 'They understand our cause in Afghanistan and Iraq because tyranny for them is still a fresh memory.' By this point, troops from all seven joining nations had served in either Afghanistan or Iraq – as had personnel from Albania, Croatia and Macedonia, all of whom would follow into the alliance in the coming years.[54]

From the start, there was a quiet understanding that the former Soviet Baltic states might be the most vulnerable to the Kremlin. In the run-up to their accession, several Russian aircraft approached their borders, prompting Estonia, Latvia and Lithuania – none of which had their own combat jets – to request NATO fighters to defend their airspace. The resulting mission was described as 'air policing', with the implication that the small number of aircraft deployed by the alliance were primarily to defend against potential terror threats as much as against aggressive Russian warplanes.

As the new Eastern NATO members were welcomed into the alliance, NATO leaders were keen to make it clear they still viewed Russia as a partner rather than a threat.[55] Foreign Minister Lavrov was deliberately invited to the flag-raising ceremony at NATO headquarters, and also pre-warned of the Baltic jet deployment. 'I think the Russian Federation has very well understood that NATO has . . . no ulterior motives by air-policing its airspace,' said de Hoop Schaeffer.[56] Alliance officials expected Lavrov to skip the foreign ministers' meeting and were positively surprised by his attendance. For many of the Eastern European delegates, how Russia felt scarcely mattered. Bulgarian Foreign Minister Solomon Isaac Passy was openly in tears, more than happy afterwards to recommit his country to supporting the US in the Middle East. 'Iraq needs our help,' he said.[57]

Enthusiasm for an increased NATO peacekeeping role in Iraq faded sharply as violence rose across that country. Afghanistan was now NATO's explicit top priority. 'It's better [to] succeed at one operation than fail at two,' one alliance official said. By the time NATO leaders met in Istanbul in June 2004, the alliance's aspirations in Iraq had been stripped back to a training mission.[58] By the end of 2004, there were almost twenty PRTs fanning out across Afghanistan. By 2008 that figure would reach twenty-six, roughly half run by the Americans and half by other nations under NATO. Their initial aim focused on fast-impact projects such as roadbuilding, restoring water supplies, and anything else likely to win hearts and minds. Despite some successes, many initiatives were woefully inefficient. There were reports of clinics without doctors; generators that could not be fixed; bridges washed away by the first annual flood. But Kabul was growing fast, its population rising from two million in 2001 to twice that eight years later, fuelled by international aid, NGO expansion and a returning Afghan diaspora looking to invest.[59] In the countryside, a quietly resurgent Taliban forced the postponement of elections to October. Still, when the 2002 elections came they would prove relatively successful, at least compared to those that followed. Karzai took a majority of the votes, his margin slim enough that there was little appetite among international powers to investigate claims of corruption and ballot-box stuffing.

*

Another election outside NATO's borders was about to have an even longer-lasting impact, putting Ukraine at the top of the global news agenda for the first time in the new century. Ukraine's 'Orange Revolution' was the second 'colour revolution' in a former Soviet state within two years. The first, the Georgian

'Rose Revolution' in November 2003, saw former Soviet Foreign Minister Eduard Shevardnadze ousted by pro-Western opposition leader Mikheil Saakashvili, who stormed a parliamentary session after days of protests, red roses in his hand.

In July 2004, President Leonid Kuchma shocked Ukrainians by announcing his government had dropped its aspirations to join both NATO and the European Union – a step he called 'pragmatic'. Analysts in Kyiv described it as a reaction not only to his treatment by the West at the Prague summit but also to mounting pressure from the Kremlin.[60] Kuchma's anointed successor, Prime Minister Viktor Yanukovych, widely expected to win the October 2004 election, was seen as even more in Russia's pocket. Then, in September, opposition leader Viktor Yushchenko fell ill, doctors eventually diagnosing poisoning with dioxin.[61]

Many in Ukraine blamed Russia for the poisoning. Using mobile phones and the still very clunky internet, activists described mass vote-rigging in elections, with busloads of voters taken around the country to cast their votes on multiple occasions. The result was hundreds of thousands of protesters taking to the streets and a rerun of the election.[62] The subsequent Yushchenko victory was less of a pro-democratic fairytale than its supporters hoped. But it set Ukraine back on a path towards the West. 'It's not just getting rid of Kuchma and this criminal government,' said Aleksander Zakletsky, a graduate student. 'We want to be with the West and be sure to be able to work in freedom.'[63] Such feelings were far from universal, particularly among Russian-speaking Ukrainians. A poll the following year showed 50 per cent opposed to joining the alliance.[64]

Since the start of the millennium the Kremlin had lost allies in Yugoslavia, Georgia and Ukraine – and would lose another to a 2005 'Tulip Revolution' in Kyrgyzstan. Within Russia, Putin now clamped down. Oligarch Mikhail Khodorkovsky, until 2004 Russia's richest man and chief of oil firm Yukos, was now in jail in Siberia. In 2006 journalist and Kremlin critic Anna

Politkovskaya would be gunned down in her apartment block in Moscow. Former KGB officer Alexander Litvinenko would be murdered in London that same year, struck down by radioactive poison in his tea.

But by then, NATO's attention had been firmly wrenched from Europe to the dusty mountains of southern Afghanistan. The alliance was finally going to have its chance to run the Afghan war, agreeing to take over combat forces across the country from summer 2006. It would prove challenging, bloody and controversial, and unlike anything the alliance had previously attempted.

23

Afghanistan: NATO's Longest War (2006–2010)

'A textbook case of how to screw up a counterinsurgency.'

Captain Leo Docherty, September 2006[1]

NATO's 2006 expansion in Afghanistan was a key part of the Bush administration's 'war on terror' strategy that year, which it hoped would see the US finally reducing troops both there and in Iraq.[2] As a concept, it was already hitting challenges: the year would see Iraq spiral deeper into vicious sectarian warfare and Afghan violence soar. Five years after 9/11, member nations still wanted to achieve very different things with their Afghan missions, often with further divisions between military and civilian elements.

As always, some were driven by national prestige, others by fear of what might go amiss. The Dutch parliament struggled to authorise the deployment of its 1,100-strong contingent to southern Afghanistan, divided over whether they would conduct combat operations or not. Given that the US troops they were replacing were already in action against the Taliban, that prompted an immediate row with Washington, as well as calls from Secretary General de Hoop Scheffer for his countrymen to approve the deployment faster.[3]

For Britain, due to deploy 4,000 new troops, Afghanistan provided an opportunity to demonstrate what it could do – and a chance to banish recent criticism over UK struggles to control southern Iraq after the 2003 invasion. In Bosnia in 1997 and

Kosovo two years later, the UK-led Allied Rapid Reaction Corps had won plaudits in managing highly complex deployments. Now it would take command of the entire NATO-led ISAF mission as it extended its remit across the entire country through 2006. That meant multiple NATO nations moving into areas in which they had not operated before, with stabilising Kandahar and its surroundings judged particularly vital.

To hear the British discuss the Afghan mission, an observer might have been deceived into thinking their twin focuses of the HQ in Kabul and a combat deployment into the southern Helmand province reflected a deliberate NATO strategy. Nothing would be further from the truth. Britain had wanted to send its troops to Kandahar, but Canada had got there first. Now, NATO and its leaders would find themselves effectively competing with a host of UK and other national government departments, each with very different concepts of what they wanted to achieve in the areas they were allocated. 'There were five or six different plans all going [on],' said British Brigadier Ed Butler, commanding Britain's 16 Air Assault Brigade deploying into Helmand. 'Every nation had their own development department, foreign office and security services, all having their own plans and ideas.'[4]

Such rivalry and confusion was not unknown in NATO, but Afghanistan would take it to new levels. To complete matters further, the NATO commander for the initial takeover would not be American – with all the crossovers and access that that brought – but British. In Sierra Leone in 2001, then-Brigadier David Richards, now taking over NATO operations in Afghanistan as a lieutenant general, had won a reputation as a maverick who benefited from good luck. Often out of communication with London for critical decisions, he had led a British military force that defeated Sierra Leonean rebels who threatened to overwhelm the capital, and launched a risky special forces rescue mission to free a team of captured British troops, succeeding with only one fatality. Commanding NATO forces in Afghanistan would be very different. Richards would report directly to NATO's civilian and military leadership, with the US continuing to lead its own separate ENDURING FREEDOM counterterrorism operation in parallel. From the start, it was clear there would be challenges.[5] Existing NATO agreements and plans left Richards with no significant reserves of troops for times of crisis, nor a helicopter to get himself around the country. When asked how the UK strategy integrated with that of the alliance, Richards later recalled a senior British civil servant saying, 'What NATO plan?'[6]

In May, Richards assumed command of ISAF in Kabul ahead of a phased series of takeovers that would see it extend its remit beyond the capital to more peaceful northern regions before taking command in the more violent south in August. Early signs were mixed. The next month, disagreements between Britain and US commanders in Helmand caused a thirty-six-hour delay in a major operation to clear areas that would shortly be handed over to NATO from ENDURING FREEDOM.[7] Mounting Taliban attacks, some suggested, might be directly aimed at breaking NATO cohesion and the commitment of European nations. 'I think it is an attempt by the Taliban to pre-empt the changeover ... to NATO command,' said Barnett Rubin, a political scientist at New York University. 'They are trying to show that there is war in the south and that the British, Dutch, Canadian or any other forces will have to take casualties and fight, not just patrol and build schools. They hope this will have an impact on internal politics in those countries.'[8]

It was already having some effect. In July, the Belgian parliament voted against sending its troops to Afghanistan, prompting an embarrassed call from its defence chief to Richards in Kabul.[9] As NATO assumed command, officials painted it as the start of a brave new phase for both the country and the alliance. In the week after raising the alliance flag in Kandahar, attacks killed four British and three Canadian soldiers. 'Teamwork ... means people carry on with the mission,' said NATO spokesman Mark

Laity in a podcast. 'Not unaffected, but certainly equally determined.'[10] In fact, team unity was under constant pressure. SACEUR US Marine General James Jones told Richards the secretary general was very 'angry' about a *Guardian* interview that talked of 'anarchy' in Afghanistan. Richards said that was not what he had said – the 'anarchy' he was talking of was the lack of coordination between NGOs and contractors. This did not appear to make matters better.[11]

Visiting Kabul in mid-2006, British Defence Secretary John Reid gave a quote that both he and the British government would spend years attempting to explain. 'We are in the south to help and protect the Afghan people to reconstruct their economy and democracy,' he said. 'We would be perfectly happy to leave again in three years' time without firing one shot.' Both Reid and his successors would attempt to explain this comment as an expression of hope rather than an expectation. Lieutenant Colonel Stuart Tootal, commanding the 3 Para battle group that represented 16 Brigade's primary combat element in Helmand, would later argue that there had been a near-complete lack of proper intelligence. 'There was a definite feeling that it was going to be a peaceable operation,' he said. 'That it was a pretty straightforward mission. Whenever anyone raised issues or concerns, the reaction was: "Oh, you're rather over-egging it." '[12] A British brigade would normally have three battle groups – roughly triple the combat force being sent to Helmand – but expectation of trouble was sufficiently light that a smaller force had been agreed.

With hindsight, the choice of Helmand for the UK contingent was probably unwise – in the days of the British Empire it had always had a reputation for fighting against the British, and those stories continued to be told into the 2000s. When one British officer asked in early 2006 how the Helmand population remembered their shared history, he was told that the British were still hated.[13] Nor was this the only complication. From 2002 onwards Pakistan's intelligence services had been reported recruiting Afghan refugees in border areas and sending them back to fight for the resurgent Taliban.[14] As fighting flared around Kandahar in April 2006, witnesses talked of new heavy machine guns and Chinese-made Kalashnikovs.[15] But not all Taliban fighters were from this hard-core element. In many areas, those fighting were locals, raised by tribal leaders to drive out local police units blamed for corruption, extortion and sexual assaults.[16]

NATO's strategy to expand the police force would always struggle. One early British patrol in Helmand found itself attacked by the very police they were supposed to support, apparently because they believed the NATO troops had come to take their opium stocks. Meeting Afghan police in the summer of 2006, British parachute Major Adam Jowett found them dishevelled and high on drugs, their officers nowhere to be found. Desertion rates were rising. To complicate matters further, although they did not understand it at the time the British were also facing fighters loyal to the former governor of Helmand, Shah Mohammad Akhundzada, whom British officials had fired from his role for his alleged involvement in the opium trade. His replacement as provincial governor, Mohammad Daoud, launched a half-hearted attempted to eradicate Helmand's poppy crop. It would prove predictably ineffective and was beset by corruption: less than 10 per cent of the annual harvest was destroyed – but at the cost of alienating local communities and farmers.[17]

NATO planners talked of relying more on economic development than firepower. But almost none of that was happening, and the fighting soon intensified, resulting in increasingly acrimonious relations between British civilian and military officials.[18] The British had planned to concentrate on the provincial capital of Lashkar Gah – still relatively peaceful – and initiate development projects that would eventually fan out into the more lawless and less developed areas. Instead, Afghan officials persuaded the British to move into Sangin and other centres in northern

Helmand. Later research by British Army officer and cultural adviser Mike Martin would conclude that the British were being manipulated by local political forces, and that the 'militants' they were attacking were often simply local rival warlords. 'The British . . . did not have enough knowledge . . . to understand who the "government" were and who the "Taliban" were,' Martin later wrote. 'The communities did not understand why British soldiers were suddenly arriving in their villages, and the British had no idea as to who their friends or enemies were.'[19]

With no plan to bring development to those areas, what the British brought instead was firepower. 'It's a pretty clear equation – if people are losing homes and poppy fields, they will go and fight,' British Captain Leo Docherty told *Sunday Times* reporter Christina Lamb, shortly before quitting the army in frustration. 'We've been grotesquely clumsy.'[20] An eventual British withdrawal from Musa Qala in October 2006 was opposed by the Americans, who saw it as a retreat for ISAF. In Sangin and elsewhere, similar deals were struck, British troops remaining on the ground but ceasing their patrols. Such agreements would collapse in 2007, with the Taliban occupying Musa Qala, many of these areas being fought over for years.[21]

*

Despite the distractions of Helmand, Richards and ISAF attempted to remain focused on their priorities near Kandahar, where Afghan Taliban had built up multiple entrenched positions enabling them to threaten the main highway to Kabul. Some officials feared that might be a precursor to an assault on the city of Kandahar itself, whose loss would be a catastrophic blow just as ISAF was getting started. MEDUSA, jointly led by the US and Canadians, was a brigade-sized operation with roughly triple the combat force of the British Helmand mission intended to break that stranglehold. Having refused to send troops to Iraq, the government in Ottawa was much more willing to resource the Afghan mission. But there had been little public discussion of how challenging it might be.[22]

The Canadians were expected to now take heavily contested ground. The offensive that began on 2 September was more organised than the British actions in Helmand, with much more allocated firepower. After an initial firefight following a Taliban ambush that lasted three hours, a US jet dropped a bomb on a Canadian infantry company which failed to explode. The next morning, a US A–10 tank-busting aircraft inadvertently strafed the same unit. Of nearly forty men in the worst-hit platoon, only eight were left standing. Survivors described the scene to a reporter as 'a kind of slow-motion horror film – bleeding men everywhere, some crawling, some moaning'. 'We were fired up and ready to go and suddenly my platoon was in ruins,' said Private Greg Bird.[23] On the first day of the offensive, a British Nimrod surveillance aircraft also crashed, killing fourteen, and officials in Whitehall warned another major incident could end UK public's already flagging appetite for the war.

When NATO ambassadors visited a few days later, Canadian commander Brigadier General David Fraser presented what ISAF commander Richards called a 'bleak picture, factually correct but oversold and likely to . . . frighten rather than encourage nations'. Richards expressed disappointment that both the Canadian commander and his government were not prepared to continue the attack. The following days brought a change of heart and a renewed Canadian push forward.[24] 'What was at stake was our credibility in the international community, our credibility as a NATO fighting force, NATO's credibility, the government's credibility and the reputation of Canadian Armed Forces,' Fraser later wrote.[25]

US forces were called in to help. Their commander, Colonel Stephen Williams, was tasked with attacking Taliban positions around a tiny cluster of villages named Pashmul on 12 September, near where the Canadians had been hit. For six days they blasted his favourite song – AC/DC's 'Back in Black' – covering the noise of armoured vehicles crossing the river in order to charge through cornfields to the Taliban bunkers. The Taliban fighting positions were sophisticated for a guerrilla war, covered with metal roofs and ventilation pipes to protect from shelling – but the firepower deployed by the alliance had been deliberately overwhelming. The Taliban had used the village school – built with US aid money – as a weapons store. It lay in ruins, struck by US jets during the assault. Williams estimated the number of dead Taliban fighters at 150 to 200 after ten days of fighting, including seven or eight senior commanders. NATO forces had dropped leaflets beforehand telling inhabitants to leave the area, but UN and Afghan authorities said forty to fifty civilians were killed.[26]

The cost to the Canadians had also been high, particularly for the initial troops caught up in the burst of 'friendly' fire – a journalist who visited them immediately afterwards described some of them as 'emotional wrecks, too fragile to speak of what transpired. Others leak anger from every pore.' But most wanted to keep going. 'Now that your friends died, you don't want to walk away for nothing,' said one turret gunner.[27] By mid-October, Canada had lost thirty-four soldiers in 2006 alone.[28] But operations around Kandahar were regarded as successful. Both British and Canadian officials were talking about 'the heaviest fighting since Korea' with an element of pride. In Helmand young soldiers and their officers were on an adrenaline-fuelled rollercoaster of excitement: grieving at the loss of comrades while simultaneously experiencing fear of being overrun and occasional guilt at the appalling damage they were wreaking on Afghan towns.

One former officer in Helmand in summer 2006 recalls a deliberate policy called 'Spike to Strike', in which patrols would be sent out to 'spike' insurgent activity so the attackers could be killed in the resulting airstrikes.[29] A British Army doctor, tasked to win 'hearts and minds' by treating the local population, complained furiously that almost all his patients were victims of allied bombs, missiles and bullets. The more junior soldiers, British Major Adam Jowett later wrote, were less likely to care, at least at the time. 'They were enjoying the fighting and the awesome display of power of exploding bombs and strafing runs. They were too young, and too detached, to consider the bigger picture.'[30]

During its six months in Helmand in 2006, Britain's 16 Brigade fired half a million rounds of small arms and 13,000 artillery and mortar rounds, losing thirty-three soldiers killed in action. Allied helicopters flew over a hundred casualty evacuations, carrying out 170 injured.[31] Recriminations would bounce around for years to come. David Richards and brigade commander Ed Butler would recount savage rows made more complex by the command chain – Richards working to NATO directly; Butler also answerable to his commanders and political leadership in Whitehall. Both Butler and 3 Para commanding officer Tootal would leave the British Army shortly after.[32]

*

Rory Stewart, a former British official and later politician who had travelled extensively in Afghanistan, concluded that the entire military attempt to 'fix' southern districts like Kandahar and Helmand wrecked what was up to that point in fact a gradually stabilising country. 'It was simply not possible for foreigners to go into southern Afghanistan and totally rebuild the political, economic and security structures,' he said, arguing US and NATO actions simply supercharged the Taliban. He believed a 'more modest mission' focused on what was already working – particularly rebuilding and economic growth in the country's north– would have worked much better.[33]

As 2006 came to an end, the rest of Afghanistan did indeed remain relatively peaceful, grabbing fewer headlines. But the consensus among commanders and officials was that more troops were needed, along with more activity and better planning – and, as in Vietnam four decades earlier, more confirmed 'enemy kills'. NATO now had some 20,000 non-US troops in Afghanistan, almost 15 per cent fewer than Richards had been promised. The US had another 21,000 personnel, some part of the NATO force, others reporting directly to US commanders. With the US forces in Iraq reaching more than 130,000, multiple NATO nations were committed in both countries, straining their armies to their limits.[34]

Having 'kicked over a hornet's nest' in 2006, Western commanders now believed only an even greater military effort could get matters back on track. In January 2007, new NATO Secretary General de Hoop Scheffer described the alliance as 'stepping up its game in Afghanistan on all fronts'. But European nations were reluctant to send more troops, so even the Polish battalion – intended to act as the 'strategic reserve' Richards had long wanted – found themselves immediately at the front.[35] At the start of February, command of ISAF passed to four-star US General Dan McNeill, who had previously led coalition forces in Afghanistan shortly after 9/11. Going forward, the NATO mission would always be led by the senior US officer in the country, which dramatically changed the dynamic as far as NATO was concerned.[36] McNeill and his successors continued to brief and liaise with the North Atlantic Council, just as Richards had, but their primary responsibility and reporting line was now to the Pentagon and White House. It significantly increased the ability of ISAF to call for US troops and made it much easier for high-value US forces in Afghanistan – such as special forces or aircraft – to serve the NATO military mission. But it significantly reduced the ability of the alliance and its leaders to genuinely shape the operations on the ground.

Reversing the previous year's losses in Helmand was now a major aim. In March 2007, ISAF launched its largest ever offensive in the province: British forces backed by troops from the US 82nd Airborne Division and overwhelming US air power (ISAF would never have its own embedded air force, and foreign jets operating over Afghanistan were commanded throughout by a US-led coalition based at US Central Command in Qatar rather than through NATO).[37] As British troops moved to retake Sangin, Helmand residents compared their even more firepower-heavy tactics to those of previous Soviet occupiers, further increasing local resistance.[38] Conflict was also spreading across the country. A new phrase was attributed to the Taliban, although its source remains unclear: 'You may have the watches, but we have the time.' The subtext was simple: the Taliban already believed they could outlast the Western allies, and as soon as NATO or the US left they would take back what they viewed as theirs. As Churchill had observed over a century before: 'Time in this area is measured in decades, not months or years.'[39]

*

By summer 2008 NATO's next commander, US General David McKiernan, had 65,000 troops from thirty-nine nations under his command – but the war appeared to be going even worse.[40] As Britain's paratroopers returned again to Helmand, new brigade commander Mark Carleton-Smith correctly predicted the Taliban would attempt to 'fix us in bases and restrict movement and then pick us off with landmines'. Britain had more troops in the province than ever before, with more fighting than at any point during the previous two years. From the headquarters in Lashkar Gah, brigade battle captains in their mid-twenties ran the battle on screens, working twelve hours on, twelve off, in a detached yet traumatising war of drone footage, strikes, observed firefights and the retrieval of dead and injured soldiers. 'Running and the gym is what stops people going mad in "Lashkatraz",' wrote journalist Sam Kiley. 'Men and women grimly drive themselves to masochistic heights of self-flagellation on rowing machines . . . having briefly forgotten the guilt, and jealousy, that goes with not being on the front line.'[41] This did not necessarily produce good judgement. Mike

Martin, serving in Helmand at the time, concluded much of the information the British Army was using to make decisions was wrong.[42]

At the beginning of September, the British were able to announce one major victory: the hugely complex moving of a 200-ton Chinese-made turbine to the hydroelectric power station at the Kajaki Dam, transported through some of the most heavily mined and attacked roads in Helmand.[43] But it would not be installed – it was instead left to rust in containers over the next decade.[44]

Helmand and Kandahar were no longer the only violent hotspots in the country. US troops were also now being sucked into other areas, including the mountainous Korengal immortalised in news stories and documentaries. With US forces split between Iraqi and Afghan battlefields, some US units found themselves spending fifteen months in the country, almost three times that of soldiers from other NATO nations such as Britain. 'I've done my killing for the week,' one exhausted US captain told a reporter after a sleepless night. He acknowledged that of the roughly twenty people he believed they had just killed, mostly with airstrikes, 'some are probably civilians . . . I'm ready to go home.' [45]

By October 2008, McKiernan and his ISAF team had concluded the rising civilian casualty rate was one of their largest barriers to success – with a tacit acknowledgement that the numbers killed might have been dramatically understated. 'Our military forces are here to protect the civilian population, not to damage them,' said McKiernan's British deputy, Lieutenant General Jonathan Riley.[46] Most national contingents were now attempting to balance what they could realistically achieve with safeguarding their forces. Carleton-Smith told his senior officers: 'If we suffer casualties for no great effect here, there could be a very great effect on the home front . . . Families will be shattered – and public support for what we are trying to achieve could fail.'[47]

Through 2008, Taliban or pro-Taliban forces entrenched themselves in rural areas around several Afghan capitals. In Kandahar, the Canadians had largely pulled out of nearby countryside, and within the city were unable to contain a prison breakout. By the following year, their control was so weak that Afghan policemen were unable to walk the streets even in plain clothes without being assassinated, while attendance at girls' schools dried up. In Ghanzi, a Polish-led battle group was reinforced to a full brigade, but the Taliban dominated everywhere outside the city.[48]

In September 2008, US Chairman of the Joint Chiefs of Staff Admiral Mike Mullen told Congress: 'I'm not sure we're winning.' The same month, Canadian Prime Minister Stephen Harper announced his forces would pull out of Kandahar by September 2011, while the British called for more US reinforcements in Helmand. In Kabul the British ambassador warned: 'The security situation is getting worse, so is corruption, and the government has lost all trust . . . Foreign forces are ensuring the survival of the regime which would collapse without them.'[49]

*

The start of 2009 brought a new US president, Barack Obama, who shared the analysis of many across NATO that the Bush administration had dropped the ball in Afghanistan by focusing on Iraq. That May, the administration announced the early release of General McKiernan and his replacement by General Stan McChrystal. He had been a legend while head of the US Joint Special Operations Command, devastating the insurgency in Iraq, and proved equally effective on his arrival in Afghanistan. As NATO's new commander on the ground, he swiftly clamped down on alcohol consumption by NATO officers in his HQ. Next, he moved to stop an overuse of firepower. Different national contingents continued to pursue different approaches in their respective areas – but as attacks against them worsened, almost all were turning more heavily to airstrikes. 'Gentlemen,

we need to understand the implications of what we are doing,'
McChrystal said. 'Airpower contains the seeds of our own
destruction.' So many mistakes had been made, he believed, that
the margin of error had collapsed. 'If every soldier is authorised
to make one mistake, then we lose the war,' he told them.[50]

McChrystal's boss in the US command chain, Central
Command chief General David Petraeus, now thought the 'war
on terror' might be endless. 'I don't think you can win this war,'
Petraeus told journalist Bob Woodward. 'This is the kind of
fight we're in for the rest of our lives and probably our kids' lives
as well.'[51] Even among those who did not believe in such a scenario, it was clear the fight would continue for years. In Britain,
David Richards's first act on becoming head of the British Army
was to declare the entire focus of Britain's land forces would be
on successive campaigns in Helmand.[52] Even as the focus of
NATO's press conferences and the NAC in Brussels increasingly switched to other topics – such as Russia's war with
Georgia, and the 2008 financial crisis – most officials at NATO's
civilian HQ and SHAPE were working on Afghanistan. Successive SACEURs remained responsible for finding new
European ISAF troops and briefing the NAC most weeks on
progress in the war. With hindsight, NATO officials at the time
would describe such briefings as far too optimistic.[53]

US and NATO officials believed several things were necessary for the Afghan situation to improve. The first, a significant
improvement in the combat capability of the Afghan army –
and its greater integration in allied operations – was already
underway, with much military activity now designed to upskill
accompanying Afghan forces. The second requirement for success, holding Pakistan to account for its support of the insurgency
and persuading it to stop, was something de Hoop Scheffer had
been pushing since 2008. It would never truly be achieved,
coming up against the commitment of successive governments
in Islamabad to maintain influence in Afghanistan through
whatever means.[54] The third – that Afghanistan's upcoming

election be seen as both democratic and successful – would see catastrophic failure. As UN and foreign election monitors watched ballots coming in, they concluded massive and often incompetent fraud had taken place. Entire blocks of ballot papers had been filled in without being taken from their booklets; others had clearly been signed with the same hand and pen. A second run-off was suggested, delayed, then ultimately cancelled. 'Everyone was just determined to continue the fiction that this is a sovereign government,' said one Western diplomat.[55]

McChrystal's efforts to get NATO forces to display what he called 'courageous restraint' also enjoyed only limited success. Media reports amplified complaints from Western soldiers on the ground, particularly after units suffered losses.[56] McChrystal's influence on foreign forces also showed its limits. Some British officers complained that the way their army approached six-month tours encouraged aggressive action: British units timetabled for deployments got heightened recruiting interest, with many soldiers judging a 'good deployment' to be one with lots of action. Commanders whose units fired large numbers of rounds were more likely to get gallantry decorations, while those who kept their sectors peaceful could expect much less recognition.[57] Meanwhile, troops from nations whose governments urged them to avoid casualties at all costs remained incentivised to reach for airstrikes and heightened firepower. In the early hours of 4 February 2009, a German commander near Kunduz called in US airstrikes on two stolen fuel trucks eight miles from a German base, worrying they could be used as mobile bombs. More than a hundred Afghans died in the resulting explosion, and despite initial claims they were mostly insurgents it rapidly became clear that this was not the case.[58]

Nevertheless, McChrystal's instructions made a difference. US and coalition troops killed 828 civilians in 2009 – but that fell to 449 in 2010, and 369 the following year (although some questioned the accuracy of those figures). Special operations raids against suspected Taliban commanders rose fivefold between February 2009 and December 2010 – accompanied by a similar uptick in drone strikes in the border areas of Pakistan.[59] NATO itself agreed a new headline strategy for Afghanistan at its summit in Strasbourg in April 2009. It committed the alliance to a multi-year, multi-pronged approach, including building Afghan security forces and civilian government capability.[60] The post-summit headlines, however, were all about limited troop commitments. 'No one will say this publicly, but we are . . . all talking about our exit strategy,' said one senior European diplomat. 'It may take a couple of years, but we are all looking to get out.'[61]

NATO's 2010 southern Afghanistan offensive, Operation MOSHTARAK – 'Together' in Dari – was both its largest yet and, with hindsight, something of a last throw of the dice when it came to major combat operations by the alliance in the country. ISAF's southern Afghanistan regional commander, British Major General Nick Carter, was determined not just to clear the Taliban from their last major urban centres in Helmand, but in doing so to demonstrate a clear narrative of a strengthening, internationally backed Afghan state delivering greater security and prosperity. Noting that most embedded journalists invariably focused their reporting on the fiercest fighting, Carter demanded British and NATO press handlers overcome their concerns over health and safety to get the BBC's security correspondent, Frank Gardner – a wheelchair user after being gunned down by Saudi militants – to the NATO operations room in Kandahar to ensure audiences in the UK, Afghanistan and globally received the 'bigger picture'.[62]

Newly stabilised areas were to receive immediate government services, with heavy weapons under tight control. It was the kind of more sophisticated approach that might have worked in 2001, 2003 or even 2006, but by 2010 it was just too late. Polling in the region showed Helmand residents were even angrier at foreign forces now than they had been before the operation. Most believed more young men were now flocking to join the

Taliban, with more than 70 per cent saying they wanted NATO forces out. The use of airstrikes and artillery alongside international efforts to stop poppy cultivation continued to be particularly unpopular.[63]

Elsewhere in Afghanistan, things looked significantly better. Despite the election controversy, US-funded opinion polls suggested the Afghan government itself was becoming increasingly popular across much of the country. The Taliban continued to gain traction in rural areas, but many people fled into the cities. In the decade to 2010, Afghanistan's urban population grew by almost 4.5 per cent per year, the fastest of any major country in South Asia.[64] As those who opposed the Taliban fled rural areas, militant control there deepened, with more areas of the map appearing to come under their control. Kandahar remained insecure, and bombings were increasing in Kabul. And yet more girls were going to school across the country, and more Afghans were embracing a globalised world that included a very different Middle East in the urban centres of Dubai and Qatar.

As 2009 turned into 2010, McChrystal enjoyed a reputation unlike any other US general – *Newsweek* described him as a 'Jedi'. But his relationship with the administration was rocky. At one stage, having publicly rejected suggestions from Vice President Joe Biden for a much lighter-touch approach with fewer troops, he was summoned to meet Obama on Air Force One.[65] For McChrystal, previously a mostly secret warrior, the media attention was something new. Around himself, the US general had gathered a team unlike that of any US or NATO commander before or since. Dubbed 'Team America', they alienated some and were praised by others, a close-knit team of senior US, UK and Afghan officials who acted as his personal 'brains trust' and advisers to help him run the war.

Then, in summer 2010, 'Team America' inadvertently ended its own service. Joined by journalist Michael Hastings for what was supposed to be a short trip – an encounter unexpectedly extended by the eruption of an Icelandic volcano and the resulting dust cloud – several of those around McChrystal were quoted being remarkably critical and disrespectful of other US officials, all quoted verbatim in *Rolling Stone* magazine. Within days McChrystal was out, replaced by David Petraeus, who moved from the Central Command role to be based in Kabul. He appeared more interested in engaging with the alliance than McChrystal had, officials said.[66] Beyond that, there was little immediate change.

A Pentagon investigation would later clear McChrystal of making any of the derogatory comments himself, although he had been present when many were made and had reportedly laughed at one in front of the reporter.[67] NATO's 'Forever War' would continue, most expected, throughout the 2010s – and the US would continue to dictate the actions of a falling number of foreign troops.

The wider world, meanwhile, was about to change rather more abruptly than anybody realised. Within months, the 'Arab Spring' would upend the Middle East, hurling NATO into another war in Libya. In Europe a more assertive Kremlin was tearing up the rulebook, ultimately drawing the alliance's attention back from distant sandy battlefields to the defence of its own borders.

Part 6:
Renewed Confrontation

24

Putin, Pirates, Cyber Attacks and Georgia (2007–2011)

'There was this idea that there had been an end of history and the priority was counterterrorism, and obviously that was wrong.'

'Central European diplomat, 2023[1]

As NATO troops fought in Afghanistan from summer 2006, Vladimir Putin's Kremlin began to be more assertive and aggressive at home and abroad. The death of political opponents and military rebuilding would be accompanied by more aggressive public statements, and a willingness to take risks outside Russia's borders.

For NATO, the Munich Security Conference in February 2007 was the chance to discuss the next 'strategic concept' for the alliance. Secretary General de Hoop Scheffer predicted success in Afghanistan would be followed by further NATO expansion, coming closer to honouring the ambitions of Ukraine and Georgia. With the NATO–Russia Council now five years old, the speech was also intended to pay tribute to a supposedly still-growing partnership with the Kremlin.[2]

Instead, Putin hijacked the summit agenda to push a very different worldview. He used his speech at the conference to rail against NATO expansion and missile defence, accusing Western forces of undermining the Russian state. Allied leaders including German Chancellor Angela Merkel and US Defense Secretary Robert Gates, as well as several members of Congress, sat through it stony-faced. US Senator Lindsey Graham described the speech as 'unnecessary bravado', while Senator Joseph Lieberman called it 'confrontational', with 'rhetoric [that] takes us back to the Cold War'.[3] In a hastily inserted paragraph in his own address, de Hoop Scheffer said he could not hide his 'disappointment' in Putin's speech.[4] US Secretary of Defense Gates attempted to dilute Putin's comments with humour: 'One Cold War was enough,' he said to laughter.[5]

Putin was not finished. As NATO foreign ministers met in Oslo on 26 April 2007, he announced that Russia would suspend its compliance with the Conventional Forces in Europe treaty, prompting more criticism from NATO and Western leaders.[6] That night, in what may not have been a coincidence, violence erupted in the Estonian capital Tallinn.

Earlier that evening, civic authorities had begun to remove a large Soviet-era war memorial from the centre of the city.[7] The response was almost instantaneous – and, Estonia's intelligence services later concluded, deliberately orchestrated. As the first workmen prepared to dismantle the statue, a crowd of up to a thousand Russian-speaking youths gathered, hurling bricks, scaffolding poles and petrol bombs. At least 300 were arrested, with dozens hurt and one civilian dead. Russian officials had warned for weeks that moving the statue would be 'blasphemy'. In Oslo for the NATO meeting, Sergey Lavrov described the act as 'disgusting', warning of 'serious consequences for our relations with Estonia'. Estonia was unapologetic – by the following day, the statue had been moved and the government in Tallinn remained defiant. As angry mobs besieged her embassy in Moscow, Estonia's ambassador had to be protected from an angry crowd. 'These actions are unacceptable and must be stopped immediately,' NATO said in a statement. With an EU–Russia summit suddenly perceived in danger, European policymakers encouraged both sides to back down. Merkel called Putin directly and spoke at least twice to Estonian Prime Minister Andrus Ansip. De Hoop Scheffer and EU policy chief Javier Solana talked with

Estonian President Toomas Hendrik Ilves. The priority, European officials said, was 'de-escalation'.[8]

As European leaders tried to calm things down, mounting problems were reported with Estonia's internet, disrupting its daily newspapers, government sites and banking. Identifying the source of the attacks was far from easy,[9] but they coincided with a suspension of rail routes from Russia – ostensibly over a need for track repairs – and a Putin speech that further intensified his anti-Western rhetoric. Without naming Estonia, he warned that desecrating war memorials was 'sowing discord and new distrust between states and people'.[10] NATO's Computer Information Systems Services Agency – the NCSA – was called in to help despite being only three years old, the incidents quickly judged the start of a long-predicted era of 'cyber warfare'.[11]

It was a pattern of behaviour the Kremlin would repeat steadily over the following fifteen years, right up to the invasion of Ukraine – escalating matters rhetorically and physically, then pulling back to reach an accommodation with the West, or at least keep relations open. It was a tactic the West would only belatedly adapt to, despite repeated calls from European states to take a tougher line with Russia. The entry of members from 2004 was already changing the alliance. New delegations to NATO from Eastern and Central Europe brought with them greater female representation and often younger, more assertive diplomats. If they had something that they wished to get agreed, these nations were more willing than older members to block alliance decisions as a negotiating tactic. A disagreement over budgets, for example, was enough to delay the deployment of NATO's AWACS aircraft to Afghanistan by more than a year.[12] With more countries wanting a say, meetings had to be run more tightly – and there was less time for alcohol-heavy lunches to deliver backroom deals.

*

As 2008 began, Kosovo declared independence from Serbia and was recognised by Western states, a move Kremlin officials warned would open a 'Pandora's box' of unintended consequences.[13] NATO leaders hoped they might soon be rid of Putin – the Russian constitution barred him from a third presidential term. But by the time he joined NATO leaders for a summit in Bucharest in March that year, it was clear he intended to simply appoint himself prime minister, moving his deputy Dmitry Medvedev into the presidency while continuing to dominate decision-making.

In his own final NATO summit, Bush was keen to get alliance agreement in Bucharest on both missile defence of Eastern Europe and membership for Ukraine and Georgia. Normally, such debates are cleared up well before the meeting. Bush, however, kept pushing the issue through to the final dinner. Germany's Angela Merkel, new French President Nicolas Sarkozy, Hungary's Viktor Orbán, Italy's Silvio Berlusconi and the leaders of the Benelux nations remained implacably opposed. The Germans and the French argued repeatedly that neither Ukraine nor Georgia was stable enough to join – and asking them would simply upset Russia. That reflected wider divisions within Ukraine – a Gallup opinion poll in May 2008 found 43 per cent of adults there viewed NATO as a 'threat'.[14]

As the NATO leaders gathered in the Romanian capital, rumours swirled that Putin had threatened to cancel what would be his first and only visit to a NATO meeting if Georgia and Ukraine had credible last-minute chances of being welcomed in.[15] That was something NATO officials were desperate to avoid – also on the agenda was a critical plan for supplies for NATO forces in Afghanistan to move through Russian territory.[16] Putin came and the deal was struck. But the decision to simultaneously open the door to Ukraine and Georgia, while denying a practical path to membership, infuriated Russia anyway – and, at least with hindsight, left the former Soviet states largely unprotected. In a private meeting in Bucharest,

Putin was reported to have told Bush that he didn't see Ukraine as a 'real nation state'. In his public speech to NATO members Putin described any future NATO membership for Ukraine and Georgia as a 'direct threat' to Russia and again cast doubt on the sovereignty of Ukraine, suggesting many Ukrainians – particularly in Crimea – were actually 'Russians'.[17] It was, of course, a sign of things to come – but it would be Georgia that would first find itself under direct threat.

*

The exact order of events that led to the five-day Russian war with Georgia in August 2008 remains shrouded in confusion and controversy, each side still blaming the other. Ever since the fall of the Soviet Union in 1991, sizeable Russian-speaking areas of the northern Georgian provinces of South Ossetia and Abkhazia had been under the control of separatists loyal to Moscow and protected by Russian troops. The result was referred to as a 'frozen conflict', itself complicating any efforts to bring Georgia into NATO. As the US and most other Western states recognised Kosovo as independent on 18 February 2008, Russia's parliament suggested both South Ossetia and Abkhazia deserved similar independence from the Georgian state.[18] From that point, tensions began to rise, along with speculation of a potential Russian military intervention.

According to Georgia, in the early hours of 7 August, Russian-backed separatist forces in South Ossetia began a major artillery barrage as a precursor to moving deeper into Georgian territory. Georgian Foreign Minister Eka Tkeshelashvili called US Deputy Secretary of State Matthew Bryza, informing him the Tblisi government believed it was about to be attacked. Acting on instructions from more senior US officials, Bryza made it clear Washington advised against any Georgian military action against the Russian forces. 'We have to defend our villages,' replied Tkeshelashvili, implying that Georgian troops might launch their own attacks.[19]

OSCE monitors were soon recording multiple artillery shells hitting the South Ossetian capital, Tskhinvali, and other separatist-held territory. Monitors said they were unable to confirm any firing by Russian forces, calling into question the official Georgian government account and suggesting it may have been Georgia that fired first. By mid-morning on 8 August, reports suggested advancing Georgian troops were well on the way to permanently evicting Russia and the separatists from South Ossetia entirely.[20] For a brief moment it looked as though Georgia might indeed be about to win a swift victory over the Kremlin and get Russian forces off its territory for the first time since 1991.

Putin was headed to Beijing to meet Bush and other world leaders for the opening of the 2008 Olympics. He ordered an immediate military retaliation, the first airstrikes hitting the Georgian capital Tblisi as the Olympic opening ceremony began. The speed of the response would lead some to suspect it was already well prepared. Over the following five days Russian troops briefly seized considerable parts of Georgia, then pulled back to hold the entire territories of South Ossetia and Abkhazia, considerably more than they and the separatists had controlled before. Before they did so, Russian forces made a point of weakening and humiliating Georgia's military, towing away US-built Humvees, crushing police cars with armoured vehicles and blowing up a naval vessel.[21] As blindfolded Georgian prisoners of war were paraded in the streets, the US Air Force flew several hundred Georgian troops back home from Iraq – although it is unclear whether any of those troops arrived before the fighting ceased. The Georgia war put the alliance in a difficult position. De Hoop Scheffer was quick to condemn the Kremlin, while some alliance members now wanted increased support to Georgia.[22] Overall, members were even more reluctant to allow Georgia to enter NATO, particularly as several privately believed it had been Georgia's actions that had sparked the war. Either way, there was now no appetite at all to admit a country that could find itself so readily at war with Putin's Kremlin. As one analyst put it: 'Russia has successfully burnt Georgia's NATO card.'[23]

In September, NAC ambassadors visited Tblisi to see the damage caused by Russian attacks. Alongside increased support to Georgia from individual nations, a new Georgia–NATO Commission was created. Multiple alliance members pledged to rethink their relationship with the Kremlin – but little really changed.[24] According to US officials, long-range Russian bombers now resumed flying periodically across the North Atlantic, a return to a Cold War military posture not seen since the one-off flights that followed the Kosovo conflict in 1999.

The year 2008, de Hoop Scheffer told the Royal United Services Institute, had been a tough one for the alliance – both in terms of fighting in Afghanistan and events in Europe. 'These two theatres alone would seem more than one can handle at any given time,' he said. One US official warned that, after events in Georgia, NATO's most exposed members were nervous of the Kremlin in a way they had not been in years. 'I think it would be fair to say the Baltic [states] and some of the other nations are looking at Georgia and saying: "What if this happens to me?" the US official said. 'We have to build confidence there.'[25]

*

In fact, confidence in Western nations was already taking another dramatic hit. Two days before NATO defence ministers came together in London on 17 September 2008, the Bush administration decided to allow Wall Street bank Lehman Brothers to go bankrupt, prompting the largest financial crisis in human history. No NATO member would come through unscathed. Russia also saw its economic boom unravel, with the collapse in energy prices alarming foreign investors already unsettled by the Georgia war. NATO's smallest member, Iceland, faced perhaps the greatest storm, its banks holding debts many times the size of the national economy. As they and its currency collapsed at the start of October, Iceland announced it was talking to Russia about a potential bailout. It was less than two months since the Georgia war, and the announcement raised eyebrows across NATO. 'The Icelandic government will need to ask themselves and the Russians a lot of questions before they accept,' said Carlo Gallo, senior Russia analyst at Control Risks global consultancy.[26]

The shocking events of the month were far from over. Iceland's Finance Minister, Árni Mathiesen, told British Finance Minister Alistair Darling that Iceland simply did not have the money to repay millions of pounds to UK savers who had been attracted by the high interest rates of Icelandic banks. The British minister could not believe his ears. Later that night he blocked Iceland's Landsbanki from repatriating assets out of the UK using the only legal instrument available: counterterrorism legislation. Icelanders were furious.[27]

As Icelandic officials headed to Moscow for talks, whether the island would remain a Western ally suddenly felt in question. By 12 October, Iceland had been forced to open International Monetary Fund negotiations and its currency was no longer tradable.[28] But according to one rumour, the Russian ambassador in Iceland had jumped the gun in agreeing to the talks, and the Kremlin – now facing its own economic pain as oil prices collapsed– did not want to take on further financial risk.[29] By November 2008 it was clear a Russian bailout would not happen. By then NATO was preoccupied with two further questions: what to do about Ukraine, stuck in its own political and economic crisis, and what approach newly elected US President Barack Obama would take with the alliance.

As the flagship of Russia's Black Sea Fleet, the *Moskva*, returned to Sevastopol in Ukraine after blockading Georgia during the August war, crowds of Russian-speaking Crimea residents lined the dockside and chanted 'Russia, Russia, Russia.' Following the

Georgia conflict, Ukraine's President Yushchenko said protecting his country's sovereignty would require stronger Ukrainian defence and better relations with NATO – membership if possible.[30] When alliance defence ministers met in November 2008 in Estonia, the question of whether to speed up Ukrainian admission was top of the agenda. European members remained divided, Germany and France still unquestionably opposed.[31] Bush administration officials suggested both Georgia and Ukraine should join quickly. The Europeans rejected the proposal.[32]

*

Inaugurated in January 2009, Barack Obama wanted to get European allies more committed to Afghanistan and to achieve a 'reset' on relations with the Kremlin. His pre-election pledge to close Guantánamo Bay played well in Europe, with several European nations offering to assist. When it came to Russia, Obama based his strategy around engaging president-to-president with Medvedev directly, hoping to sideline Putin as prime minister.[33] Shortly after his inauguration, the new administration offered to back off on deploying missile defences in Eastern Europe if Russia would help stop Iran developing long-range weapons.[34]

Following events in Georgia, officials from Eastern and Central Europe were more aggressive in their warnings about Russia. Such concerns were only magnified by Russia's major ZAPAD exercises in its western military region and Belarus in late 2009. The scenario imagined an invasion of Belarus and nearby Russia from neighbouring Poland and Lithuania. In response, Russian forces simulated an assault into nearby NATO territory in both nations including the firing of nuclear capable ballistic missiles. Repeated rumours would allege that included at least one mock nuclear strike on NATO territory, although evidence for that remains extremely limited.[35]

According to a US diplomatic cable later leaked to WikiLeaks, the secretary general told the NAC the exercises were 'provocative and inappropriate', but that it was important the alliance did not respond in a way that would initiate a 'downward spiral' in relations with the Kremlin. Eastern and Central European delegates as well as Canada described the alliance response as weak.[36]

*

The man chosen to lead NATO into the 2010s, former Danish Prime Minister Anders Fogh Rasmussen, was determined to be a much more assertive secretary general than his predecessor. 'I am here as a reformer,' he told the *New York Times*. 'I want to modernise, transform and reform . . . In a rapidly changing security environment, we have to make sure NATO is able to make rapid moves. Otherwise NATO will not maintain its relevance.' Rasmussen was the first former head of government to lead NATO since Belgium's Paul-Henri Spaak in the 1950s. His appointment was seen by some to reflect a frustration with the more 'managerial' low-key approach of de Hoop Sheffer, and a renewed desire for more of a diplomatic 'superstar' at the top of the alliance.

There were fewer meetings, and those that did take place were shorter and sometimes abruptly to the point. National ambassadors to NATO expressed mixed feelings, some worrying they were being sidelined. At one ministerial meeting, Rasmussen even made a point of not inviting the ambassadors themselves to the evening dinner, a naked display of power seen as intended to remove any doubts who was boss. Rasmussen appointed former US Secretary of State Madeleine Albright to lead a group of twelve experts to build NATO's first new strategic concept in more than a decade. It was intended to both layout alliance priorities and showcase NATO in the world, but only after pointed and public consultation with civil society in member nations and other 'stakeholders' such as Russia. Albright and her team would report directly to Rasmussen, again leaving some ambassadors feeling sidelined.[37]

Rasmussen pledged that NATO's 'transformation' extended to rebuilding the alliance's entire command structure, moving away from Cold War structures to something much more flexible.[38] He was also explicitly supportive of the Obama-era 'reset' with the Kremlin, following the example of his immediate predecessors in keeping Russia as a partner rather than potential foe. As they built the new strategic concept, Albright's team visited Russia to persuade the Kremlin that NATO's priority was now more focused on deterring terror attacks and rogue states rather than anything based in Europe.[39]

After Obama and Medvedev signed a new nuclear arms control agreement in April 2010, Rasmussen suggested a reworked Conventional Forces in Europe treaty. Russian officials said they were open to the concept – providing the future of missile defence was also on the table. Obama had quietly agreed to drop the idea of putting US rockets in Poland and the Czech Republic. Now, Rasmussen suggested a truly joint system with the Kremlin. 'If we could build a missile defence system to cover from Vancouver to Vladivostok, Russia could see the missile shield was not a threat,' Rasmussen told reporters.[40]

NATO's focus, alliance leaders were clear, remained unquestionably 'out of area', with Afghanistan clearly top priority. The alliance now had two further significant missions east of Suez. At Iraq's military academy at Ar Rustamiyah in Baghdad, NATO trainers coordinated with Iraqi and US forces to build what they hoped would be the next generation of Iraqi commanders. As in Afghanistan, it was a partnership with the US military. Italy's Carabinieri paramilitary police also trained their Iraqi counterparts under the NATO flag.[41] From August 2009, NATO warships in the Indian Ocean also commenced operation OCEAN SHIELD, which would become a seven-year mission to protect civilian shipping from

Somali pirates.[42] What had initially been a relatively localised problem around Somali waters was now spreading across the Indian Ocean, as young Somalis on skiffs armed with boarding ladders, grappling hooks and automatic weapons became increasingly bold in attacks against commercial vessels. NATO's warships would join those of multiple other forces, waters including those of the EU, Russia, China and Iran, in patrolling the vast waters, attempting to respond to attacks as fast as possible but sometimes arriving hours after vessels had been seized.[43]

This was unlike any previous mission for the alliance – but for multinational seafarers, the NATO and other warships could prove a vital lifeline. On several occasions, crews on hijacked vessels would lock themselves in secure safe rooms deep within their ships for hours on end as armed attackers roamed the ship, hoping for a warship to scare away the pirates. Such tactics would become less effective over time, however, as those seizing realised that once they had taken hostages, foreign military forces would usually hold back.[44] By the end of 2010, the Indian Ocean piracy crisis was costing the global economy $7 billion a year and providing a ready excuse for increasingly ambitious non-Western nations to station warships across the region.[45]

Within NATO itself, one long-running division was about to somewhat be put to rest. In March 2009, President Nicolas Sarkozy announced France would rejoin the alliance's military command structure at its sixtieth anniversary celebrations the following month. That move would prove more critical than many expected, opening the door to NATO's Libya intervention two years later.

*

For all the efforts to keep relations strong, trust between the West and Russia was visibly eroding. In June 2010, the FBI broke up what it described as a significant Kremlin-controlled espionage ring operating on US soil. In the largest post-Cold War spy swap, the ten Russians detained were exchanged for four suspected Western spies in Russia – including Sergei Skripal, reported to be a former MI6 informant now offered amnesty in Britain.[46] European nations too were nervous of Russian spies. Two years earlier Estonia had been horrified to discover that the head of its National Security Agency, a former police official named Herman Simm, appeared to have been passing secrets to a Russian handler.[47] That scandal, together with the Georgia war, prompted months of ferocious lobbying by all three of the Baltic states for both NATO and the Pentagon to create credible defence plans in the event of an attack by Russia – no easy feat, given that the only foreign forces in the Baltics were four NATO air-policing jets based at Lithuania's Amari Air Base. In May 2010, several Eastern European nations concluded their own bilateral defence deals with the US separate to the alliance, worried that NATO lacked the intelligence-sharing and planning capabilities to genuinely protect them in a crisis.[48] Russia's military, meanwhile, lost no opportunity to demonstrate its extended reach and occasional disregard for life. After a Russian-flagged tanker was seized by Somali pirates that summer, the Russian Navy stormed the vessel. According to a somewhat enigmatic statement from the Russian defence ministry, none of the pirates were believed to have survived. Whether they were executed by the Russians or simply cast adrift was left perhaps deliberately unclear.[49]

Events in Afghanistan and Pakistan now gave engagement with Russia a new urgency. Convoys through Pakistan across the Khyber Pass were being targeted in Taliban attacks, raising the risk of NATO forces being starved of fuel and anything else that could not be resupplied by air.[50] That made resupply through Russia even more important. Following meetings with Merkel and Sarkozy in mid-October 2010, Medvedev announced he would attend the NATO Lisbon summit the next month. 'We are in the same boat when it comes the real threats of the 21st century,' said Merkel. Sarkozy called Russia a 'friend, a friendly country'. 'The fact that NATO membership for countries like Ukraine has been put on the backburner also helps ease tension,' said analyst Thomas Gomart.[51]

Unveiled at that summit, NATO's new strategic concept pronounced the Atlantic area 'at peace', while allies committed to ongoing engagement with Afghanistan beyond a now-confirmed end of NATO combat operations in 2014. Medvedev and alliance leaders committed themselves to a new start in relations, beginning with discussions on shared missile defence and a commitment to allow more Afghan supplies to pass through Russian territory.[52] In a joint press conference with the Russian president, Secretary General Rasmussen asserted that NATO and Russia were no longer 'threats to each other'. The missile-defence deal, Merkel said, 'could be proof that the Cold War has finally come to an end'. The Baltic states remained sceptical. So did Poland, still grieving from the plane crash in Russia earlier that year that killed President Lech Kaczyński, his wife and ninety-four others in an incident Polish officials would later blame on the Russian state.[53]

Within weeks of Rasmussen's joint press conference with Medvedev, the so-called 'Arab Spring' would kick off in Tunisia. It would bring mayhem and conflict to Libya and Syria, setting in motion a return to East–West tensions that would doom NATO and Obama administration efforts to keep viewing Russia as a partner.

25

Unexpected Revolutions (2011–2013)

'When the so-called civilised community, with all its might,
pounces on a small country . . . I do not like it.'

Vladimir Putin on Libya, April 2011[1]

Until violence began in Libya in February 2011, there seemed
little prospect of NATO being dragged into the social media-
fuelled revolts that had just toppled governments in Tunisia and
Egypt. Within NATO, there was little real appetite for another
major war. Afghanistan, Iraq and now the counter-piracy mission were already consuming more resources than many allies
wished.

In Afghanistan, Kandahar remained a top 2011 priority
for General Petraeus and his team.[2] Elsewhere in the south, a
'surge' of US troops kept up efforts to evict the militants
from some rural areas.[3] In Europe, the Afghan war was
more unpopular than ever. In January 2011, the German
parliament voted to begin withdrawing its troops from
Afghanistan later in the year, infuriating US officials. In the
Indian Ocean the NATO and associated allied counter-
piracy missions were also struggling to achieve much effect.
The first weeks of 2011 saw the greatest level of pirate activity
yet, hijackers seizing oil tankers and freighters and deploying
them as giant 'motherships' from which to launch attacks on
other vessels. By mid-February they held twenty-nine vessels

and some 600 hostages, with shipping experts warning the situation was becoming unsustainable.[4]

*

While the Egyptian and Tunisian revolutions had seen violence, at no stage had that approached anything that might start a war. Having backed Egypt's President Hosni Mubarak and his Tunisian counterpart Zine El Abidine Ben Ali for years, the US and its allies withdrew support as their positions became untenable, ushering in provisional governments that both the West and the protesting activists hoped would deliver greater democracy and accountability. But it was soon clear that protests in Libya against Muammar Gaddafi were producing violence on a completely different scale. By 22 February there were several hundred dead, with bodies lying in the streets, and Qatar-based satellite channel Al Jazeera – a major cheerleader for the Egyptian and Tunisian revolutions – reported Libyan jets and attack helicopters bombing civilian areas.[5] Whether those airstrikes ever took place has never been proven, but the reports of them helped drive demands for international action. Anti-Gaddafi rebels seized control in several cities, but broadcasts from his son Saif made it clear the regime was not going down without a fight 'to the last man and . . . woman'.[6] On 24 February the North Atlantic Council met, while in New York the US and its allies circulated a UN Security Council resolution referring Libya to the International Criminal Court.[7]

The speed of events in Egypt and Tunisia delivered a momentum for action that would have been hard to predict at the end of 2010. Ironically, some of those keenest for intervention, including France and Britain, were among those most recently associated with the Libyan leader. Italy, perhaps the country to which Gaddafi had been closest in Europe, was among the first to abandon him. On 26 February the Italian government announced it was suspending a 2008 treaty with Libya in which the Tripoli government had agreed to limit migration across the

Mediterranean in return for a 'non-aggression pact' with Rome. It was a critical move, opening the door to foreign forces using Italian bases to hit Libya.[8]

In London, a packed public meeting hosted by MPs in Parliament demanded immediate British and allied intervention. Speakers talked of creating a 'stable, democratic oil-producing country at the heart of the Middle East' – with almost no one mentioning the failure to achieve that in Iraq almost exactly eight years earlier. Political advisers talked of Libyan dissidents briefing British Prime Minister David Cameron and France's Nicolas Sarkozy, lobbying for a 'no-fly zone' that would open the door to a wider military campaign to destroy Gaddafi's troops and deliver rebel victory.[9] All eyes once again turned to Washington, where cautious senior officials warned an intervention or even 'just' a no-fly zone would be complex to implement, long-running and resource-heavy.

The Obama administration was reluctant to enmesh itself, wanting a multinational alliance-based approach for any action. That put NATO centre-stage.[10] 'Our message today is: NATO is united, NATO is vigilant and NATO is ready to act,' said Rasmussen as alliance defence ministers agreed to increase forces in the Mediterranean, adding that any action would require a 'clear legal mandate'.[11] In reality, the alliance was little more unified on Libya than it had been on Iraq. On 10 March, France became the first major nation to recognise the disorganised Libyan rebels fighting Gaddafi as the legitimate government; a step that even Britain – the next-most enthusiastic for intervention – was not yet prepared to take. US Defense Secretary Gates warned NATO's deliberations would extend to planning for a no-fly zone – 'but that's the extent of it'. German officials talked bluntly of not wanting 'to get involved in a war in North Africa'.[12]

On 18 March, with Gaddafi's advancing forces within a hundred miles of the rebel-held stronghold of Benghazi, the UN Security Council authorised 'all necessary measures' to protect civilians – with abstentions from Russia, Germany, India, Brazil and China. Even with military action potentially only hours away, it was unclear what role the US or alliance would end up taking. Britain, France and the US briefly dropped the idea of any operation being NATO-led, worried that it would look too like another purely Western intervention in an Islamic nation. Britain and France might lead it separately, some suggested, ideally in conjunction with the Arab League.[13]

In Paris on 19 March, Sarkozy, Cameron, US Secretary of State Hillary Clinton and representatives of several other nations agreed on an ad hoc 'coalition of the willing'. French jets conducted their first strikes shortly afterwards, followed by an enormous barrage of more than 130 Tomahawk cruise missiles. Almost all were fired from US ships and planes, a handful launched by Britain. The result was the near-complete destruction of Libya's air defences, with strikes also conducted against Gaddafi's troops advancing on Benghazi. Joining the offensive were Danish and Canadian jets, with other countries still deciding their involvement. While US officials suggested further American military action might be limited to hitting air defences, Sarkozy pledged to get much more involved. 'As of now . . . French aircraft are ready to intervene against [Libyan] tanks and armoured vehicles threatening unarmed civilians,' he said, saying such action was necessary to stop Gaddafi's 'murderous madness'.[14]

Ultimately, it was Italy that forced NATO involvement, warning that if the operation was not led by the alliance, it might reconsider the availability of its bases.[15] Whether NATO wanted it or not – and several key nations still did not – it was the only viable option on the table. The US had been bounced into supporting the Libya intervention through Sarkozy's unilateral action. Now it was keen to cease its coordination activities as fast as possible and hand the remainder of the war over to NATO planners.

As hard as it tried to rein in its involvement, the US

administration found itself repeatedly drawn back in. France and Britain found themselves struggling to secure the Arab support they had hoped for, with Obama forced to call at least one leader in the Gulf to ensure his nation delivered on its commitment of fighter jets.[16] On 23 March, five days into the war, the NAC agreed to take responsibility for the no-fly zone, creating NATO's Operation UNIFIED PROTECTOR. But Germany and Turkey blocked a proposal to extend the alliance's role to enforcing a parallel 'no-drive zone' to safeguard rebel areas. That move was an embarrassment to the US, which had already briefed that NATO would take over both tasks. Obama had pledged that any US involvement would pull back in 'days not weeks'. Instead, the US found itself delivering logistic and other support – including armaments and, later in the war, Predator drones – to the allied campaign for its duration.[17]

Over the course of April 2011, it became clear that removing Gaddafi would take much longer than initially predicted. As NATO foreign ministers met in Berlin, the alliance pledged its willingness to maintain operations 'as long as necessary' to safeguard civilians in the country.[18] 'As long as regime forces continue attacking their own people, we will intervene to protect them,' said Lieutenant General Charles Bouchard of Canada, NATO's operational commander for the mission. In reality, most strike missions were flown by Britain and France, with only Norway, Denmark and Canada also willing to strike targets on the ground. Other nations involved, including the Netherlands, Sweden, Qatar and the UAE, were only flying 'reconnaissance' or 'no-fly zone' missions against Gaddafi's entirely inactive air force.[19] Britain and France also found themselves delivering much of the direct coordination, particularly of strikes on the ground, in part due to worries targeting information might be leaked to Libya by sources in Italy or other nations if the entire alliance structure was involved.[20]

Throughout the war's first months, the frontline moved back and forth along Libya's Mediterranean coast. By mid-May,

Gaddafi and his son had been indicted by the International Criminal Court, and senior officials were fleeing one by one.[21] In August a loose coalition of tribal fighters from the mountain regions seized Tripoli, sending Gaddafi fleeing. On 20 October 2011 fighters finally found the man who once styled himself 'king of the kings of Africa' hiding in a drainpipe. Jerky footage showed him begging for his life – and then, shortly afterwards, dead, beaten and shot.[22]

According to a story circulating in Western intelligence circles, when Medvedev saw the footage, he was reputed to have said, 'We're next.'[23] Medvedev, however, was already being sidelined. In September, Putin had announced he would run again as Russian president in the 2012 elections, moving Medvedev either back to the prime ministership or another role.[24] Like Medvedev, he was worried Western intervention to topple autocratic rulers might become a habit and was determined to nip it in the bud. With civil war now also underway in Syria, the Kremlin made it clear it would back the regime of Bashar Al Assad to the hilt as it began a brutal crackdown that would last more than a decade.

As violence in Syria escalated in November 2011, the US quietly moved a carrier battle group into the eastern Mediterranean, raising speculation of potential US action against Assad. Almost immediately a Russian task force including its only aircraft carrier sailed for the same area.[25] The Cold War was not yet back on in earnest, but the world was clearly changing.

*

The Obama administration had no intention of being dragged into Syria if it could help it. Relieved the Libya war was over, it hoped a new government there could be supported without the need for outside forces. Having initially increased troop numbers dramatically in Afghanistan immediately after taking office, Obama hoped to step back there too, supporting a broader 'pivot' from decades of US focus on the Middle East and Europe to confront a rising China.

In June 2011, Obama had set 31 December 2014 as the last day for US combat operations in Afghanistan. Meeting in Chicago in May 2012, NATO leaders agreed to meet that timetable, bringing the conflict to what Obama called a 'responsible end' and handing most of the fighting against the Taliban to the country's own security forces.[26] The alliance was not pulling out of Afghanistan entirely. A new NATO mission, RESOLUTE SUPPORT, would continue training Afghan troops until shortly before the full US withdrawal in 2021.[27] Already, though, this was proving challenging. Western forces faced rising and demoralising 'green-on-blue' attacks, in which Afghan soldiers or police turned their weapons on US or NATO allies. By the end of 2012 such attacks were occurring at the rate of almost one a week, killing dozens of allied troops.[28] Taliban leaders talked of creating a 'golden gap' between the foreign forces and Afghans.[29] 'There's no doubt insider attacks have undermined trust and confidence,' said Secretary General Rasmussen.[30]

Throughout 2012 and 2013 the US kept up negotiations with the Karzai government, making it clear that Washington intended any post-2014 military action to be counterterrorist in nature, no longer attempting to defeat the Taliban nationwide. After years of fighting, the US now preached that 'diplomacy' and a peaceful settlement were what would finally bring peace.[31] Pro-Western Afghans voiced concern that they might be abandoned, while the Taliban mounted ever more spectacular attacks, particularly in Kabul.

A number of high-profile scandals made matters worse: the reported burning of a Qur'an by US soldiers; other US service personnel urinating on dead Afghans; and the killing of sixteen Afghan villagers by a single US soldier, Robert Bales. The NATO strategy for 2012–13 envisaged embedding Western forces in Afghan units, something that now required some allied troops to act as 'Guardian Angels', constantly ready to fire on nearby Afghan soldiers. By the autumn commanders were talking about keeping significant Western forces on the ground as no longer being 'necessary', or even justifiable. 'We can ask troops who are here to build a better Afghanistan, but we cannot ask them to expose themselves to risk for those tasks,' said UK Defence Secretary Philip Hammond. 'We can only ask them to expose themselves to risk for Britain's national security, which is what they signed up to do.'[32]

Only the Eastern and Central Europeans truly viewed their Afghan experience as a success. As Estonian Defence Minister Urmas Reinsalu told his country's troops the following year: 'Thanks to your contribution . . . everyone knows how good Estonian soldiers are in battle.'[33]

There was better news from the Indian Ocean, where 2012 saw a dramatic reduction in successful pirate attacks on larger ships, attributed to a dramatic rise in use of private armed security. The handful of deployed NATO and foreign warships, meanwhile, were sometimes able to persuade armed attackers to surrender smaller vessels without firing a shot. 'It is lovely to be able to tell the original crews from Iran and Pakistan that they are able to go home,' said the commander of a Danish NATO warship whose tour in the region had been repeatedly extended throughout 2011–12.[34]

In Europe itself, the financial crisis and fight to save the euro single currency was hurting military spending[35] – something NATO Deputy Secretary General Alexander Vershbow described as 'corrosive to the alliance'. NATO–EU relations, briefly so successful in the early 2000s, had become 'dysfunctional', he said.[36] European military shortcomings highlighted by the war in Libya were also becoming more apparent. According to US officials, the two most credible European members – France and Britain – were now struggling to even deliver the basics. Stepping up operations against militants in Mali, France found itself relying on the US for military airlift and intelligence. Britain, some Obama administration officials briefed, had reduced defence spending to the point that the US believed it should axe its independent nuclear deterrent in order to retain a credible and effective conventional force.[37] Few in NATO yet perceived Russia as any kind of serious threat. France was building two helicopter-carrying warships for the Russian Navy; Germany and Eastern European states continued to increase their dependence on Russian gas.[38] In Britain police claimed there were no signs of official Russian involvement as a string of oligarchs and Kremlin critics turned up dead.[39]

In February 2012, Putin announced a \$700 billion increase in Russian military spending, part of a dramatic effort to modernise its forces and make up for perceived shortcomings in the Georgia war.[40] The decision brought some bafflement in several alliance capitals. 'Why in the world would you actually be arming yourself for a conflict with us?' said a NATO diplomat. 'Isn't that all a monumental waste of resources?'[41] Some would later look back on the 2000s and early 2010s and wonder whether the Eastern and Central European nations should have been listened to a little earlier by other NATO nations when they warned Russia might again become a threat. 'At the time, people said, "Just because you had bad experiences with Russia in the past doesn't mean you should be worried now,"' said one Eastern European diplomat. 'But it turns out that we were right.'[42]

Throughout 2012, what had started as a popular revolution within Syria increasingly resembled not just an outright civil war, but a Cold War-style proxy confrontation. For decades, the Kremlin had armed the Assad dynasty to the teeth, giving it the ability to pulverise rebel enclaves with overwhelming barrages of artillery and bombing raids. The US and Western allies were much slower to deliver weapons, but gradually they and their Gulf allies too found themselves sucked deeper into the war, while Turkey watched nervously across its border and expressed concern that Kurdish militants and jihadist fighters – as well as the Syrian state itself – now threatened Ankara directly.

In June 2012 the shooting down of a Turkish jet near their joint border by Syrian air defences briefly looked like it might open the door to greater NATO action there. Syria claimed the aircraft was well within its airspace, while Turkish authorities said it was still within their territory. Following an Article 4 NAC meeting, Rasmussen described it as 'unacceptable' and pledged alliance support if necessary. Behind the scenes the picture was more complicated. 'Politically, the alliance is taking Turkey at its word,' said one official. In reality, officials told journalists the Turkish aircraft might have been on a spying mission over Syria.[43] Already, there was nervousness in Western capitals that a war between Syria and Turkey might swiftly drag in Russia. NATO, however, was still focused on treating the Kremlin as a partner. When foreign ministers met in April 2013, most alliance members expressed hope that Assad could be managed in cooperation with Putin and not through confrontation. 'We can all see that the situation in Syria is getting worse,' said Rasmussen, talking of the importance of 'keeping momentum' in dialogue with Russia.[44]

*

As 2013 began, the Obama administration too still hoped to achieve a permanent Russia 'reset' that would ensure lasting cooperation. In March, the US cancelled several parts of the Bush-era Europe missile shield that had so upset the Kremlin, announcing the allocated US anti-ballistic missile rockets would instead be sent to Asia to protect against North Korea. US officials suggested it could prove a turning point back to positive relations.[45] But Putin wasn't interested – and found a new way to needle the US. In June 2013, US National Security Agency contractor Edward Snowden fled to Moscow via Hong Kong after leaking large numbers of US classified files that revealed widespread US global eavesdropping.[46] Russia now offered him asylum.

The US president had finally had enough, cancelling his

scheduled bilateral meeting with Putin at the G20 summit in Saint Petersburg. Given the initial hopes of the Obama presidency, it was a significant decision. The 'reset' under Medvedev was now being abandoned – and US officials felt Putin was no longer seriously engaging with them on other levels, including on a new deal on atomic arms. 'Snowden was obviously a factor, but this decision was rooted in a much broader assessment and deep disappointment,' said a senior US official.[47]

Within a month a new crisis erupted. In August 2012, Obama had told reporters that any significant movement or attack with chemical arms in Syria would 'change my calculus'. Now reports of small-scale chemical attacks began to emerge from the frontline.[48] On 21 August 2013 a strike in the Damascus suburb of Ghouta went beyond anything seen before. Within minutes footage of writhing bodies and poisoned corpses – as well as of the munitions themselves – were circulating widely on social media. On 29 August the US government stated there was a 'high degree of probability' that chemical weapons had been used. US intelligence estimated upwards of 1,400 people had been killed, including more than 400 children. Syrian and Russian claims the attack had been executed by the opposition were considered 'highly unlikely'.[49]

As Russia and China made it clear they would block any Security Council resolution, the US and key allies – including France and Britain – suggested they might strike without one. Analysts raised comparisons to Kosovo – but this time NATO was largely sidelined. Then, allied unity took another unexpected hit. The same day the US government announced it believed chemical weapons had been used, British Prime Minister David Cameron unexpectedly lost a parliamentary vote approving military action.[50] Initially, it looked as though France and the US would still conduct their strikes. At his monthly press conference on 2 September, Rasmussen described the chemical attacks as 'inexcusable and unacceptable'. Following intelligence briefings from member nations, he said he was personally convinced the Damascus government was behind them. But any action, he said, would be for individual member states – without a UN resolution, NATO's commitments were limited to defending Turkey.[51]

Then, equally unexpectedly, US Secretary of State John Kerry and his Russian counterpart Lavrov agreed a deal to allow UN weapons inspectors 'unfettered access' to Syria's chemical weapons. The military action was first delayed and then entirely cancelled, and some wondered whether the US and Russia were again headed for more friendly relations.[52] Among Western military commanders, there was a feeling of relief. US-led attacks on Syria would have brought a real risk of inadvertently killing Russian personnel. In the eastern Mediterranean, allied warships and their Russian counterparts – as well as submarines – had been tracking each other in close proximity. Should missiles have been fired, no one really knew what might have happened next.[53]

*

NATO members nearer Russia now had their own concerns. As the worries of immediate US intervention in the Middle East faded, Russia began its largest military drills in western Russia and Belarus since the fall of the Berlin Wall. Officially, Russia's defence ministry said only 10,000 troops had been mobilised for ZAPAD 2013, but external analysts estimated more than seven times that number were involved.[54]

The alliance had its own drills ready in response. Officially, STEADFAST JAZZ – the largest post-Cold War NATO drill to date, commencing at the start of November 2013 and involving 6,000 troops – was to test the NATO Response Force's ability to respond to a crisis anywhere in the world. The scenario, alliance officials repeatedly told reporters, was not designed around any potential foe. The Baltic states, in contrast, happily presented it equally explicitly as a response to a growing Russian threat. Latvia said Russian military aircraft had approached its territory thirty-seven times in 2013 alone, compared with once or twice a year five years earlier. 'These are the first exercises where we really train to defend our territory,' said Latvian Defence Minister Artis Pabriks.[55]

With hindsight, the Kremlin was not just worried about a military conflict with NATO. It was more concerned that the alliance, and even more the European Union, were now turning parts of Russia's 'near abroad' – including Ukraine – unstoppably towards the West. As Russian officials continued to work with Western counterparts on apparently friendly terms to handle Syria, Putin and those around him prepared a major political and economic effort to retain Kremlin control of the countries around its borders.

26

The Return of War to Europe
(2012–2015)

*'Everything that has happened since 1989
has been predicated on the fundamental assumption
that you don't change borders by force, and that's
now out the window. Political leaders need to
recognise that the old rules no longer apply.'*

**Estonian President
Toomas Hendrik Ilves, April 2014[1]**

Launched in 2009, the EU's Eastern Partnership was intended
to build deeper links with six former Soviet nations – Belarus,
Azerbaijan, Armenia, Moldova, Georgia and Ukraine. By 2013,
Belarus had explicitly rejected that advance in favour of closer
relations with the Kremlin, and Azerbaijan was going slow over
a reluctance to discuss human rights. Armenia, Moldova and
Ukraine, however, agreed to sign multiple deals with EU leaders at a November 2013 conference in Vilnius. It was a move
some pundits described as a permanent embrace of Europe,
and the Kremlin would prove determined to prevent it.

In September 2013, after a meeting with Putin suspected to
have included a range of subtle threats, Armenian President
Serzh Sargsyan declared Armenia would walk away from years
of EU negotiations and join a Kremlin-run customs union with
Kazakhstan and Belarus. Protests in the capital were not enough
to reverse the decision. Next, senior Russian officials warned
Moldova it would 'freeze' under a Russian gas boycott if it

established closer ties with the EU, with key exports to Russia also suddenly blocked. Moldova held the line – as, perhaps predictably, did Georgia. All eyes now turned to Ukraine, which European officials said was in receipt of the 'best ever' terms ever offered to a country outside the EU. In August, Russia imposed heightened customs inspections along the border, effectively halting Russia–Ukraine trade for almost a week. The Kremlin warned such steps could become permanent if Ukraine signed the EU deals, with one official warning such action could be 'suicidal'.[2]

The once unashamedly pro-Kremlin Ukrainian President Viktor Yanukovych, ousted by the 'Orange Revolution' in 2004, had clawed his way back into power first as prime minister then as president from 2010. His trade deal negotiations with the EU had taken months. Meeting European leaders in Vilnius to sign, he suddenly claimed he had changed his mind. EU officials openly acknowledged the summit as a failure, calling for a 'period of reflection' – but their statement, designed to avoid further confrontation, did not mention Russia at all.[3] NATO's comments were blander still. Rasmussen congratulated Georgia and Moldova on reaching their Eastern Partnership agreement, as well as Azerbaijan for its more limited deal.[4]

*

Western nations might be willing to give up Ukraine's membership of the Eastern Partnership to retain good relations with the Kremlin, but for many within Ukraine the rejection of the deal felt like the wrenching of their futures away from the West and a return of centuries of Russian dominance. Almost immediately, pro-European 'Euromaidan' demonstrators gathered in central Kyiv and other western Ukrainian cities, the beginnings of another 'colour revolution'. By mid-February 2014, Ukraine's pro-European protesters were clashing nightly with Yanukovych's 'Berkut' militia. After several nights of the worst violence in Ukraine since independence, European negotiators helped broker a 21 February deal in which the president agreed an interim power-sharing structure. But that unravelled overnight as Yanukovych fled Kyiv for the predominantly Russian-speaking city of Kharkiv, announcing he had been ousted in a *coup d'état*. In an echo of events in 1991, protesters and opposition politicians in the capital found themselves abruptly and unexpectedly in charge, but feared Yanukovych might try to split the country between the predominantly pro-European west and Russian-speaking east.[5]

Putin appeared to have focused immediately on a much more specific threat. For the second time in a decade pro-Western protesters were taking charge in Kyiv – and this time they might not be readily dislodged. If any new Ukrainian government turned the country back towards the West, Russia would lose face. But, more seriously, it might permanently lose access to the predominantly Russian-speaking Crimean Peninsula and the Sevastopol naval base. Home to Russia's Black Sea Fleet since Catherine the Great, that city and its port were critical to Kremlin access to the Mediterranean and indeed to backing Syria.

On the night of 21 February 2014, according to later official Russian accounts, Putin summoned his national security team. Firstly, Russian military forces were sent to 'rescue' Yanukovych and bring him into Russia. Secondly, military actions would be undertaken to bring Crimea directly under Kremlin control.[6] None of this was initially known in NATO or most Western capitals. As SACEUR US Air Force General Philip Breedlove spoke to Russian Chief of the General Staff Valery Gerasimov on 24 February, both expressed their 'concerns' about events in Ukraine. While Putin remained publicly silent on events, Russia's Foreign Ministry accused Kyiv of using 'dictatorial and sometimes terrorist tactics' to seize control and stifle dissent among Russian-speaking Ukrainians.[7] Within hours unexpected military movements were reported in Crimea, troops without insignia seizing key locations including government offices and the airport. Simultaneously, in Russian regions bordering Ukraine, Russia's military began a series of 'snap military drills', moving units up to combat readiness. As NATO defence ministers met the following week it became clear a land grab was underway – and that the era of rapprochement with Russia might be firmly over. In Brussels, at SHAPE and elsewhere, officials raced to come up with policies and contingency plans. 'Crimea came out of a clear blue sky,' said British General Richard Shirreff, Deputy SACEUR at the time, describing the Russian takeover as a 'hugely professional operation'. 'There was no intelligence warning.'[8]

*

By the first week of March, the Obama administration was convinced they were witnessing a Russian military intervention, but officials told journalists they still did not truly understand its scale or intent. 'There will be costs,' Obama told a hastily arranged press conference.[9] From Russia, Yanukovych called for Russian military assistance – although it was not quite clear whether he intended to return to power. As NATO foreign ministers met in an emergency session, Russia's parliament voted to use military force to protect Russian civilians in Crimea. Ukraine in turn called up its reserves, warning a full-scale invasion might be imminent.[10]

In Brussels, Poland demanded Article 4 NAC discussions on the security of its eastern flank.[11] On 5 March the alliance suspended all staff-level engagement with the Kremlin. A plan for a Russian warship to join the escort of a US chemical weapons-destroying vessel to Syria was also dropped.[12] Neither that, nor talk of crippling economic sanctions, however, appeared to deter Putin. On 16 March, Crimean authorities held a referendum in which more than 80 per cent of respondents were said to have voted to secede from Ukraine and join the Russian Federation. The move brought yet more condemnation from Rasmussen and the West.[13] Even before Crimea, NATO commanders had begun to realise they needed to focus much more on potential crisis management in Europe, holding a series of 2013 command post exercises in Latvia as well as STEADFAST JAZZ. Now, that process would accelerate.

For Eastern European states already in the alliance, NATO membership brought considerable comfort. 'It's good to be in NATO right now,' said Estonian analyst Kadri Liik, suggesting that if that were not the case they might be facing similar Russian action. In mid-March, US F–16s arrived in Poland along with F–15s in Lithuania, followed shortly by Vice President Biden on a tour of Eastern Europe designed to show unambiguous American support. US airborne early warning aircraft were now patrolling over Poland and Romania, with warships heading for the Black Sea. On 16 March cyber attacks hit multiple NATO websites, although alliance officials said no essential systems were affected. A group calling itself the 'cyber berkut' claimed responsibility, implying they were acting in support of pro-Russian Ukrainians.[14]

The NAC was divided over whether to take a tougher line. British Foreign Secretary William Hague told reporters the alliance was 'not looking at military options here – this is not a Crimean War'.[15] Critics worried such language would simply embolden an unapologetic Putin. Ukrainian officials asked for direct support from the alliance, including communications equipment, vehicles, ammunition and intelligence. Almost all activity taking place, however, remained purely bilateral. Visiting Washington in mid-March, Rasmussen was not even invited to meet the US president but described events in Ukraine as the 'gravest threat to European security since the Cold War'.[16]

By the end of March, Russia had around 75,000 personnel mobilised along the border. SACEUR Breedlove suggested they might be intending a full-scale invasion, punching all the way across Ukraine to link up with Russia's 'peacekeepers' in Moldova's Transdneistr region. Ukraine was prepared for war, and accused the Kremlin of stirring up discontent and violence in Russian-speaking eastern districts, particularly Donbass and Luhansk.[17] NATO had expected 2014 to be dominated by the end of combat operations in Afghanistan, counterterrorism and cyber security. Suddenly, it was obvious its focus was about to shift back, perhaps permanently, to Russia. The Baltic states and Poland made it clear they wanted the permanent presence of alliance ground forces on their soil. Their irritation at the slow pace of alliance action was becoming unmistakable. 'The pace of NATO increasing its military presence for sure could be faster,' said Polish Prime Minister Donald Tusk.[18]

But the overall direction was becoming obvious. The US would bolster its presence in Eastern Europe, and in time other European allies would follow suit. Ukraine would receive additional support, but nothing that would decisively change the conflict on the ground. 'The American people are not going to war with Russia over Ukraine,' said one senior US official.[19]

NATO's foreign ministers instructed the SACEUR to plan to increase alliance military activity in Eastern Europe from the end of April 2014.[20] Most of the initial 'boots on the ground' would prove to be American, showing for the umpteenth time in NATO history that only the US could truly act at speed. First to deploy would be 600 US paratroopers from the 173rd Infantry Brigade Combat Team based in Italy, split into 150-troop detachments and spread across the Baltic states and Poland by the end of April.[21] By the start of May ships from NATO's Standing Maritime Force were also in the Baltic, joined by several thousand troops from across the alliance for the Estonia-based STEADFAST JAVELIN drill that continued into June. The exercise had been planned before the annexation of Crimea, but was made much larger afterwards, involving more than 600 foreign troops, a handful of US M1A2 Abrams tanks, four British Eurofighter Typhoons and several US A–10 tank busters, the latter demonstrating their ability to take off and land from Eastern European roads.[22] The overarching message was intended to be unequivocal: if push came to shove, NATO – and particularly the US – would fight to keep the Baltics free. Their governments demanded nothing less, even as some analysts raised doubts over how credible a defence the West could put up in the event of a surprise attack.

Clashes now began in eastern Ukraine, with troops loyal to the new government in Kyiv struggling against Russian-speaking separatist fighters they suspected were being reinforced by regular Russian troops. Larger Russian forces remained poised on the Russian side of the border, some crossing into Ukrainian territory to support the new 'separatist republics'. By early summer, fighting was brutal and widespread across areas of eastern Ukraine.

In early June 2014, the US announced it was deploying teams of special forces to each Baltic state – although the Pentagon was keen to stress that this was a 'persistent' rather than 'permanent' presence so as not to violate the 1997 NATO–Russia Founding Act.[23] Then, on 14 July, a Russian-made Buk missile launcher inadvertently shot down Malaysia Airlines flight MH17, killing all 298 onboard. Pro-Kremlin media denied involvement, but social media researchers identified the launcher on the ground and Western governments were left in little doubt that the blame lay with Russian-backed separatists. NATO members expressed their outrage, while Kremlin propagandists would spend much of the next decade attempting to muddy the waters over who had really brought down the Malaysian plane.

Within the Baltic states, NATO's air-policing mission was enlarged to include a detachment of Danish F–16s in Estonia but it remained a largely symbolic presence.[24] A visit from Obama in Tallinn was overshadowed by the beheading of US journalist Steven Sotloff by Islamic State. Throughout the summer, the forces of ISIS had been on their own offensive across the Middle East, seizing whole swathes of Iraq and Syria. It inevitably pulled US attention back to that region, prompting some worries Europe might be ignored again. As he visited, however, Obama offered all three Baltic states the assurances they craved. 'Countries like Estonia and Latvia and Lithuania are not post-Soviet territory,' Obama said. 'You are sovereign

and independent nations with the right to make your own decisions.' International borders, Obama continued, should not be
redrawn 'at the barrel of a gun' – and if anybody tried to do so
in the Baltic region they would face 'the NATO alliance and
the armed forces of the United States of America'.[25]

From 4 September 2014, NATO leaders gathered in New-
port, Wales, to discuss the longer-term response and welcome
Jens Stoltenberg as the new secretary general. Some found the
summit disappointing, although alliance nations formally committed each member to reaching the 2 per cent of GDP defence
spending target by 2024, the first time this had been done since
the Cold War. There was also a promise from France – after
months of diplomatic pressure from its other allies – to cancel
the delivery of its two helicopter carriers to the Kremlin. New
Ukrainian President Petro Poroshenko, his troops fighting to
keep Russian forces from seizing the coastal industrial town of
Mariupol, received commitments of non-lethal aid and training, although membership was still as far away as ever. Now it
was effectively at war with Russia, the Ukrainian delegation did
not even bother to raise the topic of joining the alliance.[26]

The priority, some in NATO said, was to make sure that
the West played firmly to its strengths and was not pulled too
deeply into confronting the Kremlin. Given long enough, a
demographically weakened Russia might collapse in any case,
undermined by its ageing population, low birth rate and limited
economic prospects beyond energy. As one senior diplomat put
it: 'The longer game is almost completely in our favour if we
don't screw it up in the short term – if we don't go to war.'[27]
Eastern and Central European nations remained unconvinced.
They wanted immediate support. As the meeting concluded,
another series of drills – the hastily arranged STEADFAST
JAVELIN 2 – began in the Baltic states. In total 2,000 soldiers
from nine countries carried out drills across the Baltic states,
Poland and Germany.[28]

As they did so, Estonia accused Russia of kidnapping one of

its intelligence officials. The Kremlin claimed Eston Kohver was attempting to carry out an intelligence operation in western Russia when he was arrested. The Estonians said he had been seized from within Estonia and smuggled across the border. Mark Galeotti, Russian specialist at New York University, suggested the apparent kidnapping was 'sending a message to smaller countries of NATO along [the Russian] border that they should realise that NATO is a beast that is very good at doing one thing – responding to an overt military act . . . – but is not so good at dealing with a whole variety of other ways that Russia can bring pressure'. Keen to avoid any escalation, Estonia's National Security Adviser Eerik-Niiles Kross talked down prospects of the alliance becoming involved. 'We consider this a bilateral issue,' he said. 'This is our guy, our border, our fight. We have been dealing with the Russians for a very long time and I think we are quite capable of dealing with this one too.'[29]

Barely a week later Russian border guards in the Bering Sea detained a Lithuanian vessel they accused of illegal fishing. The detention prompted protests from both the Vilnius government and the European Union. Once again NATO appeared sidelined.[30] 'There has been no request for NATO to . . . take any responsibility for the problem,' said Jens Stoltenberg on 1 October.[31]

*

From Texas, 700 soldiers and twenty Abrams tanks now headed to Europe in the first such reinforcement of the continent by the Pentagon since 1989. 'The purpose is to be a very visible demonstration of commitment to our allies,' said Captain Jon Farmer. 'We may take slightly longer to deploy than lighter forces, but there's nothing like a tank if you really want to achieve effect.'[32]

Three days after Christmas 2014, NATO's combat operations in Afghanistan came to their official end. The Taliban described the NATO withdrawal as proof that 'the infidel powers who thought they would turn Afghanistan into their strategic colony' had been 'pushed to the brink of defeat'. Attending the flag-lowering ceremony in an indoor basketball court at the international military headquarters in Kabul, alliance and Afghan officials talked up the progress being made. From 42,000 five years earlier, there were now only 17,000 allied troops in country – and that figure was planned to fall to fewer than 13,500, including 5,000 American troops. Further fighting – and most expected plenty – would be the responsibility of the 350,000-strong Afghan security forces. In 2014 alone the Afghans had lost 5,000 personnel, almost twice the total NATO losses throughout the thirteen years of war so far.

Standing in for newly elected President Ashraf Ghani, Afghanistan's civilian National Security Adviser Hanif Atmar paid tribute to NATO forces for their efforts and their losses. 'We will never forget your sons and daughters who have died on our soil,' he said. 'We do not want or expect that you will support us indefinitely. However, we need your partnership and support now more than ever.'[33] In a written statement, Obama described it as the 'responsible conclusion' of the US-led intervention, although he acknowledged the country was still 'a dangerous place'. Without firepower and helicopters, the Afghan commanders would continue to be pushed back. In the cities, suicide bombings were on the rise, reaching levels never seen during the war. 'Our commitment to Afghanistan endures,' pledged US General Jon Campbell, the final commander of ISAF. 'We are not walking away.'[34]

As 2015 began, so did NATO's new RESOLUTE SUPPORT training mission in Afghanistan – still led, like ISAF, by the top US commander in the country. By the middle of the year it was clear the Taliban were continuing to take territory, almost capturing the regional capital of Kunduz in the north, and only pushed back by heavy US airstrikes. Reluctantly, the Obama administration acknowledged it would not be able to withdraw troops from Afghanistan entirely by the end of his presidency in 2016.[35] Russia's focus, meanwhile, was firmly moving towards Syria.

By mid-2015 the Assad government was still losing ground, despite the mounting presence of Iranian Islamic Revolutionary Guard Corps (IRGC) fighters and advisers, other pro-Iranian militia including the Lebanese-based Hezbollah, and growing numbers of Russian mercenaries. In June, IRGC commander Quassem Soleimani visited Putin in Moscow, lobbying the Kremlin to intervene more seriously.[36] At the end of September, Russian aircraft and warships began missile strikes in support of the Assad government. They claimed to be targeting Islamic State militants, but Western officials said their targets appeared to be primarily the mainstream US- and Turkey-backed Syrian opposition.[37] Hundreds of thousands of refugees were fleeing Syria and pouring into Europe. By March 2016, NATO Supreme Allied Commander Breedlove was accusing the Assad government and the Kremlin of deliberately inciting such vast movements through indiscriminate bombing. Breedlove accused Putin directly of 'weaponising' the issue to 'break' the Western alliance.[38]

Despite the return of tensions with the Kremlin, European military spending had fallen in the three years to 2015. 'It is clear that the European Union can no longer adequately respond to Russia's demonstrations of power, so it's comforting that at least the United States is finally stepping up,' said Roman Kuźniar, a professor at the University of Warsaw's Institute of International Relations.[39] It would not remain comforting for long. Donald Trump, millionaire businessman and star of reality TV programmes including *The Apprentice*, was running for president of the United States – and he was about to develop strong feelings about the future of the alliance.

27

Enter Donald Trump (2016–2019)

*'Even discussing the idea of leaving NATO – let alone actually
doing so – would be the gift of the century for Putin.'*

Former SACEUR Admiral James Stavridis, 2019[1]

What Trump thought about NATO was not immediately obvious. On Twitter, his only mention of the alliance before he ran for office was a single 2012 tweet criticising it for not inviting Israel to a meeting.[2] In August 2015 he said he 'didn't care' whether Ukraine ever secured membership. Relations with Russia, he said, had been 'destroyed' under the Obama administration, and he implied that he would fix them.[3]

Then, in March 2016, the now-frontrunner Republican candidate gave an interview to the *Washington Post* in which he described the alliance as a waste of money. 'NATO was set up when we were a richer country,' he said. 'NATO is costing us a fortune . . . I think the distribution of costs has to be changed. I think NATO as a concept is good, but it's not as good as when it was first evolved.' Later that day he made similar comments to CNN's Wolf Blitzer at a televised town hall rally. Each time he returned to the topic, Trump doubled down. At an April rally in Wisconsin, he told the crowd: 'Here's the problem with NATO: it's obsolete. This is a big statement to make when you don't know that much about it, but I learn quickly.'[4]

Initially, senior alliance officials attempted to avoid engaging. NATO was trying to focus on Montenegro, which had just joined the alliance, and was now starting negotiations with Macedonia to do the same. NATO ministers were also discussing a potential naval mission to the Mediterranean to tackle people-smuggling, while new headquarters were opening in Eastern Europe.[5] Preparations were underway for a major Warsaw leaders' summit, which would put considerable meat on the bones of alliance efforts to shore up defences against Russia.

Politics within NATO states were clearly getting complicated. Multiple terror attacks in Europe and the refugee crisis had supercharged the right wing in several countries, as well as pushing up the odds that Britain might quit the European Union in its June 2016 referendum. Speaking to the *Guardian* before that vote, Jens Stoltenberg described a 'strong UK in a strong Europe' as 'good for the UK and good for NATO. I don't have a vote – it's up to the people of Britain to decide,' he said. But he pointed to an era of 'unprecedented security challenges, with more terrorism, instability, and an unpredictable security environment . . . A fragmented Europe will add to instability and unpredictability.'[6]

Despite dozens of similar interventions from international figures encouraging Britain to 'remain', 52 per cent of Britons voted to quit the European Union. Some of the coverage was histrionic. US ambassador to NATO Douglas Lute described the UK vote as potentially the largest 'inflection point . . . for the alliance since the fall of the Berlin Wall and the dissolution of the Soviet Union'. One senior foreign policy expert suggested the EU had been so badly damaged that NATO was 'the last European institution standing'. Days after the referendum, NATO leaders gathered in Warsaw to discuss the future defence of the alliance's eastern flank, now also looking to project post-Brexit unity in a hurry. 'Militarily, this summit will be about strengthening forces along the eastern front,' said Michal Baranowski at the German Marshall Fund. 'Politically, it's a Brexit summit.'[7]

As NATO summits go, the Warsaw meeting was as 'pre-cooked' as they come, featuring the pre-agreed announcement of four new battle groups to be based in the three Baltic states plus Poland, led by Britain, Canada, Germany and the US. Jens Stoltenberg stressed that Britain leaving the EU would make no difference to its NATO commitment, while British Defence Secretary Michael Fallon said the fact the UK would lead the Estonia deployment showed Britain 'leading' in NATO.[8] With an eye on Trump, Stoltenberg announced non-US members were finally growing their defence spending – up 3 per cent in 2016, building on a much smaller rise the previous year. 'I believe that we have turned the corner,' he said. Obama, keen to mitigate the damage Trump was already doing, told NATO members that 'in good times and bad, Europe can count on the United States'.[9]

While NATO had suspended practical collaboration with Russia, the diplomatic channel remained open – including limited meetings of the NATO–Russia Council, which met immediately after the main summit concluded, albeit only with Russia's ambassador to the alliance rather than a minister.[10] NATO leaders described the new forces moving to Eastern Europe as 'the biggest reinforcement to our collective defence in a generation' – although finding the troops had not been easy. France was rumoured to have declined the opportunity to lead a battle group, reluctant to pull too many troops from its own soil where they were fulfilling counterterrorism duties, as well as West Africa, where they were battling jihadist militants even more directly.

Less than two weeks after Warsaw, Trump repeated his criticisms of the alliance, suggesting the US might abandon some allies altogether if they had not 'paid their bills'.[11] 'We are going to take care of this country first,' Trump added, 'before we worry about everyone else in the world.' In a statement, Stoltenberg said he did not wish to 'interfere' with the US election, but added, 'Solidarity among allies is a key value for

NATO. Two world wars have shown that peace in Europe is also important for the security of the United States.'[12] Even some of Trump's fellow Republicans were appalled. Republican Representative Adam Kinzinger – a former Air Force pilot – called his words 'disastrous . . . ill-informed' and 'dangerous'. Philip Gordon, Obama's former top National Security Council aide for Europe, described it as the first time that anyone 'anywhere on the political spectrum [in the US] would question whether we would uphold Article 5'.[13]

*

The Obama administration had another worry: Russian intelligence, US officials increasingly believed, was trying to help Trump win, part of what appeared a wider strategy to polarise the West. From summer 2015 onwards, the US National Security Agency detected signs of Russian 'digital intrusions' that appeared to access voter registration rolls. In July 2016, emails hacked from a Democratic National Committee server by suspected Russian hackers were leaked to WikiLeaks. At the start of October, US National Intelligence chief James Clapper and Homeland Security Secretary Jeh Johnson officially accused Russia of trying to interfere in the US election. Barely an hour later a Hollywood website released a tape of Trump boasting that his fame and celebrity allowed him to 'grab women by the pussy'.

Neither would stop Trump defeating Hillary Clinton to win the White House on 8 November 2016.[14] Republican campaigner Steve Bannon, who worked to get Trump elected, watched the victorious candidate field calls from world leaders including Putin. 'It's finally dawning on him,' he later recalled thinking, 'that this is the real deal. This is a guy totally unprepared . . . Trump hasn't spent a second getting ready for this moment.'[15]

A major rearguard action was already underway to stop the new president destroying the alliance. From the start Eastern European governments and NATO officials made it clear to

Trump they shared his concerns over European states failing to suitably contribute on defence, and hoped they could win him over on the value of the alliance. That meant glossing over some of his inaccuracies – there had never been a system whereby member states 'pay their bills' to the alliance, and the language Trump used to describe the US–Europe imbalance would rarely be strictly accurate. That the US was taking a disproportionate amount of the weight of defending the alliance, however, nobody could deny – the US made up 70 per cent of alliance military spending. 'We understand that security is not a one-way street,' said Estonian Defence Minister Hannes Hanso. 'You can't only be a consumer – you need to do your bit.'[16]

Stoltenberg was determined to be professional. In his congratulatory note to Trump, he said he was looking forward to working with the new president.[17] In his first call with him a week later, he went further and 'thanked' him for raising the topic of defence spending during the campaign.[18] But writing in the *Observer*, Stoltenberg warned, 'Going it alone is not an option, either for Europe or for the United States.' It was as much a riposte to the European Union as to Trump. A few days earlier European Commission President Jean-Claude Juncker had been almost gleeful in his prediction that the US would abandon Europe and that a joint European defence programme – and the long-talked-of 'European army' – was the only answer.[19]

Some Eastern European nations were now voting with their wallets. According to British research firm IHS, arms purchases by the Baltic states had doubled in the three years since 2014 and were expected to increase even more markedly in the coming years. 'They are scared to death of Russia,' said US General Raymond Thomas, head of the Pentagon Special Operations Command, confirming that dozens of US special forces were now deployed in the region. 'They are very open about that. They're desperate for our leadership.'[20]

Trump's incoming Defense Secretary, former US Marine

General Jim Mattis, like Stoltenberg, told the president that he was right to push European nations to spend more on defence. 'We need to let them know that we are not going to keep telling American parents they have to care more about protecting European kids than Europeans care,' he said. But he also told him the alliance was vital, and that if it did not exist something similar would be needed. Appealing to the president-elect's sense of spectacle, he compared NATO to one of Trump's 'big tall buildings'. If it did not already exist, he told the president, then Trump would almost certainly want to build it. Mattis reminded Trump that the only time Article 5 had been triggered was when Trump's own hometown of New York was attacked – and that alliance nations 'had been bleeding' in Afghanistan.[21]

Known by his call sign of 'Chaos' or 'Mad Dog', Mattis had served as NATO's supreme commander transformation in Norfolk, Virginia, as well as commander of the Middle East-focused US Central Command – only to be fired by Obama for being perceived as too hawkish on Iran. At his congressional confirmation hearing in January 2017, Mattis gave a full-fledged endorsement of the alliance – but echoed SACEUR Breedlove in warning that the Kremlin was attempting to 'break it'.[22] Mattis and Chairman of the Joint Chiefs of Staff General Joseph Dunford wanted to assert Washington's 'bedrock commitment' to the alliance. 'You can have your NATO,' Trump is said to have told Mattis. 'But you become the rent collector.'[23] At the defence ministers' meeting the next week, Mattis made Trump's point repeatedly. 'I owe it to you all to give clarity on the political reality in the United States, and to state the fair demand from my country's people in concrete terms,' he told the alliance ministers. '. . . Each of your capitals needs to show its support for our common defence.' 'We got the message,' said one European diplomat. 'Pay up or be . . . [expletive].'[24]

*

From February 2017, some 4,000 NATO troops and more than a hundred vehicles, including artillery and tanks, began taking up positions in Estonia, Latvia, Lithuania and Poland. The deployments of the first enhanced Forward Presence battle groups at least guaranteed some positive headlines for the alliance. In the Baltic states the British-, Canadian- and German-led eFP detachments – which included representatives from the majority of other allied nations – largely replaced the US troops that had been rotated through from 2014. The US continued to lead the battle group in Poland. Troops arriving knew the mission would be very different to Afghanistan, but there was still a clear sense of excitement. Many traded copies of *War with Russia*, a speculative novel written by British Lieutenant General Richard Shirreff, who had retired as Deputy SACEUR in March 2014, worried that NATO was unprepared to properly defend its eastern flank.

The spring series of military drills across the Baltic states – as well as the NATO LOCKED SHIELDS cyber exercise in Estonia run by the new NATO cyber centre there – received worldwide coverage. 'If you want to avoid a war, prepare for one,' one female Estonian soldier told a US TV crew.[25] Within the Baltics, though, there was some disappointment that most Americans were leaving – allied to a quietly held belief that European troops could not deliver the same degree of security, or at least deterrence. But there was relief the Europeans were finally entering the game. While British, French and Danish troops largely kept themselves to their base at Tapa in central Estonia, their periodic appearances at parades in Tallinn and elsewhere were largely well received. In Estonia's eastern town of Narva, those from the Russian-speaking minority said NATO troops appeared to largely avoid the town – but a mock attack as part of an exercise by the part-time Estonian Defence League had raised tensions.[26] These, NATO officials worried, were likely to be deliberately inflamed as part of Russia's worldwide campaign

of information warfare. 'Everything east of this line is mostly
Russian-speaking,' one British major told the BBC. 'Almost
all the media they receive is Russian.'[27] US investigators were
now convinced there had been direct Kremlin interference in
their 2016 election, involving false information deliberately
spread online. In Lithuania, false rumours that a German
soldier had raped a local schoolgirl also appeared to have
been deliberately spread. 'This was a clear example of information manipulation with a sense of weaponisation,' said
NATO's Assistant Secretary General for Emerging Security
Challenges, Sorin Ducaru, suggesting the intent to be disruption
to the deployment of the eFP.[28]

NATO still had 13,000 troops providing training in
Afghanistan, as well as its much smaller mission in Iraq.[29] For
those in Brussels, however, the big event was the long-awaited
opening of the new HQ, almost two decades in the works and
expected to provide a much more comfortable home compared to the ageing 1960s prefabricated headquarters, which
would become a counterterrorism courtroom.[30] Much larger
than its predecessor, the new HQ was intended to impress.
Viewed from the air, its multiple wings were designed to
resemble the interlocked fingers of a giant hand to represent
alliance unity, while the huge glass surfaces were designed to
insulate against heat and cold and collect rainwater for use
within the building. Even Trump would call it 'beautiful'.

*

The first months of the Trump administration were not easy on
anybody, with National Security Adviser Mike Flynn forced to
resign over contact with the Russian embassy. In Brussels, Stoltenberg and his team were determined to keep the president on side
if they could. For this they had multiple willing co-conspirators
within the administration itself. As they prepared for Trump's
first visit to Europe for the opening of the new NATO HQ in
April 2017, US officials worked to get a commitment from the

president to Article 5, and were sufficiently confident to brief the *New York Times* it was coming.

On the day, of course, Trump's speech contained no such promise, instead mingling references to 9/11 and the Berlin Wall with complaints about other allies not pulling their weight. European leaders were upset, US officials were simply blindsided. Trump himself appeared to have deleted the statement recommitting to Article 5 at the last minute, sources said. 'They didn't know it had been removed,' said a senior administration official.[31] The closest he got to supporting the alliance was to promise that the US would 'never forsake the friends that stood by our side' after 9/11 – a statement White House officials attempted to argue afterwards might be an implicit affirmation of Article 5. At the joint photo session most European leaders ignored the US president, clustering instead around Germany's Merkel. According to witnesses, Stoltenberg was the only person who spoke to Trump directly.[32]

As the headlines talked of chaos, the Pentagon increased its forces in Europe through the summer – and kept talking about it as much as possible. In late July, US troops joined twenty-four partner nations in the annual SABRE GUARDIAN drills across Hungary, Poland and Bulgaria, involving 35,000 troops in total. How much of this Trump was aware of remains unclear. 'My generals are all a bunch of fucking pussies,' he told a military aide later in the year. 'They care more about their allies than they do about trade deals.'[33]

At the start of August 2017, Russia kicked off even larger military exercises than in previous years. While the Kremlin said only 13,000 troops participated, some NATO officials estimated almost eight times that figure were involved. 'Russia is reminding us that the Baltic states are relatively indefensible,' said Jonathan Eyal at London's Royal United Services Institute. 'They want to see where the cracks are in NATO and where they can be widened.'[34] The year saw further terror attacks in Britain and France, and gains for far-right parties almost across the board, although nationalist Marine Le Pen was unable to gain traction to stop Emmanuel Macron taking the French presidency that May.[35] Increasingly, Western officials talked of right-wing parties being both overtly and secretly backed by Russia. That backing involved the rollout of increasingly sophisticated campaigns of social media and internet-based disinformation, as well as Russian state media channels amplifying right-wing voices.[36] As 2017 came to a close, a truck ploughed into a Christmas market in Berlin, killing twelve, while in Iraq anti-Islamic State forces prepared for their assault on Mosul. 'NATO is stronger because the world is more unstable,' said Stoltenberg at the foreign ministerial meeting in December. 'We have lived through crises and threats and instability before.'[37]

*

The first crisis of 2018 came from an unexpected quarter. On 4 March, in the southern English town of Salisbury, former Russian spy Sergei Skripal, exchanged as part of the 2010 spy swap, and his daughter were poisoned. So, inadvertently, was a police officer. Over the following week British officials announced they were increasingly certain all had been poisoned with a nerve agent. Following a phone call with Foreign Secretary Boris Johnson on 13 March, US Secretary of State Rex Tillerson told reporters, 'This is a really egregious act. It appears that it clearly came from Russia . . . It will certainly trigger a response.'[38] Hours later, Tillerson discovered via a Twitter post that he had been fired by Trump and replaced with CIA director Mike Pompeo. Some wondered whether it was due to his comments on the poisoning; other rumours suggested Trump had finally found out that the secretary of state had called the president a 'fucking moron'.[39]

For a brief moment it looked as though Prime Minister Theresa May's government might request that NATO trigger Article 5. In her statement to the House of Commons she described the incident as an 'unlawful use of force by the Russian state against the United Kingdom', requiring a 'full and robust response'.[40] The NAC expressed 'deep concern' over what it said was the 'first use of chemical weapons on alliance territory'.[41] On 27 March, Britain, EU nations and the US expelled more than a hundred Russian diplomats, including sixty from the US, in what May said was 'the largest collective expulsion of Russian intelligence officers in history'.[42] Reports a year later would suggest Trump initially questioned Russia's involvement.[43]

At the G7 meeting in Canada in June 2018, Trump argued with almost every other attendee and refused to sign off the communiqué. According to officials, Trump repeatedly trashed NATO, calling it 'as bad as NAFTA', referring to the North American Free Trade Area he hated. He also described annexed Crimea as Russian territory because 'everyone there spoke Russian'.[44] The president wrote letters to NATO leaders who had failed to live up to the 2 per cent spending pledge, implying they might be cut off from American protection. Diplomats talked of European nations being 'scared' – no US president had tried tactics like this since Nixon, and Trump was a lot more unpredictable. Even the normally positive Stoltenberg expressed concern. 'It is not written in stone that the transatlantic bond will survive for ever,' he told reporters.

The irony, one official said, was that the alliance was otherwise having a successful year. Eight NATO nations were now spending more than 2 per cent of GDP on defence, twice the number from when Trump took office. The US was putting more military resources into Europe, requesting $6.5 billion for European activity in the 2019 budget, twice that of the Obama administration in 2016.[45] US and alliance officials were in full damage-limitation mode. As NATO leaders prepared to meet again in Brussels, they decided there would be no official communiqué, rather a 'declaration' agreed between alliance officials before Trump and the other leaders even arrived in town. While the optics were messy, there were multiple success stories from the meeting – including the invitation for Macedonia to join, establishing a new joint command HQ in Norfolk, Virginia, and a pledge to further step up quick reaction forces.[46] All Trump needed to do was stay on script.

That, of course, did not happen. With hindsight, it may have been an error to invite TV cameras to a working breakfast between Trump and Stoltenberg in Brussels on 11 July. The US president launched into a diatribe against Germany, which he said was held 'captive' by dependence on Russian gas. 'Germany is totally controlled by Russia,' he said. The awkward exchange continued for more than seven minutes before US officials called a halt to proceedings. 'This is Trump's strategy,' said one diplomat. 'He raises the stakes, then he calms things down.' The second morning, Trump turned up late to a session and shocked everyone by issuing a new ultimatum. 'He said they must raise spending by January 2019 or the United States would go it alone,' said a source. As 'panic' spread around the room, Stoltenberg asked the Afghan and Georgian leaders who were present to leave while they discussed the comments. Press conferences were abruptly cancelled.[47] While Trump failed to force allies to increase defence spending in the current year, other US suggestions – including a Mattis proposal to have thirty battalions, thirty combat ships and the same number of jet squadrons prepared for combat within thirty days across the alliance – were agreed. 'He could declare victory . . . and ride off in a blaze of glory as leader of the West,' commented former US ambassador to NATO Alexander Vershbow. 'But he's rubbing salt in the wounds.'[48]

Immediately after leaving Brussels, Trump met with Putin, the US president appearing to trust the Russian leader over his own intelligence agencies on the subject of Russian tampering in the 2016 election.[49]

*

October 2018 saw yet another 'largest NATO exercise since the end of the Cold War', this time in northern Europe and involving 50,000 personnel, 10,000 vehicles, 250 aircraft and 65 ships. More than any drill so far, TRIDENT JUNCTURE was designed to show the alliance's ability to get forces fast to vulnerable areas near Russia.[50] Dozens of military vehicles from Britain and Germany moved through Denmark, crossing the Øresund Bridge into non-NATO Sweden and then re-entering alliance territory when they arrived in Norway.[51] NATO demonstrated for the first time that it had good enough relations with both Sweden and Finland to move troops through those countries in a time of crisis – a potentially invaluable option in terms of defending the Baltic states. The exercise's conclusion, however, was dominated by an unpleasant accident. Returning to port, the Norwegian frigate *Helge Ingstad* collided with a fully laden oil tanker ten times its size, tearing open her side. The Norwegian warship drifted ashore onto rocks, capsizing as the crew of 137 abandoned ship, and was later written off entirely. The Norwegian Navy lost a fifth of its anti-submarine warfare force in a single incident.[52]

Some allies appeared better at managing Trump than others. In mid-September 2018, Polish President Andrzej Duda visited Washington DC to request a US armoured division be permanently based in Poland, suggesting the Warsaw government might pay $2 billion to make it happen and name it after Trump. 'I hope that we will build Fort Trump in Poland together, Mr President,' he told a press conference. The flattery was to prove initially effective. Asked whether he agreed with Duda over the potential threat from Russia, Trump was unexpectedly forthcoming. 'I do,' he said. 'I think Russia has acted aggressively . . . I am with the president. I feel he's right.'

Within the alliance itself, some expressed concern over the Polish request as an unnecessarily provocative breaching of the NATO–Russia Founding Act. Polish officials said the 1997 agreement was 'moot' following Russia's actions in Ukraine.[53] When Russian forces blocked Ukrainian vessels transiting the Azov Sea in November 2018, Russia attracted widespread international condemnation. The Trump administration, however, held back from the more aggressive sanctions demanded by other nations and the Kyiv government. In December 2018, US Defense Secretary Jim Mattis resigned, saying his differences of opinion with the president over how the US treated its allies were just too great.[54]

*

As 2019 began, the *New York Times* reported Trump had privately told officials several times that he wanted to pull out of the alliance altogether. What had been intended as a heads of government conference in Washington for April 2019 to celebrate the alliance's seventieth anniversary was now downgraded to a foreign ministers' meeting, in part over concerns the president might choose to quit the alliance publicly.[55] NATO and European officials engaged in a concerted diplomatic fightback. 'NATO provides reliability in an unreliable world,' wrote German Defence Minister Ursula von der Leyen. 'We will help our weakest ally just as we have helped our strongest by invoking Article 5 . . . after September 11, 2001.'[56] In Washington both sides of the aisle found themselves making a case they never believed they would need to – that the US should stay in NATO.[57]

Russian rearmament continued to accelerate. At the end of January 2019, the US pulled out of the Intermediate Nuclear Forces treaty, citing Russia's latest cruise missile as breaching its conditions. The following day Russia also quit the agreement, blaming the US for its breakdown.[58] Inadvertently or by design, it gave the alliance another opportunity to assert its unity. NATO expressed support for the US move, while also recommitting to asking North Macedonia to join, the door to its accession opened by a deal with Greece to finally recognise its name.[59] The Munich Security Conference the same month showcased divisions once again, as US Vice President Mike Pence publicly clashed with Angela Merkel over whether European states should withdraw from the nuclear deal with Iran.[60]

More harmoniously, Stoltenberg's term in office was now extended until 2022, and his years of effort to win over the US president appeared to be paying off. At the very least, the president was now saying more positive things about both the alliance and its civilian leader. 'The relationship with the secretary general has been outstanding,' said Trump as Stoltenberg visited Washington in April 2019, adding that he had supported his extension '100 per cent'. 'I think tremendous progress has been made. If you look at the charts in the different things . . . it's a rollercoaster ride down in terms of payment. And since I came to office it is a rocketship up.' Stoltenberg thanked Trump for his 'strong commitment to NATO, to our alliance, and to our transatlantic bond, and especially for your strong leadership on burden-sharing.' By the end of 2019, he said, NATO allies would have added 100 billion to their military spending since the president took office.[61]

When Stoltenberg addressed both houses of Congress the following day – the first NATO secretary general ever to do so – he was blunter about the potential dangers to the alliance and received a standing ovation that was widely interpreted as a rebuke for Trump. 'We have to be frank,' Stoltenberg said. 'Questions are being asked on both sides of the Atlantic about the strength of our partnership . . . We have overcome our disagreements in the past, and we must overcome our differences now, because we will need our alliance even more in the future.'[62] Stoltenberg avoided mentioning the latest divisive issue – a Turkish purchase of a Russian S–300 air-defence system that would shortly see Turkey thrown out of the F–35 Joint Strike Fighter programme over worries critical data would go directly to the Russian military.[63]

Within the alliance, some argued Stoltenberg was not doing enough to hold Trump or Recep Tayyip Erdoğan to account. Others, however, believed that without his relentless efforts to keep the US president engaged and happy, NATO might have been lost in its entirety. 'He saved NATO,' said one Eastern European diplomat.[64]

Early in November, France's Emmanuel Macron delivered his own criticism of the alliance, telling the *Economist* that the loss of American leadership was leading to the 'brain death' of NATO. 'You have no coordination whatsoever of strategic decision-making between the United States and its NATO allies,' he said. Europe was on the 'edge of a precipice' and must 'wake up' and begin thinking strategically as a geopolitical power, or '[we will] no longer be in control of our destiny'. Asked if he believed in the ongoing effectiveness of Article 5, Macron said he didn't know. 'What will Article 5 mean tomorrow?' he asked rhetorically.[65] The comments brought immediate and unusual criticism from Angela Merkel. Macron, she said, had used 'drastic words that [were] not my view of cooperation in NATO . . . even if we have problems and need to pull together'.[66] Arriving in London for the reorganised leaders' summit in December 2019, Trump told reporters Macron's comments had been 'very insulting'. 'That is a very, very nasty statement,' he said, dismissing France as 'not doing well economically at all'.[67]

It set the tone for another mixed summit. On a practical level, the meeting achieved most of what alliance officials wanted, also allowing them to highlight that it was now the fifth year of rising defence investment. Allies recommitted themselves to Article 5; declared space the fifth 'operational domain' for NATO alongside land, air, sea and cyber; and stepped up counterterrorism activities as well as efforts to secure energy and telecommunications infrastructure. And yet, of course, little of that made the headlines. In a throwback to previous eras, the conference agreed that a panel of 'experts' would study the current state of NATO and make recommendations – essentially, a riposte to Macron's 'brain death' comment. But the panel would not report back for almost a year.

In Washington, Trump faced impeachment hearings over his alleged threat to Ukraine's President Zelensky to make US support for the Kyiv government contingent on Ukraine investigating alleged corruption involving former Vice President Joe Biden's son. Back in London, Turkey was threatening to block the NATO defence plans for the Baltic. 'Disagreements will always attract more attention than when we agree,' said Stoltenberg. 'What we proved today is that NATO delivers on substance.'[68] As the summit came to an end, video emerged of Canada's Justin Trudeau discussing Trump, mocking him for turning up forty minutes late to his own press conference. 'You just watch his team's jaws drop to the floor,' said Trudeau, unaware he was being filmed. During his own press conference, British Prime Minister Boris Johnson claimed not to know about the video and managed without mentioning Trump at all.[69]

As NATO leaders returned home, an unidentified virus out of China was already quietly spreading in every alliance nation. By the time the pandemic eased, the world would be back in a much deeper era of great power confrontation, with the alliance suddenly seen as more vital than at any point in decades.

28

The World Crisis of the 2020s

'Honestly, the 2020s have been bonkers . . .
and we are only at year three.'

Berlin-based engineering manager
Andreas Klinger, March 2023[1]

For NATO, 2020 would prove unpredictable from the start. Three days into January, Trump ordered a drone strike on Iranian Revolutionary Guard commander Qasem Soleimani as his convoy passed through Baghdad International Airport, in retaliation for attacks against the US embassy and another US base that had killed an American contractor. NATO had 500 troops on its Iraqi training mission, divided between the Green Zone in Baghdad and the Kurdish-controlled north – but neither the alliance nor its members had any prior warning of the US action. As Iranian-backed militia vowed revenge, several contributing nations such as Canada, Germany and Croatia moved some of their personnel to safer locations, both in and outside Iraq.[2] As the Iraqi parliament voted to evict US troops entirely – and officials in Washington made it clear they would not leave – some feared renewed and heightened war.[3] When tensions eased somewhat the following month, some briefly suggested NATO might take over more operations within the country.[4] Once again, however, this would come to little – there was simply not the appetite in member capitals.

The rest of the Middle East also posed other challenges to

the alliance. Libya was now in a state of civil war, NATO's membership divided over who the legitimate government should be. In Syria, Russian and Turkish forces were increasingly at loggerheads, with Turkey again calling for Article 4 discussions at the end of February.[5]

In Afghanistan the war dragged on. Trump had ordered commanders to significantly reduce US forces from their current 12,000 troops. Some of those US forces remained assigned to the ongoing NATO RESOLUTE SUPPORT mission, which had 8,700 troops in total, while other US and foreign forces outside NATO command focused on other missions. After hefty US encouragement, Ghani's government was now openly talking to the Taliban, the ongoing NATO presence seen as one of several levers keeping Afghanistan's security forces in the game. Several European nations, however, were again openly keen to quit the country.[6] America and NATO's longest war was eighteen years old – soldiers entering service born after 9/11 were now serving in the same conflict as their fathers. Since 2001 the US had spent more than $132 billion on Afghan reconstruction – a figure, when adjusted for inflation, higher than that to rebuild Europe after World War Two. And that number did not include military operations, with the overall cost of the conflict estimated at several trillion dollars. Addressing a congressional committee in January 2020, the US Special Inspector General for Afghan Reconstruction John Sopko criticised an entire generation of allied officials, saying they had talked up success where there was none and classified inconvenient bad news or facts to keep them secret. 'The entire conflict,' Sopko said, had an 'odour of mendacity . . . and hubris . . . There is a disincentive, really, to tell the truth. We have created an incentive to almost require people to lie.'[7]

As late as 2018 some Western commanders on the ground in Afghanistan still talked in terms of decisive years and fighting seasons. By early 2020 that confidence was gone. Either the West would need to continue limited support to the Afghan government for the foreseeable future or abandon it outright. At the end of February 2020, Stoltenberg headed to Afghanistan for the signing of NATO's joint declarations between the US, Afghanistan and the Taliban, which he described as beginning to 'end decades of devastating conflict and pave the way for negotiations'. NATO intervention had achieved much, he said, including rising life expectancy and living standards, female education, falling infant mortality and growing urban prosperity. 'The challenge now is to preserve these gains,' he said.[8]

*

With intermittent fighting continuing in eastern Ukraine, NATO's new focus for the 2020s was unquestionably Europe.

With February came the first tanks, vehicles and personnel of a planned US deployment of 20,000 for America's largest show of force on the continent since REFORGER in the 1980s. The DEFENDER 2020 drill was designed to test the ability of the alliance to move large forces across Europe's rail network, as well as obstacles such as rivers. 'We anticipate there will be some snags,' said Supreme Allied Commander Europe USAF General Tod Wolters.[9] On the sidelines of the Munich Security Conference, Jens Stoltenberg managed a quick bilateral meeting with Russian Foreign Minister Sergey Lavrov. It would be one of the last face-to-face meetings for some time to come.[10] As US troops unloaded their vehicles at Bremerhaven on the North Sea coast of Germany in late February, international health officials warned that the Covid-19 'influenza' already raging in the Chinese city of Wuhan might go global. But it was already far too late: the virus was already spreading within every member state.

Northern Italy, with its network of flights between its industrial centres and those of China, would be the first seriously hit. As cases began to skyrocket, Italy started quarantining northern towns at the end of February.[11] On 7 March a US Navy sailor based in Naples became the first US service member to

test positive, with US authorities promising a thorough investigation to limit further spread.[12] By the middle of the month, the
death toll in Italy was above 2,000 and rising exponentially,
with several hundred also dead in Spain. The US, Germany,
Canada and Israel imposed partial or complete closure of their
borders, airlines cancelled flights and stock markets nosedived
on a scale not seen since the 2008 financial crisis.[13] The military
effects were similarly rapid. The Pentagon announced that
multiple exercises, including DEFENDER, were now being
cancelled or significantly scaled back,[14] while multiple other
nations withdrew troops from what they saw as non-essential
tasks around the world.

Already, the first of what would become half a million allied
military personnel were being drawn into the pandemic effort,
doing everything from driving ambulances to building field
hospitals, staffing test centres and delivering communications
and analysis.[15] Within days several billion people – the majority
of humanity – were living under tight restrictions, and it was
clear the world was entering an unprecedented era.

On Wednesday 18 March, NAC ambassadors met to discuss the crisis in an otherwise largely empty chamber. External
meetings at NATO headquarters had already all but ceased.
Many staff continued to come to work – particularly from the
national delegations – to access classified information. But they
were mostly banned from directly meeting.[16] Staff at the Brussels headquarters described the atmosphere as unreal. The next
day, Belgium joined France, Spain and Italy in declaring a total
lockdown. NATO set up an administrative taskforce for the
crisis, its first priority being to maintain operations of the headquarters and military missions overseas. At the end of the week,
Stoltenberg launched the alliance's annual report, but it received
almost no attention. 'NATO's ability to conduct operations has
not been undermined,' he said. 'Our forces remain ready, and
our work goes on.'[17] As Stoltenberg addressed the media, Kremlin and Chinese officials confirmed a virtual meeting between

Putin and Xi Jinping, agreeing unspecified cooperation in the face of the pandemic.[18]

*

As the UN called for a potential global ceasefire through the outbreak, it was already apparent the pandemic might instead increase international tensions. US National Security Adviser Robert O'Brien was already privately accusing the Chinese authorities of deliberately keeping international travel open even as they imposed domestic lockdowns. Their aim, he said, appeared to be to allow the virus to spread internationally before it spread in China, particularly to Shanghai and Beijing. 'They're attempting to take advantage of Covid to gain a geo-political advantage over the United States and the free world,' an aide later quoted him as saying, warning that the US faced a 'fight' to maintain its status and position.[19]

Whatever the reality, the West did not start the battle well. Initially, nervous countries made almost exclusively national decisions with minimal reference to NATO, the EU or any other international structures. At the end of March, Ursula von der Leyen – now European Commission president – acknowledged that the EU had 'looked into the abyss' at the start of the crisis, before then recovering some 'positivity and cohesion'.[20] For the first time since World War Two, a major global crisis was now underway in which American leadership was either lacking, unwanted or simply mocked. Trump, it had been clear from February, was extremely reluctant to shut down the US economy in an election year, before switching gear to blame the authorities in Beijing for what he called the 'China virus'.

There was no shortage of stories damaging to allied unity. Trump was reported to have offered 'large sums of money' for access to a supposed vaccine being developed by a German firm, encouraging it to move its research facilities to the United States in order to develop it 'for the US only'.[21] A French team in China, there to buy personal protective equipment, described rival American purchasers as 'hijacking' their shipment, outbidding them in cash by the airport runway.[22] Nor was the US the only culprit. Several individual European states banned exports of essential medical equipment, followed by an EU-wide mid-March decision to do the same which infuriated developing states and non-EU nations like Serbia, which immediately turned highly publicly to China for supplies.[23]

Italian Prime Minister Giuseppe Conte's government had already angrily criticised Western allies for their lack of help. Now, they approached Russia. On 21 March, Putin offered immediate support in the form of mobile disinfection vehicles and military specialists. Within hours the first Russian transport aircraft were flying across NATO air space to a base outside Rome.[24] The spectacle of Russian military vehicles thundering through Italy adorned with the slogan 'From Russia with Love' took NATO closer to its own 'abyss'. 'This is a big success story for Putin,' said one diplomat within the alliance. 'I think the Italians have fallen into a trap.' Italian officials said the country had no choice and were backed up by some other European allies.[25] 'Italian embassies all around the world have been working to find support,' said another European diplomat. 'Russia was generous enough to help out.'[26]

Russia, European officials now believed, was deliberately fanning Western divisions over Covid. European Union researchers tracked at least eighty examples of disinformation from Russian outlets in the first weeks of the pandemic. That included blaming the outbreak on US-funded biological laboratories in Eastern Europe, and early efforts to delegitimise any future vaccines. As well as making up their own stories, pro-Kremlin news and social media feeds were increasingly amplifying any conspiracy theory they could find, officials said.[27]

Chinese officials and news outlets now appeared engaged in their own efforts to muddy the waters concerning the origin of the virus. Some suggested it might have originated in the

US, spread to China by a military team taking part in a sporting festival.[28] Short-term official Western appetite to criticise Beijing publicly was limited, whether for spreading disinformation or failing to alert the world earlier about the virus. In the opening weeks of the pandemic, almost every nation still desperately needed Chinese medical supplies. NATO's Euro-Atlantic Disaster Response Coordination Centre already existed to facilitate allies supporting each other in a time of crisis. Now, it was operating twenty-four hours a day, coordinating requests for and offers of assistance. In total, around 1,500 tons of medical supplies and assistance would be transported from East Asia and between different allied nations, as well as 350 flights transporting medical personnel.[29] By late March the alliance had a solid stream of positive headlines, primarily on medical supply shipments to Italy and Spain.[30] 'Our transatlantic family has not seen an adversary like this before,' said Stoltenberg as NATO foreign ministers met for their first ever virtual meeting on 2 April. 'But I'm convinced that we will prevail together.'[31]

Russia's aid to Italy also proved less game-changing than initially feared. According to Italian newspaper *La Stampa*, the majority of supplies delivered proved unusable, and the Russian troops finally withdrew at the start of May, their deployment having achieved little.[32] As Stoltenberg met NAC ambassadors in May 2020, officials present said he expressed frustration at how the alliance had performed so far through the outbreak. Being better prepared for future waves, he was said to have instructed alliance officials, would be critical to alliance credibility.[33] Shortly after, Russian Foreign Minister Lavrov told reporters that the Kremlin was prepared to suspend military exercises in regions bordering NATO territory if the alliance would do the same. The suggestion was rejected by the alliance, with Eastern European nations, in particular, viewing it as just another gambit.[34] Predictably, that 'rejection' was amplified profusely on Russian websites, television and social media feeds.[35]

*

Throughout the first weeks of the pandemic alliance military forces around the world had essentially locked down where they were. For NATO troops stationed in Eastern Europe or Afghanistan, that meant a temporary block on going home, interacting with the local population, or anything else not immediately vital.

Over time, a degree of normality returned – troops found ways of exercising in the open, quarantine before travelling overseas became the norm, and laptops were distributed for working virtually. NATO's IT agency rushed devices all over Europe, cutting down delivery times from weeks to days.[36] Navies were particularly desperate to keep warships uninfected. Off the east coast of the US, the aircraft carrier *Harry S. Truman* – the last uninfected operational carrier in the US Navy – sailed back and forth off the coast, American commanders refusing to let her into port until they knew they could get another counterpart safely out to sea.[37] By early May, some normal service had resumed – including a foray by US Navy destroyers and a British frigate into the Arctic to 'assert freedom of navigation' and demonstrate the ability to operate despite the virus.[38]

In Afghanistan the gradual withdrawal of NATO's 15,000 troops was now underway.[39] By June 2020, US General Scott Miller – commanding US and NATO forces, but predictably taking his main cues from the US president – had pulled back the number of US troops stationed there to fewer than 9,000, with a plan to reduce them to 4,500 by the election that November. If re-elected, Trump pledged to have all US forces home by Christmas. Within Afghanistan itself officials reported that young men were flocking to join the Taliban, exactly what many had predicted once a US withdrawal was publicly announced. 'The mindset is: Americans are leaving,' said one high-ranking government official. 'The Taliban are coming today or tomorrow. Everybody is trying to align somehow with them.'[40]

NATO's June 2020 meeting of defence ministers was dominated by another dispute, this time between France and Turkey over a Mediterranean naval confrontation. French officials said Turkish warships escorting ships the French accused of arms smuggling had pointed weapons at their vessels, while the Turks accused the French vessels of dangerous manoeuvres. Two weeks later, France announced it was withdrawing from NATO's SEA GUARDIAN mission in the Mediterranean, accusing the alliance of failing to properly enforce an arms embargo and allowing Turkey to ship arms to the government in Tripoli. Tensions between Ankara and Paris continued to simmer, with Turkish authorities arresting several Turkish nationals they accused of spying for the French.[41] That was not the only row. According to the *Wall Street Journal*, Trump now wanted to suddenly remove around 30 per cent of US troops from Germany.[42] By now the more grandiose 'Fort Trump' scheme that would have seen Poland pay for US troops stationed there appeared to have broken down, and no one really knew how the redeployments might work out.[43]

Other confrontations also raising alarm included a dramatic rise in tensions between China and Taiwan, as well as war between Armenia and Azerbaijan over the disputed region of Nagorno-Karabakh. In Belarus, popular protests briefly looked like they might finally push long-standing Kremlin ally Aleksandr Lukashenko out of office, before a Russian-backed crackdown left him if anything even more dependent on the Kremlin. It had been, clearly, a year unlike any other. But of the 113 NATO-organised or affiliated military exercises scheduled to take place in 2020, well over half – eighty-eight – were able to go ahead in some form, albeit often significantly reduced, while NATO member states held more than a hundred major manoeuvres of their own.[44] These included a string of US and British drills in Ukraine, some run directly in conjunction with NATO as part of the Partnership for Peace. Their message was intended to be simple: while Ukraine might not be an alliance member, Western states would still have its back in time of war. 'Our national leaders have sent a clear message by allowing us to stand here today,' said US Colonel Michael Hanson. 'They are telling the world that by working together . . . we are partners in peace and stand ready to ensure freedom.'[45]

By the end of 2020, the World Health Organisation estimated more than three million had died worldwide because of the pandemic.[46] Another analysis a year later significantly increased that estimate, suggesting nearly 15 million excess deaths over 2020 and 2021, although how many were directly due to Covid – or, indeed, to lockdown-related causes – remains impossible to know.[47] Across the European Union, GDP fell by more than 6 per cent, a larger slump than during the global financial crisis.[48] In the second quarter of 2020, US GDP contracted by, astoundingly, almost 30 per cent, the worst crash in its history. By the end of 2021, however, it had returned to growth, and was larger once again than at the start of 2020. From one in ten Americans being out of work at the end of April 2020, its economy – and many others – now faced a worker shortage once again.[49]

NATO itself would experience a similar rebound in its fortunes – but only after the complete unravelling of its two decades of effort in Afghanistan.

*

Within NATO headquarters and a host of alliance capitals, Trump's November 2020 election defeat brought clear sighs of relief. Many, including Trump's former National Security Adviser John Bolton, believed firmly he might quit the alliance in totality if elected for a second term. Even voted out, some worried Trump might still withdraw all US forces unilaterally from Afghanistan before leaving the White House in January 2021. 'No NATO ally wants to stay any longer than necessary,' Stoltenberg said. 'But . . . the price for leaving too soon or in an uncoordinated way would be very high.'[50]

Trump left the troops in place, postponing the decision for Biden to take. But Trump's final days in office were more chaotic than even critics predicted, with almost all his senior officials resigning in the immediate aftermath of the storming of the US Capitol by his supporters. Testing the transatlantic alliance further would be among Putin's first priorities as the world re-emerged from a second winter of Covid-19 infections in spring 2021.

*

At the end of March 2021, NATO brought together foreign ministers in Brussels for the first major in-person diplomatic gathering in more than a year. It was a major logistical effort. As the summit began, twenty Polish medical personnel began giving Covid vaccines to more than 3,500 NATO headquarters staff, including those from national delegations that had not received doses from their governments, part of a plan to deliver a 'virus-free' summit of national leaders for June.[51] With the EU still lagging in its own vaccine rollouts, it was a not uncontroversial move. NATO found itself fielding questions on whether it was depriving the vulnerable of shots, while Stoltenberg was asked directly whether the US should be encouraged or forced by the alliance to show greater 'solidarity' and export its own supplies. Decisions on vaccine sharing, he said, would continue to be made bilaterally, although there was 'dialogue' on the topic within the NAC.[52]

Already, however, the virus was fading from the headlines. Within days of the March 2021 ministerial meeting, Russia commenced its first dramatic military mobilisation along the borders of Ukraine. Among Eastern and Central European nations, it was seen as a classic Kremlin ploy to test the new

Biden administration – and NATO's most exposed members in Eastern and Central Europe were not particularly happy with the results. At the end of the second week of April, after two weeks of Russian military build-up, Biden proposed a face-to-face summit with his Russian counterpart, with US officials promising the president was willing to talk tough.[53] Those more sceptical of the Kremlin, however, worried that it looked as though Russia's military posturing was being rewarded by a meeting with the president.[54]

As NATO leaders gathered in Brussels in the second week of June 2021, that looming US–Russia summit overshadowed other discussions. Criticism of Biden's decision to meet the Russian leader continued behind the scenes, although he told reporters most NATO leaders supported it. Biden, Stoltenberg and other alliance leaders were keen to present a united front – even Erdoğan was perceived as coming more on side, with the prospect of further Russian arms purchases diminished. Biden described NATO as 'critically important for US interests', referring to Article 5 for the first time as a 'sacred obligation'.[55]

The Biden–Putin Geneva meeting itself was unshowy in the extreme, the two leaders addressing the press briefly before their discussions and holding separate press conferences afterwards. Biden criticised Russian military posturing and cyber attacks, and suggested Russia would be less isolated if it improved its behaviour – but warned he was not confident that would happen.[56] Within weeks NATO's Eastern members were complaining of a new crisis on their borders: refugees from Africa and the Middle East attempting to cross into Lithuania and Poland from Belarus. Western officials accused Belarusian President Lukashenko – and, in the background, Putin – of once again weaponising the movement of vulnerable people fleeing war.[57] At the request of Poland and Lithuania several NATO allies sent engineering troops to help build barriers along the borders, while the EU lobbied airlines to cancel flights from the Middle East and Africa to Belarus.[58]

*

In Afghanistan, the endgame was approaching. For years, some had warned withdrawal could lead to rapid Afghan governmental collapse. In early 2021, the last US and NATO commander in the country, US General Scott Miller, advised that 2,500 troops was the bare minimum necessary to avoid that outcome. Biden did not believe that would be enough. During the election campaign, Biden had talked of leaving a limited force behind to concentrate on counterterrorism, the same strategy he had pushed throughout the Obama administration. Now, he was concerned that would not be enough to prevent a Saigon-like unravelling and wanted the US to leave on its own terms. 'Our presence . . . should be focused on the reason we went in the first place: to ensure Afghanistan would not be used as a base from which to attack our homeland again,' he said in April 2021, announcing that all US troops would be out by the 9/11 twentieth anniversary. 'We accomplished that objective.'[59]

Among many who had committed years to NATO's Afghan effort, the decision to give up so abruptly was unpopular from the start. Former British diplomat Rory Stewart argued that ongoing but limited US and Western support would have kept the Afghan government in power. Former British ISAF commander David Richards later expressed a similar view. But European states had neither the appetite nor the capability to continue in Afghanistan once the US left, and once that decision had been made there was no turning back.[60]

Two weeks after Biden's words the Taliban began a nation-wide offensive. By mid-June 2021, significant elements of the Afghan army and police were refusing to fight. On a single day, 21 June, eight northern districts fell, five without resistance.[61] At the start of July, a US intelligence assessment warned that Kabul could fall within six months. Within two weeks, only 650

US personnel were left in Afghanistan, primarily defending the embassy. At the end of the month, the Taliban attacked the regional capitals of Lashkar Gah, Kandahar and Herat, and it became clear even the six-month estimate was hugely optimistic.[62] 'It's true the Afghan army lost its will to fight,' said former Afghan General Sami Sadat later. 'But we ultimately stopped fighting because our partners already had.'[63] By mid-August, Kabul was choked with refugees. The Pentagon announced 3,000 troops would be flown in to protect the US embassy and airport, with a separate British evacuation mission also readied – the endgame was imminent, with the plan to have Western nations out by 31 August.

On 15 August, Taliban elements reached the outskirts of the city, and the acting US ambassador ordered the closure of the US mission. He did not tell the Afghan authorities. Nor did Ghani tell the US of his own decision to flee by helicopter to Uzbekistan later that same day. 'I would have been hanged in front of the eyes of the people of Afghanistan and this would have been a dreadful disaster in our history,' the Afghan president later said.[64] Everything the alliance had worked for was now collapsing, but this was no longer NATO's war – its trainers had by now all been withdrawn. Some NATO civilian and military staff remained in country, attempting to extract those who had worked directly for the alliance. At a press briefing on 17 August in Brussels, Stoltenberg was asked by journalists whether it was the 'worst débâcle' in alliance history. 'We are going back again twenty years,' said Afghan journalist Lailuma Sadid, pleading with him not to recognise the Taliban without solid commitments on women's rights. 'How is that possible?' she asked, almost in tears.[65]

Many veterans of Afghanistan similarly wondered what the effort had been for. The US and its allies had lost 3,812 personnel in Afghanistan over two decades, thirteen of them US soldiers killed in a bomb blast on the airport perimeter in the final days. Of those, 2,461 were American, with more than

1,000 from other NATO nations, over half British and Canadian. In several countries, veterans' welfare organisations reported a spike in anguished and desperate calls questioning the value of their service.[66] Stoltenberg described the decision to end the military presence as 'extremely difficult'. 'I share your pain, I share your frustration,' he said. 'There are lessons that need to be learned . . . and we will do that. But the main focus today is to get people out.'[67]

On 18 August, as NATO foreign ministers held their own extraordinary meeting on Afghanistan, NATO's Military Committee gathered with representatives of the other troop-contributing nations. Immediately afterwards, new Military Committee Chair and former Dutch defence chief Admiral Bauer made a personal video statement addressed to the million NATO personnel who had passed through the country. 'Doing what your democratic governments have asked you to do . . . is never in vain,' he said. 'For those who are struggling, please reach out to a buddy or a veterans' organisation to get the help you need and very much deserve . . . Your service in Afghanistan has irreversibly changed the country, just as it has irreversibly changed you.'[68] In the early hours of 30 August 2021, the last US flight left Kabul. The final soldier to board was US Lieutenant General Chris Donahue, commanding the US 82nd Airborne Division whose soldiers were the last to leave the perimeter. Within eight months he would be in Europe, one of the first additional US troops to deploy there after Russia's full-scale invasion of Ukraine.[69]

*

From the start, it was clear that both Moscow and Beijing saw the collapse of Western intervention in Afghanistan as a propaganda victory, a chance to signal to both Taiwan and Ukraine that they too would ultimately be abandoned. 'The US desperate withdrawal plan shows the unreliability of US commitments to its allies,' proclaimed the Chinese Communist Party-run

Global Times. Russian Foreign Ministry spokeswoman Maria Zakharova called it 'the result of another historic Washington experiment'.[70]

That the Kremlin was taking a tougher line on Ukraine was not in doubt. In July 2021, Putin had written a long article on Ukraine in which he appeared to question its historic right to exist. 'We will never allow our historical territories and people close to us living there [in Ukraine] to be used against Russia,' he wrote. By October, Putin was doubling down on such comments, describing Western 'military expansion' in Ukraine as a threat to Russia. Ukrainian officials reported that nearby Russian equipment set up during the Kremlin's autumn 2021 ZAPAD military drills had not been removed. Shortly after, Russian troops began once again massing again around the border.[71]

Biden's officials were determined to leave no doubt that the US and its allies would not intervene militarily to defend Ukraine. As late as November 2021, they refused to provide hand-held Stinger anti-aircraft missiles to the Kyiv government. 'The answer was: "No, that's impossible,"' Ukrainian Defence Minister Oleksii Reznikov later recalled.[72] As the US publicly warned an invasion was 'imminent' in mid-February 2022, Ukraine's ambassador to Britain admitted many of his countrymen felt 'abandoned' by the West. 'We are not a member of the family,' Vadym Prystaiko said of NATO. 'We cannot expect someone to come and save us . . . We just want to remind everybody . . . we don't want this war.'[73]

Putin was taking no chances on deterring Western intervention. As he prepared to invade in February 2022, he warned any direct foreign military intervention would lead to 'consequences they have never seen'. For anyone in doubt over what he meant, he put Russia's nuclear deterrence forces on high alert.[74] As late as 2020, there had been discussions in Germany and elsewhere of withdrawing from the 'nuclear sharing' agreement created by SACEUR Lauris Norstad under the Eisenhower administration that stored US atomic bombs in multiple NATO states for their forces to use in time of war.[75] Now, that was replaced by mounting speculation over what action the US or the alliance might have to take if Russia broke the nuclear taboo that had held since 1945 and used even a single tactical atomic weapon against Ukraine.

The speed of events had taken everyone by surprise and yet for NATO it was, of course, in many ways a return to its beginning.

Part 7:
The Road to 2049

29

From Vilnius to Washington (2023–2024)

> *'We have for ten or twenty years been telling the world about Russia. Now the world believes us.'*
>
> **Lithuanian policeman, Vilnius summit, July 2023**[1]

Lithuanians left no doubt where they stood on Ukrainian alliance membership. On the streets around the Vilnius summit, yellow and blue Ukrainian flags outnumbered those of NATO and the hosts themselves, while advertisements on the sides of buses proclaimed: 'While you are waiting for this bus, Ukraine is waiting to become a NATO member.' 'We understand that they [the Ukrainians] are fighting for our freedom as well,' said thirty-seven-year-old Vilnius resident Karolina Vitoniene, attending a pro-Ukraine demonstration with her daughter. 'Each of us remembers what it's like to live under occupation or knows the stories from their families.'[2]

With the meeting taking place barely 30 kilometres from Belarus, now reportedly home to Russian tactical nuclear rockets, the organisers had little appetite for risk. More than 1,000 troops from sixteen NATO allies were moved to Lithuania specifically for the summit. At the airport, a dozen German Patriot missile launchers were aimed pointedly towards both Belarus and the nearest Russian territory in Kaliningrad, 151 kilometres away. Along Lithuania's new boundary fence, the number of guards was tripled. The most likely threat, officials said, was an attempt to rush the border with more migrants or a display of military might. Another option was a high-profile display of the new atomic arms or further nuclear rhetoric from the Kremlin.[3]

Villagers near the border appeared more reassured than alarmed by the NATO spectacle. Sixty-seven-year-old Edvard Rynkun told Reuters neither Belarus nor Russia 'had the guts' to attack Lithuania given its alliance membership. 'If Lithuania was alone, I would feel differently,' he said. 'If not for the NATO membership, things here could already be the same as Ukraine,' agreed his neighbour.[4] For those planning the summit, maintaining that credibility was the primary objective. 'This will be a landmark, successful summit for this alliance,' promised NATO Deputy Secretary General Mircea Geoană as it opened. Its aim, he said, was to act as a 'bridge' between the initial post-Ukraine decisions of the previous year's summit in Madrid, and NATO's seventy-fifth-anniversary summit in Washington in July 2024.[5]

That 2024 leaders' meeting would likely be Stoltenberg's last as NATO chief, as well as the last of the first Biden term, coming amid a US election that could restore Trump to the White House. Meeting the secretary general a few weeks before Vilnius, Biden congratulated him on doing an 'incredible job'. 'NATO allies have never been more united,' the president told him in front of reporters.[6] In fact, of course, the preparations for Vilnius involved at least as much politicking as any other summit.

Within Ukraine itself, the second summer of full-scale fighting brought brutal, slogging battles, German Leopard tanks, US Bradley armoured personnel carriers and British Challengers entering action for the first time. Despite periodic territorial gains by both Ukraine and Russia, major frontline shifts were limited – although allied and Ukrainian officials denied it was a 'stalemate'. The strain was showing on all sides. Barely two weeks before Vilnius, Russian Wagner Group mercenaries under former Kremlin catering contractor Yevgeny Prigozhin appeared to mutiny, seizing a military HQ in Rostov-on-Don and advancing to within 200 kilometres of Moscow. What Prigozhin called a 'march for justice' appeared the most serious threat yet to Putin's rule – but the Wagner advance was halted the same day it began, following an agreement apparently brokered by Belarus's Lukashenko. That deal would supposedly see Wagner's fighters – many of them former convicts, judged to be among the most effective Russian fighters – relocate into Belarus itself. By mid-July, Lukashenko was openly using the reported presence of Wagner to taunt the alliance, claiming only his influence was holding the mercenaries back from attacking Poland.[7]

*

In the weeks before the summit, efforts intensified to resolve the Sweden–Turkey impasse. Stoltenberg's shuttle diplomacy was joined by a concerted US effort to find ways to sweeten Ankara, including pledging support to modernise Turkey's US-made F–16s. That prompted separate negotiations with Greece, which also wanted better US arms. As Biden prepared to fly to Europe, he told CNN that a package to satisfy both governments was still being pulled together. 'It's still in play,' he said.[8]

Hungary had also so far failed to ratify Swedish membership. It was one of many topics on which Viktor Orbán's administration disagreed with other members, as Orbán maintained his own dialogue with the Kremlin and Beijing. But given his budding relationship with Erdoğan, if Turkey could be persuaded to fall in line, most alliance watchers believed Hungary would follow suit. Stoltenberg had arranged a meeting between Erdoğan and Swedish Prime Minister Ulf Kristersson in Vilnius for Monday 10 July, the day before the other leaders met. The Turk appeared to throw another curveball as he arrived, suggesting for the first time that Turkey might now require progress on its accession to the European Union before granting Swedish membership.[9] But hours later, a visibly relieved Stoltenberg was able to announce a Turkish agreement to let Sweden in, provisionally at least, although the date remained a mystery. Diplomats reported a sense of caution.

'Champagne will have to wait until the ratifications are there,' the Swedish prime minister said, adding that, instead, the Swedish delegation 'gathered in a conference room and had a beer'.[10] Others were blunter. 'We avoided a wreck,' said one diplomat. 'But nothing was really resolved.'[11]

*

Papering over the differences with Erdoğan made it easier to agree the ambitious regional defence plans outlined a year earlier in Madrid. Initially requested in 2018, the more detailed updates put forward in Vilnius were now ready some twenty months earlier than initially planned.[12] They represented the most ambitious expansion in NATO's military posture since Lisbon in 1952 – albeit with similar doubts over whether they might be fully implemented.

The first covered the High North and Atlantic, coordinated by NATO's new Joint Force Command in Norfolk, Virginia. The second covered the Baltic to the Alps, led by NATO's Allied Joint Force Command from Brunssum in the Netherlands – currently under an Italian general – and regarded as the most likely flashpoint in any crisis. The third covered the south-east of the Black Sea to the Mediterranean, commanded as usual by the HQ in Naples. Both the northern and Mediterranean plans were overseen by the senior US naval officers in those regions, in many ways a return to the former Cold War structures. Each plan outlined national responsibilities in each of NATO's five 'domains' of warfare – land, sea, air, space and cyber – both for long-term defence and in the event of attack by Russia or a terror group. Instead of exercising against imaginary scenarios in the future, officials said most major future NATO exercises would be designed around these plans.

'If all the investment is made by the nations and they have the formations we ask for, we will have full executability,' said Military Committee Chairman Admiral Bauer, warning this could all take a 'considerable amount of years'.[13] For US

General Darryl Williams, commanding all US Army forces in Europe and Africa – and simultaneously 'double-hatted' as head of NATO's land forces – the Russia plans brought back memories of his Cold War days in Germany, where as a young artillery officer he knew exactly where his guns should be and what targets they might hit. 'We look forward to a time here very quickly, where we'll be able to get that kind of clarity,' he said – but he warned the demands on the three US brigades in Europe were already becoming punishing.[14]

Other forces were also getting stretched. Ever since the invasion began, the number of Russian aircraft probing Baltic airspace had risen steadily. More than fifty were intercepted by NATO jets in Estonia alone between March and July 2023, the most active the two sides had ever been. 'I am expecting a lot of work,' said Spanish Eurofighter pilot Lieutenant Elena Gutiérrez, newly arrived in the country. 'It's what we train for every day.'[15]

*

Stoltenberg wanted summit leaders to agree a new formulation of words describing the 2 per cent target of GDP spending on defence as a 'floor rather than a ceiling'. Not everyone agreed this was really new, but the intent was to inject a much greater sense of urgency. A month before Vilnius, Germany finally committed to the 2 per cent. Given the size of Germany's economy, this would have made it the largest military spender in Western Europe.[16] Before long, however, there were reports the pledge had quietly vanished from Germany's draft budget law, and that the target might yet be abandoned.[17] According to NATO's own figures, ten nations out of thirty-one now spent more than the target figure – up from three in 2014 – although some were accused of creative accounting to make the numbers work. For the first time in recent decades, European defence spending from 2014 had grown faster than that of the US.[18] Whether that might be enough for Trump if he returned to

office – or whether he was aware of it at all – was impossible to
know. In Trump's first term, the NATO relationship had been
saved by the fact that most of his senior officials believed firmly
in its value. Now facing a range of criminal and civil charges,
the former president made it clear he would go to war against
the US 'deep state' if re-elected.

In a March 2023 campaign video entitled 'Preventing World
War Three', Trump pledged to 'finish the process we began . . .
of fundamentally re-evaluating NATO's purpose and NATO's
mission'.[19] 'In a second Trump term, we'd almost certainly withdraw from NATO,' said former adviser John Bolton, now one of
his stiffest critics.[20] As Vilnius began, US Democratic Senator
Tim Kaine and Republican counterpart Marco Rubio attached
an amendment to the upcoming US defence budget making it
impossible for any future president to quit the alliance without
congressional approval.[21] They were not just worried about
Trump: Vivek Ramaswamy, the thirty-eight-year-old biotech
entrepreneur emerging as another Republican rising star, was at
least as sceptical as his rival over NATO's value.[22]

In 2022 the speed of the US response to Ukraine had briefly
banished allied worries over long-term US commitment
sparked by the Afghanistan collapse. Now, some described the
Biden White House as perhaps the 'last traditionally transatlantic administration'.[23] Others, primarily from Eastern and
Central Europe, muttered quietly that even Biden's team were
too close to embracing 'appeasement' with the Kremlin. In particular, they blamed Washington and Germany for their
slowness in providing Ukraine with arms. 'It's been a missed
opportunity,' said one Central European official, saying that
heavy weapons and F–16 jets should have been delivered much
sooner in the war.[24]

US forces in Europe had swelled by around a fifth since the
Ukraine invasion to more than 100,000. The 2022 Madrid
summit had seen a host of US commitments: a permanent garrison and corps headquarters in Poland; a brigade combat team

rotating through Romania; two more destroyers based in Spain; UK-based F–35s; and air defence units in Germany and Italy. The US offer for Madrid included more forces rotating through the Baltic states, but nothing permanently based there.[25] In Vilnius, US officials quietly signalled they would not offer further permanent forces beyond those already promised. 'They are simply not prepared to do more,' a non-US diplomat said of the United States, describing the current US administration as 'the best we are going to get. The geopolitical centre of the world is shifting to Asia . . . We have to finally step up.'[26]

*

As their worries over lasting US commitment grew, NATO members on the eastern flank were bilaterally negotiating with major European states and Canada for troops in a way the alliance had never really seen before.

In Madrid, NATO nations had agreed that NATO's eFP battle groups on the eastern flank should be tripled in size to brigades in time of crisis. Now, multiple Eastern members argued that the time had already come, and they lobbied the nations already providing troops to deliver more. 'In any crisis, it might not be possible to move up forces quickly,' said one Baltic official, warning the Baltic states could be cut off if Russian forces pushed through from Belarus to link up with the Russian enclave in Kaliningrad, closing the so-called 'Suwałki Gap'. 'It's important that more are already on the ground.'[27]

Germany and Lithuania now wanted to use this challenge to demonstrate what greater European leadership might look like. On 26 June, two weeks before Vilnius, senior NATO officials and NAC ambassadors were invited to the demonstration day of Lithuania's GRIFFIN STORM military drills. While Stoltenberg and others sat in shirtsleeves in a tent under the baking sun, a German general explained how his troops had travelled by sea, road and air to reinforce the eFP. Then tanks, artillery and armoured vehicles tore across the sandy scrubland and forests to their front. 'It was quite something,' said a European diplomat later, 'watching German troops where they had committed some of the greatest atrocities.'[28]

The Vilnius and Berlin governments announced that Germany would base up to 4,000 soldiers permanently in Lithuania. It would offer a much more serious deterrent to any Russian land grab, protecting the Suwałki Gap. Germany had been publicly offering the scaled-up brigade since mid-2022, negotiating directly with Lithuania over new bases and housing for its troops. But the sudden move still irritated some other members of the alliance, who said they had not known it was coming.[29] Two days later, Canada announced a similar deal to enlarge the Canadian-led eFP battle group in Latvia. At the Vilnius summit, German, Lithuanian, Canadian and Latvian leaders would talk enthusiastically of their partnerships, presenting both decisions as significantly strengthening NATO's ability to protect its Eastern members.

Doing so inherently highlighted the failure of other nations to follow suit. As he headed to Vilnius, British Prime Minister Rishi Sunak was asked whether Britain would send more troops to the eFP in Estonia. He declined to comment, saying only that the UK had a 'long track record' of supporting the government in Tallinn, and that Estonia remained 'extremely grateful'.[30] Estonian officials talked down any splits, pointing out that Britain already had a brigade permanently on readiness to travel to Estonia, and had demonstrated its commitment by temporarily doubling the size of the eFP force in early 2022 immediately before the Ukraine invasion. There was no point in British and other allied troops sitting unnecessarily in the country 'getting bored', they argued.[31] German officials, for their part, argued that they were simply doing what was necessary to keep the continent defended, repaying the debt they owed to other Western states for defending West Germany for almost fifty years. 'Germany stands by its commitment . . . as

Europe's biggest economy, to stand up for the protection of the Eastern flank,' Defence Minister Boris Pistorius said.[32]

Germany's national security state, however, was now facing its own strains – particularly following reports that a senior official in its BND intelligence agency might have been passing secrets to the Kremlin. Officials said the alleged breach – first said to have been detected by an allied intelligence agency – had dented the confidence of other nations over sharing information with Berlin.[33] Some warned that Germany simply remained too open towards the Kremlin – officials in Berlin had issued more than 80,000 visas to Russians since the invasion of Ukraine, potentially a further factor in Lithuania's decision to suspend the Schengen agreement during the summit allowing free movement across European borders.[34] Suggestions Berlin might drop its 2 per cent pledge altogether also didn't help.

Having countries horsetrading directly over where troops would be based was also controversial. Putting too many troops in one place, some alliance officials noted diplomatically, risked the alliance being blindsided by a Russian move elsewhere. 'It's not all about presence,' Stoltenberg told reporters. 'It's all about the ability to have early warnings and indications, and then react . . . if there is a need.'[35]

*

As with almost every other major summit, when NATO's leaders came together for the first day in Vilnius, on Tuesday 11 July 2023, most of the deals had already been made and any divisions papered over, at least for the duration of the meeting. The largest outstanding issue, as it had been in Bucharest in 2008, was what to do about Ukraine.

Interviewed on his way to Lithuania, Biden warned there was no 'unanimity' over bringing the Kyiv government into NATO 'in the middle of the war'. If Ukraine were to join the alliance now, he said, the US and every other member could find themselves immediately pulled into the conflict. Ukraine should be offered a 'rational path' to qualify for NATO, he believed, but it would not happen quickly – and other conditions needed to be met, including those on democratic reform.[36] The comments deepened existing Ukrainian irritation. In the run-up to the summit Zelensky had briefly threatened not to come unless significant progress was seen imminently. Having seen a draft of the statement from the meeting itself on the first day, he took to Twitter to describe the lack of a timetable for Ukraine joining as 'absurd'.

Ukraine did gain concessions that it badly wanted, including the creation of a Ukraine–Russia Council with the alliance, and separate security pledges from the G7 and on long-wanted F–16s. Biden also announced Ukraine would now get US cluster munitions from US stores to help it on the battlefield. Russian media jumped on the reported disagreements, highlighting and exaggerating every one they found, to the annoyance of some at the top of the alliance. 'The summit was a success,' one senior official said – but he described Biden's comments as 'not helpful' when NATO was in a 'communications war' with Russia. Another Western diplomat suggested the alliance needed to 'fix and double down on a communication strategy to explain all the good things we are doing'. Some complained the US had unnecessarily muddied the waters with its cluster munitions offer – at the summit, multiple European leaders repeated long-held views that the weapons should be banned under international law because they often lingered on the battlefield and hurt civilians.[37] US officials said the weapons were a necessary option – Western artillery stocks were now increasingly exhausted.

For all the noisy expressions of support and pledges that Ukraine's future was in NATO, the communiqué text contained little beyond what had already been stated in Bucharest in 2008. Ukraine would join 'when allies agree and conditions are met', it stated, without giving any particular details on the latter. Attendees described Ukrainian membership as 'punted' down the road to the next summit in Washington.[38] On the sidelines of the summit, some were openly upset. 'What should I tell my son?' Ukrainian activist Daria Kaleniuk asked US National Security Adviser Jake Sullivan at a public event. 'That President Biden and NATO didn't invite Ukraine . . . because he's afraid of Russia?' Sullivan said her insinuations over US motives were 'unfounded and unjustified'. In what appeared to be a rebuke to the mounting complaints from Kyiv, he suggested the 'American people' deserved 'a degree of gratitude' for their support so far throughout the war.[39] Coming alongside similar comments from Poland and Britain, it was a rare but perhaps growing signal of mounting irritation with Kyiv.

The final meeting between Biden and Zelensky was an opportunity to set that record straight – and, predictably, both pronounced themselves firmly on the same page. 'Of course there were differences, and it's nice to read about them,' said another diplomat. 'But the important thing is that everyone remains agreed on the fundamentals.'[40]

How true that was depended on what you believed the fundamentals were. In Vilnius, NATO signed a partnership agreement with Japan, building on similar deals with New Zealand, Australia and South Korea whose leaders and officials were now a semi-permanent fixture at major NATO meetings. In the preceding months there had been much talk of NATO opening its first Asian liaison office in Tokyo. Officials said it would be a small operation with only a few staff, building connections with partners in the region. But it was vetoed by France, who argued that the alliance should keep its attention firmly locked on Europe.[41] Stoltenberg said the proposed Asian office remained on the table, and would be discussed again – another issue potentially 'punted' down the road to Washington in 2024. 'This is not about NATO becoming a global military alliance,' said Stoltenberg. 'But this is about recognising that this region faces global challenges, and the rise of China is part of that.'[42]

*

For all the differences on Ukraine and Asia, Vilnius showed the alliance as united as it had been throughout the first Cold War on the need to protect and defend existing NATO territory. But with allies so enmeshed in the Ukraine conflict, and Russia facing perhaps its most serious defeat in recent history, the risks were very different. As delegates returned from Vilnius, Ukrainian officials claimed they might soon be in a position to push forces into Russian-held Crimea, being already within striking distance of Sevastopol and Russia's Black Sea Fleet.[43] Shortly after, former Russian President Dmitry Medvedev – once seen as a potential liberal, now among the most outspoken hardliners in the Kremlin – warned again that if Kyiv began taking territory considered Russian there would be 'no other way out' beyond launching atomic arms.[44]

During the Cold War, many had assumed that if war started it would be colossal from the outset, despite all the efforts to plan for other options. In the 2020s, many feared any escalation might be much more accidental. Within NATO's Joint Force Command Brunssum, officials in its twenty-four-hour operations room described their main role as stopping the Ukraine war spreading to alliance territory.[45] Another top priority was building air defences, moving from systems intended to bring down a handful of rockets from rogue states to something more sophisticated, able to defend against the kind of massed air and missile attacks hitting Ukraine since 2022.[46]

When the first missile of the war struck alliance territory in Poland in November 2022, killing two farm workers, NATO officials talked of the world 'holding its breath'.[47] The rocket, Poland and the alliance soon reported, appeared to have come from Ukrainian air defences, although the Kyiv government continued to say otherwise.[48] Gradually, however, attacks were getting closer to NATO's borders. In summer 2023, Russian drones attacked the Ukrainian port of Reni, only 200 metres away from Romania across the Danube. Cosmin Popa, a Bucharest-based security analyst, described the strike as an 'indirect attack' against not only Romania but the alliance. 'Things will continue to get worse,' he warned, unless there is a 'clear and determined reaction from the West [to] show Putin there are limits beyond which he cannot cross.'[49]

As July 2023 drew to a close, Ukrainian intelligence officials reported the Wagner Group forcing new recruits to sign a contract agreeing to fight in Poland and Lithuania if ordered.[50] When Reuters returned to the Lithuania–Belarus border, the pre-summit complacency was gone. Russian media had released pictures of Wagner fighters training local troops just across the border, while the sound of helicopters and firing was clearly audible from NATO's territory. 'Everyone says that something will happen,' said Agata Moroz, mayor of the village of Kołpin-Ogrodniki, unable to hold back tears as she spoke to a reporter about her worries for her military son and disabled husband.[51]

NATO's first three-quarter-century had started with worries of imminent war on both sides of the world. It looked increasingly like it might finish with the same.

30

Surviving the NATO Century (2024–2049)

'This may be the most dangerous time the world has seen in decades.'

Jamie Dimon, CEO, JP Morgan, October 2023[1]

At some point in 2049 the leaders of NATO – if it still exists – will likely gather in Washington (if that also remains) to celebrate the alliance reaching its centenary. Should they fail to be there, there are three likely potential reasons. The first is that NATO has collapsed; the second is that it has been superseded by something else; and the last is that it has finally failed to stop the catastrophic war Ernest Bevin, Jack Hickerson and Theodore Achilles built it to prevent.

Aside from the brief face-off in Kosovo in 1999, NATO's post-Cold War decades have avoided the kind of 'war scares' of Berlin, Cuba or 1983. But such moments may be coming, and there are many places in the world that could go badly wrong. China has repeatedly vowed to bring Taiwan back under mainland control by 2049, the same year as the NATO anniversary, which also marks the centenary of the communist civil war victory there. US planners already worry that any war with China might be accompanied by a Russian attack in Europe, creating simultaneous crises on both sides of the world to impose the greatest strain on allied forces. 'The new global environment is fundamentally different than anything experienced in the past, even in the ... the Cold War,' warned a 2023 congressional report on the US global strategic posture. 'Today the United States is on the cusp of having not one, but two nuclear peer adversaries each with ambitions to change the international status quo by force if necessary: a situation which the United States did not anticipate and for which it is not prepared.'[2] The same could be said of the alliance.

For the first time since 1989, the 2020s have seen a new world war move alarmingly back into the realm of possibility – not just the apocalyptic prospect of a full atomic exchange, but the potential of a multi-front confrontation lasting months or years. Summer 2023 saw the US Navy holding its largest global conflict simulation in decades, putting commanders and forces in the field through a hypothetical conflict ranging from the Atlantic to the Pacific, Mediterranean and Arctic.[3] For the first time since the Cold War ended, global nuclear arsenals are increasing in almost every major nation that already has them, led by a particularly dramatic increase in the Chinese stockpile. Dan Smith, director of the Stockholm International Peace Research Institute tracking global conventional and atomic arms, warned the 2020s were on the edge of 'drifting into one of the most dangerous periods in human history.'[4]

*

In many ways, of course, such an era is well within the traditional comfort zone of the alliance. NATO's first civilian chief Hastings Ismay described it as a collective insurance policy against 'measureless catastrophe'.[5] Even in the unlikely event a pro-Western or more liberal government takes power in Moscow in the coming years, NATO allies will not tear up their Russia-facing defences as they did after the Berlin Wall came down. 'There will be more joint plans and more joint exercises,' said Norwegian Foreign Minister Anniken Huitfeldt. 'Whatever happens, it [NATO] is not going to have the downturn that we had in the 1990s. We know that it's an unstable situation.'[6]

Making more detailed predictions is a dangerous game. At the end of September 2023, NATO Military Committee Chairman Admiral Robert Bauer visited Israel's border with the Gaza Strip as Israeli troops and officials showed off high-tech systems to detect incoming danger. Israel believed its cutting-edge network cameras, drones, artificial intelligence analysis and automated weapons systems made a surprise attack impossible.[7] They were wrong – eight days after Bauer's visit, Hamas fighters from Gaza poured across that border without warning, using drones to take out key surveillance and control points, overrunning critical headquarters and slaughtering hundreds of soldiers and civilians.[8] As Israel mobilized 300,000 reservists in a matter of days and began a counteroffensive into Gaza, NATO and Western officials talked of a collective 'soul-searching' over whether they were truly doing enough to protect the most exposed alliance members from similar events in Eastern Europe. Russian-backed media around the world, meanwhile, were doing everything they could to tap into outrage over events in Gaza and present the West – and NATO nations in particular – as hypocritical, complicating the geopolitics of an already complex era.

So far, every year of the 2020s has brought NATO and its members at least one unpredicted strategic shock – first Covid-19, then the collapse in Afghanistan, Ukraine invasion and finally the Gaza war. 'Regardless of how well-connected we might be with sophisticated technologies or how much better we become at collecting and sharing information, surprise will continue to occur in the future – perhaps even more frequently,' wrote Australian Major General Mick Ryan, one of the leading voices in the study of contemporary conflict, in 2022. 'This is because we are witnessing transformations in military technology and operations at a rapid pace, driven by the changes in geopolitics, technology and broader society.'[9]

Clearly, some of the West's enemies believe the US and its allies lack the strength that they once had. 'The old order is swiftly disintegrating, and strongman politics is again ascendant among the world's great powers,' wrote Chinese academic Zheng Yongnian the same year, outlining what he described as the final unravelling of the post-World War Two global order. 'Countries are brimming with ambition, like tigers eyeing their prey, keen to find every opportunity among the ruins.'[10]

Officials at NATO headquarters and within its member states say they are now tracking potential threats, dangers and crises on a scale that would scarcely have been thought imaginable a few years ago. When the largest alliance command post exercise in recent decades, STEADFAST JUPITER, kicked off in October 2023, its planners acknowledged the scenario required repeated updating to keep track of real-world events.[11] That included efforts from potential adversaries aimed at testing NATO, with Poland accusing low-flying military helicopters from Russia's ally Belarus of deliberately breaching Polish airspace at the start of August 2023.[12] In October, less than twenty-four hours after the start of the Hamas offensive into Israel, Estonia and Finland reported the gas pipeline and data cable linking them under the Gulf of Finland had been wrenched out of position.

'We don't have the luxury of choosing only one threat and one challenge,' said Secretary General Stoltenberg as defence ministers met against the backdrop of unexpected war in Gaza, renewed crisis in Kosovo, and multiple other threats.[13] US Defense Secretary Lloyd Austin talked of the US needing to 'walk and chew gum at the same time', acknowledging that Washington would have to stand behind multiple allies at once.[14] US officials are probably right that Washington can manage simultaneous conflicts in the Middle East and Ukraine, but managing a much larger war involving Russia and China would be a very different prospect.

If it is to succeed, NATO must craft a credible narrative of deterrence that is simultaneously resilient, appealing and realistic. As NATO's Commander Multinational Corps North East, German Lieutenant General Jürgen-Joachim von Sandrart, puts it: 'Our ultimate goal is to preserve this world of ours that is so worth living in: our idea of liberal, good governance, freedom and security and well-being.' But, he added: 'We live in extraordinarily challenging times.'[15] Italian General Guglielmo Luigi Miglietta, Commander, Allied Joint Force Command in Brunnsom – who would theoretically lead a NATO's central front in the event of conflict – is prone to quoting the Roman historian Vegetius and his maxim: 'He who desires peace should prepare for war.'[16] Full-scale combat, however, is not the only threat.

Even without a major conflict, Russia has proved itself adept at finding non-military ways to undermine its enemies. Russia-linked social media feeds and news outlets have looked to build resentment against Ukrainian refugees in Poland, supported 'Yellow Vest' protesters in France, and backed far-right and anti-establishment groups across the world. 'Food, migration and energy have all become weapons,' said NATO Military Committee Chair Bauer. 'They have been throughout history, and they will be in the future.'[17] The Baltic states began weaning themselves off Russian energy in the late 2000s, while Germany has done the same following 2022 – although a new Turkish-Bulgarian pipeline may yet offer the Kremlin another way of selling its oil and gas into Europe. European politics itself looks increasingly challenging, with a host of pro-Putin political parties jostling for influence and power in multiple member nations.

For the first time since the Cold War, alliance messaging includes public talk of atomic weapons. 'NATO will remain a nuclear alliance for as long as nuclear weapons exist,' said Stoltenberg. 'While we take Russia's threats seriously, we will not be intimidated.'[18] NATO's Nuclear Planning Group has met repeatedly since the invasion of Ukraine to consider alliance atomic posture, attended by every nation aside from France which manages its nuclear forces entirely separately from NATO. Amid a new bout of Russian nuclear warnings in September 2022, roughly six months into the invasion, the alliance took the unusual step of publicly highlighting its annual

STEADFAST NOON atomic drills.[19] 'If the US and NATO aim to deter Russia from further sabre-rattling over Ukraine and other partners, they may need to be willing to signal their own nuclear resolve,' wrote NATO Defence College researcher Michael Cohen a few months later.[20]

Quietly, that is already happening. The US is upgrading its nuclear weapons storage facilities within Europe, including what appeared to be preparations to enable the return of US nuclear weapons to Britain for the first time since the 2000s.[21] In 2022, France made a point of sending three of its four ballistic missile submarines to sea simultaneously to demonstrate their wartime preparedness and resilience.[22]

Another recent NATO paper examines the 1962 Cuban missile crisis, concluding that maintaining diplomatic channels remains critical to deterrence and avoiding accidental escalation. It quotes John F. Kennedy's advice that 'nuclear powers must avert those confrontations which bring an adversary to a choice of either a humiliating retreat or a nuclear war.'[23] All that remains good guidance. But any modern nuclear confrontation will take place in a much less monolithic world than that of the Cold War, with more moving pieces, new technologies and international players.

Every major face-off between NATO members and the Kremlin since 1945 – particularly Berlin in 1961, Cuba in 1962 and the largely hidden crisis of 1983 – has revealed sometimes alarming inconsistencies in command chains, and very different views of who should be doing what and who they might report to. If and when a series of new confrontations come, it seems almost inevitable there will be similar confusions.

To what extent Western or global society is prepared for perhaps several periods of tension as great as the Cuban missile crisis remains unclear. Should such confrontations happen, however, NATO will almost certainly find itself pulled in.

*

How the war in Ukraine ends – and what relationship post-war Kyiv governments enjoy with the alliance – will itself shape NATO's future. Nordic and Eastern European diplomats increasingly talk of a new post-war 'European security structure' in which a hard alliance border runs from Norway and Finland in the Arctic, down through the Baltic states and Poland around Belarus and then – providing Kyiv enters the alliance – along wherever the post-war Russia Ukraine border then sits. That might still leave Moldova, Georgia and other former Soviet states in the Caucasus and Central Asia in a 'grey zone', but it would forever lock most of Ukraine into the Western world while any Russian-held areas would be under lasting Kremlin dominance. Those who favour Ukraine's entry into NATO believe it offers the best prospect of preventing another Russian attack in future. Those who oppose it argue it will simply increase the chances of a wider war.

History will judge both the West's long-running indecision on Ukraine as well as whatever final choice is made, but there is unlikely to be any easy fix for Europe's future security. When Stoltenberg's Chief of Staff Stian Jenssen suggested at an August 2023 panel in Norway that Ukraine might have to give up claims to some areas of its territory as part of a deal to enter the alliance, it provoked an immediate backlash from both the Kyiv government and much of the eastern flank. He was forced to withdraw the comments and apologise, while Stoltenberg and the alliance publicly confirmed the official line that such decisions were Ukraine's.[24]

How much agency Ukraine truly has will depend on how things play out on the battlefield. As the summer fighting season drew to a close in late 2023, the Kyiv government had recaptured roughly half of all territory seized by Russia at the beginning of the war, US officials said.[25] According to British military intelligence, long-range rockets supplied by the UK and other allies alongside increasing use of drones had largely forced the Russian Black Sea Fleet to quit Sevastopol and

Crimea for safer waters in the Azov Sea.[26] But progress along the main frontlines was slow, held back by obstacles and mine-fields, as well as the endless battle for supplies. Ukrainian forces on the frontline complained of a crippling shortage of shells for their Western-supplied artillery, leaving them dependent on Soviet-era systems dating back to World War Two. Many NATO nations had now all but exhausted their own pre-conflict stocks, simultaneously struggling with what some called growing domestic 'war fatigue'.[27] 'Public opinion has moved away from the war . . . because it has coincided with the increase in inflation and an industrial and production crisis which has worsened living conditions in Western democratic countries,' warned Italian Defence Minister Guido Crosetto.[28]

Some Ukrainian officials blamed the West for only giving them enough weapons to survive but not to win. One senior Ukrainian general lamented to a journalist from the *Economist* that, for all the technological advances of the last hundred years, his forces on the ground were stuck in a World War One-style stalemate consuming huge volumes of material and lives.[29] NATO's battle to ensure such scenes do not unfold elsewhere in Europe is different to Ukraine's in many ways, and it is likely to continue well past the end of the current conflict.

*

Former secretary general Ismay always told fellow NATO leaders that the alliance should avoid 'washing its dirty linen in public', keeping internal divisions both manageable and private[30] – but with an ever-growing number of members, that is clearly getting harder. The most recent NATO 'panel of experts' report on the future of the alliance – commissioned at the 2019 London summit, and published the following year during the pandemic – identified a loss of internal political cohesion as one of the greatest threats.[31] The months following the July 2023 Vilnius summit saw a considerable spike in internal disagreements. Ahead of elections, Poland's right-wing Law and Justice Party government – previously one of the strongest backers of Ukraine – abruptly dropped support for Kyiv, describing Zelensky's government as a dangerous 'drowning man' that might drag down its allies.[32] Shortly after, Slovakia elected a right-wing government under former Prime Minister Robert Fico, also ceasing its Ukraine support.[33] Perhaps most worrying of all for both Ukraine and NATO's European members, US political support appeared to be diminishing, with Congress struggling to agree more military aid and opinion polls showing support for further weapons shipments to Ukraine declining amongst both Republicans and Democrats.[34] As of autumn 2023, Turkey and Hungary had yet to sign off Sweden's membership of the alliance, with relations between Ankara and the West if anything continuing to deteriorate. In Syria, US forces shot down a Turkish drone they said was menacing both them and their nearby Kurdish allies.[35]

Few doubt that the Ukraine war has weakened Russia, but the current chaotic world still offers the Kremlin plenty of opportunities to disrupt NATO members and their allies while growing Moscow's influence. The Wagner mutiny in June 2023 showcased both how damaged Putin was, but also how resilient he remained – particularly after Wagner Group founder Yevgeny Prigozhin and several of his key lieutenants were killed in a plane crash blamed by Putin on the passengers playing with a grenade while high on drink and drugs. Former senior US intelligence official Fiona Hill described the Russian leader as presenting himself 'more and more in the tradition of the imperial czars', determined to reassert Moscow's sphere of influence while casting himself as the only bulwark against domestic chaos.[36]

Whether Putin survives or not, defeat in Ukraine could make Russia more nationalist and angry. Estimates in the Baltic states and Eastern Europe on how long it might take Russia to rebuild its military after the war range from two years to as much as twenty – one reason many of those countries are so invested in damaging the Kremlin military industrial complex as much as possible during the current conflict. 'Every loss Russia suffers in Ukraine is one which it will have to replace after the war,' wrote the Foreign Policy Research Institute in July 2023, arguing that this bought the rest of Europe time to shore up its own defences.[37] The end of fighting in Ukraine, therefore, may simply be the start of a new phase of confrontation.

Moscow's ever-evolving relationship with Beijing is also difficult to predict, although some credit Chinese pressure with pushing Russia away from even more aggressive atomic rhetoric in autumn 2022. At time of writing, Putin had failed to convince Xi Jinping to throw China's industrial might behind Russia in Ukraine, but is gaining more traction with North Korea. Estonia's intelligence services reported Pyongyang delivering as many as 350,000 shells in late 2023, warning Russia could keep up its current weight of fire within Ukraine for at least a year while the US and allies scrambled to arm both Kyiv and Israel.[38]

Defeat in either theatre, some US officials worry, might open the door to further aggression elsewhere, particularly from China. 'Beyond Europe, we know that our allies and – perhaps most importantly – our adversaries and competitors are watching,' said Biden in late October 2023. 'If we walk away and let Putin annex Ukraine's independence, would-be aggressors around the world would be emboldened to try the same.'[39] A leaked 2023 memo from the head of US Air Mobility Command warned of war over Taiwan as soon as 2025, while other Taiwanese and US officials talked of 2027 as a more likely date.[40]

According to officials, NATO first began discussing potential allied responses to an invasion of Taiwan in late 2022, with similar parallel talks taking place within the G7 and EU. The aim, those involved said, was to ensure maximum unity in times of crisis, whether on sanctions or a military response.[41] Some talk of European nations sending a joint task force to support

US efforts in the event of an invasion of Taiwan – NATO itself, most believe, would remain focused on defending Europe.

*

From the very start, NATO and its leading members have struggled to balance the need to build credible defences with the wider demand of delivering prosperity and economic growth. As Ukraine has shown, the technological and logistical challenges of modern international confrontation can be enormous. In 2022, the alliance began work on its new Defence Production Action Plan, designed to align and resource their defences against ever-growing threats. 'Every country is now trying to ensure their defence equipment, their processes, their spare parts and supply chains are ready for whatever the eventuality might be, 'said Assistant Secretary General for Defence Investments Wendy Gilmour. 'That means everything is being done at once.'[42]

The 2020s have seen rapid growth in multiple new areas of conflict. In the opening stages of fighting in Ukraine, the Kyiv government bought together 300,000 IT specialists to defend the country's own digital infrastructure and attack Russian systems – a battle that has raged throughout the war and remains largely secret. It also set up a new government app allowing millions of Ukrainians to do everything from filing official documents and tax returns to providing intelligence on enemy positions.[43] NATO's Deputy Secretary General Mircea Geoană argued the Ukraine war showed there was no 'false choice' between high-tech new systems like artificial intelligence-operated drones and the old-fashioned military 'mass' of artillery, machine guns, tanks and personnel. The alliance, he said, needed to stay on top of both.[44]

After the Hamas surprise attack on Israel, alliance officials said they had stepped up efforts to get the balance right, as well as to make sure human insight was not lost. A senior official described the challenge as being to 'team up the humans and the software to create an augmented effect while not losing control of the situation.[45] One NATO effort to keep pace on tech, commencing operations after Vilnius, was DIANA: the Defence Innovation Accelerator for the North Atlantic, headquartered at Imperial College in London. Geoană described it as designed to help start-up firms across alliance nations deliver critical systems like cloud computing and AI. 'We are basically an ecosystem of innovation that has no rival,' he said of alliance nations. 'There's nothing more fundamental for our alliance – and the free world – than to maintain our technical edge.'[46] July 2023 also saw the opening of NATO's latest Centre of Excellence for space technology in the French city of Toulouse, which will work alongside NATO's military space headquarters at Ramstein air base in Germany. With outer space and low earth orbit both becoming militarised, NATO's 2021 summit communiqué included a clause noting that an attack on the space infrastructure or resources of a member nation might be considered enough to trigger Article 5 in the future.[47]

Modern high-tech confrontation can bring new complications, particularly in areas where private companies increasingly offer capabilities most alliance governments cannot match. In Ukraine, billionaire Elon Musk's Starlink satellites were key to retaining civilian and military access to the internet despite Russian strikes and jamming – but Musk refused to increase their coverage to support Ukrainian military operations in Crimea.[48] Many of these unorthodox challenges have not been faced before by the alliance, and some believe they should be wargamed more fully before a more serious crisis comes.

The alliance knows it needs to be much nimbler to keep track of an ever-faster world. Late 2023 saw the publication of NATO's first official doctrine for combating unmanned drones, stripping back an almost unreadable 600-page 'handbook' to a 'more coherent' document of less than 100 pages that took into account the most recent lessons from Ukraine.[49] Still, many within the alliance complain that huge swathes of its structures remain remarkably ineffective, and question whether NATO itself can ever prove a driver of innovation compared to private companies and individual nations.[50]

Democratic countries clearly have their strengths, but making them resilient enough to deter or fight a Ukraine-scale war is no easy task. It is no longer impossible to imagine a long-running war across the Baltic states and Poland, 'Much of our societies are unprepared to deal with the reality of war,' said Katarzyna Pisarska, chair of the Warsaw Security Forum. 'They are prepared to live through short-term crises and go back to normal. The problem here is that there is no return to normal.'[51]

Ironically, among the most prepared NATO nations for this kind of challenge are those joining it most recently: specifically, Sweden and Finland. Despite their neutral Cold War status, both maintained significant conscript and professional militaries through to the modern era. In Finland the majority of men still do national service, allowing it to potentially mobilise enormous reserves of manpower, and meaning that most business and civic leaders have military experience. Shaped by its experience fighting Russia during World War Two, Finland's stated approach has always been to aspire to be impossible to safely occupy, its troops prepared to hide in forests and urban areas to attack an invading army. Having abolished conscription in 2010 Sweden reintroduced it in 2017, for both men and women – although it only takes in a few thousand each year, a fraction of those of fighting age. Sweden also now maintains a permanent garrison on its Baltic island of Gotland, seen as critical to control of regional sea routes in any conflict.[52]

In focus groups conducted more broadly across mainland Europe by the Friends of Europe think tank, opposition to conscription was widespread. The further from the eastern flank, the less willing to fight interviewees were. 'No person should have an obligation to serve in the armed forces,' said a young Dutchman, arguing that those who sent soldiers to war were not the ones who took the risk. 'A conflict means a complete failure of your government to protect your dignity and human rights, and that of others.' That did not mean most were pacifist: many interviewees favoured increasing defence spending to 2 per cent of GDP, some to 5 per cent. Most broadly agreed that NATO had proved vital to the defence of Europe – although many criticised the European failure to end dependence on the US. Some even suggested they would rather see conscription conducted on an EU-wide basis rather than by individual states, thereby deepening a European identity across the bloc. 'At the moment NATO is irreplaceable,' said a participant from Portugal. 'That is not to say that couldn't change in the future.'[53]

NATO's mainland European members are increasingly public in their view that integrating the EU more deeply into the defence of Europe is a necessary part of the future of the alliance. The US appears sympathetic to that view, with talk that the next secretary general after Stoltenberg might be European Commission president and former German defence minister Ursula von der Leyen.[54] By late 2023, European Union officials were discussing changing bloc-wide budget regulations to make it easier for member states to spend more on defence – a move that could prove more effective at boosting European arms purchases than NATO's unending but often unsuccessful efforts on that issue over several decades.[55]

For all that, however, there were again reports that Germany would only reach its target of 2 per cent of GDP through 'creative accounting', with Britain accused of using similar tactics by including military pensions to inflate its numbers. Shortly after standing down as UK defence minister in summer 2023 – and having failed to secure support from European NATO members to himself become secretary general – Ben Wallace accused the alliance of moving at a 'snail's pace' before the Ukraine invasion when it came to building genuine military capacity. 'We have to catch up,' he said.[56]

*

Few officials openly talk of NATO 'failing' in a crisis – and for many the prospect remains almost unthinkable. Scratch the surface, however, and it is clear the most exposed members are quietly hedging their bets, doing everything they can to make the alliance work while ensuring they have backup plans should it fail.

In early summer 2023, the UK-led Joint Expeditionary Force (JEF) – also including Denmark, Finland, Estonia, Iceland, Latvia, Lithuania, the Netherlands, Sweden and Norway – conducted a month-long exercise in a nuclear bunker in Iceland. Officials talked of the JEF offering simpler, faster military options short of full-scale NATO action, allowing the deployment of up to 10,000 high-readiness personnel to a potential conflict region 'without consensus' if needed. Under the terms of the JEF agreement, elements of the force can be deployed rapidly to any member nation that requests its presence, providing two other participating countries agree – no one has a veto.

'NATO when it does act will mean business,' said one JEF headquarters officer, sticking with the official position that the alliance remains at the heart of all European military thinking. 'We just want the responsiveness to get ahead of that.' As another put it, member nations increasingly liked 'having multiple security constructs because the world is a complicated place'.[57] Eastern and Central European officials are a little blunter. Whatever happens, they say they would resist any Russian attack with a 'coalition of the willing'. Even if NATO itself did not 'turn up' because the NAC failed to reach agreement, they hope some elements within the alliance could still be very useful. For example, the NATO Allied Rapid Reaction Corps HQ in Britain – which led previous NATO deployments in the Balkans and Afghanistan – could 'kick out' personnel from unwilling nations so that it could fight.[58]

The JEF and ARRC are both British-led – but many believe that going forwards, mainland European and EU-based structures will become the most important.[13] For now, most assume that whether or not NATO itself joins the fight, whoever holds the SACEUR role – ever since Eisenhower, the top US officer in Europe – would be the senior commander in any war. Another isolationist like Trump in the White House, however, could throw that permanently into doubt. Two of the largest air and naval exercises in summer 2023 were pointedly German-led, in both cases including extensive US forces. Britain was also scheduled to play a major part in 2024's STEADFAST DEFENDER, assembling 40,000 alliance troops from the Arctic to the Black Sea in what would be the largest drill since 1989.[59] Such training will likely continue to grow – but if real conflict ever comes, it will be more complex than any drill.

*

If Russia ever makes a serious military move onto NATO soil, Estonia's eastern border city Narva, by far the largest Russian-speaking settlement in alliance territory, is a likely target. It is a location that has marked the frontline between East and West for almost a millennium, with two ancient Russian and Danish-built fortresses facing each other across a gorge and river. Its population have few doubts that they may be amongst the first – although likely not the last – to pay the price if peace breaks down between NATO and its neighbour. Putin's 2022 invasion of Ukraine sent shockwaves through the town, with reports of panic buying. Its aftermath deepened divisions both within already conflicted Russian speakers in the region, and between them and the Estonian-speaking population and officials. Estonia's authorities cut back access to Russian media, while Narva adopted the tagline 'Europe starts here' to affirm the city's loyalty. 'We live in a democratic society – those who don't want this have already left,' said Tatjana Stolfart, city council member for the previously Russian-leaning Center Party, which distanced itself dramatically from Putin after the invasion.[60]

But a year later, with two pro-Kremlin politicians gaining
local votes, outgoing Narva mayor Katri Raik warned the
region increasingly resembled 'eastern Ukraine before the
war'.[61] Tensions were further inflamed by the removal of a
World War Two Soviet war memorial, as well as a ban on public
events marking holidays related to 'Russian war propaganda'.
Narva's police chief was unapologetic.[62] For Estonian Independence Day 2023, heavily armed Estonian troops paraded through
the town, followed by unarmed NATO counterparts from the
eFP.[63]

Nervousness over entangling the West in these centuries-old
confrontations was a key motivator for those opposing NATO
expansion after the Cold War. Former US diplomat to Moscow
George Kennan, approaching a hundred years of age as the
1990s ended, described the move to admit Eastern and Central
European states as a 'a fateful error', a comment quoted by US
presidential candidate and unashamed isolationist Vivek
Ramaswamy during the 2023 Republican primaries.[64] Kennan
was probably right that few in the West really understood the
responsibilities they were taking on, nor how much they might
antagonise many within Russia. But he was wrong when he suggested Russia's Yeltsin-era democracy was as advanced and
sustainable as that of the former Warsaw Pact countries that
now wanted alliance membership.

From the perspective of the 2020s, countries like Hungary,
Poland, Romania and Bulgaria definitely have their issues – but
that could equally be said of any of the more established democracies, including the US, France and Britain. Expecting any
member to keep quiet in the modern alliance is unrealistic.
Having fought their way into NATO, the most vulnerable
nations will likely prove ever more unapologetic about what
they want and think – and can switch opinion sharply when
new governments come to power. 'We don't comment on things
we consider moderately important,' said Estonian Foreign Ministry Secretary General Jonatan Vseviov. 'We've concluded the

risks of being silent on critically important matters far outweigh the risk of angering some PR adviser somewhere else.'[65]

Meeting fellow NATO leaders in Paris in 1957, then-President Dwight D. Eisenhower told them that NATO's formative years had taken place 'in a fast-flowing current of the great stream of history', and that 'heroic efforts' were necessary to keep the world at peace and alliance nations free.[66] That pace is now as great as it has ever been, and alliance leaders know their greatest challenges will often be unpredictable or unexpected.

Visiting Moscow in 2009, then-Secretary General Anders Fogh Rasmussen predicted a brave new world of NATO-Russia cooperation that by 2020 would see their forces working side-by-side routinely on counter-piracy and peacekeeping.[67] Instead, the 2020s are already proving amongst the most dangerous the alliance has yet faced.

By the time NATO celebrates its centenary in 2049, mankind may have colonies on the moon, artificial intelligence may have changed the world and the alliance may or may not have had to fight a major war. All that does seem certain is that if it is to continue to defend a disparate collection of democratic nations, NATO will have to find ways to navigate plenty of internal and external disagreements.

The history of NATO has never been predictable – and there is still everything to play for in the years to come.

Notes and acknowledgements

The contract to write this book was signed in September 2022. The timing was not ideal – I had just started a full-time role as part of my reserve military service. I wrote and researched furiously through the evenings and weekends, then headed to Brussels as soon as that job ended for a meeting of alliance foreign ministers. For the remainder of 2023, I have written this alongside my weekly Reuters column, and I'm grateful to the Reuters editorial management team for allowing me time to get it done. I am also indebted to my agent, Antony Topping at Greene and Heaton, for helping to put this project together.

I'm writing these final words in my cabin on a cruise ship in the Indian Ocean in November 2023. Without particularly intending, the wrapping up of this book has coincided exactly with my first visit back to Asia after breaking my neck seventeen years ago reporting on Sri Lanka's civil war. Since then, I've been largely paralysed from the shoulders down – this book has been written almost entirely with voice recognition software, and I'm grateful to both the Wildfire team and assistant Alba Andresen for their help in going through the final proofs.

Deterring Armageddon is my first full-length books, and it is built on the work of many others. From the start, those that built NATO wanted to capture lessons for future generations. One of Eisenhower's first actions on appointment as SACEUR was to recall to military service US Army Lieutenant Colonel Roy Lamson, a history professor who had served as an official military historian during World War Two. If NATO's new military command structure worked as intended, Eisenhower told him, it would be a model for future cooperation, adding: 'Even if it fails, we should know the reasons why.'[1]

Lamson oversaw the initial classified history of SHAPE and NATO's entire military structure, written annually until 1956 and now declassified in full. NATO's first Secretary General Hastings Ismay put his name to another invaluable report, 'NATO: The First Five Years', published in 1954 and in fact put together mostly by Eve Curie, daughter of the scientist Marie.[2] Jack Hickerson and Theodore Achilles also left their own extensive accounts of NATO's creation in the Truman presidential oral history archive, in the case of Achilles supplemented by his own small but detailed personally published memoir.

The opening historical chapters of this book draw heavily from that material, as well as a range of biographies, autobiographies and declassified material primarily from the UK, US and alliance archive itself. Sessions of the North Atlantic Council are only declassified after 50 years, but up until the 1970s detailed accounts of their deliberations have generally been released by the US State Department as part of its excellent and exhaustive Foreign Relations of the United States series of documents, which have also acted as a major source for this book. Details are in the references, which also contain links to work by multiple generations of modern NATO archivists. I have also drawn on multiple works of both contemporary and recent histories – with works by Max Hastings, Mary Elise Sarotte, William Hitchcock, Mike Martin, Timothy Sayle, Lawrence Kaplan, Bob Woodward, Taylor Dowling, Calder Walton, Iain MacGregor, Al Murray, David McCullough, Brian Collins, Carter Malkasian, Sandy Gall, Julian Lindley-French, Sean Maloney, Ben Barry, Fiona Hill, George Packer, Aaron Donaghy, Bridget Kendall and others particularly valuable.

I am also indebted to several generations of top-flight international journalists. I have quoted extensively from the *New York Times*, *Washington Post*, Reuters, Associated Press and other outlets, particularly when their reporting included behind-the-scenes comments from diplomatic sources that might otherwise have been lost forever. Similarly, the oral history archives of multiple presidential libraries, as well as the National Security Archive run by George Washington University, which has collated a spectacular range of US and foreign interviews and documents.

While much more recent material is based on my own reporting and interviews, either for Reuters or this book, I am once again hugely thankful for the work of other more recent journalistic colleagues from a range of outlets – *Politico, Deutsche Welle* and the Estonian public broadcaster ERR have been particularly valuable. So, of course, is the NATO website itself, with an exhaustive transcript of press conferences by NATO leadership going back to the end of the 1990s.

I am also grateful to those who have given me their time for interviews, as well as the NATO press office and international delegation staff who facilitated my various visits. I'm particularly grateful to Secretary General Jens Stoltenberg and Military Committee Chairman Admiral Robert Bauer for their time, as well as the NAC ambassadors and other current and former officials who took time to speak to me, whether anonymously or on the record. Apologies to those I didn't get to speak to given pressures of availability and time.

NATO's past continues to be fought over. Two court cases currently underway may well shape future understanding of NATO's inventions in Kosovo and Libya. The first is the prosecution for war crimes at The Hague of former Kosovo president and Kosovo Liberation Army senior leader Hashim Thaci, accused of complicity in massacres of Serbs in 1998 and 1999. If he were found guilty, it might prompt re-examination of the US and NATO's 'case for war' in 1999.[3]

Potentially even more explosive could be former French President Nicolas Sarkozy's scheduled trial in 2025 on charges of illegally receiving money from the Gaddafi dynasty in the run up to the 2007 French elections. The former French leader denies those allegations, which if proven would cast his pivotal role in pushing NATO and the West towards regime change in Libya in 2011 under a much more complex light.[4]

The present day has also continued to deliver shocks and newsworthy developments right up until the last moment – the Gaza war in October 2023 prompted a particularly heavy rewrite of the final chapter. I remain extremely grateful to the Wildfire team – particularly my editor Philip – for these last minute changes. I also thank my research assistants Alba Andreson, Sarah Westedt and Jessica Dorsch. They contributed extremely useful material, and have helped make the book a pleasure to write.

Any mistakes are, of course, entirely mine. All efforts have been made to make the book as current as possible at the time of publication.

As the Greek captain of the cruise ship carrying me back to Asia put it a few days ago, having sailed through the once again conflict-ridden Red Sea: 'The world is on fire, and we do not know what we will wake up to the next day.' For readers in the future, this book may simply feel a prequel to more dramatic events to come – for now, there is nothing left to do but wish the reader good luck in the coming years, and hope the lessons from the past do not get forgotten.

Peter Apps
Colombo, Sri Lanka, 19 November 2023

References

Introduction

1 SHAPE historians, 'SHAPE History: Volume 3, The New Approach', undated but circa 1954/5, page 5
2 André de Staercke (editor), *NATO's Anxious Birth: the Prophetic Vision of the 1940s*, 1985, page 109
3 Ibid., page 156
4 Interview with the author
5 Bob Woodward, *Rage*, 2020, Kindle location 2
6 Lauris Norstad oral history interview, Eisenhower Presidential Library

1. 'A Sense of Threat and Fear' (2022–2023)

1 Joint Press Conference, US Department of Defense, 16 February 2023
2 'UK and NATO allies tested in freezing conditions on winter exercise', *Forces News*, YouTube, 16 February 2023
3 'Ukraine war has given Estonian military confidence in its forces', Forces.net, 23 February 2023
4 'Tensions with Russia propel Baltic states towards NATO', *Washington Post*, 7 October 2002
5 Joint Press Conference, NATO website, 28 June, 2023
6 'Fear of Russia brings new purpose and unity to NATO', *New York Times*, 14 January 2022
7 'Minutes of the fourth meeting of the US–UK–Canada security conversations', 29 March 1948, Foreign Relations of the United States (henceforth FRUS), 1948, Western Europe, Volume 3, Document 61
8 Hastings Ismay, *The Memoirs of Lord Ismay*, 1960, page 456
9 'Address by President Truman', 4 April 1949, US Presidency Project, University of California at Santa Barbara
10 'How the midwives of NATO prevailed over the doubters', *New York Times*, 23 April 1999

11 'Press conference by the secretary general', NATO website, 1 April 2019

12 'Russia's war and "imperialist dreams" can't pay off, says Estonia', *Euronews*, 12 December 2022

13 'NATO's 2022 strategic concept', NATO website, June 2022

14 Interview with the author

15 'As Russia pounds Ukraine, NATO countries rush in Javelins and Stingers', *New York Times*, 4 March 2004

16 Interview with the author

17 'UN says Ukraine civilian death toll likely considerably higher than 8500 counted', *The Hill*, 12 April 2023

18 'Russia scrubs Mariupol's Ukraine identity, builds on death', *Associated Press*, 23 December 2022

19 'Troop deaths and injuries in Ukraine near 500,000, US officials say', *New York Times,* 8 August 2023

20 'Russia Hides Its War Toll. We Pieced Together the Clues', *New York Times*, 25 February 2024

21 Interview with the author

22 'Memorandum of conversation', 27 March 1975, Ford Presidential Archive

23 Interview with the author

24 'Something was badly wrong: when Washington realised Russia was actually invading Ukraine', *Politico*, 24 February 2023

25 'Fear of Russia brings new purpose and unity to NATO', *New York Times*, 14 January 2022

26 'Sending US combat troops to Ukraine not on the cards right now', *Politico*, 8 December 2021

27 'Deluded Europe can't see that it's finished', *Telegraph*, 25 August 2023

28 'NATO leaders call on Russia to stop "senseless war"', NATO website, 25 February 2022

29 'SACEUR remarks', SHAPE website, 9 January 2023

30 'Russia lost the battle for Kyiv with its hasty assault on a Ukrainian airport', *Los Angeles Times*, 10 April 2022

31 'Doorstep statement', NATO website, 24 March 2022

32 'Remarks by President Biden', White House website, 24 March 2022

33 'A new US-led international group will meet monthly to focus on aiding Ukraine', *New York Times*, 26 April 2022

34 Interview with the author

35 Interview with the author

36 'Global military expenditures hit record high, with Europe above Cold War levels', *Radio Free Europe*, 24 April 2023

37 'Shrinking US Stinger missile supply faces restocking challenges', *Reuters*, 26 April 2022

38 Babel.ua interview with Ukrainian Defence Minister Reznikov, 20 February 2023

39 'With demand high in Ukraine, US Army ramps up artillery production', *Defense News*, 26 January 2023

40 'Ukraine is firing artillery shells faster than NATO members can replace them', *Vice*, 15 February 2023

41 'SACEUR speech', SHAPE website, 9 January 2023

42 'NATO on the precipice', *Politico*, 24 February 2023

43 'The Baltics hunker down for the long game against Russia', *Foreign Policy*, 22 September 2022

44 'Never underestimate Russia, top NATO military official warns', *Politico*, 3 July 2023

45 Interview with the author

2. A Very Political Alliance (2023)

1 Interview with the author

2 'Secretary general press conference', NATO website, 4 April 2023

3 Figures from WorldData.info, retrieved 5 July 2023

4 'In NATO's new North, fresh chances to contain Moscow', *Reuters*, 3 July 2023

5 'Erdoğan says Turkey opposed to Finland–Sweden NATO membership', *Al Jazeera*, 13 May 2022

6 'Erdoğan to back Finland NATO bid', *Al Jazeera*, 17 March 2023

7 'Burning of Qur'an in Stockholm funded by journalist with Kremlin ties', *Guardian*, 27 January 2023

8 'NATO members prepare for annual summit in Lithuania', *LBC/Press Association*, 9 July 2023

9 Interview with the author

10 Witnessed by the author

11 'NATO headquarters', NATO website, 19 April 2023

12 'NATO diversity and inclusion report', NATO website, 2020, page 7

13 'Remarks by Former NATO Secretary General Lord Robertson', Council on Foreign Relations, 25 February 2009

14 Ibid.

15 Interview with the author

16 Hastings Ismay, 'The Memoirs of Lord Ismay', page 461

17 Telegram from the mission to the North Atlantic Treaty Organisation to be Department of State, 23 January 1969, FRUS 1969–1976, Volume XLI, Western Europe, NATO, 1969–1972, Document 4

18 'Mrs Kirkpatrick says NATO is greatest post-war success', *New York Times*, 1 May 1984

19 Interview with the author

20 Telegram from the embassy in Belgium to the Department of State, 19 December 1961, FRUS 1961–1963, Volume XIII, Western Europe and Canada, Document 120

21 Interview with the author

22 Interview with the author

23 'Comparison of the military capabilities of NATO and Russia as of 2023', statista.com

24 Interview with the author

25 'Joint press conference', NATO website, 17 March 2023

26 'NATO warns Russia could target undersea pipelines and cables', *Politico*, 3 May 2023

27 'New NATO force model', NATO website, 29 June 2022

28 Stephen E. Ambrose, *Eisenhower Volume 1: Soldier, General of the Army, President Elect*, 1983, pages 506, 507

29 SHAPE Historians, 'SHAPE History: volume 3, the new approach, 1953–1956', NATO archives, PDF page 22

30 'Estonia's PM says country would be "wiped from map" under existing NATO plans', *Financial Times*, 22 June 2022

31 Interview with the author

32 'NATO's new plans will help to better defend "every inch" of Allied territory', *Stars and Stripes*, 10 May 2023

33 'Secretary general foresees a growing activist role in crises', *New York Times*, 23 June 1998

34 Interview with the author

35 Interview with the author

36 Interview with the author

37 'Speech by NATO secretary general to the Imperial Defence College', NATO website, 1 November 1957

38 Interview with the author

39 Interviews with the author

40 'Poland to ramp up defence budget to 4 per cent of GDP', *Deutsche Welle*, 30 January 2023

41 'NATO treads a fine line on Ukraine membership', *Politico*, 4 April 2023

42 'War in Ukraine has changed Europe forever', *New York Times*, 26 February 2023

3. From the Ruins of Dunkirk (1945–1948)

1 George Orwell, 'The Atomic Bomb and You', *Tribune*, 19 October 1945

2 Quoted in Lord Ismay, 'NATO: The First Five Years', NATO archive, page 4

3 Report to Winston Churchill on 'Operation UNTHINKABLE', 22 May 1945, UK National Archives

4 'Operation UNTHINKABLE', *UK National Archives* website, 28 April 2014

5 Field Marshal Bernard Law Montgomery of Alamein, *The Memoirs of Field Marshal Montgomery,* 1958, Kindle location 6204

6 Andrew Adonis, *Ernest Bevin: Labour's Churchill*, 2020, Kindle location 824, 844

7 Ibid., Kindle location 3677

8 Ibid., Kindle location 3694

9 David McCullough, *Truman*, 1992, Kindle location 597

10 Ibid., Kindle location 602, 603

11 Ibid., Kindle location 595

12 Lord Ismay, 'NATO: The First Five Years', NATO archive, page 4

13 *Encyclopaedia Britannica*, entry on the Soviet army

14 Bernard Law Montgomery, *The Memoirs of Field Marshal Montgomery*, 1958/2006, Kindle location 6877

15 Ibid., Kindle location 6898

16 Odd Arne Westad, *The Cold War: A World History*, 2017, Kindle location 76

17 'A post-war war: the years of 1944–1963 in Poland', the Warsaw Institute Review, 1 October 2018

18 Al Murray, *Command: How the allies learned to win the Second World War*, 2022, Kindle location 2094, 2051, 2072

19 George Kennan, 'Long Telegram', 22 February 1946, Wilson Center Digital Archive

20 McCullough, *Truman*, Kindle location 644

21 Ibid., Kindle location 645

22 Bernard Law Montgomery, *The Memoirs of Field Marshal Montgomery,* Kindle location 11140

23 'Strong foreign policy is Washington programme', *New York Times*, 25 August 1946

24 Henry A. Wallace, 'Madison Square Garden speech', 12 September 1946, American Social History Project

25 Document collection on the Wallace speech, Truman Presidential Library

26 Robert Gildea, *France Since 1945*, 2002, Kindle location 6

27 Jean Chauvel, 'Commentary: From Algiers to Bern (1944–1952)', extract on the Dunkirk treaty on the EU's CVCE website

28 Alan Bullock, *Ernest Bevin: Foreign Secretary*, pages 360, 357

29 Bullock, ibid., page 358; Chauvel, ibid., extract on the Dunkirk treaty on the EU's CVCE website.

30 Robert Gildea, *France Since 1945*, Kindle location 7

31 Jean Chauvel, 'Commentary: From Algiers to Bern (1944–1952)', extract on the Dunkirk treaty, CVCE website

32 Ibid.

33 Georges Bidault, 'From One Resistance to Another', extract on the Dunkirk Treaty on CVCE website

34 Pathé News report on Treaty of Dunkirk, uploaded to YouTube by Pathé archive 2014

35 Jean Chauvel, 'Commentary: From Algiers to Bern (1944–1952)', extract on the Dunkirk Treaty

36 Ibid.

37 Alan Bullock, *Ernest Bevin: Foreign Secretary*, page 374

38 Ernest Bevin to Parliament, 22 January 1948, Hansard

39 Andrew Adonis, *Ernest Bevin: Britain's Churchill*, Kindle location 4158

40 US National Archives, 'The Truman Doctrine', 12 March 1947

41 Odd Arne Westad, *The Cold War: A World History*, Kindle location 93

42 Robert Gildea, *France Since 1945*, Kindle location 13

43 Odd Arne Westad, *The Cold War: A World History*, 2017, Kindle location 98

44 'Speech by NATO secretary general', NATO archive, 1 November 1957

45 Hastings Ismay, 'NATO: The First Five Years', page 9

46 Timothy Andrews Sayle, *Enduring Alliance: A History of NATO and the Postwar Global Order*, 2019, Kindle location 20

47 John D. Hickerson, oral interview with Truman Presidential Archive, 1972

4. Airlift and Alliance (1948–1949)

1 'Memorandum by the Director of office for European affairs to the Secretary of State', 8 March 1948, FRUS 1948, Western Europe, Volume III, Document 31

2 John Hickerson, oral interview, Truman Presidential Archive

3 Theodore Achilles, oral history interview, Truman Presidential Archive

4 William Edwards, oral history interview, Truman Presidential Archive

5 Theodore Achilles, oral history interview, Truman Presidential Archive

6 'Memorandum by the Director of the Office of European Affair to the Secretary of State', 19 January 1948, FRUS 1948, Western Europe, Volume III, Document 33

7 'Memorandum by the director of policy planning staff to the Secretary of State', 20 January 1948, FRUS 1948, Volume III, Document 35

8 'Memorandum of conversation by the Director of the Office of European Affairs', 21 January 1948, FRUS 1948, Western Europe, Volume III, Document 7

9 Hickerson and Achilles, oral interviews, Truman Presidential Archive

10 'Foreign Affairs debate', House of Commons, 22 January 1948, Parliamentary Hansard Records

11 'The ambassador in France to the Secretary of State', 22 September 1948, FRUS 1948, Western Europe, Volume III, Document 20

12 'The ambassador in France to the Secretary of State', 19 February 1948, FRUS, Western Europe, Volume III, Document 19

13 Hastings Ismay, 'NATO: The First Five Years', page 8

14 'Memorandum from the Director of the Office of European Affairs to the Secretary of State', 8 March 1948, FRUS, Western Europe, Volume III, Document 31

15 'Memorandum of conversation', 11 March 1948, FRUS, Western Europe, Volume III, Document 34

16 Oral history interview with William Heimlich, undated but likely 1990s, National Security Archive, George Washington University

17 'Address by President Truman to Congress', 17 March 1948, FRUS, Western Europe, Volume III, Document 48

18 'Joint Message by the French Minister of Foreign Affairs and the British Secretary of State for Foreign Affairs to be Secretary of State', 17 March 1948, FRUS, Western Europe, Volume III, Document 50

19 'Minutes of the Third Meeting of the United States–UK–Canada Security Conversations', 24 March 1948, FRUS, Western Europe, Volume III, Document 57

20 Achilles, oral history interview, Truman Presidential Archive

21 'Report by the Executive Secretary of the National Security Council', 13 April 1948, FRUS, Western Europe, Volume III, Document 71

22 'The ambassador in the United Kingdom to the Secretary of State', 16 April 1948, FRUS, Western Europe, Volume III, Document 72

23 'The ambassador in the United Kingdom to the Under Secretary of State', 17 April 1948, FRUS, Western Europe, Volume III, Document 73

24 John Hickerson, oral interview, Truman Presidential Archive

25 Hickerson and Achilles, oral interviews, Truman Presidential Archive

26 Interview with Edloe Donnan, National Security Archive, George Washington University

27 Interview with Gail Halvorsen, National Security Archive, George Washington University

28 'The United States military governor for Germany to the Department of the Army', 10 July 1948, FRUS, Germany and Austria, Volume II, Document 577

29 'Minutes of the First Meeting of the Washington Exploratory Talks on Security', 6 July 1948, FRUS, Western Europe, Volume III, Document 112

30 'Minutes of the Second Meeting of the Washington Exploratory Talks on Security', 6 July 1948, FRUS, Western Europe, Volume III, Document 113

31 Theodore Achilles, oral interview, Truman Presidential Archive

32 'Ernest Bevin and the creation of NATO', UK National Archives, 4 April 2019

33 Hastings Ismay, 'NATO: The First Five Years', page 18

34 Interview with Sir Freddie Laker, National Security Archive, George Washington University

35 Theodore Achilles, oral history interview, Truman Residential Archive

36 John Hickerson, oral history interview, Truman Presidential Archive

37 William I. Hitchcock, *The Age of Eisenhower: America and the World in the 1950s*, 2018, Kindle location 40

38 Theodore Achilles, *Fingerprints on History: The NATO Memoirs of Theodore Achilles*, Kent State University, 1992, pages 22–23

39 Hastings Ismay, 'NATO: The First Five Years', page 18

40 Achilles, oral history interview, Truman Presidential Archive

41 Achilles, oral history interview, Truman Presidential Archive

42 'Ernest Bevin and the creation of NATO, UK National Archives, 4 April 2019

43 Achilles, oral history interview, Truman Presidential Archive

44 US State Department transcript of broadcast, *The United States in World Affairs*, 18 March 1949 (embargoed for 20 March), Truman Presidential Archive

45 Hastings Ismay, 'NATO: The First Five Years', page 11

46 Andre de Staercke (ed), 'NATO's Anxious Birth', page 64

47 Achilles, oral history interview, Truman Presidential Archive

48 William Edwards, oral history interview, Truman Presidential Archive

49 Andre de Staercke (ed), 'NATO's Anxious Birth', page 53

50 Achilles, oral history interview, Truman Presidential Archive

51 Hickerson, oral history interview, Truman Presidential Archive

52 Theodore Achilles, *Fingerprints in History: the NATO Memoirs of Theodore Achilles*, pages 33–34

53 Timothy Andrews Sayle, *Enduring Alliance: A History of NATO and the Postwar Global Order*, Kindle location 27

54 'A letter from 1949 indicates Estonia wanted to be a NATO founding member', *Estonian World*, 29 March 2023

5. Putting the 'O' in NATO (1949–1951)

1 Ismay, 'NATO: The First Five Years', page 30

2 North Atlantic Council Communiqué, 17 September 1949, NATO archive

3 Minutes, NATO Military Committee, 6 October 1948

4 British Movietone News, 'Operation Bulldog', 1949, uploaded to YouTube 21 July 2015

5 Kenneth W. Conduit, 'History of the Joint Chief of Staff: The Joint Chiefs of Staff and National Policy 1947–1949', 1996, Joint Chiefs website, PDF page 135

6 'CIA organised secret army in Western Europe', *Washington Post*, 14 November 1990

7 'Memorandum By the Standing Group to the North Atlantic Military Committee Transmitting the Strategic Concept for the Defence of the North Atlantic Area', 19 October 1949, NATO archive

8 Seth A. Johnston, *How NATO Adapts: Strategy and Organization in the Atlantic Alliance Since 1950*, 2017, Kindle location 831

9 'Communiqué for the Press', 18 November 1949, NATO archive

10 'The Under Secretary of the Army to the Secretary of State', 10 April 1950, FRUS, Western Europe, Volume III, Document 36

11 Rand Corporation, 'Assessing the conventional balance in Europe, 1945–75'

12 Viscount Slim, oral history, US Department of Defense oral history archive

13 'Schuman Declaration', 9 May 1950, European Union website

14 Hastings Ismay, 'NATO: The First Five Years', page 30

15 Max Hastings, *The Korean War*, 1987, Kindle location 1040

16 Calder Walton, *Spies: The Epic Intelligence War between East and West*, 2023, Kindle location 196

17 Theodore Achilles, *Fingerprints on History* . . ., page 36

18 Ann M. Sperber, *Murrow: His Life and Times*, 1986, page 341

19 Timothy Andrews Sayle, *Enduring Alliance* . . ., Kindle location 28

20 Achilles, *Fingerprints on History* . . . , page 28

21 Seth A. Johnston, *How NATO Adapts* . . ., Kindle location 6039

22 Achilles, *Fingerprints on History* . . ., page 41

23 Address given by Winston Churchill to the Council of Europe, 11 August 1950, EU website CVCE

24 Achilles, *Fingerprints on History* . . ., page 41

25 Ibid., pages 39–42

26 Timothy Andrews Sayle, *Enduring Alliance* . . ., Kindle location 29

27 Nigel Hamilton, *Monty: The Field Marshall, 1944–1976*, 1986, page 775

28 Lauris Norstad, oral history interview, Eisenhower Presidential Archive

29 Ibid.

30 Dwight D. Eisenhower, *The Eisenhower Diaries*, 1981, page 178

31 'With Ike, rumours were steamier than facts', *Washington Post*, 1 March 1998

32 Ismay, 'NATO: The First Five Years', page 35

33 Seth A. Johnston, *How NATO Adapts . . .*, Kindle location 1262

34 SHAPE Historians, 'Shape History: Volume 1', page 67

35 Ismay, 'NATO: The First Five Years', page 37

36 Alan Bullock, *Ernest Bevin: Foreign Secretary*, page 835

37 Tributes to Ernest Bevin collated by Anthony Broxton, Tides of History website

6. The Eisenhower 'Spiral of Strength Going Upwards' (1951–1952)

1 William I. Hitchcock, *The Age of Eisenhower . . .*, Kindle location 49

2 'Memorandum prepared in the Department of State for the President', 5 January 1951, FRUS, European Security, Volume III, Part 1, Document 214

3 Nigel Hamilton, *Monty: The Field Marshal, 1944–1976*, page 774

4 Dwight D. Eisenhower, *The Eisenhower Diaries*, page 185

5 'Truman wrote of '48 offer to Eisenhower', *New York Times*, 11 July 2003

6 Eisenhower Presidential Library, 'Eisenhower Diaries', 1 January 1950

7 Dwight D. Eisenhower, *The Eisenhower Diaries*, page 175

8 Stephen E. Ambrose, *Eisenhower Volume 1: Soldier, General of the Army, President Elect*, 1983, page 496

9 William I. Hitchcock, *The Age of Eisenhower . . .*, Kindle location 40

10 Achilles, *Fingerprints on History . . .*, page 43

11 Georgie Elsey to Truman, with attached minutes of meeting with Eisenhower, 6 February 1951, Truman Presidential Archive

12 Eisenhower, *The Eisenhower Diaries*, page 194

13 Georgie Elsey to Truman, with attached minutes of meeting with Eisenhower, 6 February 1951, Truman Presidential Archive

14 Ambrose, *Eisenhower, Volume 1 . . .*, page 504

15 Ibid., page 503

16 Ibid., pages 504–507

17 Ibid., page 502

18 Remarks of Representative John F. Kennedy before the Senate Committee on Foreign Relations, 22 February 1951, John F. Kennedy Presidential Library and Museum

19 'How SHAPE took shape', NATO website

20 SHAPE Historians, 'SHAPE History: Volume 1', page 71

21 Nigel Hamilton, *Monty: The Field Marshall, 1944–1976*, page 790

22 SHAPE Historians, 'SHAPE History: Volume 1', pages 80–81

23 Ibid., page 81

24 Nigel Hamilton, *Monty: The Field Marshal, 1944–1976*, page 790

25 'Foundation of SHAPE', NATO YouTube channel

26 Eisenhower, *The Eisenhower Diaries*, page 189

27 SHAPE Historians, 'SHAPE History: Volume 1', page 129

28 Nigel Hamilton, *Monty: The Field Marshal, 1944–1976*, page 793

29 SHAPE Historians, 'SHAPE History: Volume 1', page 147

30 Ambrose, *Eisenhower, Volume 1 . . .*, page 498

31 Ibid., page 521

32 Eisenhower, *The Eisenhower Diaries*, page 202

33 Ibid., page 204

34 Ambrose, *Eisenhower: Volume 1 . . .*, page 513

35 Vladimir Pechatnov, *The Soviet Union and the World, 1944–53*, from Melvyn
    P. Leffler and Odd Arne Westad (Eds), *The Cambridge History of the Cold War:
    Volume 1*, Kindle location 110

36 Ambrose, *Eisenhower: Volume 1 . . .*, page 509

37 Eisenhower, *The Eisenhower Diaries*, page 208

38 Ibid., page 205

39 Ismay, 'NATO: The First Five Years', page 38

40 Ibid., page 40

41 William I. Hitchcock, *The Age of Eisenhower: America and the World in the
    1950s*, Kindle location 57, 58

7. Massive Retaliation, Massive Divisions (1952–1958)

1 J. Robert Oppenheimer, 'Atomic Weapons and American Policy', Foreign
   Affairs, 1 July 1953

2 Gregory Pedlow, 'NATO Strategy Documents, 1944–69', NATO website, page 16

3 Lauris Norstad, oral history interview, Eisenhower Presidential Library

4 'Working group on civil organisation in time of war', 5 July 1952, NATO
   archive

5 Theodore Achilles, *Fingerprints on History . . .*, pages 44–46

6 Ismay, 'The Memoirs of Lord Ismay', page 460

7 Achilles, *Fingerprints on History . . .*, page 46

8 Ismay, 'Memoirs of Lord Ismay', page 461

9 'Truman says NATO steadily lessens the peril of war', *New York Times,* 5
   April 1952

10 Ismay, 'NATO: The First Five Years', pages 59, 62

11 Forward to the NATO International Staff Archives Section, NATO web-
    site, March 2001

12 Achilles, *Fingerprints on History*, page 2

13 'Ridgeway held the likely choice as Eisenhower's successor', *New York Times*,
    9 April 1952

14 Montgomery, *The Memoirs of Field Marshal Montgomery*, Kindle location 8876

15 Nigel Hamilton, *Monty Volume Two: Master of the Battlefield, 1942–1944*, 1986,
    page 824

16 Gill Bennett, 'The decision to build a British atomic bomb', 8 January
    1947, British government website

17 Brian Cathcart, *Test of Greatness: Britain's Struggle for the Atomic Bomb*, 1994,
    page 267

18 David M. Blades and Joseph M. Siracusa, *A History of US Nuclear Testing and
    its Influence on Nuclear Thought, 1945–1963*, 2014, page 47

19 Boeing website, 'B–52 Stratofortress', 2023

20 John Bullard, 'History of the Redstone Missile System', 1965

21 William I. Hitchcock, *The Age of Eisenhower: America and the World in the
    1950s*, page 82

22 Ibid., page 104

23 Ibid., page 103–105

24 'NATO Leaders: Lord Ismay', NATO website, retrieved 2023

25 '25 years after East German revolt, strains linger', *New York Times*, 18 June
    1978

26 Charles Wheeler interview, National Security Archive, George Washing-
    ton University

27 Hitchcock, *The Age of Eisenhower . . .*, pages 104–107

28 'Soviet announces a test explosion of hydrogen bomb', *New York Times*, 20
    August 1953

29 Timothy Andrews Sayle, *Enduring Alliance: A History of NATO and the Post-
    war Global Order*, page 35

30 Gregory Pedlow, '*The Evolution of NATO Strategy, 1949–69*', NATO web-
    site, page XII

31 Hitchcock, *The Age of Eisenhower . . .*, page 11

32 'The Deputy Under Secretary of State to the Assistant Secretary of
    Defence for International Security Affairs', 30 July 1953, FRUS, Western
    European Security, Volume V, Part 1, Document 227

33 'Notes prepared by the Assistant Secretary of State for European
    Affairs on the Restricted Session of the North Atlantic Council', 16
    December 1953, FRUS, Western European Security, Volume V, Part 1,
    Document 245

34 Details of discussions between Eisenhower and Montgomery from Nigel Hamilton, *Monty Volume Two: Master of the Battlefield, 1942–1944*, page 830

35 'NATO Leaders: Alfred M. Gruenther', NATO website

36 Ibid.

37 'Molotov proposal to Malenkov and Khrushchev', 26 March 1954, translation in Wilson Centre Digital Archive

38 John Colville, *The Fringes of Power: Downing Street Diaries, 1939–1955*, 1985, page 640

39 Timothy Andrews Sayle, *Enduring Alliance: A History of NATO and the Postwar Global Order*, pages 37–49

40 Theodore Achilles, *Fingerprints on History . . .*, pages 56–58

41 Telegram from the US delegation at the North Atlantic Ministerial Meeting to the Department of State, Paris, 16 December 1955, FRUS, 1955–1957, Western European Security and Integration', Volume 4, Document 11

42 'Điện Biên Phu: Battle to Remember', *New York Times*, 3 May 1964

43 'Egypt nationalises Suez canal company', *New York Times*, 27 July 1956

44 '11% rise reported in Suez Canal use this year', *New York Times*, 1–19 April 1956

45 Telegram from the embassy in the United Kingdom to the Department of State, 27 July 1956, FRUS, Suez crisis, Volume XVI, Document 2

46 Telegram from the embassy in France to the Department of State, 27 July 1956, FRUS

47 'Memorandum of a Conference with the President', White House, 27 July 1956, 8.30 a.m., FRUS, 1955–1957, Suez crisis, Volume XVI, Document 3

48 Telegram from the Department of States to the embassy in the United Kingdom, 30 August 1956, FRUS, 1955–1957, Suez crisis, Volume XVI, Document 4

49 Tim Weiner, *Legacy of Ashes: The History of the CIA*, 2007, page 144

50 'Protest in Poland', *New York Times*, 30 June 1956

51 Interview with Charles Wheeler, National Security Archive, George Washington University

52 'Memorandum of a Conference with the President', White House, 27 October 1956, 11 a.m., FRUS, 1955–1957, Suez crisis, Volume XVI, Document 387

53 Timothy Andrews Sayle, *Enduring Alliance: A History of NATO and the Postwar Global Order*, page 49

54 Interview with Charles Wheeler, National Security Archive, George Washington University

55 'Memorandum of a conversation, Ambassador Dillon's Residence, Paris', 10 December 1956, 9.45 a.m., FRUS, 1955–1957, Suez crisis, Volume XVI, Document 643

56 Timothy Andrews Sayle, *Enduring Alliance: A History of NATO and the Post-war Global Order*, pages 50–52

57 Account found in the document 'Telegram from the United States Delegation at the North Atlantic Council Ministerial Meeting to the Department of State', 13 December 1956, 11 a.m., FRUS 1955–57, Western European Security and Integration, Volume IV, Document 47

58 Account found in the document 'Telegram from the United States Delegation at the North Atlantic Council Ministerial Meeting to the Department of State', 13 December 1956, 11 a.m., FRUS 1955–57, Western European Security and Integration, Volume IV

8. Sputnik, *Nukes and Charles de Gaulle (1957–1960)*

1 'Memorandum from the Assistant Secretary of State for European Affairs to Acting Secretary of State', 27 May 1958, FRUS, Western Europe, Volume VII, Document 12

2 Ismay, *Autobiography . . .*, page 462

3 General Lord Ismay. 'Rules for NATO Conduct', London, 4 June 1957, NATO Speeches, Updated 20 December 2001

4 'Alfred M Gruenther, 84, is dead; ex-military commander of NATO', *New York Times*, 31 May, 1983

5 NATO Leaders, 'Lauris M. Norstad', NATO website

6 'Present for the beginning: a Khrushchev remembers', *New York Times*, 25 September 2007

7 'History of the Joint Chiefs of Staff, Volume 7: The Joint Chiefs of Staff and National Policy, 1957–60', 1986, page 17

8 'Memorandum of Discussion at the 348th Meeting of the National Security Council, Washington', 12 December 1957, FRUS, Western European Security and Integration, Volume 4, Document 69

9 SHAPE Historians, 'SHAPE History: 1958', pages 62–65

10 'Memorandum of Conference with the President, Washington', 28 October 1957, FRUS, 1958–60, Western European Security and Integration, Volume VI, Document 60

11 Timothy Andrews Sayle, *Enduring Alliance: A History of NATO and the Post-war Global Order*, page 65

12 Max Hastings, *Abyss: The Cuban Missile Crisis 1962*, 2022, Kindle location 87

13 Robert Gildea, *France Since 1945*, Kindle locations 38–40

14 Julian T. Jackson, *A Certain Idea of France: The Life of Charles de Gaulle*, 2018, Kindle locations 465–471

15 SHAPE Historians, 'SHAPE History: 1958', pages 4–5

16 Robert Gildea, *France Since 1945*, Kindle location 49

17 'Memorandum of Conference with President Eisenhower', 3 July 1958, FRUS, 1958–60, Western Europe, Volume VII, Part 2, Document 32

18 Ibid.

19 Ibid.

20 'Memorandum of conversation', 5 June 1958, FRUS, 1958–60, Western Europe, Volume II, Part 2, Document 34

21 Nigel Henderson, *Monty Volume 2 . . .*, pages 850–902

22 Sayle, *Enduring Alliance . . .*, page 79

23 US State Department Historian, 'The Berlin Crisis', State Department website

24 FRUS, 1958–1960, Berlin crisis, 1958–59, Volume VIII, Document 40

25 Telegram from the Mission to the North Atlantic Treaty Organisation and European Regional Organisations to the Department of State, 17 November 1958, FRUS 1958–60, Berlin crisis, 1958–1959, Volume VIII, Document 43

26 Sayle, *Enduring Alliance . . .*, Kindle location 111

27 'Joint Chiefs of Staff and National Policy, 1957–1960', page 126

28 'Memorandum of Conference with President Eisenhower', 12 December 1958, FRUS 1958–60, Western Europe, Volume VIII, Part 2, Document 79

29 Letter from President Eisenhower to President de Gaulle, 20 October 1958, FRUS 1958–60, Western Europe, Volume VIII, Part 2, Document 63

30 Telegram from the Department of State to the embassy in France, 25 October 1958, FRUS 1958–60, Western Europe, Volume VII, Part 2, Document 64

31 Telegram from Secretary of State Dulles to the Department of State, 15 December 1958, FRUS 1958–60, Western Europe, Volume VII, Part 2, Document 82

32 Telegram from Secretary of State Dulles to the Department of State, 16 December 1958, FRUS 1958–60, Western European Integration and Security, Canada, Volume 7, Part 1

33 Julian Jackson, *A Certain Idea of France: The Life of Charles de Gaulle*, pages 483–500

34 Telegram from the Mission at the North Atlantic Treaty Organisation and European regional organisations to the Department of State, 10 March 1959, FRUS 1958–60, Western European Integration and Security, Canada, Volume VII, Part 1, Document 199

35 Sayle, *Enduring Alliance*, Kindle location 84

36 Ibid., Kindle location 112

37 'Memorandum of Conference with President Eisenhower', 9 June 1959, FRUS 1958–60, Western European Integration and Security, Canada, Volume VII, Part 2, Document 214

38 Max Hastings, *Abyss: the Cuban Missile Crisis 1962*, Kindle location 91

39 Colin Powell, *A Soldier's Way: An Autobiography*, 1995, Kindle location 67

40 Hitchcock, *The Age of Eisenhower*, Kindle locations 417–422

41 Ibid., Kindle locations 423–427

42 Alan Gevinson, 'De Gaulle's Visit to the National Press Club', National Press Club archives, date uncertain, Library of Congress

43 Hitchcock, *The Age of Eisenhower*, Kindle location 463

44 NATO communiqué, 19 May 1960

45 'Memorandum of Conference with President Eisenhower', 24 August 1959, FRUS 1958–60, Western European Integration and Security, Canada, Volume VII, Document 221

46 Hitchcock, *The Age of Eisenhower*, Kindle locations 469–471

9. Testing Kennedy in Berlin (1961)

1 Telegram from the Mission to the North Atlantic Treaty Organisation and European Regional Organisations to the Department of State, 18 December 1961, FRUS 1961–1963, Volume XIII, Western Europe and Canada, Document 118

2 Arthur M. Schlesinger Jnr, *A Thousand Days: John F. Kennedy in the White House*, 1965, Kindle location 2246

3 Gregory W. Pedlow, 'The Evolution of NATO Strategy, 1949–1969', official NATO publication, 1997

4 Iain MacGregor, *Checkpoint Charlie: the Cold War, the Berlin Wall and the Most Dangerous Place on Earth* 2019, Kindle location 69

5 Max Hastings, *Abyss: the Cuban Missile Crisis 1962*, Kindle location 127

6 'Memorandum of conversation', 1 February 1961, FRUS 1961–1963, Volume XIII , Western Europe and Canada, Document 93

7 NATO Declassified, 'Dirk Stikker', NATO website

8 Arthur M. Schlesinger Jnr, *A Thousand Days: John F. Kennedy in the White House*, Kindle location 5116–5137

9 'Memorandum of conversation', 21 February 1961, FRUS 1961–1963, Volume XIII, Western Europe and Canada, Document 95

10 'Memorandum of conversation', 15 March 1961, FRUS 1961–1963, Volume XIII, Western Europe and Canada, Document 96

11 Oral history interview with General Lauris Norstad, Eisenhower Presidential Library, pages 33–34

12 Policy Directive, FRUS 1961-1963, Volume XIII, Western Europe and Canada, Document 100

13 'Memorandum of conversation', 5 April 1961, FRUS 1961–1963, Volume XIV, Berlin Crisis, 1961–1962, Document 14; Macmillan's doubts are quoted in Sayle, *Enduring Alliance*, Kindle location 113

14 Sayle, *Enduring Alliance*, Kindle location 111-122

15 Schlesinger, *A Thousand Days . . .*, Kindle location 4830

16 Speech to the Canadian Parliament, 17 May 1961, page 3, JFK Presidential Library

17 'Memorandum from Henry Kissinger of the National Security Council Staff to President Kennedy', FRUS 1961–1963, Volume XIV, Berlin Crisis, 1961–1962, Document 13

18 Schlesinger, *A Thousand Days . . .*, Kindle location 1866

19 Sayle, *Enduring Alliance*, Kindle location 103

20 'Memorandum of conversation', 31 May 1961, FRUS 1961–1963, Volume XIV, Berlin Crisis, 1961–62, Document 30

21 Presidential comments to North Atlantic Council, 1 June 1961, JFK Presidential Library

22 'Memorandum of conversation between the President and President Nikita Khrushchev', 4 June 1961, JFK Presidential Library

23 Dean Rusk, oral history interview 4, page 28, JFK Presidential Library

24 Gregory Pedlow, 'NATO and the Berlin Crisis of 1961: Facing the Soviets While Maintaining Unity', page 2

25 Donald A. Carter, 'The US Military Response to the 1960–1962 Berlin Crisis', pages 2–3

26 Gregory Pedlow, 'NATO and the Berlin Crisis of 1961: Facing the Soviets While Maintaining Unity', page 3

27 Ibid., pages 5–7

28 Donald A. Carter, 'The US Military Response to the 1960–1962 Berlin Crisis', pages 3–4

29 Ibid., pages 3–5

30 'Iain MacGregor, *Checkpoint Charlie . . .*, Kindle location 80

31 Gregory Pedlow, 'NATO and the Berlin Crisis of 1961: Facing the Soviets While Maintaining Unity', page 4

32 'Memorandum from President Kennedy to Secretary of State Rusk', 14 August 1961, FRUS 1961–1963, Volume XIV, Berlin Crisis, 1961–1962, Document 109

33 Telegram from the Mission at Berlin to the Department of State, Berlin, 16 August 1961, FRUS, 1961–1963, Volume XIV, Berlin Crisis, 1961–1962, Document 114; Donald A. Carter, 'The US Military Response to the 1960–1962 Berlin Crisis', pages 4–8

34 Telegram from the Mission at Berlin to the Department of State, 16 August 1961, FRUS 1961–1953, Volume XIV, Berlin Crisis, 1961–1962, Document 115

35 Telegram from the Mission at Berlin to the Department of State, 16 August 1961, FRUS 1961–1963, Volume XIV, Berlin Crisis, 1961–1962, Document 117

36 Record of Meeting of the Berlin Steering Group, 17 August 1961, 17 August 1961, FRUS 1961–1963, Volume XIV, Berlin Crisis, 1961–1962, Document 118

37 Donald A. Carter, 'The US Military Response to the 1960–1962 Berlin Crisis', pages 4–8

38 'Troops dispatched by JFK', *Berlin Observer: The Newspaper of Berlin Command*, 15 August 1961

39 Donald A. Carter, 'The US Military Response to the 1960–1962 Berlin Crisis', pages 4–8

40 Gregory Pedlow, 'NATO and the Berlin Crisis of 1961: Facing the Soviets While Maintaining Unity', pages 7–11

41 Telegram from the Department of State to the embassy in Germany, 17 September 1961, FRUS 1961–1963, Volume XIV, Berlin Crisis, 1961–1962, Document 153

42 Donald A. Carter, 'The US Military Response to the 1960–1962 Berlin Crisis', pages 7–8

43 MacGregor, *Checkpoint Charlie* . . . , Kindle locations 80-85

44 Max Hastings, *Abyss: the Cuban Missile Crisis 1962*, Kindle location 126

45 'Nuclear Test Ban Treaty', JFK Presidential Archive

46 Max Hastings, *Abyss: the Cuban Missile Crisis 1962*, Kindle location 129

47 Gregory Pedlow, 'NATO and the Berlin Crisis of 1961: Facing the Soviets While Maintaining Unity', page 12-13

48 'Memorandum Prepared in the Department of State', 9 November 1961, FRUS 1961–1963, Volume XIV, Berlin Crisis, 1961–1962, Document 205

49 Timothy Andrews Sayle, *Enduring Alliance* . . ., Kindle location 128-130

50 Ibid., Kindle location 130

51 'Memorandum of conversation', 12 December 1961, FRUS 1961–1963, Volume XIV, Berlin Crisis, 1961–1962, Document 238

52 Telegram from the Mission to the North Atlantic Treaty Organisation and European Regional Organisations to the Department of State, 18 December 1961, FRUS 1961–1963, Volume XIII, Western Europe and Canada, Document 118

53 Telegram from the embassy in Belgium to the Department of State, 19 December 1961, FRUS 1961–1963, Volume XIII, Western Europe and Canada, Document 120

54 Telegram from the Secretary of State Rusk to the Department of State, 15 December 1961, FRUS 1961–1963, Volume XIII, Western Europe and Canada, Document 117

10. Cuba (1962)

1 George Ignatieff, *The Making of a Peacemonger: the Memoirs of George Ignatieff*, Kindle location 3145

2 Letter from the President's military representative to President Kennedy, FRUS 1961-1963, Volume XIII, Western Europe and Canada, Document 131

3 'Telegram from the mission at Berlin to the Department of State', FRUS 1951–1962, Volume XV, Berlin Crisis 1961–1963, Document 31

4 Graham Allison and Philip Zelikow, *Essence of Decision: Explaining the Cuban Missile Crisis*, 1999, pages 94–95

5 Instructions for the Permanent Representative to the North Atlantic Council, undated (1962), FRUS 1961–1963, Volume XIII, Western Europe and Canada, Document 142

6 'The Jupiter Missiles and the Endgame of the Cuban Missile Crisis', Wilson Center,

7 Lauris Norstad, oral history interview, Eisenhower Presidential Library, pages 50–51

8 'The French Spy Scandal', *Life* magazine, 26 April 1968, page 38

9 Ibid., page 36

10 Paper Prepared for the National Security Council by the Department of State Operations Centre, 27 April 1961, FRUS 1951–1953, Volume X, Cuba, January 1961–September 1962

11 Iain MacGregor, *Checkpoint Charlie . . .* , Kindle locations 89-91

12 Max Hastings, *Abyss: the Cuban Missile Crisis 1962*, Kindle location 118

13 Dean Rusk, oral history interview, JFK Presidential Library, page 32

14 William J. Perry, *My Journey at the Nuclear Brink*, 2015, Kindle locations 1–2

15 Dean Rusk, oral history interview, JFK Presidential Library, page 38

16 Interview with Robert McNamara for 2003 documentary *The Fog of War*, transcribed on the Alpha History website

17 Kenneth Jack, 'Forgotten missiles of the Cuban missile crisis', US Naval Institute News, 21 October 2012

18 Hastings, *Abyss . . .,* Kindle locations 214–280

19 Ibid., Kindle locations 199–202

20 Ibid., Kindle locations 236–239

21 Ibid., Kindle location 256

22 Oral history interview with Dean Acheson, JFK Presidential Archive, pages 23-29

23 Hastings, *Abyss . . .,* Kindle location 262

24 Ibid., Kindle location 257

25 Ibid., Kindle location 273

26 Ibid., Kindle location 326

27 Notes on Meeting with President Kennedy, 21 October 1962, FRUS 1961–1963, Volume XI, Cuban Missile Crisis and Aftermath, Document 36

28 Telegram from the President to SACEUR, 22 October 1962, JFK Presidential Archive

29 Telegram from the Department of State to the embassy of the United Kingdom, 22 October 1962, FRUS 1961–1963, Volume XI, Cuban Missile Crisis and Aftermath, Document 39

30 Oral history interview with Dean Acheson, JFK Presidential Archive, pages 30–33

31 'Memorandum for the Record', FRUS, 1951–1963, American Republics; Cuba 1961 1962, Volumes X–XII, Document 152

32 US embassy in West Germany telegram to the Secretary of State, 22 October 1962, George Washington University National Security Archive

33 Hastings, *Abyss* . . ., Kindle location 293

34 Chester Cooper, 'Memorandum for the Record, Mission to London', 29 October 1962, George Washington University National Security Archive

35 Telegram for the President from General Norstad, 22 October 1962, JFK Presidential Library

36 Hastings, *Abyss* . . ., Kindle location 273–275

37 United Kingdom delegation to NATO Paris telegram 1632 Foreign Office, 'Cuba', 22 October 1962, George Washington University National Security Archive

38 US embassy Belgium telegram 636 to State Department, 'Cuba', 23 October 1962, George Washington University National Security Archive

39 George Ignatieff, *The Making of a Peacemonger: the Memoirs of George Ignatieff*, Kindle location 3145

40 'Memorandum for the Record', FRUS, 1951–1963, American Republics; Cuba 1961 1962, Volumes X/XI/XII, Document 352

41 Chester Cooper, 'Memorandum for the Record, Mission to London', 29 October 1962, National Security Archive, George Washington University

42 Hastings, *Abyss* . . ., Kindle location 284

43 Ibid., Kindle locations 300–304

44 Ibid., Kindle location 315

45 Ibid., Kindle location 326

46 'The critical implications of the Cuban missile crisis on a divided Germany and Berlin', Britannica.com, undated

47 Hastings, *Abyss* . . ., Kindle location 337

48 Cable from Federal Republic of Germany embassy, Washington, 27 October 1962, reproduced in 'Konrad Adenauer and the Cuban Missile Crisis: West German Documents', page 630

49 Hastings, *Abyss . . .*, Kindle location 405

50 Hastings, ibid, Kindle location 411; Recollections of Vadim Orlov, National Security Archive, George Washington University, 1 January 2002

51 Letter from Chairman Nikita Khrushchev to President Kennedy, 27 October 1962, JFK Presidential Archive

52 Rusk, oral history interview, JFK Archive, page 51

53 Hastings, *Abyss . . .*, Kindle location 414

54 Ibid., page 416

55 'Exceptional Circumstances: Canada's Maritime Response to the Cuban Missile Crisis', Canadian Armed Forces Directory of History and Heritage, 2022, Pages 44-47

56 'Cold War Royal Navy diesel submarine officer during the 1960s and 1970s', Cold War Conversations podcasts

57 'Remembering the Cuban missile crisis', European Leadership Network, 11 November 2014

58 'The critical implications of the Cuban missile crisis on a divided Germany and Berlin', Britannica.com, undated

59 Hastings, *Abyss . . .*, Kindle location 291

60 Sayle, *Enduring Alliance*, Kindle location 136

61 Telegram from the Joint Chiefs of Staff to CINCLANT, 22 October 1962, FRUS 1961–1963, American Republics, Cuba 1961–1962; Cuban Missile Crisis and Aftermath, Volumes X–XII, Microfiche Supplement

62 'Exceptional Circumstances: Canada's Maritime Response to the Cuban Missile Crisis', Canadian Armed Forces Directory of History and Heritage, 2022, Pages 44-47

63 Summary Record of the Seventh Meeting of the Executive Committee Meeting of the National Security Council, 27 October 1962, JFK Presidential Archive

64 Telegram from the Mission to the North Atlantic Treaty Organisation and European Regional Organisations to the Department of State, 25 October 1962, FRUS 1961–1963, Volume XVI, Eastern Europe; Cyprus; Greece; Turkey, Document 380

65 Telegram from Secretary of State Rusk to the Department of State, 15 December 1962, FRUS 1961–1963, Volume XII, Western Europe and Canada, Document 159

66 'Memorandum of conversation', 14 November 1962, FRUS 1961–1963, Volume XIII, Western Europe and Canada, Document 157

67 Dean Acheson, 'NATO in the light of the October crisis', 5 November 1962, page 3, JFK Presidential Library

11. The Shadow of Vietnam (1963–1974)

1 Jamie Shea, 'NATO history lesson – the 1960s', NATO website, 3 March 2009

2 Ibid.

3 'The Pâques Affair', NATO declassified, viewed 2023

4 'The French Spy Scandal', *Life* magazine, 26 April 1968, page 36

5 'The Pâques Affair', secret internal NATO report, NATO archive, 25 March 1964

6 Remarks of President Kennedy to the National Security Council, January 22, 1963, FRUS 1961–1963, threats slip in Maryland based on Volume XIII, Western Europe and Canada, Document 168

7 'Hotline established between Washington and Moscow', November 16 2009, HISTORY, A&E Television Networks

8 Lawrence Kaplan, *NATO United, NATO Divided*, 2004, Kindle location 654

9 Ignatieff, *Makings of a Peacemonger*, Kindle location 3247

10 'Memorandum of conversation', 25 February 1963, FRUS 1961–1963, Volume 13, Western Europe and Canada, Document 177

11 President John F. Kennedy's trip to Germany, JFK Presidential Archive, 1 March 2022

12 'Memorandum from the President's Special Assistant for National Security Affairs to Secretary of State Rusk and Secretary of Defence McNamara', 21 November 1963, FRUS 1961–1963, Volume XII, Western Europe and Canada, Document 217

13 'Memorandum of conversation', 6 November 1964, FRUS 1964–1968, Volume 14, Soviet Union, Document 68

14 NATO declassified, 'Manlio Brosio', NATO website

15 Rusk, oral history interview 4, Johnson Presidential Archive, pages 15–16

16 Sayle, *Enduring Alliance*, Kindle location 172

17 Max Hastings, *Vietnam: An Epic History of a Divisive War, 1945–1975*, 2018, Kindle location 347

18 Quoted by Jonathan Colman, 'A Battalion Would Be Worth a Billion', in *A Special Relationship*, Manchester University Press, 2004

19 'Memorandum of conversation', 26 September 1966, FRUS 1960–1968, Volume XII, Document 207

20 Sayle, *Enduring Alliance*, Kindle locations 283–293

21 Transcript of de Gaulle's press conference, 21 February 1966, EU website CVCE

22 Ignatieff, *Making of a Peacemonger*, Kindle location 3247

23 John L. Hess, 'US Forces begin their withdrawal', *New York Times*, 1 July 1966

24 'History of SHAPE – SHAPE finds a new home', SHAPE website

25 'NATO takes over new headquarters in Brussels', *New York Times*, 17 October 1967

26 Gregory Pedlow, 'The Evolution of NATO Strategy, 1949–1969', pages 28–29

27 Telegram from the Mission to the North Atlantic Treaty Organization, 17 December 1966, FRUS 1964–1968, Volume XIII, Western Europe, Document 232,

28 Sayle, *Enduring Alliance*, Kindle location 180

29 Telegram from the Mission to the North Atlantic Treaty Organization, 17 December 1966, FRUS 1964–1968, Volume XIII, Western Europe, Document 232

30 Sayle, *Enduring Alliance*, Kindle locations 220–224

31 Intelligence Memorandum No. 2049/68, 4 November 1968, FRUS 1964–1968, Volume 13, Document 334

32 Sayle, *Enduring Alliance*, Kindle locations 218–222

33 'The Future Tasks of the Alliance', NATO archive, December 1967

34 Telegram from the Mission to the North Atlantic Treaty Organisation to the Department of State, 23 January 1969, FRUS 1969–1976, Volume XLI, Western Europe, NATO, 1969–1972, Document 4

35 Melvin Laird, Department of Defense oral history interview 3, 29 October 1986, page 3

36 Remarks to the North Atlantic Council, 24 February 1969, Nixon Foundation

37 Informal record of a private meeting of the Council with President Nixon in the State Department, Friday 11 April 1969, NATO archive

38 Luke A. Nichter, *Richard Nixon and Europe: the Reshaping of the Postwar Atlantic World*, 2015, Kindle location 7

39 'Memorandum from the President's Assistant for National Security Affairs to President Nixon', 2 June 1969, FRUS 1969–1976, Volume 41, Western Europe; NATO, 1969–1972, Document 19

40 Luke A. Nichter, *Richard Nixon and Europe . . .*, Kindle location 13

41 'Memorandum of conversation', Nixon Foundation

42 Alexander Haig, DoD oral history interview, page 22

43 Luke A. Nichter, *Richard Nixon and Europe . . .*, Kindle location 27

44 'NATO boss sang anti-NATO songs as a youth', The Local, 6 August 2015

45 'Memorandum from the Assistant Secretary of State for European Affairs to Secretary of State Rogers', 15 November 1971, FRUS 1969–1976, Volume 41, Western Europe; NATO, 1969–1972, Document 75

46 'Memorandum from the Assistant Secretary of State for European Affairs to Secretary of State Rogers', 15 November 1971, FRUS 1969–1976, Volume 41, Western Europe; NATO, 1969–1972, Document 75

47 Minutes of a Defence Programme Review Committee Meeting, 4 August 1971, FRUS, 1969–1976, Volume 41, Western Europe; NATO, 1969–1972, Document 70

48 Interview with Henry Kissinger, National Security Archive

49 'Memorandum from the President's Assistant for National Security Affairs to secretary of State Rogers', 9 March 1972, FRUS 1969–1976, Volume 41, Europe; NATO, 1969–1972, Document 80

50 'Nixon accord with Soviet embittered NATO officials', _New York Times_, 26 July 1972

51 Ibid.

52 Ibid.

53 Luke A. Nichter, _Richard Nixon and Europe . . ._, Kindle locations 31–33

54 'Conference at Helsinki – the facts in brief', _New York Times_, 3 July 1973

55 Minutes of Senior Review Group Meeting, 31 January 1973, FRUS 1969–1976, Volume E-15, Part 2, Documents on Western Europe, 1973–1976, Document 5

56 'Memorandum from President Nixon to the President's Assistant for National Security Affairs', 10 March 1973, FRUS 1973–1976, Volume E-15, Part 2, Documents on Western Europe, 1973–1976, Document 9

57 Text of Kissinger's speech on 'US Relations With Europe', _New York Times_, 24 April 1973,

58 Sayle, _Enduring Alliance_, Kindle location 246

59 Ibid., Kindle location 249

60 'Memorandum from Philip Odeen of the National Security Council staff to the President's Assistant for National Security Affairs', 9 June 1973, FRUS 1969–1976, Volume E-15, Part 2, Documents on Western Europe, 1973–1976, Document 22

61 'Nixon and Brezhnev – Personal Partners in _détente_', Nixon Foundation, 2010

62 'Memorandum of conversation', 30 July 1973, FRUS 1969–1976, Volume E-15, Part 2, Documents on Western Europe, 1973–1976, Document 27

63 Transcript of telephone conversation between President Nixon and the President's Assistant for National Security Affairs, 9 August 1973, FRUS 1969–1976, Volume E-15, Part 2, Documents on Western Europe, 1973–1976, Document 31

64 Sayle, _Enduring Alliance_, page 255

65 Telegram from US Mission to NATO to Secretary of State, 26 October 1973, US National Security Archive, George Washington University

66 Sayle, _Enduring Alliance_, Kindle location 258

67 'Memorandum from the President's Deputy System for National Security Affairs to President Nixon', 24 March 1974, FRUS 1973–1976, Volume E-15, Part 2, Documents on Western Europe, 1973–1976, Document 55

68 Sayle, *Enduring Alliance*, Kindle location 259

69 'Nixon in Brussels today for talks with NATO chiefs', 26 June 1974, *New York Times*

70 Sayle, *Enduring Alliance*, Kindle location 260

71 Donald Rumsfeld, oral history interview, Ford Presidential Library

72 'Memorandum for the President's File prepared by President's Assistant for National Security Affairs', 9 August 1974, FRUS 1969–1976, Volume E-15, Part 2, Documents on Western Europe, 1973–1976, Document 72

73 Walter S. Poole, 'The Decline of *Détente*', Cold War Foreign Policy Series, Historical Office, Office of the Secretary of Defense, page 23

74 Drew Middleton, 'Haig takes over as head of NATO', *New York Times*, 16 December 1974

75 Alexander Hague, DoD oral history interview, page 38

12. Back to the Brink (1975–1980)

1 'Memorandum of conversation', 27 March 1975, Ford Presidential Archive

2 Telegram from the embassy in Greece to the Department of State, 15 August 1974, FRUS 1969–1976, Volume 30, Greece; Cyprus; Turkey, 1973–1976, Document 20

3 'Memorandum of conversation', 24 February 1975, Ford Presidential Library

4 'Memorandum for the Record', 4 February 1975, FRUS 1969–1976, Volume E-15, Part 2, Documents on Western Europe, 1973–1976, Document 144

5 'Lisbon says coup is foiled after barracks raid', *New York Times*, 12 March 1975

6 Conversation Between President Nixon and the President's Assistant for National Security Affairs, 3 February 1973, FRUS 196–1973, Volume E-15, Part 2, Documents of Western Europe, 1973–1976, Document 6

7 'Memorandum of conversation', 27 March 1975, FRUS 1969–1976, Volume E-15, Part 2, Documents on Western Europe, 1973–1976, Document 149

8 Telegram 2395 from the embassy Portugal to the Department of State, 26 April 1975, FRUS 1969–1976, Volume E-15, Part 2, Documents on Western Europe, 1973–1976, Document 152

9 'NATO annual opinion tracker', NATO website, May 2023

10 'Memorandum of conversation', 12 August 1975, FRUS 1969–1976, Volume E-15, Part 2, Documents on Western Europe, 1973–1976, Document 158

11 'Memorandum Prepared in the Department of State', 10 October 1975, FRUS 1969–1976, Volume E-15, Part 2, Documents on Western Europe, 1973–1976, Document 164

12 The Embassy in Portugal to Department of State, 26 November 1975, FRUS 1969–1976, Volume E-15, Part 2, Documents on Western Europe, 1973–1976, Document 167

13 James Oliver and Nicholas Gilby, 'The secret British plan to keep it is Communists from power', *Observer*, 2 October 2022

14 Hastings, *Vietnam . . .*, Kindle location 884–886

15 'President to ask NATO if Portugal should be kept in', *New York Times*, 24 May 1975

16 '35 states meet in Helsinki to ensure peace in Europe', *New York Times*, 31 July 1975

17 Interview with Gerald Ford, National Security Archive, George Washington University

18 'Little gain since Helsinki accords, Eastern and Western aides agree', *New York Times*, 20 September 1976

19 Alexander Haig, DOD oral history interview, 2 May 1996, pages 34, 39, 42

20 'The Republican Primaries: Key Issues', Ford Presidential Library website

21 'Carter pledges an open foreign policy', *New York Times*, 24 June 1976

22 Sayle, *Enduring Alliance*, Kindle location 265

23 Address by Vice President Mondale, 24 January 1977, FRUS 1977–1980, Volume 1, Foundations of Foreign Policy, Document 16

24 'Mondale pledges US won't cut NATO funds', *New York Times*, 25 January 1977

25 'Prague is now insisting Charter 77 appeal violates constitution', *New York Times*, 25 February 1977

26 Sir Michael Alexander, British diplomatic oral history interview, Churchill College, Cambridge

27 Michael Getler, 'US broadcasts reach Soviet jails', *Washington Post*, 7 April 1977

28 Aaron Donaghy, The Second Cold War – Carter, Reagan and the Politics of Foreign Policy, 2021, Kindle location 35

29 'President bids NATO respond forcefully to Russians' build-up', *New York Times*, 11 May 1977

30 Edward Keefer, 'Harold Brown: Offsetting the Soviet Military Challenge', Secretaries of Defense Historical Series, 2017, page 426

31 'Conceding defeat in Europe', *Washington Post*, 4 August 1977

32 'Pershings put Moscow on six-minute warning', *New York Times*, 27 February 1983

33 Interview with the author

34 Aaron Donaghy, *The Second Cold War . . .*, Kindle location 60

35 Edward Keefer, 'Harold Brown: Offsetting the Soviet Military Challenge, Secretaries of Defense Historical Series', 2017, pages 444–448

36 Walter Pincus, 'Neutron killer warheads buried in the ERDA budget', *Washington Post*, 6 June 1977,

37 Sayle, *Enduring Alliance*, Kindle location 270

38 'Neutron bomb controversy strained alliance and caused splits in the administration', *New York Times*, 9 April 1978

39 Taylor Downing, *1983: The World at the Brink*, 2018, Kindle locations 136–140

40 Edward Keefer, 'Harold Brown: Offsetting the Soviet Military Challenge', Secretaries of Defense Historical Series, 2017, pages 349–440

41 'NATO extends 3% rise in annual spending to '85', *New York Times*, 16 May 1979

42 Donaghy, *The Second Cold War*, Kindle locations 82–84; Why did Soviets invade Afghanistan? Documents of a history lesson for Trump', *New York Times*, 29 January, 2019

43 William Burr, 'False warnings of Soviet missile attacks during 1979–1980 led to actions by US strategic forces', National Security Archive, George Washington University, 1 March 2012

44 Telegram from the Embassy in Afghanistan to the Department of State, FRUS 1977–1980, Volume 12, Afghanistan, Document 98

45 NATO statement, 15 January 1980

46 Donaghy, *The Second Cold War*, Kindle location 77

47 Ibid., Kindle location 98

48 William Burr, 'False warnings of Soviet missile attacks during 1979–1980 led to actions by US strategic forces', National Security Archive, George Washington University, 1 March 2012

49 'NATO favouring Soviet dialogue, demands a pull-out in Afghanistan', *New York Times*, 27 June 1980

50 'General Haig unhurt as car is target of bomb on road to NATO office', *New York Times*, 26 June 1979

51 William Inbolden, 'The Peacemaker: Ronald Reagan, the Cold War and the World on the Brink', 2022,, Kindle location 44

52 Presidential directive/NSC–59, 25 July 1980, National Security Archive, George Washington University

53 'Carter directive modifies strategy for a nuclear war', *Washington Post*, 6 August 1980

54 'Pope helped to bring Poland its freedom', *New York Times*, 6 April 2005

55 'US to supply NATO with radar planes', *New York Times*, 9 December 1980

56 'NATO warns Soviet invasion of Poland would end *détente*', *New York Times*, 12 December 1980

57 'NATO is meddling in Poland, Soviet paper implies', *New York Times*, 29 December 1980

13. The Gloves Come Off (1981–1982)

1 Quoted in President's Foreign Intelligence Advisory Board, 'The Soviet "War Scare",' 15 February 1990, Declassified to US National Archives 2012

2 William Inbolden, *The Peacemaker: Ronald Reagan, the Cold War and the World on the Brink*, 2022, Kindle location 22

3 Presidential News Conference, 29 January 1981, US Presidency Project

4 Caspar Weinberger, oral history interview, Ronald Reagan Oral History Project, Miller Centre of Public Affairs, University of Virginia, page 10

5 'NATO chief says *détente* has sapped West's resolve and been exploited by the Kremlin', *New York Times*, 23 February 1981

6 Ben B. Fischer, 'The 1983 war scare in US-Soviet relations', CIA Centre for the Study of Intelligence, undated but circa 1996, Declassified 2011, National Security Archive, George Washington University, page 5; Thomas R. Johnson, 'American Cryptology During the Cold War, 1945–1989, Book IV: Cryptologic Rebirth, 1981–1989', Center for Cryptologic History, National Security Agency, 1999, Declassified 2011, National Security Archive, George Washington University, page 318

7 Robert Kaiser, 'Reagan's defence spending could turn into economic nightmare', *Washington Post*, 25 April 1981

8 John F. Lehman, *Oceans Ventured: Winning the Cold War at Sea*, Kindle location 100

9 Yuri Andropov speech to KGB members, 25 March 1981, Ukrainian KGB archives, translation held in National Security Archive, George Washington University

10 'Soviet concepts for initial military operations against NATO in Europe', CIA archive, February 1977

11 Ben B. Fischer, 'The 1983 war scare in US-Soviet relations', CIA Centre for the Study of Intelligence, undated but circa 1996, Declassified 2011, National Security Archive, George Washington University

12 Undisclosed transcripts published by Allen: Richard Allen, 'The day Reagan was shot', *Atlantic* magazine, April 2001

13 Alan Peppard, 'Command and Control: Tested and Under Fire', *Dallas Morning News*, 13 May 2015. Peppard interviewed several key players that day including Bush and Allen

14 News summary, *New York Times*, 5 April 1981

15 'Europeans demonstrate against NATO missiles', *New York Times*, 5 April 1981

16 'NATO ministers get the hard sell', *New York Times*, 12 April 1981

17 'NATO defense aides issued joint warning to Soviet on Poland', *New York Times*, 9 April 1981

18 'Haig, in Europe, is pressed to agree to nuclear arms talks', *New York Times*, 3 May 1981

19 'NATO hardens view on Soviet activities, questions *détente*', *New York Times*, 6 May 1981

20 'Mitterrand says West must step up efforts for world security', *New York Times*, 4 June 1981

21 'Bonn needs the business even more than the gas', *New York Times*, 16 August 1981

22 'American-owned cars set afire in West Germany', *New York Times*, 2 September 1981

23 'Violence in Berlin marks Haig's visit', *New York Times*, 14 September 1981

24 'US general safe in raid in Germany', *New York Times*, 16 September 1981

25 'Red Brigades kidnapped an American general in Verona', *New York Times*, 18 December 1981

26 Lehman, *Oceans Ventured . . .*, Kindle locations 102, 72–76

27 Ibid., Kindle locations 85–86

28 'Majority in a British survey oppose US nuclear stands', *New York Times*, 8 November 1981

29 '100,000 in Milan peace March', *New York Times*, 1 November 1981

30 'Brezhnev asserts Soviet doctrine rules out preventative nuclear war', *New York Times*, 4 November 1981

31 'Greece says it wants to ban the US nuclear arms on its soil', *New York Times*, 12 November 1981

32 'Big Madrid rally opposes NATO entry', *New York Times*, 16 November 1981

33 'Reagan to propose missile terms for Europe ahead of Soviet talks', *New York Times*, 17 November 1981

34 Ronald Reagan, *The Reagan Diaries*, 2007, Kindle location 50

35 'West Europeans are enthusiastic; Soviet accuses president of "ploy"', *New York Times*, 19 November 1981

36 'Brezhnev revives missile-freeze bid pending US talks', *New York Times*, 24 November 1981

37 'West Germans sign huge pipeline deal with Soviets and get just what they wanted', *Christian Science Monitor*, 23 November 1991

38 Institute of National Remembrance, 'Polish month: December 1981', Polish government website

39 Ronald Reagan, *The Reagan Diaries*, Kindle location 57

40 'Split among allies runs deeper than sanctions', *New York Times*, 3 January 1982

41 'NATO Declaration on Events in Poland', 11 January 1982, NATO website

42 'Greece is said to tie [i.e. link] stand on Poland to other issues', *New York Times*, 13 January 1982

43 '205 held, 14 hurt in Polish protest on price increases', *New York Times*, 1 February 1981

44 'Poland's slump endangering economics of the Soviet Bloc', *New York Times*, 8 January 1982

45 Mark Harrison, 'How much did the Soviets really spend on defence? New evidence from the close of the Brezhnev era', Warwick Economic Research Paper Number 662, 2002, page 12

46 Ronald Reagan, *The Reagan Diaries*, Kindle location 69

47 'NATO chief seeks a rise in arms outlays by the Europeans', *New York Times*, 15 February 1982

48 Ronald Reagan, *The Reagan Diaries*, Kindle location 75

49 'How the US almost betrayed Britain', *Wall Street Journal*, 2 April 2012

50 'Crisis brings to fore problems facing NATO', *New York Times*, 1 May 1982

51 'Two Soviet sites reported in crisis area', *New York Times*, 14 April 1982

52 'Crisis brings to fore problems facing NATO', *New York Times*, 1 May 1982

53 'NATO backs Britain, Weinberger declares', *New York Times*, 6 May 1982

54 'Reagan readied US warship for Falklands war', US Naval Institute News, 27 June 2012

55 'Bombs hit US bases in West Germany', *New York Times*, 2 June 1982

56 'Reagan off on European trip today', *New York Times*, 2 June 1981

57 'President urges global crusade for democracy', *New York Times*, 9 June 1982

58 'Reagan suggests a limit on troops for 2 alliances', *New York Times*, 10 June 1982

59 Ronald Reagan, *The Reagan Diaries*, Kindle location 87

60 '200,000 are drawn to a Bonn protest', *New York Times*, 11 June 1982

61 'Spain says British move could divide the West', *New York Times*, 11 June 1982

62 'Allies ask: if Carter was bad, is Reagan worse?', *New York Times*, 25 July 1982

63 'GIs in West Germany meet rising wall of bias', *New York Times*, 25 June 1982

64 'New man for NATO', *New York Times*, 15 August 1982

65 'NATO manoeuvres failed to impress some witnesses', *New York Times*, 15 September 1982

14. Dancing Blindly on the Edge (1983)

1 President's Foreign Intelligence Advisory Board, 'The Soviet "War Scare"', 15 February 1990, US National Archive, page xii

2 Ibid., page vii

3 'Warsaw Pact leaders meet', *New York Times*, 5 January 1983

4 'The Emergence of Andropov', *New York Times*, 27 February 1983

5 Quotes from Wolf's autobiography on page 11 of Ben Fischer, 'A Cold War Conundrum: the 1983 Soviet War Scare', undated but approximately 1996, US National Security Archive

6 Suzanne Moore, et al., 'How the Greenham Common protest changed lives', *Guardian*, 20 March 2017

7 'Bush says the US is "deadly serious" weapons curbs', *New York Times*, 5 February 1983

8 'Bush, in London, challenged by nuclear foe', *New York Times*, 10 February 1983

9 'Britain's nuclear battle', *New York Times*, 11 January 1983

10 'Kohl takes his case to the middle class', *New York Times*, 27 February 1983

11 'Kohl and his coalition win decisively in West Germany', *New York Times*, 7 March 1983

12 'NATO on "moral high ground", general says', *New York Times*, 20 March 1983

13 Reagan, *The Reagan Diaries*, Kindle location 130

14 Downing, *1983: The World at the Brink*, page 110

15 'NATO ministers endorsed the US position on missiles', *New York Times*, 24 March 1983

16 Downing, *1983: . . .*, page 113

17 'NATO urges quick Soviet response to US plan', *New York Times*, 31 March 1983

18 Quoted by Robert Kozloski, '1983 Revisited', United States Naval Institute, 31 May 2013

19 'Warsaw Pact jogs NATO on a treaty', *New York Times*, 8 April 1983

20 State Department Cable from Secretary of State to US embassy Moscow, "Soviet protests on overflight rejecting" and related cables, 6 May 1983, National Security Archive, George Washington University

21 Ben Fischer, 'A Cold War Conundrum: the 1983 Soviet War Scare', page 23

22 President's Foreign Intelligence Advisory Board, 'The Soviet "War Scare"', 15 February 1990, US National Archive, page 6

23 Taylor Dowling, *1983: . . .*, Kindle locations 140–143

24 Declassified British documents discussed in Aaron Bateman, 'Revisiting the British reaction to Reagan's "Star Wars"', *Physics Today*, 20 February 2019

25 Jamie Bradburn, 'In 1983 Gorbachev took a stroll in small-town Ontario that helped shape the future of the Soviet Union', Canadian news site TVO, 2 September 2022

26 'Foreign ministers of NATO reaffirmed plans for missiles', *New York Times*, 11 June 1983

27 'Soviet invokes German partition in warning Kohl on new missiles', *New York Times*, 6 July 1983

28 President's Foreign Intelligence Advisory Board, 'The Soviet "War Scare"', 15 February 1990, US National Archive, page 16

29 Ibid., page 65

30 'Averell Harriman, US ambassador to the Soviet Union during the war, visits Moscow', 2 June 1983

31 Memorandum of Conversation, 2 June 1983, National Security Archive, George Washington University

32 Ibid.

33 'A little give, a little take at Madrid', *New York Times*, 22 July 1983

34 Commander in Chief US Army Europe, 'REFORGER '83 After Action Report', 6 March 1984, National Security Archive, George Washington University

35 Interview with Marshal Sergei Akhromeyev, 10 January 1990, National Security Archive, George Washington University

36 Dowling, *1983: . . .*, Kindle location 185

37 'Angry charges at Russians: "barbaric", "criminal", "cruel", *New York Times*, 3 September 1983

38 'NATO allies seem to favour curbs on flights to Moscow', *New York Times*, 8 September 1983

39 Commander in Chief US Army Europe, 'REFORGER '83 After Action Report', 6 March 1984, National Security Archive, George Washington University

40 Dowling, *1983: . . .*, Kindle location 210-214

41 Interview with Marshal Sergei Akhromeyev, 10 January 1990, National Security Archive, George Washington University

42 President's Foreign Intelligence Advisory Board, 'The Soviet "War Scare"', 15 February 1990, US National Archive, page 68

43 Dowling, *1983: . . .*, Kindle location 228

44 'Vast crowds hold rallies in Europe against US arms', *New York Times*, 23 October 1983

45 Interview with Marshal Sergei Akhromeyev, 10 January 1990, National Security Archive, George Washington University

46 UK TV interview, quoted by Taylor Dowling, *1983: . . .*, Kindle locations 238–40

47 'ABLE ARCHER Exercise Scenario', undated but likely 2006, National Security Archive, George Washington University

48 Nate Jones, *Able Archer '83: The Secret History of the NATO Exercise that Almost Triggered Nuclear War*, Kindle location 33

49 President's Foreign Intelligence Advisory Board, 'The Soviet "War Scare"', 15 February 1990, US National Archive, pages 70–75

50 UK TV interviews, quoted by Taylor Dowling, *1983: . . .*, Kindle locations 247–254

51 'History of the Headquarters, 7th Air Division, 1983–1984', National Security Archive, George Washington University

52 FLASHBACK TV interviews quoted by Taylor Dowling, *1983: . . .*, Kindle location 245

53 Ibid., Kindle location 265

54 Gregory Pedlow, 'ABLE ARCHER '83: Information from SHAPE Historical Files', 28 March 2013 National Security Archive, George Washington University

55 Nate Jones, *Able Archer '83: The Secret History of the NATO Exercise that Almost Triggered Nuclear War*, Kindle location 37

56 Lieutenant General Leonard Perroots, 'End of Tour Report Addendum', January 1989

57 'First US missiles arrived by plane at British base', *New York Times*, 15 November 1983,

58 'Soviet breaks off early in Geneva on nuclear arms', *New York Times*, 24 November 1983

59 'NATO ministers firm on missiles', *New York Times*, 8 December 1993,

60 Lieutenant General Leonard Perroots, 'End of Tour Report Addendum', January 1989,

61 Nate Jones, *Able Archer '83: The Secret History of the NATO Exercise that Almost Triggered Nuclear War*, Kindle location 44

62 Dowling, *1983: . . .*, Kindle location 270

63 'Memorandum for the Deputy Assistant to the President for National Security Affairs', 8 December 1983

15. Endgame (1984–89)

1 'American in Bonn finds cloud in NATO's future', *New York Times*, 5 January 1984

2 'British report first cruise missiles are all operational', *New York Times*, 2 January 1984

3 'Gas arriving in France', *New York Times*, 5 January 1984

4 Calder Walton, *Spies*, Kindle location 446, 449, 450

5 William Inbolden, *The Peacemaker: Ronald Reagan, the Cold War and the World on the Brink*, 2022, Kindle location 260

6 'NATO manoeuvres in Norway', *New York Times*, 7 January 1984

7 'Soviet is holding big naval games', *New York Times*, 4 April 1984

8 Interview with the author

9 'NATO nations submit plan on averting war', *New York Times*, 25 January 1984

10 'Trudeau assailed over NATO remark', *New York Times*, 2 February 1984

11 'A visit to Budapest, 2–4 February 1984', Margaret Thatcher Foundation

12 'Bush says talks with Chernenko gave promising signal on future', *New York Times*, 15 February 1984

13 'Chernenko gives a gloomy survey of US-Soviet ties', *New York Times*, 9 April 1984

14 'Soviet fighter pilots say they will shoot down air intruders', *New York Times*, 8 April 1984

15 'MiGs shoot at army copter or not West German–Czech border', *New York Times*, 21 April 1984

16 'Allies in Europe seek a bigger role', *New York Times*, 26 February 1984,

17 'Seven European aides meet to bolster NATO ties', *New York Times*, 13 June 1984

18 'Nudging NATO is a touchy issue', *New York Times*, 24 June 1984

19 William Inbolden, *The Peacemaker: Ronald Reagan, the Cold War and the World on the Brink*, 2022, Kindle location 291

20 'NATO leaders languid air masks iron resolve', *New York Times*, 12 January 1984

21 'The biggest British Army exercise', *Forces News*, 2 May, 2019

22 Interview with the author

23 'US tries to fight Allied resistance to nuclear arms', *New York Times*, 14 February 1985

24 'Gorbachev starts a visit to Britain with Soviet group', *New York Times*, 16 December 1984

25 Margaret Thatcher, *The Downing Street Years*, 1993, pages 459–463; Margaret Thatcher Foundation website

26 'Allies back "Star Wars" studies, not deployment', *New York Times*, 10 February 1985

27 'Spain says it would bar US a-arms', *New York Times*, 15 February 1985

28 'Belgian Parliament backs deployment of missiles', *New York Times*, 21 March 1985

29 'US and Soviet generals discuss killing of American army major', *New York Times*, 16 April 1985

30 'Gorbachev ready for Reagan talks, freezes missiles', *New York Times*, 8 April 1985

31 'US and Soviet generals discuss killing of American army major', *New York Times*, 16 April 1985

32 'Gorbachev offensive: splitting allies', *New York Times*, 4 October 1985

33 'NATO chief welcomes Soviet proposals', *New York Times*, 8 October 1985

34 'Why has Reagan yielded to Europe?', *New York Times*, 6 January 1986

35 'West Europe cool to the removal of US medium-range missiles', *New York Times*, 25 February 1986

36 'Spain votes to remain in NATO in dramatic victory for González', *New York Times*, 13 March 1986

37 'Gorbachev says Libya raid may hurt US–Soviet ties', *New York Times*, 19 April 1986

38 'Chernobyl fuels nuclear anxieties in Europe', *New York Times*, 18 May 1986

39 'East–West accord reached on a plan to cut the risk of war', *New York Times*, 22 September 1986

40 'Shultz briefs NATO allies on talks', *New York Times*, 14 October 1986

41 'Soviet bloc commandos said to infiltrate West', *New York Times*, 2 November 1986

42 NATO ministers back cuts in US–Soviet atomic arms, but warn of spending effect', *New York Times*, 6 December 1986

43 'Soviet proposal on missiles finds support in Western Europe', *New York Times*, 2 March 1987

44 'Reagan announces new US proposal on mid-range arms', *New York Times*, 4 March 1987

45 'Hard choices over missiles', *New York Times*, 27 March 1987

46 'West in quandary over Gorbachev offer to get rid of missiles', *New York Times*, 16 April 1987

47 'Commander of NATO is opposed to ridding Europe of all missiles', *New York Times*, 21 April 1987

48 'Shultz responds tartly to NATO chief's criticism', *New York Times*, 21 June 1987

49 'NATO chief warns of "euphoria" on arms', *New York Times*, 18 September 1987

50 'A cautious Europe cheers US–Soviet moves on arms', *New York Times*, 20 September 1987

51 'Treaty leads sightseers to US base', *New York Times*, 9, June 1988

52 'NATO backs level of arms spending', *New York Times*, 11 June 1988

53 'The US says Soviets may pull troops out of Hungary', *New York Times*, 9 July 1988

54 'Thatcher honours Solidarity shrine', *New York Times*, 5 November 1988

55 'The Gorbachev visit: excerpts from speech to UN on major Soviet military cuts', *New York Times*, 8 December 1988

56 'Western officials term troop cuts significant', *New York Times*, 8 December 1988

57 Final communiqué, Brussels meeting, 9 December 1988, NATO website

58 *AP*, full text of Gorbachev speech, 8 December 1988

59 'Baker, outlining worldview, assesses plan for Soviet bloc', *New York Times*, 28 March 1989

60 Imre Pozsgay interviewed by Brian Hanrahan, 'Hungary's role in the 1989 revolutions', BBC News, 9 May 1989

61 Manfred Wörner, address to the North Atlantic Council, 4 April 1989, NATO website

62 'Excerpts from joint communiqué from NATO summit meeting', *New York Times*, 31 May 1989

63 Sergey Radchenko, 'I do not want Red Square to look like Tiananmen Square', Foreign Policy, 4 June 2014, National Security Archive, George Washington University

64 UPI, 'China reduces official Tiananmen death toll to about 200', 14 June 1989

65 'Warsaw accepts Solidarity sweep and humiliating losses by party', *New York Times*, 9 June 1989

66 'Bush, in Polish press interview, urges a pullout of Soviet troops', *New York Times*, 4 July 1989

67 'Gorbachev spurns the use of force in Eastern Eur/short-range ope', *New York Times*, 7 July 1989

68 'Baker announces NATO agreement on aircraft cuts', *New York Times*, 13 July 1989

69 'Soviet arms official criticises West's plans', *New York Times*, 14 July 1989

70 'Leaders back financial aid for East Europe', *New York Times*, 16 July 1989

71 'Baltic citizens link hands to demand independence', *New York Times*, 24 August 1989

72 Lawrence Kaplan, *NATO United, NATO divided*, Kindle location 1664

73 'US voicing fears that Gorbachev will divide West', *New York Times*, 16 September 1989

74 'Top NATO civilian sees role for both alliances in the 1990s', *New York Times*, 13 October 1989

75 Interview with the author

76 M. E. Sarotte, 1989: *The Struggle to Create Post-Cold War Europe*, 2015, Kindle location 55

77 'NATO and the Warsaw Pact; as threat of war recedes, US and Soviets face pressure for troop cuts', *New York Times*, 11 November 1989

78 'NATO officials see role in transition of Europe', *New York Times*, 17 November 1989

79 M. E. Sarotte, *1989: The Struggle to Create Post-Cold War Europe*, 2015, Kindle locations 67, 76

80 'Bonn aides in Washington say moralising missiles is a dead issue', *New York Times*, 19 November 1989

81 'Vladimir Putin's formative German years', BBC News, 27 March 2015

16. Driving Fast Through Fog (1990–1991)

1 'Study of war changes with Europe', *New York Times*, 16 January 1990

2 Ibid.

3 'Europe's military chiefs meet in a step to reduce tensions', *New York Times*, 16 January 1990

4 Telephone conversation with Chancellor Helmut Kohl, 26 January 1990, George H. Bush Presidential Library

5 Meeting with Manfred Wörner, 24 February 1990, Bush Presidential Library, page 3

6 'Baker and West German envoy discuss reunification issues', *New York Times*, 3 February 1990

7 Record of conversation between Gorbachev and Baker in Moscow, 9 February 1990, National Security Archive

8 M. E. Sarotte, *Not One Inch: America, Russia and the Making of Post-Cold War Stalemate*, 2021, Kindle location 87

9 'Poland favours one Germany in NATO', *New York Times*, 15 February 1990

10 'Accord seen on full Soviet pullout from Hungary', *New York Times*, 4 March 1990

11 Statement by press secretary on the restoration of Lithuanian independence, 11 March 1990, George H. Bush Presidential Library

12 Telephone call to Chancellor Helmut Kohl, 20 March 1990, George H. Bush Presidential Library

13 'Europeans near a consensus on East Bloc ties', *New York Times*, 2 April 1990

14 'To a fading US bugle, Rhineland sings a dirge', *New York Times*, 1, April 1990

15 Meeting with Foreign Minister Eduard Shevardnadze, 6 April 1990, George H. Bush Presidential Library

16 Meeting with President Mitterrand, 19 April 1990, George H. Bush Presidential Library

17 'Military voice being heard on Lithuania, Soviet aide says', *New York Times*, 15 April 1990

18 'NATO adopts plan to revamp itself for German unity', *New York Times*, 4 May 1990

19 'Bush sees revamped NATO as core of Europe's power', *New York Times*, 5 May 1990

20 Meeting with Manfred Wörner, 7 May 1990, George H. Bush Presidential Library

21 'Verbatim record of the North Atlantic Council meeting with the participation of heads of state and government', 5 July 1990, NATO archive

22 Conversation with Manfred Wörner, 5 July 1990, George H. Bush Presidential Library

23 Meeting with Manfred Wörner, 7 May 1990, George H. Bush Presidential Library

24 'Verbatim record of the North Atlantic Council meeting with the participation of heads of state and government', 5 July 1990, NATO archive

25 'An alliance for a new age: has NATO donned a velvet glove?', *New York Times*, 7 July 1990

26 Ibid.

27 'Iraqi army invades capital of Kuwait in fierce fighting', *New York Times*, 2 August 1990

28 'NATO, bereft of a military role, redefines itself as the West's political galvaniser', *New York Times*, 9 August 1990

29 'Operation ANCHOR GUARD', NATO-funded website Freedom Anatomy,

30 US Transportation Command, 'So many, so much, so far, so fast', Joint Chiefs of Staff website

31 'Four allies give up rights in Germany', *New York Times*, 13 September 1990

32 'What is the need for NATO now? Where do East Bloc nations fit in?', *New York Times*, 20 November 1990

33 'US and Soviet reach agreement on a new arms pact', *New York Times*, 4 October 1990

34 'What is the need for NATO now? Where do East Bloc nations fit in?', *New York Times*, 20 November 1990

35 'NATO is struggling to redefine itself', *New York Times*, 24 September 1990

36 'Bonn, rejecting protests, will send jets to Turkey', *New York Times*, 4 January 1991

37 Anonymous interview with author

38 'NATO sending jets to the Turks in Gulf face-off', *New York Times*, 3 January 1991

39 'Crowds in European cities protest a war in the Gulf area', *New York Times*, 13 January 1991

40 'Protests in Lithuania continue, turning peaceful', *New York Times*, 10 January 1991

41 'Soviet tanks roll in Lithuania', *New York Times*, 13 January 1991

42 Colin Powell, *A Soldier's Way: An Autobiography*, 1995, Kindle location 646

43 'Soviet commandos stage Latvia raid, at least five killed', *New York Times*, 21 January 1991

44 'Soviet envoy in US voices worry and conduct of war', *New York Times*, 27 January 1991

45 'In Cotswold town, chance to relive finest hour as B-52s return', *New York Times*, 3 February 1991

46 'Warsaw Pact agrees to dissolve its military alliance by March 31', *New York Times*, 26 February 1991

47 'New uncertainties said to invigorate NATO', *New York Times*, 26 February 1991

48 Colin Powell, *A Soldier's Way . . .*, Kindle location 660

49 'NATO is planning to cut US forces in Europe by 50 per cent', *New York Times*, 29 May 1991

50 'US and France are at odds over a NATO army', *New York Times*, 28 May 1991

51 'US, wary of European corps, seeks assurance on NATO role', *New York Times*, 20 October 1991

52 'NATO agreed to expand a rapid reaction force', *New York Times*, 14 April 1991

53 M. E. Sarotte, *Not One Inch . . .*, Kindle location 171

54 'NATO tries to ease security concerns in Eastern Europe', *New York Times*, 7 June 1991

55 'Europeans warn on Yugoslav split, US deplores moves', *New York Times*, 26 June 1991

56 'Yugoslav army uses force in the breakaway republic, Europe presses for debate', *New York Times*, 28 June 1991

57 Alastair Finlan, *The Collapse of Yugoslavia, 1991–1999*, Kindle location 24

58 'Summit in London; toward a smaller world', *New York Times*, 18 July 1991

59 'Bush and Gorbachev sign nuclear arms pact', *Politico*, 31 July 2018

60 M. E. Sarotte, *Not One Inch . . .*, Kindle location 172

61 'EC nations recognise independence of Baltic republics', *Washington Post*, 28 August 1991

62 Robert O'Neill, 'An alliance for this new Europe', *International Herald Tribune*, reprinted in the *New York Times*, 2 September 1991

63 M. E. Sarotte, *Not One Inch . . .*, Kindle location 183–185

64 'Ukrainian nationhood: daunting reality', *New York Times*, 23 September 1991

65 'Ukrainian leader gets encore visit with Bush', *New York Times*, 26 September 1991

66 'Remarks by President Bush on reducing US and Soviet nuclear weapons', *New York Times*, 28 September 1991

67 M. E. Sarotte, *Not One Inch . . .*, Kindle location 177

68 NATO chronology, 1991, NATO website, last updated 8 November 2001

69 'NATO summit meeting ends with warning to Soviet republics over nuclear arms', *New York Times*, 9 November 1991

70 M. E. Sarotte, *Not One Inch . . .*, Kindle location 186

71 NATO chronology, NATO website

72 'Yeltsin says Russia seeks to join NATO', *New York Times*, 21 December 1991

73 Ibid.

17. Into the Balkans (1992–1994)

1 'Speech by the secretary general', NATO website, 10 September 1993

2 'Russians marching to Croatia armed with promise of peace', *New York Times*, 17 March 1992

3 'Only NATO can do the job – or can it?', *New York Times*, 16 January 1993

4 'Sweden's sonar is quiet after Soviet collapse', *New York Times*, 13 February 1992

5 'Memorandum of conversation', NATO archive, 1 February 1992

6 M. E. Sarotte, *Not One Inch . . .*, Kindle location 207

7 'At East–West crossroads, Western Europe hesitates', *New York Times*, 25 March 1992

8 'NATO and European warships blockade Yugoslavia', *New York Times*, 21 November 1992

9 'US talks of using military to get food past the Serbs', *New York Times*, 7 July 1992

10 'NATO seeks options to big troop deployment for insuring delivery of aid to Bosnia', *New York Times*, 14 August 1992

11 'NATO to help UN on Yugoslav plans', *New York Times*, 16 December 1992

12 'Allies to use threats of action on flight ban as way to press Serbs', *New York Times*, 19 January 1993

13 'Russia declares it plans to join Bosnia airdrop', *New York Times*, 3 March 1993

14 'US pressing NATO for a peace force to patrol Bosnia', *New York Times*, 11 March 1993

15 'Enforcing a flight ban over Bosnia', *New York Times*, 12 July 1993

16 'NATO agrees to enforce flight ban over Bosnia ordered by UN', *New York Times*, 3 April 1993

17 'NATO jets in Bosnia told to shoot as last resort', *New York Times*, 12 April 1993

18 'NATO adrift? Allies worry over Bosnia impasse', *New York Times*, 14 May 1993

19 'UN is authorising allied air strikes against the Serbs', *New York Times*, 5 June 1993

20 'UN calls them "safe areas"; Bosnians, a sick joke', *New York Times*, 11 July 1993

21 'Enforcing a flight ban over Bosnia', *New York Times*, 12 July 1993

22 'Serbs pound a UN position in Sarajevo', *New York Times*, 26 July 1993

23 'US may attack Serbs even without NATO', *New York Times*, 2 August 1993

24 'NATO to join US in planning airstrikes against Serb forces', *New York Times*, 3 August 1993

25 'Defying NATO, Serbs assault key Sarajevo outpost', *New York Times*, 5 August 1993

26 M. E. Sarotte, *Not One Inch . . .*, Kindle location 223

27 Ibid., Kindle location 228–30

28 Ibid., Kindle location 231

29 Ibid., Kindle location 233

30 Ibid., Kindle location 233

31 'East Europe weeks for the West's welcome wagon', *New York Times*, 29 August 1993

32 'NATO says alliance is unlikely to grow soon', *New York Times*, 2 September 1993

33 'Speech by the secretary general to the IISS in Brussels', NATO website, 10 September 1993

34 'Official US retranslation of Yeltsin letter on NATO expansion', 15 September 1993, National Security Archive

35 'Allies at odds with US on Bosnia command', *New York Times*, 12 September 1993

36 'The forgotten lessons of *Black Hawk Down*', *New York Times*, 3 October 2018

37 'Bosnia's desperate gamble: winter in time of war', *New York Times*, 3 October 1993

38 'Bonn tries to calm East Europeans on NATO', *New York Times*, 10 October 1993

39 M. E. Sarotte, *Not One Inch . . .*, Kindle location 241

40 'Promises made, promises broken?', *War on the Rocks*, 22 November 2019

41 'Russia warns NATO on expanding East', *New York Times*, 26 November 1993

42 'Promises made, promises broken?', *War on the Rocks*, 22 November 2019

43 Fiona Hill and Clifford G. Gaddy, *Mr Putin: Operative in the Kremlin*, 2015, Kindle location 84

44 'US officials allege that Russians are working on biological arms', *Washington Post*, 8 April 1994

45 'Letter to the NATO secretary general from the UK national security adviser', UK government website, 13 April 2018

46 'NATO membership for Russia doubted', *New York Times*, 10 September 1994

47 'Heavy shelling and fire fights rake Sarajevo', *New York Times*, 7 January 1994

48 'Dispute grows over UN troops in Bosnia', *New York Times*, 20 January 1994

49 'World leaders express shock and outrage at blast', *New York Times*, 6 February 1994

50 'NATO gives Serbs a ten-day deadline to withdraw guns', *New York Times*, 10 February 1994

51 'Serbs welcome Russian troops with jubilation', *New York Times*, 21 February 1994

52 'NATO craft down four Serb warplanes attacking Bosnia', *New York Times*, 4 March 1994

53 'Manfred Worner, 59, NATO leader, is dead', *New York Times*, 14 August 1994

54 'US jets down four Bosnian Serb planes to enforce "no-fly zone"', *Los Angeles Times*, 1 March 1994

55 'Prices plummet, life turns normal and Sarajevans rush to sell goods', *New York Times*, 23 March 1994

56 'NATO jets bomb Serbs besieging Bosnian haven', *New York Times*, 11 April 1994

57 'NATO's modest air operation in Bosnia crosses major political frontier', *New York Times*, 11 April 1994

58 'US planes bomb Serbian positions for a second day', *New York Times*, 12 April 1994

59 'Serbian troops step up pressure on UN', *New York Times*, 15 April 1994

60 Ibid.

61 'On this day, 16 April 1994', Fleet Air Arm Officers' Association website

62 'NATO warns Serbs to ceasefire or face bombings', *New York Times*, 23 April 1994

63 'UN tanks kill nine Serbs in Bosnia', *Washington Post*, 2 May 1994

64 George Packer, *Our Man: Richard Holbrooke and the End of the American Century*, 2019, Kindle location 292–302

65 'After six months, peace fades away again in Sarajevo', *New York Times*, 8 August 1994

66 'UN forces mull how to finesse a Bosnia pull-out', *Los Angeles Times*, 6 September 1994

67 'Jet attacks Bosnian town, ten deaths reported', *New York Times*, 10 November 1994

68 'Move on Bosnia by US alarms allies in NATO', *New York Times*, 12 November 1994

69 'NATO keeps Bosnia arms blockade as US drops role', *New York Times*, 16 November 1994

70 'NATO jets hit missiles as Serbs gain in Bosnia', *New York Times*, 24 November 1994

71 'NATO turns from force to diplomacy in Bosnia', *New York Times*, 3 December 1994

72 'Bill Clinton says he feels "terrible" for pushing a 1994 agreement that resulted in Ukraine giving up its nuclear weapons', Business Insider, 5 April 2023

18. 'Where Angels Fear to Tread' (1995–1998)

1 'Secretary general foresees a growing activist role in crises', *New York Times*, 23 June 1998

2 Lawrence Kaplan, *NATO United, NATO divided: The Evolution of an Alliance*, 2004, Kindle location 1859

3 'Bosnian troops frayed by fighting and disputes', *New York Times*, 17 January 1995

4 'NATO disputes UN reports of possible arms airlift to Bosnia', *New York Times*, 1 March 1995

5 'America used Islamists to arm the Bosnian Muslims', *Guardian*, 22 April 2002

6 'Fighting in Bosnia draws UN warning', *New York Times*, 28 March 1995

7 'UN overrules new calls for airstrikes against Serbs', *New York Times*, 9 May 1995

8 'US lobbied allies for weeks before NATO attack on Serbs', *New York Times*, 26 May 1995

9 NATO timeline, 'May 1995', NATO website

10 'Nations with peacekeepers in Bosnia stand firm', *New York Times*, 28 May 1995

11 'Serbs killed a Bosnian leader and take more hostages', *New York Times*, 29 May 1995

12 'US force may help UN troops to regroup', *New York Times*, 1 June 1995

13 'US jet on mission for NATO is shot down over Bosnia', 3 June 1995

14 Scott O'Grady, *Basher Five-Two: The True Story of F–16 Fighter Pilot Captain Scott O'Grady*, 1998, Kindle location 632

15 Ibid., Kindle location 1154

16 'UN moves heavy guns near Sarajevo', 9 June 1995

17 Ibid., 9 June 1995

18 'Costly collapse in Bosnia looms unless UN can prove effective', *New York Times*, 9 July 1995

19 International Criminal Tribunal for the Former Yugoslavia, transcript, 4 July 1996

20 'As usual, Serbs call the shots', *New York Times*, 12 July 1995

21 International Criminal Tribunal for the Former Yugoslavia, transcript, 4 July 1996

22 Human Rights Watch, 'The fall of Srebrenica and failure of UN peace-keeping', 15 October 1995

23 Ibid.

24 'US and NATO face unhappy choices for UN force in the Balkans', *New York Times*, 12 July 1995

25 International Criminal Tribunal for the Former Yugoslavia, transcript, 4 July 1996

26 'NATO diplomats question plans for air raids', *New York Times*, 23 July 1995

27 'Western generals personally warn Serb commander', *New York Times*, 24 July 1995

28 'US says France raided Bosnian Serb stronghold', *New York Times*, 25 July 1995

29 'The powers prepare to blink at a new Croatian war', *New York Times*, 4 August 1995

30 'Bosnian Serb chief says US envoys took "risky" road', *New York Times*, 21 August 1995

31 'US officials say Bosnian Serb face NATO attack if talks stall', *New York Times*, 28 August 1995

32 'Shelling killed dozens in Sarajevo', *New York Times*, 29 August 1995

33 SENSE Tribunal Reports, 'The second Markale massacre myth', 16 January 2007, the Wayback Machine archive

34 'Military aides uncertain about air attacks' effects', *New York Times*, 31 August 1995

35 Tim Ripley, *Operation Deliberate Force: the UN and NATO campaign in Bosnia 1995*, 1999, Kindle location 192

36 'NATO resumes bombardment of Serbs', *New York Times*, 6 September 1995

37 Tim Ripley, *Operation Deliberate Force . . .*, Kindle location 193

38 'NATO secretary general questioned in Belgian scandal', *New York Times*, 1 March 1995

39 'The Dayton keys to peace', *New York Times*, 17 November 2015

40 Brigadier Ben Barry, *The Road from Sarajevo: British Army Operations in Bosnia, 1995–1996*, 2001, Kindle location 1097, 1630

41 'Bosnia questions: where are exits?' *New York Times*, 2 December 1995

42 'The crisis in former Yugoslavia', NATO Joint Force Command Naples webpage

43 'Bosnia proving ground for NATO contenders', *New York Times*, 9 December 1995

44 Brigadier Ben Barry, *The Road from Sarajevo: British Army Operations in Bosnia, 1995–1996*, Kindle location 1886

45 Mike Jackson, *Soldier: The Autobiography of General Sir Mike Jackson*, 2007, page 199

46 'Bid to foil a Sarajevo transfer is ended by a NATO threat', *New York Times*, 7 March 1996

47 Mike Jackson, *Soldier: The Autobiography of General Sir Mike Jackson*, page 205

48 'Bosnia limits war crimes arrests after NATO delivers two suspects', *New York Times*, 13 February 1996

49 'After 50 years, GIs and Russians meet again', *New York Times*, 12 March 1996

50 'NATO picks Spanish Foreign Minister for secretary general', *New York Times*, 10 December 1995

51 'Solana: off to a good start in momentous times for NATO', *New York Times*, 7 February 1996

52 'US and France face off on control of NATO Southern Command', *New York Times*, 2 October 1996

53 'Rift in NATO over control is delaying restructuring', *New York Times*, 3 December 1996

54 'US backs NATO growth', *New York Times*, 5 February 1996

55 'Opening statement by the secretary general', 3 June 1996, NATO website

56 'Clinton aides say US might back NATO force in Bosnia in '97', *New York Times*, 26 September 1996

57 'US held likely to keep troops in Bosnia', *New York Times*, 14 November 1996

58 'Muslim rioters in Bosnia attack a US army column', *New York Times*, 15 November 1996

59 'Secretary general statement to the press', 10 December 1996, NATO website

60 'US tries to speed integration of Russia in NATO', *New York Times*, 7 September 1996

61 'US pushes bigger NATO despite qualms on Russia', *New York Times*, 10 October 1996

62 'Russia accepts eastward growth of NATO, but only inch by inch', *New York Times*, 4 March 1997

References

63 'Yeltsin tells Russians that depending on the NATO issue paid off', *New York Times*, 27 March 1997

64 'Russia drops major demand on limiting NATO forces', *New York Times*, 3 May 1997

65 'Russia agrees to NATO plan pushed by Clinton to admit nations from Eastern Bloc', *New York Times*, 15 May 1997

66 'Bedfellows of every stripe in NATO fray', *New York Times*, 21 April 1998

67 'Leak caused NATO to drop Bosnia effort on fugitives', *New York Times*, 24 April 1998

68 'Senate approves expansion of NATO by vote of 80 to 19; Clinton pleased by decision', *New York Times*, 1 May 1998

69 'A new NATO for a new Europe and a new era', *New York Times*, 7 July 1997

70 'NATO leaders begin Madrid talks', *New York Times*, 8 July 1997

71 'NATO troops kill a Soviet suspect in war atrocities', *New York Times*, 11 July 1997

72 'US links top Bosnian Serbs to attacks', *New York Times*, 26 July 1997

73 'NATO plans to disarm paramilitary forces in Bosnia', *New York Times*, 9 August 1997

74 'NATO troops raided Serb hardliners in a Bosnian city', *New York Times*, 21 August 1997

75 'To American peacekeepers in Bosnia, danger is just beginning', *New York Times*, 16 September 1997

76 'NATO is weighing the need for troops in Bosnia after midyear', *New York Times*, 2 December 1997

77 'GIs warm to Bosnia', *New York Times*, 4 January 1998

78 'US back Baltic membership in NATO, but not any time soon', *New York Times*, 12 January 1998

79 'Resistance to Serbia turns violent in Kosovo', *New York Times*, 17 February 1997

80 'It's risky to talk tough on Kosovo', *New York Times*, 10 March 1998

81 'New Serb assault on Albanian rebels', *New York Times*, 1 June 1998

82 'First Bosnia, now Kosovo', *New York Times*, 10 June 1998

83 'NATO jets patrol skies near Serbia in show of force', *New York Times*, 16 June 1998

84 'Milošević pledges steps to hold off attacks from NATO', *New York Times*, 17 June 1998

85 'Security Council tells Serbs to stop Kosovo offensive', *New York Times*, 24 September 1998

86 'US is urging NATO to step up plans to act against Yugoslavia', *New York Times*, 24 September 1998

87 'Allies inch toward action against Serbs', *New York Times*, 25 September 1998

88 'Milošević accepts Kosovo monitors, averting attack', *New York Times*, 14 October 1998

89 'Kosovo crisis strained relations between the US and Europe', *New York Times*, 10 November 1998

90 'Report of plot to kill tycoon leaves Yeltsin to call inquiry', *New York Times*, 21 November 1998

19. Kosovo (1999)

1 PBS Frontline Interviews, 'General Klaus Naumann', PBS website

2 'US and EU denounce massacre in Kosovo as NATO ponders next move', *New York Times*, 18 January 1999

3 'US weighs its reaction to massacre in Kosovo', *New York Times*, 17 January 1999

4 'The terrible lessons of Bosnia: will it help Kosovo?', *New York Times*, 1 February 1999

5 'Clinton seriously considering GIs in Kosovo', *New York Times*, 5 February 1999

6 'US official sees "collision course" in Kosovo dispute', *New York Times*, 10 March 1999

7 'Three fragments of Soviet realm joining NATO's ranks today', *New York Times*, 12 March 1999

8 'NATO assures five neighbours that fear Serbian attack', *New York Times*, 25 March 1999

9 PBS Frontline, 'Richard Holbrooke interview', PBS website

10 Rebecca Grant, 'Aerospace power and the Kosovo crisis', US Air Force Association, 1999, pages 8–9

11 'How Dutch F-16 AMs shot down a MiG–29', F–16.net website

12 'NATO opens broad barrage against Serbs', *New York Times*, 25 March 1999

13 'UN secretary general offers implicit endorsement of raids', *New York Times*, 25 March 1999

14 Rebecca Grant, 'Aerospace power and the Kosovo crisis', US Air Force Association, 1999, pages 8–9

15 'NATO launches daytime strike', *New York Times*, 27 March 1999

16 'US stealth fighter is down in Yugoslavia as NATO orders attack on Serb army units', *New York Times*, 28 March 1999

17 PBS Frontline, 'General Michael Short interview', PBS website

18 'NATO had signs its strategy would fail Kosovans', *New York Times*, 1 April 1999

19 Rebecca Grant, 'Aerospace power and the Kosovo crisis', US Air Force Association, 1999, page 10

20 'Captured soldiers to face trial', *Guardian*, 1 April 1999

21 Mike Jackson, *Soldier . . .*, page 242

22 PBS Frontline, 'General Michael Short interview', PBS website

23 'Jamie Shea, NATO's persuasive force', *Washington Post*, 10 June 1999

24 'NATO website zapped', *New York Times*, 1 April 1999

25 Rebecca Grant, 'Aerospace power and the Kosovo crisis', US Air Force Association, 1999, page 10

26 'Allies hit troops and bridge', *New York Times*, 2 April 1999

27 Rebecca Grant, 'Aerospace power and the Kosovo crisis', US Air Force Association, 1999, page 12

28 PBS Frontline, 'General Michael Short interview', PBS website

29 'Joint chiefs doubted air strategy', *Washington Post*, 5 April 1999

30 'NATO says train was hit not once but twice', *New York Times*, 14 April 1999

31 'Civilians are slain in military attack on a Kosovo road', *New York Times*, 15 April 1999

32 PBS Frontline, 'General Michael Short interview', PBS website

33 'Civilians are slain in military attack on a Kosovo road', *New York Times*, 15 April 1999

34 PBS Frontline, 'General Wesley Clark interview', PBS website

35 'NATO confronts a new role: regional policeman', *New York Times*, 22 April 1999

36 'City rolls out the red carpet for NATO summit', *Washington Post*, 23 April 1999

37 'With fanfare, first attack copters arrive', *New York Times*, 22 April 1999

38 Rebecca Grant, 'Aerospace power and the Kosovo crisis', US Air Force Association, 1999, page 12

39 'NATO raids send notice to Milošević', *New York Times*, 22 April 1999

40 'NATO to discuss ground troops in Kosovo', *Washington Post*, 23 April 1999

41 PBS Frontline, 'Sandy Berger interview', PBS website

42 'How Kosovo strained Blair's special relationship', *Guardian*, 17 September 2000

43 'NATO widens security "map"', *Washington Post*, 25 April 1999

44 'NATO summit ends with restoration vow', *Washington Post*, 26 April 1999

45 PBS Frontline, 'Kosovo war chronology', PBS website

46 'US military acted outside NATO framework during Kosovo conflict, France says', *New York Times*, 11 November 1999

47 PBS Frontline, 'General Klaus Naumann interview', PBS website

48 'Human Rights Watch report on Kosovo war', Human Rights Watch, 2000

49 'NATO confident in their bombs, allies still plan for winter', *New York Times*, 5 May 1999

50 'How Kosovo strained Blair's special relationship', *Guardian*, 17 September 2000

51 'How Kosovo strained Blair's special relationship', *Guardian*, 17 September 2000

52 'Kosovo land threat may have won war', *Washington Post*, 19 September 1999

53 'NATO was closer to ground war in Kosovo than is widely realised', *New York Times*, 7 November 1999

54 'Kosovo land threat may have won war', *Washington Post*, 19 September 1999

55 Mike Jackson, *Soldier: The Autobiography of General Sir Mike Jackson*, page 255

56 'Clinton's remarks: we have achieved a victory', *New York Times*, 11 June 1999

57 'Allies begin effort to rebuild Kosovo', *New York Times*, 11 June 1999

58 Mike Jackson, *Soldier: The Autobiography of General Sir Mike Jackson*, page 260

59 Wesley K. Clark, *A Time to Lead . . .*, Kindle location 3460

60 Mike Jackson, *Soldier: The Autobiography of General Sir Mike Jackson*, page 219

61 'UN Security Council Resolution of 1244', UN website, 10 June 1989. The resolution includes no reference to NATO at all.

62 'US leaders are shocked but accept Russian story', *New York Times*, 12 June 1999

63 Mike Jackson, *Soldier: The Autobiography of General Sir Mike Jackson*, pages 258–262

64 Sean M. Maloney, *Operation Kinetic: Stabilising Kosovo*, Kindle location 2770

65 'Kremlin instability in Moscow: who is giving orders?', *New York Times*, 13 June 1996

66 Wesley K. Clark, *A Time to Lead: . . .*, Kindle location 3181

67 Sean M. Maloney, *Operation Kinetic: Stabilising Kosovo*, Kindle location 3486

68 Ibid., Kindle location 3486

69 Ibid., Kindle location 3562, 3587

70 Wesley K. Clark, *A Time to Lead . . .*, Kindle location 3481

71 Mike Jackson, *Soldier: The Autobiography of General Sir Mike Jackson*, pages 270–273

72 'Singer James Blunt "prevented world war three" ', BBC News, 14 November 2010

73 'Secret Russian troop deployment thwarted', *Washington Post*, 25 June 1999

74 Wesley K. Clark, *A Time to Lead . . .*, Kindle location 3503

75 'Role agreed for Russian troops', BBC News, 19 June 1999
76 Sean M. Maloney, *Operation Kinetic: Stabilising Kosovo*, Kindle location 2770
77 Ibid., Kindle location 2797
78 'The April 1999 Russian Federation Security Council Meeting on Nuclear Weapons', Nuclear Threat Initiative website (NTI), 31 May 1999
79 'Why Putin keeps talking about Kosovo', Foreign Policy, 3 March 2022

20. Into a New Century (1999–2001)

1 Mark Laity, 'Pre-empting war in Macedonia', RUSI Whitehall Paper, 2008, page 1
2 'NATO extends control over Kosovo', *Washington Post*, 19 June 1999
3 'Kosovo Albanians give Russian troops no peace', *New York Times*, 16 August 1999
4 Sean M. Maloney, *Operation Kinetic: Stabilising Kosovo*, Kindle location 4085
5 'Despite the GIs, Kosovo town is purged of Serbs', *New York Times*, 5 August 1999
6 'NATO appoints British defence chief to its top civilian post', *New York Times*, 5 August 1999
7 'German general's Kosovo peacekeepers are fighting crime', *New York Times*, 21 December 1999
8 Sean M. Maloney, *Operation Kinetic: Stabilising Kosovo*, Kindle location 4243
9 'Imitating NATO: a script is adapted for Chechnya', *New York Times*, 28 September 1999
10 'Kosovo inquiry confirms US fears of war crimes court', *New York Times*, 3 January 2000
11 Human Rights Watch report on Kosovo war', Human Rights Watch, 2000
12 'US soldier gets life for killing Kosovo girl', ABC, 1 August 2000
13 'GIs in Kosovo face a barrage of complaints', *New York Times*, 29 January 2000
14 'Bus ambush in Kosovo costs NATO faith of Serbs', *New York Times*, 4 February 2000
15 'Seven killed and nine hurt in Kosovo rampage, worst since war', *New York Times*, 5 February 2000
16 'NATO-led troops caught in battle over Kosovo town', *New York Times*, 14 February 2000
17 'NATO says Milošević incites violence covertly in Kosovo', *New York Times*, 23 February 2000
18 'Not enough troops in Kosovo, NATO says', *New York Times*, 26 February 2000

19 'Torn Mitrovica reflects West's trials in Kosovo', *New York Times*, 27 February 2000

20 'Kosovo's unquenched violence dividing US and NATO allies', *New York Times*, 12 March 2000

21 'Europe's dim view of US is evolving into frank hostility', *New York Times*, 9 April 2000

22 'Putin nears Russian victory', *Washington Post*, 27 March 2000

23 'Putin in major test wins vote for accord on nuclear arms', *New York Times*, 11 April 2000

24 'Ratko Mladić: the full story of how the general evaded capture for so long', *Guardian*, 2 April 2013

25 'UN war crimes prosecutor declines to investigate NATO', *New York Times*, 3 June 2000

26 'Kosovo buffer zone becomes sensitive issue', Radio Free Europe, 21 May 2001

27 'US troops say Kosovo duty sharpens their skills', *New York Times*, 18 January 2001

28 'Allies questioning Bush stand say US Kosovo role is crucial', *New York Times*, 16 January 2001

29 Mark Laity, *Preventing War in Macedonia: Pre-emptive Diplomacy for the 21st Century*, page 8

30 Ibid., page 1

31 'West is alarmed as warfare grows in Balkans again', *New York Times*, 17 March 2001

32 'Rebels hope to shift borders in Balkans, diplomats say', *New York Times*, 19 March 2001

33 'Macedonia backs away from war', CNN, 7 May 2001

34 Mark Laity, *Preventing War in Macedonia: Pre-emptive Diplomacy for the 21st Century*, pages 20–21

35 'Rumsfeld outlines to NATO fast track for missile shield', *New York Times*, 8 June 2001

36 'Bush trip aimed at winning over Europeans', *New York Times*, 9 June 2001

37 'The US–Europe split casts a long shadow on Bush tour', *New York Times*, 15 June 2001

38 'Putin urges Bush not to act alone on missile shield', *New York Times*, 17 June 2001

39 'Macedonia expands attacks against rebels', *New York Times*, 9 June 2001

40 'Peacekeepers in Kosovo seize 19 Macedonia rebel suspects', *New York Times*, 12 June 2001

41 'Macedonia seeks NATO troops to help disarm Albanian rebels', *New York Times*, 15 June 2001

42 Mark Laity, *Preventing War in Macedonia: Pre-emptive Diplomacy for the 21st Century*, pages 26–28

43 'Macedonian talks are moved away from heated emotions', *New York Times*, 28 July 2001

44 'NATO begins placing troops in Macedonia', *New York Times*, 19 August 2001

45 Interview with the author

46 Mark Laity, *Preventing War in Macedonia: Pre-emptive Diplomacy for the 21st Century*, pages 53–60

47 Ibid., pages 60–64

48 Ibid., pages 64–74

49 'US in supporting role for NATO force in Macedonia', *New York Times*, 8 September 2001

21. 9/11 and its Aftermath (2001)

1 'Being NATO's secretary general on 9/11', George Robertson, NATO website, 4 September 2011

2 Ibid.

3 Nicholas Burns, 'NATO commemoration of September 11', NATO website, 11 September 2002

4 George Robertson, 'Being NATO's secretary general on 9/11', NATO website, September 4, 2011

5 Bob Woodward, *Bush at War*, 2003, Kindle location 268–271

6 Ibid., Kindle location 268

7 Ibid., Kindle location 328

8 Nicholas Burns, 'NATO commemoration of September 11', NATO website, 11 September 2002

9 Interview with the author

10 'Statement by the North Atlantic Council', NATO website, 11 September 2001

11 Bob Woodward, *Bush at War*, Kindle location 735

12 'Reflections on 9/11', NATO YouTube channel, 2011

13 'Bush says "time is running out"; US plans to act largely alone', *New York Times*, 7 October 2001

14 'Ex-NATO head says Putin wanted to join alliance early on in his rule', *Guardian*, 4 November 2021

15 Interview with the author

16 George Robertson, 'Being NATO's secretary general on 9/11', NATO website, 4 September 2011

17 'Allies say attack was directed at all; NATO commits to supporting US', *New York Times*, 14 September 2001

18 Nicholas Burns, 'NATO commemoration of September 11', NATO website, 11 September 2002

19 Bob Woodward, *Bush at War*, Kindle location 730–795

20 Ibid., Kindle location 1610

21 'In Europe, a pause to ponder Washington's tough talk', *New York Times*, 16 September 2001

22 'NATO, though supportive, has little to offer militarily', *New York Times*, 20 September 2001

23 'So far, Europe breathes easier over freehand given the US', *New York Times*, 29 September 2001

24 'NATO says US has proof against bin Laden group', *New York Times*, 3 October 2001

25 Bob Woodward, *Bush at War*, Kindle location 1209

26 Ibid., Kindle location 1041

27 'Timeline: Blair's last ten days', *Guardian*, 21 September 2001

28 Bob Woodward, *Bush at War*, Kindle location 1565

29 Ibid., Kindle location 1776

30 'Putin softens his stance against NATO expansion', *New York Times*, 4 October 2001

31 Bob Woodward, *Bush at War*, Kindle location 839

32 Ibid., Kindle location 2313

33 'NATO quickly gives the US all the help that it asked', *New York Times*, 5 October 2001

34 'Bush says "time is running out"; US plans to act largely alone', *New York Times*, 7 October 2001

35 'US and UK bomb targets in Afghanistan', *New York Times*, 8 October 2001

36 'Statement by NATO secretary general', NATO website, 8 October 2001

37 'NATO's chief stresses international resolve', George W Bush White House archive, 10 October 2001

38 Bob Woodward, *Bush at War*, Kindle location 4462

39 'Challenged White House takes steps to bolster bloc fighting terror', *New York Times*, 7 November 2001

40 'Turkey to send forces to Afghanistan', *New York Times*, 1 November 2001

41 '"BBC liberated Kabul" says Simpson', *Guardian*, 13 November 2001

42 Carter Malkasian, *The American War in Afghanistan: A History*, 2021, Kindle location 74

43 'NATO is vital for the challenges of the new century', *New York Times*, 10 November 2001

44 'UK, US forces on airbase mission', CNN, 16 November 2001

45 'Security Council authorises International Security Force for Afghanistan; welcomes UK's offer to be the initial lead nation', UN website, 20 December 2001

46 'Is NATO "relevant" in era of US power?', *New York Times*, 6 December 2001

47 'In spat over NATO and Russia, Powell fends off Rumsfeld', *New York Times*, 8 December 2001

48 'Facing Pact's end, Putin decides to grimace and bear it', *New York Times*, 14 December 2001

49 Interview with the author

22. The Schisms of Iraq (2002–2005)

1 Interview with the author

2 Carter Malkasian, *The American War in Afghanistan . . .*, Kindle locations 80–82

3 'US officials tried to assure Europeans on NATO', *New York Times*, 3 February 2002

4 'Europe seethes as the US flies solo in world affairs', *New York Times*, 23 February 2002

5 'Rumsfeld's "old" and "new" Europe touches on uneasy divide'. Radio Free Europe, 24 January 2003

6 'Putin chooses the West', *New York Times*, 14 February 2002

7 'Final communiqué, ministerial meeting of the North Atlantic Council', NATO website, 14 May 2002

8 'NATO countries approve pact giving Russia role of a partner', *New York Times*, 14 May 2002

9 'US suspects Ukraine of selling radar to Iraq', *New York Times*, 24 September 2002

10 'Ukraine invites investigation of radar sale', *New York Times*, 27 September 2002

11 'NATO: solidarity with Russia, cold shoulder to Kuchma', Radio Free Europe, 22 November 2002

12 'NATO looking ahead to mission makeover', *Washington Post*, 5 November 2002

13 'Baltic report', Radio Free Europe, 6 December 2002

14 'Putin questions US terror allies', *New York Times*, 23 November 2002

15 'US asks NATO nations to offer forces for an Iraq campaign', *New York Times*, 5 December 2002

16 'Robertson says NATO "morally obliged" to back war, *Guardian*, 26 December 2002

17 Bob Woodward, *Plan of Attack*, 2004, Kindle location 275

18 'NATO rebuffs US in debate over aid for a war with Iraq', *International Herald Tribune*, 22 January 2003

19 'Robertson to stand down as NATO chief', *Guardian*, 22 January 2003

20 'Latvia's oil dries up as Russia alters flow', *New York Times*, 21 January 2003

21 'New allies back US Iraq policy', *New York Times*, 6 February 2003

22 'France, Germany and Belgium trigger one of the biggest crises in alliance history', *International Herald Tribune*, 11 February 2003

23 'Three members of NATO and Russia resist US on Iraq plans', *New York Times*, 10 February 2003

24 'US backs deal to salvage NATO aid for Turkey', *New York Times*, 13 February 2002

25 'Decision sheet of the defence planning committee', NATO website, 16 February 2003

26 'Press conference by NATO secretary general', 16 February 2003

27 'NATO to deploy defensive assistance to Turkey', NATO website, 19 February 2003

28 'Remarks at photo opportunity', NATO website, 19 February 2003

29 'Questions and answers with NATO secretary general Lord Robertson at the European Institute, Washington DC', NATO website, 20 February 2003

30 'NATO chief says alliance needs role in Afghanistan', *New York Times*, 21 February 2003

31 'Navy SEALS easily seized two oil sites', *New York Times*, 22 March 2003

32 'Europe; allies once again?', *New York Times*, 5 April 2003

33 'Anti-Americanism in Greece is reinvigorated by war', *New York Times*, 7 April 2003

34 'Chirac calls Bush as France seeks to mend relations', *Washington Post*, 16 April 2003

35 'Press briefing', NATO website, 16 April 2003

36 Carter Malkasian, *The American War in Afghanistan . . .*, Kindle location 110

37 'Germany's long military mission in Afghanistan', *Deutsche Welle*, 25 March 2021

38 'Afghan report', Radio Liberty, 12 June 2003

39 'NATO takes control of Afghanistan peace mission', *AP/Guardian*, 11 August 2003

40 'NATO takes control of peace force in Kabul', *New York Times*, 12 August 2003

41 Interview with the author

42 'Afghan report', Radio Free Asia, 18 June 2004

43 'Speech by secretary general', NATO website, 12 November 2003

44 'A new NATO chief takes over', *New York Times*, 6 January 2004

45 'NATO: a bruised alliance marches on', *International Herald Tribune*, 30 January 2004

46 'General urges NATO to send Afghanistan more troops', *New York Times*, 28 January 2004

47 'At US urging, NATO acts to bolster Afghan rebuilding role', *New York Times*, 7 February 2004

48 'Mission for NATO: an alliance against the traffic in humans', *New York Times*, 4 March 2004

49 'Madrid train attacks', BBC website, 11 March 2004

50 'Spain's new leade this r may send more troops to Afghanistan', *New York Times*, 23 March 2004

51 'Eight are killed as ethnic fighting flares in Kosovo', *New York Times*, 17 March 2004

52 'Kosovans survey the damage of ethnic violence', *New York Times*, 21 March 2004

53 'Seven former communist countries join NATO', *Washington Post*, 30 March 2004

54 Ibid.

55 Interviews with the author

56 'Seven former communist countries join NATO', *Washington Post*, 30 March 2004

57 'NATO welcomes seven new members', *New York Times*, 2 April 2004

58 Ibid.

59 Carter Malkasian, *The American War in Afghanistan . . .*, Kindle locations 97–99

60 'Ukraine changes mind about joining NATO and the European Union', BBC News, 26 July 2004

61 'Liberal leader from Ukraine was poisoned', *New York Times*, 12 December 2004

62 'Pro-West leader appears to win Ukraine election', *New York Times*, 27 December 2004

63 'Kyiv protesters look beyond vote', *Washington Post*, 5 December 2004

64 'NATO chief talked up Ukraine ties', *New York Times*, 28 June 2005

23. *Afghanistan: NATO's Longest War (2006–2010)*

1 Sandy Gall, *War Against the Taliban: Why it All Went Wrong in Afghanistan*, 2012, Kindle location 89

2 'Bush predicts a year of progress in Iraq and Afghanistan', *New York Times*, 4 January 2006

3 'NATO's future on the line', *New York Times*, 11 January 2006

4 Sandy Gall, *War Against the Taliban: Why it All Went Wrong in Afghanistan*, Kindle location 101

5 General David Richards, *Taking Command*, 2014, Kindle locations 185–86

6 Ibid., Kindle location 184

7 Ibid., Kindle location 209

8 'US airstrikes rise in Afghanistan as fighting intensifies', *Washington Post*, 18 June 2006

9 General David Richards, *Taking Command*, Kindle locations 217–18

10 'Kabul podcast', NATO website, 7 August 2006

11 General David Richards, *Taking Command*, Kindle location 219

12 Sandy Gall, *War Against the Taliban . . .*, Kindle location 85

13 Mike Martin, *An Intimate War: An Oral History of the Helmand Conflict*, 2014, Kindle location 159

14 Sandy Gall, *War Against the Taliban . . .*, Kindle location 77

15 'Dozens reported killed in attack on Taliban', *New York Times*, 16 April 2006

16 Mike Martin, *An Intimate War: An Oral History of the Helmand Conflict*, Kindle locations 134–135

17 Ibid., Kindle location 153

18 Sandy Gall, *War Against the Taliban . . .*, Kindle location 100

19 Mike Martin, *An Intimate War: an Oral History of the Helmand Conflict*, Kindle location 160

20 Sandy Gall, *War Against the Taliban . . .*, Kindle location 91

21 Mike Martin, *An Intimate War . . .*, Kindle location 165

22 'Canada leader accused of trying to deemphasise danger to troops', *New York Times*, 25 April 2006

23 'What really happened when Canadians died in 2006 firefight', *Toronto Star*, 30 September 2006

24 General David Richards, *Taking Command*, Kindle location 238

25 'Operation Medusa: the Furious Battle that Saved Afghanistan from the Taliban', Vancouver City News, 20 May 2018

26 'After Afghan battle, a harder fight for peace', *New York Times*, 3 October 2006

27 'What really happened when Canadians died in 2006 firefight', *Toronto Star*, 30 September 2006

28 'Afghan attack brings total of Canadians killed to 42', *New York Times*, 16 October 2006

29 Interview with the author

30 Adam Jowett, *No Way Out: the Searing True Story of Men Under Siege*, 2018, Kindle location 521

31 'Operation Herrick 4', paradata.org.uk

32 Sandy Gall, *War Against the Taliban . . .*, page 111

33 'Rory Stewart on what went wrong in Afghanistan' *Yale News*, 9 November 2021

34 'US and NATO commanders seek more troops in Afghanistan', *International Herald Tribune*, 17 January 2007

35 'NATO slow to respond on Afghan force level', *New York Times*, 26 January 2007

36 'US general takes charge of NATO operations in Afghanistan', *New York Times*, 4 February 2007

37 'NATO mounts largest attack on Taliban in the south', *New York Times*, 7 March 2007

38 Mike Martin, *An Intimate War . . .*, Kindle location 166

39 'Ten years of Afghan war: how the Taliban go on', *Newsweek*, 2 October 2011

40 'Afghans' toll shakes generals', *New York Times*, 18 October 2008

41 Sam Kiley, *Desperate Glory: At War in Helmand with Britain's 16 Air Assault Brigade*, Kindle location 196

42 Mike Martin, *An Intimate War . . .*, Kindle location 182

43 'Britain delivers turbine in Afghan rebel stronghold', *Reuters*, 2 September 2008

44 'Afghanistan waste exhibit A: Kajaki Dam, more than 300 million spent and still not done', ProPublica, 19 January 2016

45 'Battle Company is out there', *New York Times*, 24 February 2008

46 'Afghans' toll shakes generals', *New York Times*, 18 October 2008

47 ''Battle Company is out there', *New York Times*, 24 February 2008

48 Carter Malkasian, *The American War in Afghanistan . . .*, Kindle locations 209, 212

49 Ibid., Kindle locations 213–215

50 'Stan McChrystal's long war', *New York Times*, 18 October 2009

51 Carter Malkasian, *The American War in Afghanistan . . .*, Kindle location 221

52 General David Richards, *Taking Command*, Kindle location 287

53 Interviews with the author

54 Carter Malkasian, *The American War in Afghanistan . . .*, Kindle location 224

55 'Afghanistan: anatomy of an election disaster', *Guardian*, 20 October 2009

56 Carter Malkasian, *The American War in Afghanistan . . .*, Kindle location 226

57 Interviews with the author

58 'German probe to Kunduz airstrike was adequate, rules court', *Deutsche Welle*, 16 February 2021

59 Carter Malkasian, *The American War in Afghanistan . . .*, Kindle location 226

60 'NATO expands its role in Afghanistan', NATO website, April 4, 2009

61 'Europeans offer few new troops for Afghanistan', *New York Times*, 4 April 2009

62 General Carter remarks at 'How Mainstream Media and Social Media Shape Military Decision Making', Oxford Media Network event, 22 March 2023

63 'Operation Moshtarak: Lessons Learned', International Council on Security and Development, March 2010

64 'Leveraging urbanisation in Afghanistan', World Bank report, 2016

65 'Obama meets top Afghan commander', *New York Times*, 2 October 2009

66 'Obama publishes account of firing General McChrystal', *Rolling Stone*, 17 November 2020

67 'McChrystal cleared of nasty remarks', *Politico*, 23 September 2010

24. Putin, Pirates, Cyber Attacks and Georgia (2007–2011)

1 'Putin criticises West for Libya incursion', *New York Times*, 26 April 2011

2 'Speech by NATO secretary general', NATO website, 9 February 2007

3 'US undermines global security, Putin declares', *International Herald Tribune*, 10 February 2007

4 'Speech by NATO secretary general', NATO website, 9 February 2007

5 'Gates counters Putin's words on US power', *New York Times*, 12 February 2007

6 'Putin picks up a bargaining chip with suspension of treaty', *New York Times*, 26 April 2007

7 'The Bronze Soldier crises of 2007', International Center for Defense Studies, August 2020

8 'EU and NATO seek to quell Russia–Estonia spat', *New York Times*, 3 May 2007

9 'Russia accused of unleashing cyber war to disable Estonia', *Guardian*, 17 May 2007

10 'Putin cites Third Reich in veiled criticism of US', *New York Times*, 9 May 2007

11 'Russia accused of unleashing cyber war to disable Estonia', *Guardian*, 17 May 2007

12 Interviews with the author

13 'Russia warns West Kosovo independence looms', *Reuters,* 10 February 2008

14 'That time Ukraine tried to join NATO and NATO said no', *Washington Post,* 4 September 2014

15 'NATO allies oppose Bush on Georgia and Ukraine', *New York Times,* 3 April 2008

16 'Putin tells NATO: "let's be friends"', *Reuters,* 4 April 2008

17 'A fateful summit 15 years ago hangs over the NATO meeting in Vilnius', *Washington Post,* 10 July 2023

18 'Kosovo Is Recognized but Rebuked by Others', *New York Times,* 19 February 2008

19 'Georgia offers fresh evidence on war's start', *New York Times,* 15 September 2008

20 'Georgia claim on Russian war called into question', *New York Times,* 6 November 2008

21 'Russia takes first steps towards Georgia pullback', NBC News, 19 August 2008

22 'EU, NATO chief urged Russia to halt Georgia advance', *Reuters,* 11 August 2008

23 'The US won't push NATO to admit Georgia', *New York Times,* 18 August 2008

24 'Statement of the North Atlantic Council', 19 August 2008

25 'Gates urges cautious NATO stance on Russia after Georgia conflict', *New York Times,* 19 September 2008

26 'Wounded Iceland takes over top bank, seeks Russian loan', *Reuters,* 7 October 2008

27 'Terror law used for Iceland deposits', *Financial Times,* 8 October 2008

28 'Iceland returns to Russia after IMF deal', *Reuters,* 13 October 2008

29 Conversations with the author, 2008

30 'Russian actions reignite tensions over strategic port in Ukraine', *New York Times,* 24 August 2008

31 'NATO's table, Ukraine and a test of Russian ties', *New York Times,* 11 November 2008

32 'US presses NATO on Georgia and Ukraine', *New York Times,* 25 November 2008

33 'Europe is ready to work with Obama', *New York Times,* 3 January 2009

34 'Obama offered a deal to Russia in secret letter', *New York Times,* 2 March 2009

35 'Does Russia really include limited nuclear strikes in its large-scale military exercises?', *Survival Online,* International Institute for Strategic Studies, 15 February 2018

36 US State Department cable from 23 November 2009, published by WikiLeaks/Norwegian newspaper Aftenposten

37 'A reformer in the NATO henhouse', *New York Times*, 15 October 2009

38 'Remarks from secretary general', NATO website, 23 February 2010

39 'Remarks of Madeleine Albright', NATO website, 11 February 2010

40 'US seeks to revamp NATO treaty in Europe', *New York Times*, 29 April 2010

41 'NATO training Mission Iraq', SHAPE website

42 'Operation OCEAN SHIELD', NATO Maritime Command website

43 'NATO extends anti-piracy mission of Somalia', *Reuters*, 24 April 2009

44 'Somali piracy is back with a $1.7 billion problem after shipping firms lower vigilance', CNBC, 3 May 2017

45 '"Citadel Room" Foils Pirate Attack', US Naval Institute Blog, 26 October 2010) 'Somali piracy is back with a $1.7 billion problem after shipping firms lower vigilance', CNBC, 3 May 2017

46 'Spy swap: US and Russia handover agents in full media glare', *Guardian*, 9 July 2010

47 'Estonia spy case rattles nerves at NATO', *New York Times*, 25 November 2008

48 'East Europe feels ignored by NATO, report says', *New York Times*, 16 May 2010

49 'Military says pirates did not reach land', *AP/Moscow Times*, 12 May 2010

50 'Another strike on NATO convoy in Pakistan; vehicles set ablaze', CNN, 6 October 2010

51 'Russia accepts invitation to attend NATO summit meeting', *New York Times*, 19 October 2010

52 'NATO leaders agreed to new start with Russia', *New York Times*, 21 November 2010

53 'Vladimir Putin was responsible for plane crash that killed Polish president, says Polish defence minister', *Independent*, 15 December 2017

25. Unexpected Revolutions (2011–2013)

1 'Putin criticises West for Libya incursion', *New York Times*, 26 April 2011

2 'Security in Kandahar city', NATO website, 24 February 2011

3 'Karzai seeks end to NATO reconstruction teams', *New York Times*, 6 February 2011

4 'Somali pirates grow bolder, world response lags', *Toronto Star*, 9 February 2011

5 'Fresh violence rages in Libya', Al Jazeera, 22 February 2011

6 'Muammar Gaddafi fires on his own people', *Daily Telegraph*, 21 February 2011

7 'Following US sanctions, UN Security Council to meet on Libya', *New York Times*, 26 February 2011

8 'US and Allies weigh Libya no-fly zone', *New York Times*, 27 February 2011

9 'With Libya, is intervention talk back in style?', *Reuters*, 4 March 2011

10 'Obama bolsters relief effort at Libyan border', *New York Times*, 7 March 2011

11 'NATO ready to support international efforts on Libya', NATO website, 10 March 2011

12 'NATO steps back from military intervention in Libya', *New York Times*, 10 March 2011

13 'As UN backs military action in Libya, US role is unclear', *New York Times*, 18 March 2011

14 'Allied strikes sweep Libya as West intervenes in conflict', *Guardian*, 11 March 2011

15 'Confusion over who leads Libya strikes, and for how long', *New York Times*, 22 March 2011

16 'Obama seeks to unify allies as more airstrikes rock Tripoli', *New York Times*, 23 March 2011

17 'NATO agrees to take command of no-fly zone in Libya', *New York Times*, 25 March 2011

18 'NATO to maintain high operational tempo as long as necessary', NATO website, 14 April 2011

19 'The pace of attacks in Libya conflict is dividing NATO', *New York Times*, 12 April 2011

20 Interviews with the author

21 'Libya's Gaddafi under pressure but with nowhere to go', *Reuters*, 19 May 2011

22 'Gaddafi's last words as he begged for mercy: "What did I do to you?"', *Guardian*, 23 October 2011

23 Interview with the author

24 'Key Syrian city takes on the tone of a civil war', *New York Times*, 2 October 2011

25 'Russian warships head for Syria', NavyRecognition.com, November 2011

26 'NATO leaders agree on a framework to wind down Afghan mission', 21 May 2012

27 'Resolute Support Mission in Afghanistan', NATO website, 30 May 2022

28 'Afghanistan: green-on-blue attacks in context', Institute for the Study of War, 31 October 2012

29 'Afghanistan: "green-on-blue" killings explained', Newsweek, 27 August 2012

30 'NATO withdrawal from Afghanistan could be speeded up, says Rasmussen', *Guardian*, 1 October 2012

31 Carter Malkasian, *The American War in Afghanistan: a History*, Kindle location 345

32 'Troops may come home early from Afghanistan', Sky News, 14 September 2012

33 'Afghanistan was a turbulent NATO proving ground for the Baltic states', Foreign Policy Research Institute, 20 December, 2021

34 'NATO – Taking on the Pirates', NATO YouTube channel, April 2012

35 'NATO's shrinking resources', *New York Times*, 16 May 2012

36 'Shrinking Europe military spending under scrutiny', *New York Times*, 22 April 2013

37 Ibid.

38 'Pipeline has allowed Germany to take a stronger line with Russia over Ukraine but other EU members cannot afford confrontation', LSE website, 18 November 2014

39 '14 suspected hits on British soil', *Buzzfeed News,* 15 June 2017

40 'Putin promises big Russian build-up', *Washington Post*, 20 February 2012

41 'NATO stages exercise as rearming Russia worries some allies', *Reuters*, 1 November 2013

42 Interview with the author

43 'Backed by NATO, Turkey steps up warning to Syria', *New York Times*, 27 June 2012

44 'Doorstep statement by secretary general', NATO website, 23 April 2013

45 'US cancels part of missile defence that Russia opposed', *New York Times*, 16 March 2013

46 'Edward Snowden leaves Hong Kong for Moscow', *Guardian*, 23 June 2013

47 'Obama drops Putin meeting', *New York Times*, 7 August 2013

48 'Off the cuff Obama line put US in bind on Syria', *New York Times*, 4 May 2013

49 'Government assessment of the Syrian government's use of chemical weapons on August 21, 2013', White House website, 30 August 2013

50 'Blow to Cameron's authority as MPs rule out British assault on Syria', *Guardian*, 30 August 2013

51 'Monthly press conference by the NATO secretary general', NATO website, 2 September 2013

52 'US and Russia agreed chemical weapons deal', *Guardian*, 14 September 2013

53 Interviews with the author

54 'Russia's Zapad 2013 military exercise', The Jamestown Foundation, December 2015

55 'NATO's Steadfast Jazz exercise gets underway', NATO website, 2 November 2013

26. The Return of War to Europe (2012–2015)

1 'Eastern Europe frets about NATO's ability to curb Russia', *New York Times*, 23 April 2014

2 'Russia putting a strong arm on neighbors', *New York Times*, 22 October 2013

3 'The EU seeks "time for reflection" after Vilnius summit failure', Euractiv, 29 November 2013

4 'Statement by the NATO secretary general', NATO website, 29 November 2013

5 'With president's departure, Ukraine looks forward to a murky future', *New York Times*, 23 February 2014

6 'Putin says he decided to take Crimea just hours after Yanukovych's ouster', Radio Free Europe, 9 March 2015

7 'Kremlin says Ukrainian instability threatens Russian interests', *New York Times*, 25 February 2014

8 Interview with the author

9 'With military moves seen in Ukraine, Obama warns Russia', *New York Times*, 1 March 2013

10 'Ukraine mobilises reserve troops, threatening war', *New York Times*, 1 March 2015

11 'US effort to broker Russia–Ukraine diplomacy fails', *New York Times*, 5 March 2014

12 'Remarks by NATO secretary general', NATO website, 5 March 2014

13 'NATO secretary general condemns moves to incorporate Crimea into Russian Federation', NATO website, 18 March 2014

14 'NATO websites hit in cyber attack linked to Crimea tension', *Reuters*, 16 March 2014

15 'Russian aggression puts NATO in spotlight', *New York Times*, 18 March 2014

16 'NATO weighs assistance for Ukraine to dissuade further moves by Moscow', *New York Times*, 19 March 2014

17 'NATO general warns of further Russian aggression', *Washington Post*, 23 March 2014

18 'NATO orders end to practical and military cooperation with Russia', *New York Times*, 1 April 2014

19 'Military cuts render NATO less formidable as a deterrent to Russia', *New York Times*, 26 March 2014

20 'NATO commander says he sees potent threat from Russia', *New York Times*, 2 April 2014

21 'US sends troops to Eastern Europe', *Politico*, 22 April 2014

22 'Steadfast Javelin kicks off in Estonia', NATO website, 2015

23 'After Ukraine, US trains more special forces in Eastern Europe', *Reuters*, 11 June 2014

24 'Darkened by a bloody history, Baltics hope to be bolstered by NATO', NPR, 15 July 2014

25 'From Estonia, Obama talks tough on Islamic State and Russia', NPR, 3 September 2014

26 'NATO plans a special force to reassure Eastern Europe and deter Russia', *New York Times*, 5 September 2014

27 'NATO's new missions won't solve Ukraine, Iraq crises', *Reuters*, 7 September 2014

28 'NATO stages major military exercise in Latvia after Wales summit', *Reuters*, 6 September 2014

29 'Estonia "spy" dispute could be Russia making anti-NATO mischief', NPR, 14 September 2014

30 'EU protests Russia's forced capture of Lithuanian fishing boat', *Moscow Times*, 1 October 2014

31 'Press conference by the coming secretary general', NATO website, 1 October 2014

32 'US sends "iron horse" tanks to NATO's nervous Baltic frontline', *Reuters*, 1 October 2014

33 'NATO ends combat operations in Afghanistan after 30 years', *Guardian*, 28 December 2014

34 'NATO flag lowered in Afghanistan as combat mission ends', *Washington Post*, 28 December 2014

35 'NATO hopes to keep the base in Afghanistan, a US general says', *Washington Post*, 23 May 2015

36 'What has Russia gained from five years of fighting in Syria?', Al Jazeera, 1 October 2020

37 Ibid.

38 'NATO chief: Putin "weaponising" refugee crisis to "break" Europe', *Daily Telegraph*, 2 March 2016

39 'Eastern Europe cautiously welcomes larger US military presence', *New York Times*, 2 February 2016

27. Enter Donald Trump (2016–2019)

1 'Trump discussed pulling US from NATO', *New York Times*, 14 January 2019

2 'A guide to Trump's past comments about NATO', CBS, 12 April 2017

3 'US presidential hopeful Trump on Ukraine's possible NATO entry: "I wouldn't care"', Radio Free Europe, 16 August 2015

4 'A guide to Trump's past comments about NATO', CBS, 12 April 2017

5 'NATO to expand military presence in Europe to deter Russians', *New York Times*, 10 February 2016

6 'NATO chief says UK staying in the EU is key to fighting terrorism', *The Guardian*, 22 June 2016

7 '"Brexit" and Russia loom over Obama's final NATO summit meeting', *New York Times*, 7 July 2016

8 'UK troops to take on NATO duties in Poland and Estonia', BBC, 8 July 2016

9 'Obama tells NATO that "Europe could count on" the US', *New York Times*, 9 July 2016

10 'Press conference', NATO website, 8 July 2016

11 'Donald Trump remarks trigger NATO alarm bells in Europe', NBC News, 21 June 2016

12 'Donald Trump sets conditions for defending NATO allies against attack', *New York Times*, 20 July 2016

13 'Trump's NATO comments "unprecedented"', *Politico*, 21 July 2016

14 Bob Woodward, *Fear: Trump in the White House*, 2018, pages 45–48

15 Ibid., Kindle location 66

16 'Europe to US: ignore Donald Trump, we need NATO', *Politico*, 1 April 2016

17 'NATO secretary general congratulates US president-elect Donald Trump', NATO website, 9 November 2016

18 'Readout of phone call with US president-elect Donald Trump', NATO website, 18 November 2016

19 'Trump warned by NATO chief that "going it alone is not an option"', *Guardian*, 13 November 2016

20 'US lending support to Baltic states fearing Russia', *New York Times*, 1 January 2017

21 Bob Woodward, *Rage*, Kindle location 2

22 'Placing Russia first among threats, Defense nominee warns of Kremlin attempts to "break" NATO', *Washington Post*, 12 January 2017

23 Bob Woodward, *Fear: Trump in the White House*, Kindle location 102

24 'Defense Secretary Mattis issues new ultimatum to NATO allies on defense spending', *Washington Post*, 15 February 2017

25 Journeyman Pictures, 'Estonian wargames: how NATO is preparing Estonia for war', YouTube, 20 July 2017

26 Interview with the author

27 *Army: Behind the New Front Lines* series one; episode two, 'The New Cold War', BBC, 18 October 2017

28 'Lithuania pushes back on fake news', DW, 23 February 2017

29 'Press conference by NATO secretary general', NATO website, 25 May 2017

30 'From 1960s prefab to glass palace: NATO to finally move home', *Reuters*, 25 May 2017

31 'Trump national security team blindsided by NATO speech', *Politico*, 5 June 2017

32 'In NATO speech, Trump is vague about mutual defence pledge', *New York Times*, 25 April 2017

33 Bob Woodward, *Rage*, Kindle location 37

34 'Russia kicks off huge Zapad 2017 military exercises with Belarus', NBC, 2 August 2017

35 'Europe has to reform: how the far right grew in 2017', Al Jazeera, 22 December 2017

36 'Europe's far right enjoys backing from Russia's Putin', NBC, 12 February 2017

37 'Doorstep statement by NATO secretary general', NATO website, 5 December 2017

38 'UK seeks allies' support after Russian spy, daughter poisoned with nerve agent', ABC News, 14 March 2018

39 'Secretary of State fury at Trump required intervention from Pence', NBC News, 4 October 2017

40 'Statement on Salisbury incident response', British government website, 14 March 2018

41 'Statement by the North Atlantic Council on the use of a nerve agent in Salisbury', NATO website, 4 March 2018

42 'Western allies expel scores of Russian diplomats over attack', *Guardian*, 27 March 2018

43 'No children or ducks harmed by attacks, say health officials', *Guardian*, 18 April 2019

44 'Trump trashed NATO at G7', *Guardian*, 28 June 2018

45 'As summit nears, NATO allies have one main worry', *New York Times*, 26 June, 2018

46 'US officials scrambled behind the scenes to shield NATO deal from Trump', 9 August 2018

47 'How Trump's NATO summit meltdown unfolded', *Guardian*, 12 July 2018

48 'Trump won't take yes for an answer at NATO', *Washington Post*, 11 July 2018

49 'Trump–Putin summit is over. The head-scratching? Not so much', *New York Times*, 16 July 2018

50 'NATO secretary general briefs on exercise Trident Juncture', NATO website, 24 October 2018

51 'UK forces test military mobility', video produced by Allied Joint Force Naples, 11 October 2018

52 'Warnings and confusion preceded Norwegian frigate disaster', Defense News, 11 November 2018

53 'US considering building "Fort Trump" in Poland', *Politico*, 19 September 2018

54 Bob Woodward, *Fear: Trump in the White House*, 2018, pages 140–143

55 'Trump discussed pulling US from NATO, aides say amid new concerns over Russia', *New York Times*, 14 January 2019

56 'The world still needs NATO', *New York Times*, 18 January 2019

57 'Congressional leaders to invite NATO chief to speak', *New York Times*, 11 March 2019

58 'Russia pulls out of the INF treaty in "symmetrical" response to US move', *New York Times*, 2 February 2019

59 'Press conference' NATO website, 15 February 2019

60 'Pence calls on European states to withdraw from Iran nuclear deal', CNN, 16 February 2019

61 'Remarks by NATO secretary general and US president', NATO website, 3 April 2019

62 'NATO: good for Europe and for America', NATO website, 3 April 2019

63 'NATO chief addresses Congress, appeals to Trump in anniversary speech', *Washington Post*, 3 April 2019

64 Interview with the author

65 'Macron warns Europe NATO is becoming brain dead', *Economist*, 7 November 2019

66 'Macron criticised by US and Germany over NATO "brain death" claims', *Guardian*, 7 November 2019

67 'Trump blasts Macron for "very nasty statement" on NATO', *Reuters*, 3 December 2019

68 'Press conference', NATO website, 4 December 2019

69 'Trump abruptly exits NATO gathering after embarrassing video emerges', *New York Times*, 4 December 2019

28. The World Crisis of the 2020s

1 Andreas Klinger, Twitter post, 23 March 2023

2 'Some NATO troops begin leaving Iraq', *New York Times*, 7 January 2020

3 'US is not willing to withdraw troops from Iraqi, says Pompeo', *Guardian*, 10 January 2020

4 'Round table with NATO secretary general at the Munich Security Conference', NATO website, 15 February 2020

5 'Press point by NATO secretary general', NATO website, 28 February 2020

6 'NATO eyes troop reductions in Afghanistan as US draws down', *New York Times*, 7 February 2020

7 'Afghan war plagued by "mendacity" and lies, Inspector General tells Congress', *Washington Post*, 15 January 2020

8 'NATO secretary general visits Afghanistan', NATO website, 29 February 2020

9 'As soldiers arrived for Defender 2020, European infrastructure will be tested', Army Times, 26 February 2020

10 'Bilateral meeting', NATO TV, February 2020

11 'US sailor in Italy tests positive for coronavirus', Navy Times, 7 March 2020

12 Ibid.

13 'Coronavirus latest: 16 March at a glance', *Guardian*, 16 March 2020

14 'Soldiers in Europe for Defender 2022 return home amid pandemic', Army Times, 16 March 2020

15 'NATO's response to the Covid-19 pandemic', NATO website, March 2021

16 'NATO allies take stock of response to Covid-19 outbreak', NATO website, 19 March 2020

17 'Press conference by NATO secretary general', NATO website, 19 March 2020

18 'Russia's Putin, China's Xi discussed coronavirus, agree medical cooperation: Kremlin', *Reuters*, 19 March 2020

19 Woodward, *Rage*, Kindle location 332-3

20 'EU faced "abyss" at start of coronavirus crisis', *Politico*, 28 March 2020

21 'Germany confirms that Trump tried to buy firm working on coronavirus vaccine', *Politico*, 15 March 2020

22 'US hijacking mask shipments in Russia coronavirus protection', *Guardian*, 3 April 2020

23 'How Russia, China and EU vie to win over Serbia', *Guardian*, 13 April 2020

24 'Russian army to send coronavirus help to Italy after Putin phone call', *Reuters*, 22 March 2020

25 'Russian aid to Italy leaves EU exposed', *Reuters*, 26 March 2020

26 'Russia sends Italy coronavirus aid to underline historic ties', *Financial Times*, 23 March 2020

27 'Russian media "spreading Covid-19 disinformation"', *Guardian*, 18 March 2020

28 'China pushes propaganda casting doubts on virus origin', *Guardian*, 13 March 2020

29 'NATO's response to the Covid-19 pandemic', NATO website, March 2021

30 'Additional medical aid arrives in Italy', NATO website, 30 March 2020

31 'Opening remarks by NATO secretary general', NATO website, 2 April 2020

32 'Russia brings army doctors home from Italy', BBC News, 6 May 2020

33 'NATO is preparing for the second corona wave', *Spiegel*, 2 May 2020

34 'Russia maintains training tempo after NATO rebuffs "offer" to freeze drills', Shepherd Media, May 2020

35 'NATO rejects Russia's offer to MUTUALLY freeze military drills amid Covid-19 pandemic', RT, 26 May 2020

36 'Covid-19 and teleworking', NATO website, 15 April 2020

37 'Too risky to come home, crew of "clean" US warship in coronavirus limbo', *Reuters*, 1 May 2020

38 'NATO Allied maritime assets operate in the Arctic', NATO website, 7 May 2020

39 'Resolute support mission', NATO website, June 2020

40 Carter Malkasian, *The American War in Afghanistan*, Kindle location 449

41 'France suspends role in NATO naval mission over tensions with Turkey', France 24, 1 July 2020

42 'Trump orders large withdrawal of US forces from Germany', *Politico*, 6 June 2020

43 'Congress moves to block Trump's Germany troop withdrawal plans', Defense News, 30 June 2020

44 'Key NATO and Allied exercises in 2021', NATO website, March 2021

45 'Rapid Trident 2020 officially kicks off', DVIDS, 17 September 2020

46 'The true death toll of Covid-19', World Health Organisation

47 'Nearly 15 million excess deaths occurred globally in 2020 and 2021', *New Scientist*, 14 December 2022

48 'The EU economy after Covid-19', Centre for Economic and Political Research, 21 October 2021

49 'How is the US economy doing following Covid-19?', World Economic Forum, February 2021

50 'NATO chief warns against troop cuts in Afghanistan', *Washington Post*, 17 November 2020

51 'NATO prepares "virus free" zone for summit', *AP*, 23 March 2021

52 Press conference, NATO website, 24 March 2021

53 'Biden proposes summit in phone call with Putin', CNBC, 13 April 2021

54 Interviews with the author

55 'Biden calls the alliance "critically important" for US interests', *New York Times*, 14 June 2021

56 'With Putin, Biden tries to forge a bond of self interest, not souls', *New York Times*, 16 June 2021

57 'In Lithuania, migrants find themselves caught in a geopolitical battle', *New York Times*, 19 July 2021

58 'Airlines move to block fights to Belarus', *New York Times*, 12 November 2020

59 Carter Malkasian, *The American War in Afghanistan*, Kindle locations 449–451

60 'Oral evidence: government policy on Afghanistan', House of Commons Foreign Select Committee, 23 November 2021

61 Carter Malkasian, *The American War in Afghanistan*, Kindle location 453

62 Ibid., Kindle location 456

63 Ibid., Kindle location 470

64 Ibid., Kindle location 460–465

65 'Press briefing on Afghanistan', 17 August 2021

66 'Germany's Afghanistan vets grapple with "second war" ', *Deutsche Welle*, 1 September 2021

67 'Press briefing on Afghanistan', 17 August 2021

68 'NATO military committee convenes special meeting', NATO website, 19 August 2021

69 US Army Europe and Africa Twitter feed, 6 February 2022

70 Carter Malkasian, *The American War in Afghanistan*, Kindle location 471

71 'Russian troop movements near Ukraine border prompt concern in US, Europe', *Washington Post*, 30 October 2021

72 'Inside the monumental, stop-start effort to arm Ukraine', *Washington Post*, 23 December, 2022

73 'Ukrainians feel they've been abandoned', CNBC, 14 February 2022

74 'Putin puts Russia nuclear deterrence forces on high alert', *Guardian*, 27 February 2022

75 'NATO Steadfast Noon and nuclear modernisation in Europe', Federation of American Scientists, 17 October 2022

29. From Vilnius to Washington (2023–2024)

1 Interview with research assistant

2 'Vilnius cheers on Ukraine at NATO summit', *Politico*, 12 July 2023

3 Interviews with the author

4 'NATO flexes muscle to protect Vilnius summit near Russia, Belarus', *Reuters*, 9 July 2023

5 'Remarks by NATO deputy secretary general', NATO website, 11 July 2023

6 'NATO chief offers Vilnius summit preview at White House', Al Jazeera, 13 July 2023

7 'Wagner troops in Belarus "want to go West" into Poland', Radio Free Europe, 23 July 2023

8 'Biden says war with Russia must end before NATO can consider membership for Ukraine', CNN, 9 July 2023

9 'Erdoğan: "Let Turkey into the EU if you want Sweden to join NATO"', *Politico*, 10 July 2023

10 'No champagne for Swedes at NATO yet, PM says', *Politico*, 11 July 2023

11 Interview with the author

12 'Remarks by NATO deputy secretary general', NATO website, 11 July 2023

13 'NATO is set to approve new defence plans at Vilnius summit', Euractiv, 4 July 2023

14 'Detailed defence plans remind senior army leaders of Cold War', Stars and Stripes, 23 June 2023

15 'RAF intercepts 50 Russian aircraft on longest NATO air policing deployment yet', *Forces News*, YouTube, 2 August 2023

16 Interviews with the author

17 'Germany walks back plan to meet NATO spending target', *Reuters*, 16 August 2023

18 'NATO details leap in member defence spending ahead of summit', *Air and Space Forces* magazine, 8 July 2023

19 'Agenda 47: Preventing World War Three', Trump campaign website, 16 March 2023

20 'Bolton: "In a second Trump term, we'd almost certainly withdraw from NATO"', The Hill, 3 August 2023

21 'With eyes on Trump, Senate votes to make NATO withdrawal harder', Defense News, 19 July 2023

22 Vivek Ramaswamy, Twitter, 5 June 2023

23 Interview with the author

24 Interview with the author

25 'US defence contributions to Europe', US DOD website, 29 June 2022

26 Interviews with the author

27 Interview with the author

28 Interview with the author

29 Interviews with the author

30 'UK resists pressure to station troops permanently in Estonia', *Politico*, 11 July 2023

31 Interviews with the author

32 'With eyes on Russia, Germany ready to station troops permanently in Lithuania', *Reuters*, 26 June 2023

33 'A Russian mole in Germany sows suspicions at home and beyond', *New York Times*, 17 February 2023

34 'German spy agencies "hobbled, toothless and dependent on allies"', *The Times*, 6 August 2023

35 'With eyes on Russia, Germany ready to station troops permanently in Lithuania', *Reuters*, 26 June 2023

36 'Biden says war with Russia must end before NATO can consider membership for Ukraine', CNN, 9 July 2023

37 'NATO's crucial summit in Vilnius nearly came off the rails and gave Russia a PR victory', CNN, 14 July 2023

38 Brussel Sprout podcast, Center for a New American Security, 24 July 2023

39 Live NATO summit updates, NBC News, 13 July 2023

40 Interview with the author

41 'NATO appears to shelve plans to open Japan liaison office in Tokyo', *Guardian*, 12 July 2023

42 'NATO leaders send mixed messages in Japan office controversy', *Reuters*, 12 July 2023

43 'Ukraine set to enter Crimea "soon"', *New York Post*, 29 July 2023

44 'Nuclear weapons on the table if Ukraine counteroffensive succeeds: Russia's Medvedev', *Politico*, 30 July 2023

45 'Multi-domain activities in the Baltic', *BALTIC AMBER* Magazine, NATO website, 26 July 2023

46 'Baltics look to NATO for air defence support in new defence plans', Euractiv, 2 May 2023

47 'Readiness is the path to peace', *BALTIC AMBER* magazine, NATO website, 26 July 2023

48 'Missile that hit Poland likely came from Ukraine's defences, say Warsaw and NATO', *Guardian*, 16 November 2022

49 'Russian drone strike on Ukrainian port "an indirect attack" on Romania, Moldova', Radio Free Europe, 25 July 2023

50 'Wagner recruiting fighters in Belarus on condition of readiness to fight in Poland, Lithuania', *Kyiv Independent*, 27 July 2023

51 'Fears in Poland's east, as Wagner Group trains across the border', *Reuters*, 20 July 2023

30. Surviving the NATO Century (2024–2049)

1 'JP Morgan's Jamie Dimon warns world facing 'most dangerous time in decades'.' BBC News, 14 October 2023

2 'America's Strategic Posture', House Armed Services Committee website, October 2023

3 'Global exercise to test US Navy's live, virtual and constructive training environment', *Defense News*, 11 August 2021

4 'States invest in nuclear arsenals as geopolitical relations deteriorate', Stockholm International Peace Research Institute, 12 June 2023

5 'Rules for NATO conduct', speech by secretary general, 4 June 1957, NATO archive

6 Interview with research assistant

7 'Israel's Intelligence Failure Is a Wake-Up Call for NATO', *Foreign Policy*, 14 October 2023

8 'The secrets Hamas knew about Israel's military', *New York Times*, 13 October 2023

9 Mick Ryan, *War Transformed*, 2022, Kindle location 3

10 'China Sees at Least One Winner Emerging From Ukraine War: China', *New York Times*, 14 March 2023

11 'Largest NATO command post exercise STEADFAST JUPITER 2023 begins', NATO website, 10 October 2023

12 'Poland says Belarus helicopters violated its airspace', Radio Free Europe, 1 August 2023

13 'NATO assures Zelenskiy of support even as world's eyes turn to Mideast', *Reuters*, 11 October 2023

14 'Secretary of Defense Lloyd J. Austin III Holds a Press Conference Following a NATO Defense Ministers Meeting, Brussels, Belgium' U.S Department of Defense, 12 October 2023

15 Jürgen-Joachim von Sandrart, 'Commanders Foreword', *Baltic Amber Magazine*, 25 July 2023

16 Guglielmo Luigi Miglietta, 'Deter and Defend: Readiness is the path to peace', *Baltic Amber Magazine*, 31 January 2023

17 Interview with the author

18 'Remarks by NATO Secretary General Jens Stoltenberg at the 18th Annual NATO Conference on Arms Control, Disarmament and Weapons of Mass Destruction Non-Proliferation', NATO website, 18 April 2023

19 'Top secret NATO exercise to take place over UK', *Sky News*, 15 October 2022

20 Michael Cohen, 'The US and NATO at a nuclear crossroads', NATO Defense College, January 2023

21 Hans Kristensen, 'Lakenheath Air Base Added To Nuclear Weapons Storage Site Upgrades', Federation of American Scientists, 4 November 2022

22 Jean-Yves Haine, 'The Cuban Missile Crisis, the Russia-Ukraine war and nuclear risks', NATO Defence College, December 2022

23 Ibid.

24 'Nato official apologises over suggestion Ukraine could give up land for membership', *Guardian*, 16 August 2023

25 'Ukraine has recaptured 50% of the territory that Russia seized, Blinken says', *Reuters*, 23 July 2023

26 'Not enough Bears: Russia's Black Sea Fleet is pulling out of Crimea', *Telegraph*, 3 October 2023

27 'British howitzers fall silent in Ukraine because of 'catastrophic' shortage of shells', *Telegraph*, 13 October 2023

28 'Italian official warns of war fatigue, limited resources for Ukraine', *Defense News*, 5 October 2023

29 'Ukraine's commander-in-chief on the breakthrough he needs to beat Russia', Economist, 1 November 2023

30 'Rules for NATO conduct', speech by secretary general, 4 June 1957, NATO archive

31 'NATO 2030: United for a New era', NATO website, 25 November 2020

32 'Poland's ruling party pivots away from Ukraine in attempt to shore up votes', *Guardian*, 21 September 2023

33 'Slovakia's pro-Russia former PM Robert Fico invited to form coalition', *Guardian*, 2 October 2023

34 'US public support declines for arming Ukraine, Reuters/Ipsos poll shows' *Reuters*, 5 October 2023

35 'US shoots down armed Turkish drone after it came too close to US troops in Syria', *AP News*, 5 October 2023

36 'Putin's war in Ukraine: a conversation with Fiona Hill and Angela Stent', Brookings Institution, 19 September 2022

37 'How long to the Baltic states have? Planning horizons for Baltic defense', Foreign Policy Research Institute, 11 July, 2023

38 'EDF colonel: Russia still has four million artillery shells left', ERR, 20 October 2023

39 'Remarks by President Biden', White House website, 20 October 2023

40 'US general's 'gut' feeling of war with China sparks alarm over predictions', *Guardian*, 2 February 2023

41 'Nato holds first dedicated talks on China threat to Taiwan', *Financial Times*, 29 November 2023

42 'NATO prepares industry plan to boost arms production', September 11 2023

43 'European Defence Study: After The War', Friends of Europe, June 2023, page 93

44 'Remarks by NATO Deputy Secretary General Mircea Geoană', NATO website, 11 July 2023

45 'Israel's Intelligence Failure Is a Wake-Up Call for NATO', *Defence News*, 14 October 2023

46 'Remarks by NATO Deputy Secretary General Mircea Geoană', NATO website, 11 July 2023

47 'Brussels Summit Communiqué', NATO website, 14 June 2021

48 'Elon Musk says he withheld Starlink over Crimea to avoid escalation' BBC News, 8 September 2023

49 'NATO to adopt first-ever counter-drone doctrine for member nations', *Defense News,* 20 October 2023

50 Interviews with the author

51 'European Defence Study: After The War', Friends of Europe, June 2023, page 34

52 'Sweden to boost military on Gotland amid Russia fears', *Reuters*, 29 April 2022

53 'European Defence Study: After The War', Friends of Europe, June 2023, page 111

54 'Joe Biden pushes for Ursula von der Leyen to be Nato chief', *Telegraph*, 4 July 2023

55 'New rules would give Europe more scope for military spending post-Ukraine invasion', *Reuters*, 7 September 2023

56 'Former UK defense chief warns big EU countries won't keep NATO spending pledges', *Politico*, 20 October 2023

57 'Deploying to a nuclear bunker with the UK-led military alliance', *Forces News*, 7 July 2023

58 Interviews with the author

59 'Nato to launch biggest military exercise since cold war', *Financial Times*, 10 September 2023

60 'In city where "Europe starts", ethnic Russians start questioning Putin's war', *New York Times*, 7 July 2022

61 'Narva mayor on county election results', ERR, 7 March 2023

62 'Some Narva residents find public meetings ban incomprehensible', ERR, 26 July 2023

63 'Estonian War of Independence commemorations in Narva', ERR, 1 March 2023

64 Vivek Ramaswamy, Twitter, 5 June 2023

65 'Our policy is aimed at getting Russia back into Russia', Estonia World, 10 July 2023

66 'Remarks at the Opening of the NATO Meetings in Paris', UC Santa Barbara, 16 December 1957

67 'NATO-Russia: Partners for the Future', Carnegie Moscow Centre, 17 December 2009

Notes and acknowledgements

1 'The origins of SHAPE', NATO website, 11 February 2021
2 'NATO: The First Five Years', Forward by the NATO International Staff Archives Section, March 2001
3 'Ex-Kosovo president pleads not guilty in the Hague', Deutsche Welle, 3 April 2023
4 'Sarkozy to face 2025 trial', France 24, 25 August 2023

Index

Index